OVERUSE IN THE CRIMINAL JUSTICE SYSTEM
LE RECOURS EXCESSIF AU SYSTÈME DE JUSTICE PÉNALE

OVERUSE IN THE CRIMINAL JUSTICE SYSTEM

On Criminalization, Prosecution and Imprisonment

LE RECOURS EXCESSIF AU SYSTÈME DE JUSTICE PÉNALE

Aux sanctions et poursuites pénales et à la détention

Edited by

P.H.P.H.M.C. van Kempen
M. Jendly

intersentia

Cambridge – Antwerp – Chicago

Intersentia Ltd
Sheraton House | Castle Park
Cambridge | CB3 0AX | United Kingdom
Tel.: +44 1223 370 170 | Fax: +44 1223 370 169
Email: mail@intersentia.co.uk
www.intersentia.com | www.intersentia.co.uk

Distribution for the UK and Ireland:
NBN International
Airport Business Centre, 10 Thornbury Road
Plymouth, PL6 7PP
United Kingdom
Tel: +44 1752 202 301 | Fax: +44 1752 202 331
Email: orders@nbninternational.com

Distribution for Europe and all other countries:
Intersentia Publishing nv
Groenstraat 31
2640 Mortsel
Belgium
Tel.: +32 3 680 15 50 | Fax: +32 3 658 71 21
Email: mail@intersentia.be

Distribution for the USA and Canada:
Independent Publishers Group
Order Department
814 North Franklin Street
Chicago, IL 60610
USA
Tel.: +1 800 888 4741 (toll free) | Fax: +1 312 337 5985
Email: orders@ipgbook.com

Overuse in the criminal justice system: On criminalization, prosecution and imprisonment
Le recours excessif au système de justice pénale : Aux sanctions et poursuites pénales et à la détention

ISBN 978-1-78068-822-0 (hardback)
ISBN 978-1-78068-839-8 (PDF)
D/2019/7849/27
NUR 828

British Library Cataloguing in Publication Data. A catalogue record for this book is available from the British Library.

In memory of Judge Michael Reilly
(1945-2016)

ACKNOWLEDGEMENTS

In editing this forty-seventh publication of the International Penal and Penitentiary Foundation I am delighted to have been joined by professor Dr Manon Jendly. She joins me in offering grateful thanks first of all to all contributors to this book, for the energy they have put into their contributions. This volume is the result of the four-day IPPF colloquium that was held in Helsinki, Finland, in June 2016. In this respect I am also indebted to professor Dr Tapio Lappi-Seppälä, Justice Ilkka Rautio and Director General Esa Vesterbacka, and their colleagues from Finland, for their support and enthusiasm in organizing the colloquium. Ms Inge de Wit deserves great appreciation for her assistance in organizing and editing the book, as does Mrs Fiorina Argante, MA, for supporting me with the enormous amount of correspondence that this project has entailed.

Piet Hein van Kempen
Secretary General International Penal and Penitentiary Foundation
Professor of Criminal Law and Criminal Procedure Law, Radboud University, Nijmegen, the Netherlands

REMERCIEMENTS

C'est un plaisir pour moi d'avoir pu compter sur l'assistance de la Dr. Manon Jendly à l'occasion de l'édition de cette quarante-septième publication de la Fondation Internationale Pénale et Pénitentiaire. Elle se joint à moi pour remercier chaleureusement tous ceux qui ont contribué à cet ouvrage, pour l'énergie qu'ils ont déployée dans leurs contributions. Ce volume est le résultat du colloque de quatre jours organisé par la FIPP à Helsinki, Finlande, en juin 2016. Je me dois également d'exprimer ma gratitude à l'égard du Dr. Tapio Lappi-Seppälä, du juge Ilkka Rautio et du Directeur Général Esa Vesterbacka pour l'aide qu'ils m'ont apportée et l'enthousiasme dont ils ont fait preuve lors de l'organisation du colloque. Mme Inge de Wit mérite également toute ma reconnaissance pour l'aide qu'elle m'a apportée dans l'organisation et la publication du livre, de même que Mme Fiorina Argante, MA, pour son soutien dans le traitement de la volumineuse correspondance générée par ce projet.

Piet Hein van Kempen
Secrétaire général de la Fondation Internationale Pénale et Pénitentiaire
Professeur de droit pénal et procédure pénale, Université Radboud, Nijmegen, Pays-Bas

CONTENTS

The American Experience with the Prosecutorial Overuse of Plea Bargaining

Overuse of Imprisonment: Statistical Analyses of Incarceration Rates Across the World

PART I

INTRODUCTORY SYNTHESIS AND ANALYSES

1ÈRE PARTIE

SYNTHÈSE ET ANALYSES INTRODUCTIVES

CRIMINAL JUSTICE AND THE *ULTIMA RATIO* PRINCIPLE: NEED FOR LIMITATION, EXPLORATION AND CONSIDERATION

Piet Hein VAN KEMPEN*

I. INTRODUCTION

The claim that it is possible to overuse the criminal justice system implies a substantive approach rather than a procedural one. In a procedural approach, the question whether the criminal justice system is violating its limits is principally concerned about whether the criminalization of conduct has been reached through proper application of the legislative process and whether prosecutions and adjudication of criminal cases take place in conformity with criminal procedure law.[1] This volume and its chapters are rather based on a substantive approach of overuse of the criminal justice system, more particularly the overuse of criminalization, criminal prosecution and criminal imprisonment.

Overuse of criminalization – or: overcriminalization – may entail an unnecessary widening of criminal liability (conduct is criminalized without sufficient necessity, offences are constructed too broadly, the statute of limitations for crimes entails overly long periods or extraterritorial jurisdiction is claimed unconvincingly) or an unnecessary deepening of criminal liability (the statutory maximum and/or minimum sentence is set too high). As for an unnecessary

* Prof. Dr. (Piet Hein) P.H.P.H.M.C. van Kempen (MLaw, PhD) is full professor of Criminal Law and Criminal Procedure Law, and Dean of the Faculty of Law of Radboud University, Nijmegen, the Netherlands. He is also a Justice *ad litem* at the Court of Appeal, 's-Hertogenbosch, The Netherlands, and Secretary General of the International Penal and Penitentiary Foundation (IPPF).

1 Cf. Michael S. Moore, 'Liberty's Constraints on What Should be Made Criminal,' in: R.A. Duff, Lindsay Farmer, S.E. Marshall, Massimo Renzo & Victor Tadros, *Criminalization: The Political Morality of the Criminal Law*, Oxford University Press: Oxford, 2014, p. 182-212 at 183.

widening of criminal liability, this may, for example, manifest itself when the legislator aims to prevent or repress certain conduct through criminalization of that conduct, when it would be more effective or useful to repress or control that conduct fully or at least primarily through operational preventive measures or adopting measures that are of an administrative or civil nature. It may also mean that the legislator has criminalized conduct where it is arguably not useful or necessary or in any event not appropriate to criminalize at all.

Overuse of prosecution primarily means that too many violations of criminal law are prosecuted. This can particularly be the case when in certain individual cases or specific categories of cases it would be more effective, fairer, more efficient or otherwise desirable to refrain from prosecution and/or to repress or control that conduct through other means than prosecution, such as negotiating justice, settlement of the case through other means, including restorative justice possibilities, or administrative fines. Overuse of prosecution can, furthermore, occur through overcharging, *i.e.* when defendants are charged for offences that are formally applicable but which do little justice to the actual behaviour and its consequences.

Finally, overuse of imprisonment can also present itself in different forms. One form is that imprisonment is applied in too many cases (too many people are sentenced to imprisonment), while another reveals itself when the courts impose overly long prison sentences. In both situations, this may have something to do with insufficient legal or practical availability or a too modest use of alternatives to imprisonment, such as conditional punishment, community service or fines. Finally, execution of imprisonment under unnecessary strict or harsh conditions could be seen as a third manifestation of overuse of imprisonment. Whereas the first two forms are of a quantitative nature, the third is of a rather qualitative character.

Generally speaking, overuse thus presents itself where the criminal justice system is employed when this is unnecessary, ineffective, inefficient, unfair or otherwise inappropriate. The three different forms of overuse – relative to criminalization, prosecution and imprisonment respectively – are of course interrelated. Overuse of criminalization can easily produce overuse of prosecution, which in turn will most probably result in too much punishment.[2] As the chapters in this volume demonstrate, overuse of criminalization, prosecution and imprisonment manifests itself in many countries, while there are various instruments and solutions to prevent or overcome overuse.

The present chapter (which constitutes Part I of this volume) will now first explore a principle which can serve as a fundament for a substantive approach to

2 See also Douglas Husak, *Overcriminalization. The Limits of the Criminal Law*, Oxford: Oxford University Press, 2013, who argues that overcriminalization is objectionable mainly because it produces too much punishment.

overuse, i.e. the *ultima ratio* or *ultimum remedium* principle (sections II, III and IV). Mainly on the basis of a selection from the results of the seven thematic chapters (see Part II of this volume) and the sixteen national chapters (in Part III of this volume), the present chapter will then continue to discuss overuse – of criminalization, prosecution and imprisonment – in the criminal justice system and solutions to tackle overuse (section V). It will end with a brief conclusion (section VI).

II. THE *ULTIMA RATIO* OR *ULTIMUM REMEDIUM* PRINCIPLE

The criminal justice system encompasses the most severe instrument at the state's disposal in times of peace. It is principally coercive in nature. It is so for the intrusiveness of its criminal investigation powers (including arrest and detention) as well as for the severity of its sanctions (including imprisonment), the aim of both of which is to uphold the firm limitations on human conduct set by criminalization. The intrinsic violation by the application of criminal law and criminal procedure of an individual's freedom and social sphere is a universal characteristic.[3] Moreover, involvement in the criminal justice process may have other adverse consequences, including the delinquent's social exclusion and stigmatization, violation of the interest of third parties such as the delinquent's family or employer and on a general scale more in extremity even the erosion of free society and human dignity. Perhaps also relevant to the principle is that application of the criminal justice system is financially very costly to society, particularly the execution of criminal punishments. Besides, the overbroad scope of criminal law and its application may undermine the efficiency and effectivity of the system as a whole. Finally, the idea that there must be limits to using criminal law and applying criminal procedure also follows from legal notions such as the harm principle, the principle of wrongfulness and the principle of fair labelling.[4]

For these and other reasons, it is a fundamental criminal justice principle that criminal law is and must be regarded as a so-called *ultima ratio* or *ultimum*

3 Piet Hein van Kempen, 'Introduction – Criminal Law and Human Rights', in: P.H.P.H.M.C. van Kempen (ed.), *Criminal Law and Human Rights, The International Library of Essays on Criminal Law*, England/USA: Ashgate, 2014, p. XI-XXXIII at XI. Cf. Panu Minkkinen, '"If Taken in Earnest": Criminal Law Doctrine and the Last Resort', 45 *The Howard Journal* 5 (2006), p. 521-536 at 521, who, thus, in our view fails to appreciate that the essential and distinctive feature that makes criminal law what it is, is not only determined by criminal punishment but also by the nature of criminal investigation powers and methods.

4 On labelling, see James Chalmers & Fiona Leverick, 'Fair Labelling in Criminal Law', 71 *The Modern Law Review* 2 (2008), p. 217-246.

remedium, sometimes also referred to as the principle of restraint.[5] This first of all means that conduct should only be criminalized and the criminal justice system only be applied as a last resort, *i.e.* if all other avenues that are less coercive than criminal law fail to sufficiently forestall or repress the harmful conduct.[6] For example, operational preventive measures and administrative or civil sanctions may encompass such less coercive alternatives to criminalization, criminal investigation, prosecution or criminal punishment including imprisonment. Moreover, the *ultima ratio* principle implies that the harmful conduct should be sufficiently serious to justify that the conduct is brought within the scope of the criminal justice system.[7] The principle acknowledges that the criminal justice system should (principally) and can (practically) only offer fragmentary protection.[8] The principle is of significance for both the question of what the scope of substantive criminal law should be (relevant for the legislator) and as to what – in case of criminal conduct – the limits ought to be to the applicability and application of criminal procedure (relevant for the legislator, police, prosecution and courts) and to imprisonment (relevant for the prosecution, courts and authorities that are responsible for the execution of sentences).

At this point, it is important to stress that the *ultima ratio* principle – as such – is merely what is says it is: a principle, not a rule. Principles entail a requirement of some dimension of morality, as Dworkin has stated. They have a rather fluid and fuzzy content and scope and an open structure. Principles indicate a direction and put argumentative weight on the considerations to be made, rather than that they impose absolute limits or exact a particular outcome.[9] All of this also applies to the *ultima ratio* principle. It does not dictate

---

5 See Morinaga's chapter on Japan.

6 See P.H.P.H.M.C. van Kempen, 'Four Concepts of Security – A Human Rights Perspective', 13 *Human Rights Law Review* 1 (2013), p. 1-23 at 19, with references to: Michael G. Faure & Marjolein Visser, 'Law and economics of environmental crime', in: Hans Sjögren & Göran Skogh (eds.), *New Perspectives on Economic Crime*, Cheltenham, UK/Northampton, USA: Edward Elgar Publishing 2004, p. 57-75 at 68; Andrew Ashworth & Jeremy Horder, *Principles of Criminal Law*, Oxford: Oxford University Press, 2013, p. 33, 52. See also Nils Jareborg, Criminalization as Last Resort (Ultima Ratio), 2 *Ohio State Journal of Criminal Law* (2005), p. 521-534. For the recognition of the principle in European law, see Sakari Melander, 'Ultima Ratio in European Criminal Law', 3 *Oñati Socio-legal Series* 1 (2013), p. 42-61.

7 Cf. European Parliament resolution of 22 May 2012 on an EU approach to criminal law (2010/2310(INI)), *Official Journal of the European Union* C 264 E/7, para I: "criminal law must be applied as a measure of last resort (ultima ratio) addressing clearly defined and delimited conduct, which cannot be addressed effectively by less severe measures and which causes significant damage to society or individuals". See also Fernando Molina, 'A Comparison Between Continental European and Anglo-American Approaches to Overcriminalization and Some Remarks on How to Deal with It', 14 *New Criminal Law Review* 1 (2011), p. 123-138 at 135.

8 See further Nils Jareborg, Criminalization as Last Resort (Ultima Ratio), 2 *Ohio State Journal of Criminal Law* (2005), p. 521-534 at 525-526. See also Lucia Zedner, 'Too much security?', 31 *International Journal of the Sociology of Law* (2003), p. 155-184.

9 These characterizations are derived from the – now classic – explanation of the distinction between principles and rules by Ronald M. Dworkin, 'The Model of Rules', 35 *The University of*

which conduct may be criminalized or when prosecution or imprisonment is acceptable, it only cautions the legislator and authorities within the criminal justice system not to overuse the system. Moreover, the principle is a moral standard that as such is not legally binding to the authorities. In that sense, the power of the principle is limited.[10] The morality of the principle can, for example, be found in the presumption that restraint in creating and applying criminal law is indispensable, for utilization of a criminal justice system is at best a necessary wrong that must be maintained and applied to repress other, more severe wrongs and to protect that freedom against even greater intrusions. Where the criminal justice system is not a necessity or not proportionate to accomplish these protective goals, the intrusion that system causes is just a wrong and in that sense an immorality. And the other way around: in that case, there is insufficient moral ground for application of the criminal justice system.

It is in line with this that Díez-Ripollés in his chapter presents, discusses and applies the objective of punitive moderation – alongside the objective of social inclusion – as an analytical framework for conducting comparative criminal policy description and evaluation of national crime control systems. He remarks that national crime control systems should make sure that crime control does not inflict more social suffering than strictly necessary and that criminalization should not go beyond what might be considered vital for protecting essential public interests, and that those subjected to criminal law enforcement bodies, be they suspects or offenders, will experience only moderate and proportional distress as a result of their behaviour.

When there is insufficient moral ground for the application of the criminal justice system, this can have serious consequences. As Rotman, in his chapter on the USA, states: overcriminalization ultimately creates a climate of unfairness that not only undermines faith in the rule of law, but may also be criminogenic by delegitimizing the criminal justice system in potential offenders' eyes, thus justifying their rationalizations to engage in criminal behaviour.

Chicago Law Review 14 (1967), p. 14-46 at 22-29. Although this distinction in our view cannot be made as categorically as Dworkin implies, Dworkin's characterizations of principles are still highly valid and useful.

10 See Douglas Husak, 'Applying Ultima Ratio: A Skeptical Assessment', 2 *Ohio State Journal of Criminal Law* (2005), p. 535-545 at 536-540. Cf. Panu Minkkinen, 2013. 'The "Last Resort": A Moral and/or Legal Principle?', 3 Oñati Socio-legal Series 1 (2013), p. 21-30 at 28, who claims that the 'ultima ratio' or 'last resort' as he names it, is "a politico-moral principle with constitutional significance" or, what he would call, "a constitutionalist principle".

III. SUPPORT FOR THE FOUR ASPECTS OF THE *ULTIMA RATIO* PRINCIPLE BY LEGALLY BINDING LAW

Though the *ultima ratio* or *ultimum remedium* principle as such – meaning: by itself – is not legally binding, it does find firm ground in both national and international positive law that is binding indeed. Several principles that are part of positive law are relevant in this respect. The following – non-exhaustive – overview is based on the different aspects of the *ultima ratio* principle.

The first two aspects concern criminal substantive law and relate to the criminalization of conduct. The most prominent axiom of the *ultima ratio* principle is that conduct should only be criminalized as a last resort. What is most obviously relevant here is the principle of necessity or subsidiarity. According to that principle, a measure may only be employed if the goal for applying it cannot be achieved through less intrusive means. Positively formulated: if there is a need to apply restrictive measures, among those measures the least intrusive instrument that may achieve the result must be applied. As far as the criminalization of conduct interferes with human rights, for example the rights to privacy and protection of property and the freedoms of expression, religion, assembly, association and movement, such interference can only be justified if it is necessary for achieving the outcome sought. As follows from the jurisprudence of, for example, the European Court of Human Rights (ECtHR)[11] and the Human Rights Committee (HRC), this also means that criminalizations that are wider in scope than is required to achieve that aim, to that extent can be held contrary to the principle of necessity.[12] More generally, and therefore not only in relation to human rights interferences, the Court of Justice of the European Union (CJEU) has stated that "when there is a choice between several appropriate measures recourse must be had to the least onerous, and the disadvantages caused must not be disproportionate to the aims pursued."[13] Furthermore, in many national jurisdictions the principle of necessity is recognized as a constitutional principle, which then usually applies in case of

11 On the case law of the ECHR, see the chapter by Pinto de Albuquerque.

12 See, *e.g.*, ECtHR 22 October 1981, *Dudgeon/The UK*, no. 7525/76, para 42-62 (especially 62); HRC, General Comment No. 27: Freedom of movement (article 12), *UN doc.* CCPR/C/21/Rev.1/Add.9, 1 November 1999, para 14: "[...] it is not sufficient that the restrictions serve the permissible purposes; they must also be necessary to protect them. Restrictive measures [...] must be the least intrusive instrument amongst those which might achieve the desired result".

13 See Sakari Melander, 'Ultima Ratio in European Criminal Law', 3 *Oñati Socio-legal Series* 1 (2013), p. 42-61 at 55, with reference to several cases, among which CJEU 13 November 1990, *The Queen/Minister of Agriculture, Fisheries and Food and Secretary of State for Health, ex parte: Fedesa and others*, Case C-331/88, para 13. More recently and in a criminal case, see CJEU 20 March 2018, *Luca Menci/Procura della Repubblica*, Case C-524/15, para 46.

interferences with constitutional rights.[14] The German Constitutional Court (Bundesverfassingsgericht, BVerfGE) even recognizes the 'ultima ratio' principle as such in consistent case law, when stating: "The criminal law is indeed not the primary means of legal protection, if only because of its strongly intervening character; its use is therefore subject to the requirements of proportionality [...]. However, it is used as a 'ultima ratio' of this protection if certain conduct beyond its prohibition is in a special way socially damaging and intolerable for the orderly coexistence of human beings, as a result of which the prevention thereof is particularly urgent."[15]

The latter part of this quote offers a positive law foundation to a second aspect of the *ultima ratio* principle, *i.e.* that the harmful conduct should be sufficiently serious to justify its criminalization. This axiom too is supported by international human rights law. This is more particular the case under the principle of proportionality *stricto sensu*, which demands that the infringement on the right is proportionate to the aim pursued, and under the requirement that this aim must be legitimate.[16] Especially where the criminalization of conduct severely interferes with human rights – for example because it involves "a most intimate aspect of private life" – there must exist "particularly serious reasons before interferences on the part of public authorities can be legitimate".[17] This also follows from the Charter of Fundamental Rights of the European Union, Article 52(1) of which holds that limitation on the exercise of the rights and freedoms recognized by this Charter "may be made only if they are necessary and genuinely meet objectives of general interest recognized by the Union or the need to protect the rights and freedoms of others". Of relevance here also, is the principle of culpability, guilt or *mens rea*, *i.e.* the principle according to which a person can only be held criminally responsible for acts or omissions for which he is blameworthy. The legislator must therefore also be careful not to establish criminal liability in situations where it cannot be reasonably and fairly expected

14 See, e.g., Kaarlo Tuori, 'Ultima Ratio as a Constitutional Principle', 3 *Oñati Socio-legal Series* 1 (2013), p. 6-20 at 9-12.

15 See BVerfGE 28 May 1993, *Schwangerschaftsabbruch II*, no. 88, 203 at 258; BVerfGE 26 February 2008, *Geschwisterbeischlaf*, no. 120, 224 at 240. See on that case law Klaus Gärditz, 'Demokratizität des Strafrechts und Ultima Ratio-Grundsatz', 71 *JuristenZeitung* 13, July 2016, p. 641-650 at 642-643; Rudolf Wendt, 'The Principle of "Ultima Ratio" and/or the Principle of Proportionality, 3 *Oñati Socio-legal Series* 1 (2013), p. 81-94.

16 See, e.g., again ECtHR 22 October 1981, *Dudgeon/The UK*, no. 7525/76, para 42-62; HRC, General Comment No. 27: Freedom of movement (Article 12), *UN doc.* CCPR/C/21/Rev.1/Add.9, 1 November 1999, para 14. Cf. Rudolf Wendt, 'The principle of "ultima ratio" and/or the principle of proportionality'. 3 *Oñati Socio-Legal Series* 1 (2013), p. 81-94 at 86.

17 See relative to the right to privacy ECtHR 22 October 1981, *Dudgeon/The UK*, no. 7525/76, para 52. See also the chapter of Ortenzi & García Basalo on Argentina, where they discuss CSJN, Judgment of 25 August 2009, *Arriola, Sebastián et al.*, Case No. 9080, about possession of drugs for personal use in the private sphere.

of a person to act lawfully.[18] The principle of culpability is broadly – but not everywhere – recognized in positive national law, then often explicitly in case law while it can also be deduced from the system of criminal laws. The principle can furthermore – to some minor extent – find ground in international human rights law under the presumption of innocence.[19]

The two other aspects of the *ultima ratio* principle regard the policy on and the use of criminal procedure powers in individual cases, including determination of punishment. Here, the most important axiom is that the criminal justice system – or more specifically, for example, criminal investigation, prosecution and punishment – should only be applied as a last resort. The axiom finds support in positive law through the aforementioned principle of necessity or subsidiarity, which is also of relevance to the use of procedural powers. Since many investigative powers interfere with, for example, privacy (e.g. searches, surveillance, collecting finger prints or DNA) or liberty (e.g. arrest and detention), the execution of such powers has to be consistent with the principle of necessity as required by the human rights to privacy and to liberty (the right against arbitrary arrest and deprivation of liberty).[20] See also Article 52(1) of the Fundamental Rights Charter EU mentioned above. The rule that procedural powers can only be applied if necessary, usually also follows from national criminal procedural law. Moreover, if a criminal procedure measure is ineffective, it can never be necessary. Furthermore, for example, the principle of legality functions as a guarantee against unreasonable use of criminal procedural powers. According to the European Court of Human Rights, the principle is an essential element of the rule of law and should "be construed and applied, as follows from its object and purpose, in such a way as to provide effective safeguards against arbitrary prosecution, conviction and punishment".[21]

The fourth aspect of the *ultima ratio* principle is that the use of criminal procedural powers can only be justifiable if the harmful conduct that is sought to be repressed is sufficiently serious or if there are at least good reasons to use these powers. Where the use of criminal investigative powers interferes with fundamental rights such as the right to privacy and the right to liberty, such use must be proportionate to the aim pursued and it must serve a legitimate aim.

---

18 See, e.g., Mordechai Kremnitzer & Tatjana Hörnle, 'Human Dignity and the Principle of Culpability', 44 *Israel Law Review* 1-2 (2011), p.115-141; Andrew Ashworth & Jeremy Horder, *Principles of Criminal Law*, Oxford: Oxford University Press, 2013, p. 74-75.

19 See, e.g., Stefan Trechsel, *Human Rights in Criminal Proceedings*, Oxford: Oxford University Press 2005, p. 157-158 and 171.

20 See, *e.g.*, ECtHR (GC) 4 December 2008, *S. and Marper/the UK*, no. 30562/04, para 101-126 (privacy), and ECtHR (GC) 5 July 2016, *Buzadji/Moldova*, no. 23755/07, para 115-123 (liberty); on the ICCPR, with further references, see S. Joseph & M. Castan, *The International Covenant on Civil and Political Rights, Cases, Materials and Commentary*, Oxford: Oxford University Press, 2013, para 16.10-16.12 (privacy) and 11.15-11.17 (liberty).

21 See, e.g., ECtHR 4 October 2016, *Žaja/Croatia*, no. 37462/09, para 90-106.

Positive law offers much less general support for a restriction on the possibilities to prosecute on the ground that the harmful conduct is of insufficient seriousness. For example, the ECtHR holds "that the assessment of the appropriateness of a criminal prosecution falls outside its supervisory competence".[22] That a prosecution may not be disproportionate to the severity of the crime does not seem to be a universally recognized principle of law, although it is recognized in some national jurisdictions in some areas of the law.[23] This is different as regards punishments. For example, Article 49(3) of the Fundamental Rights Charter EU states: "The severity of penalties must not be disproportionate to the criminal offence." With regard to the jurisprudence of the ECtHR, see Pinto de Albuquerque's chapter, which holds that the Strasbourg Court has adopted a proportionality-based approach to custodial sentences by assessing the necessity of its application – or its length – to the offence committed in the light of the circumstances of the case.[24]

IV. INTERESTS THAT DEMAND REASONABLE RATHER THAN ABSOLUTE USE OF THE *ULTIMA RATIO* PRINCIPLE

Although the *ultima ratio* principle intends to set limits to the criminalization of conduct and to the application of criminal procedure, it does not plead against the criminal justice system in general. *Ultima ratio* cannot and should not be equated to abolitionism. The principle does not fail to appreciate that the criminal justice system does have value. Even so, it must be acknowledged that the *ultima ratio* principle is not entirely unproblematic.

A first limitation of the principle is that its rationale primarily lies in the harming effects that the criminal justice system has for defendants and convicts, rather than in that system's value for crime control and protection of society. Still, whereas overuse of criminalization, prosecution and imprisonment has many serious adverse effects for society and individuals, this can be equally the case for underuse of criminal justice systems. As Rotman stresses in his chapter on the USA, underuse of the system poses problems to fairness, fosters resentment and disrespect for the law and can have a corrosive effect on the fabric of democracy and equality. Furthermore, as De Valkeneer, Dizier & Seron in their chapter on

22 ECtHR 6 November 2007, *Patsuria/Georgia*, no. 30779/04, para 42 and 85.

23 See, e.g., Prosecution guidance on minor offences, United Kingdom, at: https://www.cps.gov.uk/legal-guidance/minor-offences (last visited: 15 December 2018), or Article 7(2)(c) of the International Protection Act 2015 of Ireland.

24 See also the chapter by Lappi-Seppälä on Finland, which discusses the choice of sanction according to the "ladder model" in accordance with the principle that views imprisonment as a last resort.

Belgium point out, criminological research tends to show that it is not so much the severity of sentences that generates a deterrent effect as the certainty of being sanctioned. Thus, from the viewpoint of preventing crime, too much restraint on prosecutions may weaken the preventive effect of the criminal justice system.

Another difficulty is that the *ultima ratio* principle's call that conduct should only be criminalized and the criminal justice system only be applied as a last resort, is concerned with prevention and sanctioning of harmful behaviour. This implies a focus on the instrumental side of criminal justice (crime control) and its harmful effects, rather than on the protective value of the system for them (due process). Although administrative and civil law procedure are in many ways less intrusive than criminal law is, their capacity to protect fairness and truthfulness is usually less well developed than that of criminal procedure. Thus, adjudication of cases through administrative or civil law proceedings instead of criminal justice does not necessarily benefit the individual concerned (cf. the chapter on Japan, where Morinaga explains the historical problems with administrative law adjudication in this country). The *ultima ratio* principle may consequently push for criminal or civil enforcement, even though criminal enforcement in certain situations should be preferable from the view point of legal protection. This needs to be taken into serious consideration when discussing decriminalization and moving enforcement of legal rules from the criminal justice system to administrative or civil law procedure.

V. SELECTIONS OF RESULTS FROM THE CHAPTERS IN THIS VOLUME

As stated in the introduction of this chapter, a thematic approach to overuse in the criminal justice system is presented in Part II of this volume. Subsequently, Part III contains the national chapters. These are based on a questionnaire on overuse in the criminal justice system, to which experts from 16 countries from Africa, America (North and South), Asia, Europe and Oceania responded in 2016, 2017 and 2018. The reporting states are Argentina, Belgium, Finland, Germany, Greece, Ireland, Japan, the Netherlands, New Zealand, Nigeria, Poland, Russia, Spain, Switzerland, Taiwan and the United States of America (USA). Each of the national chapters contains a similar structure, with separate sections on overuse of criminalization, overuse of prosecution and overuse of imprisonment. The following provides a synthesis of results from the chapters, which is relevant to the *ultima ratio* principle.

V.1. GENERAL

Although the principle that criminal law is and must be regarded as a so-called *ultima ratio* or *ultimum remedium* can offer general direction when deciding on the content and scope of criminal law and the application thereof in concrete cases, it does not offer substantive criteria for precise assessment and evaluation of criminalizations, prosecution and sentencing. It is, therefore, of much interest that Díez-Ripollés in his chapter presents a more detailed conceptual framework to evaluate national crime control systems. That framework recognizes punitive moderation and social inclusion as the two principal objectives when comparing and evaluating national criminal justice systems. Díez-Ripollés not only explains the significance and content of his evaluative proposal as well as the hypotheses on which it rests, he also immediately applies it to the three defining moments of criminal intervention: criminalization, prosecution, and enforcement of sanctions. For each of these, several rules and practices are discussed in the chapter.

An equally general approach, though legal rather than theoretical, is offered in the chapter by Pinto de Albuquerque. He discusses the case law of the European Court of Human Rights that is relevant for overuse of criminal justice, particularly relative to overuse of criminalization (with specific attention for defamation and crimmigration) and overuse of imprisonment (with specific attention for abuse of pre-trial detention and disproportionate custodial sentences). One of Pinto de Albuquerque's conclusions is that the ECtHR has adopted a twofold approach in the context of the overuse of criminal justice: in some cases it controls the excessive application of criminal law and criminal sanctions with regard to specific behaviour, while in other cases it criticizes States for having adopted a lenient sentence with regard to an offender (positive obligations case law).

Of course, the use of criminalization, prosecution and imprisonment can be best avoided by tackling the root causes of wrongful behaviour and thereby preventing that application of the criminal justice system becomes necessary. Interestingly, in her chapter, Agomoh elaborately explains how the environment and traffic – being two related aspects of societal management – present an enormous challenge for the criminal justice system of Nigeria and constantly present a puzzle for policymakers. Furthermore, as Kuhn & Solcà point out in their chapter on Switzerland, the need for criminalization can in some instances also be avoided by applying technical solutions, which would however require a little political courage.

V.2. OVERUSE OF CRIMINALIZATION

Combining philosophy, political sciences, criminology, history and law, the thematic chapter of Guzmán Dalbora focuses on overuse of criminalization. It highlights how the increase of criminalizing behaviour poses challenges to the theory of law, threatens the liberal organization of society and of democracy and calls into question the legal authority of the government. Guzmán Dalbora elaborates on several punitive trends, particularly in Latin America, and offers a critical appraisal of how ideology, moral conviction and elitism influence criminal policy and practices.

If a jurisdiction is confronted with overuse of criminalization, several solutions are possible. In her chapter on Spain, García Magna discusses three ways of reducing punitive pressure: legalization, decriminalization and permissiveness or policy-based tolerance. In their chapter on Germany, Haverkamp, Cirener, Boetticher & Feest view reflection on the "ultima ratio" of criminal law as the best starting point for preventing the alarming increase in punishability of behaviour that is socially undesired but not per se earning of punishment. A further step would be abolition of criminal law entirely, *i.e.* abolitionism, to which Kuhn & Solcà call attention in their chapter on Switzerland. Meanwhile, on the basis of the experience in Taiwan, Rong-geng Li concludes that the smaller the chance that an offence harms others or the whole society, the more likely it is that it may be decriminalized.

The national chapters show many examples of both developments of further criminalization as well as tendencies towards decriminalization. See, for example, developments to relax the criminalization of the possession of drugs for personal use in the chapters on Argentina, Belgium, Germany, Ireland, Poland, Spain and Taiwan, whereas unabated repression of drugs offences is manifest in for example Finland, Japan and Russia (further increased repression). Furthermore, criminalization of sexual offences intensified in, for example, Finland, the Netherlands and Taiwan. Meanwhile, in Ireland there is discussion about decriminalization, legalization and policy around prostitution. Likewise, in some countries there is movement towards decriminalizing abortion (for example: Spain, Ireland[25], Taiwan) or euthanasia (Spain; see also the chapter on the Netherlands). Decriminalization of blasphemy is under discussion in Ireland and recently implemented in the Netherlands, whereas the chapter on Russia makes clear that the development in this jurisdiction is in the other direction, as is illustrated by the further criminalization of "offending the feelings of religious believers" (art. 148 Criminal Code, as amended in 2013) and the prosecution and

25 On 13 December 2018, the *Seanad* (the Upper House of parliament, the *Oireachtas*) followed the *Dáil* (the Lower House) in passing the *Health (Regulation of Termination of Pregnancy) Bill 2018*, as a result of which abortions will be legally available in Ireland from 1 January 2019.

sentencing of the punk music group "Pussy Riot" for "disorderly conduct motivated by religious hatred or enmity" (art. 213.2 CC). See for more examples the chapter on Russia by Gilinskiy, in which he points out that there have been many, many more such cases over the past years. There are more areas that display increasing criminalization, for example relative to terrorism (see, e.g.: the Netherlands), migration (crimmigration; see, e.g.: Germany, and the chapter by Pinto de Albuquerque), business crimes (e.g.: USA) and cybercrime or crime that has come into existence because of the commencement of new technologies (e.g.: Japan, the Netherlands, Switzerland).

Several jurisdictions more generally experience a tendency to criminalization and repression, though the intensity of these development may be very different between countries (see, for example, the chapters on the Netherlands, Russia and Spain). Often this involves the introduction of new offences or broadening of already defined crimes, but also the increase of the maximum applicable sentence to an offence (see, e.g.: the Netherlands) is a form of increasing criminalization. Interestingly, some chapters note that obligations under international law (including regional law, such as European Union law) to criminalize certain actions or omissions have increased the use of criminal law; see, for example, the chapters on Germany, Greece, Japan, the Netherlands and Poland. Meanwhile, it should be noted that the increase of criminalization is not only caused by new offences or the widening of the definitions of established ones. In some jurisdictions, criminalizations are broadened in the sense that the time limits for prosecution (statute of limitations) are extended (see, for example, the chapters on the Netherlands and Switzerland).

Even where criminal law is not overly broad (no overuse of criminalization), there may still be overuse of criminal procedural instruments. Ortenzi & García Basalo (chapter on Argentina) state that the causes thereof "are related to the provisions of the procedural codes and the administrative inadequacies of the Judiciary". For example, in several chapters it is asserted that the use of pre-trial detention is increasingly problematic; see, for example, the chapters on Argentina, Greece, the Netherlands and Nigeria (very elaborately), and the statistical chapter by Lappi-Seppälä.[26] See furthermore the chapter on the Netherlands, in which Mevis argues that the expanding possibilities for criminal investigation and the codification of possibilities to interfere with fundamental rights and liberties of citizens brings one to another point that can be qualified as 'overuse'. Examples he discusses are the weakening of the legal professional

26 See also the chapters on twenty-one countries around the world, in P.H.P.H.M.C. van Kempen (ed.), *Pre-trial detention. Human rights, criminal procedural law and penitentiary law, comparative law / Détention avant jugement. Droits de l'homme, droit de la procédure pénale et droit pénitentiaire, droit comparé*, Cambridge/Antwerp/Portland: Intersentia 2012.

privilege of doctors, lawyers and others, and the attenuation of the exclusionary rule in case of illegally obtained evidence.

V.3. OVERUSE OF PROSECUTION

The expediency principle, which offers prosecutorial discretion to determine whether or not an offender should be prosecuted and, if so, on what charge, can be a useful instrument to prevent or overcome overuse of prosecution. The principle applies in one form or another in Argentina, Belgium, Ireland, Japan (which abandoned the prosecutorial legality principle), the Netherlands (far reaching), New Zealand, Nigeria, Russia[27] and the USA. The counter principle, *i.e.* the principle of legality with respect to the prosecution of crimes, is for example applied in Finland, Germany, Greece, Poland, Spain, Switzerland and Taiwan. According to that principle, the prosecutor is obliged to pursue charges if there is probable cause and sufficient evidence for a conviction. As a result (so the chapter on Switzerland asserts), a system dominated by the principle of legality will usually produce a large number of convicts guilty of offences of little gravity, since any investigation must be continued until conviction as soon as clues allow the admission of guilt of the defendant. Many countries that apply the principle do, however, recognize a variation of exceptions and grounds for expediency and non-prosecution (see the chapters of the countries that apply the legality principle). With this, overuse can be prevented. Kuhn & Solcà (chapter on Switzerland) therefore argue for more exceptions to the legality principle, as does Rong-geng Li (Taiwan). At the same time, even if the expediency principle applies in a country, this in itself certainly does not guarantee that overuse is non-existent. For example, as follows from the chapter on Nigeria, lack of guidelines for prosecutors to help them with the decision whether or not to prosecute and with the selection of the appropriate sanction, can be the cause of both overuse and underuse of prosecution. Moreover, the de facto loss of independence of prosecutors and their embracing of politics relative to the execution of sentences and prevention measures: can be problematic as well in this regard. Haverkamp, Cirener, Boetticher & Feest consider this to be a troublesome development in Germany. The foregoing illustrates how the exact effects of the expediency principle and the legality principle much depend on the specific circumstances under which they operate. Actually, there is probably not a very significant difference in practice between a system based on the legality principle that recognizes a detailed set of exemptions and a system based on the expediency principle that is guided by precise guidelines that prescribe when prosecution is required and when it must not be applied.

27 See Article 221 of the Russian Criminal Procedure Code.

Diversion, by which a conviction is avoided, is possible in many other jurisdictions. The relatively low rate of prosecution in Japan may be a reflection of the fairly developed "diversion" scheme. However, in New Zealand for example, there is some concern that diversion has a net-widening effect, resulting in prosecutions which would not have been pursued without the scheme being in place. Meanwhile, in Ireland there is an increased focus on alternatives to prosecution. There, the so-called Adult Caution Scheme can be applied as such an alternative.

There is a variety of systems of summary proceedings; see, for example, the chapters on Argentina, Finland (fines), Ireland, Japan, the Netherlands (punishment order) and Taiwan. The same applies for negotiating justice; see, for example, the chapters on Belgium and New Zealand. See Ligeti & Robinson's contribution, in particular, for an elaborate discussion on "negotiated" – as opposed to traditional, imposed – justice as a way of dealing with an overload of case files. They argue that the minimization, sidelining or complete excision of the full trial stage, which is typical of negotiated justice mechanisms – such as out-of-court settlements, penal orders, guilty pleas and deferred prosecution agreements – raises serious questions around the quality of justice being delivered, the openness of criminal justice in general, and the communicative function of sanctioning systems. After exploring these tensions through the prism of the evolving roles of the prosecutor and the judge in the context of negotiated justice in Europe, the authors find that negotiated justice is not a solution to overprosecution as such, and that it is important not to reduce negotiated justice to a mere response to systemic overload in criminal justice systems. They point out that the increasing resort to negotiated justice has never been centered qualitatively on justice but on efficiency. Therefore, they stress that improving the transparency of negotiated justice tools is to be treated as a priority in order to facilitate a thorough, continual review of their effectiveness.

Forms of plea-bargaining are accepted in Finland (limited), Greece (certain categories of crimes), Nigeria[28], Russia[29], Spain, Taiwan and the USA. Prosecutorial overuse of plea bargaining is extensively dealt with in the chapter by Rapoza. By focusing on the criminal justice system of the United States of America, which presently "is for the most part a system of pleas, and not a system of trials", Rapoza offers a thorough and detailed exposition of the historical development, the legal procedure and the many problems of plea bargaining. The chapter finds that plea bargaining is largely based on the functional premise that

28 Not mentioned in the chapter on Nigeria, but see Sule Peter Echewija, 'Plea Bargaining and the Administration of Criminal Justice in Nigeria: A Moral Critique', 3 *IAFOR Journal of Ethics, Religion & Philosophy* 2 (2017), p. 35-47.

29 Not mentioned in the chapter on Russia, but see Ekaterina Moiseeva, 'Plea bargaining in Russia: the role of defence attorneys and the problem of asymmetry', 41 *International Journal of Comparative and Applied Criminal Justice* 3 (2017), p. 163-184.

the defendant is in fact guilty of something, with the only significant issue being how to label his offence and the degree of punishment to be imposed. Rather, the question that needs to be addressed, according to Rapoza, is how the process can be rendered fairer and more equitable; he elaborately discusses several solutions. Also one of Rapoza's many conclusions is that the use of plea bargaining undoubtedly has played a significant role in generating America's high rate of incarceration. Plea bargaining can thus be an important cause of overuse of imprisonment. Another author critical of plea bargaining – as well as of speedy trials and of violations of the rule of evidence for forfeiture proceedings – is Díez-Ripollés. He holds that such "gimmicky" criminal procedures give up essential elements of due process in exchange for alleged efficacy. Nevertheless, Lambropoulou & Tsolka regard plea-bargaining as a useful measure to solve problems of overuse in the criminal justice system in Greece.

Mediation, another possibility to avoid or mitigate prosecution, has gained a substantial role in the handling of criminal cases in Finland for example. In Poland, article 59a of the Criminal Code provided for restorative justice, but this provision was removed in 2016. This is much to the regret of Paprzycki & Wąsek-Wiaderek, who state in their chapter on Poland that it had a chance to become an effective tool to terminate many criminal proceedings concerning offences against property which are the most frequently reported offences in Poland. Also Kuhn & Solcà (chapter on Switzerland) argue for the introduction in law of restorative justice possibilities, such as mediation.

V.4. OVERUSE OF IMPRISONMENT

Overuse of imprisonment from a general perspective is first of all dealt with by Lappi-Seppälä. In his chapter on statistics of incarceration rates across the world, he offers a very thorough and detailed analysis of the major trends in the use of imprisonment across the world and over time. Individual countries form the basic unit in the analysis, but trends and differences are examined in great detail also by regions and continents. One of the many conclusions that Lappi-Seppälä draws is that statistical comparisons generally point out that neither reported crime nor victimization is systematically reflected in levels of incarceration. Rather, incarceration rates, in the end, are very much a result of political choices. Another of Lappi-Seppälä's conclusions is that income inequality as well as investments in social welfare correlate strongly with imprisonment among European countries. The same applies to social sentiments such as fear of crime, subjective punitivity and social and institutional trust.

Where in some countries short-term prison sentences are the principal cause of high prison rates (see, for example, the chapter on Ireland), in other jurisdiction long prison sentences are mainly responsible for this. In their chapter on New Zealand, Tinsley & Young argue that the overuse of imprisonment in

New Zealand can be seen to be a result of longer nominal and effective sentences imposed, which in turn has been driven by both government policy and the public mood, as affected by the media and pressure groups. See the chapter on Spain, which points at pressure groups and populist dynamics, and the chapter on Taiwan, which explains how public pressure (the "White Rose Movement") led to changed interpretations by the Supreme Court of several sexual offences. Probably also a result of this is the increasing use of life imprisonment in some countries (see particularly the chapters on Finland, Germany, Greece and the Netherlands, and the thematic chapters by Díez-Ripollés, Pinto de Albuquerque, Lappi-Seppälä and Rogan). Meanwhile, as is the case in Switzerland, the use of prison sentences may seriously vary between regions within a country or between different groups such as nationals and foreigners (see also the statistical chapter by Lappi-Seppälä). The same applies for women and men (again, see the statistical chapter by Lappi-Seppälä, and furthermore, the chapters on Ireland and Nigeria[30]). Differences may also be the result of preferential treatment of certain groups. This is, as Rotman elaborately explains in his chapter on the USA, the case for white-collar offenders.

Mandatory minimum sentencing is a feature that can be an obstacle to decrease the use of imprisonment (see, for example, the chapter on Nigeria). This is not only true for offences for which mandatory sentencing applies, it can also give rise to an uplift in the sentencing for other offences, as Rogan & Reilly note in their chapter on Ireland. It can, furthermore, cause unfair sentencing if the law does not leave any room for any exception (see the chapter on the Netherlands). Moreover, as is the case in Spain, even if courts impose penalties at their minimum limit, the rigidity of the enforcement system and the lack of non-custodial alternatives may be an obstacle to decrease the number of prisoners significantly. According to Rong-geng Li, that also applies to Taiwan, where courts ruling only on minor crimes have the discretion to reduce sentences, suspend sentences and commute sentences to a fine or community service. However, contrary to the above, according to García Magna in her chapter on Spain, limiting judicial discretion could also be positive in a sense, as it may prevent excesses in sentencing, even in the Spanish rigid system in which minimum limits are high. Which effect limiting judicial discretion has on the use of imprisonment may thus depend on whether it is used to either promote or limit lower sentencing and application of non-custodial sentences. Still, even measures to promote non-custodial sentences will not necessarily have the effect that is being pursued. For example, in Switzerland the increase in the prison population could, according to Kuhn & Solcà, also be explained by the fact that

30 See further, on 23 countries around the world: P.H.P.H.M.C. van Kempen & M.J.M. Krabbe (eds.), *Women in Prison. The Bangkok Rules and Beyond / Femmes en prison. Les règles de Bangkok et au-delà*, Cambridge/Antwerp/Portland: Intersentia, 2017.

by forcing judges to impose pecuniary penalties for convictions of less than 6 months, the system probably pushed them to increase their punitiveness by pronouncing sentences of more than 6 months imprisonment.

There are several examples of countries where the solutions to decrease imprisonment are under pressure; see, for instance, the chapter on Germany, which discusses this more elaborately. Moreover, some countries experience an increase of possibilities for further effective control of behaviour of the criminal after the execution of sanctions; see particularly the chapters on Germany and the Netherlands.[31]

Meanwhile, the severity of imprisonment sentences of course does not only rest on the length of the prison sentence, it is also determined by the conditions under which it is executed. In his chapter on Russia, Gilinskiy explains how the widespread use of torture results from a number of factors. However, also in case of less inhumane practices, incarceration does have harmful effects.

Rogan's thematic chapter focuses on efforts to minimize these effects and on the regulation of the use of imprisonment through release and other backdoor strategies. To that end, Rogan discusses the harmful effects of incarceration, the positive effects of contact with the outside world, the need for decent physical and material prison conditions, the importance of procedural fairness and accountability in prison, and release from prison as a key factor in minimizing the harms of imprisonment and reducing the size of the prison population. Her analysis is based on a wide variety of human rights standards and case law as well as on the results of social science research. The chapter is peppered with numerous findings and recommendations.

In the final thematic chapter, Sakalauskas states that the possibilities for prison leave, the presence of open prisons and general conditions for release on parole are excellent indicators of a humane and inclusion-orientated prison system (as regards open prisons, see also the chapters on Ireland). Sakalauskas illustrates – on the basis of a detailed analyses of the situation in Lithuania – how political, economic, social and cultural factors can nevertheless make it difficult to get a criminal policy adopted in which these instruments are actually applied.

Surely, the best way to avoid the negative effects for a convict of imprisonment is the use of non-custodial sentences. In some countries, the use of non-custodial sentences has a significant decreasing effect on the prison population; see, for instance, the chapters on Belgium (e.g. electronic monitoring), Finland (a widely

31 See also the contributions (particularly those of Tak and Shute, in Part III) in P.H.P.H.M.C. van Kempen & W. Young (ed.), *Prevention of reoffending. The value of rehabilitation and the management of high risk offenders / Prévention de la récidive. Valeur de la réhabilitation et gestion des délinquants à haut risque*, Cambridge/Antwerp/Portland: Intersentia, 2014.

applied policy of non-custodial solutions) and Ireland (Community Return). In order to limit the use of imprisonment, it is of great importance that such and other alternative sentences to imprisonment are available. Only then is it possible to apply the *ultima ratio* principle in the sentencing process. It is in line with this when Kuhn & Solcà stress the need to personalize sentences, i.e. that punishment is always adapted to the particular situation of the individual it affects. To achieve this, in addition to the need to broaden the range of sanctions available to courts, they propose that the system of sanctions be divided into two distinct phases. Their idea – which they work out in further detail – is to create a two-tiered criminal system, with a judge of the court deciding on the length of the sentence and a judge of enforcement of sentences who subsequently decides on the form of the sentence (type, conditions). In both phases, it is important to take the *ultima ratio* principle into consideration. Indeed, in his chapter on Finland, Lappi-Seppälä points out how the results of actually applying the principle of imprisonment only as a last resort have been very good; more durable and constructive results are achieved by criminologically informed evidence-based crime prevention techniques, and by developing alternative community sanctions to be used instead of incarceration, without any notable effects in the Finnish crime rates, when compared to the situation in the other Nordic countries.

VI. CONCLUSION: THE SIGNIFICANCE OF THE *ULTIMA RATIO* PRINCIPLE TO COUNTERING OVERUSE

To prevent or overcome overuse of criminalization, prosecution and imprisonment, the fundamental criminal justice principle that criminal law is and must be regarded as a so-called *ultima ratio* or *ultimum remedium* can offer significant guidance to the legislator and government, the prosecution, the judiciary and prison authorities.

Requirement of limitation. A first attribute of the *ultima ratio* principle is that it calls for limitation in the use of the criminal justice system. This requires that the legislator exercises restraint with criminalization of behaviour, *i.e.* in criminalizing at all, in the scope of offences, in the labelling of offences, in the period for which criminal responsibility for offences can be established (statute of limitations), in claiming extraterritorial jurisdiction and in the maximum punishment allowed for the offence. As to the prosecution, the notion of limitation implies that prosecution should not necessarily take place in every case in which it is possible and, furthermore, that it should refrain from overcharging, *i.e.* charging of defendants on the basis of offences that are formally applicable but which do little justice to the actual behaviour and its consequences. Finally, limitation as regards the judiciary – and/or possibly the prosecution – primarily entails reticence in the use of prison sentences. In cases where imprisonment is appropriate, it requires restraint in the length of the prison term and application of the lightest prison regime suitable in the case.

Requirement of exploration. A second quality of the *ultima ratio* principle is that the authorities actively search for possible alternative solutions. It is first of all the legislator and government that have to explore other solutions. Full or partial alternative solutions to criminalizing certain behaviour in order to prevent and sanction crime can be both non-legal (e.g. technical or informational) and legal (e.g., administrative or civil law regulation) in nature. It is also the legislator that will have to play a role in exploring the possibilities for a sufficiently flexible legal framework for the prosecution to exercise restraint in the prosecution of offenders and for application of alternative procedures to resolve criminal cases such as restorative justice processes. Furthermore, alternative sentences to imprisonment (non-custodial sentences) must be developed by the legislator, which might also have a role – as does the prison administration – in developing less intrusive forms of deprivation of liberty (e.g., open prisons, electronic surveillance) and restricting avoidable harms of incarceration. Which alternatives to (or options for mitigation of) prosecution and imprisonment are available within the legal framework in a concrete case must primarily be explored by the prosecution, the judiciary and the prison administration.

Requirement of consideration. Finally, the *ultima ratio* principle requires that the use of available alternative or mitigating solutions to criminalization, prosecution and imprisonment are seriously considered first. This applies in general (consideration by the legislator, government, prison administration) as well as in concrete cases (consideration by the prosecution, judiciary, prison administration). Only then will a criminal justice system that offers sufficient flexibility and possibilities to escape overuse actually be able to fully meet the standards of proportionality, necessity and fairness and thus avoid overuse.

LA JUSTICE PÉNALE ET LE PRINCIPE DE L'*ULTIMA RATIO* : EXIGENCE DE LIMITATION, D'EXPLORATION ET DE RÉFLEXION

Piet Hein van Kempen*

I. INTRODUCTION

L'affirmation selon laquelle le recours au système de justice pénale peut s'avérer excessif requiert une approche substantielle plutôt qu'une approche procédurale. Dans une approche procédurale, la question de savoir si le système de justice pénale enfreint ses limites consiste principalement à découvrir si la criminalisation du comportement a été atteinte par une application correcte du processus législatif et si les poursuites et le verdict dans les affaires pénales sont conformes au droit de procédure pénale.[1] Le présent volume et les chapitres qui le composent reposent plutôt sur une approche matérielle du recours excessif au système de justice pénale, plus particulièrement le recours excessif à la criminalisation, aux poursuites pénales et à l'incarcération.

Le recours excessif à la criminalisation (également dénommé surcriminalisation) peut engendrer un élargissement inutile de la responsabilité pénale (le comportement est criminalisé sans nécessité suffisante, les infractions sont définies trop largement, le délai de prescription des infractions est prolongé à l'excès ou une compétence extraterritoriale peu convaincante est invoquée) ou un durcisse-

* Le prof. Dr. (Piet Hein) P.H.P.H.M.C. van Kempen (MLaw, PhD) est Professeur titulaire de droit pénal et de droit de procédure pénale et doyen de la faculté de droit à l'université de Nijmegen, Pays-Bas. Il est également juge *ad litem* à la Cour d'appel de La Haye, Pays-Bas et Secrétaire général de la Fondation internationale pénale et pénitentiaire (IPPF).
Note : la langue originale de ce texte est l'anglais.

1 Cf. Michael S. Moore, 'Liberty's Constraints on What Should be Made Criminal,' in : R.A. Duff, Lindsay Farmer, S.E. Marshall, Massimo Renzo & Victor Tadros, *Criminalization : The Political Morality of the Criminal Law*, Oxford University Press : Oxford, 2014, p. 182-212 at 183.

ment inutile de la responsabilité pénale (la peine maximale et/ou minimale prévue par la loi est excessive). À l'instar de l'extension superflue de la responsabilité pénale, cela pourrait par exemple se manifester lorsque le législateur tend à prévenir ou réprimer certains comportements par leur criminalisation, alors qu'il serait plus efficace ou utile de réprimer ou contrôler totalement ou au moins partiellement ce comportement par l'adoption de mesures préventives opérationnelles ou par l'adoption de mesures de nature administrative ou civile. Elle peut également signifier que le législateur a criminalisé un comportement alors que l'utilité ou la nécessité de cette mesure est discutable ou que la criminalisation peut s'avérer tout simplement inappropriée.

Le recours excessif aux poursuites signifie que le nombre d'infractions criminelles poursuivies est excessivement élevé. Cela peut être particulièrement vrai lorsqu'il serait plus efficace, équitable, efficient ou souhaitable, pour certaines affaires individuelles ou catégories d'affaires spécifiques, de ne pas poursuivre et/ou de réprimer ou de contrôler ce comportement par d'autres moyens que des poursuites, par exemple la négociation, le règlement de l'affaire par d'autres moyens, notamment les possibilités de justice réparatrice ou des amendes administratives. Le recours excessif aux poursuites peut en outre passer par la majoration des sanctions, *c'est-à-dire* lorsque les auteurs d'actes délictueux font l'objet de sanctions applicables sur le plan formel, mais qui ne rendent que peu justice du comportement effectif et de ses conséquences.

Enfin, le recours excessif à l'incarcération peut également se présenter sous diverses formes. L'une d'elles est l'application excessive des peines d'emprisonnement (trop de délinquants sont condamnés à une peine d'emprisonnement), l'autre voit le jour lorsque les tribunaux appliquent des peines d'emprisonnement excessives. Toutes deux pourraient être liées à l'insuffisance de disponibilité légale ou pratique ou à un recours trop modeste aux peines alternatives à l'incarcération, telles que les peines avec sursis, les travaux d'intérêt général ou les amendes. Enfin, l'exécution d'une peine d'emprisonnement dans des conditions inutilement strictes ou dures pourrait être considérée comme une troisième manifestation du recours excessif à l'incarcération. Si les deux premières formes citées ont une nature quantitative, la troisième revêt un caractère plutôt qualitatif.

De manière générale, le recours excessif à la justice pénale traduit l'idée qu'elle est utilisée alors que cela n'est pas nécessaire, efficace, efficient, équitable ou que cela s'avère inapproprié d'une autre façon. Il va de soi que les trois différentes formes de surutilisation (respectivement relatives à la criminalisation, aux poursuites et à l'incarcération) sont interdépendantes. Le recours excessif à la criminalisation peut aisément déboucher sur une utilisation excessive des poursuites qui, à leur tour, résulteront plus que probablement en une sanction excessive.[2] Comme le montrent les différents chapitres qui composent le présent volume, le recours excessif à la criminalisation, aux poursuites et à l'incarcération se manifeste dans de nombreux pays alors qu'il existe des instruments et solutions permettant de prévenir et de résoudre ce problème.

Le présent chapitre (Partie I du présent volume) se penche dans un premier temps sur un principe pouvant servir de base à une approche substantielle de l'utilisation excessive, à savoir le principe de l'*ultima ratio* ou de l'*ultimum remedium* (sections II, III et IV). Il poursuit ensuite le débat sur le recours excessif à la justice pénale en prenant appui sur les résultats des sept chapitres thématiques (voir Partie II du présent volume) et des seize chapitres nationaux (Partie III du présent volume), avant d'aborder plusieurs solutions susceptibles de le réduire (section V). Il se termine par une brève conclusion (section VI).

II. LE PRINCIPE DE L'*ULTIMA RATIO* OU *ULTIMUM REMEDIUM*

Le système de justice pénale est l'instrument le plus sévère dont l'État dispose en temps de paix. Sa nature est principalement coercitive. C'est le cas pour la nature intrusive des pouvoirs d'enquête judiciaire (en ce compris l'arrestation et la détention), mais aussi pour la sévérité des sanctions (notamment l'incarcération), dont l'objectif est de faire respecter les limitations strictes du comportement humain mises en œuvre par la criminalisation. La violation intrinsèque par l'application du droit pénal et de la procédure pénale de la liberté d'un individu et de son cercle social est une caractéristique universelle.[3] L'implication dans une procédure pénale peut en outre avoir d'autres conséquences négatives, par exemple l'exclusion sociale et la stigmatisation du délinquant, la violation de l'intérêt de tierces parties (par exemple la famille ou l'employeur du délinquant) et de manière plus générale et plus extrême, l'érosion de la société libre et de la dignité humaine. Le coût extrêmement élevé pour la société du système de justice pénale, notamment l'exécution des condamnations, peut également s'avérer pertinent

2 Voir également Douglas Husak, *Overcriminalization. The Limits of the Criminal Law*, Oxford : Oxford University Press, 2013, qui argumente que la surcriminalisation est principalement discutable au vu du nombre excessif de condamnations qu'elle génère.

3 Piet Hein van Kempen, 'Introduction – Criminal Law and Human Rights', in : P.H.P.H.M.C. van Kempen (ed.), *Criminal Law and Human Rights, The International Library of Essays on Criminal Law*, England/USA : Ashgate, 2014, p. XI-XXXIII at XI. Cf. Panu Minkkinen, '"If Taken in Earnest" : Criminal Law Doctrine and the Last Resort', 45 *The Howard Journal* 5 (2006), p. 521-536 at 521, qui échoue donc selon nous à comprendre que la caractéristique essentielle et distinctive qui fait du droit pénal ce qu'il est, n'est pas seulement déterminée par la condamnation, mais aussi par la nature des pouvoirs et méthodes d'instruction judiciaire.

pour le principe de l'*ultima ratio*. De plus, la portée excessive du droit pénal et de son application peut ébranler l'efficience et l'efficacité du système dans son ensemble. Enfin, l'idée que le recours au droit pénal et l'application de la procédure pénale doivent être limités découle également de notions légales telles que le principe du moindre mal, le principe de l'illicéité et le principe du juste étiquetage.[4]

Pour ces motifs et d'autres encore, l'un des principes fondamentaux de la justice pénale est que le droit pénal est et doit être considéré comme un *ultima ratio* ou *ultimum remedium*, parfois également dénommé principe de modération.[5] Cela signifie avant toute autre chose qu'un comportement ne doit être criminalisé et que le système de justice pénale ne doit être utilisé qu'en dernier ressort, *c'est-à-dire* quand toutes les autres voies moins coercitives échouent à empêcher ou réprimer suffisamment le comportement préjudiciable.[6] Des mesures préventives opérationnelles et administratives ou des sanctions civiles peuvent par exemple constituer des alternatives moins coercitives à la criminalisation, à l'instruction judiciaire, aux poursuites ou la condamnation, y compris l'incarcération. De plus, le principe de l'*ultima ratio* implique que le comportement répréhensible doit être suffisamment sérieux pour justifier son intégration dans le périmètre du système de justice pénale.[7] Il reconnaît que le système de justice pénale doit (principalement) et peut (dans la pratique) uniquement apporter une protection partielle.[8] Ce principe est important pour déterminer à la fois la portée du droit pénal matériel (pertinente pour le législateur) et, en cas de comportement criminel, les

4 À propos de l'étiquetage, voir James Chalmers & Fiona Leverick, 'Fair Labelling in Criminal Law', 71 *The Modern Law Review* 2 (2008), p. 217-246.

5 Voir le chapitre de Morinaga consacré au Japon.

6 Voir P.H.P.H.M.C. van Kempen, 'Four Concepts of Security – A Human Rights Perspective', 13 *Human Rights Law Review* 1 (2013), p. 1-23 at 19, avec des références à : Michael G. Faure & Marjolein Visser, 'Law and economics of environmental crime', in : Hans Sjögren & Göran Skogh (eds.), *New Perspectives on Economic Crime*, Cheltenham, UK/Northampton, USA : Edward Elgar Publishing 2004, p. 57-75 at 68 ; Andrew Ashworth & Jeremy Horder, *Principles of Criminal Law*, Oxford : Oxford University Press, 2013, p. 33, 52. Voir également Nils Jareborg, Criminalization as Last Resort (Ultima Ratio), 2 *Ohio State Journal of Criminal Law* (2005), p. 521-534. Pour ce qui est de la reconnaissance de ce principe dans le droit européen, voir Sakari Melander, 'Ultima Ratio in European Criminal Law', 3 *Oñati Socio-legal Series* 1 (2013), p. 42-61.

7 Cf. résolution du Parlement européen du 22 mai 2012 sur une approche de l'UE en matière de droit pénal (2010/2310(INI)), *Journal officiel de l'Union européenne* C 264 E/7, para I : « le droit pénal doit être appliqué en dernier ressort (*ultima ratio*) à des actes clairement définis et délimités, auxquels des mesures moins strictes ne peuvent être appliquées efficacement, et qui causent un préjudice important à la société et aux individus ». Voir également Fernando Molina, 'A Comparison Between Continental European and Anglo-American Approaches to Overcriminalization and Some Remarks on How to Deal with It', 14 *New Criminal Law Review* 1 (2011), p. 123-138 at 135.

8 Voir en outre Nils Jareborg, Criminalization as Last Resort (Ultima Ratio), 2 *Ohio State Journal of Criminal Law* (2005), p. 521-534 at 525-526. Voir également Lucia Zedner, 'Too much security?', 31 *International Journal of the Sociology of Law* (2003), p. 155-184.

limites de l'applicabilité et de l'application tant de la procédure pénale (pertinente pour le législateur, la police, l'accusation et les tribunaux), que de l'emprisonnement (pertinent pour l'accusation, les tribunaux et les autorités responsables de l'exécution des peines).

À ce stade, il est important de souligner que le principe de l'*ultima ratio* est (intrinsèquement) purement et simplement ce qu'il dit être : un principe, pas une règle. Comme l'a affirmé Dworkin, les principes impliquent la nécessité d'une dimension de moralité. Leur contenu est plutôt mouvant et flou, à l'instar de leur contenu et de leur portée, et ils présentent une structure ouverte. Les principes indiquent une direction et ajoutent un poids argumentatif aux considérations qu'il convient de prendre en compte plutôt que d'imposer des limites absolues ou exactes à une issue particulière.[9] Il en va de même pour le principe de l'*ultima ratio*. Ce dernier n'indique pas quels comportements sont susceptibles d'être criminalisés ni quand les poursuites ou l'incarcération sont acceptables, il incite le législateur et les autorités du système de justice pénale à la prudence et à ne pas abuser du système. Le principe est en outre une règle morale qui ne revêt pas en tant que telle un caractère contraignant pour les autorités. En ce sens, le principe n'a qu'un pouvoir limité.[10] La moralité du principe se trouve par exemple dans la présomption selon laquelle la modération appliquée à la création et à l'application du droit pénal est indispensable, car le recours à un système de justice pénale est, dans le meilleur des cas, un mal nécessaire qui doit être conservé et appliqué pour réprimer d'autres maux plus graves et pour protéger cette liberté contre des intrusions plus grandes encore. Si le système de justice pénale n'est pas une nécessité ou n'est pas proportionné pour atteindre ces objectifs de protection, l'intrusion générée par le système est uniquement un mal et, en ce sens, une immoralité. Et inversement : dans ce cas, le fondement moral à l'application du système de justice pénale est insuffisant.

Dans la lignée de ce qui précède, dans son chapitre, Díez-Ripollés présente et applique l'objectif de la modération punitive (ainsi que l'objectif de l'inclusion sociale) comme un cadre analytique destiné à mener une description et une évaluation de politique comparative des systèmes nationaux de justice pénale. Il fait remarquer que ces systèmes doivent veiller à ne pas infliger une souffrance sociale

---

9 Ces qualifications sont dérivées de l'explication – désormais classique – de la distinction entre les principes et les règles de Ronald M. Dworkin, 'The Model of Rules', 35 *The University of Chicago Law Review* 14 (1967), p. 14-46 at 22-29. Si à notre avis, cette distinction ne peut être aussi catégorique que ce que Dworkin laisse entendre, ces qualifications n'en demeurent pas moins amplement valables et utiles.

10 Voir Douglas Husak, 'Applying Ultima Ratio : A Skeptical Assessment', 2 *Ohio State Journal of Criminal Law* (2005), p. 535-545 at 536-540. Cf. Panu Minkkinen, 2013. 'The "Last Resort" : A Moral and/or Legal Principle?', 3 Oñati Socio-legal Series 1 (2013), p. 21-30 at 28, qui revendique que l'« ultima ratio » ou « dernier ressort », comme il le qualifie, est « un principe politico-moral qui revêt une signification constitutionnelle » ou ce que nous dénommerions « un principe de constitutionnaliste ».

plus grande encore que ce qui est strictement nécessaire, que la criminalisation ne doit pas excéder ce qui pourrait être considéré comme étant vital pour protéger les intérêts publics essentiels et que ceux qui sont confrontés à des organes d'application du droit pénal, qu'ils soient suspects ou condamnés, ne subissent qu'un désagrément modéré et proportionnel au regard de leur comportement.

En l'absence de fondement moral suffisant à l'application du système de justice pénale, cela peut avoir de graves conséquences. Comme l'affirme Rotman dans son chapitre sur les États-Unis : la surcriminalisation crée *in fine* un climat d'injustice qui mine non seulement la foi dans l'État de droit, mais s'avère criminogène par la perte de légitimité du système de justice pénale aux yeux des délinquants potentiels, justifiant de ce fait leurs comportements répréhensibles.

III. SOUTIEN DU DROIT LÉGALEMENT CONTRAIGNANT EN FAVEUR DES QUATRE ASPECTS DU PRINCIPE DE L'*ULTIMA RATIO*

Bien que le principe de l'*ultima ratio* ou de l'*ultimum remedium* ne soit pas intrinsèquement légalement contraignant, il puise de solides racines à la fois dans le droit positif national et international, lesquels sont effectivement contraignants. Plusieurs principes du droit positif sont pertinents à cet égard. L'aperçu ci-après – non exhaustif – repose sur les divers aspects du principe de l'*ultima ratio*.

Les deux premiers concernent le droit pénal substantif et se rapportent à la criminalisation du comportement. L'axiome le plus connu du principe de l'*ultima ratio* est que la criminalisation du comportement ne doit intervenir qu'en dernier ressort. Le principe de nécessité ou de subsidiarité est le plus pertinent en la matière. Selon ce principe, une mesure ne peut être appliquée que si l'objectif pour lequel elle est appliquée ne peut être atteint par des moyens moins intrusifs. Formulé de façon positive : s'il est nécessaire d'appliquer des mesures restrictives, parmi ces dernières l'instrument le moins intrusif permettant d'atteindre l'objectif doit être appliqué. Lorsque la criminalisation du comportement interfère avec les droits de l'homme, par exemple les droits au respect de la vie privée et à la protection des droits de propriété ainsi que la liberté d'expression, de religion, de réunion, d'association et de mouvement, cette interférence ne peut se justifier que si elle est nécessaire pour atteindre le résultat recherché. Comme il apparaît au vu de la jurisprudence, par exemple de la Cour européenne des droits de l'homme (CEDH)[11] et du Comité des droits de l'homme (CEDH), cela signifie également que les criminalisations dont la portée est supérieure à ce qui est nécessaire pour atteindre cet objectif, peuvent dans cette mesure être décrétées contraires au prin-

11 Pour la jurisprudence de la CEDH, voir le chapitre rédigé par Pinto de Albuquerque.

cipe de nécessité.[12] De manière plus générale, et par conséquent autrement qu'en relation avec les interférences avec les droits de l'homme, la Cour de justice de l'Union européenne (CJUE) a affirmé que « lorsqu'un choix s'offre entre plusieurs mesures appropriées, il convient de recourir à la moins contraignante, et que les inconvénients causés ne doivent pas être démesurés par rapport aux buts visés. »[13] De plus, le principe de nécessité est reconnu par de nombreuses juridictions nationales comme un principe constitutionnel, qui s'applique alors habituellement en cas d'interférences avec les droits constitutionnels.[14] La Cour constitutionnelle allemande (Bundesverfassingsgericht, BVerfGE) va jusqu'à reconnaître le principe de « l'ultima ratio » en tant que tel dans sa jurisprudence constante en affirmant : « le droit pénal n'est effectivement pas le premier moyen de protection légale, fût-ce en vertu de son caractère interventionniste ; son application est par conséquent subordonnée à des exigences de proportionnalité [...]. Il est cependant utilisé en tant qu'« *ultima ratio* » de cette protection lorsque certains comportements, hors de portée de sa prohibition, sont à ce point socialement dommageables et intolérables pour la coexistence harmonieuse des êtres humains, que leur prévention est particulièrement urgente. »[15]

La dernière partie de cette citation apporte un fondement positif du droit à un second aspect du principe de l'*ultima ratio*, c'est-à-dire que le comportement préjudiciable doit être suffisamment grave pour justifier sa criminalisation. Cet axiome est lui aussi soutenu par les droits de l'homme internationaux. Il en va notamment ainsi dans le principe de la proportionnalité *stricto sensu* en vertu duquel la violation du droit doit être proportionnelle à l'objectif visé et dans l'exi-

---

12 Voir *par exemple* CEDH 22 octobre 1981, *Dudgeon/Royaume-Uni*, no. 7525/76, paragraphes 42-62 (particulièrement 62) ; HCR, Observation générale N° 27 : Liberté de circulation (article 12), *UN doc.* CCPR/C/21/Rev.1/Add.9, 1er novembre 1999, paragraphe 14 : « [...] il ne suffit pas que les restrictions servent les buts autorisés ; celles-ci doivent être également nécessaires pour protéger ces buts. Les mesures restrictives doivent constituer [...] le moyen le moins perturbateur parmi ceux qui pourraient permettre d'obtenir le résultat recherché ».

13 Voir Sakari Melander, 'Ultima Ratio in European Criminal Law', 3 *Oñati Socio-legal Series* 1 (2013), p. 42-61 at 55, contenant des références à plusieurs affaires, notamment CJUE 13 novembre 1990, *La Reine/Ministre de l'Agriculture, des Pêches et de l'Alimentation et ministre de la Santé, ex parte : Fedesa et autres*, Affaire C-331/88, par. 13. Plus récemment et dans une affaire pénale, voir CJUE 20 mars 2018, *Luca Menci/Procura della Repubblica*, Affaire C-524/15, par. 46.

14 Voir, par exemple, Kaarlo Tuori, 'Ultima Ratio as a Constitutional Principle', 3 *Oñati Socio-legal Series* 1 (2013), p. 6-20 at 9-12.

15 Voir BVerfGE 28 mai 1993, *Schwangerschaftsabbruch II*, no. 88, 203 at 258 ; BVerfGE 26 février 2008, *Geschwisterbeischlaf*, n° 120, 224 at 240. Voir à ce sujet la jurisprudence Klaus Gärditz, 'Demokratizität des Strafrechts und Ultima Ratio-Grundsatz', 71 *JuristenZeitung* 13 juillet 2016, p. 641-650 at 642-643 ; Rudolf Wendt, 'The Principle of "Ultima Ratio" and/or the Principle of Proportionality, 3 *Oñati Socio-legal Series* 1 (2013), p. 81-94.

gence de légitimité de cet objectif.[16] Tout particulièrement lorsque la criminalisation du comportement interfère gravement avec des droits de l'homme – par exemple parce qu'il implique « un aspect extrêmement intime de la vie privée » – des « motifs particulièrement graves » doivent exister « pour que des interférences de la part des autorités publiques puissent être légitimées ».[17] Cette position est également confirmée par l'Article 52(1) de la Charte des droits fondamentaux de l'UE, stipulant que les limitations de l'exercice des droits et libertés reconnues par cette Charte « ne peuvent être apportées que si elles sont nécessaires et répondent effectivement à des objectifs d'intérêt général reconnus par l'Union ou au besoin de protection des droits et libertés d'autrui ». Le principe de la culpabilité, de la faute ou du *mens rea*, est également pertinent en l'occurrence, à savoir le principe suivant lequel une personne ne peut être considérée comme pénalement responsable que des actes ou omissions susceptibles de lui être reprochés. Le législateur doit de ce fait en outre être attentif à ne pas créer de responsabilité pénale dans des situations où l'on ne peut raisonnablement et équitablement attendre d'une personne qu'elle agisse légalement.[18] Le principe de la culpabilité est largement (mais pas universellement) reconnu dans le droit national positif, mais aussi explicitement dans la jurisprudence, et il peut également être déduit du système de droit pénal. Le principe peut par ailleurs – dans une moindre mesure – trouver un certain fondement dans la présomption d'innocence contenue dans les droits de l'homme internationaux.[19]

Les deux autres aspects du principe de l'*ultima ratio* concernent la politique en matière de procédure pénale et l'utilisation de cette dernière dans des cas individuels, notamment la fixation de la peine. Dans ce cas, l'axiome le plus important est que le système de justice pénale – ou plus spécifiquement par exemple l'enquête judiciaire, les poursuites ou la condamnation – doit être appliqué en dernier recours uniquement. Cet axiome trouve sa justification dans le droit positif, par le principe susmentionné de nécessité ou de subsidiarité, également pertinent pour l'utilisation des pouvoirs procéduraux. Dans la mesure où bon nombre de pouvoirs d'investigation interfèrent par exemple avec le respect de la vie privée

---

16 Voir par exemple à nouveau CEDH 22 octobre 1981, *Dudgeon/Royaume-Uni*, no. 7525/76, paragraphe 42-62 ; HCR, Observation générale N° 27 : Liberté de circulation (Article 12), *UN doc.* CCPR/C/21/Rev.1/Add.9, 1er novembre 1999, paragraphe 14 : Cf. Rudolf Wendt, 'The principle of "ultima ratio" and/or the principle of proportionality'. 3 *Oñati Socio-Legal Series* 1 (2013), p. 81-94 at 86.

17 Concernant le droit au respect de la vie privée, voir CEDH 22 octobre 1981, *Dudgeon/Royaume-Uni*, n° 7525/76, paragraphe 52. Voir également le chapitre d'Ortenzi & García Basalo sur l'Argentine, dans lequel ils abordent CSJN, Jugement du 25 août 2009, *Arriola, Sebastián et al.*, Affaire N° 9080, concernant la possession de drogues à usage personnel dans la sphère privée.

18 Voir par exemple, Mordechai Kremnitzer & Tatjana Hörnle, 'Human Dignity and the Principle of Culpability', 44 *Israel Law Review* 1-2 (2011), p.115-141 ; Andrew Ashworth & Jeremy Horder, *Principles of Criminal Law*, Oxford : Oxford University Press, 2013, p. 74-75.

19 Voir par exemple, Stefan Trechsel, *Human Rights in Criminal Proceedings*, Oxford : Oxford University Press, 2005, p. 157-158 et 171.

(notamment les perquisitions, la surveillance, la collecte d'empreintes digitales ou d'ADN) ou la liberté (notamment l'arrestation et la détention), l'exécution de ces pouvoirs doit s'inscrire dans la lignée du principe de nécessité tel que requis par les droits de l'homme au respect de la vie privée et de la liberté (le droit à la protection contre les arrestations et les privations de liberté arbitraires).[20] Voir également l'Article 52(1) de la Charte des droits fondamentaux de l'UE mentionnée ci-avant. La règle selon laquelle les pouvoirs procéduraux ne peuvent être appliqués que lorsque cela s'avère nécessaire découle habituellement aussi de la procédure pénale nationale. Qui plus est, une mesure de procédure pénale ne peut en aucun cas être nécessaire si elle est inefficace. Le principe de légalité fait en outre par exemple office de garantie contre le recours déraisonnable aux pouvoirs de procédure pénale. Selon la Cour européenne des droits de l'homme, ce principe est un élément essentiel de l'État de droit et « ainsi qu'il découle de son objet et de son but, il doit être interprété et appliqué de manière à assurer une protection effective contre les poursuites, les condamnations et les sanctions arbitraires ».[21]

Le quatrième aspect du principe de l'*ultima ratio* est que le recours aux pouvoirs de procédure pénale ne peut se justifier que si le comportement préjudiciable que l'on cherche à réprimer est suffisamment grave ou s'il existe à tout le moins de bonnes raisons de recourir à ces pouvoirs. Quand le recours aux pouvoirs d'investigation pénale interfère avec des droits fondamentaux tels que le droit au respect de la vie privée et le droit à la liberté, cette utilisation doit être proportionnelle à l'objectif visé et elle doit servir un but légitime. Le droit positif soutient plus généralement une restriction des possibilités de poursuite au motif que le comportement préjudiciable n'est pas suffisamment grave. Par exemple, la CEDH affirme que « l'appréciation de l'adéquation de poursuites pénales n'entre pas dans son pouvoir de contrôle ».[22] Le fait que des poursuites ne peuvent être disproportionnées au regard de la gravité du délit ne semble pas être un principe universellement accepté, bien qu'il soit reconnu dans certains domaines du droit de diverses juridictions nationales.[23] Il n'en va pas de même pour ce qui est des condamnations. L'Article 49(3) de la Charte des droits fondamentaux de l'UE stipule par exemple : « L'intensité des peines ne doit pas être disproportionnée par rapport à l'infraction. » Pour ce qui est de la jurisprudence de la CEDH, le cha-

20 Voir par exemple, CEDH (GC) 4 décembre 2008, *S. et Marper*/Royaume-Uni, n° 30562/04, paragraphe 101-126 (vie privée), et CEDH (GC) 5 juillet 2016, *Buzadji/Moldova*, n° 23755/07, paragraphe 115-123 (liberté) ; à propos the PIDCP, contenant d'autres références, voir S. Joseph & M. Castan, *The International Covenant on Civil and Political Rights, Cases, Materials and Commentary*, Oxford : Oxford University Press, 2013, paragraphe 16.10-16.12 (vie privée) et 11.15-11.17 (liberté).

21 Voir par exemple CEDH 4 octobre 2016, *Žaja/Croatie*, n° 37462/09, paraphe 90-106.

22 CEDH 6 novembre 2007, *Patsuria/Géorgie*, n° 30779/04, paragraphes 42 et 85.

23 Voir par exemple, Prosecution guidance on minor offences, United Kingdom, at : https :// www.cps.gov.uk/legal-guidance/minor-offences (dernière visite : 15 décembre 2018), ou l'Article 7(2)(c) de la loi sur la protection internationale de 2015, Irlande.

pitre de Pinto de Albuquerque montre bien comment la Cour de Strasbourg a adopté une approche fondée sur la proportionnalité des peines d'emprisonnement par l'évaluation de la nécessité de son application – ou de sa durée – à l'infraction commise au regard des circonstances de l'affaire.[24]

IV. INTÉRÊTS NÉCESSITANT UN RECOURS RAISONNABLE PLUTÔT QU'ABSOLU AU PRINCIPE DE L'*ULTIMA RATIO*

Bien que le principe de l'*ultima ratio* vise à limiter la criminalisation du comportement et le recours à la procédure pénale, il ne s'oppose pas de manière générale au système de justice pénale. L'*ultima ratio* ne peut et ne doit pas être assimilé à l'abolitionnisme. Ce principe ne manque pas d'apprécier la valeur du système de justice pénale. Toutefois, même dans ces circonstances, force est de constater que le principe de l'*ultima ratio* n'est pas sans poser des problèmes.

La première limite du principe est que sa justification réside avant tout dans les effets néfastes du système de justice pénale pour les défendeurs et les condamnés plutôt que dans la valeur de ce système en matière de contrôle de la criminalité et de protection de la société. Cependant, alors que le recours excessif à la criminalisation, aux poursuites et à l'incarcération a de nombreux effets négatifs sur la société et les individus, il peut en aller de même pour une sous-utilisation des systèmes de justice pénale. Comme le souligne Rotman dans le chapitre qu'il consacre aux USA, la sous-utilisation du système pose problème en termes d'équité, il stimule le ressentiment et le manque de respect à l'égard de la loi et peut avoir un effet corrosif sur le tissu de la démocratie et de l'égalité. De plus, comme le soulignent De Valkeneer, Dizier & Seron dans leur chapitre consacré à la Belgique, la recherche en criminologie tend à démontrer que ce n'est pas tant la sévérité des peines qui génère un effet dissuasif que la certitude d'être sanctionné. Par conséquent, suivant le point de vue de la prévention de la criminalité, une limitation excessive des poursuites peut affaiblir l'effet préventif du système de justice pénale.

Une autre difficulté liée au principe de l'*ultima ratio* réside dans l'exigence que le comportement ne peut être criminalisé et le système de justice pénale appliqué qu'en dernier ressort : il en résulte une mise en exergue de la partie instrumentale de la justice pénale (le contrôle de la criminalité) et de ses effets néfastes plutôt que de la valeur de protection du système (procédure équitable). Bien que les procédures de droit administratif et civil soient en bien des façons

24 Voir également le chapitre sur la Finlande par Lappi-Seppälä, qui évoque le choix de la sanction en fonction du « modèle d'échelle », suivant le principe qui considère l'incarcération comme un dernier ressort.

moins intrusives que le droit pénal, leur capacité à protéger l'équité et l'honnêteté est généralement moins bien développée que celle de la procédure pénale. Par conséquent, le jugement de certaines affaires par des procédures administratives ou civiles plutôt que par la justice pénale n'est pas forcément bénéfique pour les personnes concernées (cf. le chapitre sur le Japon, dans lequel Morinaga explique les problèmes historiques liés à l'application du droit administratif dans ce pays). Le principe de l'*ultima ratio* peut par conséquent inciter au recours à une procédure pénale ou civile, alors même que dans certaines situations, une procédure pénale sera préférable du point de vue de la protection légale. Ces éléments doivent être pris en compte dans toute discussion sur la décriminalisation et le déplacement de l'application des règles légales du système de justice pénale vers un droit de procédure administrative ou civile.

V. SÉLECTION DE RÉSULTATS TIRÉS DES CHAPITRES DE CE VOLUME

Comme indiqué dans l'introduction du présent chapitre, la Partie II de ce volume présente une approche thématique du recours excessif au système de justice pénale. La Partie III contient ensuite les chapitres nationaux. Ces derniers s'appuient sur un questionnaire concernant le recours excessif au système de justice pénale auquel des experts de 16 pays d'Afrique, d'Amérique (du Nord et du Sud), d'Asie, d'Europe et d'Océanie ont répondu en 2016, 2017 et 2018. Les États dont il est ici question sont l'Argentine, la Belgique, la Finlande, l'Allemagne, la Grèce, l'Irlande, le Japon, les Pays-Bas, la Nouvelle-Zélande, le Nigeria, la Pologne, la Russie, l'Espagne, la Suisse, Taïwan et les États-Unis d'Amérique (USA). Chaque chapitre national suit une structure similaire, divisée en sections distinctes sur le recours excessif à la criminalisation, aux poursuites et à l'incarcération. Vous trouverez ci-après une synthèse des résultats des chapitres pertinents pour le principe de l'*ultima ratio*.

V.1. GÉNÉRALITÉS

Si le principe selon lequel le droit pénal est et doit être considéré comme un *ultima ratio* ou *ultimum remedium* peut apporter une orientation générale lorsqu'il convient de décider du contenu et de l'ampleur du droit pénal et de son application dans des cas concrets, il n'offre pas de critères substantiels d'analyse et d'évaluation de la criminalisation, des poursuites et des condamnations à la prison. Il est dès lors extrêmement intéressant que Díez-Ripollés présente dans son chapitre un cadre conceptuel plus détaillé d'évaluation des systèmes nationaux de justice pénale. Ce cadre reconnaît la modération punitive et l'inclusion sociale comme étant les deux principaux objectifs de la comparaison et de l'évaluation des systèmes de justice pénale. Díez-Ripollés explique non seulement la signification et le contenu de sa proposition évaluative et les hypothèses sur lesquelles elle repose, il l'applique aussi immédiatement aux trois moments décisifs de l'intervention pénale : la criminalisation, les poursuites et l'application des peines de prison. Plusieurs règles et pratiques sont évoquées dans ce chapitre pour chacun de ces moments.

Une approche tout aussi générale, bien que légale plutôt que théorique, est proposée dans le chapitre de Pinto de Albuquerque. Il évoque la jurisprudence de la Cour européenne des droits de l'homme pertinente dans le cas du recours excessif à la justice pénale, notamment concernant le recours excessif à la criminalisation (avec une attention spécifique à la diffamation et à la crimmigration) et à l'incarcération (avec une attention spécifique au recours abusif à la détention préventive et à la détention provisoire). Pinto de Albuquerque conclut notamment que la CEDH a adopté une approche duale dans le contexte du recours excessif à la justice pénale : dans certains cas, elle contrôle l'application excessive du droit et des sanctions pénales au regard de certains comportements spécifiques, tandis que dans d'autres cas, elle critique les États pour avoir appliqué une sentence clémente envers un délinquant (jurisprudence des obligations positives).

Il va sans dire que la meilleure façon de prévenir le recours à la criminalisation, aux poursuites et à l'incarcération consiste à lutter contre les causes fondamentales du comportement fautif et veiller de la sorte à ce que l'application du système de justice pénale devienne inutile. Il est intéressant de noter que dans son chapitre, Agomoh explique en détail en quoi l'environnement et la circulation (deux aspects connexes de la gestion sociétale) constituent un défi énorme pour le système de justice pénale du Nigeria et un casse-tête pour les décideurs politiques. De plus, comme le soulignent Kuhn & Solcà dans leur chapitre consacré à la Suisse, la nécessité de criminaliser peut aussi parfois être évitée par l'application de solutions techniques nécessitant cependant un peu de courage politique.

V.2. RECOURS EXCESSIF À LA CRIMINALISATION

Dans son chapitre thématique, Guzmán Dalbora met l'accent sur le recours excessif à la criminalisation en associant philosophie, sciences politiques, criminologie et droit. Il souligne comment la criminalisation croissante met à mal la théorie du droit, menace l'organisation libérale de la société et de la démocratie et met en cause le pouvoir légal du gouvernement. Guzmán Dalbora évoque plusieurs tendances punitives, particulièrement en Amérique latine, et il propose une appréciation critique de la façon dont l'idéologie, la conviction morale et l'élitisme influencent la politique et les pratiques pénales.

Lorsqu'une juridiction est confrontée à un recours excessif à la criminalisation, plusieurs solutions se présentent. Dans le chapitre qu'elle consacre à l'Espagne, García Magna aborde trois méthodes possibles pour réduire la pression punitive : la légalisation, la décriminalisation et la permissivité ou tolérance basée sur la politique. Dans leur chapitre sur l'Allemagne, Haverkamp, Cirener, Boetticher & Feest envisagent la réflexion sur l'« *ultima ratio* » du droit pénal comme étant le meilleur point de départ pour mettre un frein à la punissabilité sans cesse croissante du comportement socialement indésirable, mais ne méritant pas obligatoirement en soi une sanction. Une autre étape, sur laquelle Kuhn & Solcà attirent l'attention dans leur chapitre consacré à la Suisse, consisterait à abolir purement et simplement le droit pénal, que l'on dénomme également abolitionnisme. Dans le même temps, en se basant sur l'expérience de Taïwan, Ronggeng Li conclut que plus la probabilité qu'une infraction porte atteinte à autrui ou à la société dans son ensemble est faible, plus il est probable qu'elle soit décriminalisée.

Les chapitres nationaux présentent de nombreux exemples d'évolution vers un renforcement de la criminalisation et quelques tendances à la décriminalisation. Voir par exemple l'évolution vers l'assouplissement de la criminalisation de la possession de drogues à usage personnel dans les chapitres consacrés à l'Argentine, la Belgique, l'Allemagne, l'Irlande, la Pologne, l'Espagne et Taïwan, alors que la répression des délits en matière de drogue demeure sans conteste aussi stricte, voire renforcée, en Finlande, au Japon et en Russie par exemple. La criminalisation des délits sexuels s'est en outre intensifiée, par exemple en Finlande, aux Pays-Bas et à Taïwan. Dans le même temps, l'Irlande mène actuellement un débat sur la dépénalisation, la légalisation et la politique en matière de prostitution. De même, certains pays enregistrent un mouvement en faveur de la dépénalisation de l'avortement (par exemple : l'Espagne, l'Irlande[25], Taïwan) ou de l'euthanasie (Espagne ; voir également le chapitre sur les Pays-Bas). La dépénalisation du blasphème est à l'examen en Irlande et elle a récemment été adoptée aux Pays-Bas, tandis que le chapitre à propos de la Russie montre clairement que l'évolution dans cette juridiction prend la voie inverse, comme l'illustre la criminalisation renforcée de « l'offense aux sentiments des croyants » (art. 148 du Code pénal, modifié en 2013), ainsi que la poursuite et la condamnation du groupe de musique punk « Pussy Riot » pour « hooliganisme motivé par la haine religieuse » (art. 213.2 CP). Le chapitre sur la Russie rédigé par Gilinskiy souligne que les exemples de ce type pourraient avoir été beaucoup plus nombreux au cours des dernières années. D'autres domaines ont fait l'objet d'une criminalisation accrue, par exemple le terrorisme (cf. les Pays-Bas), la migration (crimmigration, cf. l'Allemagne, et le chapitre de Pinto de Albuquerque), la criminalité en col blanc (cf. les USA) et la cybercriminalité ou les infractions qui ont vu le jour dans la

---

25 Le 13 décembre 2018, le *Seanad* (la Chambre haute du parlement, l'*Oireachtas*) suivi par le *Dáil* (la Chambre basse) a adopté la Loi sur la santé *(Réglementation sur l'interruption de grossesse) 2018*, à la suite de quoi l'avortement est désormais admise en Irlande à compter du 1er janvier 2019.

foulée de l'émergence des nouvelles technologies (cf. le Japon, les Pays-Bas, la Suisse).

Plus généralement, plusieurs juridictions connaissent une tendance à la criminalisation et à la répression, même si l'intensité de cette évolution peut présenter des différences particulièrement marquées d'un État à l'autre (voir par exemple les chapitres consacrés aux Pays-Bas, à la Russie et à l'Espagne). Cela se traduit souvent par l'introduction de nouvelles infractions ou l'élargissement des délits déjà définis, mais l'augmentation de la peine maximale applicable à un délit (cf. par exemple les Pays-Bas) est une autre forme de renforcement de la criminalisation. Il est intéressant de constater que certains chapitres mettent en avant les obligations de criminalisation de certaines actions ou omissions en vertu du droit international (y compris le droit régional, par exemple le droit de l'Union européenne) comme levier du recours au droit pénal. Voir par exemple à ce sujet les chapitres consacrés à l'Allemagne, à la Grèce, au Japon, aux Pays-Bas et à la Pologne. Dans le même temps, il convient de noter que le renforcement de la criminalisation n'est pas seulement la résultante de nouveaux délits ou de l'élargissement des définitions de certains délits existants. Dans certaines juridictions, la criminalisation est étendue par l'extension dans le temps de la possibilité de poursuivre (délai de prescription) (cf. par exemple les chapitres sur les Pays-Bas et la Suisse).

Un droit pénal peu étendu (absence de recours excessif à la criminalisation) n'empêche pas l'utilisation abusive des instruments de procédure pénale. Ortenzi & García Basalo (chapitre consacré à l'Argentine) affirment que ses causes « sont liées aux dispositions des codes de procédure et à l'inadéquation administrative du pouvoir judiciaire ». Plusieurs chapitres affirment par exemple que le recours à la détention préventive devient de plus en plus problématique ; voir par exemple les chapitres sur l'Argentine, la Grèce, les Pays-Bas et le Nigeria (très détaillés), ainsi que le chapitre statistique de Lappi-Seppälä.[26] Voir en outre le chapitre sur les Pays-Bas, dans lequel Mevis affirme que les possibilités croissantes d'investigation criminelle et la codification des possibilités d'interférer avec les droits et libertés fondamentaux des citoyens mènent à une situation que l'on peut qualifier de « recours excessif ». Les exemples présentés par Mevis sont l'affaiblissement du secret professionnel des médecins, avocats et autres, ainsi que l'affaiblissement de la règle d'exclusion des preuves obtenues illégalement.

26 Voir également les chapitres consacrés à vingt et un pays dans le monde dans P.H.P.H.M.C. van Kempen (ed.), *Pre-trial detention. Human rights, criminal procedural law and penitentiary law, comparative law / Détention avant jugement. Droits de l'homme, droit de la procédure pénale et droit pénitentiaire, droit comparé*, Cambridge/Antwerp/Portland : Intersentia 2012.

V.3. RECOURS EXCESSIF AUX POURSUITES

Le principe d'opportunité, qui laisse à la discrétion des procureurs de décider de poursuivre ou non un délinquant et, dans l'affirmative, pour quel chef d'inculpation, peut s'avérer utile pour prévenir ou résoudre le recours excessif aux poursuites. Ce principe s'applique sous une forme ou une autre en Argentine, en Belgique, en Irlande, au Japon (qui a abandonné le principe de la légalité des poursuites), aux Pays-Bas (très étendue), en Nouvelle-Zélande, au Nigeria, en Russie[27] et aux USA. Le principe opposé, c'est-à-dire le principe de la légalité concernant la poursuite des délits est par exemple appliqué en Finlande, en Allemagne, en Grèce, en Pologne, en Espagne, en Suisse et à Taïwan. Selon ce principe, le ministère public est tenu de poursuivre des accusations s'il existe une présomption et des preuves suffisantes pour une condamnation. Par conséquent (c'est ce qu'affirme le chapitre consacré à la Suisse), un système dominé par le principe de la légalité produira généralement un grand nombre de condamnés coupables de délits de faible gravité, puisque toute enquête doit être poursuivie jusqu'à la condamnation dès lors que des indices permettent de reconnaître la culpabilité de l'accusé. Bon nombre de pays appliquant ce principe reconnaissent toutefois une série d'exceptions et de motifs d'opportunité et d'abandon des poursuites (voir les chapitres sur les pays qui appliquent ce principe de légalité). Ils permettent de prévenir l'utilisation excessive. Kuhn & Solcà (chapitre sur la Suisse) plaident de ce fait, à l'instar de Rong-geng Li (Taïwan), en faveur d'une multiplication des exceptions au principe de légalité. Dans le même temps, quand bien même le principe d'opportunité est appliqué par un pays, cela ne garantit pas l'absence de recours excessif. Par exemple, comme l'illustre le chapitre consacré au Nigeria, l'absence de directives visant à aider le ministère public dans sa décision de poursuivre ou non et dans l'application de la sanction adéquate peut déboucher sur un recours excessif ou insuffisant aux poursuites. De plus, la perte d'indépendance *de facto* du ministère public et l'adoption par ce dernier de politiques relatives à l'exécution des peines et des mesures préventives peuvent également s'avérer problématiques en la matière. Haverkamp, Cirener, Boetticher & Feest estiment qu'il s'agit d'une évolution préoccupante en Allemagne. Ce qui précède illustre en quoi les effets exacts du principe d'opportunité et du principe de légalité dépendent en grande partie des conditions spécifiques dans lesquelles ils sont appliqués. Dans la pratique, il n'existe sans doute pas de différence significative entre un système basé sur le principe de la légalité, qui reconnaît un ensemble détaillé d'exemptions, et un système basé sur le principe de l'opportunité orienté par des directives précises indiquant quand des poursuites sont requises et quand elles ne le sont pas.

27 Voir article 221 du Code de procédure pénale russe.

La déjudiciarisation, qui permet d'éviter la condamnation, est possible dans de nombreuses autres juridictions. Le taux de poursuite relativement faible que connaît le Japon peut refléter le programme de « déjudiciarisation » relativement poussé. Toutefois, en Nouvelle-Zélande par exemple d'aucuns se préoccupent que la déjudiciarisation ait un effet d'élargissement, de sorte que des poursuites sont menées alors qu'elles ne l'auraient pas été en l'absence d'application de ce régime. Dans le même temps, l'Irlande met de plus en plus l'accent sur les solutions alternatives aux poursuites. Le régime dénommé « Adult Caution Scheme » instauré dans ce pays peut être appliqué au titre d'alternative.

Il existe divers systèmes de procédures sommaires. Voir par exemple les chapitres consacrés à l'Argentine, la Finlande (amendes), l'Irlande, le Japon, les Pays-Bas (peine communautaire) et Taïwan. Il en va de même pour la justice négociée, voir par exemple les chapitres sur la Belgique et la Nouvelle-Zélande. Veuillez consulter notamment le chapitre de Ligeti & Robinson, qui aborde en détail la justice « négociée » — par opposition à la justice traditionnelle, imposée — comme un mode de traitement de la surcharge de dossiers. Les deux auteurs argumentent que la minimisation, le déplacement ou la suppression totale de l'étape du procès complet, qui est typique des mécanismes de justice négociée (par exemple les règlements à l'amiable, les ordonnances pénales, les plaidoyers de culpabilité et les accords de poursuites différées), soulèvent de sérieuses questions quant à la qualité de la justice ainsi rendue, à l'ouverture de la justice pénale en général et à la fonction communicative des régimes de sanction. Après avoir exploré ces tensions selon la perspective des rôles en évolution du procureur et du juge dans le contexte de la justice négociée en Europe, Ligeti & Robinson estiment que la justice négociée n'est pas une solution au recours excessif à la justice pénale en tant que tel et qu'il est important de ne pas réduire la justice négociée à une simple réponse à la surcharge systémique des systèmes de justice pénale. Ils soulignent en outre que le recours croissant à la justice négociée n'a jamais visé une justice qualitative, mais bien l'efficacité. C'est pourquoi ils plaident pour que l'amélioration de la transparence des outils de justice négociée soit traitée comme une priorité afin de faciliter un contrôle approfondi et permanent de leur efficience.

Certaines formes de négociation des peines sont acceptées en Finlande (limitée), en Grèce (certaines catégories de délits), au Nigeria[28], en Russie[29], en Espagne, à Taïwan et aux USA. Le recours excessif à la négociation de peine durant les poursuites est traité en détail dans le chapitre de Rapoza. En mettant

---

28 N'est pas mentionné dans le chapitre sur le Nigeria, mais voir Sule Peter Echewija, 'Plea Bargaining and the Administration of Criminal Justice in Nigeria : A Moral Critique', 3 *IAFOR Journal of Ethics, Religion & Philosophy* 2 (2017), p. 35-47.

29 N'est pas mentionné dans le chapitre sur la Russie, mais voir Ekaterina Moiseeva, 'Plea bargaining in Russia : the role of defence attorneys and the problem of asymmetry', 41 *International Journal of Comparative and Applied Criminal Justice* 3 (2017), p. 163-184.

l'accent sur le système de justice pénale des États-Unis d'Amérique, qui est actuellement « pour la plus grande part un système de négociations et non un système de procès », Rapoza propose une analyse approfondie et détaillée de l'évolution historique de la procédure légale et des nombreux problèmes suscités par la négociation de peine. Ce chapitre estime qu'une négociation repose largement sur le postulat fonctionnel que l'accusé est en réalité coupable de quelque chose, la seule question significative étant de savoir comment étiqueter son délit et quel niveau de peine imposer. La question à laquelle il convient plutôt de répondre, selon Rapoza, est comment rendre le processus plus honnête et plus équitable ; il se penche longuement sur plusieurs solutions. L'une des nombreuses conclusions auxquelles Rapoza aboutit est que le recours à la négociation de peine a indiscutablement joué un rôle significatif dans le taux élevé d'incarcération que connaissent les États-Unis. La négociation des peines peut par conséquent être une cause importante de recours excessif à l'incarcération. L'auteur Díez-Ripollés se montre tout aussi critique à l'égard de la négociation de peine, mais aussi envers les procès expéditifs, les violations de la règle de preuve et les procédures de confiscation. Il affirme que ces procédures pénales « fantaisistes » abandonnent des éléments essentiels du processus requis en échange d'une pseudo-efficacité. Lambropoulou & Tsolka considèrent néanmoins la négociation de peine comme étant une mesure utile pour résoudre les problèmes de recours excessif au système de justice pénale en Grèce.

La médiation, autre possibilité d'éviter ou de réduire les poursuites, a acquis une place substantielle dans le traitement des affaires pénales en Finlande par exemple. En Pologne, l'article 59a du Code pénal prévoyait une justice réparatrice, mais il a été supprimé en 2016. Au grand regret de Paprzycki & Wąsek-Wiaderek, qui affirment, dans leur chapitre sur la Pologne, que cet article pouvait devenir un outil effectif pour mettre fin aux poursuites pénales pour les délits contre les biens, qui sont précisément les délits les plus souvent signalés en Pologne. Kuhn & Solcà (chapitre sur la Suisse) plaident également en faveur de l'introduction dans le droit de possibilités de justice réparatrice telle que la médiation.

V.4. RECOURS EXCESSIF À L'INCARCÉRATION

Dans une perspective générale, le recours excessif à l'incarcération est avant tout traité par Lappi-Seppälä. Dans son chapitre consacré aux statistiques des taux d'incarcération, il propose une analyse approfondie et détaillée des principales tendances du recours à l'incarcération dans le monde et au fil des époques. Les pays forment l'unité de base de l'analyse, tandis que les tendances et les différences sont examinées en détail, également par régions et continents. L'une des nombreuses conclusions tirées par Lappi-Seppälä est que la comparaison statistique indique généralement que ni les délits signalés, ni la victimisation ne se traduisent systématiquement en taux d'incarcération. Au contraire, au final, ces derniers résultent bien plus largement de choix politiques. Une autre conclusion de Lappi-Seppälä est que les inégalités salariales ainsi que les investissements dans le bien-être social sont fortement liés à l'incarcération dans les pays d'Europe. Il en va de même pour les sentiments sociaux tels que la peur du crime, la punitivité subjective et la confiance sociale et institutionnelle.

Alors que dans certains pays les peines d'emprisonnement de courte durée sont la cause de taux d'incarcération élevés (voir par exemple le chapitre sur l'Irlande), dans d'autres juridictions, ce sont les peines de longue durée qui en sont responsables. Dans leur chapitre sur la Nouvelle-Zélande, Tinsley & Young avancent que le recours excessif à l'incarcération en Nouvelle-Zélande peut être considéré comme le résultat des peines nominales et effectives plus longues imposées, qui découlent à leur tour de la politique gouvernementale et de l'opinion publique affectées par les médias et les groupes de pression. Voir le chapitre consacré à l'Espagne, qui montre du doigt les groupes de pression et la dynamique populiste, ainsi que le chapitre sur Taïwan qui explique comment la pression populaire (le « Mouvement de la rose blanche ») a suscité une modification des interprétations par la Cour suprême de plusieurs délits sexuels. L'une des conséquences de ces pressions est aussi le recours accru à l'incarcération à perpétuité dans certains pays (voir particulièrement les chapitres sur la Finlande, l'Allemagne, la Grèce et les Pays-Bas, ainsi que les chapitres thématiques rédigés par Díez-Ripollés, Pinto de Albuquerque, Lappi-Seppälä et Rogan). Dans le même temps, comme c'est le cas en Suisse, le recours aux peines d'emprisonnement peut varier fortement d'une région à l'autre dans un même pays ou entre différents groupes tels que les ressortissants nationaux et les étrangers (voir également le chapitre statistique de Lappi-Seppälä). Il en va de même pour les femmes et les hommes (voir également le chapitre statistique de Lappi-Seppälä, ainsi que les chapitres sur l'Irlande et le Nigeria[30]). Certaines différences peuvent également résulter du traitement préférentiel de certains groupes. Comme Rotman l'explique en détail dans son chapitre consacré aux États-Unis, c'est le cas des délinquants en col blanc.

Les peines minimales obligatoires sont un élément susceptible de faire obstacle à la réduction des peines d'emprisonnement (voir par exemple le chapitre sur le Nigeria). Comme Rogan & Reilly le soulignent dans leur chapitre consacré à l'Irlande, ce n'est pas seulement le cas pour les délits auxquels une peine minimale obligatoire s'applique, il peut également donner lieu à une augmentation des peines appliquées aux autres délits. Il peut en outre générer des condamnations injustes si la loi ne laisse aucune place à des exceptions (voir le chapitre sur les

---

30 Voir en outre, sur 23 pays dans le monde : P.H.P.H.M.C. van Kempen & M.J.M. Krabbe (eds.), *Women in Prison. The Bangkok Rules and Beyond / Femmes en prison. Les règles de Bangkok et au-delà*, Cambridge/Antwerp/Portland : Intersentia, 2017.

Pays-Bas). De plus, comme c'est le cas en Espagne, même si les tribunaux appliquent les peines minimales, la rigidité du système d'application et l'absence d'alternatives non privatives de liberté peuvent former un obstacle à une réduction significative du nombre de détenus. Selon Rong-geng Li, c'est également le cas à Taïwan, où seuls les tribunaux qui se prononcent sur des délits mineurs peuvent réduire les peines, les suspendre et les transformer en une amende ou un travail d'intérêt général. Toutefois, contrairement à ce qui précède, d'après García Magna (chapitre sur l'Espagne), limiter le pouvoir discrétionnaire de la justice pourrait également être positif d'une certaine façon, par exemple parce que cela pourrait prévenir les excès dans les condamnations, même dans le système espagnol rigide dont les limites minimales sont élevées. L'incidence qu'à la limitation du pouvoir discrétionnaire des juges sur le recours à l'incarcération peut dès lors dépendre de son utilisation pour promouvoir ou limiter les faibles peines et l'application des peines non privatives de liberté. Néanmoins, même les mesures visant à promouvoir les peines non privatives de liberté n'auront pas nécessairement l'effet visé. En Suisse par exemple, selon Kuhn & Solcà, l'augmentation de la population carcérale pourrait également s'expliquer par le fait qu'en contraignant les juges à imposer des sanctions pécuniaires pour les condamnations inférieures à 6 mois, le système les pousse probablement à plus de sévérité et à prononcer des peines d'emprisonnement supérieures à 6 mois.

Il existe plusieurs exemples de pays dans lesquels les solutions utilisées pour réduire l'incarcération sont mises en cause ; voir par exemple le chapitre sur l'Allemagne qui aborde la question plus en détail. De plus, certains pays connaissent une augmentation des possibilités de contrôle effectif du comportement des criminels après l'exécution des peines ; voir notamment les chapitres consacrés à l'Allemagne et aux Pays-Bas.[31]

Dans le même temps, la sévérité des peines d'emprisonnement ne repose évidemment pas uniquement sur la longueur de la peine d'emprisonnement, elle dépend également des conditions dans lesquelles elles sont exécutées. Dans son chapitre sur la Russie, Gilinskiy explique en quoi le recours répandu à la torture dépend de plusieurs facteurs. Toutefois, même lorsque les pratiques sont moins inhumaines, l'incarcération a des effets néfastes.

Le chapitre thématique de Rogan met l'accent sur les efforts visant à minimiser ces effets et sur la réglementation du recours à l'incarcération par la libération et autres stratégies détournées. À cette fin, Rogan aborde les effets néfastes de l'incarcération, les effets positifs des contacts avec le monde extérieur, la nécessité

31 Voir également les contributions (particulièrement celle de Tak et Shute, dans la Partie III) in P.H.P.H.M.C. van Kempen & W. Young (ed.), *Prevention of reoffending. The value of rehabilitation and the management of high risk offenders / Prévention de la récidive. Valeur de la réhabilitation et gestion des délinquants à haut risque*, Cambridge/Antwerp/Portland : Intersentia, 2014.

d'appliquer des conditions d'incarcération physiquement et matériellement décentes, l'importance de l'honnêteté procédurale et de la responsabilité en prison, ainsi que la libération comme élément clé de la minimisation des effets néfastes de l'incarcération et de la réduction de la population carcérale. Son analyse repose sur une grande variété de normes en matière de droits de l'homme et de jurisprudence, ainsi que sur les résultats des recherches dans le domaine des sciences sociales. Ce chapitre est parsemé de nombreux résultats et recommandations.

Dans le chapitre thématique final, Sakalauskas affirme que les possibilités de congé pénitentiaire, l'existence de prisons ouvertes et les conditions générales de libération conditionnelle constituent d'excellents indicateurs des systèmes carcéraux humains et axés sur l'inclusion (pour ce qui est des prisons ouvertes, veuillez consulter également les chapitres consacrés à l'Irlande). Sakalauskas illustre (en se fondant sur une analyse détaillée de la situation en Lituanie) comment des facteurs politiques, économiques, sociaux et culturels peuvent néanmoins rendre l'adoption d'une politique criminelle plus compliquée si elle applique effectivement ces instruments.

La meilleure façon d'éviter l'incidence négative de l'incarcération pour les condamnés est certainement le recours à des peines non privatives de liberté. Dans certains pays, le recours à ces peines a significativement réduit la population carcérale. Voir par exemple le chapitre consacré à la Belgique (e.g. la surveillance électronique), à la Finlande (une politique de solutions non privatives de liberté est largement appliquée) et à l'Irlande (politique communautaire de retour). La disponibilité de ces peines alternatives et d'autres encore revêt une importance cruciale pour limiter le recours à l'incarcération. C'est alors seulement que le principe de l'*ultima ratio* pourra être appliqué au processus de détermination de la peine. Dans cette lignée, Kuhn & Solcà soulignent la nécessité de personnaliser les peines, c'est-à-dire que la peine doit systématiquement être adaptée à la situation particulière de la personne qu'elle affecte. Pour ce faire, outre la nécessité d'étendre la gamme de sanctions dont les tribunaux disposent, ils proposent la division du système de sanctions en deux phases distinctes. Leur idée (qu'ils exposent plus en détail) consiste à créer un système pénal à deux niveaux : le juge du tribunal fixerait la longueur de la peine, tandis qu'un juge d'application des peines déciderait ultérieurement de la forme de la peine (type, conditions). Il est important que le principe de l'*ultima ratio* soit pris en compte dans les deux phases. En effet, dans son chapitre consacré à la Finlande, Lappi-Seppälä souligne l'excellence des résultats générés par l'application effective des peines d'emprisonnement en dernier ressort seulement. Les résultats obtenus au moyen de techniques préventives éprouvées et le développement de peines alternatives d'intérêt général utilisées en lieu et place de l'incarcération sont plus durables et constructifs, sans incidence notable sur le taux de criminalité finlandais au regard de la situation dans les autres pays nordiques.

VI. CONCLUSION : DE L'IMPORTANCE DU PRINCIPE DE L'*ULTIMA RATIO* POUR CONTRER TOUT RECOURS EXCESSIF

Pour prévenir et supprimer le recours excessif à la criminalisation, aux poursuites et à l'incarcération, le principe fondamental de la justice pénale selon lequel le droit pénal est et doit être considéré comme un *ultima ratio* ou *ultimum remedium* peut largement orienter le législateur et le gouvernement, le ministère public, ainsi que les autorités judiciaires et carcérales.

Exigence de limitation. La première caractéristique du principe de l'*ultima ratio* est qu'il exige une limitation du recours au système de justice pénale. Pour ce faire, le législateur se doit de limiter la criminalisation du comportement, c'est-à-dire la criminalisation en soi, l'ampleur des délits, leur étiquetage, la période pendant laquelle la responsabilité pénale peut être établie pour les délits (délai de prescription), l'exigence d'une juridiction extra territoriale et la peine maximale autorisée pour le délit. Pour ce qui est des poursuites, la notion de limitation implique qu'elles ne doivent pas obligatoirement être menées chaque fois que c'est possible et qu'il convient d'éviter la majoration, c'est-à-dire d'accuser le prévenu sur la base de délits formellement applicables, mais qui ne font que peu justice au comportement effectif et à ses conséquences. Enfin, les limitations concernant le pouvoir judiciaire (et/ou éventuellement le ministère public) impliquent principalement des réticences au recours aux peines d'emprisonnement. Lorsque l'incarcération s'avère pertinente, sa durée doit être la plus modérée possible et son régime d'exécution le moins contraignant possible en regard du cas particulier.

Exigence d'exploration. Une seconde qualité du principe de l'*ultima ratio* réside dans la recherche active par les autorités de solutions alternatives. Il appartient avant tout au législateur et au gouvernement d'explorer d'autres solutions. Des solutions alternatives totales ou partielles à la criminalisation de certains comportements, afin de prévenir et de sanctionner les délits, peuvent être à la fois non juridiques (par exemple techniques ou informationnelles) et juridiques (par exemple réglementation administrative ou civile) par nature. Il appartient également au législateur de jouer un rôle dans l'exploration des possibilités de cadre légal suffisamment flexible pour que le ministère public puisse restreindre les poursuites et appliquer des procédures alternatives pour résoudre les affaires criminelles, par exemple les processus de justice réparatrice. De plus, les peines alternatives à l'incarcération (peines non privatives de liberté) doivent être mises au point par le législateur qui peut également jouer un rôle (à l'instar de l'administration pénitentiaire) dans le développement de formes moins intrusives de privation de liberté (par exemple les prisons ouvertes, la surveillance électronique) et la limitation des préjudices évitables causés par l'incarcération. Il appartient au ministère public, au système judiciaire et à l'administration pénitentiaire d'explorer les solutions alternatives (ou atténuantes) aux poursuites et à l'incarcération disponibles, dans le respect du cadre légal et en regard du cas particulier.

Exigence de réflexion. Enfin, le principe de l'*ultima ratio* implique que le recours à des alternatives disponibles ou à des solutions atténuantes à la criminalisation, aux poursuites et à l'incarcération soit envisagé sérieusement, en premier ressort. C'est le cas en général (réflexion par le législateur, le gouvernement, l'administration pénitentiaire) et pour les cas particuliers (réflexion du ministère public, du système judiciaire et de l'administration pénitentiaire). Alors seulement le système de justice pénale pourra offrir une flexibilité et des avenues susceptibles de pallier à son recours excessif et de la sorte répondre aux exigences de proportionnalité, de nécessité et d'équité.

PART II
THEMES

2ÈME PARTIE
THÈMES

OVERUSE OF THE CRIMINAL JUSTICE SYSTEM
Analytical Approach, Rules and Practices

José Luis Díez-Ripollés*

I. AN ANALYTICAL APPROACH

To properly assess to what extent a national crime control system overuses the punitive means at its disposal, it has to be established first what the legitimate goals are that the system must pursue through those means. Therefore, we need to adopt a precise analytical approach before being able to evaluate the abuses into which crime control actors could be falling. We deal with this topic in the following two sections.

I.1. PUNITIVE MODERATION AS AN OBJECTIVE

Current criminal policy has a strong tendency to compare different national crime control systems from the single perspective of their punitiveness. Punitive rigorousness or moderation has become the point of reference for most comparative analyses of ongoing criminal policy in different countries. Moreover, this approach has gradually gained significance as an evaluation criteria of national crime policies.

This framework assumes that national crime control systems, as they develop the necessary social interventions to obtain their preventive aims, should make sure that crime control does not inflict more social suffering than strictly necessary. It means that criminalization should not go beyond what might be considered vital for protecting essential public interests, and that those, either suspects or offenders, subjected to criminal law enforcement bodies will

* Full professor of Criminal Law, University of Málaga.

experience moderate and proportional distress as a result of their behaviour.[1] This objective is so relevant that it justifies that comparative criminal policy evaluations are guided in accordance of the degree to which different national systems come closer to an optimum of punitive moderation, notwithstanding the achievement of preventive goals.

It is important to question why, despite the strong moral and cultural dependence to which the ideas of criminal restraint or rigor are subjected to, this approach has got itself into such a big predicament.[2] Some reasons are worth mentioning. The hypothesis that most Western countries are moving towards a progressive harshening of the penal system has been very suggestive, and has permeated the criminal justice policy discussion.[3] In turn, a program aimed at reducing the punitive pressure commonly has support amongst the field of criminal policy reflection. In addition, it has influenced the conceptual clarity and strength of this view, suggesting that a few indicators can explain it. Indeed, we should not forget that from the outset it has used easily accessible indicators of punitiveness, which has certainly increased its appeal.

However, drawing up descriptive and evaluative frameworks of comparative criminal policy on lesser or higher punitiveness achieved by different national systems entails a number of significant theoretical and methodological shortcomings.

From a theoretical point of view, the objective of punitive moderation places itself in an ideologically poor context. In fact, one could consider it a humanitarian approach to criminal policy that is content with guaranteeing that any criminal justice system, regardless of the adopted criminal policy model or its intended goals, does not reach unacceptable levels of severity. Hence, it is said that it is an evaluative proposal which can only question policies that lead to an

---

1 On the idea of punitiveness see, among others, Nelken, D, "When is a society non-punitive? The Italian case", in Pratt J, Brown D, Brown M, Hallsworth S, Morrison W, *The New Punitiveness.* Cullompton: Willan Publishing, 2005, p. 219-222; Cavadino, M, Dignan, J, *Penal Systems.* London: Sage Publications. 2006, p. xii; Roché, S, "Criminal justice policy in France", in Tonry M, ed. *Crime, Punishment and Politics in Comparative Perspective.* Chicago: University of Chicago Press. 2007, p. 474-476, 494; Lappi-Seppälä, T, "Trust, Welfare, and Political Culture", in Tonry M ed. *Crime and Justice.* n. 37. Chicago: University of Chicago Press. 2008, p. 320-321; del Rosal Blasco, B, "¿Hacia el derecho penal de la posmodernidad?", *Revista electrónica de ciencia penal y criminología.* 2009, 11-08, p. 14-19.

2 See, among many others, Hinds, L, "Crime control in Western countries", in Pratt J, Brown D, Brown M, Hallsworth S, Morrison W. *The New,* cit. p. 47-65; Cavadino / Dignan, cit. p. 3-49; Downes, D, Hansen, K, "Welfare and punishment in comparative perspective", in Amstrong S, McAra L eds. *Perspectives on Punishment.* Oxford: Oxford University Press, 2006, p. 133, 143-153; Tonry. M, "Determinants of penal policies", in Tonry M, ed. *Crime, Punishment and Politics,* cit, p. 7-13; Lappi-Seppälä, T, "Trust, Welfare," cit.; Larrauri Pijoan, E, "La economía política del castigo", *Revista electrónica de ciencia penal y criminología.* 2009, 11-06, p. 1-22.

3 See about the origin and evolution of this hypothesis, Díez-Ripollés, JL, "La dimensión inclusión / exclusión social como guía de la política criminal comparada". *Revista electrónica de ciencia penal y criminología.* 2011, 13-12, p. 2-3.

increase in criminal reactions but not those which maintain or diminish such reactions.[4] This does not mean that punitive moderation is a trivial attribute or goal. On the contrary, as we shall see, it is necessarily woven into a broader and more complex criminal policy program, of which it constitutes an essential element.

Actually, assigning punitive moderation a prominent role simply correlates to the adoption of procedural justice as a criminal policy model, in this case, emphasizing the expansion and intensity of criminal reactions. Yet, I have shown elsewhere that procedural justice, without prejudice to the essential role legal safeguards have to play in any criminal justice system, does not fulfil all the necessary criteria to become a real strategy against crime, in other words, a criminal policy model.[5]

Legal and procedural guarantees erect themselves as a convincing and indispensable bulwark for the preservation of civil liberties and citizens' fundamental rights when exercising *ius puniendi*. Accordingly, procedural justice identifies well-founded principles for establishing legal interests to be protected by criminal law, for confining policing, for ascertaining the conceptual framework of criminal responsibility and its verification in criminal procedure, for shaping and for implementing the sanctions system. That is why it should be borne in mind and respected by policymakers as part of any given crime policy strategies. However, procedural justice lacks the necessary content to support a public policy such as criminal policy: this requires a strategy of social intervention which, integrated into the set of public policies, develops specific and measurable objectives aimed at preventing crime within acceptable social parameters. Procedural justice stops at the identification and strengthening of those parameters, that is to say, values, concepts and legal safeguards common to any rule-of-law-based criminal policy, and gives no indication as to which crime control strategy, among those compatible with such principles, one should select.[6]

From a methodological point of view, the discourse of punitive moderation is based on too limited indicators. In fact, the most prominent indicator it uses is the incarceration rate per 100,000. There is no doubt, however, that this indicator has many virtues: it is easily accessible from various reliable sources; it provides long-standing data sets ranging over extended time periods; it focuses on the

---

4 See Brodeur, JP, "Comparative penology in perspective, in Tonry ed. *Crime, Punishment and Politics*, cit. p. 67; Webster, CM, Doob, A, "Punitive trends and stable imprisonment rates in Canada, in Tonry M ed. *Ibidem*, p. 300-301.

5 See Díez-Ripollés, JL, "El nuevo modelo penal de la seguridad ciudadana", *Revista electrónica de ciencia penal y criminología*. 2004. 06-03, p. 31-33. Likewise Zaffaroni, R, *El enemigo en el derecho penal*, México DF: Ediciones Coyoacán, 2007, p. 184.

6 On the role of procedural justice for designing criminal policies, see Díez-Ripollés, JL, "El nuevo", cit. p. 31- 33. See also the Nordic debate contrasting offensive and defensive criminal policy, in Lahti, R, "Towards a rational and humane criminal policy", *Journal of Scandinavian Studies in Criminology and Crime Prevention*. 2000, 1, p. 147-148.

most severe punishment that a criminal law system may impose except for the death penalty; and it is usually a sanction which adequately reflects the outcome of penal policies and practices of particular criminal justice systems.[7]

Nevertheless, criminological and criminal policy literature has repeatedly revealed its limitations. Above all, for unduly focusing the evaluation of the punitiveness of a criminal justice system on the use of imprisonment and thus marginalizing other relevant indicators, such as the number of criminal proceedings and sentences, the severity of the whole system of sanctions, the intensity and frequency of alternative sanctions to prison, and the rules on accumulation of penalties, amongst others.

In addition to this, as the relative use of prison in different national systems is measured in this way, the almost exclusive use of the incarceration rate per 100,000 inhabitants leaves out other relevant indicators, such as the average length of imposed prison sentences, the number of admissions to prison, the effective average stay in prison or the number of confinements outside the penal system. Moreover, one should not forget certain practices that may distort the figures, such as the use of waiting lists for admission into prison or the use of general pardons.[8]

Nevertheless, the preceding methodological critique does not question the undoubted significance that the rate of incarceration and its associated indicators have upon the characterization of relevant aspects of a criminal justice system. What is being discussed are the unilateral visions that seek to evaluate an entire criminal justice system, or, in other words, its punitiveness, based solely on data concerning the rate of incarceration. This should not impede the point, however, that within more complex analytical models, this indicator is afforded a significant role

7 See, for all, Cavadino, M, Dignan, J, "Penal systems", cit. p. 4-5; Tonry. M, "Determinants", cit. p. 7.

8 See Balvig, F, "When law and order returned to Denmark". *Journal of Scandinavian Studies in Criminology and Crime Prevention.*2004, 5, p. 169; Hinds, L, "Crime control", cit. p. 47-48; Tonry, M, "Determinants", cit. p. 8-14; Tamarit Sumalla, JM, "Sistema de sanciones y política criminal", *Revista electrónica de ciencia penal y criminología.* 2007, 09-06, p. 6-27; Lappi-Seppälä, T, "Penal Policy in Scandinavia", in Tonry M, ed. *Crime, Punishment and Politics,* cit. p. 254-258, 266-270; Newburn, T, "Tough on crime: Penal policy in England and Wales", *Ibidem, p.* 435-436, 442-445; Snacken, S, "Penal policy and practice in Belgium", *Ibidem, p.* 145-150; Downes, D, "Visions of penal control in the Netherlands", *Ibidem, p.* 95-96, 97, 99; Levy, R, "Pardons and amnesties as policy instruments in contemporary France", *Ibidem,* Roché, S, "Criminal justice", cit. p. 502-511, 539-540; Pratt, J, "Scandinavian exceptionalism in an era of penal excess". I *British Journal of Criminology,* 2008, 48, p. 135; Nelken, D, *Comparative Criminal Justice.* Los Angeles: Sage Publications. 2010, p. 61-66.
However, there have been relevant arguments on the remarkable ability of the incarceration rate to significantly subsume all those other useful prison indicators within itself. See Webster, CM, Doob, A, cit, p. 305-309; Lappi-Seppälä, T, "Trust, Welfare", cit. p. 322-332.

I.2. SOCIAL INCLUSION AS AN OBJECTIVE

Another way of conducting a comparative criminal policy description and evaluation is by studying the capacity of the corresponding national crime control systems to promote social inclusion and to minimize the social exclusion of those who come into conflict with criminal law.[9] This perspective is broader in scope than the previous one because it touches on the very core of the preventive objectives of the corresponding criminal policy model. It is no longer a question, as in the previous approach, to ensure that the preventive strategy chosen, whatever it is, remains within the limits of punitive moderation. The inclusion/exclusion social dimension expresses two different options of preventive strategy.

The aim of the inclusive approach is that the selection of any behaviour to be punished is governed by impartial criteria on the social harmfulness of that behaviour without any bias that might discriminate against specific social groups. Besides, the social-inclusive approach intends to ensure that suspects or offenders, after having been in direct contact with the crime control system, find themselves in the same or better individual and social conditions to voluntarily conduct their lives in accordance with the law.

The exclusionary alternative considers that the selection of any behaviour to be punished must transcend the mere identification and control of socially harmful behaviours, and pursue additional controls of certain social groups. At the same time, it aims to ensure that suspects or offenders, after having been exposed to the crime control system, find themselves in individual and social conditions that make it more difficult for them to break the law or to avoid being caught.[10]

As can be seen, while decisions on criminalization affect the society as a whole (even though certain groups or collectives may or may not receive equal treatment from the criminal justice system), at the time of prosecution and sanctioning those directly under penal control as suspects, offenders and ex-offenders are the ones who are mainly affected by the criminal justice system.

My analytical proposal is based on the fundamental hypothesis that an unbiased selection of social interests to be protected under criminal law, and the maintenance of a certain level of social inclusion for suspects, offenders and ex-offenders is one of the most effective strategies for crime prevention in the mid and long term. And on the correlative hypothesis that any form of social sectarianism in the selection of social interests to be protected under criminal law, as well as an increase or consolidation of the levels of social exclusion for

9 See thoroughly on this approach, Díez-Ripollés, JL. "La dimensión", cit. p. 1-36; same author, "Social inclusion and comparative criminal justice policy", *Journal of Scandinavian Studies in Criminology and Crime Prevention*, vol. 14, 2013, p. 62-78.

10 See also, Cavadino, M, Dignan, J, "Penal systems", cit. p. xiii, 28, 338-339; Brodeur, JP, "Comparative", cit. p. 54-60, 81-82.

suspects, offenders, and ex-offenders by the crime control system, will foster greater levels of crime in the mid and long term.[11]

However, while the maximizations of either the inclusive or the exclusive criminal policy program go to a great extent in opposite directions[12], the use of the preferred inclusive program does not rule out some contents of the exclusive program. But the inclusive program is designed so that the combination that is adopted reflects an optimum level of social inclusion.

Moreover, social inclusion/exclusion and punitive moderation/ rigorousness are not two parallel dimensions. In fact, interests linked to obtaining social inclusion can sometimes lead to the establishment of more distressing criminal interventions or sanctions than those demanded by any interests linked to social exclusion. Anyway, it would be normal that social inclusion and punitive moderation maintain close and direct relationships. What happens is that the social inclusion/exclusion dimension incorporates a more complex and rich vision of criminal policy phenomena.

In any case, the two hypotheses mentioned are pending demonstration[13], which is not the goal of this work.[14] But we will only achieve progress in empirically testing the preventive performance of inclusive or exclusive models if we identify punitive rules and practices that unequivocally generate evidence of one or the other effect. Identification of those rules and practices should not be carried out on a theoretical level, but by looking for punitive rules and practices

---

11 In any case, I intend to formulate hypotheses about the effects that either an inclusive or an exclusive criminal policy model may have about setting up a more or less inclusive society in all its aspects. No doubt, the adopted criminal policy program will have an impact on society as a whole, but my approach is not intended to go so far. On the contrary, about the consolidation of an increasingly less inclusive society and the corresponding adaptation to it of criminal policy, see an overview in Brandáriz García, JA. *El gobierno de la penalidad. La complejidad de la política criminal contemporánea.* Madrid: Dykinson. 2014. p. 43-73.

12 It is evident that, concerning its intervention on suspects and offenders, the inclusive program is inspired by the penological trends, which promote the rehabilitation of offenders, and that the exclusive program is centred on the incapacitation of the offender. However, we should be cautious in identifying these criminal policy models with certain specific-prevention theories of punishment. Their objectives are more far-reaching, easily outstrip the impact on the convicted offender, and determine the configuration of the whole system of crime control. Something that is evident when making decisions on criminalization

13 See some considerations about them, in Uggen, C, Manza, J, Thompson, M, "Citizenship, democracy and the civic reintegration of criminal offenders". *Annals of the American Academy of Political and Social Science,* 605, 2006, p. 303–304. A significant recent research in Savage, J, Bennett, R, Danner, M, "Economic assistance and crime: a cross-national investigation", *European journal of Criminology,* vol. 5-2, 2008, with further references to previous researches.

14 Let me remind the reader that any program must be assessed on the basis of its success to prevent crime in accordance with socially assumable parameters. It is not enough to be able to identify and significantly reduce the frequency and severity of behaviours that are seriously harmful to society, and therefore criminal. Preventive work within socially assumable parameters entails in our Western democracies full respect for the rule of law principles and legal safeguards. See Díez-Ripollés, JL. "Dimension", cit. p. 4–5.

common in the developed Western world, either because they are enforced to a different extent, or because their possible implementation belongs to contemporary criminal policy debate. And this is an endeavour to which this study on the overuse of criminal law can collaborate.

II. OVERVIEW OF PUNITIVE RULES AND PRACTICES

Here we will list and briefly describe a set of punitive rules and practices that illustrate the ideas presented. They are grouped into three sections, which correspond to the three defining moments of criminal intervention: criminalization, prosecution, and enforcement of sanctions. Within each section, there are subgroups of rules or practices that are conceptually close or share a common area. The selection will be made taking into account the socially exclusionary effects that they are estimated to produce.

II.1. CRIMINALIZATION

a. Selecting punishable criminal behaviour

It is well known that unrestrained criminal legislative activity has been taking place for at least a couple of decades in many countries. In many cases, the phenomenon cannot be justified by an increase in socially deviant behaviours or improved prevention. Rather, it is because criminal law has become a useful instrument for achieving political and social goals that have little or nothing to do with crime prevention. In addition, this abuse of criminal law has consequences for the quality of legislative decisions: As the predominant objective is to produce certain symbolic or appeasing effects on the population, we find opportunistic and short-term laws, without regard to any rational decision based on the social reality to be intervened nor taking into account previous successful crime control interventions.

This expansion of criminal legislation has both a quantitative and a qualitative aspect. The first is expressed in the constant expansion of the scope of existing criminal provisions and in the creation of new ones, accompanied by a tightening of the penal reaction. In contrast, the processes of decriminalization, frequent at other times, are conspicuous by their absence. Furthermore, the qualitative expansion is mainly concentrated on a few behaviours: Certainly, the increasingly profound social rejection of violent behaviour expresses a clear reformist line, which also includes terrorist acts. But beyond that, it is instructive to look at the other preferred areas of intervention: Firstly, crimes of trafficking, mainly of drugs and people, and traditional property crimes, behaviours that are carried out mainly by socially disadvantaged groups such as minorities, the poor, foreigners or youth; secondly, sexual offenses, which have a limited prevalence but are suitable for imposing on the perpetrators (who are akin to contemporary witches) a disproportionate criminal reaction, which is aimed at calming various extended social anxieties and discomforts. In contrast, there are many legislative decisions that create a lenient criminal law for crimes committed by the upper-middle classes, by offenders who are socially well-integrated; this is a criminal law with escape routes such as self-regulation provisions, rewards for whistle-blowers and financial redresses, which make possible an exceptional and moderate use of prison.

This manipulation of criminal law for unrelated purposes ignores principles such as harmfulness, subsidiarity and proportionality and concentrates punitiveness on groups, who are either disadvantaged or symbolically useful. This does nothing to encourage, due to its arbitrary and socially skewed character, respect for criminal law nor, consequently, social inclusion.[15]

b. Maximum penalties

Without doubt, the death penalty, despite its persistence in a significant number of countries, some of them very prominent, is in decline worldwide. Some regions such as Europe or Latin America have virtually eradicated it, with some international regional organizations playing a very active role in this respect. However, there has been an increase in very long prison sentences. Many countries have passed legislation that permits custodial penalties in excess of 25 and even 30 years. In addition, life imprisonment is increasing, instead of being drawn back, and it is sometimes endorsed by prestigious international courts such as the European Court of Human Rights. The more severe laws on recidivism and the disproportionate reaction to certain crimes such as murder,

15 See Haffke, B. *Tiefenpsychologie und Generalprävention.* Frankfurt: Verlag Sauerlander. 1976; Tham, H, "Law and order as a leftist project?". *Punishment and society.* Vol. 3(3). 2001 p. 409-426; Díez Ripollés, JL, Prieto del Pino, AM, Soto Navarro, S, *La política legislativa penal en Occidente. Una perspectiva comparada.* Valencia: Tirant. 2005; Lappi-Seppälä, T. "Penal Policy", cit. p. 234, 246, 252, 256; Snacken, S. "Penal policy". cit. p. 150–172; Newburn, T., "Tough on crime". cit. p. 436-449; Dünkel, F, Lappi-Seppälä, T, Morgenstern, C, van Zyl Smit, D, "Gefangenenraten und Kriminalpolitik in Europa: Zusammenfassung und Schlussfolgerungen", in Dünkel, F, Lappi-Seppälä, T, Morgenstern, C, van Zyl Smit, D, *Kriminalität, Kriminalpolitik, strafrechtliche Sanktionspraxis und Gefangenenraten in europäischen Vergleich.* Band 2. Mönchengladbach: Forum Verlag Godesberg. 2010, p. 1042–1048; Díez-Ripollés, JL, García Pérez, O, coords. *La política legislativa penal iberoamericana en el cambio de siglo.* Montevideo: B de F. 2008; Díez-Ripollés, JL. "Rigorismo y reforma penal. Cuatro legislaturas homogéneas. Parte I y Parte II". *Boletín criminológico.* n. 142–143. 2013; v. Hofer, H, Tham, H, "Punishment in Sweden: A changing penal landscape", in Ruggiero, V, Ryan, M, eds. *Punishment in Europe.* Palgrave McMillan, 2013, p. 46–49.

terrorism, drug trafficking, organized crime and sexual offenses, among others, means that life imprisonment is a very real option.

Long custodial penalties and life imprisonment aim mainly to incapacitate the offender, with an offender's rehabilitation and even the principle of proportionality being alien to them. Certainly, the review of life sentences, if progress is seen in the social reintegration of the offender, commonly occurs after a tariff that is rarely less than 20 years. But what cannot be ignored is the fact that the length of already elapsed detention and the uncertainty about the review decision are factors that will discourage any effort on behalf of the prisoner in that regard. This means then that these penalties are a privileged instrument for the social exclusion of offenders through their direct segregation from society.[16]

c. *System of sanctions*

The dissocializing effects of imprisonment have long been well established. However, notwithstanding the marked differences between incarceration rates in different regions and countries, imprisonment as a form of punishment is expanding. The maximum tariff of the prison penalties provided for many different crimes is often raised, something that occasionally entails higher prison sentences than reviewable life imprisonment sentences. It is also worth mentioning the renewed prestige and application of short prison terms, until recently discarded due to their negative effects on offenders' social reintegration, but which are now being reclaimed for their strong deterrent effects.

The optimism generated by the proliferation of penalties different to prison should be tempered, although these new sanctions are mainly designed in favour of the social reintegration of the offender. First of all, we must not overlook the fact that their growth, which has only just started, has been slowed in regions such as Latin America, encompassing the consolidation of punitiveness. In addition, the net widening effect gives rise to an expansion of crime control to areas where it did not exist or existed only occasionally, rather than replacing prison sentences with these non-custodial sentences. Meanwhile, although fines in wealthier societies have been credited with enough distressing effects as to

16 See Zimring, F. *The contradictions of American Capital Punishment.* Oxford, Oxford University Press, 2003; Penal Reform International. "Alternatives to the death penalty: the problems with life imprisonment". *Penal Reform Briefing.* N.1 (2007) www.penalreform.org. p. 1–11; Díez Ripollés, JL. "La política legislativa penal iberoamericana a principios del siglo XXI", in Díez-Ripollés, JL, García Pérez, O. *La política legislativa penal iberoamericana.* cit. p. 502–503; Arroyo, L, Biglino, P, Schabas eds. *Hacia la abolición universal de la pena capital.* Valencia, Tirant lo Blanch. 2010; Garland, D. *Peculiar institution: America´s death penalty in an age of abolition.* Cambridge, Mass: Harvard University Press. 2010; Cervelló Donderis, V. *Prisión perpetua y de larga duración.* Valencia: Tirant lo Blanch. 20015. p. 59–108; ECtHR, Judgment 12 February 2008 *Kafkaris v. Cyprus,* Judgment. 9 July 2013 *Vinter y otros v. United Kingdom,* Judgment 13 November 2014 *Bodein v. France,* Judgment 3 February 2015 *Hutchinson v. United Kingdom.*

successfully replace incarceration for many crimes, its disproportionate use can produce remarkable socially exclusionary effects. This can be the case if the use of fines too often leads to default imprisonment or creates insurmountable financial burdens over time. A good example of the ambivalence of these new penalties is the electronic monitoring of offenders: This practice ranges from being a penalty that restrains the movements and activities of offenders without imprisoning them, to its use as a pervasive and insensitive tool of control of probationers and parolees, which exponentially increases the number of revocations and prison readmissions.[17]

II.2. PROSECUTION

a. *Control of public spaces*

The city is a privileged place of social interaction that facilitates the relationship between acquaintances and strangers and, if well organized, generates feelings of belonging, which is an important component of social integration. At the same time, the city can be organized to hinder or reduce social interaction between certain groups of residents, which then results in the segregation of such groups. Recently, the use of control techniques in public spaces has clearly intended to reduce any contact with those members of society whose mere appearance, lifestyle or socio-economic status makes them potential criminal suspects. These members of the community are not only excluded from certain public spaces, but limits are also placed on their mobility in the city and they are subjected to continuous monitoring.

It is noteworthy that in many countries, there has been a proliferation of gated communities: they break city networks and consequently reduce social interaction, and ensure that well-off sectors of society can voluntary segregate themselves away from the most disadvantaged groups in society. Elsewhere there are urban plans that actively promote the segregation of different social strata within the same neighbourhood, such as with gentrification, which albeit in a less

17 See Tonry, M, *Sentencing matters.* New York: Oxford University Press. 1996 p. 100-133; v. Hofer, H.. "Die elektronische Überwachung von Straftätern in Schweden", in Jehle, JM ed. *Täterbehandlung und neue Sanktionsformen. Kriminalpolitische Konzepte in Europa.* Mönchengladbach: Forum Verlag Godesberg, 2000, p. 349-358; Petersilia, J. *When prisoners come home. Parole and prisoner reentry.* New York: Oxford University Press. 2003. p. 88-92; Tamarit Sumalla, JM. "Sistema de sanciones". cit. p. 1–40; Díez Ripollés, JL. "La política legislativa penal iberoamericana a principios", cit. p. 501–504; Lindström, P, Leijonram, E, "The Swedish prison system", en Tak, P, Jendly, M, *Ibídem p.* 559–570; Harris, A, Evans, H, Beckett, K. "Drawing blood from stones: Legal debt and social inequality in the contemporary United States". *The American Journal of Sociology.* Vol. 115 n. 6, May 2010, p. 1753–1799; Aebi, M, Linde, A, Delgrande, N. "Is there a relationship between imprisonment and crime in Western Europe?. *European Journal on Criminal Policy and Research.* Vol. 21 n. 3. 2015. p. 425–446.

obvious way produces similar results. With regard to social outcasts such as beggars, loiterers and the homeless, or people devoted to small-scale drug trafficking and street prostitution, the use of exclusion techniques in these spaces is more stringent. These include bans on accessing areas such as shopping centres or quarters, historic sites, transport hubs and parks among other places, giving rise to criminal sanctions for the repeated infringement of these bans. Not to mention public places and street furniture, which have been designed to prevent or make staying or gathering there uncomfortable. The explosion in the use of CCTV in public places and in private places of public access, despite being proven useless in preventing crime, is another key element in the conversion of public space to an inhospitable environment, where spontaneous or equivocal behaviour must be avoided.[18]

b. Legal safeguards

The contemporary system of criminal liability has been built on a strict respect for the legal safeguards of any citizen under crime control. Fear that the authorities would take advantage of *ius puniendi* for curtailing individual rights was present at the very birth of modern criminal law in nineteenth century liberal societies. This fear kept conditioning the configuration of criminal law throughout the twentieth century, giving rise to ambitious programs like the continental legal theory of crime or the due process principles of American case law. This procedural justice develops citizens' trust in criminal law, whose legitimacy is acquired in this way, and is essential for its compliance. However, biased or exaggerated claims of effectiveness and efficacy, which have increasingly been applied to criminal law, have perceived legal safeguards as an obstacle. The growing reduction in these guarantees makes citizens under crime control

---

18 See Lynch. M, "From the punitive city to the gated community: security and segregation across the social and penal landscape", *University of Miami Law Review*, 56, (2001); Norris, C, McCahill, M, Wood, D, "Editorial. The growth of CCTV: a global perspective on the international diffusion of video surveillance in publicly accessible space". *Surveillance and society*, 2 (2/3), (2004); Midtveit, E, "Crime prevention and exclusion: from walls to opera music", *Journal of Scandinavian studies in criminology and crime prevention*, 6, (2005); Baumann, Z, *Modernidad líquida*. Buenos Aires: Fondo de cultura económica. 2006. 99-118, 190-192; Doherty, J., Busch-Geertsema, et al. "Homelessness and exclusion: regulating public space in European cities". *Surveillance and society*, 5 (3), (2008); Welsh, B, Farrington, D. *Making public places safer. Surveillance and crime prevention*. New York: Oxford University Press. 2009; Beckett, K., Herbert, S. *Banished. The new social control in urban America*. New York: Oxford University Press. 2010; Medina Ariza, J. *Políticas y estrategias de prevención del delito y seguridad ciudadana*. Montevideo: B de F. 2011. p. 281-323; Björklund, F, Svenonius, Q. eds. *Videosurveillance and social control in a comparative perspective*. London: Routledge. 2013; Díez-Ripollés, JL, "El control de espacios públicos como técnica de exclusión social. Algunos contrastes regionales", *Revista española de investigación criminológica*, 4, 12 (2014).

significantly reluctant to trust the legal system, something that generates social alienation.

Reflecting this attitude is the disturbing trend of international legislation, supported by national laws, to blur significant gradings of criminal liability, such as those that distinguish conspiracy or attempt from commission of a crime, with a paradigmatic example being the configuration of the mere belonging to a criminal organization or a criminal group as an autonomous crime, or those that make a clear distinction between perpetration or complicity of a crime. Also, the recognition of legal safeguards is no longer uniform as certain offenders experience significant restrictions: Violent and sexual offenders, terrorists, members of criminal groups and recidivists bear the brunt of a criminal law that is more focused on criminals than on criminal behaviours. Moreover, we should be aware of the increasing effort required for making sure that a stigmatizing society fairly considers and evaluates behavioural disturbances that affect criminal liability. The additional contribution of a gimmicky criminal procedure, which is willing to give up essential elements of due process in exchange for alleged efficacy, must be addressed: This can be seen in the proliferation of speedy trials, the generalization of plea bargaining and the international admission of violations of the rule of evidence for forfeiture proceedings.[19]

c. *Youth justice*

The differentiated approach to juvenile offenders is a characteristic feature of any inclusive criminal policy. Minors can be strongly influenced as they are still forming their personality, so they provide crime control with the opportunity to focus on recovering or ensuring their proper socialization. However, over the last few decades of the twentieth century, the perception grew that the informality and discretion common to the welfare or protectionist approach towards juvenile offenders left them defenceless against a procedure and rulings, which, although usually well-meaning but paternalistic, ignored them as citizens. A new youth

---

19 See Feeley, M, Simon, J, "The new penology: Notes on the emerging strategy of corrections and its implications". *Criminology.* Vol. 30. N. 4 (1992); United Nations General Assembly. *Resolution 55/25 of 15 November 2000. United Nations Convention against Transnational Organised Crime.* art. 2; Tyler, T. "Procedural justice, legitimacy and the effective rule of law". *Crime and justice.* Vol. 30. Chicago: University of Chicago Press. (2003). p. 283-357; Tonry, M. *Thinking about crime.* New York: Oxford University Press. 2004. p. 141-150; Díez-Ripollés, JL. "De la sociedad del riesgo a la seguridad ciudadana: un debate desenfocado". *Revista electrónica de ciencia penal y criminología.* Vol. 07-01. (2005), p. 22-31; Corrado, M.L. "Sex offenders, unlawful combatants and preventive detention". *North Carolina Law Review.* 84 (2005-2006). p. 102-103; Lappi-Seppälä, T. "Trust, welfare", cit. p.. 361-365, 375-377; Díez-Ripollés, JL. "Tendencias político-criminales en materia de drogas", in Díez Ripollés, JL. *Política criminal y derecho penal. Estudios.* 2ª edic. Valencia: Tirant lo Blanch. 2013. p. 850-852; European Parliament and Council. *Directive UE 214/42 of 3 April 2014 on the freezing and confiscation of instrumentalities and proceeds of crime in the European Union,* Articles 4–6.

justice was proposed, which recognizes that minors require legal safeguards and due process without neglecting the predominant goal of social reintegration. Unfortunately, this transformation coincided with criminal policy trends towards punitiveness and social exclusion. The result has been a distortion of the initial objectives, so that the transition to a justice model has often meant the incorporation into youth justice of objectives and intervention techniques of adults' criminal law.

Firstly, this contamination can be seen in the evolution of age limits: Contrary to international legislation that considers a child to be a person under the age of 18, most jurisdictions have retained a more reduced minimum age for making possible the application of youth justice, with the effect that reactions that are increasingly punitive in nature are applied at very early ages. At the other extreme, there is the frequent establishment of legal provisions allowing the juvenile court to refer the case to an adult court, given the personal conditions of the minor or the kind of offence. Furthermore, we must not forget the increasing questioning of the special regime for young adults. Secondly, there has been a noticeable hardening in the system of sanctions for juvenile offenders, no matter whether they are considered penalties or not. With custodial sentences being handed down in a greater number of crimes, such custodies are increasingly enforced under closed regimes, and they extend for longer periods. Finally, it is more and more common that certain juvenile offenders serve their sentence from the beginning, or at least as soon as they become young adults, in adult prisons.[20]

d. *Sentencing system*

The system of sentencing is undergoing substantial changes in a significant number of jurisdictions. Aggravating circumstances due to recidivism or repeated offending are on the increase everywhere. Concerns about the violation that such aggravating circumstances entail for the principle of punishment for the act committed, which once recommended the abolition of these circumstances or, at least, their transformation in discretionary dispositions, have lost support. Instead, ground has been yielded to legal reforms that provide an increase in the effects of aggravating circumstances as the offender repeatedly returns to commit crimes; the "three strikes and you're out" laws in the US have been at the forefront

20 See ECtHR, Judgment 16 December 1999 T. v. United Kingdom, Judgment S.C. v. United Kingdom 15 June 2004; Tonry, M, Doob, A. eds. *Youth crime and youth justice: Comparative and cross-national perspectives. Crime and justice. A review of research.* Vol.31. Chicago: The University of Chicago Press. 2004; Tonry, M. *Thinking* cit p. 150-156; Vázquez González, C. *Derecho penal juvenil europeo.* Madrid: Dykinson. 2005; Cavadino, M, Dignan, J. *Penal systems.* cit. p.199-303; Muncie, J, Goldson, B, eds. *Comparative Youth Justice.* London: Sage Publications. 2006; Committee on the Rights of the Child. United Nations. *General Comment no. 10. Children's rights in juvenile justice.* 2007. CRC/C/GC/10. p. 11-13; González Tascón, M-M. *El tratamiento de la delincuencia juvenil en la Unión europea.* Valladolid: Lex Nova. 2010. p. 119-365.

of this change. On the other hand, it does not seem an exaggeration to say that one of the most repeated patterns in numerous recent legal reforms is the reduction in the scope of judicial discretion in setting tariffs. This can be achieved by various methods, among which may be the continuous raising of the mandatory minimum for penalties to be imposed, or complex and dysfunctional sentencing guidelines that make the judge seem little more than an accountant. This distrust shown for expertise in sentencing projects its influence on the corrections system through the so-called truth-in-sentencing: Their provisions curtail the flexibility of the prison regime, and maintain a harsh serving of the sentence over a prolonged period of time, regardless of the personal conditions of the inmates.

Again, all this is nothing but a corollary of the prominence acquired by the new demands for the social segregation of offenders. They are able to disregard the principle of proportionality when what is intended is to keep the repeat offender away from social life for as long as possible, as plainly accepted by certain supreme courts. They are the ones who reject judicial expertise in sentencing, because it excessively prioritizes the offender's needs for rehabilitation as opposed to retributive and incapacity requirements. And they are the ones who are not willing to accommodate the serving of the sentence to the personal conditions of inmates, at least until they have spent some time in social isolation.[21]

e. Pre-trial and preventive detention

The detention of persons suspected of having committed an offense, as well as of those who, after serving their prison term, are still considered criminally dangerous, has experienced notable recent abuses. On the one hand, we must mention the anti-terrorism legislation enacted in many different countries after the Islamist attacks of September 2011 in the United States and which was later replicated in other places on the planet; this emergency legislation permits indefinite detention or disproportionately prolonged detention of people without charge; the persistence of Guantanamo Bay detention centre is its most

21 See Tonry, M. *Sentencing matters.* cit.; Zimring, F, Hawkins, G, Kamin, S. *Punishment and democracy. Three strikes and you're out in California.* New York: Oxford University Press. 2001; US Supreme Court. *Ewing v. California,* 538 US 11, 2003, *Lockyer v. Andrade*, 538 US 63, 2003; Whitman, J. *Harsh Justice.* New York: Oxford University Press. 2003. p. 53-56; Castiñeira, M-T, Ragues, R. "Three strikes. El principio de proporcionalidad en la jurisprudencia del tribunal supremo de los Estados Unidos". *Revista electrónica de derecho penal y criminología.* n.14. (2004), p. 59-85; Brodeur, J-P. "Comparative penology", cit. p. 55-60; Tonry, M. "Determinants", cit. *p.* 27-30; Dünkel, F, Lappi-Seppälä, T, Morgenstern, C, van Zyl Smit, D, "Gefangenenraten und Kriminalpolitik", cit. p. 1046-1048; Zysman Quirós, D. *Castigo y determinación de la pena en Estados Unidos. Un estudio sobre las United States Sentencing Guidelines.* Madrid: Marcial Pons. 2013.

conspicuous example. But we must not forget the intensive use of remand detention in a number of legal systems, which is singularly affecting the duration and reasons of detention together with the enforcement conditions. On the other hand, detentions after the completion of the sentence are going through a phase of re-legitimization. This allows authorities to legally establish new cases of dangerousness, to admit indefinite detention, and to expand the use of preventive detention to new jurisdictions

The detention of suspects, especially if no charges have been brought against them, although it may be justified in certain cases, must not only be exceptional, but also strictly linked to ensuring prosecution. Overcoming these limits erodes the trust in the criminal justice system of those affected, who become alienated from its values and internalize their rejection to criminal justice. Detentions after completion of the sentence, due to alleged criminal dangerousness, are unjustified, and especially when they can potentially be indefinite: It is unfair to take an uncertain prognosis on the already ex-offender and it means the assumption of the failure of the prison system to provide effective ways of rehabilitation. In any case, the chosen option keeps the ex-offender temporarily or permanently socially excluded.[22]

II.3. ENFORCEMENT OF SANCTIONS

a. *Prison regime*

During the last third of the twentieth century, prison regimes were inspired by two central ideas. Prison conditions should safeguard the greatest possible number of inmate rights not directly restricted by the sentence; and inmates, notwithstanding the abandonment of the treatment model in countries where it once was rooted, should have access to rehabilitation treatments and social reintegration assistance while serving their sentence. Developments in the last twenty years have gone through quite different routes: the social segregation and the incapacitation of inmates have gained rapid prominence, together with the reaffirmation of imprisonment as a retributive and deterrent measure. It has been said that the prison system resembles a waste management institution, where

22 See Corrado, M.L. "Sex offenders", cit, p. 77-122; Vervaele, J. *La legislación antiterrorista en Estados Unidos. ¿Inter arma silent leges?*. Buenos Aires: Editores del Puerto. 2007. p. 52-56, 68-75, 86-98; Viano, E. "Guantánamo: the crucible for human and constitutional rights in XXI century USA", in Tak, P, Jendly, M, *Prison policy and prisoners' rights*. Nijmegen: Wolf Legal Publishers. 2008 p. 75-129; van Kempen PH ed. *Pre-trial detention. Human rights, criminal procedural law and penitentiary law, comparative law.* Cambridge: Intersentia. 2012. p. 3-46, Part Three p. 225-819; van Kempen, P.H, Young, W. eds. *Prevention of reoffending. The value of rehabilitation and the management of high-risk offenders.* Cambridge: Intersentia. 2014. Part Three. p. 145-335.

human waste – mostly from socially disadvantaged groups, the poor and illegal foreign residents – is handled and processed.

This change in emphasis has allowed significant modifications of the penitentiary framework: the emergence of private prisons that are scarcely committed to more than inmates' custody; an increase in the capacity of new prison facilities; and the normalization of maximum security and supermax security prisons, where draconian prison regimes are enforced not just for very dangerous or disruptive inmates but are also the first destination for other offenders or those with certain sentences. The living conditions of inmates are another phenomenon to consider. Surely, prison overcrowding is a persistent reality in both rich and poor countries and, as a consequence, it is not surprising that penitentiary administration must proceed on the basis of controlled releases mainly aimed at keeping the facilities in good conditions of operation, if not, in extreme cases, it leaves inmates themselves to take over the internal management of the prison. But more revealing is the development of policies that intentionally seek to worsen the material and regime conditions of prisoners in order to reinforce the whole distressing and stigmatizing effect of any stay in prison. Also, while there has been a growth in victims' rights to have a say in the offender's sentencing and prison enforcement conditions in accordance with their interests, there has been a decrease in the inmates' abilities to protect their rights for fair living and regime conditions. Thus, it is common that inmates confront serious, sometimes insurmountable, obstacles for appealing against penitentiary decisions about living conditions, or related to the regime or discipline, not to mention the frequent denial of inmates' rights to associate or to file a collective claim. Also, by making use of the theory of inherent limitations, prison authorities deprive inmates of rights other than those related to the conviction based on organizational arguments. Finally, the widespread crisis of parole is worth noting: conditions attached to its obtaining or maintenance are increasingly stringent, revocations are rising, and certain crimes and offenders are beforehand generally not eligible.[23]

23 See Kurki, L, Morris, N. "The purposes, practices and problems of supermax prisons", in Tonry, M. ed. *Crime and justice. A review of research.* Vol. 28. 2001 p. 385-421; van Zyl Smit, D, Dünkel, F. *Imprisonment today and tomorrow. International perspectives on prisoner's rights and prison conditions.* The Hague: Kluwer Law international. 2001; Whitman, J. *Harsh Justice,* cit. p. 19-25, 56-62, 70-80; Tonry, M. *Thinking* cit. p. 156-163, 183; Jacobs, J. "Prison reform amid the ruins of prisoner's rights", in Tonry, M ed. *The future of imprisonment.* New York: Oxford University Press. 2004. p. 179-194; Simon, J. *Governing through crime.* New York: Oxford University Press. 2007 p. 141-144, 152-175; Tak, P, Jendly, M, eds. *Prison policy* cit.; US Supreme Court. *Brown v. Plata.* 563 US__2011, *Brown v. Plata* 570 US__2013.

b. *Legal and social status of offenders and ex-offenders*

Deprivation of political, civil and social rights for offenders and ex-offenders is increasingly widespread, though its intensity is different according to geographical areas and legal traditions. In other words, judicial or administrative authorities can impose disqualifications on these rights by the mere fact of a conviction, even if those disqualifications are not linked to the nature of the crime committed or the dangerousness of the offender. These disabilities can have effects after the completion of a sentence over significant periods or time, sometimes for life. Among the political rights that are affected are enfranchisement, jury service, the right to legally reside in a foreign country and eligibility for naturalization. Among the civil rights that may be affected are parental rights, adoption of children, access to public service positions or many kinds of private employment, public contracting or attaining a driving license. Offenders may also be deprived of social rights such as the eligibility for social welfare benefits, public housing or student financial aid, the access to health prevention programs or to receive compensation as a victim of a crime. These collateral sanctions until recently have not been carefully considered by legal practitioners, and offenders and ex-offenders are often only aware of them when they try to use or access them. They have been called *invisible punishments*.

Given their indiscriminate application, one can only think of it as a new dimension of social incapacitation. Offenders and ex-offenders must have a political, civil and social status inferior to other citizens; they must be placed in a permanent situation of stigmatization that keeps them on the margins of society and be governed through crime control institutions. To this end, the community involves social actors and institutions in its governance that are not originally related to crime control. The persistent exclusion of these people from social activities that are unrelated to the crime significantly hinders their social reintegration – not to mention their families – and it seems no coincidence that, given the prevalence of crime, these disqualifications are concentrated in socio-economically disadvantaged groups.[24]

24 See Mauer, M, Chesney-Lind, M. eds. *Invisible punishment. The collateral consequences of mass imprisonment*, New York: The New Press, 2002; Petersilia, J. *When prisoners come home* cit. p. 105-137; Mele, C, Miller, T. eds. *Civil penalties, social consequences*, New York: Routledge, 2005; Uggen, C, Manza, J, Thompson, M, "Citizenship, democracy", cit; Manza, J. / Uggen, C. *Locked out. Felon disenfranchisement and American democracy*. New York: Oxford University Press, 2008; Ewald, A, Rottinghaus, B, eds. *Criminal disenfranchisement in an international perspective*, New York: Cambridge University Press, 2009; Pinard, M. "Collateral consequences of criminal convictions: confronting issues of race and dignity", *New York University Law Review*, Vol. 85, (2010); Díez-Ripollés, JL. "Sanciones adicionales a delincuentes y exdelincuentes. Contrastes entre Estados Unidos de Amérića y países nórdicos europeos". *Indret*. 4, (2014); Jacobs, J. *The eternal criminal record*, Cambridge: Harvard University Press 2015, p. 246-300.

c. Police and criminal records

The police, criminal and prison records of suspects, or those who have been prosecuted or convicted of crimes have grown in substance and volume, thanks to the ubiquitous use of new electronic media. New registries, such as criminal intelligence databases or administrative infractions repositories, also take on a new role. The extension of the terms for the limitation of crimes, as well as for sealing or expungement of criminal records, together with the added difficulty of actually getting records sealed or expunged, keeps them operative for longer and longer periods. Although there are significant differences depending on the type of records and national traditions, the fact is that conviction records are becoming available in greater numbers and more easily to non-penal institutions, businesses or private organizations, and individuals. In fact, a clean criminal record is a requirement prescribed by law for a progressive number of jobs, and its demand has established itself as a good business practice. The impact on stigmatized offenders, especially sex offenders and other types of offenders that are gradually being included, is more than just about appearing on a register: they are forced, sometimes for life, to provide accurate information on their whereabouts after conviction for the purpose of public knowledge.

Criminal records and community notifications thus become the contemporary shaming penalties, as has been explicitly demanded by some scholars and legal practitioners. The rights to honour, privacy and personal data protection, as well as the social interest in the social reintegration of offenders, are cast aside. In turn, we not only find an exaggerated form of freedom of speech, but also the transfer to the community and individuals of the responsibility to assess ex-offenders' dangerousness, together with the overvaluation of social stigmatization as a social control mechanism.[25]

---

25 See Louks, N, Lyner, O, Sullivan, T, "The employment of people with criminal records in the European Union", *European Journal on Criminal Policy and Research*, 6 (1998); Petersilia, J, *When prisoners come*, cit. p. 106-112, 127-129; Petrunik, M, Deutschmann, L, "The exclusion-inclusion spectrum in state and community response to sex offenders in Anglo-American and European jurisdictions", *International Journal of Offender Therapy and Comparative Criminology*, vol 52, 5 (2008); Wacquant, L. *Punishing the poor. The neoliberal government of social insecurity*, Durham: Duke University Press, 2009, p. 208-239; Thomas, T, "European developments in sex offender registration and monitoring", *European Journal of Crime, Criminal Law and Criminal Justice*, 18 (2010); Larrauri Pijoan. E, "Legal protection against criminal background checks in Europe", *Punishment and Society*. 16 (1), (2014); Harris, A, Levenson, J, Ackermann, A. "Registered sex offenders in the United States: Behind the numbers", *Crime and Delinquency*, vol. 60 (1). (2014); Jacobs, J, *The eternal criminal record*, cit.; Fernández-Pacheco, C. "Intimidad y publicidad de los antecedentes penales. Los registros para delincuentes sexuales", en Doval Pais, A dr. *Nuevos límites penales para la autonomía individual y la intimidad*, Cizur Menor: Thomson Reuters, 2015.

III. CONCLUSIONS

The chosen analytical approach has allowed us to integrate into a single conceptual framework, both descriptive and evaluative, numerous punitive rules and practices whose actual or potential application characterizes the current evolution of contemporary criminal policy and conditions the doctrinal debate. Given that this approach is based on a clear strategic alternative to prevent crime, it can develop a discourse that identifies large areas for criminal intervention and within them, diverse rules and practices that acquire a clear sense under such an analytical approach. This sense is no longer constrained to generic considerations on whether an expansive or rigorous use of criminal instruments.

Previous formulations of this approach have focused on identifying indicators to highlight differences between different national criminal policy models according to the social inclusion / social exclusion dimension.[26] In this case, we have used one of the poles of the strategic alternative, which of social exclusion, to group together rules and practices whose progressive consolidation in our systems of penal control will mean a clear evolution towards an exclusionary criminal policy model and, consequently, to an overuse of criminal intervention means. Thus, this social inclusion / social exclusion dimension becomes useful beyond its rich ideological content when discriminating between different criminal policy models.

Selected aspects correspond largely with those already chosen to confront the exclusionary and inclusive criminal policy models, but this time, an aspect related to the selection of criminal behaviours has been added, and any of the other aspects already considered has been divided into two. In addition, they have still all been grouped according to the three most important phases of criminal intervention: criminalization, prosecution and enforcement of penalties.

At no time has there been an attempt to enter into the analysis of the political, socio-economic or criminological causes that may be influencing the evolution towards this increasingly interventionist criminal law.

However, the catalogue of rules and practices that has been identified is large, well interconnected and consistent with the analytical approach developed. In that sense, it offers important clues to the way forward to make decisions against the evolution that has been outlined.

26 See Díez-Ripollés, JL, "Social inclusion", cit., p. 68-71.

THE OVERUSE OF CRIMINAL JUSTICE IN THE CASE LAW OF THE EUROPEAN COURT OF HUMAN RIGHTS

Paulo Pinto de Albuquerque*

I. INTRODUCTION

The relationship between human rights and criminal justice has long been considered to be particularly intricate. On the one hand, human rights law may promote change in the criminal justice machinery at both the domestic and international levels. On the other hand, unsuitable national criminal law or wrongful application of the applicable criminal law and procedure provisions may interfere with treaty obligations undertaken by States in respect of human rights. It is therefore of the utmost importance that the existing bond between human rights and criminal justice be clearly defined in the context of the administration of criminal justice so that the objectives of both can be harmonised within the democratic state.[1]

In this context, the European Court of Human Rights (ECtHR) has played an important role as human rights adjudicator in the field of criminal law. An analysis of the Strasbourg case law on criminal matters reveals that the Convention obligations undertaken by the States are twofold: on one hand, the protection of the individual against the overuse of criminal justice and, on the other hand, the use of criminal law for the protection of the rights and freedoms of individuals and legal persons. The former Belgian Judge at the ECtHR, Françoise Tulkens, described these two aspects as the "the defensive role of

---

* Prof. Dr. Paulo Pinto de Albuquerque is the judge of the European Court of Human Rights in respect of Portugal and vice-president of Section IV since 1 September 2018. He is furthermore professor of criminal law at the law faculty of the Catholic University of Lisbon. He thanks Dr. Catarina Garcia for her help in the preparation of this text.

1 Stefan Trechsel, *Human Rights in Criminal Proceedings*, Oxford: Oxford U.P., 2006, p. 7-8.

human rights" and "the offensive role of human rights" in what she called "the paradoxical relationship between criminal law and human rights".[2]

This contribution aims at exploring the case law of the ECtHR in the light of the traditional "defensive role of human rights", focusing on the overuse of criminal justice against the individual and, in particular, on the overuse of criminalisation and of imprisonment. In other words, this contribution will revisit some of the cases in which the Strasbourg Court has considered the criminalisation of an act and the recourse to imprisonment to be in breach of a Convention right.

II. OVERUSE OF CRIMINALISATION

A manifestation of the overuse of the criminal justice machinery can be first found at the legislative level. When considering the criminal approach to be adopted in relation to a specific conduct, the legislature should take into account that criminal law should only be used as a last resort when no other alternative to a criminal law measure exists.

A look into the case law of the ECtHR allows us to identify various group of cases where the Strasbourg Court has criticised the legislative choice on account of the excessive or disproportionate criminalisation of a certain conduct. Examples of this situation can be found in the cases *Dudgeon v. the United Kingdom* (no. 7525/76, 24 February 1983), *Norris v. Ireland* (no. 10581/83, 26 October 1988), *Modinos v. Cyprus* (no. 15070/89, 22 April 1993) and *A.D.T. v. the United Kingdom* (no. 35765/97, 31 July 2000) with regard to private homosexual acts between consenting adults; *S.L. v. Austria* (no. 4533/09, 9 January 2003) regarding homosexual acts of adult men with consenting adolescents between 14 and 18 years of age; *Vajnai v. Hungary* (no. 33629/06, 8 July 2008) on the wearing of the red star, symbol of the international workers' movement at a demonstration; *Altug Taner Akçam v. Turkey* (no. 27520/07, 25 October 2011) concerning insults to "Turkishness"; *Mosley v. the United Kingdom* (no. 48009/08, 10 May 2011) regarding the non-compliance with the pre-notification requirement to publish news on private life; *Akgöl and Göl v. Turkey* (nos. 28495/06 and 28516/06, 17 May 2011) with regard to the participation in an unlawful but peaceful demonstration; *Wizerkaniuk v. Poland* (no. 18990/05, 5 July 2011) concerning the publication of unauthorised verbatim

2 Françoise Tulkens, 'The Paradoxical Relationship between Criminal Law and Human Rights', *Journal of International Criminal Justice* 9 (2011), p. 577-595. In this paper F. Tulkens describes the historical role of human rights, which aims at affording protection against criminal law, and contrasts it with a new role in which criminal law is called into play in order to protect human rights.

quotations; *Bayatyan v. Armenia* (no. 23459/03, 7 July 2011) on conscientious objection in the military; *Mallah v. France* (no. 29681/08, 10 November 2011) with regard to the assistance of illegal entry, circulation or stay of a foreigner in the national territory; *Gillberg v. Sweden* [GC] (no. 41723/06, 3 April 2012) concerning the misuse of office due to refusal of access to research material owed by a public university; *Stübing v. Germany* (no. 43547/08, 12 April 2012) on incest; and *Şükran Aydin and Others v. Turkey* (nos. 49197/06, 23196/07, 50242/08, 60912/08 and 14871/09, 22 January 2013) regarding the use of mother tongue in political campaign.

In this context, two issues stand out in view of their recurrence in the case law: 1) the criminalisation of defamation and 2) "crimmigration" or the practice of treating irregular migration as a security and law enforcement question. These two issues will be addressed specifically below.

II.1. CRIMINALISATION OF DEFAMATION: THE OLD QUESTION

From the reading of the case law of the ECtHR, it can be inferred that the issue of criminalisation of defamation remains unsolved. Whereas the ECtHR has frequently considered specific criminal sanctions to be in breach of freedom of expression on account of its disproportionality, namely the use of prison sentences in defamation cases, it has not adopted a clear stance against criminalisation of defamation in itself. This in spite of the more straightforward position of the Parliamentary Assembly of the Council of Europe, which opposes any use of criminal sanctions against defamation in view of their substantial – and undesirable – effect on freedom of expression.[3]

For the ECtHR the imposition of criminal sanctions to defamation offences cannot be considered an automatic breach of Article 10 of the Convention.[4] It has however stressed that it raises serious concerns regarding freedom of expression. In the *Šabanović v. Montenegro and Serbia*[5] judgment, for example, the Strasbourg Court recalled that the use of criminal law sanctions in defamation cases was not in itself disproportionate and reiterated, however, that the nature and severity of the penalties imposed were factors to be taken into account. It

3 See, for example, Parliamentary Assembly of the Council of Europe Resolution no. 1577 (2007), "Towards decriminalization of defamation", 4 October 2007 (at http://assembly.coe.int/nw/xml/XRef/Xref-XML2HTML-en.asp?fileid=17588&lang=en (last visited 23 march 2017), where the Assembly insisted on the existence of "procedural safeguards enabling anyone charged with defamation to substantiate their statements in order to absolve themselves of possible criminal responsibility."

4 *Lindon, Otchakovsky-Laurens and July v. France* [GC], no. 21279/02 and 36448/02, 22 October 2007, *Radio and Others v. France*, Appl. 53984/00, 30 March 2004; *Rumyana Ivanova v. Bulgaria*, no. 36207/03, 14 February 2008.

5 *Šabanović v. Montenegro and Serbia*, no. 5995/06, 31 May 2011.

further recalled the Resolution of the Council of Europe calling on the member States which still provided for prison sentences for defamation – even if they were not actually imposed – to abolish them without delay. In the *Šabanović* judgment the fact that the applicant had been given a suspended sentence was seen with particular concern given that it could have been transformed into a prison sentence. Moreover, in the context of the penalties applied, the amount of the fine that an applicant is ordered to pay – and, when it occurs, the accumulation with the payment of compensation to the victim[6] – is carefully examined by the ECtHR.

In the case *Raichinov v. Bulgaria*[7] the Strasbourg Court held in particular that recourse to criminal proceedings in order to protect a person's reputation or pursue another legitimate aim under paragraph 2 of Article 10 had to be based on an assessment of the proportionality of an interference with the rights protected which implied considering whether the authorities could have resorted to means other than a criminal penalty, such as civil and disciplinary remedies. In that particular case, the ECtHR concluded that the criminal proceedings against the applicant had been a disproportionate response to the incident in issue (a remark about a deputy Prosecutor-General) and that the applicant's resulting sentence (a fine and a public reprimand), while being in the lower range of the possible penalties, was still a sentence under criminal law, registered in the applicant's criminal record and therefore not necessary in a democratic society.

By contrast, situations could exist where the ECtHR accepts the need to apply a criminal sanction to defamatory statements whenever those are capable of undermining an individual's right to presumption of innocence protected under Article 6 § 2 of the Convention. In the case *Ruokanen and Others v. Finland*[8], the Strasbourg Court noted that in view of the margin of appreciation accorded to States, a criminal measure as a response to defamation could not, as such, be considered disproportionate to the aim pursued. In addition, it highlighted, however, that the imposition of a prison sentence for a press offence would be compatible with Article 10 "*only in exceptional circumstances, notably where other fundamental rights had been impaired, as for example, in the case of hate speech or incitement to violence*". In this case the ECtHR considered that a journalist who had been convicted of defamation should had verified the accuracy of a rape accusation. It further noted that, although quite severe, the penalties imposed, seen against the background of the circumstances of the case, had been proportionate in regard to the competing interests at stake. The ECtHR thus reiterated the need, in the context of defamation cases, to assess the necessity of a given specific criminal sanction on a case-by-case basis.

6 *Do Carmo de Portugal e Castro Câmara v. Portugal*, no. 53139/11, 4 October 2016.
7 *Raichinov v. Bulgaria*, no. 47579/99, 20 April 2006.
8 *Ruokanen and Others v. Finland*, no. 45130/06, 6 April 2010.

II.2. CRIMMIGRATION: A NEW TREND

Irregular migration into Europe has surged in the last two decades and, in particular, in the wake of the recent migration crisis. Europe's response to this surge has notoriously emphasised the role of criminal law in this area. On the one hand, the State criminal-law machinery, including detention, prosecution and sentencing to imprisonment terms, has been used for the purpose of immigration enforcement and, on the other hand, expulsion and deportation measures and detention for that purpose are imposed as a method of crime control.[9]

This has been called the *crimmigration* trend; a policy which perceives the migrant as the newest "enemy", a social outcast whose presence is no longer a valuable contribution to the European melting pot and its economy, but instead endangers social order, the social-security balance and the organisation of the labour market, if not the continent's ethnic and religious fabric.

No better lens through which to observe the current fusion of criminal and immigration law exists than the imprisonment and detention of migrants. The number of refugees, asylum-seekers, rejected asylum-seekers, stateless persons, trafficked persons and irregular migrants who have been jailed is at unprecedented levels in Europe. In some jurisdictions, detention is mandatory or based on presumptions in favour of detention. When the domestic legal framework is vague and open-ended, immigration authorities rely on discretionary administrative practices. Furthermore, detention is frequently applied as part of a policy to deter future asylum-seekers or to dissuade those who have commenced their claims from pursuing them. Sometimes it is even used as a punitive measure for irregular entry or presence in the country, lack of documentation or failure to comply with administrative requirements or other restrictions related to residency in the host country. The ECtHR has already had opportunity to deliberate on the issue and has reiterated in many occasions that detention of migrants has to have a legal basis in domestic law and must be necessarily demanded by the circumstances of the case.

Practice demonstrates that asylum-seekers are detained for indefinite or very prolonged periods of time, placed at best in mid-security, special detention centres, at worst in police stations and common prison facilities, but in any event treated as if they were convicted criminals. In Europe, as elsewhere, the *crimmigration* trend has led to the excessive detention of asylum-seekers. Unfortunately the Court failed to resist this trend. *Saadi v. the United Kingdom*[10] is the regrettable landmark in this trend in the Court's case-law. According to that judgment, a State may detain an asylum-seeker to prevent unauthorised entry

9 See my opinion attached to *Abdullahi and Aweys Abubakar v. Malta*, nos. 25794/13 and 28151/13, 22 November 2016, with further references to the relevant materials.

10 *Saadi v. the United Kingdom [GC]*, no. 13229/03, ECHR 2008-I.

and to expedite the asylum claim, and it is not relevant whether detention is necessary in order to prevent that irregular entry. Efficiency considerations prevail over liberty, in the Grand Chamber's view.

Quite remarkably, some Chambers of the Strasbourg Court have departed from such rationale in what has now become a silent but growing revolt against *Saadi*. In a succession of cases, various Chambers of the ECtHR held the view that detention of asylum-seekers and, in general, of migrants breaches Article 5 § 1(f) when it is applied automatically and no other less drastic measure was sought. In *Louled Massoud*[11], which concerned a detention which lasted for more than eighteen months after the determination of the applicant's asylum claim, the ECtHR found "*it hard to conceive that in a small island like Malta, where escape by sea without endangering one's life is unlikely and fleeing by air is subject to strict control, the authorities could not have had at their disposal measures other than the applicant's protracted detention to secure an eventual removal in the absence of any immediate prospect of his expulsion.*" In *Suso Musa*[12], the ECtHR cited the passage of Recommendation Rec (2003) 5 of the Committee of Ministers referring to the "*careful examination of their necessity in each individual case*", in order to conclude that it had "*reservations as to the Government's good faith in applying an across-the-border detention policy (save for specific vulnerable categories) with a maximum duration of eighteen months.*" Oddly enough, the necessity principle implicitly came into play in the assessment of the Government's good faith and the Court held that the applicant's detention up to the date of the determination of his asylum application was not compatible with the first limb of Article 5 § 1(f).

In *Rahimi*[13], a case concerning the detention pending his expulsion of an unaccompanied minor who had presented a request for political asylum, the Chamber reproached the national authorities because "*they [had] not [sought] to establish whether the applicant's placement in the Pagani detention centre had been a measure of last resort or whether another less drastic measure might have sufficed to secure his deportation*". In *Raza*[14], a case concerning the detention of an adult pending deportation, the Court noted that "*[i]t should also be observed that after his release on 15 July 2008 Mr Raza was placed under an obligation to report to his local police station at regular intervals... This shows that the authorities had at their disposal measures other than the applicant's protracted detention to secure the enforcement of the order for his expulsion.*" In *Mikolenko*[15], another case concerning the detention of an adult pending deportation, the Court concluded that the grounds for the applicant's detention, imposed with a view to his

11 *Louled Massoud v. Malta*, no. 24340/08, 27 July 2010.
12 *Suso Musa v. Malta*, no. 42337/12, 23 July 2013.
13 *Rahimi v. Greece*, no. 8687/08, 5 April 2011.
14 *Raza v. Bulgaria*, no. 31465/08, 11 February 2010.
15 *Mikolenko v. Estonia*, no. 10664/05, 8 October 2009.

deportation, did not remain valid for the whole period of his detention because the Estonian authorities had at their disposal measures other than the applicant's protracted detention in the deportation centre, since after his release he was obliged to report to the Board at regular intervals.

Such use of criminal sanctions within the framework of border controls has prompted criticism from different entities, including non-governmental organizations and international organisations.[16] In this regard, the issue paper prepared in 2010 by the Commissioner for Human Rights of the Council of Europe is noteworthy and in which he stressed that

> "the criminalisation of persons seeking international protection is a matter of substantial concern in Europe. This takes place in a number of ways – measures which make access to European territory extremely difficult for refugees, such as visa requirements, carriers sanctions, interdiction at sea, criminal sanctions on the using of false documents etc. Secondly, when asylum seekers manage to arrive in Europe, they often face further criminal sanctions – criminal charges in respect of the manner of their arrival, prohibition on employment and criminalisation of unauthorised employment when there if no functioning reception system which will permit asylum seekers to eat and have shelter. Criminal penalties for changing address without authorisation, failing to notify state authorities of changes of circumstances and detention are all increasingly common and permitted in the EU acquis."[17]

III. OVERUSE OF IMPRISONMENT

Mass incarceration is a worldwide growing concern and is deeply linked to criminal policy and sentencing practice. The UN Special Rapporteur on Torture, Juan E. Méndez, has characterised the overuse of imprisonment as "*one of the major underlying causes of overcrowding which results in conditions that amount to ill-treatment or even torture.*"[18]

According to the latest SPACE Statistics, despite some signs of decline such as the fact that the prison population rate has decreased by 7% in 2014, the ratio of

16 Among others, Alan Desmond, 'The Development of a Common EU Migration Policy and the Rights of Irregular Migrants: a Progress Narrative?', Human Rights Law Review, 2016, 16, p. 247-272.

17 Council of Europe, Commissioner for Human Rights, 'Criminalisation of Migration in Europe: Human Rights Implications', CommDH/IssuePaper(2010)1.

18 United Nations General Assembly, Interim report of the Special Rapporteur on torture and other cruel, inhuman or degrading treatment or punishment, A/68/295, 9 August 2013.

inmates being of 124 inmates per 100,000 inhabitants, overcrowding remains a problem in Europe.[19]

The root causes of prison overcrowding in Europe were recently summarised in the "White Paper on Prison Overcrowding", prepared by the Council of Europe[20]: they included penal policy and legislation leading to overuse of the penal system; the limited use of alternatives to detention on remand; length of detention on remand; and limited use of community sanctions and measures. This has led to what the Open Society Foundation has called "the most overlooked human rights crisis in our time".[21] In this regard the Parliamentary Assembly of the Council of Europe has recently observed that the high number of pre-trial detainees in Europe was an indication that the permissible grounds for pre-trial detention were being to widely interpreted in order to justify pre-trial detention for abusive purposes aiming, inter alia, to put pressure on detainees in order to coerce them into confessing to a crime, to neutralise political competitors, to intimidate civil society and to silence critical voices.[22]

The ECtHR has also highlighted the existing relationship between prison overcrowding and the excessive recourse to pre-trial. In the pilot judgments *Torreggiani and others v. Italy*[23] and *Varga and others v. Hungary*, for example, the ECtHR observed that the solution to the problem of overcrowding lied in the *"reduction of the number of prisoners by more frequent use of non-custodial punitive measures and minimising the recourse to pre-trial detention."*[24]

---

19 2014 Council of Europe Penal Statistics, at https://wcd.coe.int/ViewDoc.jsp?p=&id=2423393&Site=DC&BackColorInternet=F5CA75&BackColorIntranet=F5CA75&BackColorLogged=A9BACE&direct=true (last visited 1 March 2019).

20 Council of Europe, Directorate General Human Rights and Rule of Law, White Paper on Prison Overcrowding, 30 June 2016 (at: www.coe.int/t/DGHL/STANDARDSETTING/PRISONS/PCCP%20documents%202016/PC-CP%20(2015)%206_E%20Rev%207 %20White%20Paper%2030 %20June%202016.pdf (last visited 1 March 2019).

21 Open Society Justice Initiative, Presumption of Guilt: The Global Overuse of Pretrial Detention, 2014 (at https://www.opensocietyfoundations.org/sites/default/files/presumption-guilt-09032014.pdf (last visited 1 March 2019).

22 Parliamentary Assembly of the Council of Europe, Abuse of pretrial detention in States Parties to the European Convention on Human Rights, Summary of the Draft Resolution, 7 September 2015 (at http://assembly.coe.int/nw/xml/XRef/Xref-XML2HTML-EN.asp?fileid=21992&lang=en (last visited 1 March 2019).

23 *Torreggiani and Others v. Italy*, Appls. 43517/09, 46882/09, 55400/09, 57875/09, 61535/09, 35315/10 and 37818/10, 8 January 2013. It is important to highlight the effects of a good execution of the *Torreggiani* judgment by the Italian authorities in so far as they adopted a group of structural measures in view of complying with the judgment which resulted in an important and continuing drop in the prison population (see, in this regard, the 2014 Report on Supervision of the Execution of Judgments and Decisions (https://rm.coe.int/CoERMPublicCommonSearchServices/DisplayDCTMContent?documentId=0900001680592ae9) and the Action Plan submitted by the Italian Authorities to the Committee of Ministers (http://hudoc.exec.coe.int/ENG?i=DH-DD(2014)1143E).

24 *Varga and Others v. Hungary*, Appls. 14097/12, 45135/12, 73712/12, 34001/13, 44055/13 and 64586/13, 10 March 2015.

An integrated approach to the problem of prison overcrowding requires long-term solutions, including changes to the legal framework, practices and attitudes. Penal policies that over-criminalise and over-punish must be subjected in penalties for minor offences, an increase in punishment suspension, parole and early release possibilities, a reduction in custodial measures, diversion of mentally-ill offenders and drug-addicted offenders to therapy thus replacing the autopilot cycle of arrest, prosecution and incarceration – all these are well-known alternatives to a strict penal policy.[25]

III.1. ABUSE OF PRE-TRIAL DETENTION

The right to liberty is protected by Article 5 of the Convention and has been considered to be "*in the first rank of the fundamental rights that protect the physical security of an individual*".[26] According to the ECtHR, the list provided by Article 5 regarding the situations in which recourse to detention may occur has to be strictly interpreted.[27]

Within the framework of the Council of Europe, the Parliamentary Assembly has recently stressed the importance of the presumption of innocence in criminal proceedings and reiterated that pre-trial detention should be used only in exceptional circumstances[28], as a last resort, "*when alternative measures of restraint are insufficient to safeguard the integrity of the proceedings.*"[29] That is not, however, what the practice within many of the Contracting States of the Council of Europe has shown.

In the case *Nart v. Turkey*[30] the Court recalled that pre-trial detention of minors should be used only as a measure of last resort and added that, if such a measure was to be applied, it had to be for the shortest period of time. In that case, the Court additionally observed that the domestic authorities had not taken into consideration the applicant's age when ordering his detention. Following the same approach, in the *Güvec v. Turkey*[31] judgment the ECtHR held that the applicant's detention in an adult prison had been in contravention of the applicable regulations in force in Turkey at the material time and of the country's

25 See my opinion joined to *Mironovas and Others v. Lithuania*, nos. 40828/12, 29292/12, 69598/12, 40163/13, 66281/13, 70048/13 and 70065/13, 8 December 2015.

26 *McKay v. Uk (GC)*, no. 543/03, 3 December 2006.

27 See, for example, *Guzzardi v. Italy*, no. 7367/76, 6 November 1980.

28 The elements concerning a reductionist policy on the use of pre-trial detention as a preventive measure can be found already in Recommendation R(99) 22 concerning prison overcrowding of the Committee of Ministers of the Council of Europe.

29 See Parliamentary Assembly of the Council of Europe, Abuse of pretrial detention in States Parties to the European Convention on Human Rights, Summary of the Draft Resolution, 7 September 2015.

30 *Nart v. Turkey*, no. 20817/04, 6 May 2008.

31 *Güvec v. Turkey*, no. 70337/01, 20 January 2009.

obligation under international treaties. In addition, the ECtHR also found a violation of Article 3 of the Convention due to the fact that the applicant's detention had increased his psychological problems for which he did not receive adequate medical care. In *Kandzhov v. Bulgaria*[32] the ECtHR was called to analyse the (un)lawfulness of the applicant's arrest and detention for 72 hours for putting up two posters allegedly insulting the Minister of Justice and gathering signatures calling for the Minister's resignation. On account of those acts, criminal proceedings had been instituted against the applicant for insult and for hooliganism under the relevant provisions of the Criminal Code. The ECtHR firstly held that, at the material time, the charge of insult was a privately prosecutable offence and could not attract a sentence of imprisonment; therefore, there had been no basis for the applicant's detention and the ECtHR highlighted that the Prosecutor's Office had "*blatantly ignored the clear and unambiguous provisions of domestic law.*" In so far as the charges of hooliganism, the Court observed that the applicant's actions had not amounted to the constituent elements of that offence. His detention and arrest on that account had also been unlawful. Furthermore, in finding a violation in respect of Article 10 on account of the applicant's arrest and detention, the ECtHR reiterated the need for Governments' to "*display restraint in resorting to criminal proceedings, and the associated custodial measures, particularly where other means are available for replying to the unjustified attacks and criticism of their adversaries (see, mutatis mutandis, Castells v. Spain, judgment of 23 April 1992, § 46, Series A no. 36).*"

The ECtHR has also, on a multitude of occasions, set out its position on the length of pre-trial detention. The Strasbourg Court has, in this regard, adopted what could be called a strict approach. The ECtHR has noted that the reasonability for an accused to remain in detention must be assessed on the facts of each case. In addition, it has stated that "*Continued detention can be justified in a given case only if there are actual indications of a genuine requirement of public interest which, notwithstanding the presumption of innocence, outweighs the rule of respect for individual liberty laid down in Article 5 of the Convention.*"[33] Moreover, the ECtHR has emphasised that "*the existence and persistence of a reasonable suspicion that the person arrested has committed an offence is a prerequisite for the lawfulness of the continued detention. However, after a certain amount of time has elapsed it no longer suffices.*"[34] Furthermore, the ECtHR requires that "relevant" and "sufficient" grounds justify continued detention and that authorities have displayed "special diligence" in the conduct of proceedings.[35] Additionally, the Court requires that arguments for and against release be not "general and

32 *Kandzhov v. Bulgaria*, no. 68294/01, 6 November 2008.
33 *Kudla v. Poland*, no. 30210/96, 26 October 2000.
34 *Qing v. Portugal*, no. 69861/11, 5 November 2015.
35 *Labita v. Italy (GC)*, no. 26772/95, 6 April 2000.

abstract"[36] and imposes on the authorities the obligation to consider alternative measures of ensuring an individual's appearance on trial when considering whether he or she should be released or detained.[37] Hence, the ECtHR has on many occasions found a violation on account of the general terms adduced by authorities justifying the length of pre-trial detention and where authorities had not considered alternative measures for pre-trial detention: for example, *Ignatov v. Ukraine*[38], in which the applicant had been in pre-trial detention for nearly a year and eight months; or *Qing v. Portugal*, where the applicant stayed in pre-trial detention for one year and seven months.[39]

In the context of pre-trial detention special attention should be given to situations in which individuals were subject to criminal proceedings and, ultimately, to detention on account of abusive reasons (e.g. political grounds). The use of the criminal justice machinery in such a way is an obvious problem to the democratic values protected by the Convention and undertaken by the Council of Europe Member States. Under the Convention, rule of law and democracy are protected by Article 18, which primarily aims at prohibiting the abusive restriction of the rights established in the European Convention.[40]

There are not many examples of cases in which the ECtHR had to address Article 18 and the case law is therefore still flourishing in this regard. The first violation of Article 18 was found in 2004 in the *Gusinskiy*[41] judgment. The case concerned the arrest of a Russian and Israeli national who, at the material time, was the Chairman of the Board and majority shareholder of a Media company, which included a popular Russian television channel. He had been arrested on suspicion of fraud for which he was subsequently charged. He was released from detention in exchange for an undertaking that he would not leave the country. In addition, during his detention, the Acting Minister for Press and Mass Communications had offered to drop the criminal charges against the applicant if he would sell his Media company to Gazprom (a State-controlled company which was in dispute with the Media company about the latter's debts in its favour) at a price to be determined by Gazprom. Following the signing of such an agreement, criminal proceedings against the applicant were discontinued. Before the Strasbourg Court, the applicant argued that his detention had been unlawful and arbitrary as it had intended to force him to sell his media business on unfavourable terms and conditions. When analysing the applicant's complaint

36 *Smirnova v. Russia*, nos. 46133/99 and 48183/99, 24 July 2003.

37 *Suslov v. Russia*, no. 2366/07, 29 May 2012.

38 *Ignatov v. Ukraine*, no. 40583/15, 15 December 2016.

39 *Qing*, cited above.

40 For an in-depth analysis on how the abuse of criminal proceedings undermine democracy in the Strasbourg's Court's case-law, see Helen Keller and Corina Heri, 'Selective Criminal Proceedings and Article 18 of the ECHR. The European Court of Human Rights Untapped Potential to Protect Democracy', *Human Rights Law Journal*, Vol. 36, no. 1-6, p. 1-10, 30 June 2016.

41 *Gusinskiy v. Russia*, no. 70276/01, 19 May 2005.

under Article 18 of the Convention, the Court had to assess whether the applicant had been detained for any other purpose than that provided for in Article 5 § 1(c). The ECtHR observed that it had not been disputed that the agreement linked the termination of the criminal investigation against the applicant to the sale of his media organisation to Gazprom, a company controlled by the State. In the Court's opinion, it was not the purpose of such public-law matters as criminal proceedings and detention on remand to be used as part of commercial bargaining strategies.

More recently, the Court was called to analyse the lawfulness of the arrest and detention pending trial in two cases against Azerbaijan. In *Mammadov*[42], the ECtHR considered that the applicant, an Azeri opposition politician and blogger who had a history of criticising the Government, had been arrested and detained without any evidence to reasonably suspect him of having committed the offence with which he was charged, namely that of having organised actions leading to public disorder. The Court concluded that the actual purpose of his detention had been to silence or punish the applicant for criticising the Government and publishing information it was trying to hide. Therefore, the Court considered that the domestic authorities had not acted in good faith. In *Rasul Jafarov*[43], the ECtHR considered that the arrest and pre-trial detention of a human rights defender and also co-founder of a non-governmental organisation who had been involved in the preparation of various reports relating to human rights issues in Azerbaijan, had been unjustified in so far as a number of factors supported the argument that the actual purpose of the measures against the applicant had been to silence and to punish him for his activities as a human rights defender. In particular, his arrest and detention in 2014 had occurred in the general context of an increasingly harsh and restrictive legislative regulation of NGO activity; there had been numerous statements by high-ranking officials and articles published in pro-Government media which had accused local NGOs and their leaders, including the applicant, of being traitors and foreign agents; and several other notable human rights activists, who had also cooperated with international organisations protecting human rights, had similarly been arrested and charged.

42 *Mammadov v. Azerbaijan*, no. 4762/05, 17 December 2009.
43 *Rasul Jafarov v. Azerbaijan*, no. 69981/14, 17 March 2016.

III.2. EXCESSIVE CUSTODIAL SENTENCE

The excessive application of custodial sentences is a twofold reality in the Member States of the Council Europe: in some cases, the application of a sentence of imprisonment is disproportional in itself; in others, it is the length of that sentence that raises proportionality problems. With regard to the jurisprudence of the ECtHR, it can be considered that the Strasbourg Court has adopted a proportionality-based approach to custodial sentences by assessing the necessity of its application – or its length – to the offence committed in the light of the circumstances of the case.

The majority of cases in which the ECtHR has been called to pronounce itself on the need to apply a custodial sentence refers to the rights protected by Articles 10 (freedom of expression) and 11 of the Convention (freedom of assembly and association). Recently, in the case *Murat Vural v. Turkey*[44] the ECtHR had to assess whether the prison sentence of thirteen years to which the applicant had been convicted had been excessive and disproportionate to the offence in question under Article 10 of the Convention – pouring paint over statues of Mustafa Kemal Atatürk, the founder of the Republic of Turkey, as a political protest (under Turkish law the applicant had been initially sentenced to twenty-two years and six months' imprisonment, but on appeal the sentence had been reduced to about thirteen years' imprisonment). The ECtHR noted that although the applicant's conviction and the imposition of a prison sentence had been prescribed by a law which criminalised certain conducts considered to be insulting to Atatürk's memory and the damaging to the sentiments of the Turkish society, the thirteen years' imprisonment imposed on him had been extremely severe. The ECtHR considered that while the applicant's acts had involved a psychical attack on property, they had not warranted the imposition of a custodial sentence. The Court further reiterated what it had said in the *Akgöl and Göl* judgment, namely that peaceful and non-violent forms of expression should not be made subject to the threat of imposition of a custodial sentence.

In *Karpyuk and Others v. Ukraine*[45], the ECtHR had to analyse whether the conviction of three applicants for the organisation and participation in a mass protest in Kyiv in March 2001 had interfered with their right to freedom of assembly. The Strasbourg Court first noted that Article 11 only protected the right to "peaceful assembly" and did not cover a demonstration where the organisers and participants had violent intentions. The ECtHR stated that, even considering that a sanction for the applicant's actions in organising an obstructing gathering and inciting violence during the protest could have been warranted by the demands of public safety, the long prison sentences imposed on

44 *Murat Tural v. Turkey*, no. 9540/07, 21 October 2014.

45 *Karpyuk and Others v. Ukraine*, nos. 30582/04 and 32152/04, 6 October 2015.

the applicants had, however, not been proportionate to the legitimate aim pursued. It further considered that the sanction imposed had not only been severe, but had also a chilling effect on the applicants and other persons organising protest gatherings. In addition, to reach its conclusion, the ECtHR also took into account the fact that the applicants' conviction had resulted from a trial that had not met the requirements of Article 6 of the Convention. In *Kakabadze and Others v. Georgia*[46], the ECtHR considered that the application of thirty days of deprivation of liberty to the applicants (the most severe penalty applicable to the offences in question), had been an unreasonable and drastic penalty having regard, in particular, to the absence of any violent behaviour during an authorised picket.

The ECtHR has also considered a prison sentence of five months in which its execution had been suspended to be a disproportionate sanction to the legitimate aim pursued in the context of Article 10 of the Convention. It said so, for example, in the case *Kanellopoulou v. Greece*[47], which concerned the publication of articles which could have an adverse effect on an individual's image. In the case *Marchenko v. Ukraine*[48], the ECtHR adopted the same reasoning and stressed that the fact that a sentence is suspended *"does not alter that conclusion particularly as the conviction itself was not expunged."*

Lastly, as far as the length of a prison sentence is concerned, a special reference should be made regarding life imprisonment. In the case law of the ECtHR this issue has been addressed under Article 3 of the Convention. The principles concerning the whole life order were recently set out in *Vinter and Others v. the United Kingdom*[49] and clarified in *Murray v. the Netherlands*[50], in which the Grand Chamber of the ECtHR held that the imposition of a whole life prison sentence without the possibility of review would be in breach of Article 3. According to *Vinter*, the Convention as interpreted by the ECtHR requires from States that they have in place a mechanism offering the possibility of review of a whole life sentence at the time a sentence is imposed. In *Vinter*, the ECtHR thus acknowledged the right to parole if and when the legal requisites of parole obtain.[51] The *Vinter* approach was later followed in *Lázló Magyar v. Hungary* (no. 73593/10, 20 May 2014), in *Harakchiev and Tolumov v. Bulgaria* (nos. 15018/11 and 61199/12, 8 July 2014) and *T.P. and A.T. v. Hungary* (nos. 37871/14 and 73986/14, 4 October 2016).[52]

---

46 *Kakabadze and Others v. Georgia*, no. 1484/07, 2 October 2012.

47 *Kanellopoulou v. Greece*, no. 28504/05, 11 October 2007.

48 *Marchenko v. Ukraine*, no. 4063/04, 19 February 2009.

49 *Vinter and Others v. the United Kingdom (GC)*, nos. 66069/09 130/10 3896/10, 9 July 2013.

50 *Murray v. the Netherlands (GC)*, no. 10511/10, 26 April 2016.

51 See my opinion joined to *Hutchinson v. the United Kingdom (GC)*, no. 57592/08, 17 January 2017.

52 In opposition to the above, there are also situations where the ECtHR has criticised the domestic courts for imposing lenient criminal sanctions where the severity of the crimes committed

IV. CONCLUSION

From the above analysis it can be concluded that the ECtHR has adopted a twofold approach in the context of the overuse of criminal justice: in some cases it controls the excessive application of criminal law and criminal sanctions with regard to a specific conduct (which is most visible in the context of Articles 10 and 11 cases); and in other cases, it criticises States for having adopted a lenient sentence with regard to an offender (which will normally be the case in the context of killing or ill-treatment committed by law-enforcement agents). The two perspectives mirror the relationship between human rights and criminal law and the particular function of human rights law in the administration of criminal justice. The majority of the cases, however, demonstrate that the ECtHR has, most of the time, the role of controlling the application of excessive punishment. With regard to the particular aspect of pre-trial detention and custodial sentences, the case law of the ECtHR persists on the compliance with the principle of "last resort" and has been calling on States to consider alternative measures to detention. It further urges States to create mechanisms enabling the possibility of parole in the context of whole life prison sentences. Moreover, the ECtHR has had an important role in controlling the excessive use of criminal law in the context of irregular migration and in reminding Member States that they should not overuse criminal law as an instrument of border patrol; the "*crimmigration*" trend is an example of that.

---

required the application of a prison sentence. Examples of this can be found in *Kasap and Others v. Turkey*, no. 8656/10, 14 January 2014, where the ECtHR found a violation of Article 2 on account of the suspension of pronouncement of judgment in which an officer considered to be responsible for causing death by negligence had been sentenced to one year and eight month's imprisonment; *Derman v. Turkey*, 21789/12, 31 May 2011, concerning the complaint that criminal proceedings against police officers for torture had been ineffective on account, inter alia, that their sentenced had been suspended on the ground that it was unlikely that they would reoffend; *Shishkin v. Russia*, 18280/04, 7 July 2011, in which the applied sentence below the statutory minimum – and the suspension of its execution – in a case concerning ill-treatment by the police was considered by the ECtHR to be manifestly disproportionate to the gravity of the acts committed; *Enukidze and Girgvliani v. Georgia*, 25091/07, 26 April 2011, where the ECtHR considered that the prison sentences in respect of crimes of abduction, beating and killing by law enforcement agents and the way they had been imposed in practice had been inadequate and that the pardon granted and release on license had been too lenient and unreasonably generous and in which stressed that States had to be stringent when punishing law-enforcement officers in order to combat the sense of impunity.

OVERUSE OF CRIMINALIZATION: A PHILOSOPHICAL AND POLITICAL APPROACH ON THE LATIN-AMERICAN SITUATION

José Luis Guzmán Dalbora*

I. TERMINOLOGICAL CLARIFICATION AND CONCEPTUAL DELIMITATION

The English word "overuse" can be translated into Spanish, the lecturer's mother tongue, as "excessive use" or "overwork". Nonetheless, as this word is followed by the complement "criminalization", it seems more appropriate to translate it as "abuse".

Abuse or overuse is not just using something too much or using it excessively, but to use it in an improper, inadequate or unfair manner. Also the term "abuse", in the English language, means mistreatment, wrongdoing, and it can even mean an aggression. And this is precisely the meaning of the phrase "overuse of criminalization": an unlawful act of violence carried out by the State through its criminal laws against the citizens. Consequently, it is not merely the unnecessary use of the law to criminalize conducts or the barely quantitative censorship of this proceeding, but it is something deeper, qualitative.

There was full awareness of this fact at the founding moment of the Rule of Law, the French Declaration of the Rights of Man and the Citizen. Article 8° asserted as principle the minimal need or intervention of the state punishment: *"The law shall not provide for punishments other than those strictly and obviously*

* Tenured Professor of Criminal Law and Introduction to legal and moral philosophy, Universidad de Valparaíso (Chile). The author acknowledges the English translation of Daniella Ávila Fuentes.

necessary".[1] The mindset of the reformers of the Enlightenment understood that an unnecessary punishment accounts for something more serious than a mere excess by the legislator, who was able to overlook the law because it was not absolutely necessary. On the contrary, it had to be considered as a tyrannical act; according to Beccaria, "an *act* of violence perpetrated by *one or many* upon a private citizen"[2], and in accordance with the terminology of our time, a factual imposition rather than a legal punishment. Certainly, regardless of the individual and social effects of unnecessary punishment, in the underlying abuse, the legitimacy of the criminalization of conducts, situations or individuals and, in the end, the authority of the political-legal title by virtue of which it is established by the government[3] is at stake.

The relationship between criminal law and politics, very much alive at the dawning of the Late Modern Period, was based on a theory about the speculative origin of the right to punish, related to the social contract, the consent of all the members of a community, a will that can be conceived as the implicit assumption of all the public determination that limit the freedom, the honour or people's rights in order to guarantee the exercise of freedom of the other and the peaceful coexistence in the community. It is worth noting that the same men, who laid the foundations for contemporaneous criminal law, may well have yielded to the temptation to denature the ideological root of the *ius puniendi* by considering the need of the punishment as a mere empirical demand required by the corresponding political decision. It would have been sufficient for them to accommodate to Europe conditions by the end of the old regime, when the subsistence criminality increased, resulting from the economic crisis, the rise in the prices and the lack of food. Nonetheless, in spite of becoming crueller with the conventional criminality, the Enlightenment criminal reform reduced dramatically the extension of the felonies and diminished the intensity of the punishments.[4]

The excess of criminalization has once again become a subject in our times. It is certainly not an exclusive topic of these days, since its origins go back to the

---

1 Clause repeated in article 15 of the Declaration of the Rights of Man and of the Citizen of 1793, headed by the French Constitution that same year. Cfr. Jorge Del Vecchio, *Persona, Estado y Derecho*, Madrid: Instituto de Estudios Políticos, 1957, p. 95 and 105.

2 *Dei delitti e delle pene*, Torino: Einaudi, 3rd ed., 1965, p. 104. We italicize the phrase «or many» to denote that the abuse may come from a democratically elected assembly.

3 Similar, Luiz Luisi, 'Principle of Minimum Intervention', in: Luiz Luisi, Manuel de Rivacoba, José Luis Guzmán and Sergio Politoff, *Política criminal y reforma penal*, Santiago of Chile: Editorial Jurídica ConoSur, 1996, p. (7-24) 7-8.

4 Paradigm of which is the French Penal Code of 1791. Cfr. our translation and introductory note of this Code in: *Revista de Derecho penal y Criminología*, Madrid, 3rd season, number 1, 2009, p. 481-517.

mid-twentieth century and even to the second half of the nineteenth century[5] as a phenomenon first induced by the industrialization and then, by the actual or suspected dangers of the post-industrial society. Nonetheless, it seems that it has worsened all over the western world, no matter how developed the country, and jurists, criminologists and sociologists pay attention to it because they sense an abuse.

There are different points of view to examine it. Crime policy will notice the personal and collective consequences of the excess of the law, that are considered to be criminogenic and one of the factors of the last and unprecedented rise in the prison populations.[6] Legal sociology may relate it to anomic processes within societies undergoing the effects of "globalisation" or, more generally, to an ambivalence inherent to this instant in history.[7] The non-positivist criminology will point out that a project of strong control of the human behaviour and the punishment of the people excluded from the labour market[8] hides behind globalization understood as the reorganization of the economic power and the weakening of the public powers. The jurist may give a detailed description of the problem in his country or in several States, by comparing the vast amount of punitive manifestations. Finally, the philosopher of law will try to find out the source in the legal metaphysics, as well as to clarify its corollaries in the conception of values that gives life to the political system.

This last approach has been adopted by many, such as Husak, in the United States, on what he calls "overcriminalization", which, in his view, involves the concept of rule of law, and by Zaffaroni in Argentina, who believes he can speculate that the irrationality of the present political speech on criminal matters

5 Carlo Enrico Paliero, *"Minima non curat praetor". Ipertrofia del Diritto penale e decriminalizzazione dei reati bagatellari*, Padova: Cedam, 1985, p. 12-36, remembers the expression of Peter Noll in the seventies: *legal tide*.

6 The Americas has two of the world's countries with the highest percentage of imprisonment by reference groups of one hundred thousand inhabitants, the United States of America with six hundred and ninety-three prisoners (2014), and Chile, with two hundred and forty-five (2016). Cfr. *International Centre for Prison Studies*, World Prison Brief (at: www.prisonstudies.org/country/united-states-america and www.prisonstudies.org/country/chile [last visited: 16 May 2016]. A general overview of Latin America in 2012 is offered by Manuel Iturralde, 'O governo neoliberal da insegurança social na América Latina: semelhanças e diferencias com o Norte Global', in: Vera Malaguti Batista (ed.), *Loïc Wacquant e a questão penal no capitalismo neoliberal*, Rio de Janeiro: Revan, 2012, p. 169-195.

7 Cfr. Alfonso Serrano Gómez and Alfonso Serrano Maíllo, 'El aumento de la firmeza en la respuesta al delito a nivel legislativo en España (1995-2007), in: Helmut Kury and Alfonso Serrano Maíllo (org.), *Punitividad y victimización en la experiencia contemporánea. Estudios*, Madrid: Dykinson, 2009, p. (295-316) 314-315.

8 Thus, the reference works of David Garland, *A cultura do controle*, Rio de Janeiro: Revan, 2008, p. 422-423, Jock Young, *A sociedade excludente*, Rio de Janeiro: Revan, 2002, p. 22-28, and Loïc Wacquant, *Punir os pobres*, Rio de Janeiro: Revan, 2007, p. 62-65.

poses a risk for the future of democracy in the Hispanic America.[9] We will address the issue of overuse of criminalization from the same approach, although with nuances as regards to the two aforementioned authors, because we are interested in highlighting the challenge posed by the increase in criminal characters to the theory of law and the threat that tends to a liberal organization of the life in relationships.

II. OVERVIEW OF THE PRIMARY CRIMINALIZATION IN THE IBERO-AMERICAN CONTINENT

The philosophy of criminal law consists of considering the criminal law in an abstract and omni-comprehensive manner. In this sense, it is the set of general doctrines in the criminal field that can be claimed as having an absolute nature.[10] Nonetheless, this branch of the philosophy of law does not draw back from the teaching that knowledge starts from experience, which accounts for, namely, that even the *a priori* legal concepts are characterised by relating a concept with a certain material. Consequently, in order to test some philosophical-legal hypothesis on the overuse of criminalization in Latin America, it seems necessary to have a brief description of the legal situation that, out of reasons of space, we have to narrow down to a small sample of countries.

It should be borne in mind that, with a few exceptions, the instability of their Codes and the punitive legislation in general[11] has been a constant sign of the criminal law in the States of the continent. From the late nineteenth century, not long after a new criminal code had been approved, it is already thought to replace it for another one or, if the global reform project does not work, the current Code will be modified or complemented with partial reforms or special acts, often not related to the guiding principles of its articles.

This reformist uneasiness, which spoils the guarantee of rationality and stability that we consider to be inherent to the Code, has increased in the last thirty years, both in the countries that prepared new Criminal Codes, such as Peru and Colombia, as well as in those which keep the old ones. Peru sanctioned

9 Cfr. Douglas Husak, *Sobrecriminalización. Los límites del Derecho penal*, Madrid: Pons, 2013, p. 64-73, and Eugenio Raúl Zaffaroni, 'La globalización y las actuales orientaciones de la política criminal', in Eugenio Raúl Zaffaroni, *En torno de la cuestión penal*, Montevideo-Buenos Aires: B. de F., 2005, p. 179-214.

10 Cfr. José Luis Guzmán Dalbora, *Elementi di Filosofia giuridico-penale*, Napoli: Editoriale Scientifica, 2015, p. 15.

11 Cfr. Luis Jiménez de Asúa, *Tratado de Derecho penal*, 7 vols., Buenos Aires: Losada, t. I, 2nd ed., 1956, p. 1292.

a Code, which was new and modern in different levels, in 1991.[12] Nonetheless, almost from the time it entered into force it was subject to several modifications, both of its rules, in general, as well as the crimes, in particular. As a result, the principles have distorted, the punishments have dramatically increased, reintroduction of recidivism and the excessive criminalization of teenagers, the actions against sexual freedom, guns, terrorism and drugs, among others.[13] On the other hand, over twenty years, Colombia has had two Codes, one in 1980 and the once in force from 2000. If the first code was harshly accused of being classist, the second one was not inspired precisely by the principle of necessity of the penalty. On the contrary, it added sixty new crimes and also criminalized around fifteen conducts that to that time had been sanctioned as misdemeanours or minor offences. Four years later, the country resumed the path of the punitive expansion and decoding with an extremely hard reform that added even more crimes, many of them said to be in violation of the legality principle.[14]

Countries with older Codes certainly do not free from the legal tide. The Argentinean Code, which dates back from 1921, has undergone around nine hundred reforms throughout its ninety-five years in force. Only during the period 2000 to 2006 there were twenty-seven amending laws, many of which consisted in extending the known crimes or add up new ones. With an average of ten legal alterations per year, it is understood that there is the profound awareness in this country of the loss of certainty of the legislation and the inability of the legislator that seems to believe that criminal law is the only means there is to face social conflicts.[15] On the other hand, the Brazilian Criminal Code, dating back to 1940, but that had its general part replaced in 1984, has been surrounded since 1990 by a legion of special acts that entailed a swarm of crimes regarding the most different matters (environment, telecommunications, genetic engineering, etc.), "most of them unnecessary and inconsistent with the actual social demands and

---

12 Cfr. José Luis Guzmán Dalbora, *El nuevo Código penal del Perú (1991)*, in: *Doctrina penal*, Buenos Aires, year 14, numbers 55-56, June-December of 1991, p. 631-731.

13 Cfr. José Hurtado Pozo, *Manual de Derecho penal. Parte general*, I. Lima: Grijley, 3rd ed., 2005, p. 129-133, and Felipe Villavicencio Terreros, *Derecho penal. Parte general*, Lima: Grijley, 2014, p. 23. The latter speaks of "overcriminalization in the criminal law". Between 2000 and 2006, 162 amendments were made to articles of Code of 1991, records José Urquizo Olaechea, 'La reciente política legislativa penal en el Perú', in: José Luis Díez Ripollés and Octavio García Pérez (eds.), *La política legislativa penal iberoamericana en el cambio de siglo*, Madrid-Montevideo: Edisofer and B. de F., 2008, p. (325-381) 331.

14 The fact that this maximum criminal law has been imposed by the Government of the United States of America is stated. See Fernando Velásquez Velázquez, *Derecho penal. Parte general*, Medellín: Comlibros, 4th ed., 2009, p. 433-443. Additionally, Juan Oberto Sotomayor Acosta, 'Las recientes reformas penales en Colombia: un ejemplo de irracionalidad legislativa', in: *La política legislativa penal iberoamericana en el cambio de siglo*, cit., p. (75-118) 93.

15 Cfr. César Fortete, 'Las reformas penales en Argentina. La otra inflación', in Helmut Cury and Alfonso Serrano Maíllo, *Punitividad y victimización en la experiencia contemporánea. Estudios*, cit., p. (237-261) 238, and Alejandro Slokar, 'La reciente política legislativa penal en Argentina', in *La política legislativa penal iberoamericana en el cambio de siglo*, cit., p. (1-24) 12-16.

others prepared in such a manner that, compromising the seriousness of the criminal legislation, reach, sometimes, paradoxical and hilarious connotations".[16]

Chile is a paradigm in this scenario. We can understand that throughout its existence the old Criminal Code of 1874 has undergone several reforms. However, it is noteworthy that most of the amendments, including the most important and serious ones, have been performed over the last twenty-five years, time when the country recovered democracy after a long-term military dictatorship. Just a few of these innovations were of a decriminalization nature, such as the suppression of the offence of contempt in 2005, ordered to the State by the Inter-American Court of Human Rights[17], and turning the offence of practices contrary to free competition into an administrative offence (2003), decision which actual or latent reasons are not known, but that in fact backed up the illegal activities of the monopolies and oligopolies in the country. As a counterpart, a significant number of crimes has stretched the criminal system, especially in sexual matters (wherein crimes against minors are highlighted: sodomy, young adults prostitution, production of virtual pornography, possession of pornographic material and others), drugs (including the possession of small quantities of soft drugs, equivalent to hard drugs, and the punishment for public or private consumption of any drug), terrorism, guns, possession (with an emphasis on stealing things of negligible value, burglary in someone else's home, stealing of things of different values), domestic abuse and other matters related to conventional crimes. There is also the excess of having criminalized the cloning of human beings, an unlikely hypothesis given the technological underdevelopment in the country. But perhaps the most serious situation regarding this punitive spiral took place in the juvenile criminal law. A special law issued in 2005 allows to criminally prosecute children older than 14 but younger than 18 for whatsoever felony, as adults, and also for misdemeanours typical to adolescence, such as petty theft, small amount damage and public disorders. Considering the characteristics of the youth and the teachings of criminology regarding how soft, diffuse and recessive offences are in youngsters, we are talking here of overuse of criminalization.[18]

---

16 Luiz Luisi, 'El principio de intervención mínima', cit., p. 14. Cfr., also, Juárez Tavares, 'La reforma penal en Brasil', in: *La política legislativa penal iberoamericana en el cambio de siglo*, cit., p. 46-74.

17 Cfr. José Luis Guzmán Dalbora, 'El caso de Chile (influencia de las decisiones de la Corte y la Comisión Interamericanas de Derechos humanos en el Derecho penal chileno)', in: Kai Ambos, Ezequiel Malarino and Christian Steiner (eds.), *Sistema interamericano de protección de los derechos humanos y Derecho penal internacional*, Bogotá: Konrad-Adenauer Stiftung, t. III, 2013, p. 135-164.

18 Abuse that exists in other countries of the Americas, except the important case of Brazil, which still works with the tutelary system. Cfr. Manuel Iturralde, 'O governo neoliberal da insegurança social na América Latina: semelhanças e diferencias com o Norte Global', in: *Loïc Wacquant e a questão penal no capitalismo neoliberal*, cit., p. 188.

Certain criminal law schools and the uncritical rise of European punitive models[19] have been held liable for the legislative instability, the abrupt changes of Codes. However, underneath this purely legal explanation that cannot illustrate why the phenomenon of primary criminalization has increased in recent years, when the criminal schools no longer influence reforms and legislators do not bother to listen to the experts, there are more in-depth conditions. In spite that some Ibero-American countries have reached an economic development, its social structure is somehow still old, facing a powerful oligarchy with an enormous amount of poor, ignorant people that can be manipulated by the local elites.[20] A concrete way of criminal instrumentalization is the ideology of citizen safety, heir to the national safety of the military dictatorships.[21] It was readily available for the increase of crimes and stronger punishments, typical of societies of unequal distribution of richness and exclusive, from the social standpoint. In turn, neo-liberalism has not been the cause of the legislative abuse, even less in countries that did not reach a true industrialization and that only know the ugliest side of post-modernity, but it is a factor that contributes to intensify the triumphant march of the punitive scope of the intersubjective relationships.[22] The combination of these two aspects together, a despotic punitive ideology and a sectarian economical organization, are on the basis of most of the recent reforms, especially of those affecting offences against life, health, sexual freedom and property. The leading role of conventional criminality is strengthened by other

19 Cfr. Jiménez de Asúa, *Tratado de Derecho penal*, cit., p. 1294-1129. Extensively on the influence of the different political-criminal currents in Europe, Eugenio Raúl Zaffaroni, *Los Códigos penales de Latinoamérica*, México: Suprema Corte de Justicia de la Nación e Instituto Latinoamericano de las Naciones Unidas para la Prevención del Delito y el Tratamiento del Delincuente, 2000, *pássim*.

20 Rightly underlined is this relevant factor, the poverty of the population, causes of which are not attacked, and crime is not prevented either, becoming tough against the criminalized demonstrations of social conflicts produced by misery, Agustín Pérez Carrillo, 'Política legislativa en la prevención del delito', in: José Luis Díez Ripollés, Ana María Prieto del Pino and Susana Soto Navarro (eds.), *La política legislativa penal en Occidente. Una perspectiva comparada*, Valencia: Tirant lo Blanch, 2005, p. (216-251) 219-220.

21 Please refer to José Luis Guzmán Dalbora, 'Una especial versión del autoritarismo penal en sus rasgos fundamentales: la ideología de la seguridad ciudadana', *Revista Brasileira de Ciências Criminais*, São Paulo, year 11, January-March of 2003, p. 66-78, José Luis Díez Ripollés, 'El nuevo modelo penal de la seguridad ciudadana', *Revista Electrónica de Ciencia Penal y Criminología*, Granada, 06-03, 2004 (at: www.criminet.ugr.es/recpc) (last visited: 17 may 2004), *pássim*, and Eugenio Raúl Zaffaroni, 'Politique criminelle et droits d l'homme en Amerique Latine : de la sécurité nationale à la sécurité civique', *Archives de Politique Criminelle*, 1992, p. 77-86. In subsequent works, Zaffaroni relates it to urban safety and warns of its possible evolution towards an ideology of total safety. Cfr. *Derecho penal. Parte general*, Buenos Aires: Ediar, 2nd ed., 2002, p. 353-354.

22 In the same vein, Manuel Iturralde, 'O governo neoliberal da insegurança social na América Latina: semelhanças e diferencias com o Norte Global', in: *Loïc Wacquant e a questão penal no capitalismo neoliberal*, cit., p. 177.

factors[23], of which it is worth noting an unreflecting confusion between the legal requirements and the moral requirements and, accordingly, the classification as offence of actions of genuine exercise of freedom of the individuals, but disliked by the power of the hegemonic groups. As the latter, however, have never been able to resist the pressure of foreign powers that operate in a direct manner or by way or international organisms, makes sense that within the arsenal of offences there are some that are very unlikely to cause damage to third parties, such as drug consumption and the possession of pornography, other ones disrespecting the principle of legality, such as unlawful enrichment of public officers and the unauthorised possession of weapons, and the other ones giving in to the defence of the national sovereignty, such as punishment for conspiracy to commit certain offences and bribery of foreign public officials in international transactions.[24]

III. METAPHYSICAL MEANING, POLITICAL BACKGROUND AND LEGAL CONSEQUENCES OF THE OVERUSE OF CRIMINALIZATION

Overuse of criminalization has a special meaning for Metaphysics of Law, meaning which agrees with the absolutism in the scope of values. This absolutism is linked to the political background of said legislative current in which hides a fearful punitive authoritarianism, such as that claimed by the Enlightenment. And these two elements revealed by the legal philosophy shows us a set of harmful consequences for the scientific management and the practical application of this area of the legal system.

Indeed, overuse compromises the identity of the Law within the framework of the systems of social guarantees, especially its difference vis-à-vis morals and collective conventionalisms. Originally, these systems – Law, morals, customs, even religion – used to be an undifferentiated whole. The unfolding of culture and the dominium of reason allowed noticing that the possibility of behaving in a

23 For instance, the demagogic use and the journalistic exaggeration of common crime, with the purpose of magnifying fear of crime among people, fear that must not be confused with the objective reality of the problem of public safety, which is significant in some States of the continent, for example, Venezuela, Brazil, El Salvador, Guatemala and Mexico. For the case of Mexico, cfr. Moisés Moreno Hernández, *Política criminal y reforma penal*, México: Editorial Ius Poenale, 1999, p. 91-94.

24 On the laws that have extended the Criminal Law to a myriad of social relations, some are due not only to the reformulation of the State, the privatization of companies and public services, and other demands of neoliberal globalization, but also to international programmatic norms, that require the State a better protection of the fundamental rights of individuals, not necessarily to criminalize their violation. Cfr. Juárez Tavares, 'La reforma penal en Brasil', in: *La política legislativa penal iberoamericana en el cambio de siglo*, cit., p. 48-49.

manner against the norms "adopts different forms, modalities and degrees".[25] Now, this delimitation process, which had two historical landmarks, the most important one in the eighteen century, and another one, less-far-reaching, in the sixties and the first seventy years of the twentieth century, experiences a countermarch because of the modern plethora or crimes and, over all, the confrontation to some crimes that punish private conducts rather than events that harm the rights of third parties.

The loss of identity in the legal system is due to the fact that the legislative elephantiasis necessarily causes an anomic criminal law. From the different meanings the term anomy has in sociology of law[26], three are considered here: anomy as the abundance of norms that end up annulling in a de facto manner some or many of them; anomy as the product of contradictory norms that belong to the same normative order; finally, anomy as contradiction between legal norms and other (moral or social). We will deal with the two first senses below. Right now, let´s focus in the last one.

At present there are many examples of anomy regarding legal norms that contradict moral norms or social conventionalisms. One which is quite evident is that playing the role of legal good attempting to steal the area of freedom of the individuals in the privacy of the erotic game: the so called "sexual integrity". This one has inspired reforms in Chile and Argentina, among other countries, and allowed to mutilate the sexual self-determination of youngsters, invade the intimacy of their elders, vent its anger on the solitude of some, meddle in the fantasy of others and, finally, scrap the rationality of the punitive system. This is certainly not a legal concept. Taking it literally, sexual integrity is absurd. No one, not even the most experienced person in this area can refer to himself/herself as integral. The complexity of the sexual drive turns into a chimera the fact that sometime there would be an integrity with all its parts well assembled in the psychical and social economy of a personality; in other words, there has never been and there will never be a human being who is complete from a sexual standpoint. On the other hand, as sexual integrity is not a synonym for health, concept which is medically different and legally unrelated to the result of the sexual offences, for scientific consideration can only be used the meaning of fairness, probity and purity consistent with integrity. Certainly, the legal pseudo concept is based on moral feelings. It is specifically that mixture of perspectives which has destroyed the legal ontology by taking the carnal act for a price with teenagers, preparation of pornographic material with non-existent children and

25 Max Ernst Mayer, *Filosofía del Derecho*, Barcelona: Labor, 1937, p. 96.

26 See Ana Lucia Sabadell, *Manual de Sociologia jurídica. Introdução a uma leitura externa do Direito*, São Paulo: Revista dos Tribunais, 6th ed., 2013, p. 73-86, and 'Actualidad de la anomia y su repercusión en el Derecho penal', in: José Urquizo Olaechea (dir.), *Modernas tendencias de Dogmática penal y Política criminal. Libro Homenaje al Dr. Juan Bustos Ramírez*, Lima: Idemsa, 2007, p. 897-910.

the possession of child pornography[27] as an offence. There is a serious cost and it is paid twice, whether because of the venom of disorientation regarding the norms inoculated to the individuals, or because of the lack of orientation of the community itself, uncertainty that the abusive criminal law channels towards a cohesion based on the feeling of revenge and other primitive drives against the hatred wrongdoer.[28] Nonetheless, this is the logical consequence of the absolutism in values which makes these and other rules, characteristic of which is to pose universal values, unconditioned and mandatory for everyone, both for the ones that believe in them as well as for those who do not.

Underlying any ideology, any program, even simple political ends, there is a conscious or unconscious value option, an axiological system, which requires a certain legal conception. Indeed, the absolutism in values is projected in a supra-individualist legal conception, in which the individual is not the subject of the human ends, but the whole or that which is presented to people as an essential requirement for the whole. All in all, power rather than the legal safety, and even less the dignity of all human aspect has, is the idea of the law regarding these conceptions. Authoritarianism is the political track of the absolutist mindset and its supra-individualist vocation, the government of the domination power. As much as authoritarianism appears to be democratic, is the only one capable of finding in any social problem a matter worth of being faced with punishment. Moreover, it does not penalise conducts because they are themselves and according to the *extra-penal* law acts contrary to the value requirements of the community, but because it criminalizes them to be considered as disvalues because they are punished.[29] Such an attitude, typical of voluntarism, rejects as a principle that criminal law is of a guarantor or merely punitive in nature. Quite the contrary, voluntarism assumes that it has the undeniable virtuality of creating

27 Rightly, in Spain, Díez Ripollés states a "sexual freedom beleaguered" by the will of "protection of *sexual integrism*", which replaces the positive conception of the free exercise of sexuality by a two-faced and biased one, disguised with the "new magic word" sexual integrity. *Delitos y penas en España*, Madrid: Catarata, 2015, p. 125 and 129. By the way, the punitive integrism goes beyond the field of sexuality, although always from a value-based absolutism that we immediately note in the text. Cfr. Antonio García-Pablos de Molina, *Introducción al Derecho penal*, Madrid: Editorial Centro de Estudios Ramón Areces, 3rd ed., 2005, p. 595. And it is one of factors responsible for the excessive increase of incarceration rates, as noted by Massimo Pavarini, *Un arte abyecto. Ensayo sobre el gobierno de la penalidad*, Buenos Aires: Ad-Hoc, 2006, p. 148-149.

28 Cfr. Eugenio Raúl Zaffaroni, *El enemigo en el Derecho penal*, Bogotá: Grupo Editorial Ibáñez, 2006, p. 94. Demonstrations of inhumanity legally encouraged against sexual offenders are analysed in the cited work of Wacquant, p. 360-377. The stigmatization of the pervert evokes the criminal practices of Nazi totalitarianism.

29 Cfr. Daniel Pastor, *Recodificación penal y principio de reserva de Código*, Buenos Aires: Ad-Hoc, 2005, p. 61-62. In the polar opposite, there is the opinion that if there is no consensus on the positive values in a society, the criminal law will help to build consensus and strengthen the community. Cfr. Jesús María Silva Sánchez, *La expansión del Derecho penal. Aspectos de la política criminal en las sociedades postindustriales*, Madrid: Cívitas, 2nd ed., 2001, p. 41-42.

their own initiative of legal goods and, consequently, an illegality of their own. Hence, it is disgusted with the subsidiary character of the felonies system in the protection of the legal rights, the principle that the criminal law is the *ultima ratio* of a legally organised society. By relinquishing of the social requirement of the punishment, by inventing legal rights there were there are no dominant values collected from the non-criminal areas of the law, this new voluntarism appears as it is, legal politicism and political authoritarianism. Politicism, the complete subordination of law in each of its moments —creation, interpretation and application of the legal norms— to specific political ends, the ones required by those in power, is one of the most evident features of the modern overuse of criminalization.[30] It is its immediate cause, since "the supremacy of political objectives in the criminal justice leads to an unlimited criminal coercion, as is practiced by the logics of efficiency".[31] In turn, authoritarianism does not rely on the architectonic capability of the reason, but it cultures the power that configures fear, for which reason it will throw its legislation to the depths of the irrational, leaving only the compulsory aspect of the law. As it has to increase its strength precisely because it recognises the weakness of the own political legitimacy, it will overuse the power granted by the law with no further interest than the immediate political success of the operation, although this operation covers a contempt for the social structure that leads to criminality. It is thus proven that this political tendency is not only dangerous for the liberalism it claims to defend, but also a threat for the subsistence of the democracy as a way of government.[32]

The coherence of the legal system rests on the rationality of the legislative technique. Voluntarism, on the contrary, is an inextinguishable source of anomie in the two first meanings of the term. Indeed, overuse of criminalization shall render into contradictory legal norms, whether because they logically overlap or intertwine among themselves, whether because some contradict the values

30 Although without using the term, which suits the fascist and Nazi mindset, jurists, criminologists, and historians have pointed it out as a characteristic of the criminal law of the security of citizens and political populism. Cfr. José Luis Díez Ripollés, 'El nuevo modelo penal de la seguridad ciudadana', cit., p. 10-12, David Garland, *A cultura do controle*, cit., p. 57, y Tzvetan Todorov, *Los enemigos íntimos de la democracia*, Barcelona: Galaxia Gutemberg, 2012, p. 148-151.

31 René van Swaanignen, *Perspectivas europeas para una criminología crítica*, Montevideo-Buenos Aires: B. de F., 2011, p. 299.

32 On the risk for the Liberal Criminal Law, cfr. Cornelius Prittwitz, *Strafrecht und Risiko*, Frankfurt am Main: Vittorio Klostermann, 1993, p. 248-250. The political delegitimization of the politicized criminal law can be found in numerous studies of the phenomenon, whether related to the deideologization of traditional political parties, or to the increase of inequality in society. Cfr. Juan Oberto Sotomayor Acosta, 'Las recientes reformas penales en Colombia', in José Luis Díez Ripollés and Octavio García Pérez (eds.), *La política legislativa penal iberoamericana en el cambio de siglo*, cit., p. 89. For Europe, see summary of Charlotte Vanneste, 'Penalidad y desigualdad: nueva actualidad de los informes entre penalidad y economía. El ejemplo de Bélgica', *Revista de Derecho penal y Criminología*, year V, number 5, June of 2015, p. (67-80) 70.

encapsulate within other norms. The logical antinomies can be worked out by the legal dogma. Hence, no jurist will uphold that if three different laws punish armed robbery, the illegal possession of guns and the evasion of prisoners from jail, the individual who freed the prisoner by intimidating with an unregistered fire gun to the prison guard by taking his away, should be accountable for all three felonies. This is an apparent merger of criminal laws, in which only one applies, the one that punishes helping prisoners to escape. Nonetheless, in practice a wide spectrum of possible felonies renders the prosecutor the power of merging them, at his discretion, against the accused, which makes an efficient defence[33] to become complex and expensive and, in certain cases, an illusion. This without mentioning that the parthenogenesis of the criminal actions can reach the point of producing anomie in another sense, that in which no one really knows which are the criminal laws or how to apply the ones in force in accordance with its legitimate meaning, which entails one of the two situations: either the laws become inefficient or their efficiency depends not on the courts, but on the police.[34]

Even worse for the criminal science and the task of the courts are the axiological antinomies, namely, when an article imposes a disproportionate penalty to rape with homicide in terms of the two crimes making up this legal unity legal, as if raping and murdering a person were the same as raping one and murdering several. The axiological antinomies lack of scientific solution. They are, then a source of mishaps in the legal application, its arbitrariness will not go unnoticed in the community and will contribute to weaken in it its trust and attachment to the law. "An unrestrained voluntarism", as overuse of criminalization seems to be, "is nothing else than arbitrariness, and the realm of arbitrariness is, in turn, the realm of contradiction and, all the same, the end or the denial of the Law and the Science of Law".[35]

---

33 More laws actually means to grant more discretionary power to prosecutors, argues Husak, *Sobrecriminalización*, cit., p. 64-72.

34 Situation in which the police becomes the power that underpins the Law, as Walter Benjamin glimpsed in his shocking study 'Para la crítica de la violencia', in: *Ensayos escogidos*, México: Ediciones Coyoacán, 3rd ed., 2006, p. (169-201) 182-183.

35 Manuel de Rivacoba y Rivacoba, 'La racionalidad del ordenamiento como presupuesto de la Dogmática jurídica en materia penal', in: Manuel de Rivacoba y Rivacoba, *Nueva crónica del crimen*, Valparaíso: Edeval, 1981, p. (187-211) 193.

IV. POLITICAL LEGITIMIZATION AND CRIMINAL SYMBOLISM

We started by claiming that overuse of criminalization calls into question the legal authority of the government, if it is true that the overuse degrades authority into mere power, and the subjective right to punish, to an institutionalised violence. We would like to conclude our work with this issue.

Constitutions have not been able to stop excess. This may not surprise us since Constitutions are documents which are more or less open to debate of whatsoever position regarding the requirement of the punishment, even if we imagine that any Constitution dared to enshrine the minimal intervention principle. An example of their inadequacy is given by the modest acceptance of the principle of offensively in the constitutional jurisprudence and the legal weakening of this maxim in the modern reform of penal law in Italy.[36] Instead, the problem of the legal legitimacy of these legal practices must be studied from the political law, that is, the total set of norms organizing the political life of a social unity, fundamental character of which depends upon the legal validity of all the fields of the law, wherein the criminal lawyer should adhere to the precepts reality of said organisation and, underlying it, to the conception to which is accountable to and gives it its basis.[37]

Certainly, the liberal criminal law, criminal-legal expression of the political doctrine of liberalism, is aware that the more complex and richer a culture is, "the more and different nucleus of objects that values and preserves, with the corresponding more amount and diversity of possible criminal conducts".[38] Nonetheless, they are not willing to criminalize them without considering it. If they did it, they would be ignoring the contradictions between the social and cultural structures that give rise to the crimes or a significant part of crimes.[39] Along with this irrational gesture there would be the political sin of covering the social life under a mantle of distrust on the freedom of people, thus giving a

---

36 Cfr. Vittorio Mannes, *Il principio di offensività nel Diritto penale*, Torino: Giappichelli, 2005, p. 79-106 and 121-107, in which the author mentions the current «moral crusades» of Criminal Politics in his country. A comprehensive summary in Spanish of the Italian situation, Carlos Cabezas Cabezas, 'El principio de ofensividad y su relación con los delitos de peligro abstracto en la experiencia italiana y chilena. Un estudio comparado', *Revista de Derecho*, Universidad Católica del Norte, Antofagasta (Chile), year 20, number 2, 2013, p. (85-120) 105-108.

37 Manuel de Rivacoba y Rivacoba, 'Orden político y orden penal', *Revista Chilena de Derecho*, Facultad de Derecho de la Pontificia Universidad Católica de Chile, vol. 22., number 2 (monographic work: «*Derecho penal y Criminología*»), May-August of 1995, p. 201-212.

38 Manuel de Rivacoba y Rivacoba, *Elementos de Criminología*, Valparaíso: Edeval, 1982, p. 137.

39 A provision that raises as a major obstacle to decriminalization is that which consists of using criminal law as an apparent solution for a social problem. This is the symbolic criminal law, another abuse of the moment, which must not be confused with the criminal symbolism mentioned *infra*, text and note 43. Cfr. Raúl Cervini, *Los procesos de decriminalización*, Montevideo: Universidad, 1993, p. 69.

deathblow to the axis of said political doctrine. That is why Willem Pompe, one of the members of the old Utrecht University, upheld that the level of trust in human beings and in society in general, is directly proportional to the intensity of the criminal intervention, and that scarce trust causes a more punitive society and vice versa.[40] However, in the political law, the problems related to legitimacy are rendered into a question of legal validity. And since the authoritarianism inherent to the overuse of criminalization is merely irreconcilable with a liberal criminal law, it does not surprise us that the American criminal lawyers, more aware of the political dependence on the punitive matters, today pose the same question Beccaria raised in an emphatic assertion two hundred fifty years ago, whether is over use is indeed criminal law or, on the contrary, mere direct coercion, or just violence.[41]

Anyone who does not wish to go along the path of challenging the legal validity of dispositions raised from the liberticide discretion has to at least be aware of the political cauldron in which they are prepared. They will also have to become aware of the symbolic reduction that the criminal law is experiencing as the walls of the political building that had saved an emergency room collapse. The crime current flows into the trivialisation of the valuation meaning of crime among individuals. The social representation caused by the legislative impotence is – allow me to quote a sentence, which may be out of context, but not too much, by the Chilean poet, Nicanor Parra – *"Here not even the law of the jungle gets any respect!"*.[42]

That being the case, society will have lost the most significant values, the criminal law will not be able to show, from a symbolic standpoint, the importance of the ideals of life in the community, which is in what the legal rights consist of, and criminal penalties will lack of its limited aptitude of containing the occurrence of crimes within tolerable limits.[43]

40 Cfr. René van Swaanignen, *Perspectivas europeas para una criminología crítica*, cit., p. 112.

41 Eugenio Raúl Zaffaroni, 'El Derecho penal liberal y sus enemigos', in: *En torno de la cuestión penal*, cit., p. (153-177) 153-159.

42 *Nuevos sermones y prédicas del Cristo de Elqui*, in: *Obras completas & algo †*, Barcelona: Galaxia Gutemberg, 2 vols., t. II, p. (33-75) 60.

43 On the genuine symbolic nature of the Punitive Law, see Manuel de Rivacoba y Rivacoba, *Función y aplicación de la pena*, Buenos Aires: Depalma, 1993, p. 83-84, and José Luis Díez Ripollés, 'El Derecho penal simbólico y los efectos de la pena', in *Modernas tendencias en la Ciencia del Derecho penal y en la Criminología*, Madrid: Universidad Nacional de Educación a Distancia, 2001, p. (108-130) 108-109, 111-112 and 122-123.

V. BIBLIOGRAPHY

Cesare Beccaria, *Dei delitti e delle pene*, Torino: Einaudi, 3ª ed., 1965;

Walter Benjamin, 'Para la crítica de la violencia', en: *Ensayos escogidos*, México: Ediciones Coyoacán, 3ª ed., 2006, p. 169-201;

Carlos Cabezas Cabezas, 'El principio de ofensividad y su relación con los delitos de peligro abstracto en la experiencia italiana y chilena. Un estudio comparado', *Revista de Derecho*, Universidad Católica del Norte, Antofagasta (Chile), año 20, número 2, 2013, p. 85-120;

Raúl Cervini, *Los procesos de decriminalización*, Montevideo: Universidad, 1993;

Código penal francés de 1791, traducción y nota introductoria de José Luis Guzmán Dalbora, in *Revista de Derecho penal y Criminología*, Madrid, 3ª época, número 1, 2009, p. 481-517;

Jorge Del Vecchio, *Persona, Estado y Derecho*, Madrid: Instituto de Estudios Políticos, 1957;

José Luis Díez Ripollés, *Delitos y penas en España*, Catarata, Madrid, 2015; 'El Derecho penal simbólico y los efectos de la pena', in *Modernas tendencias en la Ciencia del Derecho penal y en la Criminología*, Madrid: Universidad Nacional de Educación a Distancia, 2001, p. 108-130;

José Luis Díez Ripollés, 'El nuevo modelo penal de la seguridad ciudadana', *Revista Electrónica de Ciencia Penal y Criminología*, Granada, 06-03, 2004 (at: www.criminet.ugr.es/recpc);

César Fortete, 'Las reformas penales en Argentina. La otra inflación', in Helmut Cury y Alfonso Serrano Maíllo, *Punitividad y victimización en la experiencia contemporánea. Estudios*, Madrid: Dykinson, 2009, p. 237-261;

Antonio García-Pablos de Molina, *Introducción al Derecho penal*, Madrid: Editorial Centro de Estudios Ramón Areces, 3ª ed., 2005;

David Garland, *A cultura do controle*, Rio de Janeiro: Revan, 2008;

José Luis Guzmán Dalbora, *Elementi di Filosofia giuridico-penale*, Napoli: Editoriale Scientifica, 2015;

José Luis Guzmán Dalbora, 'El caso de Chile (influencia de las decisiones de la Corte y la Comisión Interamericanas de Derechos humanos en el Derecho penal chileno)', in: Kai Ambos, Ezequiel Malarino y Christian Steiner (eds.), *Sistema interamericano de protección de los derechos humanos y Derecho penal internacional*, Bogotá: Konrad-Adenauer Stiftung, t. III, 2013, p. 135-164;

José Luis Guzmán Dalbora, *El nuevo Código penal del Perú (1991)*, in: *Doctrina penal*, Buenos Aires, año 14, números 55-56, junio-diciembre de 1991, p. 631-731;

José Luis Guzmán Dalbora, 'Una especial versión del autoritarismo penal en sus rasgos fundamentales: la ideología de la seguridad ciudadana', *Revista Brasileira de Ciências Criminais*, São Paulo, año 11, enero-marzo de 2003, p. 66-78;

José Hurtado Pozo, *Manual de Derecho penal. Parte general*, I. Lima: Grijley, 3ª ed., 2005;

Douglas Husak, *Sobrecriminalización. Los límites del Derecho penal*, Madrid: Pons, 2013;

Manuel Iturralde, 'O governo neoliberal da insegurança social na América Latina: semelhanças e diferencias com o Norte Global', in: Vera Malaguti Batista (ed.), *Loïc Wacquant e a questão penal no capitalismo neoliberal*, Rio de Janeiro: Revan, 2012, p. 169-195;

Luis Jiménez de Asúa, *Tratado de Derecho penal*, 7 vols., Buenos Aires: Losada, t. I, 2ª ed., 1956;

Luiz Luisi, 'El principio de intervención mínima', in: Luiz Luisi, Manuel de Rivacoba, José Luis Guzmán y Sergio Politoff, *Política criminal y reforma penal*, Santiago de Chile: Editorial Jurídica ConoSur, 1996, p. 7-24;

Vittorio Mannes, *Il principio di offensività nel Diritto penale*, Torino: Giappichelli, 2005;

Max Ernst Mayer, *Filosofía del Derecho*, Barcelona: Labor, 1937;

Moisés Moreno Hernández, *Política criminal y reforma penal*, México: Editorial Ius Poenale, 1999;

Carlo Enrico Paliero, *"Minima non curat praetor". Ipertrofia del Diritto penale e decriminalizzazione dei reati bagatellari*, Padova: Cedam, 1985;

Daniel Pastor, *Recodificación penal y principio de reserva de Código*, Buenos Aires: Ad-Hoc, 2005;

Massimo Pavarini, *Un arte abyecto. Ensayo sobre el gobierno de la penalidad*, Buenos Aires: Ad-Hoc, 2006;

Agustín Pérez Carrillo, 'Política legislativa en la prevención del delito', in: José Luis Díez Ripollés, Ana María Prieto del Pino y Susana Soto Navarro (eds.), *La política legislativa penal en Occidente. Una perspectiva comparada*, Valencia: Tirant lo Blanch, 2005, p. 216-251;

Cornelius Prittwitz, *Strafrecht und Risiko*, Frankfurt am Main: Vittorio Klostermann, 1993;

Manuel de Rivacoba y Rivacoba, *Elementos de Criminología*, Valparaíso: Edeval, 1982;

Manuel de Rivacoba y Rivacoba, *Función y aplicación de la pena*, Buenos Aires: Depalma, 1993;

Manuel de Rivacoba y Rivacoba, 'La racionalidad del ordenamiento como presupuesto de la Dogmática jurídica en materia penal', in: Manuel de Rivacoba y Rivacoba, *Nueva crónica del crimen*, Valparaíso: Edeval, 1981, p. 187-211;

Manuel de Rivacoba y Rivacoba, 'Orden político y orden penal', *Revista Chilena de Derecho*, Facultad de Derecho de la Pontificia Universidad Católica de Chile, vol. 22., número 2 (monográfico: "Derecho penal y Criminología"), mayo-agosto de 1995, p. 201-212;

Ana Lucia Sabadell, *Manual de Sociologia jurídica*. Introdução a uma leitura externa do Direito, São Paulo: Revista dos Tribunais, 6ª ed., 2013;

Ana Lucia Sabadell, 'Actualidad de la anomia y su repercusión en el Derecho penal', in: José Urquizo Olaechea (dir.), *Modernas tendencias de Dogmática penal y Política criminal. Libro Homenaje al Dr. Juan Bustos Ramírez*, Lima: Idemsa, 2007, p. 897-910;

Alfonso Serrano Gómez y Alfonso Serrano Maíllo, 'El aumento de la firmeza en la respuesta al delito a nivel legislativo en España (1995-2007), in: Helmut Kury y

Alfonso Serrano Maíllo (org.), *Punitividad y victimización en la experiencia contemporánea. Estudios*, Madrid: Dykinson, 2009, p. 295-316;
Jesús María Silva Sánchez, *La expansión del Derecho penal. Aspectos de la política criminal en las sociedades postindustriales*, Madrid: Cívitas, 2ª ed., 2001;
Alejandro Slokar, 'La reciente política legislativa penal en Argentina, in José Luis Díez Ripollés y Octavio García Pérez (eds.), *La política legislativa penal iberoamericana en el cambio de siglo*, Madrid-Montevideo: Edisofer y B. de F., 2008, p. 1-24;
Juan Oberto Sotomayor Acosta, 'Las recientes reformas penales en Colombia: un ejemplo de irracionalidad legislativa', in: José Luis Díez Ripollés y Octavio García Pérez (eds.), *La política legislativa penal iberoamericana en el cambio de siglo*, Madrid-Montevideo: Edisofer y B. de F., 2008, p. 75-118;
René van Swaanignen, *Perspectivas europeas para una criminología crítica*, Montevideo-Buenos Aires: B. de F., 2011;
Juárez Tavares, 'La reforma penal en Brasil', in: José Luis Díez Ripollés y Octavio García Pérez (eds.), *La política legislativa penal iberoamericana en el cambio de siglo*, Madrid-Montevideo: Edisofer y B. de F., 2008, p. 46-74;
Tzvetan Todorov, *Los enemigos íntimos de la democracia*, Barcelona, Galaxia Gutemberg, 2012;
José Urquizo Olaechea, 'La reciente política legislativa penal en el Perú', in: José Luis Díez Ripollés y Octavio García Pérez (eds.), *La política legislativa penal iberoamericana en el cambio de siglo*, Madrid-Montevideo: Edisofer y B. de F., 2008, p. 325-381;
Charlotte Vanneste, 'Penalidad y desigualdad: nueva actualidad de los informes entre penalidad y economía. El ejemplo de Bélgica', *Revista de Derecho penal y Criminología*, Buenos Aires, año V, número 5, junio de 2015, p. 67-80;
Fernando Velásquez Velázquez, *Derecho penal. Parte general*, Medellín: Comlibros, 4ª ed., 2009;
Loïc Wacquant, *Punir os pobres*, Rio de Janeiro: Revan, 2007;
Jock Young, *A sociedade excludente*, Rio de Janeiro: Revan, 2002;
Eugenio Raúl Zaffaroni, *Derecho penal. Parte general*, Buenos Aires: Ediar, 2ª ed., 2002;
Eugenio Raúl Zaffaroni, *El enemigo en el Derecho penal*, Bogotá: Grupo Editorial Ibáñez, 2006;
Eugenio Raúl Zaffaroni, 'El Derecho penal liberal y sus enemigos', in: *En torno de la cuestión penal*, Montevideo-Buenos Aires: B. de F., 2005, p. 153-177;
Eugenio Raúl Zaffaroni, 'La globalización y las actuales orientaciones de la política criminal', in: Eugenio Raúl Zaffaroni, *En torno de la cuestión penal*, Montevideo-Buenos Aires: B. de F., 2005;
Eugenio Raúl Zaffaroni, *Los Códigos penales de Latinoamérica*, México: Suprema Corte de Justicia de la Nación e Instituto Latinoamericano de las Naciones Unidas para la Prevención del Delito y el Tratamiento del Delincuente, 2000;
Eugenio Raúl Zaffaroni, 'Politique criminelle et droits d l'homme en Amerique Latine: de la sécurité nationale à la sécurité civique', *Archives de Politique Criminelle*, 1992, p. 77-86.

OVERPROSECUTION AND NEGOTIATED JUSTICE IN EUROPE

Katalin LIGETI* & Gavin ROBINSON**

I. INTRODUCTION

As judicial authorities face increasingly complex criminal legislation and ever-mounting workloads, to such an extent that the judicial apparatus risks losing its capacity to properly fulfil its function and maintain credibility, legislators and prosecutors are looking to various possibilities to filter out less exigent cases, to accelerate criminal proceedings or to launch new tools to make good on and prevent future wrongdoing without engaging the power of the criminal law at all.

One way of dealing with the overload of case files consists in resorting to forms of "negotiated" – as opposed to traditional, imposed – justice, such as out-of-court settlements, penal orders, guilty pleas and deferred prosecution agreements. Such alternative routes first and foremost enable prosecutors and judges to handle certain cases more quickly and without having to comply with all of the burdensome trappings of a full criminal trial, in theory assuaging fears of loading criminal justice systems beyond breaking point. Yet the minimization, sidelining (or complete excision) of the full trial stage which is typical of negotiated justice mechanisms raises serious questions around the quality of justice being – swiftly – delivered, the openness of criminal justice in general, and the communicative function of sanctioning systems.[1]

In this chapter, we explore these tensions through the prism of the evolving roles of the prosecutor and the judge in the context of negotiated justice in Europe.

We begin by reflecting, in Part II, on the main causes of overprosecution, before discussing its ramifications for the very viability of European criminal

* Professor of European and International Criminal Law, University of Luxembourg.
** Postdoctoral researcher: Criminal Law & IT Law, University of Luxembourg.
1 Ligeti & Tosza (2019), 25.

justice systems – such as the highly problematic overuse of pre-trial detention. The term "overprosecution" will be used interchangeably with "overuse of prosecution" to mean the (quantitatively) excessive resort to prosecution rather than any (qualitative) misuse or abuse of prosecutorial power.

Part 2 closes by situating the turn to negotiated justice mechanisms amongst a broader set of developments aiming principally to streamline criminal justice via strengthened prosecutorial power and a gradual shift toward more horizontal, transactional forms of dispute resolution. The term "negotiated justice" is construed as encompassing any scenario wherein a defendant in criminal proceedings consents, expressly or implicitly, to waive their right to a full public trial in return for some form of benefit compared to the envisaged outcome at such a full public trial (most typically, a formal sentence discount) having engaged in negotiations with the prosecution service, with or without the oversight or involvement of a judge.[2]

In Part III, we tackle the standard account of negotiated justice tools as legal transplants from the realms of common law into continental systems, before highlighting three elements which are shared across national mechanisms and systems: the avoidance of a full trial, the putatively more lenient outcome thereby secured, and some level of negotiation or bargaining between prosecutor and defendant. A discussion of the evolving roles of prosecutor and judge ensues, before we offer some closing remarks on the future of negotiated justice in Europe.

II. CAUSES AND CONSEQUENCES OF OVERPROSECUTION

II.1. CAUSES

The overuse of prosecution may be considered a side-effect of substantive overcriminalisation, meaning the expansion of the scope of criminal law beyond the classical notion of a crime. Several key examples of this trend stand out. Likely the most widespread is the increasing prevalence in our modern societies of statutory or "regulatory offences": from taxation to the protection of the environment or migration, criminal law is employed more and more often in order to sanction and deter non-compliance with administrative obligations or

2 Whilst admitting that negotiated justice does not have one fixed meaning, Gless and Zurkinden (2017) similarly identify a common understanding of the term as "the result generated by an exchange process of reciprocal concessions replacing the classic criminal trial'; in Ligeti & Franssen (eds), 119.

orders issued by administrative authorities.[3] Such an extension of the role of criminal law, especially in cases where non-compliance or contravention may be commonplace – for example, incomplete or incorrect declarations to the tax authorities or road traffic offences – paves the way for the overuse of prosecution.

Other important factors are the growing criminalisation of behaviour, acts or omissions which constitute (mere) dangerous conduct; in other words, shifting criminalisation from "effect" to "endangerment". The absorption into national criminal justice systems of complex new categories of crimes set out in EU and international criminal law, further proliferating the quantity and range of potential options on offer for prosecutors, is another key driver. In some places, aggressive criminal justice ("war on crime") policies in response to economic or social issues which are perceived to require urgent and strong attention in the form of (more) convictions and stiffer sentences and penalties have further cranked the pressure up on the criminal justice system to deliver a demonstrable response.[4]

Many of the above forces can be observed at work in the arena of white-collar crime, where the sheer complexity of economic and financial operations has posed an existential challenge to the traditional trial format through not only the inflated costs of investigations and criminal proceedings, but also the damaging repercussions that criminal sanctions may have on all stakeholders, such as punished entities' employees and shareholders, and the national or global economy as a whole: the "too big to jail" phenomenon.[5]

At criminal policy level, a key driver of overprosecution in Europe has been the application of a strict interpretation of the legality principle to the effect that where evidence is sufficient and a case does not unequivocally suffer from a procedural defect (prescription period elapsed; accused unidentifiable; etc.), as a rule prosecution must proceed. This stance has compounded the overcriminalisation phenomena outlined above: where opportunities for prosecutorial discretion – as evinced traditionally in common law systems – are less, the introduction of more and broader criminal offences logically translates to increased levels of prosecution.

Lastly, the strengthening of fair trial rights, in particular to a jury trial, to confrontation, and to litigate on the exclusion of evidence have created a paradox effect whereby trials become longer and more expensive, further adding to the

---

3 For example, on complex cases of environmental crime in Germany; see F. Saliger (2012), para 542. On the use in Sweden of summary penal orders, issued by the prosecutor, in relation to environmental law see Bastidas Venegas & Bergstrom (2019), 137.

4 In the US, the War on Drugs and sentence multipliers for weapons offences stand out; more recently in Europe, waves of public pressure for action on corruption and other corporate crimes has provoked *inter alia* the adoption in recent years of deferred prosecution agreements in the UK and France, discussed *infra* at 3.2.

5 For an overview of criminal law and alternatives thereto in the context of the enforcement of economic and financial crime laws in Europe and the US, see Ligeti & Tosza (2019), Ch.1.

backlog of criminal cases before courts.[6] Going to trial, as a result, becomes less "attractive" to both accused and prosecutor and less feasible for the system as a whole.[7]

II.2. CONSEQUENCES

The immediate consequence of overprosecution is the overloading of court dockets and a drain on the resources of the criminal justice system in general[8], from human and financial resources right up to the burgeoning caseloads faced by prosecutors and trial judges.[9]

The locus of delay may shift around between systems: whilst in inquisitorial traditions, the preliminary investigation tends to be the strongest drain on time and resources, in adversarial systems it is the trial (usually by jury).[10] In concrete terms, the centrality of the preliminary investigation also compounds civil law jurisdictions' longstanding problem of the overuse of pre-trial detention, both in terms of excessive resort to detention and the duration thereof.[11]

Outcomes, however, are very similar across European systems: an overload of work slows the justice system down, causing a failure in most cases to deliver a fair procedure without undue delay, raising the potential of violations of the fundamental right enshrined in Article 6(1) of the European Convention on Human Rights.[12] In addition to delay, the probity of proceedings can also be indirectly affected by such oversaturation. For instance, informal practices may

6 Bradley in Luna & Wade (eds) (2012), 97–101.

7 For example, when Italy was moving in the 1990s towards an adversarial procedure in which written evidence would be replaced by oral evidence at trial, the reform retained a simplified 'trial by dossier' procedure in order to assuage serious concerns over time and resource drain; see Hodgson (2015), 227, who notes that "(i)t would seem that the introduction of improved procedural defense rights immediately triggers the establishment of procedures through which these rights can be waived".

8 This problem was highlighted nearly 15 years ago in the outcomes of a comparative academic study of six European criminal justice systems; see J.-M. Jehle & M. Wade, *Coping with Overloaded Criminal Justice Systems: The Rise of Prosecutorial Power Across Europe* (Springer, 2005).

9 See the report of the European Commission for the Efficiency of Justice, 'Length of court proceedings in member states of the Council of Europe based on the case law of the European Court of Human Rights, adopted in December 2018, citing "court congestion" as the first cause of delay (before proceedings start) for all proceedings; and "insufficient number of prosecutors" as an origin of delay in criminal proceedings; 4.

10 Thaman in Luna & Wade (eds) (2012), 156–157.

11 In turn, in the EU context concerns have been raised around the adverse impact of the overuse of pre-trial detention on mutual trust (a prerequisite to the proper execution, for example, of European Arrest Warrants) due to the potential that long periods of pre-trial detention hold for breaches of detainees' fundamental rights. See Sellier & Weyembergh (2018), 87.

12 The first sentence of Article 6(1) ECHR reads: "In the determination of his civil rights and obligations or of any criminal charge against him, everyone is entitled to a fair and public hearing within a reasonable time by an independent and impartial tribunal established by law".

develop in order to dispense with less serious cases, such as the informal or *de facto* exercise of prosecutorial discretion by means of inertia, for instance by delaying the closing of an investigation until an offence is time-barred, or simply not undertaking any actual investigative measure during the investigative stage in order to obtain a preliminary dismissal for lack of evidence.

Beyond such – ill-advised – prosecutorial coping mechanisms, one knock-on effect of the overloading of criminal justice systems has been the opening, either formally or informally (in practice), of "vents" at the prosecution level that allow for the disposal of cases either unilaterally (decision taken by prosecutor alone) or multilaterally[13], in concert with the accused and/or the victim.

Unilateral prosecutorial disposal of a case may be either based on grounds prescribed by law (across European criminal justice systems) or on an evaluation of whether prosecution is opportune or not (traditionally, in jurisdictions permitting discretionary prosecution). Across European systems, the core of mandatory grounds for the unilateral disposal of a case by the prosecutor is almost uniform.[14] By contrast, calibrations of the so-called "public interest drop" vary across criminal justice systems. In countries which traditionally adhere to discretionary prosecution[15], proceedings may be dropped where the prosecutor considers that prosecution is not opportune. In other European jurisdictions, which have traditionally adhered to the legality principle, in practice the most frequent grounds for discretion are where the offence is deemed to be of minor importance, where the suspect has considerably contributed to clarifying the commission of the offence and the interest in doing so overrides the interest in prosecution, and where the suspect is of a young age. Lastly, dropping the least important of the offences (in cases of multiple or related offences) is also envisaged in some systems if the perpetrator has already been sentenced, is expected to be sentenced, or where adding one more offence would not alter the maximum sentence.

Meanwhile, multilateral disposal of proceedings – entailing the agreement (or at least absence of objection) of either the accused or both the accused and

---

(Emphasis added). See also Council of Europe, Recommendation Rec(2000)19, The Role of Public Prosecution in the Criminal Justice System, 6 October 2000; 24(c): 'public prosecutors should in particular ... seek to ensure that the criminal justice system operates as expeditiously as possible'.

13 See F. Tulkens, 'Negotiated Justice' in M. Delmas-Marty & J. R. Spencer (eds), *European Criminal Procedures,* (Cambridge University Press, 2002).

14 Mainly: where there is a lack of evidence, the perpetrator is unknown, the prosecution is time-barred, the act allegedly committed is no longer a criminal offence, amnesty, death of the suspect/accused, the victim did not make a request for prosecution (where required by law), or where prosecution would constitute a violation of the *ne bis in idem* principle. See K. Ligeti, 'Pre-trial procedures in the European Union' in K. Ligeti (ed), *Toward a Prosecutor for the European Union. Vol. 2: Draft Rules of procedure* (Hart Publishing, forthcoming 2019).

15 For instance, Luxembourg, the Netherlands and the UK.

the victim to the discontinuation of proceedings – shows an even greater variety of approaches and mechanisms across European criminal justice systems. In general, however, "diversion" from prosecution almost always entails agreement by the accused to (a) specific condition(s) ("conditional disposal"[16]; most commonly, payment of a fine) and/or victim-offender conciliation or mediation (often directly linked to compensation of the victim by the offender).

For example, s.153(a) of the German *Strafprozessordnung* (StPO) provides that the public prosecution office may (provisionally, and later definitively) decline to take misdemeanours to court, where "these are of such a nature as to eliminate the public interest in criminal prosecution and if the degree of guilt does not present an obstacle", so long as both court and accused consent to the attached conditions which may include *inter alia* the performance a specified service in order to make reparations for damage caused by the offence; payment a sum of money to a non-profit-making institution or to the Treasury; performance of some other service of a non-profit-making nature; compliance with duties to pay a specified amount in maintenance; making a serious attempt to reach a mediated agreement with the aggrieved person (perpetrator-victim mediation). Similar – but not identical – provisions apply to "provisional terminations of criminal proceedings" for misdemeanours.[17]

The degree to which the accused and/or the victim actually engage in negotiations in such scenarios (as opposed to complying with the will of the prosecutor) is too context-dependent, and perhaps too opaque to be summarised here. In theory, however, it does seem plausible that some level of negotiation will generally contribute in practice to the settled terms being acceptable to all parties. This applies *a fortiori* in systems where the prosecutorial decision to drop a case constitutes *res judicata* and may be challenged by, for instance, the person or authority who reported the offence, any person whose rights may have been prejudiced, or the victim.[18]

Another important type of procedural "vent" which has increasingly been made available to prosecutors in several European systems is the penal order, whereby the prosecutor files a request at the court for approval of a sanction – usually a fine. This outcome (a formal conviction) is a key factor distinguishing the penal order model from conditional disposals, where (notwithstanding attached conditions) the case is ultimately dismissed. So too is the necessary,

16 Although these forms of disposal are clearly distinguished from one another in terms of both outcome and procedure, in many jurisdictions conditional disposals were introduced alongside the public interest drop, with both intended to ease caseload pressures; see Luna & Wade (2010), 1446.

17 Cited from the official English translation of the StPO, available at https://www.gesetze-im-internet.de/englisch_stpo/.

18 Private prosecutions by the victim may ensue in some systems, such as France, Germany, Finland, and Belgium.

corollary involvement of a court in approving the punitive outcome of a penal order; with conditional disposals, as mentioned above, the procedure usually stops at prosecutor level. All the same, the two routes may often work in a very similar manner[19] in practice where the input of the overloaded court – as well as that of the accused – in reality amount to a decision to either "take it or leave it".[20] This is not to say that there is never room for some level of negotiation between the accused or her defence team and the prosecutor in conditional disposals or penal orders – but this will depend on the national system, the context and circumstances of the case at hand, and the interplay or relationship between these two interlocutors.

By way of contrast, a markedly greater amount of negotiation may be said to take place, in either (or both) an informal and formalised basis – such as before a judge – in the context of existing procedures which aim to defer prosecution, to shorten trial proceedings, or to dispense with the need for either a preliminary investigation or trial altogether, whether in return for an admission of guilt on the part of the accused (plea bargaining) or independently of any such admission. Given their emphasis on the "negotiated" aspect of the "justice" that they render, in what follows the focus shall in the main be on this last range of practices.

III. NEGOTIATED JUSTICE IN EUROPE: TRENDS, FORMS AND TENSIONS

III.1. FROM THE COMMON LAW TO THE CONTINENT

While in the Anglo-American systems the existence and acknowledgement of such mechanisms is not new, the increasing interest of Continental systems in "negotiated justice" still constitutes to some extent a novelty. The expansion of diversion and negotiated justice is a growing trend in continental criminal justice systems that, in various forms, have introduced different procedural devices which result in a consensual "escape from the trial" – meaning the avoidance, with the consent of the defendant, of fully-fledged court proceedings.[21] A selective overview of the common features of these devices is provided below at III.2.

19 Jehle (2004), 7.

20 Thaman in Luna & Wade (2012), 161.

21 For example, the palette of negotiated justice options continues to grow in France, where "initially timid, the movement is deepening; *justiciables* (citizens and companies), judges and lawyers are confronted with a real change of paradigm and culture. From a conflictual starting point, criminal justice is becoming more and more transactional". See V. De Senneville, 'La révolution de la justice pénale négociée', *Les Echos*, 26 June 2018. Authors' own translation.

It would of course be an oversimplification to ascribe the growth of negotiated justice mechanisms in Europe to the urgent need to unlock clogged criminal justice systems. In particular as concerns efforts to introduction and acceptance of the use of perpetrator-victim negotiations and measures of restorative justice, fading recourse to the criminal trial and the rise of a transactional form of justice has reflected a broader shift towards organising society in a more egalitarian way.[22] In certain cases, even prosecutor-dominated procedures have tracked the growth of restorative justice: compensation paid by perpetrators to victims of road traffic offences, for example, may be preferable to the traditional outcome of imposed, top-down criminal justice: payment of a fine to the state and the victim going empty-handed.

The consensus, nonetheless, is that the adoption of diversion programmes and forms of negotiated justice has most often been justified and promoted through arguments of efficiency and procedural economy.[23] The sheer pressure exerted by this imperative to streamline criminal justice systems is such that even those systems which have not traditionally permitted prosecutorial discretion have opened avenues for a model that is in essence alien to them. This transformation[24], which has created tensions with long-standing principles of criminal justice, provoking resistance and criticism (discussed below at III.3), is part of a broader picture of convergence between common law and civil law systems. Indeed, neither the inquisitorial nor the accusatorial system of criminal justice exists today in pure form in Europe. As Spencer wrote nigh on two decades ago in 2002, "although there are unquestionably two different traditions, the borrowings between the two have been so extensive that it is no longer possible to classify any of the criminal justice systems in Western Europe as wholly accusatorial or wholly inquisitorial".[25]

---

22 "(I)n a society which has become more egalitarian, more complex and less coherent, regulation based on an authoritarian model has lost its natural legitimacy (…) From the point of view of socio-criminology, negotiated justice draws on a number of theories, in particular interactionist theories, the movement for victim support and the model of restorative justice"; F. Tulkens (2002), 646–648.

23 See R. Vogler & B. Huber (eds), *Criminal Procedure in Europe*, 11; S. Sun Beale, *Prosecutorial Discretion in Three Systems: Balancing Conflicting Goals and Providing Mechanisms for Control*, in M. Caianiello & J. Hodgson (eds), *Discretionary Criminal Justice in a Comparative Context*, Carolina Academic Press, 2015, 51.

24 As stressed by Jehle (2004), "There is almost no country in Europe which follows the principle of legality without exception. Almost nowhere are all criminal offenders prosecuted in order to be convicted by a court. Mostly one finds either diversion from the criminal justice system or discretion at police and/or prosecution service level"; 14.

25 Spencer (2002) identifies seminal steps of this *rapprochement* at the national levels on either side of the historical common/civil law divide. Key examples include the introduction in England and Wales of a public prosecutor in the mid-1980s (shifting the focus of the criminal justice system away from the trial toward a regulated, filtering pre-trial stage akin to continental traditions) whilst the shared concern of improving the situation of the defendant (chiefly through the rights to legal advice at an earlier stage of proceedings and to information) has

Subject to that proviso, the efficiency rationale underlying the turn to negotiated justice may nonetheless be perceived and nuanced differently in the two sets of systems, owing to their different starting points. When discretion is already granted *ab initio* with regard to the decision whether to prosecute or not, negotiated justice represents an additional tool to administrate and fine-tune specific prosecutorial policy; in systems based on the legality principle, on the other hand, negotiated justice may primarily function as a pressure relief device and a gateway to introduce some prosecutorial discretion – albeit legitimately, in the course of agreed reforms – through the backdoor.

III.2. FORMS OF NEGOTIATED JUSTICE IN EUROPE

Negotiated justice mechanisms assume different forms and show different features across the various criminal justice systems. Three recurrent characteristics may nonetheless be identified:

- the *avoidance of a full public trial*;
- the *alternative outcome being more lenient* than otherwise envisaged should the case proceed to a full trial;
- the *consent or acquiescence of the accused* to such an outcome, necessitating some degree of negotiation between the parties.

The avoidance of a full public trial

Depending on the form and outcome of negotiated justice in play, the trial stage may be either avoided entirely or systematically simplified, accelerated or otherwise curtailed. The Dutch *transactie,* a "transaction" resulting in a conditional disposal of criminal proceedings, is an example of avoidance of the trial stage: the procedure ends with the prosecutor. A long-established practice of systematic acceleration of the trial, meanwhile, is found in Spain where proceedings may be shortened in accordance with a range of options, including the *conformidad* procedure whereby a trial is routinely opened only to be swiftly closed via a guilty plea.[26]

More recently, a third route has emerged in relation to corporate defendants: the deferred prosecution agreement ('DPA'). With DPAs, now available in the

resulted in reforms from the 1960s into the 1990s and beyond, bringing criminal justice systems closer together in the process; 15–19. Important "(e)xternal pressures toward a common approach" have meanwhile emerged through Europeanisation: most fundamentally, the deepening influence of the European Convention on Human Rights and the European Union on national criminal justice systems. See M. Delmas-Marty and J.R. Spencer (eds), *European Criminal Procedures* (CUP, 2004) 5 *et seq.*

26 On the Spanish system of "plea agreements", see L. Bachmaier in Caianiello & Hodgson (2015). Point cited here at 100.

UK[27] and in France in relation to limited categories of offences[28], there is no final disposal of prosecution; the opening of proceedings is merely temporarily avoided ('deferred') for a period of time set in the terms of an agreement between prosecutor and corporate entity. In their country of origin (the US), most DPAs stipulate a public statement of facts and the acceptance of responsibility, along with undertakings to bring in external monitors in order to monitor an entity's compliance with the terms of the agreement.[29] Those terms may be very wide-ranging, comprising for instance restitution to be paid to wronged parties, future personnel decisions or the disclosure of expenses and fees charged to customers.[30] Should the corporate entity fail to honour the terms of the DPA, its prosecution may ensue.[31] Additionally, DPAs may contribute to the opening of criminal proceedings against natural persons, by including in their terms the full cooperation of the targeted entity with ongoing investigations into – most likely – its employee(s).[32]

A more lenient outcome

In return for accepting not to proceed to trial, across all European systems the accused receives a more lenient outcome than would otherwise materialise should such a trial go ahead and a conviction – as anticipated – be secured. Whereas the advantages for the prosecutor and the criminal justice system as a whole are more easily summarised as the procedural (and therefore resource) savings made by escaping a full trial, the type of "benefit" which defendants may extract through negotiation varies across jurisdictions and procedures.[33] Depending on the system and mechanism, penalties in relation to which it is possible to agree diminished punishment may be limited to those of a financial nature, or also include custodial sanctions.

27 Crime and Courts Act 2013, Schedule 17, 'Deferred Prosecution Agreements'. The UK system does not include non-prosecution agreements, 'NPAs', which are struck between the prosecutor and the defence without the filing of charges or judicial oversight.

28 The French version of the DPA, the *convention de judiciaire d'intérêt public* ('CJIP') was introduced by Article 2 of the so-called *"loi Sapin II", Loi no. 2016-1691 du 9 décembre 2016 relative à la transparence, à la lutte contre la corruption et à la modernisation de la vie économique*.

29 Mazzacuva (2014), 257.

30 See R.E. Barkow (2009), 'The Prosecutor as Regulatory Agency', Section II.

31 Moreover, in the UK system where the terms of a DPA were previously approved by the Crown Court, the statement of facts contained therein is to be treated as "proof by formal admission"; UK Crime and Courts Act 2013, Schedule 17, s.13(2).

32 UK Crime and Courts Act 2013, Schedule 17, s.5(3)(f): "The requirements that a DPA may impose on P include, but are not limited to, the following requirements – (…) to co-operate in any investigation related to the alleged offence".

33 With the obvious exception of DPAs in the UK and France, where the – temporary – benefit for the target corporation is by definition the conditional (and provisional) avoidance of prosecution.

Some negotiated justice tools provide for a standardised sentence discount in primary law[34], whilst in others a more lenient sentence flows *de facto* from practice, sometimes facilitated by sentencing guidelines.[35] An indirect route to leniency may also be secured for example via the exclusion of accessory sanctions from subsequent proceedings, or an undertaking not to include the outcome in the criminal record of the accused may be available. Conditional suspension or discontinuation of prosecution may also be possible, as may mediation and reparation or reconciliation schemes involving a third actor: the victim.

Plea agreements in particular have in recent decades become a central plank of negotiated justice across the European jurisdictions, and illustrate well the variety of balancing acts which distinct criminal justice systems have come to perform in order to accommodate the march of procedural efficiency within legal-institutional traditions. Whereas in England and Wales (and of course the United States) charge bargaining and even "fact bargaining"[36] may be commonplace, European forays into plea bargaining have tended to limit what may be offered to (and sought by) the accused to discounts on the sentence which will eventually be handed down, rather than any adjustment of charges or facts.[37] This pattern is "closely linked to the principle of legality, providing less leeway for the prosecution to amend and drop charges"[38], and the quintessentially civil law ideal of searching for material truth rather than admitting an agreed version of

34 See the examples of Spanish fast-track proceedings and Italian penal orders, discussed *infra*.

35 In 2017, a major worldwide study of trial waiver systems found that "(w)hile some jurisdictions essentially bind judges to the sentence agreed upon by the parties (...), in many others the parties do not agree on a specific sentence, but it is understood that a discount will be applied by the judge"; Russell & Hollander (2017), 318. In England and Wales (where the prosecutor has unfettered discretion to negotiate with the defendant on sentence discounts as well as charges and facts), the Sentencing Guidelines Council (SGC) issued guidance in 2007 which recommends: a one-third discount for a guilty plea at the first opportunity, a one-quarter discount for a guilty plea after the trial date is set; a one-tenth discount for a guilty plea at the door of court/after trial begun. The Court of Appeal had previously indicated in *R v Buffrey* 14 Cr. App. R (S) 511 that while there was no absolute rule as to what the discount should be, as general guidance the Court believed that something of the order of one-third would be an appropriate discount. See Crown Prosecution Service, *Sentencing – Overview*, available at https://www.cps.gov.uk/legal-guidance/sentencing-overview.

36 Hodgson (2015) gives an example of "fact bargaining": an informal pre-trial pact to maintain that the alleged victim was slapped rather than punched, thereby lowering the seriousness of the facts considered in court by judge(s) and jury. The pact is honoured when, at the apposite moment of the trial, both parties stick to this version of events. As Hodgson notes, a certain level of trust between prosecution and defence is required for this practice to take hold.

37 'Negotiated agreements' in Germany, for example, "may only comprise the legal consequences that could be the content of the judgment and of the associated rulings, other procedural measures relating to the course of the underlying adjudication proceedings, and the conduct of the participants during the trial"; see s257(c) of the StPO (official English translation available at https://www.gesetze-im-internet.de/englisch_stpo/.

38 See the "comparative study" of plea agreements in Council of Europe states in the judgment of the European Court of Human Rights in *Natsvlishvili and Togonidze v Georgia*, App. No 9043/05 (Judgment of 29 April 2014), paras 62-65 (quoted text: para 65).

the truth. In by and large eschewing the use of charge bargaining, European systems also reflect concerns that tolerating such methods may *inter alia* incentivise the notorious practices of "overcharging" detected in the United States, whereby "the authorities compel the accused to plead guilty for something the accused actually did not do in order to avoid trouble he does not deserve".[39]

Over time, some individual systems have formalised and tinkered with the organically-established "going rate" for discounts via guilty pleas in response to observed practices in the aim of both fostering the consistency of judgments and boosting the rate of pleas. An interesting example is provided by Spain, where the *conformidad* system held out no real benefit for the accused until successive reforms brought greater speed and efficiency to standard *conformidad* (in 1988) and then introduced a new type of fast-track proceedings (in 2002; for offences carrying up to 3 years' imprisonment) wherein guilty pleas automatically lead to the reduction of the sentence by one third.[40] A significant rise in plea agreements in fast-track proceedings has ensued.[41] Statutory reductions can also be found in the field of penal orders: for example Italy, where the fine which would otherwise have been appropriate following trial proceedings is halved should a penal order be issued.[42]

The question of permissible outcomes is inherently bound up too with the material scope of negotiated justice mechanisms, which naturally varies between European criminal systems. Deferred prosecution agreements (where the "benefit" for the target entity consists simply of an escape from trial and potential conviction), for example, are limited in the UK and in France to core offences of corporate crime such as fraud, bribery, money laundering, *trafic d'influence* and tax evasion.[43] In general, penal orders correspond and are limited to offences which are punishable by fine only[44]: in Germany, where the penal order originated, this has been the case since the 1970s, with the exception of a 1993 reform which allowed suspending a prison sentence of up to one year.[45] In France, meanwhile, an *ordonnance pénale* is available for misdemeanours (*contraventions*)[46] and certain *délits*[47] but not the most serious category, *crimes*.

39 Mylonopoulos in Sieber et al (2018), 102–103.
40 Article 801, Spanish *Código penal.*
41 L. Bachmaier in Caianiello & Hodgson (2015), 99.
42 Article 459(2), Italian *Codice di procedura penale.*
43 Schedule 17, Part 2, Crime and Courts Act 2013 (UK) and Article 41-1-2-I, French *Code de procédure pénale* as amended. The scope of French CJIPs was extended to tax fraud in October 2018; see W. Garcin, 'Le Parlement adopte définitivement le renforcement de l'arsenal contre la fraude fiscale', *Le Figaro*, 10 October 2018.
44 Thaman (2010), 339.
45 See Vivell (2006), 42–43.
46 Article 524, French *Code de procédure pénale* ('CPP'). The maximum fine is of €3,000; Article 131-13, French *Code pénal.*
47 Article 495, French *Code de procédure pénale. Délits* covered include types of theft, traffic offences, drug use and counterfeiting (Article 495-II). The prosecutor must be satisfied *inter alia*

Over time and reflecting different societal perceptions of the workings of the criminal justice system, some national approaches to out-of-court settlements and penal orders have also evolved in distinctive ways. For example, the Dutch *transactie* (formally a civil law agreement whereby non-prosecution is secured in exchange, usually, for payment of a sum of money) was first introduced for misdemeanours in 1926, but gradually extended – in the twin aims of minimising the effects of a criminal trial on suspects and streamlining the overburdened criminal justice system – first to serious crimes of a socio-economic nature in 1951 and then to felonies carrying a maximum sentence of up to 6 years' imprisonment in 1983. After a shifting and hardening of public opinion decreed that the *transactie* was "not real punishment", a reform in 2008 introduced a new prosecutorial penal order (*strafbeschikking;* removing the civil law character of the *transactie* and requiring an admission of guilt)[48], applicable to the same offences as had been the *transactie.*[49]

As regards plea bargaining, most inquisitorially-rooted systems in which it takes place tend to limit its use to less serious cases. The Italian '*patteggiamento*'[50], an agreement on the sentence first introduced in 1981, can only be used for offences which result in a maximum penalty of 5 years once the discount (up to a third of the envisaged sentence) is applied.[51] In Spain, guilty pleas are formally valid for offences carrying an upper limit of 6 years' imprisonment.[52] The French *comparution sur reconnaissance préalable de culpabilité* ('CRPC'), introduced in 2004, may be used for all *délits* (which carry a maximum sentence of 10 years' imprisonment), excepting certain specified *délits* consisting of attacks on "personal integrity" and sexual offences when the latter are punished with a prison sentence of more than 5 years.[53] For example, the CRPC procedure will in principle be available for all cases of repeated nuisance telephone calls or electronic messages[54], whereas an aggravating circumstance might tip sexual

that the allegations are "simple and established" and that the seriousness of the facts do not merit a term of imprisonment (Article 495-I); the victim may insist on going to trial (Article 495-III-2).

48 Article 257, Dutch *Wetboek van Strafvordering.* The position of the defendant vis-à-vis penal orders is discussed *infra.*

49 Brants in Sieber et al (2018), 62–66.

50 Formally, *l'applicazione della pena su richiesta delle parti*; Article 444, Italian *Codice di procedura penale* ('CPP').

51 Article 444.1, Italian CPP. The previous general limit of 2 years' imprisonment was raised to 5 years' imprisonment in 2003; Article 1, *Legge* 12.6.2003.

52 Despite this, however, guilty pleas are accepted in practice in more serious cases by tolerating a "fake" trial; see Bachmaier in Caianiello & Hodgson (2015), 105.

53 Article 495-7, French CPP.

54 Maximum penalty of one year's imprisonment and €15,000; Article 222-16, French CPP.

assaults other than rape out of its range.[55] In Poland, meanwhile, serious risks of non-compliance with the "reasonable time" criterion in Article 6 ECHR[56] led in 1998 to the introduction of a new procedure whereby the prosecutor is able to apply to the court, with the defendant's consent, for a conviction without oral hearing in relation to a misdemeanour with a maximum of 10 years' imprisonment.[57] A notable exception to the general trend persists in Germany, where both serious and minor offences are covered. Commentators have attributed this broad coverage to the fact that – unlike, notably, in France or in Italy – such practices were first left to develop informally without legislative brakes before eventually the law caught up.[58] To circumscribe their existing – and moreover, entrenched – use would likely have caused great friction amongst lower court judges and practitioners.[59]

The different forms of consent

Amongst the negotiated justice tools examined here, penal orders generally entail the smallest degree of negotiation between accused and prosecutor. As mentioned above (at II.2), in practice the issuing of a penal order can, in large part due to the lack of a hearing, resemble unilateral prosecutorial sanctioning. Some level of informal bargaining may, however, have already taken place; for instance, fieldwork in Germany has reported that the prosecutor may suggest a level of fine to the defendant if they agree not to object to the penal order.[60] Although in some systems the mere absence of any objection on the part of the defendant suffices to imply agreement to a penal order[61], the norm is to accord defendants a fairly short period[62] in which to indicate either acceptance thereof or opposition thereto. In most systems, the judge may still reject a penal order if they believe the procedure should proceed to a normal trial[63]; their role in the process is discussed below (at III.3).

55 Sexual assaults other than rape are punished by up to 5 years' imprisonment and a fine of €75,000 (Article 222-27, French CPP), but these rise to 7 years and € 100,000 respectively where, for instance, where the defendant used or threatened to use a weapon (Article 222-28-5, French CPP), removing the possibility of a CRPC.

56 Peters et al (2008), 151.

57 Article 335, Polish Code of Criminal Procedure.

58 Hodgson (2015), 227.

59 Weigend & Iontcheva Turner (2014), 81–82. The German incarnation of plea bargaining is discussed further *infra* at 3.3.

60 Dubber (1997), 560.

61 See for example Articles 525 (no mention of acceptance of *prévenu*) and 527, para 4 (according 30 days in which to oppose the penal order), French *Code de procédure pénale.*

62 Thaman has reported (2010) a range in European systems of between 7 days (Lithuania) and 30 days (France); 340.

63 Thaman (2010), 340.

To return to the defendant's point of view, the stipulation of very short timeframes for acceptance or rejection (or a decision not to object) raises the important point of legal representation. Logically, where both outcomes are legally possible an individual who risks receiving a penal order would tend to angle for a conditional disposal – which of course entails no sanction. Despite the challenges of having to weigh up whether to accept a penal order or to try to secure more leniency in a matter of days or weeks without any legal representation, depending on the system this may well be the reality for less fortunate defendants due to limitations of the right to a court-appointed lawyer to cases above a seriousness threshold which penal orders will rarely meet.[64] In Germany, for example, the court will mandate the appointment of counsel only where a suspended prison sentence of up to one year is sought by the prosecutor.[65] For all other possible punitive outcomes[66], some defendants may struggle to understand the consequences of their decision without independent legal advice.

In contrast to penal orders, plea agreements in most European systems are entered into by defendant and prosecutor before being validated by a judge.[67] Important and contrasting exceptions to this pattern exist in Italy where (like in the United States) judges are generally prohibited from participating in negotiations, and in Germany where the court plays a central role in them. The differing ambits of the judge vis-à-vis the prosecutor in the context of a range of negotiated justice tools are discussed *infra* at 3.3. To keep the focus here on the defendant's predicament when faced with the prosecutor offering benefits in return for a trial waiver, it is worth recalling the primary legislation defining – as discussed above – maximum (or automatic) sentence discounts as well as a cap on the seriousness of offences which may be subject to negotiations. In this way, negotiations are to a certain extent structured in advance by the legislator. After this pre-trammelling, but before the judicial scrutiny stage, there is ample opportunity for prosecutors to exert heavy pressure on defendants to cede to

64 Thaman (2012), 164.

65 Articles 408b and 407(2), German StPO.

66 A fine, a warning with sentence reserved, a driving ban, forfeiture, confiscation, destruction, making something unusable, announcement of the decision, and imposition of a regulatory fine against a legal person or an association; withdrawal of permission to drive, where the bar does not exceed two years; prohibition of the keeping or care of, trade in or other professional contact with animals of any kind or of a certain kind for the duration of one to three years; Article 407(2), German StPO.

67 *Natsvlishvili and Togonidze v Georgia*, para 69.

offered terms[68], especially given that in most systems the judge cannot amend the agreement but only reject it.[69]

Although adequate legal representation is obviously a key safeguard in this context, a minority of European systems include mandatory access to a lawyer for plea negotiations[70]; in others, the regular rules relating to legal representation apply.[71] Notably, a wide-ranging worldwide study recently found that defendants entering trial waivers without representation tended to arise more often in the context of minor offences, despite the potentially long-term impact of convictions for minor offences carrying no custodial sentence.[72] Legal representation may be particularly helpful in systems where the timing of prosecutors' offers is designed to extract maximum resource savings for the criminal justice system: in England and Wales, for example, the earlier the plea the greater the benefit[73] – incentivising swift decision-making.[74] In Spain, where it has been reported that prosecutors offer reduced sentences mere moments before trial, the Madrid Bar responded by circulating amongst its lawyers a sample request for additional time for consideration of trial waiver offers.[75]

III.3. THE EVOLVING ROLES OF PROSECUTOR AND JUDGE

From a prosecutorial perspective, the negotiated justice tools discussed heretofore represent first and foremost a means to more effectively allocate investigative and prosecutorial resources. In certain cases, their introduction may offer an intermediate option between the unconditional prosecutorial dismissal of a case

68 "It is undeniable that the will of the defendant is conditioned by a number of factors, including the uncertainty about the outcome of the trial, the fear of being convicted, the message conveyed by the prosecutor that choosing to go to trial will have worse consequences, or the situation of pre-trial detention"; Bachmaier (2018), 240.

69 *Natsvlishvili and Togonidze v Georgia*, para 69.

70 For example under the French *CRPC* (guilty plea) procedure; "The person cannot waive their right to be assisted by a lawyer" (Article 495-8, French *Code de procédure pénale*).

71 *Natsvlishvili and Togonidze v Georgia*, para 71.

72 Fair Trials International (2017), 88.

73 See Sentencing Council (2017), *Reduction in Sentence for a Guilty Plea: Definitive Guideline*, under 'Key Principles', "The purpose of this guideline is to encourage those who are going to plead guilty to do so as early in the court process as possible. Nothing in this guideline should be used to put pressure on a defendant to plead guilty"; 4. Available at https://www.sentencingcouncil.org.uk/wp-content/uploads/Reduction-in-Sentence-for-Guilty-Plea-definitive-guideline-SC-Web.pdf.

74 In particular in the context of serial or "routine" offences and low-level street criminality (drug dealing, theft), the option of a "consensual" solution may constitute "damage limitation", especially in simple cases where the suspect has been caught red-handed, is a recidivist or could be subject to additional consequences in the occasion of a formal conviction – such as deportation – where the sanction applied hits a certain threshold.

75 Fair Trials International (2017), 92.

and its prosecution, triggering a fully-fledged criminal trial. This is not to imply that the drive toward the simplification and acceleration of criminal justice has necessarily unburdened prosecutors – indeed, a new form of performance pressure may emerge, more in keeping with the prosecutor's newfound "crime regulator" outlook.[76] In such visions of a managerialised criminal justice system, the role of the judge is often portrayed as diminished, diluted or virtually wholly displaced, with copious critical literature – above all in the United States – referring to *de iure* or *de facto* "prosecutorial sentencing".[77]

Amongst the different forms of negotiated justice in Europe which are explored here, judicial influence on or control of prosecutor-driven sanctioning ranges from the non-existent (*transactie* or *strafbeschikking*) to light review (penal orders) through intermediate control to a full review of the material circumstances of the case and the ordering of the taking of new evidence (plea bargaining systems). Assessing the input of judges and courts in each negotiated justice tool in theory and in practice is a crucial factor in seeking the contours of the evolving rapport between judge and prosecutor, and ultimately to appraising the quality of justice thereby rendered.

Drawing on extensive comparative fieldwork, Luna and Wade reported that although some penal order systems require court review, "this is often pro forma, with the prosecutor acting as a veritable judge before the judge".[78] Importantly, the judge cannot amend the penal order but has a binary choice between accepting or rejecting it, with the latter option triggering a full trial. The German *Strafbefehl* has served as a model for other systems, bringing with it a requirement of court review and approval before a conviction is pronounced.[79] However, important exceptions do exist: the Dutch shift away from the *transactie* toward the *strafbeschikking* has drawn criticism *inter alia* because it has increased the punitiveness of the system (it culminates in a formal conviction) without

---

76 As Hodgson (2015) notes, the prioritisation of speed, efficiency and resource considerations entails the adoption of "methods (...) drawn from the world of business and the language of productivity, (...) alien to those in the judicial world"; 22. Regarding Germany, see Weigend & Iontcheva Turner (2014): "Under a system of quantitative benchmarks of performance, prosecutors and judges felt impelled to process more complex cases in less time"; 86–87, and references cited.

77 For instance, in the context of discussing deferred prosecution agreements Epstein (2011) has posited that "the (American) criminal justice system will grind to a halt if the settlement of criminal cases is barred, so that all cases must be litigated to final judgment"; in Barkow & Barkow (eds), 39. In the United States, there are virtually no more criminal trials at federal level; entrenched plea bargaining has combined with expansions of crimes being treated at federal level and mandatory sentences to the effect that "the federal prosecutor has become the federal sentencer" (Hodgson, 2015, 228).

78 Luna & Wade (2010), 1450.

79 Luna & Wade (2010), 1449–1450.

introducing a semblance of judicial oversight or review.[80] Indeed, it is the public prosecutor who must, in some cases (for instance, a fine of more than € 2,000) "hear" the suspect before issuing the penal order.[81] Although the suspect may file an objection to the penal order within 14 days of being made aware of it, triggering a hearing before a court, the legislation expressly provides that no appeal is possible where the suspect has waived his right to do so in writing or "by voluntarily complying with the punishment order".[82] The rapidity of some Dutch procedural routes combined with the fact that penal orders are often issued at an early stage in the investigation means that the suspect (like the victim) "simply have to trust the prosecutor".[83]

As noted above (at III.2), the involvement of the judge in plea bargaining situations is in most systems limited to validating the agreement struck between prosecutor and accused. The introduction (or formal recognition) of consensual procedures has inevitably sparked tensions with basic principles of continental criminal justice systems (such as the legality principle) and the inquisitorial ideal of the judicial search for the substantive truth – an ideal which is *prima facie* incompatible with a judicial role which is confined to arbitrating between competing versions of agreed *versions* of the truth.

The German settlement perhaps best reflects the delicate – and arguably unresolved – accommodation of deep-seated conceptions of the judicial process with the modern drive toward ever-greater efficiency. Most fundamentally, the official introduction of the *Verständigung*[84] has not negated the court's statutory duty to carry out a "free evaluation of evidence".[85] Not even a full confession made by the defendant in open court can of itself remove the judge's obligation to "discover the truth".[86] This duty also renders (at least in theory) any pre-arranged

80 Blom & Smit (2006); "(T)he *strafbeschikking* is a formal sanction which is not imposed by a judge but by the prosecutor. There is no court involvement at all"; 253.

81 S.257c(2), Dutch *Wetboek van Strafvordering*, English translation.

82 S.257e(1), Dutch *Wetboek van Strafvordering*, English translation.

83 Expressing doubt as to whether the regime is fully compliant with Article 6(1) ECHR, see Brants (2018), 74–75.

84 The *Verständigung* (agreement) was formally introduced via § 257(c) of the German StPO in 2009; various forms of negotiated justice (*Absprache*, *verfahrensbeendende Abstimmung*, *informelles Rechtsgespräch*) had, however, been informally employed since the 1970s. On the 2009 reform, see Weigend in Bloy et al. (2010), 831. In 2013, the German Federal Constitutional Court (*Bundesverfassungsgericht*) held that the new provisions were compatible with the German Constitution, considering, *inter alia*, their contribution to ensuring that criminal proceedings are completed in reasonable time. With regard to the criticisms advanced by the German doctrine, see *ex multis*: B. Schünemann in Hanack et al. (2002), 525 ff; Schlothauer (1998), 133.

85 "The court shall decide on the result of the evidence taken according to its free conviction gained from the hearing as a whole" (s.261, official English translation of StPO).

86 Weigend (2008), 44.

agreement on the facts ineffective[87], since the judge remains obliged to ground its verdict on its own fact-finding – which may extend, as per standard German proceedings, to ordering the taking of new evidence.[88]

Moreover, and in stark contrast to the majority of plea bargaining systems in place in Europe, the German judge is able to negotiate directly with both defence lawyers and prosecutor and to suggest an upper and lower sentence limit.[89] A further peculiarity of the *Verständigung*, mentioned above, is the absence of statutory limits on the offences to which it may apply or the sanctions it may deliver. However, judges must keep in mind the *Schuldprinzip* which, the *Bundesverfassungsgericht* has stressed, "may not depart – not even downward – from its purpose to provide just punishment commensurate with culpability".[90] It has been reported that in practice, in most cases the court actually indicates the penalty it is prepared to hand out if a confession is provided immediately, and the penalty that would materialise should the matter proceed to a full trial.[91] The difference between the two penalties is known as the *Sanktionsschere* or "sanction spread"; although not normally more than one third[92], the flexibility of the procedure by its very nature renders compatibility with the *Schuldprinzip* in particular "highly problematic"[93], whilst misgivings abound as to whether all defendants who confess under such circumstances could have been convicted as charged at trial.[94]

The compatibility of plea bargaining with national constitutional provisions has also been questioned in France and Portugal with contrasting results. After the French law due to introduce the *Comparution sur reconnaissance préalable de culpabilité* (CRPC) procedure was challenged by parliamentarians, the *Conseil constitutionnel*[95] deemed it to be in conformity with the French constitution. The

---

87 Furthermore, charge bargaining is expressly forbidden: "The verdict of guilt, as well as measures of reform and prevention, may not be the subject of a negotiated agreement"; s.257c(1), German StPO.

88 S.257c(1), referring to s. 244(2), German StPO: "In order to establish the truth, the court shall, *proprio motu*, extend the taking of evidence to all facts and means of proof relevant to the decision."

89 S. 257c(3), German StPO.

90 BVerfG, Judgment of 19 March 2013, paras 53–54, as translated by Weigend & Iontcheva Turner (2014), 85.

91 Altenhain, Dietmeier & May (2013), 122–136.

92 *Ibid*, 130–131.

93 Gless & Zurkinden (2017), 128, citing Weigend & Iontcheva Turner (2014), 85.

94 Weigend & Iontcheva Turner (2014), 93. According to the authors, in 2013 the German *Bundesverfassungsgericht* failed to engage deeply with this fundamental constitutional question. Further to the relationship between guilt and bargaining, Weigend and Iontcheva Turner also argue that the court failed to examine judges' "practical abandonment of their duty to inquire thoroughly into the facts", preferring to focus instead on a range of formal rules (mainly, transparency, publicity and a full documentation of negotiated proceedings) as guarantors of constitutionality; 95.

95 French *Conseil constitutionnel*, Décision no. 2004-492 DC, 2 March 2004.

request for an *a priori* constitutionality review rested on the contention that the CRPC disregarded the right to a fair trial and violated the presumption of innocence, equality before justice and the public nature of deliberations.[96]

In rejecting the first two (and strongest) complaints, the *Conseil constitutionnel* relied extensively on the role of the judge in CRPC proceedings. With regard to the separation of powers and a fair trial, its decision thus referred to the duty of the judge (or the president of the *Tribunal de Grande Instance*) to verify the "reality of the facts and their legal qualification"[97] before including along with their approval of the agreed sanctions their observations on the justifications therefor, "with regard to the circumstances of the offence and the personality of the perpetrator".[98] Together with the inclusion of the (mandatory) defence counsel and related safeguards, and account taken of the limited scope of application of the CRPC (with regard to offences and sanctions, as noted above at III.2) the theoretical centrality of the judge in proceedings was adjudged to be sufficient to ensure constitutionality – subject to the proviso that the procedure take place publicly.[99]

A decade later and in a different civil law system, as hinted at above the Portuguese Supreme Court took a very different view of a practice akin to plea bargaining which had recently sprung up organically in that country, inspired by the German experience.[100] In several cases, judges accepted confessions (operating *de facto* as a guilty plea) at trial whilst adhering to the maximum sentence previously agreed between prosecutor and accused. When a disgruntled defendant (claiming that his expectations had been violated by the eventual outcome at trial) appealed his convictions to the Supreme Court, it took the opportunity to ban such agreements outright.[101] The court held confessions secured on agreement to be inadmissible by virtue provisions of the Portuguese Code of Criminal Procedure rendering null and void "evidence obtained by torture, coercion, or, in general, infringement of the physical or moral integrity of persons"[102]; and in particular "evidence obtained, even with the person's consent, of a promise a legally inadmissible advantage".[103] To accept such agreements in the absence of any legislative grounding would, the court held, clearly violate the

96 *Ibid*, para 105.
97 Article 495-9 para 2, French *Code de procédure pénale.*
98 Article 495-11 para 1, French *Code de procédure pénale.*
99 *Conseil constitutionnel*, cit., para 118 and subsequently incorporated into Article 459-2, French *Code de procédure pénale.* Arguing that in practice the role of defence counsel is essential to ensuring fulfilment of the criteria ascribed to the judge, and questioning whether prosecutorial tactics and later legislative amendments have since undermined the *Conseil constitutionnel*'s reasoning, see Hodgson (2012), Section II.C.
100 See Costa Ramos (2014), 5.
101 Judgment of the *Supremo Tribunal de Justiça*, 4 October 2013, 224/06.7GAVZL.C1.S1
102 Article 126(1), Portuguese *Código de Processo Penal* (authors' translation).
103 Article 126(2)(2), Portuguese *Código de Processo Penal* (authors' translation).

loyalty principle, the legality principle, the demands of legal certainty and the principle of equality before the law, since the outcomes of such agreements would depend on the discretion of prosecutors and courts which may in turn vary from place to place.[104]

In a sense, the Portuguese Supreme Court had a relatively free hand insofar as the impugned agreements were both entirely unregulated and still a new development of limited impact. In scenarios where such practices are entrenched, settled legislation is in place and significant numbers of convicts are serving time pursuant to consensual deals, the right balance between promoting efficiency and coercive bargaining practices may be more difficult to strike.[105] In this regard, Fair Trials International has warned that although in many jurisdictions the judge has in one form or another a duty to be satisfied that trial waivers are entered into voluntarily, "no specific mechanism for ensuring this is provided in practice".[106] Future empirical and qualitative research into the true role of the judge in differently-calibrated plea agreement systems would thus appear necessary.[107]

We turn lastly to the distinct role of the court in the context of deferred prosecution agreements. In the UK system, the court's approval of a DPA is obtained in a two-step process: a preliminary hearing after the commencement of negotiations between prosecutor and the target entity, and a final hearing after the parties have agreed terms. Both hearings are geared towards ensuring that a DPA is likely to be in the interests of justice, and that its terms are fair, reasonable and proportionate.[108] Whereas the first hearing is of a strictly private nature and deliberations in the latter hearing may also be held in private, the declaration approving a DPA and the reasons for doing so are made in open court, before the

104 Costa Ramos (2014), 5.

105 See the judgment of the European Court of Human Rights in *Natsvlishvili and Togonidze v Georgia*, App. No 9043/05 (Judgment of 29 April 2014). For strong criticism in particular of the Strasbourg court's narrow focus on formal aspects of the true voluntariness of guilty pleas (thereby ensuring compatibility with the right to a fair trial enshrined in Article 6 ECHR) whereas the alternative to bargaining would – considering local circumstances in Georgia – almost certainly be an *unfair* trial, see Bachmaier (2018), esp. 248–249.

106 Fair Trials International (2017), para 100.

107 In this vein, Fair Trials International (2017) have invited states to "audit" *inter alia*: "Do judicial authorities provide meaningful review of procedure and evidence to verify the integrity of investigations and the effectiveness of defendants' trial waivers, with the ability to reject or delay trial waivers or to require trial or other, further, proceedings where evidence relied on by prosecuting authorities is particularly unreliable or in need of further vetting (for example, in cases involving a single witness, or those requiring forensic testing)?"; para 147.

108 Ss. 7–8, Schedule 17, Crime and Courts Act 2013. Nestled between the open-ended options provided to the prosecutor regarding content of a DPA (as discussed above at III.2) is one concrete restraint: the amount of any financial penalty agreed between the prosecutor and (the target entity) "must be broadly comparable to the fine that a court would have imposed on (the target entity) on conviction for the alleged offence following a guilty plea"; s.5(4).

prosecutor in principle publishes the DPA, the court's declaration and the reasons attached to relevant stages of proceedings.[109]

Comparable transparency requirements apply to the next juncture at which the court may be called into action by the prosecutor: to rule on the balance of probabilities – thus, a civil standard of proof is applied by a criminal court – on whether the target entity has failed to comply with the terms of the DPA.[110] The court may invite the prosecutor and target entity to agree proposals to remedy the breach once it is established; should this prove unfeasible leading to termination of the DPA, the statement of facts contained therein is to be treated as "proof by formal admission" in ensuing criminal proceedings.[111]

All of the four DPAs concluded to date have been secured by the Serious Fraud Office (SFO), in relation to conduct such as conspiracy to corrupt, false accounting and failure to prevent bribery and resulting in fines paid (or sums repaid) by target entities of approximately £670m. No breaches of the terms of the DPAs have yet been reported; nor have criminal prosecutions been initiated on the basis of information obtained via the mechanism. In November 2018, the first ever DPA ended successfully 3 years after it had taken effect.[112]

In the newer French DPA system, which focuses strongly on corruption offences, the *juge d'instruction* transfers proceedings which may give rise to a *convention judiciaire d'intérêt public* (CJIP) to the public prosecutor.[113] The latter enters into negotiations with (counsel of) the target entity; if agreement is reached, the prosecutor seizes the *Président du tribunal de grande instance* via a request detailing a precise summary of facts alleged and legal qualifications, before the judge examines – at a public hearing – procedural regularity, the lawfulness of the fines stipulated and the proportionality of compliance measures requested.[114] Judicial control of the CJIP is therefore based on less open criteria than in the UK DPA system, which revolves around fairness and reasonableness; within this legislative setting, it is particularly difficult to imagine the French judge questioning the judgment of the national anticorruption agency.

The first CJIP was concluded in June 2018 when the French National Financial Prosecutor (PRF) reached agreement with the *Société Générale* bank. The bank had been the subject of a preliminary investigation into suspected corruption of foreign public officials; the terms of the CJIP included the payment of €250m to the public treasury and a commitment to improve anti-corruption

---

109 S. 7(4); ss.8(5)–(7), Schedule 17, Crime and Courts Act 2013.

110 S. 9, Schedule 17, Crime and Courts Act 2013.

111 Schedule 17, s.13(2), Crime and Courts Act 2013.

112 The six terms imposed on the target entity, Standard Bank, were 1. Cooperation; 2. Compensation; 3. Disgorgement of profits; Financial Penalty and 5. Corporate Compliance Programme. See https://www.sfo.gov.uk/2018/11/30/uks-first-deferred-prosecution-agreement-between-the-sfo-and-standard-bank-successfully-ends/.

113 Article 180-2, French *Code de procédure pénale.*

114 Article 411-1-2-II, French *Code de procédure pénale.*

mechanisms within the bank.[115] The US Department of Justice, with whom the PRF had coordinated the investigation, received the same figure as part of a separate DPA across the Atlantic – in what seems likely be an *avant-goût* of more globalised criminal enforcement to come.

IV. CONCLUSIONS

Negotiated justice is not a solution to overprosecution as such, especially insofar as the latter derives from structural causes such as extensive criminalisation or an overly-strict application of the principle of mandatory prosecution. Systemic reforms, such as decriminalisation or the introduction of adequate criteria for the exercise of prosecutorial discretion remain thus the most appropriate means to ensure the respect of the principle of equality. Moreover, it is important not to reduce negotiated justice to a mere response to systemic overload in criminal justice systems, not least because empirically-grounded proof of its efficiency is scarce. Its rise has at times gone hand-in-hand with restorative justice movements and has reflected broader shits toward less hierarchical and more egalitarian societies where opposing sides talk on equal terms. In this sense, changed societal paradigms are bringing negotiations as a response to the overloaded inertia of criminal justice systems.

That being so, it is difficult to disagree with the contentions of those who posit that despite its epithet, growing resort to negotiated justice has never been centred qualitatively on *justice* but on efficiency[116] - at least from where the individual citizen caught up in the cogs of the freshly-oiled justice machine is sitting.[117] From their perspective, the serious concerns around negotiated justice that we have evoked here demand careful appraisal. In the worst-case scenario, excessive limitation of judicial control in negotiated procedures may invite abuse of the prosecutorial power, for instance by encouraging the launch of weakly-grounded prosecution in the sole aim of pushing the defendant to settle, heightening the risk of wrongful conviction or disproportionate punishment. Matters of wilful abuse aside, poor investigative practices at prosecutor or police

115 *Communiqué de presse, Cour d'appel de Paris,* 4 June 2018, available at https://www.economie.gouv.fr/files/files/directions_services/afa/Communique_CJIP_SG_LIA_-_4_juin_2018.pdf

116 Gless & Zurkinden (2017), 119.

117 Cf. Mylonopoulos (2018), who argues in the context of plea bargaining that "(t)he principles of the criminal trial must therefore be assessed on a macroscale basis, i.e. with regard to the total social profit of the bargaining; (...) Bargaining must be assessed not only in relation to the rights of the particular and concrete person who stands accused but also in relation to the rights of all other people who participate in the criminal justice system as accused or as civil parties"; 96–97.

level may also remain undetected where the light of the trial process is absent or dimmed.

Important issues not substantially addressed here include the unresolved controversy around limitations on the right to appeal which incorporated into negotiated justice tools. Nor have we seen fit to provide a holistic analysis of the professional ethics of European prosecutors in whom negotiated justice tools express strong levels of trust.[118] Technological changes, too, undoubtedly have an important role to play in the present[119] and near future; might developments in Regtech, for instance, even effectively eliminate a root cause of overprosecution – the complexity of criminal cases and quite simply "too much evidence"?

Whatever form it takes, negotiated justice need not work "behind closed doors". Where this is so, defendants cannot refer to other instances of negotiated justice, in most cases the media and general public cannot monitor them[120], there is no guarantee that justice has been done and, moreover, the sanctioning system is shorn of its communicative power.[121] For these reasons, improving the transparency of negotiated justice tools is to be treated as a priority in order to facilitate thorough, continual review of their effectiveness.

V. BIBLIOGRAPHY

K. Altenhain, F. Dietmeier & M. May, *Die Praxis der Absprachen in Strafverfahren* (Nomos, 2013).

L. Bachmaier, 'The Principle of Legality, Discretionary Justice and Plea Agreements: The Practice in Spain' in M. Caianiello & J.S. Hodgson (eds), *Discretionary Criminal Justice in a Comparative Context* (Carolina Academic Press, 2015), 89–113.

L. Bachmaier (2018), 'The European Court of Human Rights on Negotiated Justice and Coercion', *European Journal of Crime, Criminal Law and Criminal Justice* 26: 236–259.

A.S. Barkow & R.E. Barkow (eds), *Prosecutors in the Boardroom: Using Criminal Law to Regulate Corporate Conduct* (NYU Press, 2011).

R.E. Barkow, 'The Prosecutor as Regulatory Agency', in A.S. Barkow & R.E. Barkow (eds), *Prosecutors in the Boardroom: Using Criminal Law to Regulate Corporate Conduct* (NYU Press, 2011).

V. Bastidas Venegas & M. Bergström, 'Sweden' in K. Ligeti & S. Tosza, *White Collar Crime* (Hart, 2019).

118 See for example, comparing the discretion of prosecutors in England and Wales and France through an analysis of their institutional and professional settings, Hodgson (2017).

119 Cf. Brants (2018), who has recently expressed concerns about the computerisation of "quasi-judicial" decision-making, overseen by "unauthorized functionaries".

120 F. Tulkens (2002) in Delmas-Marty & Spencer (eds), 680.

121 Ligeti & Tosza (2019), 25.

M. Blom & P. Smit, 'The Prosecution Service Function within the Dutch Criminal Justice System' in J.-M. Jehle & M. Wade, *Coping with Overloaded Criminal Justice Systems: The Rise of Prosecutorial Power Across Europe* (Springer, 2005), 237–256.

R. Bloy, M. Böse, T. Hillenkamp, C. Momsen & P. Rackow (eds), *Gerechte Strafe und legitimes Strafrecht: Festrschrift für Manfred Maiwald zum 75. Geburstag* (Duncker & Humblot, 2010).

C. Bradley, 'The Prosecutor's Role: Plea Bargaining and Evidentiary Exclusion' in E. Luna & M. Wade (eds), *The Prosecutor in Transnational Perspective* (Oxford University Press, 2012).

C. Brants, 'Prosecutorial Sanctions in the Netherlands' in Sieber et al (eds), *Alternative Systems of Crime Control: National, Transnational, and International Dimensions* (Duncker & Humblot, Berlin, 2018). 59–75.

M. Caianiello & J.S. Hodgson (eds), *Discretionary Criminal Justice in a Comparative Context* (Carolina Academic Press, 2015).

F. Calvez & N. Regis (2018), European Commission for the Efficiency of Justice (CEPEJ), 'Length of court proceedings in the member states of the Council of Europe based on the case law of the European Court of Human Rights', CEPEJ(2018) 26.

V. Costa Ramos (2014), 'Is there plea bargaining in the Portuguese Legal System?', *ABA Section of International Law, 2014 Fall Meeting - Buenos Aires, Argentina*. Available at http://carlospintodeabreu.com/public/files/COSTA_RAMOS_Plea_Bargaining_and_the_Role_of_the_Lawyer_Portugal.pdf.

Council of Europe, Recommendation Rec(2000)19, *The Role of Public Prosecution in the Criminal Justice System*, 6 October 2000.

M. Delmas-Marty & J. R. Spencer (eds), *European Criminal Procedures* (Cambridge University Press, 2002)

M.D. Dubber (1997), 'American Plea Bargains, German Lay Judges, and the Crisis of Criminal Procedure', *Stanford Law Review* 49(3): 547–605.

Fair Trials International & Freshfields Bruckhaus Deringer LLP (2017), *The Disappearing Trial: Towards a rights-based approach to trial waiver systems*. Available at https://www.fairtrials.org/publication/disappearing-trial-report

S. Gless & N. Zurkinden, 'Negotiated Justice – Balancing Efficiency and Procedural Safeguards' in K. Ligeti & V. Franssen (eds), *Challenges in the Field of Economic and Financial Crime in Europe and the US* (Hart, 2017), Ch. 6.

E. Hanack, H. Hilger, V. Mehle & G. Widmaier (eds), *Festschrift für Peter Rieß zum 70. Geburstag am 4. Juni 2002* (De Gruyter, 2002).

J. Hodgson, 'Guilty Pleas and the Changing Role of the Prosecutor in French Criminal Justice' in E. Luna & M. Wade (eds), *The Prosecutor in Transnational Perspective* (Oxford University Press, 2012).

J. Hodgson (2015), 'Plea Bargaining: A Comparative Analysis', *International Encyclopedia of the Social & Behavioral Sciences* (2nd Edition), Vol. 18: 226–231.

J. Hodgson, 'The Democratic Accountability of Prosecutors in England and Wales and France: Independence, Discretion and Managerialism' in M. Langer & D.A. Sklansky (eds), *Prosecutors and Democracy: A Cross-National Study* (Cambridge University Press, 2017).

J.-M. Jehle (2004), 'Discretionary powers of public prosecution: opportunity or legality principle – Advantages and disadvantages', Report for *Conference of Prosecutors General of Europe*, 5th Session (organized by the Council of Europe in co-operation with the Prosecutor General of Lower Saxony), Celle, 23–25 May 2004.

J.-M. Jehle & M. Wade, *Coping with Overloaded Criminal Justice Systems: The Rise of Prosecutorial Power Across Europe* (Springer, 2005).

M. Langer & D. A. Sklansky (eds), *Prosecutors and Democracy: A Cross-National Study* (Cambridge University Press, 2017).

K. Ligeti (ed), *Toward a Prosecutor for the European Union. Vol. 2: Draft Rules of procedure* (Hart, forthcoming 2019).

K. Ligeti & V. Franssen (eds), *Challenges in the Field of Economic and Financial Crime in Europe and the US* (Hart, 2017).

K. Ligeti & S. Tosza (eds), *White Collar Crime. A Comparative Perspective* (Hart, 2019)

E. Luna & M. Wade (2010), 'Prosecutors as Judges', *Washington & Lee Law Review* 67: 1413–1532.

E. Luna & M. Wade (eds), *The Prosecutor in Transnational Perspective* (Oxford University Press, 2012).

F. Mazzacuva (2014), 'Justifications and Purposes of Negotiated Justice for Corporate Offenders: Deferred and Non-Prosecution Agreements in the UK and US Systems of Criminal Justice', *The Journal of Criminal Law* 78: 249–62.

J. Peters, B. Aubusson de Cavarlay, C. Lewis & P. Sobota (2008), 'Negotiated Case-ending Settlements: Ways of Speeding up the (Court) Process', *European Journal on Criminal Policy and Research* 14: 145–159.

J. Russell & N. Hollander (2017), 'The Disappearing Trial: The global spread of incentives to encourage suspects to waive their right to a trial and plead guilty', *New Journal of European Criminal Law* 8(3): 209–222.

F. Saliger, *Umweltstrafrecht* (Vahlen, 2012).

A. Sellier & A. Weyembergh (2018), 'Criminal procedural laws across the European Union – A comparative analysis of selected main differences and the impact they have over the development of EU legislation', Study requested by the LIBE Committee of the European Parliament, PE 604.977.

U. Sieber, V. Mitsilegas, C. Mylonopoulos, E. Billis & N. Knust (eds), *Alternative Systems of Crime Control: National, Transnational, and International Dimensions* (Duncker & Humblot, Berlin, 2018).

R. Schlothauer, *Vorbereitung der Hauptverhandlung mit notwendiger Verteidigung und Pflichtverteidigung* (Müller Verlag, 1998).

B. Schünemann, 'Die Absprachen im Strafverfaren – Von ihrer Gesetz und Verfassungswidrigkeit, von der ihren Versuchungen erliegenden Praxis und vom dogmatisch gescheiterten Versuch des 4. Senats des BGH, sie im geltenden

Strafprozeßrecht zu verankern', in E. Hanack et al. (Hrsg.), *Festschrift für Peter Rieß zum 70. Geburstag am 4. Juni 2002* (De Gruyter, 2002).

S. Sun Beale, 'Prosecutorial Discretion in Three Systems: Balancing Conflicting Goals and Providing Mechanisms for Control', in M. Caianiello & J. Hodgson (eds), *Discretionary Criminal Justice in a Comparative Context* (Carolina Academic Press, 2015).

S.C. Thaman (ed), *World Plea Bargaining: Consensual Procedures and the Avoidance of the Full Criminal Trial* (Carolina Academic Press, 2010).

S.C. Thaman, 'A Typology of Consensual Criminal Procedures: An Historical and Comparative Perspective on the Theory and Practice of Avoiding the Full Criminal Trial' in S.C. Thaman (ed), *World Plea Bargaining: Consensual Procedures and the Avoidance of the Full Criminal Trial* (Carolina Academic Press, 2010), 297–396.

S.C. Thaman, 'The Penal Order: Prosecutorial Sentencing as a Model for Criminal Justice Reform' in E. Luna & M. Wade (eds), *The Prosecutor in Transnational Perspective* (Oxford University Press, 2012).

F. Tulkens, 'Negotiated Justice' in M. Delmas-Marty & J.R. Spencer (eds), *European Criminal Procedures,* (Cambridge University Press, 2002).

D. Vicoli, 'Critical Aspects on the Italian Features Concerning "Negotiated Justice"' in M. Caianiello & J.S. Hodgson (eds), *Discretionary Criminal Justice in a Comparative Context* (Carolina Academic Press, 2015), 141–155.

A. Vivell, *Das Strafbefehlsverfahren nach Eröffnung des Hauptverfahrens (§ 408a StPO): Eine kritische Untersuchung und Analyse* (Peter Lang, 2006).

R. Vogler & B. Huber (eds), *Criminal Procedure in Europe* (Duncker & Humblot, Berlin, 2008).

T. Weigend, 'The Decay of the Inquisitorial Ideal: Plea Bargaining Invades German Criminal Procedure' in J. Jackson, M. Langer & P. Tillers (eds), *Crime, Procedure and Evidence in a Comparative and International Context: Essays in Honour of Professor Mirjan Damaška* (Hart Publishing, 2008).

T. Weigend, Verständigung in der Strafprozessordnung – auf dem Weg zu einem neuen Verfahrensmodell, in R. Bloy et al. (Hrsg.), *Gerechte Strafe und legitimes Strafrecht: Festschrift für Manfred Mainwald zum 75. Geburstag,* (Dunker & Humblot, 2010).

T. Weigend & J. Iontcheva Turner (2014), 'The Constitutionality of Negotiated Criminal Judgments in Germany', *German Law Journal* 15(1): 81–106.

THE AMERICAN EXPERIENCE WITH THE PROSECUTORIAL OVERUSE OF PLEA BARGAINING

Phillip RAPOZA*

I. INTRODUCTION

Trial by jury in criminal cases, which is guaranteed by the United States Constitution, has largely been replaced by plea bargaining, a practice that has become the primary means by which the overwhelming majority of criminal prosecutions are resolved in both Federal and state courts. The American experience with the prosecutorial overuse of plea bargaining is reflected not simply in the frequency with which criminal cases are concluded by means of a negotiated guilty plea. Rather, structural features of the legal framework, such as legislatively enhanced criminal penalties and mandatory minimum sentences of incarceration, promote and drive the use of plea bargaining. They do so by altering the balance of power in plea negotiations in the prosecutor's favor, to the detriment of the defendant. Moreover, they effectively shift control of the sentencing process from judges to prosecutors, who have the power to determine the charges that are brought against the defendant. As a result, for the most part, plea negotiations do not take place on a level playing field. Nevertheless, plea negotiations promise to be an enduring feature of the American criminal justice system. Consequently, the ongoing challenge will be to ensure that, to the extent possible, plea bargaining is rendered more fair and equitable and that increased transparency and accountability are brought to the process.

* Hon. Phillip Rapoza is the President of the International Penal and Penitentiary Foundation and the former Chief Justice of the Massachusetts Appeals Court. He is also the international reserve judge on the Supreme Court Chamber of the Extraordinary Chambers in the Courts of Cambodia and the former head international judge on the Special Panels for Serious Crimes in Timor-Leste.

II. THE CURRENT STATUS OF PLEA BARGAINING

The United States Supreme Court has stated that the American criminal justice system, as it now stands, "is for the most part a system of pleas, and not a system of trials."[1] In describing that reality, the Court noted that plea bargaining "is not some adjunct to the American criminal justice system; it *is* the criminal justice system."[2] Consequently, the Court observed, "the negotiation of a plea bargain, rather than the unfolding of a trial, is almost always the critical point for a defendant."[3]

The use of plea bargaining in the United States has evolved over time. When the American legal system first took shape, trials and not negotiated guilty pleas were the means by which criminal cases were most frequently brought to a conclusion.[4] Indeed, "[d]uring most of the history of the common law, pleas of guilty were actively discouraged by English and American courts. For centuries, litigation was thought 'the safest test of justice'."[5]

The United States Constitution guarantees the right to trial by jury in criminal cases in Article III, Section 2, which provides that "[t]he trial of all crimes, except in cases of impeachment, shall be by jury." The Bill of Rights further recognizes the right to a speedy and public trial by an impartial jury in all criminal prosecutions. In addition, the Bill of Rights guarantees that a defendant has the right, at trial, to the assistance of counsel who can confront and cross-examine his accusers and present evidence on his behalf.[6] Plea bargaining, on the other hand, is not mentioned in the Constitution, although the Supreme Court has consistently upheld the use of negotiated guilty pleas, describing the practice as "inherent in the criminal law and its administration."[7]

The role of plea bargaining has expanded over the years for largely practical reasons relating to the growth in the number of criminal cases before the courts.[8]

---

1 *Lafler* v. *Cooper*, 566 U.S. 156, 170 (2012).

2 *Missouri* v. *Frye*, 566 U.S. 134, 144 (2012) (emphasis in original) (citation omitted).

3 *Ibid.*

4 *See* Albert W. Alschuler, 'Plea Bargaining and its History', 13 *Law & Society Review* 2 (1979) pp. 211-245 at pp. 221-232 (hereinafter: Alschuler, 'Plea Bargaining and its History').

5 Albert W. Alschuler, 'The Prosecutor's Role in Plea Bargaining', 36 *University of Chicago Law Review* 1 (1968) pp. 50-112 at p. 50 (hereinafter: Alschuler, 'The Prosecutor's Role in Plea Bargaining').

6 "In all criminal prosecutions, the accused shall enjoy the right to a speedy and public trial, by an impartial jury . . . and to be informed of the nature and cause of the accusation; to be confronted with the witnesses against him; to have compulsory process for obtaining witnesses in his favor, and to have the assistance of counsel for his defense." Sixth Amendment.

7 *Brady* v. *United States*, 397 U.S. 742, 751-752 (1970).

8 For a discussion regarding the evolution of plea bargaining, *see* George Fisher, *Plea Bargaining's Triumph: A History of Plea Bargaining in America*, Stanford, CA: Stanford University Press, 2003 (hereinafter: Fisher, *Plea Bargaining's Triumph*].

Noting "the enormous increase in the workload of the often understaffed prosecutor's offices" the Supreme Court has explained that "[i]f every criminal charge were subjected to a full-scale trial, the States and the Federal Government would need to multiply by many times the number of judges and court facilities."[9] As a result, "[w]hatever might be the situation in an ideal world, the fact is that the guilty plea and the often concomitant plea bargain are important components of [the] criminal justice system [in the United States]."[10] Indeed, the Supreme Court has gone so far as to describe plea bargaining as "not only an essential part of the process but a highly desirable part" stating that, "[p]roperly administered, it is to be encouraged."[11]

The growth of plea bargaining thus has not been premised on it being a better mechanism than a jury trial to ensure that justice is done or that fairness is observed in the disposition of criminal charges. Rather, its increased use has been rooted in the desire to resolve a growing number of criminal cases in a more expeditious, economical and final manner than could be accomplished by way of jury trials or, for that matter, jury-waived trials.[12] Consequently, plea bargaining has replaced a "noble clash for truth" with a resolution achieved in the form of what one observer has called a "skulking truce."[13] The paradigmatic shift from trials to pleas produced the desired result of moving more cases more quickly, but in the process the profile of the American criminal justice system radically changed. As a result, at the present time approximately 94% of all state convictions and 97% of all Federal convictions are the result of guilty pleas, the overwhelming majority of which involve plea bargains.[14]

---

9 *Santobello* v. *New York*, 404 U.S. 257, 260(1971).

10 *Bordenkircher* v. *Hayes*, 434 U.S.357, 361-362(1978) citing *Blackledge* v. *Allison*, 431 U.S. 63, 71 (1977).

11 *Santobello* v. *New York*, *supra* note 9 at 260-261.

12 Cynthia Alkon, 'The U.S. Supreme Court's Failure to Fix Plea Bargaining: The impact of Lafler and Frye', 41 *Hastings Constitutional Law Quarterly* (2014) pp. 561-621 at pp. 589-590 (hereinafter: Alkon, 'The U.S. Supreme Court's Failure to Fix Plea Bargaining'); The defendant's admission of guilt plays a different role in non-common law systems of justice. "In Continental legal systems someone who is accused of a serious crime may confess, but he will nevertheless go to trial. Confession shortens the trial by affecting the quality of the evidence, but confession does not eliminate the trial. For most purposes it hardly mattered that the common law treated confession as a waiver of trial, by contrast with the Continental practice of viewing it as merely evidence of the most cogent kind." John H. Langbein, 'Understanding the Short History of Plea Bargaining', 13 *Law & Society Review* 2 (1978) pp. 261-272 at pp. 267-268 (citations omitted) (hereinafter: Langbein, 'Understanding the Short History of Plea Bargaining').

13 Fisher, *Plea Bargaining's Triumph*, *supra* note 8 at Prologue, p.1.

14 Bureau of Justice Statistics, U.S. Department of Justice, Sourcebook of Criminal Justice Statistics Online (at: http://www.albany.edu/sourcebook/pdf/t5222009.pdf) (last visited: 16 April 2018); *See also* United States Sentencing Commission, 2016 Sourcebook of Federal Sentencing Statistics - Sentencing Information: Guilty Pleas and Trial Rates: Figure C (at: https://www.ussc.gov/research/sourcebook-2016) (last visited: 16 April 2018).

III. HISTORICAL ASPECTS OF PLEA BARGAINING

The use of plea bargaining developed in the mid-nineteenth century and, by the beginning of the twentieth century, it was "the dominant method of resolving criminal cases."[15] As the country's population grew, the use of guilty pleas and plea bargains served as a response to increasing caseloads and the limited resources available to deal with them. By the 1920s "plea bargaining had become a central feature of the administration of justice."[16]

The evolution of the jury trial from what historically had been a fairly summary proceeding to one of greater complexity also played a role in the increased use of plea bargaining.[17] The rise of a more vigorous adversarial system and the development of the law of evidence caused the common law jury trial "to undergo a profound transformation."[18] Once trial by jury became a more demanding endeavor, however, "it could no longer be used as the exclusive dispositive proceeding for cases of serious crime."[19] Indeed, the transformation of the jury trial "left the trial system clogged" and the alternative of a plea bargain provided an even more expeditious option for the disposition of a criminal case than even a jury-waived bench trial.[20]

After immigration had passed its peak in the early 20th Century, population growth continued to burden the American criminal justice system. The so-called baby boom generation following World War II created new challenges and produced a society with a significantly higher proportion of young people.[21] Moreover, the 1960s and 1970s saw a steep increase in the amount of crime.[22] At the same time, the Supreme Court began the process of expanding the rights of criminal defendants in a series of decisions often referred to as the "due process revolution" or more colloquially, the "Warren Revolution," named after the Court's chief justice, Earl Warren. This period of legal development produced a tremendous amount of additional criminal litigation.[23]

Eventually, criminal law reforms moved in the direction of getting, as the term went, "tough on crime." America also declared a so-called "war on drugs"

15 Alschuler, 'Plea Bargaining and its History', *supra* note 4 at p.211.

16 *Ibid.* at p. 232; *See also* Douglas D. Guidorizzi, 'Should We Really "Ban" Plea Bargaining?: The Core Concerns of Plea Bargaining Critics', 47 *Emory Law Journal* (1998) pp. 753-783 at pp. 758-759 (hereinafter: Guidorizzi, 'Should We Really "Ban" Plea Bargaining?').

17 Langbein, 'Understanding the Short History of Plea Bargaining', *supra* note 12 at p. 265 n. 7.

18 Langbein, 'Understanding the Short History of Plea Bargaining', *supra* note 12 at p. 262.

19 *Ibid.* at p. 265.

20 *Ibid.* at p. 267.

21 Alschuler, 'Plea Bargaining and its History', *supra* note 4 at p. 236.

22 *Ibid.*

23 Alschuler, 'Plea Bargaining and its History', *supra* note 4 at pp. 238-239.

that significantly increased the number of criminal cases in the courts.[24] In addition, the process of "overcriminalization" greatly expanded the reach of the law, resulting in a proliferation of new offenses that criminalized activity that previously had not been the subject of prosecution.[25] At the same time, sentences were enhanced for a large number of offenses relating to drugs and alcohol, as well as for crimes involving firearms, domestic violence and sexually dangerous offenders, to name but a few.[26] Similarly, defendants charged as repeat offenders were subjected to substantially increased sentences for the commission of subsequent offenses.[27]

In addition to enhancing the maximum penalties for a variety of crimes, legislatures at both the Federal and state level enacted statutes providing for new and increased mandatory minimum prison sentences for a wide range of offenses, especially drug law violations.[28] In cases involving crimes for which there is a mandatory minimum sentence of incarceration, the judge has no discretion to impose a sentence that is less than the minimum committed sentence provided by law for the offense charged. Considering that it is the prosecutor who decides what charges will be brought before the grand jury for indictment, the ability to bring charges calling for mandatory minimum terms of imprisonment thus increased the clout of prosecutors seeking to extract guilty pleas from defendants.[29] In return for the defendant pleading guilty to a lesser offense than the one mandating a minimum incarcerated sentence, the

---

24 *See* Mona Lynch, *Hard Bargains: The Coercive Power of Drug Laws in Federal Court*, New York: Russell Sage Foundation, 2016, at pp. 109-130 ("Inducing the Plea: Strategic Uses of Legal Power"); *See also* Elizabeth Hinton, *From the War on Poverty to the War on Crime: The Making of Mass Incarceration in America*, Cambridge, Massachusetts: Harvard University Press, 2016.

25 "Since the late 19th Century, the number of federal offenses has risen steadily, accelerating during the New Deal and virtually exploding since the 1970s." Ted Cruz, *Reduce Federal Crimes and Give Judges Flexibility*, Brennan Center for Justice (April 27, 2015) (hereinafter; Cruz, *Reduce Federal Crimes and Give Judges Flexibility*) (at: https://www.brennancenter.org/analysis/reduce-federal-crimes-and-give-judges-flexibility) (last visited: 16 April 2018); See also, Erik Luna, 'The Overcriminalization Phenomenon', 54 *American University Law Review* 3, pp. 703-743 (2005); Harvey Silverglate, *Three Felonies a Day*, New York: Encounter Books, 2011 (discussing the growth in federal criminal legislation that has exposed the "unwary innocent" to prosecution).

26 Richard A. Oppel, Jr., 'Sentencing Shift Gives New Leverage to Prosecutors', *The New York Times* (25 September 2011) (at: www.nytimes.com/2011/09/26/us/tough-sentences-help-prosecutors-push-for-plea-bargains.html) (last visited: 16 April 2018).

27 *Ibid.*

28 *See*, Michael Tonry, *Sentencing Matters*, Oxford: Oxford University Press (1996) "Mandatory Penalties" at pp. 134-164 (hereinafter: Tonry, *Sentencing Matters*); Cruz, *Reduce Federal Crimes and Give Judges Flexibility, supra* note 25 (noting the problem of "the ratcheting up of mandatory minimum sentences over the last several decades . . . The current draconian mandatory minimum sentences sometimes result in sentencing outcomes that neither fit the crime nor the perpetrator's unique circumstances. This is especially true for nonviolent drug offenders.")

29 Tonry, *Sentencing Matters, supra* note 28 at p. 135 ("The record is clear from research in the 1950s, the 1970s, the 1980s, and the 1990s that mandatory penalty laws shift power from judges to prosecutors . . .")

prosecutor could now recommend a more lenient sentence than what would be imposed were the case to proceed on the basis of the more serious charge.[30]

The development of plea bargaining over time, however, was not free from controversy.[31] Although the practice continued to grow as the 19th Century drew to a close, it was still subject to judicial criticism based on the inviolability of the right to trial by jury.[32] Similar opposition from the legal profession eventually waned, however, "[a]s America's dependency on pleas of guilty increased, [and] attitudes changed."[33]

Even with the wider acceptance of negotiated guilty pleas, the practice was not without its critics. Concerns about its application continued to be expressed, with "[m]ost of the criticisms [coming] from the hawks of the criminal process rather than the doves."[34] More recent reservations about plea bargaining fall along similar lines, with the practice being criticized by "hawks" for rewarding those who are guilty with lower sentences and by "doves" for punishing those who are innocent with imprisonment. Although those divergent views reflect different perspectives, both indicate a concern that the plea bargaining process as currently practiced results in defendants receiving sentences other than what they deserve.[35]

IV. CONTOURS OF THE PLEA BARGAIN

The common representation of American criminal justice, being twelve jurors sitting together to determine the fate of a defendant, is seriously outdated.[36] The more appropriate image is one of a defendant and his attorney standing before a judge, with the prosecutor informing the court of a plea agreement that has been

30 *Ibid.* at p. 150 (noting that in one study "there were clear indications that prosecutors used mandatory provisions tactically to induce guilty pleas. . . [A]mong defendants who were fully charged with applicable mandatory sentence charges and who were convicted at trial 96 percent received the full mandatory minimum sentence; by contrast, 27% of those who pled guilty pled to charges bearing no mandatory minimum or a lower one.")

31 See generally, Alschuler, 'Plea Bargaining and its History,' *supra* note 4 at pp. 224-226.

32 *Ibid.* at p. 227.

33 Alschuler, 'The Prosecutor's Role in Plea Bargaining,' *supra* note 5 at p. 51.

34 Alschuler, 'Plea Bargaining and its History,' *supra* note 4 at p. 232.

35 Guidorizzi, 'Should We Really "Ban" Plea Bargaining?', *supra* note 16 at pp. 753-754.

36 "The criminal justice system in the United States today bears little relationship to what the Founding Fathers contemplated, what the movies and television portray or what the average American believes." Jed S. Rakoff, 'Why Innocent People Plead Guilty', *The New York Review of Books* (20 November 2014) (hereinafter: 'Why Innocent People Plead Guilty') (at: www.nybooks.com/articles/2014/11/20/why-innocent-people-plead-guilty/) (last visited: 16 April 2018).

reached by the parties.[37] Understood by all, but not publicly stated, is the fact that the process leading to the defendant's guilty plea is largely controlled by the prosecutor through negotiations that are conducted in private, outside the presence of the judge and without judicial oversight. As one Federal judge has put it, "the power to determine the terms of the plea bargain is, as a practical matter, lodged largely in the prosecutor, with the defense counsel having little say and the judge even less."[38]

Although in large part absent from the process leading to a defendant's guilty plea, the judge has a nonetheless important role to play, considering that "a guilty plea is a grave and solemn act, to be accepted [by the court] only with care and discernment."[39] In pleading guilty, a defendant waives his right to a trial and serves as a witness against himself, thus also waiving his right against self-incrimination. The judge must thus inquire of the defendant to ensure that the waiver of his right to trial (with or without a jury) and the waiver of his other constitutional rights are not only voluntary, but also "knowing, intelligent acts done with sufficient awareness of the relevant circumstances and likely consequences."[40] The judge must also confirm that there is a factual basis for the defendant's admission of guilt.[41] That determination, however, is not based on an independent judicial inquiry into the facts, but on a summary agreed to by the parties and generally recited to the judge by the prosecutor. Such proceedings are not geared to look behind or, even less, to renegotiate the agreement proposed by the parties.

In the United States the plea bargaining process thus takes place between the prosecutor and the defendant and for the most part does not include the judge, who cannot engage in plea bargaining.[42] Although there is some variation among state courts, the general practice is reflected in Rule 11 of the Federal Rules of

37 "Bargaining with unrepresented defendants is largely a thing of the past." Albert W. Alschuler, 'The Defense Attorney's Role in Plea Bargaining', 84 *The Yale Law Journal* (1975) pp. 1179-1314 at p. 1270. (hereinafter: Alschuler, 'The Defense Attorney's Role in Plea Bargaining').

38 Rakoff, 'Why Innocent People Plead Guilty', *supra* note 36.

39 *Brady* v. *United States*, *supra* note 7 at 748.

40 *Ibid.* See, e.g. Federal Rule of Criminal Procedure 11(b)(2): "Before accepting a plea of guilty... the court must address the defendant personally in open court and determine that the plea is voluntary and did not result from force, threats or promises (other than the promises in a plea agreement)."

41 *See, e.g.* Federal Rule of Criminal Procedure 11(b)(3): "Before entering judgment on a guilty plea, the court must determine that there is a factual basis for the plea."

42 *See* Albert W. Alschuler, 'The Trial Judge's Role in Plea Bargaining, Part I', 76 *Columbia Law Review* 7 (1976) pp. 1059-1154(hereinafter: Alschuler, 'The Trial Judge's Role in Plea Bargaining') (noting at p. 1059 that "[t]he general consensus seems to be that trial judges should not participate in the pretrial negotiations that currently lead the overwhelming majority of American criminal defendants to plead guilty rather than exercise the right to trial."); *See also*, Jenia Iontcheva Turner, 'Judicial Participation in Plea Negotiations: A Comparative View', 54 *The American Journal of Comparative Law* 1 (2006) pp. 199-267 (hereinafter: Turner, 'Judicial Participation in Plea Negotiations') (noting at p. 199 that "In plea bargaining. . . the role of the

Criminal Procedure, which reserves the negotiation of a plea agreement to the parties and states that "[t]he court must not participate in these discussions."[43] The judge, however, is not bound by the terms of the plea bargain and may accept or reject the agreement.[44] In circumstances where the court rejects a plea agreement, however, the judge must inform the parties of that fact and advise the defendant that he may withdraw his guilty plea, understanding that if he does not, "the court may dispose of the case less favorably . . . than the plea agreement contemplated."[45]

V. PLEA BARGAINING AND THE "MUTUALITY OF ADVANTAGE"

Against this procedural backdrop, the United States Supreme Court has suggested that a plea bargain is similar to an enforceable contract in which the parties exchange concessions from which they reap corresponding benefits.[46] In *Brady* v. *United States* the court ruled that plea bargains are constitutional, observing that a negotiated plea amounts to an agreement from which both sides profit, reflecting what the Court described as a "mutuality of advantage."[47] Indeed, the Supreme Court has subsequently stated, "[t]he potential to conserve valuable prosecutorial resources and for defendants to admit their crimes and receive more favorable terms at sentencing mean that a plea agreement can benefit both parties."[48] As the court concluded in *Brady*, "we cannot hold that it is unconstitutional for the State to extend a benefit to a defendant who in turn extends a substantial benefit to the State."[49]

In a plea bargain, the fate of both the prosecution and the defense thus rests largely with the parties, who can choose either to exercise their procedural rights or to negotiate them away in return for a perceived benefit. What makes the

judge is essentially passive. . . The judge's role is limited to reviewing the bargain once it is presented. Many jurisdictions, including the federal, expressly prohibit judges from participating in or commenting on the plea negotiations.").

43 Federal Rule of Criminal Procedure 11(c)(1).

44 Federal Rule of Criminal Procedure 11(c)(3)(A).

45 Federal Rule of Criminal Procedure 11(c)(5).

46 A negotiated plea agreement cannot be breached and "[w]hen a plea rests in any significant degree on a promise or agreement of the prosecutor, so that it can be said to be part of the inducement or consideration, such promise must be fulfilled." *Santobello* v. *New York*, *supra* note 9 at 262.

47 *Brady* v. *United States*, *supra* note 7 at 752.

48 *Missouri* v. *Frye*, *supra* note 2 at 144.

49 *Brady v. United States*, *supra* note 1 at 753.

interaction a bargain lies in what each side is prepared to give up in return for what it considers to be a satisfactory result.[50]

As to benefits realized, it is fair to say that the use of plea bargaining has become an essential tool for prosecutors hoping to process more cases with less preparation and at less cost than required for a full investigation and trial, while at the same time guaranteeing convictions and avoiding acquittals.[51] Similarly, plea bargaining can serve the interests of defendants. Although negotiated pleas ensure a high rate of conviction, they also mitigate harsh statutory penalties and provide defendants with a degree of leniency that might not otherwise be available.[52] In considering whether a plea agreement in fact reflects a "mutuality of advantage", however, it is necessary to consider not only the results the parties hope to achieve, but also what each side agrees to sacrifice in order to obtain the benefits of the bargain.

By entering into a negotiated plea, the prosecutor makes concessions that would not be required were he to go to trial. These generally relate to how the prosecutor will exercise his considerable discretion in both bringing charges and subsequently prosecuting them.[53] In the course of plea negotiations, the prosecutor may agree to dismiss or reduce charges (called charge bargaining) or to recommend a reduced sentence (called sentence bargaining), or both, in return

---

50 "Courts enforce plea agreements as they do other contracts. They treat such compromises as voluntary; consider each party as the best judge of its own interests; and reckon bargained-for sentences as adequate substitutes for the outcomes of adversarial adjudication." Jacqueline E. Ross, 'The Entrenched Position of Plea Bargaining in United States Legal Practice', 54 *The American Journal of Comparative Law* (2006) pp. 717-732 at p. 732.

51 "The benefit received by the prosecution is the avoidance of uncertainty, delay and expense of trial." Eleanor J. Ostrow, 'The Case for Preplea Disclosure', 90 *The Yale Law Journal*, No. 7 (1981) pp. 1581-1622 at p. 1593 (hereinafter: Ostrow, 'The Case for Preplea Disclosure'); Oren Gazal, 'Partial Ban on Plea Bargains', University of Michigan Law School Law & Economics Working Papers Archive, Art. 59 (2005) pp. 1-73 (hereinafter: Gazal,, 'Partial Ban on Plea Bargains') (observing at p. 53 that "when prosecutors try to plea bargain before compiling enough evidence [they] bargain in order to save resources needed for investigation and preparation of the case.") (at: http://repository.law.umich.edu/law_econ_archive/art59) (last visited: 16 April 2018); *See also*, Guidorizzi, 'Should We Really Ban Plea Bargaining?', *supra* note 16 at p. 765.

52 "The benefits most often obtained by the defendant are a favorable sentence recommendation, dismissal of charges and the opportunity to plead to a lesser included offense." Ostrow, 'The Case for Preplea Disclosure', *supra* note 51 at p. 1593.

53 It is not uncommon for the prosecutor to inform the defendant that "unless the case can be promptly resolved by a plea bargain, he intends to charge the defendant with the most severe offenses he can prove. . . .If, however, the defendant wants to plead guilty, the prosecutor will offer him a considerably reduced charge – but only if the plea is agreed to promptly (thus saving the prosecutor valuable resources). Otherwise, he will charge the maximum, and while he will not close the door to any later plea bargain, it will be to a higher level offense than the one offered at the outset of the case." Rakoff, 'Why Innocent People Plead Guilty', *supra* note 36.

for a defendant's guilty plea.[54] Regardless of the form of bargaining used, the sentence ultimately recommended by the prosecutor amounts to a discounted version of a higher sentence that could be proposed but for the negotiated plea. In sum, in return for the defendant's willingness to plead guilty the prosecutor agrees to exercise his discretion in such a way as to extend a measure of leniency to the defendant.

The defendant, on the other hand, gives up a significant array of rights by agreeing to plead guilty pursuant to a negotiated agreement. As the Supreme Court noted in *Brady* v. *United States*, "the plea is more than an admission of past conduct; it is the defendant's consent that judgment of conviction may be entered without a trial – a waiver of his right to trial before a judge or a jury."[55] The defendant's negotiated plea also involves the waiver of a number of other rights implicated in a trial.[56] By pleading guilty, the defendant waives the presumption of innocence and the corresponding right to demand that the prosecutor prove his guilt at trial beyond a reasonable doubt. Similarly, he gives up the right to have the evidence evaluated by a jury of his peers, whose verdict would require unanimity. By his plea, the defendant sacrifices other rights as well, including the right to confront the witnesses against him, the right to present evidence and witnesses on his own behalf, and the right to remain silent throughout the proceedings. Moreover, in cases where claims could be raised to suppress evidence from an illegal search or seizure or to dismiss charges based on the conduct of the police or the prosecution, the defendant who pleads guilty waives

54 *Charge bargaining* occurs when the prosecutor agrees to a defendant pleading guilty to a lesser charge or to only some of the charges that have been filed against him. For example, a defendant charged with distributing drugs in a school zone may plead guilty to the less serious charge of simple drug distribution, with the prosecutor dismissing the school zone aspect of the case and proposing a lesser sentence in line with the reduced charges. "Often armed with an extensive menu of crimes, each with their own sentencing ranges, federal prosecutors can wield their discretionary charging power to great effect by threatening the most serious charges that theoretically (if not realistically) can be proved. If the accused succumbs to the threat and pleads guilty . . . the prosecutor agrees to bring lesser or entirely different charges that carry a lower sentencing range." Cruz, *Reduce Federal Crimes and Give Judges Flexibility*, *supra* note 25.
Sentence bargaining involves the defendant pleading guilty to the original charges brought against him, with the prosecutor, in turn, proposing a sentence more lenient than what might be expected following conviction at trial. *See* Guidorizzi, 'Should We Really Ban Plea Bargaining?' *supra* note 16 at p. 756; *See also*, Fisher, *Plea Bargaining's Triumph*, *supra* note 8 at p. 12, pp. 21-22 and pp. 33-34.

55 *Brady* v. *United States*, *supra* note 7 at 748.

56 *Boykin* v. *Alabama*, 395 U.S. 238, 243 (1969) (ruling that when a defendant pleads guilty, he foregoes not only a fair trial, but also other accompanying constitutional guarantees such as the Fifth Amendment privilege against self-incrimination, the Sixth Amendment right to confront one's accusers, and the Sixth Amendment Right to trial by jury); See Ostrow, 'The Case for Preplea Disclosure', *supra* note 51 at p. 1582 n. 6 ("Pleading guilty also deprives defendants of a large number of other rights" including the right to challenge an unlawful search or coerced confession and the right to attack an insufficient indictment or the composition of grand jury.) (citations omitted).

his right to have those issues decided by the court. In addition, a negotiated plea is final in nature, with the defendant also foregoing his right to appeal.

The fact that the prosecutor and the defendant may have agreed to a plea bargain, however, does not mean that the value of the bargain is the same to both sides. Indeed, it is worth asking whether it is possible to assert that a genuine "mutuality of advantage" exists without also considering whether the parties face a similar "mutuality of risk," which it is also the purpose of plea negotiations to avoid.

It should be noted that any risks facing the prosecutor with respect to a particular criminal case are of an entirely different character than those faced by the defendant. While the availability of witnesses, considerations with respect to victims, problematic evidentiary issues or even legal difficulties may pose challenges to the successful prosecution of a case, they do not confront the prosecutor with the same, very significant risks that face the defendant whose personal liberty, if not his life, is at stake. Indeed, from the prosecutor's perspective, in the majority of situations plea bargaining is simply a less time-consuming way to process more cases at less cost. Speed and efficiency in securing guilty verdicts are thus advantages of plea bargaining, especially in light of the resource constraints facing the prosecution. Put another way, as far as the prosecutor is concerned, plea bargaining is good business. Unlike for the defendant, who plea bargains hoping to avoid incarceration or to minimize his term of imprisonment, for the prosecutor plea bargaining is nothing personal.

Although the Supreme Court has discerned a "mutuality of advantage" in the plea bargaining process, the facts of the situation suggest otherwise. It is difficult to see how mutual the advantage really is when the risks facing the parties are of a very different kind and the negotiating process is not conducted on a level playing field. Put another way, in the typical case in which the defendant goes to jail and the prosecutor returns to his office, it is "the prosecutor [who] has all the advantages."[57]

VI. PLEA BARGAINING: IS THE PLAYING FIELD LEVEL?

The Supreme Court has candidly observed that "by tolerating and encouraging the negotiation of pleas, this Court has necessarily accepted as constitutionally legitimate the simple reality that the prosecutor's interest at the bargaining table is to persuade the defendant to forego his right to plead not guilty."[58] The Court has also explained that although a plea agreement requires a defendant to waive that

57 Rakoff, 'Why Innocent People Plead Guilty', *supra* note 36.
58 *Bordenkircher* v. *Hayes*, *supra* note 10 at 364.

important constitutional right, "acceptance of the basic legitimacy of plea bargaining necessarily implies rejection of any notion that a guilty plea is involuntary in a constitutional sense simply because it is the end result of the bargaining process."[59]

The Court thus has asserted that a defendant's waiver of his right to plead not guilty does not, by itself, impugn the "basic legitimacy" of the plea negotiations that gave rise to his guilty plea. It is noteworthy, however, that a premise for that conclusion was the Court's expectation that the defendant's waiver would result from "the give-and-take negotiation common in plea bargaining between the prosecution and defense, *which arguably possess relatively equal bargaining power*."[60] The question thus worth asking is whether, in the plea bargaining process as currently practiced, the prosecutor and the defendant "possess relatively equal bargaining power" in any meaningful way. The evidence strongly suggests that they do not.

Comparing plea bargaining to contractual negotiations suggests a non-existent degree of parity between the prosecutor and the defendant in the negotiation of a plea agreement. As one commentator, who is also a sitting Federal judge, has put it: "The Supreme Court's suggestion that a plea bargain is a fair and voluntary contractual arrangement between two relatively equal parties is a total myth. It is much more like a 'contract of adhesion' in which one party can effectively force its will on the other party."[61] A former Federal judge has similarly stated that with respect to such negotiations: "[t]here is nothing remotely like fair bargaining between equal parties with equal resources or equal information."[62] She further observed that "to call the process 'plea bargaining' is a cruel misnomer."[63]

The process of plea bargaining is heavily weighted in the prosecutor's favor and a defendant has little bargaining power with which to affect the outcome.[64]

59 *Ibid.* at 363.

60 *Ibid.* at 362 (emphasis added) (quoting *Parker* v. *North Carolina*, 397 U.S. 790, 809 (1970). It is worth noting that the opinion in *Parker* "predates the changes in legislation giving prosecutors more power in charging and plea bargaining, and predates the dramatic increase in incarceration rates nationwide." Alkon, 'The U.S. Supreme Court's Failure to Fix Plea Bargaining', *supra* note 12 at p. 594 n.213.

61 Rakoff, 'Why Innocent People Plead Guilty', *supra* note 36; "The plea bargaining system is premised on the assumption that there is relatively equal bargaining power between the accused and the state. Nothing, of course, could be further from the truth." Cruz, *Reduce Federal Crimes and Give Judges Flexibility*, *supra* note 25.

62 Nancy C. Gertner, 'Why the Innocent Plead Guilty: An Exchange', *The New York Review of Books* (8 January 2015) (at: www.nybooks.com/articles/2015/01/08/why-innocent-plead-guilty-exchange/) (last visited: 16 April 2018).

63 *Ibid.*

64 *See* Cynthia Alkon, 'An Overlooked Key to Reversing Mass Incarceration: Reforming the Law to Reduce Prosecutorial Power in Plea Bargaining', 15 University of Maryland Law Journal of Race, Religion, Gender and Class 2 (2015) pp. 191-208 at pp. 194-198 (hereinafter: Alkon,'An Overlooked Key to Reversing Mass Incarceration').

The terms of engagement are largely decided by the prosecutor who has the authority, through the grand jury, to determine exactly what charges the defendant will face, thus controlling the applicability of statutory provisions involving both higher and mandatory minimum sentences. The prosecutor similarly has the power to dismiss or not to prosecute charges after they have been brought, essentially allowing him to reduce the penal consequences that a defendant will face at the time of sentencing.

The potentially coercive effect of such practices is onerous in and of itself, but it is even more so with respect to certain defendants, such as those unable to make bail and who are held in custody awaiting trial or disposition of their case.[65] In plea bargaining those cases, in return for a guilty plea, the prosecutor can recommend a sentence of "time served" while awaiting trial, or a committed sentence involving a minimal amount of additional time in custody. It goes without saying that defendants who are being held awaiting the disposition of their case are thus highly motivated to plead guilty, especially if waiting for an eventual trial will result in even more time in custody.[66]

Indeed, the pressure to plead guilty exists even for defendants in custody who are not in fact guilty, considering that their change of plea can serve as the key to the door of their jail cell. Such tactics may not be "coercive" in the sense that they do not involve torture or physical mistreatment to force a guilty plea from a defendant. At the same time, however, it can hardly be said that a prosecutor and a defendant already in custody "possess relatively equal bargaining power."

Plea bargaining is thus very different from the kind of arm's length transaction that typifies the negotiation of a contract. The power to ratchet up or down the sentencing risk to which the defendant is exposed, knowing the coercive effects of such manipulations, means that the prosecutor can essentially determine the extent of the penal dilemma from which the defendant seeks to extricate himself by plea bargaining. It is true that a defendant can decline a plea bargain and take his case to trial, thus putting the prosecutor to the burden of proving his case. But doing so exposes the defendant to the likelihood of a significantly higher sentence if found guilty, a prospect that risk-averse

65 At midyear 2016, the number of inmates held in county and local jails in the United States was 740,700, of which 65 % were awaiting court action on a current charge and 35 % were already serving a sentence or were convicted offenders awaiting sentencing. Bureau of Justice Statistics, *Jail Inmates in 2016* (February 2018) (at: https://www.bjs.gov/content/pub/pdf/ji16_sum.pdf) (last visited: 16 April 2018).

66 Ostrow, 'The Case for Preplea Disclosure', *supra* note 51 at p. 1593 (citing the pressure "felt by the indigent defendant who cannot make bail when arrested on charges unlikely to bring a punishment more serious than probation or a minimal prison sentence. Under these circumstances, the defendant may spend more time in jail before trial than he would if he pleaded, and that prospect may exert great pressure on the defendant to plead guilty.").

defendants are understandably anxious to avoid.[67] In such a case, a plea bargain resulting in a lower sentence, or one of time already served in the case of a defendant held in pre-trial custody, can benefit a defendant by ensuring the certainty of a less severe punishment in a way that going to trial does not. Indeed, the phenomenon whereby defendants who are convicted following a trial routinely receive harsher sentences than those who plead guilty has been labelled the "trial penalty."[68]

Although a defendant might thus realize some advantage from his guilty plea, that should not overshadow the fact that the bargaining process has become increasingly weighted in the prosecutor's favor. Indeed the degree to which a guilty plea benefits a defendant is in direct proportion to the risks with which he is presented by a legal framework that strengthens the hand of the prosecutor. Put another way, the more severe the risk faced by the defendant, the greater his incentive to plead guilty upon terms proposed by the prosecutor. Plea negotiating on the part of a defendant is basically an exercise in risk avoidance and the higher the risk of incarceration, the greater the incentive on the part of the defendant to avoid that prospect.

The success of plea bargaining, at least from the prosecutor's perspective, is thus necessarily dependent on criminal penalties being both severe enough and certain enough that the majority of defendants will plead guilty rather than run the risk of a higher sentence after a conviction following trial.[69] Harsh sentencing schemes thus benefit the prosecution by enhancing the possibility of an even more severe sentence being imposed after trial and, as a result, increasing the likelihood of a defendant pleading guilty to avoid that possibility. Higher sentences provide the prosecutor with greater leverage in negotiations with the defendant and put him in a much stronger position to dictate the terms of the plea bargain. The current legal framework of increased punishments for an

---

67 "Threatening trial is often the only real power that a defendant has to put leverage on the prosecutor to make a better deal or dismiss the case. However, under current laws, many defendants cannot risk trial due to mandatory minimums, enhancements, or threats to file the charge as a felony." Alkon, 'An Overlooked Key to Reversing Mass Incarceration', *supra* note 64 at p. 208; *See also* Alkon, 'The U.S. Supreme Court's Failure to Fix Plea Bargaining', *supra* note 12 at pp. 605-608; "The plea bargaining system plainly rests on the fact that defendants convicted at trial usually receive more severe sentences than defendants convicted by guilty plea." Alschuler, 'The Defense Attorney's Role in Plea Bargaining', *supra* note 37 at p. 1205.

68 According to Judge Gertner, "the court [should] frankly characterize enhanced trial sentences for what they are, an improper penalty for going to trial, a substantial burden on the rights the Constitution provides." Gertner, *supra* note 62; "[N]ow everyone acts with the assumption that the case should end with a plea. When you have that attitude, you penalize people who have the nerve to go to trial." Professor Rachel Barkow, quoted in Oppel, *supra* note 26; "Plea bargaining rests on the constitutional fiction that our government does not retaliate against individuals who wish to exercise their right to trial by jury." Timothy Lynch, 'The Case Against Plea Bargaining', *Regulation* (Fall, 2003) pp. 24-27 at p. 26; *See also* Candace McCoy, 'Plea Bargaining as Coercion: The Trial Penalty and Plea Bargaining Reform', 50 *Criminal Law Quarterly* 67 (2005).

69 Oppel, *supra* note 26.

expanding array of crimes thus inexorably shifts the balance of power in plea negotiations toward the prosecutor.[70]

The growing number of criminal statutes has also given prosecutors the opportunity to "overcharge" defendants in terms of both the number and the severity of offenses, providing them yet more leverage in the plea bargaining process.[71] Prosecutors are in a position to file the maximum number of available criminal charges to enhance the defendant's risk of conviction should he go to trial. Where such further charges implicate both more severe sentences as well as mandatory minimum prison terms, the possibility of conviction after trial also includes the greatly enhanced risk, and in some cases the certainty, of a longer period of incarceration.

The prosecutor's "ability to shape whatever charges are brought can effectively dictate the [defendant's] sentence.... Put another way, it is the prosecutor, not the judge, who effectively exercises the sentencing power, albeit cloaked as a charging decision."[72] As one former Federal judge has put it, by his choice of what charges to pursue "[t]he prosecutor sentence(s) the defendant, not the judge, with far less transparency and no appeal."[73] In such circumstances, it is difficult to affirm either that the parties possess, in the words of the Supreme

70 Albert W. Alschuler, 'A Nearly Perfect System for Convicting the Innocent', 79 *Albany Law Review* 3 (2015/2016) pp. 919-940 (hereinafter: Alschuler, 'A Nearly Perfect System for Convicting the Innocent') (describing at p. 925 as "fiction" the view "that today's post-trial sentences are those that would be imposed in the absence of plea bargaining." Rather, "longer sentences exist on the books largely for bargaining purposes."); "When Congress creates new crimes and increases sentences, it speaks, not of doing justice, but of giving 'tools' to prosecutors." (citation omitted) Albert W. Alschuler, 'Lafler and Frye: Two Small Band-Aids for a Festering Wound', 51 Duquesne Law Review (2013) pp. 673-707 at p. 703 (hereinafter: 'Lafler and Frye: Two Small Band-Aids'); "The bodies of law, state and federal, that claim to define crimes and sentences do not really do what they claim. Instead, those bodies of law define a menu – a set of options law enforcers may exercise, or a list of threats prosecutors may use to induce the plea bargains they want." William J. Stuntz, 'Plea Bargaining and Criminal Law's Disappearing Shadow', 117 *Harvard Law Review* 8 (2004) pp. 2548-2569 at p.2569; "[D]efendants who do take their case to trial and lose receive longer sentences than even Congress or the prosecutor might think appropriate, because the longer sentences exist on the books largely for bargaining purposes." Rachel E. Barkow, 'Separation of Powers and the Criminal Law', 58 *Stanford Law Review* 989 at p. 1034 (2006), quoted in *Missouri* v. *Frye*, *supra* note 2 at 144.

71 For a discussion of the practice of overcharging, *see* Alschuler, 'The Prosecutor's Role in Plea Bargaining', *supra* note 5 at pp.85-112.

72 Rakoff, 'Why Innocent People Plead Guilty', *supra* note 36. A former Federal judge has similarly summarized the current situation as follows: "Judges have lost discretion and that discretion has accumulated in the hands of prosecutors, who now have the ultimate ability to shape the outcome. With mandatory minimums and other sentencing enhancements . . . prosecutors can often dictate the sentence that will be imposed." Oppel, *supra* note 26 (quoting from Paul Cassell, former Federal judge and prosecutor).

73 Gertner, *supra* note 62; "In the current era dominated by pleas instead of trials, federal prosecutors are not merely law enforcers. They are the final adjudicators in the vast majority of cases." Rachel E. Barkow, 'Institutional Design and the Policing of Prosecutors: Lessons from Administrative Law', *New York University Public Law and Legal Theory Working Papers*. Paper 69.

Court, "relatively equal bargaining power" or that plea bargaining takes place on a level playing field.

VII. THE INNOCENCE FACTOR: WHEN DOES PLEA BARGAINING BECOME COERCIVE?

There are those who might ask if there really is a problem when a guilty person admits his culpability and pleads guilty without the need for a trial. After all, doesn't plea bargaining produce a generally acceptable result for all concerned? The question, however, suggests a certain amount of naiveté about both plea bargaining as it is currently practiced and the results it has come to produce.

In the universe of plea bargaining, guilty pleas do not emerge from the void fully developed, but in large part take shape through the deliberate actions of the prosecutor. In that regard, however, the prosecutor's authority to act is not without restriction. The Supreme Court recognized in *Brady v. United States* that the practice of plea bargaining is subject to certain limits, noting that "[o]f course, the agent of the State may not produce a plea by actual or threatened physical harm or by mental coercion overbearing the will of the defendant."[74] Such reassurances, however, relate only to the most egregious forms of conduct that could be considered coercive. Put simply, the described actions are in and of themselves objectionable, especially when perpetrated by the State, and any plea they produce must be considered inherently suspect and unacceptable in a court of law.

The Supreme Court's analysis in *Brady*, however, went on to discuss coercion more broadly. In that case the defendant had challenged, on several grounds, his conviction following a change of plea to guilty. Pertinent to the issues under discussion here, the Court considered whether the voluntariness of the defendant's plea could have been affected by "the possibility of a heavier sentence following a guilty verdict after trial."[75] In addressing that consideration, the Court stated that "even if we assume that Brady would not have pleaded guilty except

(2008) pp. 1-54 at p. 3 (at: http://lsr.nellco.org/cgi/viewcontent.cgi?article=1068&context=nyu_plltwp) (last visited: 16 April 2018); "In this plea bargaining system, prosecutors have extraordinary power, nudging both judges and juries out of the truth-seeking process. The prosecutor is now the proverbial judge, jury, and executioner in the mine-run of cases." Cruz, *Reduce Federal Crimes and Give Judges Flexibility*, *supra* note 25.

74 *Brady v. United States*, *supra* note 7 at 750.

75 *Ibid.* at 749. In *Brady*, the possible heavier sentence was the death penalty. Subsequent to the defendant's guilty plea, in *United States* v. Jackson, 390 U.S. 570 (1968) the Supreme Court prohibited the imposition of the death penalty pursuant to the statute under which Brady was charged. In *Brady*, however, the Court ruled that a plea of guilty is not invalid merely because it was offered to avoid the possibility of the death penalty, as long as the plea of guilty met the standard of voluntariness, having been made by a defendant fully aware of the consequences of

for the death penalty provision [of the statute], this assumption merely identifies the penalty provision as a 'but for' cause of his plea. That the statute caused the plea in this sense does not necessarily prove that the plea was coerced and invalid as an involuntary act."[76] Consequently, even if a defendant would not have entered into a plea bargain "but for" the possibility of a more severe sentence being imposed after a trial, it cannot be said that his plea was involuntary in a constitutional sense unless that fact were established by additional evidence.

Running as a subtext throughout the Supreme Court's opinion in *Brady*, however, is the expectation that a defendant who offers a guilty plea will be represented by competent counsel.[77] In underscoring the importance of legal representation for the defendant at the guilty plea stage, the Court highlighted counsel's role in alleviating the pressures implicit in plea bargaining.[78] Asserting that the defendant in the case before them was represented throughout by competent counsel, the Court concluded that "nothing in the record impeaches Brady's plea or suggests that his admissions in open court were anything but the truth."[79] The Court nevertheless warned that "[w]e would have serious doubts about this case if the encouragement of guilty pleas by offers of leniency substantially increased the likelihood that defendants, advised by competent counsel, would falsely condemn themselves."[80] The Court revisited the issue, although in a more affirmative manner, in *Bordenkircher* v. *Hayes*: "Defendants advised by competent counsel and protected by other procedural safeguards are presumptively capable of intelligent choice in response to prosecutorial persuasion, and *unlikely to be driven to false self-condemnation*."[81]

In the time that has passed since both *Brady* and *Bordenkircher* were decided, a significant body of evidence has developed confirming that the apprehension expressed by the Supreme Court has become a reality: that a substantial number of innocent defendants in fact *do* plead guilty in return for leniency. As matters now stand, "[p]erhaps the greatest concern is that, at least as currently practiced

---

the plea. *Brady v. United States*, *supra* note 7 at 749-755. The Court went on to conclude that Brady's plea had been intelligently made and the fact that it did not anticipate the Court's subsequent ruling in *Jackson* did not call into question the reliability of the plea. *Ibid.* at 756-758.

76 *Ibid.* at 750.

77 *Ibid.* at 750, 751, 754, 757 and 758.

78 *Ibid.* at 754. The Court observed, somewhat obliquely, that it had *not* previously held that "the possible coercive impact of a promise of leniency could *not* be dissipated by the presence and advice of counsel." The Court went on to note that in *Miranda* v. *Arizona*, 384 U.S. 436 (1966) it similarly had *not* held "that the possibly coercive atmosphere of the police station could *not* be counteracted by the presence of counsel or other safeguards." (emphasis added).

79 *Ibid.* at 758.

80 *Ibid.* at 758.

81 *Bordenkircher* v. *Hayes*, *supra* note 10 at 363 (emphasis added). One commentator has referred to such assertions as reflecting "the Court's almost idyllic view of how the criminal justice system operates." Alkon, 'The U.S. Supreme Court's Failure to Fix Plea Bargaining', *supra* note 12 at p. 595.

in the United States, plea bargaining can be so coercive as to lead some innocent people to plead guilty."[82] Indeed, plea bargaining has been described as "a nearly perfect system for convicting the innocent."[83]

The "serious doubts" of the type referred to by the Supreme Court in *Brady* would, perhaps, be of less concern if one were to operate on the assumption that all defendants who plead guilty are, in fact, guilty of the charges brought against them. That assertion, however, is in no way supported by the evidence. The National Registry of Exonerations (NRE) has collected an extensive body of post-*Brady* documentation concerning all known exonerations of innocent criminal defendants in the United States from 1989 to the present.[84] The NRE reports that, as of March 2018, 18% of the cases in which those convicted were later exonerated involved defendants who had pleaded guilty (387 out of 2,182).[85] In cases involving drug crimes, the proportion of exonerations for wrongful convictions based on guilty pleas is significantly greater, with a rate as high as 66%.[86] Just as troubling, if not more so, is the fact that as of October 15, 2016, the NRE reported that of all defendants convicted of crimes and later exonerated because they were innocent, 47% were African Americans, a rate three times higher than their representation in the general population.[87] Although that statistic is not limited to cases involving plea bargains, it strongly suggests a disproportionate representation of African Americans among those exonerated for convictions based on guilty pleas.

Unquestionably, such statistics should trigger the "serious doubts" described in *Brady* v. *United* States relative to the possibility of plea bargaining substantially increasing the likelihood that innocent defendants seeking leniency will plead

---

82 Jenia I. Turner, 'Plea Bargaining', in Erik Luna (ed.), *Reforming Criminal Justice*. Vol. 3, *Pretrial and Trial Processes*, Phoenix: Arizona State University (2017) pp. 73-99 at p. 75 (hereinafter: Turner, 'Plea Bargaining').

83 Alschuler, 'A Nearly Perfect System for Convicting the Innocent', *supra* note 69 (concluding at p. 940 that "bargaining almost certainly multiplies the number of wrongful convictions.").

84 The National Registry of Exonerations, *Our Mission* (at: https://www.law.umich.edu/special/exoneration/Pages/mission.aspx) (last visited: 16 April 2018).

85 National Registry of Exonerations, *Exoneration Detail List* (at: www.law.umich.edu/special/exoneration/Pages/detaillist.aspx) (last visited: 16 April 2018).

86 National Registry of Exonerations, *Innocents Who Plead Guilty* (24 November 2015) (at: https://www.law.umich.edu/special/exoneration/Documents/NRE.Guilty.Plea.Article1.pdf)(last visited: 16 April 2018).

87 Samuel R. Gross,, co-author. *Race and Wrongful Convictions in the United States*, (M. Possley and K. Stephens, co-authors). National Registry of Exonerations, Newkirk Center for Science and Society (2017) pp. 1-32 at p. 1. (at: https://repository.law.umich.edu/cgi/viewcontent.cgi?referer=http://scholar.google.com/&httpsredir=1&article=1121&context=other) (last visited: 16 April 2018) Although not limiting itself to cases involving guilty pleas, the report notes: "Judging from the cases we know, a substantial majority of innocent people who are convicted of crimes in the United States are African Americans." *Ibid.*

guilty.[88] With NRE statistics establishing that 18% of all exonerations involved convictions resulting from guilty pleas, we are presented with the harsh reality that *almost one in five innocent defendants who were later exonerated actually pleaded guilty*. The work of the NRE thus strongly supports the view that plea bargaining "almost certainly multiplies the number of wrongful convictions."[89]

The relatively high proportion of exonerated defendants who pleaded guilty clearly challenges the view that plea bargaining merely processes the cases of guilty persons more expeditiously. Rather, it strongly suggests that the pressure to plead guilty under the current legal framework is so compelling that in a relatively high proportion of cases even those who are not in fact guilty as charged will nevertheless plead guilty in order to avoid the risk of more onerous sanctions should they be convicted following trial. "The huge disparity between [a possible] post-trial sentence and the plea sentence presumably leads the defendant, though innocent, to accept the deal."[90]

In such circumstances, a defendant's decision to accept a plea bargain may in some sense represent a rational choice, but "the pressure of the situation may cause an innocent defendant to make a less-than-rational appraisal of his chances for acquittal and thus decide to plead guilty when he not only is actually innocent but also could be proven so."[91] Large sentencing differentials thus present a "duress problem" that "may disproportionately harm innocent defendants."[92] A significant factor giving rise to this problem is that in plea bargaining, "the

88 *Brady* v. *United States*, *supra* note 7 (expressing at 758 "serious doubts about this case if the encouragement of guilty pleas by offers of leniency substantially increased the likelihood that defendants, advised by competent counsel, would falsely condemn themselves.").

89 Alschuler, 'A Nearly Perfect System for Convicting the Innocent', *supra* note 69 at p. 940. To the extent that prosecutors are especially keen to bargain when the case is weakest, that fact may lead not only to wrongful convictions, but also to "grossly disparate treatment for identical offenders – assuming, for the moment, that they are offenders." Alschuler, 'The Prosecutor's Role in Plea Bargaining,' *supra* note 5 at p. 60. Moreover, "[e]ven if defendants are guilty of *some* offense, incomplete investigations, inadequate disclosure, limited adversarial testing, perfunctory judicial oversight, and sizeable plea discounts can lead defendants to plead guilty to crimes different from the ones they committed." Turner, 'Plea Bargaining', *supra* note 82 at p. 75 (emphasis in original).

90 Robert E. Scott and William J. Stuntz, 'Plea Bargaining as Contract', 101 *The Yale Law Journal* 8, Symposium: Punishment (1992), pp. 1909-1968 at p. 1960 (hereinafter: Scott and Stuntz, 'Plea Bargaining as Contract').

91 Rakoff, 'Why Innocent People Plead Guilty', *supra* note 36.

92 Scott and Stuntz, 'Plea bargaining as Contract', *supra* note 90 at p. 1961; "The harsh penalties associated with conviction at trial provide the prosecutor with significant leverage to persuade defendants to plead guilty. In some cases, this may result in innocent defendants being faced with a choice where the cost of pleading guilty outweighs the risks of going to trial. Risk-averse defendants will accept the state's offer and plead guilty. The incentives inherent in plea bargaining, therefore, create an increased risk of innocent defendants receiving punishment." Guidorizzi, 'Should We Really Ban Plea Bargaining?', *supra* note 16 at pp. 771-772.

dynamic of the parties' interaction makes it harder for innocent defendants to identify themselves."[93]

In large part, the criminal justice system, which originally was designed to determine who is guilty and who is not, now operates from a very different perspective. Plea bargaining is largely based on the functional premise that the defendant is in fact guilty of something, with the only significant issue being how to label his offense and the degree of punishment to be imposed. It is also worth noting that as the use of plea bargaining has reached historically high levels, the United States has achieved one of the highest rates of incarceration in the world, with approximately 2.25 million inmates currently being held in Federal or state prisons or other correctional facilities.[94] Without question a number of factors may contribute to that striking statistic, but undoubtedly the use of plea bargaining has played a significant role in generating America's high rate of incarceration.[95]

VIII. HOW EFFECTIVE IS THE "EFFECTIVE ASSISTANCE" OF COUNSEL?

It is no longer tenable to assert that in the course of plea negotiations the prosecution and defense "possess relatively equal bargaining power."[96] The role of defense counsel in negotiations leading to a guilty plea, however, is nonetheless an important one. As a guilty plea involves the waiver of a defendant's constitutional right to a trial, among other rights, the Supreme Court has endeavored to ensure that "pleas of guilty are voluntarily and intelligently made

93 Scott and Stuntz, 'Plea bargaining as Contract', *supra* note 90 at p. 1949. "And by permitting prosecutorial manipulation of broad mandatory sentencing statutes, [current legal] doctrine reduces prosecutors' incentives to separate innocent for guilty defendants at the charging stage." *Ibid.* at p. 1967.

94 As of 2016, approximately 1.51 million prisoners were incarcerated in Federal or state prisons. Bureau of Justice Statistics, "Prison Inmates in 2016" (February 2018) (at: https://www.bjs.gov/content/pub/pdf/p16_sum.pdf) (last visited: 16 April 2018). Approximately 741,000 inmates were held in county and local jails or other correctional facilities, either serving a sentence or awaiting trial or disposition of their case. Bureau of Justice Statistics, "Jail Inmates in 2016" (February 2018) (at: https://www.bjs.gov/content/pub/pdf/ji16_sum.pdf) (last visited: 16 April 2018).

95 "Harsh mandatory minimum sentences for nonviolent drug crimes have contributed to prison overpopulation and are both unfair and ineffective relative to the public expense and human costs of years-long incarceration." Cruz, *Reduce Federal Crimes and Give Judges Flexibility*, *supra* note 25; Alkon, 'An Overlooked Key to Reversing Mass Incarceration', *supra* note 64 (referring at p. 194 to "the often coercive atmosphere of plea bargaining that contributes to mass incarceration."); *See generally*, Michael Tonry, 'Remodeling American Sentencing: A Ten-Step Blueprint for Moving Past Mass Incarceration', 13 Criminology & Public Policy 4 (2014) pp. 503-533 (hereinafter: 'Remodeling American Sentencing').

96 *Bordenkircher* v. *Hayes*, *supra* note 10 at 362.

by competent defendants with adequate advice of counsel."[97] Just as a defendant is entitled to the effective assistance of counsel to guarantee his right to a fair trial, he is entitled to the same effective assistance of counsel in deciding whether or not to waive his right to trial and to plead guilty.[98]

In safeguarding the integrity of guilty pleas, the Court has thus stated that "the negotiation of a plea bargain is a critical phase of litigation for purposes of the Sixth Amendment right to effective assistance of counsel."[99] "Anything less," the Supreme Court has said, "might deny a defendant effective representation of counsel at the only stage when legal aid and advice would help him."[100]

That point was pressed home in the case of *Lafler* v. *Cooper*, in which the defendant, on the advice of his lawyer, rejected a prosecutor's offer of a favorable plea bargain.[101] Instead, he went to trial, following which he was convicted on all counts and received a mandatory minimum sentence that was three and a half times longer than the sentence proposed in the prosecutor's plea offer. The trial itself was fair and free from error, but the defendant claimed that he would not have gone to trial at all had he been properly advised by his lawyer to accept the original plea bargain.

Lafler thus did not involve a claim that defense counsel's incompetence had led to a guilty plea that the defendant later sought to withdraw. Rather, the defendant claimed that he was ill-advised by counsel to reject the offered plea bargain and, as a result, he had gone to trial and suffered the consequence of a longer sentence following conviction. Even though the trial itself was free from error, the Supreme Court ruled that the defendant was entitled to more than just a fair trial, concluding that even a fair trial does not wipe clean the deficient performance of counsel during plea negotiations.[102] Affirming that the constitutional guarantee to the effective assistance of counsel applies to plea bargaining as a critical pretrial stage, the Court declared that "[t]he favorable sentence that eluded the defendant in the criminal proceeding appears to be the sentence he or others in his position would have received in the ordinary course,

97 *Brady* v. *United States*, *supra* note 7 at 758.

98 In articulating the right of a defendant to the effective assistance of counsel at the guilty plea stage, the Court has asserted that counsel must inform the defendant of possible consequences of the plea, such as deportation. *Padilla v. Kentucky*, 559 U.S. 356 (2010). Similarly, the Court has stated that counsel must inform the defendant of any plea offers made by the prosecutor and explain the advantages and disadvantages of accepting the offer. *Lafler v. Cooper*, *supra* note 1 at 163 and *Missouri v. Frye*, *supra* note 2 at 145.

99 *Padilla v. Kentucky*, *supra* note 98 at 373.

100 *Missouri v. Frye*, *supra* note 2 at 144 (citation omitted).

101 "[A]ll parties agree the performance of [defendant's] counsel was deficient when he advised [the defendant] to reject the plea offer on the grounds he could not be convicted at trial." *Lafler v. Cooper*, *supra* note 1 at 163. Defense counsel asserted that the prosecution would be unable to establish intent to murder because the victim had been shot below the waist. *Ibid.* at 156.

102 *Ibid.* at 169-170.

absent the failings of counsel."[103] In sum, the Court concluded that just as a defendant is entitled to the effective assistance of counsel to ensure a fair trial, he is entitled to the same effective assistance during plea negotiations. Having determined that counsel's assistance was ineffective and that the defendant was prejudiced as a result, the Court ruled that the proper remedy was to order the prosecutor to reoffer the plea agreement.[104]

The immediate reaction to the Supreme Court's opinions in the companion cases of *Lafler* and *Frye* reflected a degree of optimism as to the future of plea bargaining. One commentator observed that "the Court has brought law to the shadowy plea-bargaining bazaar."[105] Another enthusiastically proclaimed that "[t]he Supreme Court's decision in these two cases constitute the single greatest revolution in the criminal justice process since *Gideon* v. *Wainwright* provided indigents the right to counsel."[106] As the passage of time provided greater perspective, however, the reactions were far less strident. One assessment explained that the opinions in *Lafler* and *Frye* had taken only a "tiny step" in the direction of improving the plea bargaining process.[107] Another suggested that *Lafler* and *Frye* "are unlikely to create meaningful change in how plea bargaining works because they focus on one narrow issue in the context of plea bargaining: single instances of bad lawyering. These cases do not address the larger structural issues that create serious concerns for defendants in plea bargaining."[108]

In concluding that a defendant is entitled to the effective assistance of counsel at the plea bargaining stage, the Supreme Court confirmed the importance of plea bargaining in the American criminal justice system. It remains to be seen, however, whether the Court's decision in that regard will have a meaningful impact on how plea negotiations are conducted. Although the Supreme Court has recognized the need for competent counsel during plea bargaining, that fact will not, in and of itself, correct the unequal bargaining

---

103 *Ibid.* at 167-168.

104 *Ibid.* at 174. The Court did not, however, order the specific performance of the original plea agreement. It ruled that if the defendant accepted the reoffered plea agreement, the trial court could then vacate the convictions and resentence the defendant pursuant to the plea agreement, vacate some of the convictions and resentence him accordingly or, in its discretion, leave the trial convictions and sentence undisturbed. In a dissenting opinion joined by Justice Thomas and, in part, by Chief Justice Roberts, Justice Scalia argued that "even though [the defendant] has received the exorbitant gold standard of American justice – a full-dress criminal trial," the majority had raised "plea bargaining from a necessary evil to a constitutional entitlement." *Ibid.* at 186.

105 Stephanos Bibas, 'Taming Negotiated Justice', 122 *Yale Law Journal Online* 35 (2012) in Penn Law: Legal Scholarship Repository (at: http://scholarship.law.upenn.edu/cgi/viewcontent.cgi?article=1454&context=faculty_scholarship) (last visited: 16 April 2018).

106 Adam Liptak, 'Justices'Ruling Expands Rights of Accused in Plea Bargains', *The New York Times*, 21 March 2012 quoting Wesley M. Oliver (at: https://www.nytimes.com/2012/03/22/us/supreme-court-says-defendants-have-right-to-good-lawyers.html) (last visited: 16 April 2018).

107 Alschuler, 'Lafler and Frye: Two Small Band-Aids', *supra* note 70 at p. 707.

108 Cynthia Alkon, 'The U.S. Supreme Court's Failure to Fix Plea Bargaining', *supra* note 12 at p. 562.

power that exists between the prosecutor and the defendant during plea negotiations. As long as serious structural issues in the legal framework of plea bargaining go uncorrected, the question remains how effective the assistance of defense counsel can really be in a process that continues to be dominated by the prosecutor.

IX. PLEA BARGAINING AND THE WAY FORWARD

Despite the many challenges it presents, plea bargaining is unlikely to disappear from American criminal practice.[109] The relevant question is thus not whether plea bargaining will have the same central role in the future that it currently enjoys. Rather, the question that needs to be addressed is how the process can be rendered more fair and equitable or, as one observer has phrased it, "less awful."[110] Put another way, "[s]cholars and practitioners should accept plea bargaining as a natural part of the adversarial system and shift the debate to appropriate remedies that address the problems of plea bargaining."[111]

Although the Supreme Court has come to recognize the significant role of plea negotiations in the American criminal justice system, the Court appears to have concluded that "sufficient procedural protections and competent defense lawyers are all that is needed to protect the fairness of the plea bargaining process."[112] The Court has thus focused on the constitutional requirements of the guilty plea itself, including the defendant's right to the effective assistance of competent counsel during plea negotiations. What the Court's constitutional jurisprudence has not addressed, however, are "the serious structural issues that call into question the fundamental fairness of plea bargaining."[113] Nor has the Court answered the question of how effective even competent counsel can be

109 "[P]lea bargaining has triumphed . . . . The battle has been lost for some time." Fisher, *Plea Bargaining's Triumph*, *supra* note 8 at Prologue, p.1. Professor Alschuler has remarked that "The view of plea bargaining the Supreme Court took in 1970 [in *Brady* v. *United States*] rested on wishful thinking, but I do not imagine the Court will change its mind." Alschuler, 'A Nearly Perfect System for Convicting the Innocent', *supra* note 70 at p. 940.

110 "[T]he time for a crusade to prohibit plea bargaining has passed. Instead, the time may have come for criminal justice scholars to abandon the search for ways to make the criminal justice system fair and principled. Their principal mission today should be to make it less awful. Improving the plea bargaining process should be one of their goals." Alschuler, 'Lafler and Frye: Two Small Band-Aids', *supra* note 70 at pp. 706-707.

111 Guidorizzi, 'Should We Really Ban Plea Bargaining?', *supra* note 16 at p. 754.

112 Alkon, 'The U.S. Supreme Court's Failure to Fix Plea Bargaining' *supra* note 12 at pp. 595-596.

113 *Ibid.* at p. 620; "[P]lea bargains are . . . the product of a seriously flawed bargaining structure." Scott and Stuntz, 'Plea Bargaining as Contract', *supra* note 90 at p. 1910.

when the legal framework of the plea bargaining process is so heavily weighted in the prosecutor's favor.[114]

Tackling such "serious structural issues" will need more than reliance on constitutional litigation because meaningful change will require reforms that the Supreme Court has shown no inclination to mandate on a constitutional basis. Rather, consideration must be given to the regulation of plea bargaining in such a way as to bring greater fairness to the process and to render it more equitable, even though the necessary reforms have not yet had their "constitutional moment" before the Court. As a result, for the foreseeable future, the prospects for reform will need to rely on legislative and executive efforts as well as regulation within the judicial branch itself.

As invigorating as it might be to propose the abolition of plea bargaining (a now unlikely prospect) or to suggest "crashing the system" by urging all defendants to request trials, the way forward will require a more deliberate approach focusing on specific structural issues.[115] Although there is no silver bullet for the challenges under consideration, the following sections address some of the more serious structural issues affecting the plea bargaining process.

IX.1. LIMITING THE ROLE OF ENHANCED AND MANDATORY MINIMUM SENTENCES

Perhaps foremost among the larger structural issues is the considerable role of enhanced and mandatory sentencing schemes. Steps to limit their effect on plea bargaining could include the outright repeal of such laws; narrowing their scope and severity to the extent that they remain in effect; and amending such laws as may remain to authorize a level of sentencing discretion on the part of judges.[116] Reducing their impact, however, will require legislative as well as executive action at both the Federal and state levels.

Although a meaningful effort to undertake such sentencing reform has being lacking to date[117], "[a] bipartisan consensus against mandatory minimum

114 "Until the Court is ready to grapple with the structural issues preventing fairness in plea bargaining for defendants, criminal courts around the country will continue business as usual, and defendants will continue to accept plea bargains that may not be a good choice but may be their only choice under the circumstances." Alkon, 'The U.S. Supreme Court's Failure to Fix Plea Bargaining', *supra* note 12 at p. 621.

115 *See e.g.* Guidorizzi, 'Should We Really Ban Plea Bargaining', *supra* note 16 at pp. 772-781. *See also* Michelle Alexander, 'Go to Trial: Crash the Justice System', *The New York Times Sunday Review* (10 March 2012) (hereinafter: Alexander, 'Go to Trial: Crash the Justice System') (at: www.nytimes.com/2012/03/11/opinion/sunday/go-to-trial-crash-the-justice-system.html) (last visited: 16 April 2018).

116 See, e.g., Tonry, 'Remodeling American Sentencing', *supra* note 95 at pp. 516-517. See also, Alkon, 'An Overlooked Key to Reversing Mass Incarceration', *supra* note 64 at pp. 205-207.

117 "So far, initiatives undertaken by legislatures and executive branch officials have been meager . . ." Tonry, 'Remodeling American Sentencing', *supra* note 95 at p. 526.

sentencing appears to be emerging across [the] country."[118] Indeed, in the shadow of America's experience with mass incarceration, "broad-based support" has been expressed by both liberal and conservative critics of plea bargaining for reining in the use of enhanced and mandatory minimum sentences.[119] Nevertheless, until recently, such support has not been matched with the political will to enact necessary reforms.[120] Significant recent developments in the United States Congress, however, suggest that a legislative consensus may be growing as to the need for criminal justice reform.[121] The possibility of bipartisan collaboration in that regard is reflected in a bill entitled the Sentencing Reform and Corrections Act ("Act") currently pending in the United States Senate.[122]

The motivation behind the bill, it should be noted, is not to reform plea bargaining *per se*, but rather to address the problem of mass incarceration by taking steps to reduce the Federal prison population. Recognizing the link between enhanced and mandatory minimum sentences and the growth of the prison population, the bill restricts their use. The bill thus reduces, but does not eliminate, enhanced and mandatory minimum sentences for certain non-violent drug offenders.[123] Moreover, it provides a "safety valve" allowing judges a certain amount of flexibility in an increased number of drug cases to impose sentences

118 R. Michael Cassidy and Hon. Robert L. Ullmann, 'Sentencing Reform: The Power of Reason', 97 *Massachusetts Law Review* 4 (July 2016) pp. 80-83 at p. 80 (hereinafter: Cassidy and Ullmann, 'Sentencing Reform: The Power of Reason')

119 Tonry, 'Remodeling American Sentencing', *supra* note 95 at p. 526.

120 Cassidy and Ullmann, 'Sentencing Reform: The Power of Reason', *supra* note 118 (noting at p. 81 that legislative concerns about "[n]ot wanting to appear soft on crime" have resulted in "little stomach" for reform); *See also*, Alkon, An Overlooked Key to Reversing Mass Incarceration', *supra* note 64 (citing at p. 206 the issue of "practical political constraints").

121 "The urgency of criminal justice reform has become a rare matter of bipartisan consensus in Washington." 'A bill to reduce the federal prison population is necessary – but far from sufficient', *The Washington Post,* (October 15, 2017) (at: https://www.washingtonpost.com/opinions/a-bill-to-reduce-the-federal-prison-population-is-necessary--but-far-from-sufficient/2017/10/15/ecb793f2-ae06-11e7-be94-fabb0f1e9ffb_story.html?utm_term=.14c2688f8547) (last visited: 16 April 2018).

122 S. 1917 – Sentencing Reform and Corrections Act of 2017 (Introduced on 4 October 2017 by Senator Chuck Grassley and ten Republican and Democrat senators. Latest action: ordered to be reported favorably without amendment by the Committee on the Judiciary) (at: https://www.congress.gov/bill/115th-congress//senate-bill/1917/text) (last visited: 16 April 2018).

123 *Ibid. Title I – Sentencing Reform: Sec. 101. Reduce and restrict enhanced sentencing for prior drug felonies* in which the mandatory minimum term of imprisonment for certain felony drug offenses is reduced from 20 to 15 years. The section also reduces the mandatory term of life imprisonment for certain repeat drug offenders ("three strike rule") to a term of imprisonment for not less than 25 years; See also *Sec. 103. Limitation on application of the 10-year mandatory minimum* in which the mandatory minimum term of imprisonment for certain drug offenders without a prior conviction for a serious drug felony or a serious violent felon is reduced from 10 to 5 years. The bill also permits certain nonviolent offenders sentenced prior to the enactment of the act to petition courts for a review and reduction of their sentences consistent with the Act's reduced sentencing provisions (*Sec. 101).*

that are lower than the mandatory minimum term of imprisonment.[124] In limiting the impact of enhanced and mandatory minimum sentences for certain lower level drug offenses and allowing a measure of judicial discretion in sentencing, the proposed legislation begins to address one of the most troubling structural issues affecting the plea bargaining process.[125] Although it would not entirely resolve the challenges the issue presents, it would mitigate their effect, which would be a solid step in the right direction.

Were such proposals to be enacted into law, they would amount to a significant departure from sentencing policies that for decades have driven the plea bargaining process, especially with respect to lower level drug offenses. It goes without saying, however, that whether or not these provisions will become law remains a very open question.[126] Whatever challenges the Federal legislative process may present, however, the Act reflects a new, consequential perspective on sentencing and has the potential to serve as a model for similar reform at the state level.[127]

---

124 *Ibid.* at *Title I – Sentencing Reform: Sec. 102. Broadening of existing safety valve.* At the same time, however, the bill creates new mandatory minimum sentences for interstate domestic violence offenses, certain terrorism-related crimes and the trafficking of fentanyl-laced heroin. *Ibid.* at *Title I – Sentencing Reform: Sec. 106. Mandatory minimum sentences for domestic violence offenses; Sec. 107. Minimum term of imprisonment for certain acts relating to the provision of controlled goods or services to terrorists or proliferators of weapons of mass destruction; Sec. 109. Fentanyl.* Although such provisions suggest that it would be premature to predict the demise of mandatory minimum sentences, the serious crimes to which the new penalties apply are fewer in number and scope than the numerous drug offenses currently subject to mandatory minimum sentences. Consequently, if enacted, these new sentencing provisions are less likely to affect significantly the overall size of the Federal prison population, which is the focus of the legislation. Moreover they are less likely to have the same broad impact on the plea bargaining process as does the use of mandatory minimum sentences for lower level drug offenses.

125 The pending legislation follows in the footsteps of other recent efforts such as the proposed Smart Sentencing Act of 2015, which would have lowered minimum mandatory sentences in cases involving nonviolent drug offenders, cutting them in half and giving judges more flexibility in determining the appropriate sentence based on the unique facts and circumstances of each case. Cruz, *Reduce Federal Crimes and Give Judges Flexibility*, *supra* note 25.

126 The current bill must first be approved by both the Senate and the House of Representatives, after which it must be signed into law by the President, a process easy to describe but often difficult to accomplish "In 2016, the Sentencing Reform and Corrections Act never received a vote due to opposition from, among others, then-Sen. Jeff Sessions. As attorney general, Mr. Sessions has since made his opposition to sentencing reform clear by advocating for prosecutors to pursue the harshest penalties possible." *See* 'A bill to reduce the federal prison population is necessary – but far from sufficient', *The Washington Post, supra* note 121.

127 By way of example, in April, 2018, the Massachusetts legislature enacted a 121-page bill calling for far-reaching changes in the state's criminal justice system, which the governor signed into law. Among other provisions, it repeals mandatory minimum sentences for certain low level drug offenses. Bob Salsburg (Associated Press), *Massachusetts Legislators Back Revamp of State's Criminal Justice Laws,* 4 April 2018 (at: https://www.boston.com/news/local-news/2018/04/04/massachusetts-legislators-back-revamp-of-states-criminal-justice-laws) (last visited: 16 April 2018); Steve LeBlanc (Associate Press), *Baker Signs Sweeping Criminal Justice Overhaul Bill,*

IX.2. PRE-PLEA DISCOVERY AND DISCLOSURE OF EXCULPATORY AND IMPEACHMENT EVIDENCE

"[T]the primary obstacle to conviction by plea is the defendant's own perception of his chance of acquittal."[128] In order to weigh the risks and benefits of going to trial a defendant must thus have enough information to make a meaningful assessment of his situation. Moreover, in order to assist his client effectively, defense counsel must have access to sufficient discovery to evaluate the strengths and weaknesses of the prosecutor's case.[129]

The opportunity for discovery at the plea bargaining stage, however, is severely limited.[130] At that juncture the defendant "is not entitled to prosecutorial disclosure of the evidence available to convict him. [He] is thereby deprived of the information he most needs for a rational evaluation of his chances of acquittal."[131] Moreover, as a matter of constitutional law, at the plea bargaining stage defendants are not entitled to either witness impeachment information or, more than likely, exculpatory evidence.[132] The eventual availability of such information in the course of pre-trial discovery, however, does not resolve the

---

(13 April 2018) (at: https://www.boston.com/news/local-news/2018/04/13/baker-signs-sweeping-criminal-justice-overhaul-bill) (last visited: 16 April 2018).

128 Ostrow, 'The Case for Preplea Disclosure', *supra* note 51 at pp. 1581-1582.

129 "The extent to which a defense attorney can learn the strength of the prosecutor's case against his client has an important influence on the plea-negotiation process." Alschuler, 'The Defense Attorney's Role in Plea Bargaining', *supra* note 37 at p. 1224; "Full disclosure promotes more accurate assessments on both sides and produces bargains that more accurately mirror the likely outcome of a trial." John G. Douglass, 'Can Prosecutors Bluff – *Brady* v. *Maryland* and Plea Bargaining', 57 *Case Western Reserve Law Review* 3 (2007) pp. 581-592 at p. 582 (hereinafter: Douglass, 'Can Prosecutors Bluff').

130 Judge Rakoff has referred to "the information-deprived defense lawyer" who is at "a considerable informational disadvantage to the prosecutor." Rakoff, *supra* note 36; "In the federal and many state systems, discovery rules are highly restrictive or do not require discovery early enough for plea negotiations . . . Many discovery rules are designed to give defendants information in time for effective use at trial, not for effective use in plea bargaining." Stephanos Bibas, 'Plea Bargaining Outside the Shadow of Trial', 117 *Harvard Law Review* 8 (2004) pp. 2463-2547 at p. 2531 (hereinafter: Bibas, 'Plea Bargaining Outside the Shadow of Trial').

131 Ostrow, 'The Case for Preplea Disclosure', *supra* note 51 at p. 1582.

132 The extent to which the prosecutor has a constitutional duty to disclose exculpatory and impeachment evidence to the defendant, both before trial and before the entry of a negotiated guilty plea, has been addressed by the Supreme Court in two opinions separated by almost forty years. In *Brady* v. *Maryland*, decided in 1963, the Supreme Court held that a prosecutor's pretrial failure to disclose exculpatory evidence favorable to a defendant violated due process where the information was material "either to guilt or to punishment." The Court also stated that the principle underlying its ruling was the "avoidance of an unfair trial to the accused." *Brady* v. *Maryland*, 373 U.S. 83, 86-87 (1963). In 2002, the Court decided *United States* v. *Ruiz*, in which it addressed the prosecutor's disclosure responsibilities at the plea bargaining stage. During plea negotiations, the prosecutor in *Ruiz* agreed to provide exculpatory evidence relative to the defendant's "factual innocence," but refused to provide impeachment evidence relating to witnesses (which would have been required had the defendant gone to trial). The Court stated: "We must decide whether the Constitution requires [the] pre-guilty plea disclosure of

defendant's information deficit during plea negotiations, considering that plea bargaining often begins prior to the completion of pre-trial discovery, if not before the pre-trial discovery process has even begun.[133] Consequently, "the parties bargain blind-folded."[134] The resulting peril is even greater for defendants who are innocent and for whom access to exculpatory and other evidence is even more critical.[135]

In such circumstances, a strong case can be made to require that the prosecutor provide sufficient discovery prior to plea negotiations "[t]o ensure that innocent defendants do not plead guilty and to improve the fairness of plea bargains."[136] One observer has provided a useful outline for such discovery:

---

impeachment information. We conclude that it does not." *United States* v. *Ruiz*, 536 U.S. 622, 629 (2002). In so ruling, the Court decided that the disclosure of such information is necessary to ensure the fairness of a trial, but not to ensure the voluntariness of a guilty plea. *Ibid.* Because of the facts in *Ruiz*, the Court did not specifically rule on the disclosure of exculpatory evidence at the plea bargaining stage. "While prosecutors do not have a responsibility to disclose impeachment evidence in the plea-bargaining context, the Court has not directly spoken with respect to exculpatory evidence." Murray, 'Prosecutorial Responsibility and Collateral Consequences', supra note 131 at p. 22. The Court's decision in *Ruiz* not to order the disclosure of impeachment evidence during plea negotiations, however, was based on "reasoning [that] would apply with almost as much force to classic *Brady* exculpatory material." Bibas, 'Plea Bargaining Outside the Shadow of Trial', *supra* note 130 at p. 2494 n. 125. That said, the decision in *Brady* retains "symbolic power [that] may be its greatest virtue." Douglass, 'Can Prosecutors Bluff', *supra* note 129 at p. 592. *Brady* essentially poses the question whether confidence in a guilty verdict following trial is undermined when the defendant has been deprived of exculpatory evidence. "After a guilty plea, *Brady* should lead us to ask the same question." *Ibid.* at p. 589.

133 Bibas, 'Plea Bargaining Outside the Shadow of Trial', *supra* note 130 at p. 2494.

134 Bibas, 'Plea Bargaining Outside the Shadow of Trial', *supra* note 130 at p. 2495.

135 "[L]ack of discovery and, in particular, lack of access to exculpatory information held by the prosecutor can contribute to innocent defendants pleading guilty." Peter A. Joy and Kevin C. McMunigal, 'Innocent Defendants Pleading Guilty', 30 *Criminal Justice* 45 (Spring 2015) (Washington University in St. Louis School of Law Legal Studies Research Paper No. 15-11-02) Case Legal Studies Research Paper No. 2015-23, pp. 45-47 at p.46 (hereinafter: Joy and McMunigal, 'Innocent Defendants Pleading Guilty') (at: https://ssrn.com/abstract=2686810) (last viewed: 16 April 2018); "[The argument] that *Brady*-like disclosure during plea bargaining helps to protect innocent people from being coerced into pleading guilty . . . is both correct and immensely important to anyone concerned about justice in our system . . . [A]s a general rule, nondisclosure disproportionately harms the innocent since, almost by definition, guilty defendants know more about the facts surrounding the crime than do those who are factually innocent." Douglass, 'Can Prosecutors Bluff', *supra* note 129 at pp. 581-582.

136 Turner, 'Plea Bargaining', *supra* note 83 at p. 96; "The obvious remedy is to liberalize discovery. Discovery rules designed for plea bargaining would provide more information earlier." Bibas, 'Plea Bargaining Outside the Shadow of Trial', *supra* note 130 at p. 2531; "Mitigating the coercive effect of the plea-bargaining process will require empowering the defense. And one way to do that is to reduce the informational asymmetry between prosecutors and defense counsel." Cruz, *Reduce Federal Crimes and Give Judges Flexibility*, *supra* note 25; "In short, disclosure of evidence is critical to the fairness of the guilty plea process." Ostrow, 'The Case for Preplea Disclosure', *supra* note 51 at p. 1583.

> [D]iscovery rules should be amended to require prosecutors to disclose to the defense, before a guilty plea, at a minimum, the following types of evidence: (1) impeachment and exculpatory evidence, without regard to its materiality; (2) witness names and statements, redacted as necessary to protect witnesses from risk of harm; and (3) police reports, again redacted as needed to protect the safety of witnesses.[137]

The importance of such discovery, especially as to exculpatory evidence, is independent of whether its disclosure is constitutionally mandated.[138] In addition to promoting more accurate case assessments, access to pre-plea discovery is important because "how informed a defendant is at the critical moment of plea-bargaining is relevant to the justness and fairness of the individual plea itself, not to mention the entire plea-bargaining norm."[139] Put another way, disclosure of a sufficient amount of case information at the plea bargaining stage "is the first step to ensuring that parties are negotiating fair, well-informed and factually based plea bargains and that innocent defendants are not coerced into pleading guilty."[140] In addition, by providing a defendant with the opportunity to assess his chances of acquittal, evidentiary disclosure prior to plea negotiations helps "to make meaningful the consent on which the legitimacy of plea bargaining rests."[141] In sum, a guilty plea should not only be voluntary in a constitutional sense; it must also be the product of informed consent.

Although providing pre-plea discovery of the type described is by no means the rule, the practice has been adopted in a sufficient number of states to suggest that it can be implemented "at a reasonable cost and without undue hardship to

---

137 Turner, 'Plea Bargaining', *supra* note 82 at pp. 96-97.

138 "Congress should pass legislation that requires the government – whether constitutionally required or not – to disclose material exculpatory evidence before the accused enters into any plea agreement. This reform will reduce the risk of false guilty pleas by helping ensure that the accused is better informed before sealing his or her fate." Cruz, *Reduce Federal Crimes and Give Judges Flexibility, supra* note 25; "In our view, adding such a discovery requirement, especially one requiring disclosure of *Brady* material . . . would significantly increase the potential . . . to reduce the risk of innocent people pleading guilty." Joy and McMunigal, 'Innocent Defendants Pleading Guilty', *supra* note 135 at p. 47.

139 Brian M. Murray, 'Prosecutorial Responsibility and Collateral Consequences', *Temple University Beasley School of Law, Legal Studies Research Paper Series* – Research Paper No. 2016-3 (2016) pp. 1-44 at p. 31 (at: https://papers.ssrn.com/sol3/papers.cfm?abstract_id=2703664) (last visited: 16 April 2018); "[In plea bargaining,] wide disparities or variations in each party's information threaten equity and fairness." Bibas, 'Plea Bargaining Outside the Shadow of Trial', *supra* note 130 at p. 2531; In circumstances where a defendant pleads guilty without first receiving access to exculpatory information, "[t]he question should be whether undisclosed exculpatory evidence undermines confidence in the judgment of guilty entered as a result of that guilty plea. In other words, we should ask whether the evidence raises a reasonable probability that an innocent person has pleaded guilty." Douglass, 'Can Prosecutors Bluff', *supra* note 129 at p. 584.

140 Turner, 'Plea Bargaining', *supra* note 82 at p. 97.

141 Ostrow, 'The Case for Preplea Disclosure', *supra* note 51 at p. 1583.

witnesses."[142] Indeed, "most observers agree that some measure of prosecutorial disclosure is a condition of the validity of guilty plea convictions. Disagreement exists primarily over the appropriate scope of disclosure."[143] In whatever way those disagreements come to be resolved, any step to ensure greater disclosure of case information during plea bargaining would be another step in the right direction.

IX.3. JUDICIAL INVOLVEMENT AT THE PLEA BARGAINING STAGE

As already noted, state court judges generally do not participate in plea negotiations and Federal judges are specifically barred from doing so by the Federal Rules of Criminal Procedure.[144] Considering the adversarial nature of the American criminal justice system, it should come as no surprise that plea bargaining has largely been left to the parties, to the exclusion of the judge. Moreover, the judge's passive role relative to the process is consistent with the perception of the plea bargain as a contract between the prosecutor and the defendant.[145] Limitations on judicial participation, however, also reflect a concern that "[g]reater involvement could interfere with the judge's impartiality and place undue pressure on a defendant to accept a plea deal."[146]

142 Turner, 'Plea Bargaining', *supra* note 82 at p. 97. Moreover, states such as North Carolina and Texas have adopted what has been described as "open-file pre-plea discovery," apparently without unduly impairing the use of plea bargaining to dispose of criminal cases. *Ibid.* Moreover, "[i]f introducing a disclosure duty is likely to affect the number of guilty pleas in justifiable and insubstantial ways, it is also likely to cause no substantial increase in delay in the plea process." Ostrow, 'The Case for Preplea Disclosure', *supra* note 51 at p. 1618. In *United States* v. *Ruiz*, however, the Supreme Court suggested that as a practical matter, requiring the pre-plea disclosure of information would necessitate more work on the part of the prosecutor, "depriving the plea bargaining process of its main resource-saving advantages. Or it could lead the Government instead to abandon its heavy reliance upon plea bargaining." *United States* v. *Ruiz*, *supra* note 132 at 632. Although it is unclear the extent to which the Court's ruling in *Ruiz* was rooted in such practical considerations, the Court discounted the effects of a defendant's information deficit on the decision to plead guilty, limiting itself to the observation that requiring pre-plea disclosure would achieve "comparatively small a constitutional benefit." *Ibid.* As already noted, however, the benefit of providing appropriate discovery at the plea bargaining stage is independent of whether its disclosure is constitutionally mandated. *See*, *supra* note 138.

143 Ostrow, 'The Case for Preplea Disclosure', *supra* note 51 at p. 1606.

144 "An attorney for the government and the defendant's attorney... may discuss and reach a plea agreement. The court must not participate in these discussions." Federal Rule of Criminal Procedure 11(c)(1).

145 Turner, 'Judicial Participation in Plea Negotiations', *supra* note 42 at p. 266.

146 *Ibid.* at p. 199; "[T]he proposal that trial judges not take part in the bargaining process . . . is designed to render the process less coercive." Alschuler, 'The Trial Judge's Role', *supra* note 42 at p. 1153; The concern reflected in Rule 11 is "that defendants might feel coerced by the judge into pleading guilty and that plea bargaining judges might not be able to objectively assess the voluntariness of the guilty pleas." Daniel S. McConkie, 'Judges as Framers of Plea Bargaining', 26

Whatever concerns might exist about judicial involvement at the plea bargaining stage, however, the duress currently experienced by defendants during plea negotiations derives from the prosecutor's almost total control over the process. As a result, "there is reason to believe we have overestimated the costs of judicial participation in plea negotiations and underestimated its benefits."[147] Indeed, "judicial bargaining in an appropriately limited form is no more coercive than prosecutorial bargaining, and... the bargaining process can operate in a fairer, more straightforward manner when judges take an active part."[148]

A number of thoughtful proposals have been suggested to give the judge a more active role in plea bargaining.[149] In the main they involve advancing the judge's involvement to an earlier stage in the process, rather than limiting judicial participation to an after-the-fact review of an already-negotiated plea agreement.[150] Moreover, they range from direct participation in plea negotiations to what might be described as more of an oversight role in the process.[151] In considering alternate ways of proceeding, useful guidance also can be gleaned

Stanford Law & Policy Review (2015) pp. 61-117 at p. 72 (hereinafter: McConkie, 'Judges as Framers of Plea Bargaining').

147 Turner, 'Judicial Participation in Plea Negotiations', *supra* note 42 at p. 200.

148 Alschuler, 'The Trial Judge's Role in Plea Bargaining', *supra* note 42 at p. 1060. Professor Alschuler goes on to cite additional benefits of an expanded judicial role in the plea bargaining process, stating that it "would offer defendants a clear and tangible basis for reliance in entering their guilty pleas; it would, at least on occasion, permit effective regulation of the extent of the penalty that our criminal justice system imposes for exercise of the right to trial; it would facilitate the introduction of new procedural safeguards; it would be likely to affect the tone and substance of the bargaining process in a variety of useful ways; and most, importantly, it would restore judicial power to the judges." *Ibid.* at p. 1154.

149 The discussion of judicial involvement in plea bargaining is usually framed in terms of a judge's participation in plea bargaining, generally subject to recusal should negotiations fail and the case go to trial. In Federal court (and potentially in other jurisdictions) the availability of a magistrate provides an alternate way to involve a judicial neutral without incurring the later need for recusal. See, e.g. Rakoff, 'Why Innocent People Plead Guilty', *supra* note 36.

150 "Plea bargaining discussions are conducted largely on the basis of what the parties believe judges would do at sentencing, but judges have no early opportunity to dispel them of any misconceptions." McConkie, 'Judges as Framers of Plea Bargaining', *supra* note 146 at p. 64; "Judges can provide a neutral assessment of the merits of the case and prod the defense attorney or the prosecutor to accept a fairer resolution. They can also offer a more accurate estimate of the expected post-plea and post-trial sentences, which is especially valuable in systems of indeterminate sentencing. Finally, the involvement of an impartial party can render the bargaining process more transparent and more acceptable to the public." Turner, 'Judicial Participation in Plea Negotiations', *supra* note 42 at p. 200.

151 *See*, e.g., Rakoff, 'Why Innocent People Plead Guilty', *supra* note 36 (refer criminal cases to a magistrate who would meet separately with the prosecutor and defense counsel, conduct recorded proceedings that are placed under seal, review the particulars regarding evidence and issues, potentially interview witnesses and possibly the defendant (subject to appropriate safeguards), and finally make a non-binding recommendation regarding the disposition of the case); McConkie, 'Judges as Framers of Plea Bargaining', *supra* note 146 at p. 61 (create a "public, court-supervised advocacy procedure" to allow judges to help frame the parties' sentencing discussion, to include a pre-plea presentence report, issuance by the judge of two proposed

from the experience of those jurisdictions that already permit some degree of judicial participation at the plea bargaining stage.[152]

Although variations exist among the proposals for greater judicial involvement in plea negotiations, significant common elements are present: (1) introducing a neutral and presumptively more objective party into the plea bargaining process; (2) promoting greater accountability for case preparation and evaluation on the part of both the prosecutor and defense counsel; (3) ensuring a more thorough inquiry into the facts of the case; (4) safeguarding the accused, including defendants who are innocent, from pressures to accept unfair plea bargains; and (5) making plea negotiations more transparent and fostering greater public confidence in the integrity of the process.[153]

Some of the listed elements might appear aspirational in nature, but they help illustrate what greater judicial involvement in plea bargaining has the potential to accomplish. "Though judicial involvement is not likely to eliminate all risks of plea bargaining, it is likely to minimize some of the gravest dangers of the practice: that a plea bargain does not reflect the true facts of the case, is unfair to the defendant, or is inconsistent with the public interest."[154] An expanded role for judges with respect to plea bargaining thus need not be a cure-all to be of significant value. Moreover, in whatever way judicial involvement in plea bargaining might be structured, a broader judicial role is clearly warranted.[155]

---

sentences, one for a guilty plea and one for a trial conviction, all done "without involving the judge in the parties' plea discussions"); Joy and McMunigal, 'Innocent Defendants Pleading Guilty', *supra* note 135 at p. 47 (require prosecutors and defense counsel to meet with a magistrate to discuss the case and the evidence, although expressing reservations about the time and resources available in state courts to engage in "the sort of plea negotiation sessions Judge Rakoff envisions").

152 *See* Turner, 'Judicial Participation in Plea Negotiations', *supra* note 42 (comparing judicial involvement in plea bargaining in Germany, Florida and Connecticut with a proposal reflecting the author's selection of best practices from each, including judicial discussion with the parties as to both post-plea and post-trial sentences and the factual basis for the possible plea, open file disclosure to the defense unless good cause shown, judicial access to the investigative file, oral presentation by the parties, pre-plea probation report, use of a different judge for a trial should plea negotiations fail and appellate review of judge's remarks for bias).

153 "[P]lea bargaining has been kept in the shadows because of Rule 11's overly strict injunction against judicial participation in those discussions." McConkie, 'Judges as Framers of Plea Bargaining', *supra* note 146 at p. 117.

154 Turner, 'Judicial Participation in Plea Negotiations', *supra* note 42 at p. 202; Judge Rakoff has observed as follows: "I am under no illusions that this suggested involvement of judges in the plea-bargaining process is a panacea. But would not any program that helps to reduce the shame of sending innocent people to prison be worth trying?" Rakoff, 'Why Innocent People Plead Guilty', *supra* note 36.

155 "Federal criminal procedure has generally rested on at least two assumptions: first, that trials determine guilt or innocence and second, that judges preside over the proceedings. Plea bargaining's triumph over criminal procedure has conclusively thrown out the first assumption. But the second need not be thrown out as well." McConkie, 'Judges as Framers of Plea Bargaining', *supra* note 146 at p. 117.

IX.4. EXPANDING AND SUSTAINING THE PUBLIC DISCUSSION ABOUT PLEA BARGAINING

As long as the discussion about plea bargaining is restricted to judges, lawyers and law professors, the prospects for reform will remain dim. The political will needed to effect change will be energized only if concerns about negotiated guilty pleas reach a broader, more public audience. It is thus noteworthy that the Sentencing Reform and Corrections Act calls for a National Criminal Justice Commission, the purpose of which is to conduct a comprehensive review of the American criminal justice system.[156] The last such study was conducted over fifty years ago by the President's Commission on Law Enforcement and Administration of Justice, established in 1965. It goes without saying that the criminal justice landscape, especially as relates to plea bargaining, has undergone significant changes since then and a reexamination is long overdue. Indeed, previous proposals for such a bipartisan commission have been widely supported by a range of relevant groups, including both civil rights organizations and police associations.[157]

The Act calls for Federal, state and local governments along with elements of civil society to "come together to review evidence and consider how to improve the criminal justice system."[158] Following its comprehensive review, the commission is to make recommendations for Federal criminal justice reform to the President and Congress and disseminate its findings nationwide.[159]

If brought into existence, such a commission would provide an important forum for discussing plea bargaining reform, a debate that has already begun to extend beyond the courthouse and the academy and has entered the public arena.[160] A commission focused on criminal justice issues can thus supply an

156 S. 1917 – Sentencing Reform and Corrections Act of 2017 *supra* note 123 at *Title III – National Criminal Justice Commission Act: Sec. 304. Purpose of the Commission.*

157 'A bill to reduce the federal prison population is necessary – but far from sufficient', *The Washington Post, supra* note 122.

158 S. 1917 – Sentencing Reform and Corrections Act of 2017 *supra* note 123 at *Title III – National Criminal Justice Commission Act: Sec. 302. Findings.*

159 *Ibid.* at *Title III – National Criminal Justice Commission Act: Sec. 304. Purpose of the Commission.*

160 See, e.g. Dirk Olin, 'The Way We Live Now: Crash Course; Plea Bargain', *The New York Times Magazine* (29 September 2002) (at: www.nytimes.com/2002/09/29/magazine/the-way-we-live-now-9-29-02-crash-course-plea-bargain.html) (last visited: 16 April 2018); Alexander, 'Go to Trial: Crash the Justice System', *supra* note 115; 'The Kings of the Courtroom: How prosecutors came to dominate the criminal justice system', *The Economist* (4 October 2014) pp. 33-34; Dylan Walsh, 'Why U.S. Criminal Courts Are So Dependent on Plea Bargaining', *The Atlantic* (May 2017) (at: https://www.theatlantic.com/politics/archive/2017/05/plea-bargaining-courts-prosecutors/ 524112/) (last visited: 16 April 2018); Emily Yoffe, 'Innocence is Irrelevant', *The Atlantic* (September 2017) (at: https://www.theatlantic.com/magazine/archive/2017/09/ innocence-is-irrelevant/534171/) (last visited: 16 April 2018).

even more prominent platform for the kind of national dialogue that will be needed to generate support for necessary reforms in the plea bargaining process.

X. CONCLUSION

There is little question that American criminal justice has become a system of pleas rather than a system of trials. Moreover, it appears certain that plea bargaining will remain an enduring feature of criminal practice in the United States. What is not certain, however, is the form plea bargaining will take as attempts are made to address the challenges that it presents.

The Supreme Court has acknowledged the central role of plea bargaining in America's justice system and has ruled that it constitutes a critical stage in criminal proceedings. As a result, the Court has recognized that the constitutional right of defendants to the effective assistance of counsel extends not only to trials but also to plea negotiations. As welcome as the Court's ruling might be, to date it has had little impact on the prosecutorial overuse of plea bargaining.

Although the Supreme Court has helped to shine a light on plea bargaining, it has focused primarily on the sufficiency of procedural protections and competent defense lawyers to ensure that negotiated guilty pleas are entered into voluntarily, knowingly, and with an awareness of the consequences. In doing so, the Court has focused on the constitutional requirements of guilty pleas themselves but has failed to address the serious structural issues in the negotiating process that produces such pleas. Noteworthy in this regard is the Court's failure to revisit the concern it expressed in *Brady* v. *United States* about the possibility of prosecutorial offers of leniency substantially increasing the likelihood of innocent defendants pleading guilty. With the available evidence demonstrating that almost one in five innocent defendants who were later exonerated actually pleaded guilty, the need for corrective action is clear.

The challenge in the future will be to enhance the fairness of plea bargaining by bringing about necessary reforms, even those that are not constitutionally mandated. As a result, legislative and executive action rather than constitutional litigation may provide a better basis for rendering the plea bargaining process more equitable by, for example, addressing the structural issue of enhanced and mandatory minimum sentences. Similarly, rules of court may be adjusted to provide greater access to exculpatory evidence and other case information as part of the plea bargaining process, allowing the parties to better evaluate the strengths and weaknesses of the case. At the same time, steps can be taken to achieve the potential benefits of properly structured judicial involvement in plea negotiations. Proceeding along these lines will go a long way toward promoting not only fairness and equity in plea bargaining, but also increased transparency and accountability in the process.

As the discussion about plea bargaining gains a wider audience beyond the courthouse and the academy, thoughtful approaches to plea bargaining reform will continue to emerge. A more robust public debate is to be encouraged and the possibility of a national commission to conduct a comprehensive review of the American criminal justice system, including the plea bargaining process, should be applauded. Whatever further dialogue about plea bargaining is thus generated, the focus should be on what is fair and equitable and not simply on what is constitutionally required. In that regard, it is worth reflecting on the admonition that, with respect to plea bargaining, "[w]e should not allow what is familiar to become what is right."[161]

Only time will tell whether a heightened awareness of the challenges presented by plea bargaining, especially the prosecutorial overuse of the practice, will help promote necessary reforms in the process by which the American justice system disposes of the overwhelming majority of its criminal cases. Let us hope that it does.

XI. POSTSCRIPT

Following the submission of this chapter to the publisher, President Donald J. Trump signed into law the "First Step Act" on 21 December 2018.[162] The act (the name of which is an acronym for the "Formerly Incarcerated Reenter Society Transformed Safely Transitioning Every Person Act") was passed with overwhelming bipartisan support in both the United States Senate (87 to 12 on 18 December) and the House of Representatives (358 to 36 on 20 December).[163] Hailed as "the most far-reaching overhaul of the criminal justice system in a generation," the First Step Act deals with both prison reform and changes in sentencing practices at the Federal level.[164] As such, it provides for substantial changes "to the tough-on-crime prison and sentencing laws that ballooned the Federal prison population and created a criminal justice system that many

161 Alschuler, 'Lafler and Frye: Two Small Band-Aids', *supra* note *70* at p. 707.

162 Public Law No: 115-391 (at: https://www.congress.gov/bill/115th-congress/senate-bill/756/text) (all websites referred to in this Postscript were last visited on: 22 February 2019).

163 For legislative history, see "All Actions S.756 – 115th Congress (2017-2018) (at: https://www.congress.gov/bill/115th-congress/senate-bill/756/all-actions).

164 John Wagner, 'Trump signs bipartisan criminal justice bill amid partisan rancor over stopgap spending measure', *The Washington Post* (21 December 2018) (at: https://www.washingtonpost.com/politics/trump-to-sign-bipartisan-criminal-justice-bill-amid-partisan-rancor-over-stopgap-spending-measure/2018/12/21).

conservatives and liberals view as costly and unfair."[165] With respect to those individuals who are already incarcerated, the act calls for improved prison conditions along with expanded educational and job training opportunities to prepare lower risk offenders for re-entry into society. Involvement in such programs will not only allow participating prisoners to earn increased time credits toward a reduction of their sentences, but also provide a pathway to forms of supervised pre-release such as halfway houses and home confinement with electronic monitoring.[166] The act also takes steps to reduce certain enhanced sentences for some nonviolent drug offenses. One example is the reduction of the "three strikes" penalty for drug felonies from life in prison to 25 years. At the same time the act provides judges with greater discretion in the application of mandatory minimum sentences, while also limiting sentencing disparities in certain drug cases both prospectively and retroactively.[167] Although the new law is not as broad in scope as the previously proposed Sentencing Reform and Corrections Act[168], as its name suggests, it is a "first step" in the right direction. Moreover, it has helped to coalesce a broad-based coalition in support of criminal justice reform. As one reform advocate has stated, "We've already started talking about the second step."[169]

---

165 Nicholas Fandos, 'Senate Passes Bipartisan Criminal Justice Bill', *The New York Times* (18 December 2018) (at: https://www.nytimes.com/2018/12/18/us/politics/senate-criminal-justice-bill.html).

166 See, S. 756 (Enrolled Bill) Title I – Recidivism Reduction; Title V – Second Chance Act of 2007 Reauthorization; and Title VI – Miscellaneous Criminal Justice (at: https://www.congress.gov/bill/115th-congress/senate-bill/756/text. See also, 'Criminal justice reform: A first step', *The Economist* (15 December 2018) (at: https://www.economist.com/united-states/2018/12/15/congress-discovers-a-bill-with-bipartisan-support-that-the-president-will-sign).

167 See, S. 756 (Enrolled Bill) Title IV – Sentencing Reform (at: https://www.congress.gov/bill/115th-congress/senate-bill/756/text).

168 *Supra* note 122.

169 Deborah Barfield Berry and Eliza Collins, 'Criminal justice bill passes House, heads to President Trump for his signature', *USA Today* (20 December 2018) quoting Holly Harris, executive director of the Justice Action Network (at: https://www.usatoday.com/story/news/politics/2018/12/20/criminal-justice-reform-bill-passes-congress-goes-president-trump/2373992002/).

OVERUSE OF IMPRISONMENT

Statistical Analyses of Incarceration Rates Across the World

Tapio LAPPI-SEPPÄLÄ*

I. INTRODUCTION

An unprecedented expansion of penal control has occurred in recent decades in different parts of the world. Since the mid-1970s, North American imprisonment rates have increased nearly fivefold. Many other countries followed from the 1980s onwards, in Africa, Asia, Europe, South America and Occania. This has resulted to high imprisonment rates and severe overcrowding. In 2016, more than two out of three countries have an occupancy rate of over 100%. In the worst cases, the number of prisoners exceeds the number of prison places by three to one.

This text gives an overview of major trends in the use of imprisonment across the world. Trends and differences in imprisonment rates are examined both cross-sectionally and over time.

Imprisonment rates. In the following, the use of imprisonment is examined mainly in terms of imprisonment rates / 100,000 population. Imprisonment rates indicate how many of its residents the state keeps in prison on any given day (Stock-statistics). The main data-source is the World Prison Brief database (WPB). The database is hosted by the Institute for Criminal Policy Research (ICPR), at Birkbeck University of London.[1] The WPB holds statistics for 223 independent countries and dependent territories. For most countries, there is also

* Dr. Tapio Lappi-Seppälä (PhD) is the Director General of the National Research Institute of Legal Policy in Finland. Alongside his current position, he has been acting as a part-time professor in criminology and sociology of law at the University of Helsinki.

1 The database was originally launched in 2000 using data compiled by Roy Walmsley, Director of the World Prison Brief, and hosted by the International Centre for Prison Studies (ICPS) in

data on specific categories of prisoners, including juveniles, persons detained in pre-trial or prior to sentencing, female prisoners and foreigners. Other sources include the Council of Europe data from the SPACE I project. It allows more exact comparisons between European countries by providing standardized (adjusted) figures through the use of identical counting methods.[2] The third source of information includes national time-series, dating back to the early 1960s or early 1980s.[3]

Besides stock-based imprisonment rates, the use of imprisonment can also be measured by the number of people admitted to prison (flow-statistics), or by the length of served prison terms. Both measures provide complementary information about a country's prison profile. On the other hand, imprisonment rates (as stock-statistics) are a function of the number of entries and the duration of stay. It thus tells more than either of these two options alone and is the most complete basic indicator for the use of imprisonment.

Overcrowding and prison conditions. The intensity of imprisonment and the scale of punitivity is dependent not only on the number of people held in prisons, but also on the conditions under which the inmates live. One indicator of prison conditions is overcrowding. In this connection, overcrowding is measured by occupancy rate. An occupancy rate that exceeds 100% means that the number of prisoners exceeds the official prison capacity. The main drawback with this measure is that it depends heavily on national/local standards.[4] Countries that allow four prisoners in one cell may report "free space", while countries with single-cell accommodation as the norm may report overcrowding with much less "objective" overcrowding. Neither does this measure take into account differences in time to be spent in cells, nor any other prison conditions. For that purpose,

---

King's College University of London. In 2014 the project was merged with ICPR in 2014). For data description, see Coyle et al 2017 p. 6-8 and for the data www.prisonstudies.org/.

2 Adjustments are needed since the number of prisoners may be counted differently in different countries. Adjusted figures exclude from national (raw) figures persons placed in juvenile institutions, in drug treatment or mental health facilities, and immigrants and foreigners detained on the basis of immigration laws (see SPACE I 2015).

3 For sources, see Lappi-Seppälä 2017.

4 There is no agreement on international standards of what constitutes prison overcrowding. The Council of Europe Prison Rules have no provisions for the minimum space in the EPR. The commentary to Rule 18 of the European Prison Rules indicates that the CPT considers 4 square meters per person as a minimum requirement in shared accommodation and 6 square meters for a single-occupancy prison cell, but also notes that the CPT has never laid down such a norm directly. In fact, indications are that the CPT would consider 9 to 10 square meters as a desirable size for a cell for one prisoner. The CPT has emphasized that the acceptable minimum space also depends on the quality of the space and the time to be spent in the cells. See UNODC handbook 2013 p. 10 with references.

other measures would be needed.[5] All in all, the following figures in overcrowding will be in most cases absolute minimum figures. Following more normative criteria – for example those imposed by the CPT – ratings for prison overcrowding would most probably look much worse.

Individual countries form the basic unit in the analyses, but trends and differences are examined also by regions and continents. Regional comparisons may be conducted either with unweighted or weighted country data. When regional means are calculated with unweighted values, each country appear with the same weight in the calculations. This approach treats countries (and their penal policies) as units. They describe the "average criminal political approach" in the region as presented in national penal policies. However, unweighted regional mean are less suitable to give information about the average number of prisoners in the region, since small and large countries share the same weight in the calculus. In order to take into account these differences in size, values should be weighted by population size. Weighted figures enable comparisons between regions that wish to know whether Western Europe holds more or less prisoners relative to population compared to the Caribbean, for instance. Both measures are used below, depending on the focus of interest.

Changes may be measured either by rates (for example an increase from the level of 150 prisoners/pop to 200 prisoners/pop), or by percentages (in this case an Increase of 33%). Both have their merits, and research literature is not in agreement of the preferred method (see for the discussions between Zimring and Webster & Doob contributions in Reitz 2017). When countries with large level-differences in incarceration are compared, it is advisable to use both methods, as is done also in the following.

II. OVERVIEW

II.1. THE USE OF IMPRISONMENT

Imprisonment rates by countries are presented in Figure II.1. Only countries with population over 100,000 are included.

On the top of the scale remains the US with over 680 prisoners/100,000 pop. The lowest figures of around 10-20 can be found in the smaller (mostly Western) African countries, as well as in some miniature states (Liechtenstein, San Marino,

5 Other substantial criteria would refer for example to spatial density (sq meters /person), social density (number of persons in one space), privacy (the amount of time individuals can spend on their own), overall material conditions, sanitation, health services, nutrition, etc. (see for example the structure of the CPT-reports) For the development of comparative indicators for prison conditions, see Karstedt 2010.

Figure II.1. Prisoner rates by countries 2016

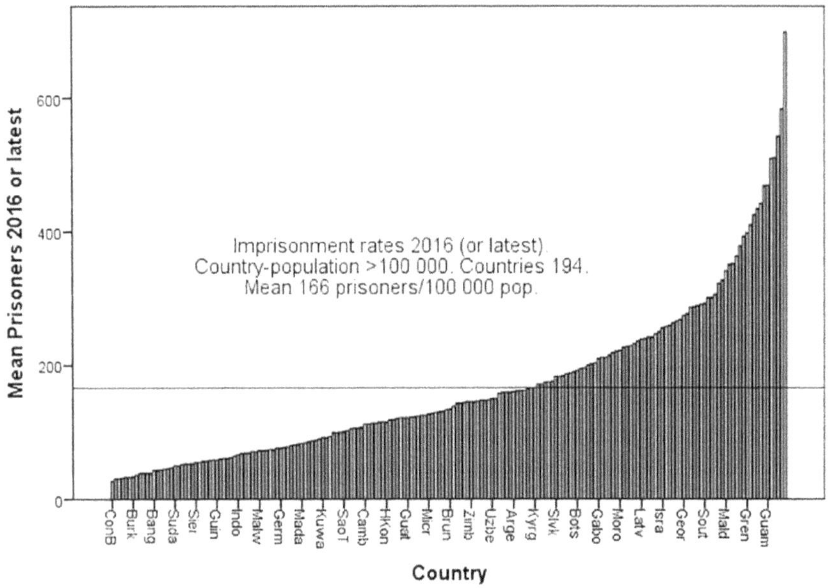

Faeroe Islands, Tuvalu, Nauru, Timor Leste). The overall mean lies around 152 prisoners / 100,000. Leaving out miniature states with populations less than 100,000, the overall mean lies around 166 (194 countries).

Regional averages are displayed in Figure II.2 with both unweighted and weighted values. However, in order to absorb undue influence of small miniature states from the unweighted measurement (such as the Channel Islands), states with less than 100,000 inhabitants are excluded.

Average unweighted prisoner rates vary in Europe (mean 145) from 58 in Scandinavia to over 260 in Europe/Asia (= Russia and the former Soviet Union region). In Africa (mean 107) the figures range from 64 in Western Africa to 200 in Southern Africa. The highest overall figures are to be found in the Americas (mean 280) ranging between 216 and 402.

The overall profile with weighted values remains the same. However, there are also visible differences. Regional means have been lifted up by large countries with high imprisonment rates in Former Soviet Europe (by Russia), South Africa (by South Africa) and North America (by the USA). In Asia regional rates have been decreased by the influence of highly populated low-imprisonment countries of India and Bangladesh.

Third way to measure the scale of imprisonment is to count the raw (absolute) number in inmates in each country and sum the values within each regions (Figure II.3).

Figure II.2. Mean imprisonment rates by continents and regions 2016. Unweighted values

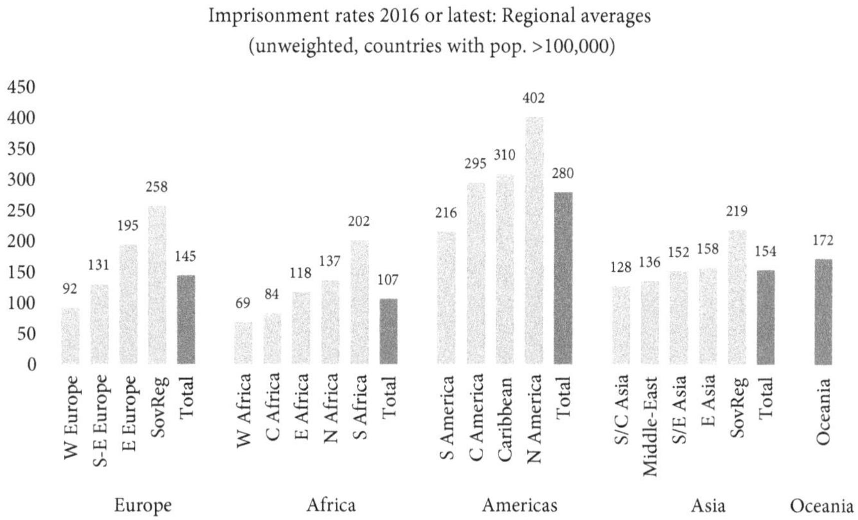

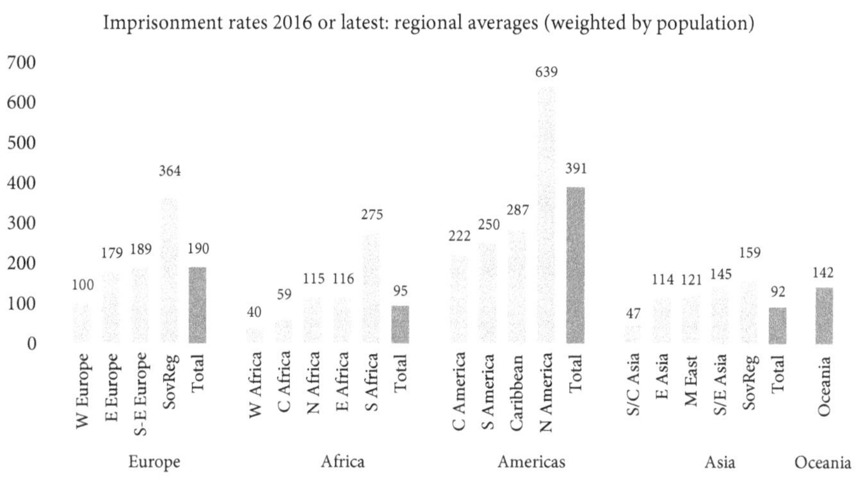

Highly populated countries dominate the regional picture. In term of absolute number, both Asia (3.9 M prisoners) and Americas (3.8 M) hold the largest prison populations. In the Americas, the US holds the top position both in relative (rates; 680) and absolute prison populations (over 2.2 M). The high total number of Asian prisoners originate from China (1.7 M), India (420,000) and Thailand (320,000). European total figures are dominated by the Russian Federation (650,000), and South America by Brazil (610,000). In this comparison, the total prison population in Oceania remains negligible.

Figure II.3. Total number of prisoners by continents and regions

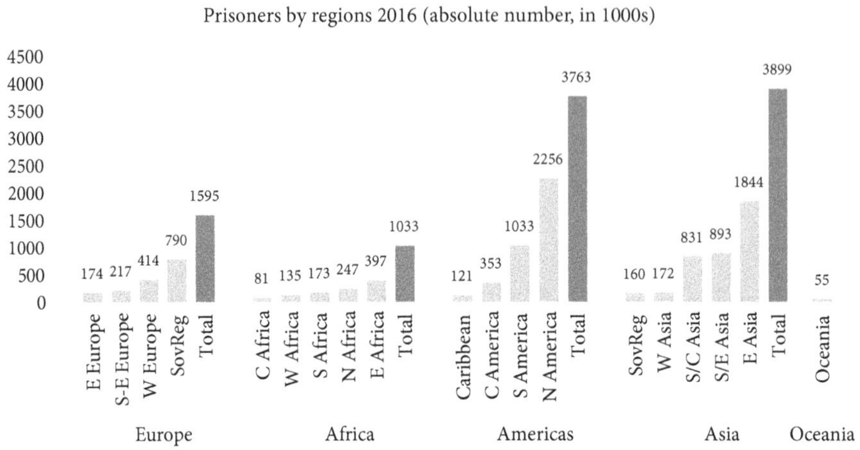

II.2. OCCUPANCY AND OVERCROWDING

Figure II.4 shows the distribution of countries according to occupancy rate. An occupancy rate of 100% means that all prison places are in use. Rates exceeding 100% indicate that prisoners have been inhabited more densely than the official enforcement policy would allow. However, a responsible prison policy would place the norm not to be exceeded a little lower than 100% (as is done in the figure).

More than two out of three countries have an occupancy rate of over 100%. The average (mean) global occupancy rate is 131%, exceeding the overall capacity by one third. In worst cases the number of prisoners exceeds the number of prison places by three to one.

The degree of overcrowding varies between regions and between continents (Figure II.5).[6] With the exception of Northern parts, all African and American regions suffer from overcrowding. Considerably overcrowded countries can also be found in South Central Asia.

It must be emphasized that occupancy rates provide only a rough and partly misleading picture of prison conditions. The concept itself is subject to national norms and definitions. Overcrowding problems are most easily avoided by using four-bed cells (as in one Russian prison near St Petersburg, see Dünkel 2017 p. 639), than by following the single-bed rule. In addition, occupancy rates say

6 Due to space limitations most the regional comparisons to follow are based on unweighted values, however excluding small states with population below 100,000. This measure represents a sort of compromise between totally unweighted and population weighted measurements.

Figure II.4. Occupancy rate by countries 2016

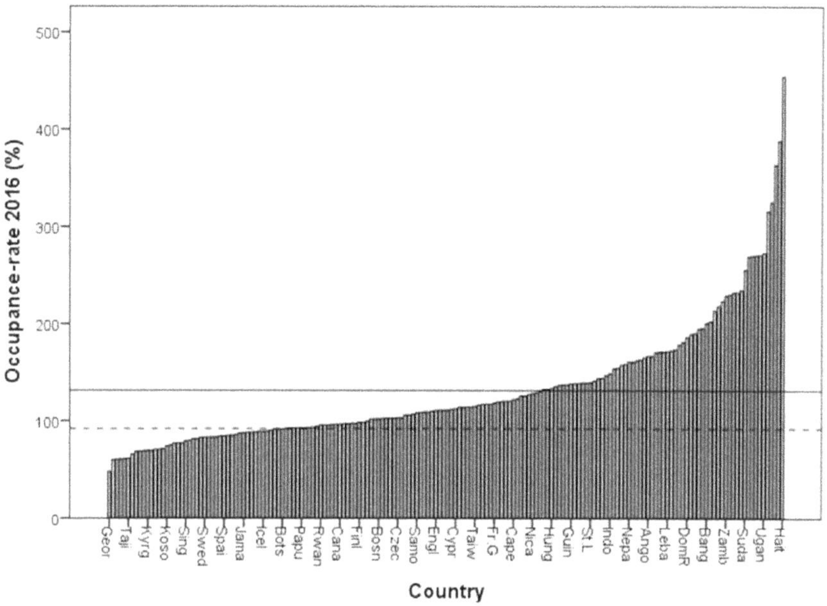

Figure II.5. Occupancy rates by continents and regions (Unweighted, pop >100,000)

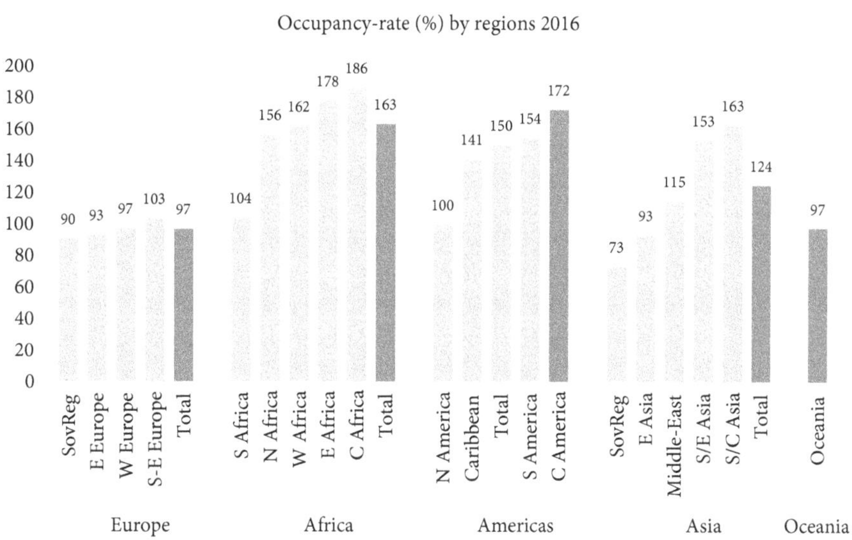

very little about other conditions and treatment in prisons. For that purpose, other measures are needed.

III. PRISONER GROUPS

III.1. PRE-TRIAL AND REMAND PRISONERS

The figures in the previous section also included prisoners in pre-trial detention. Figures III.1 and III.2 display separately the share of pre-trial prisoners of the whole prison population by countries (Figure III.1) and by sub-regions (Figure III.2).

Figure III.1. Pre-trial prisoners by countries and sub-regions 2016

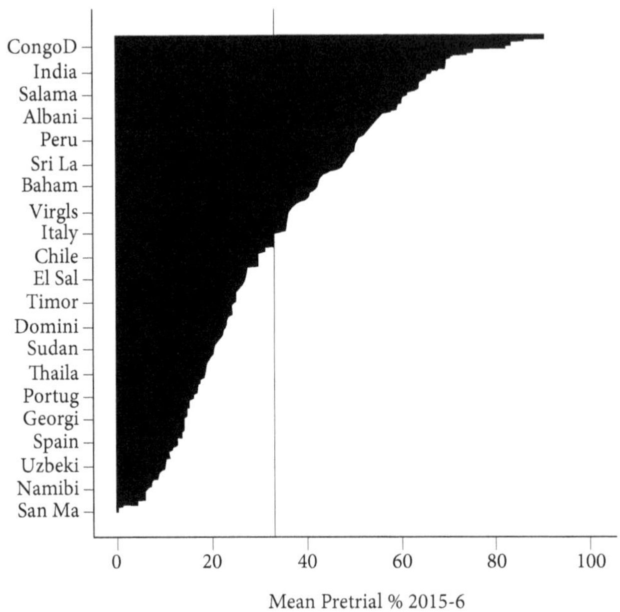

There is enormous proportional variation in the use of remand as a share of the total use of imprisonment in different countries. In the most extreme cases the share of pre-trial prisoners is close to 100%. In a substantial number of countries the share of pre-trial prisoners exceeds 60% of the total prison population.

Regional patterns emerge, too: Most African regions report exceptionally large numbers of pre-trial detainees (over 50%) while in Asia and Europe their share stays around 15-25%.

Figure III.3 compares the share of pre-trial detainees against prisoner rates (above panel) and occupancy level (below panel) with country level data.

The number of pre-trial detainees does not seem to explain the overall use of imprisonment. If anything, there seems to be a negative association between these two: a decrease in the share of pre-trial detainees corresponds to more

Figure III.2. Pre-trial prisoners (%) by continents and regions (Unweighted, pop > 100,000)

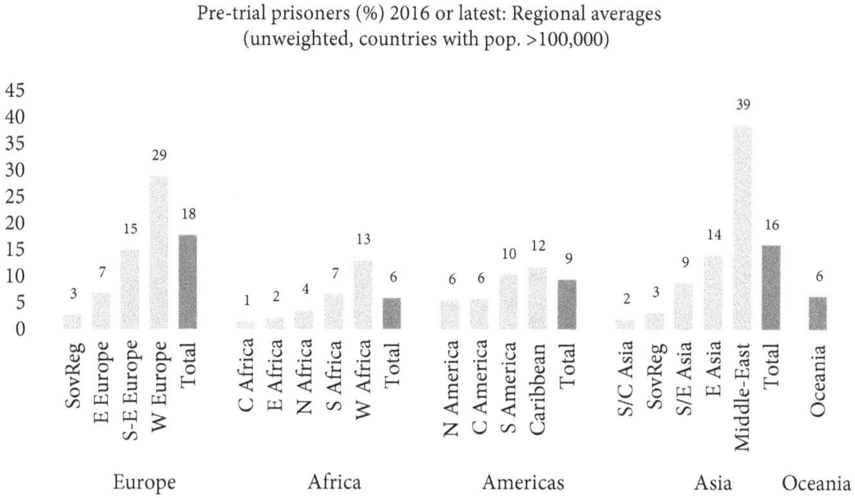

prisoners. However, occupancy level seems to be positively associated with the share of pre-trial detainees: The higher the share of pre-trial detainees, the higher the occupancy level.

These associations grew even stronger in regional analyses. Several African regions report high pre-trial shares and fairly low incarceration levels but very high overcrowding levels. In some countries and regions, overcrowding is closely associated with the overuse of pre-trial detention. This seems to be the case especially in most parts of Africa, South America and South-Central Asia. In these areas, targeted actions for reducing the use and length of pre-trial detention would work effectively against overcrowding.

III.2. FEMALE PRISONERS

Female prisoners. Figures III.4 and III.5 display the share of female prisoners of the whole prison population by countries and by regions.

The share of female prisoners varies on a country level from 1 to 25%. The share of female prisoners seems to be considerably higher in the Asian regions (8.1% in the whole of Asia, with Maldives 22%, Hong Kong 20%, and Thailand 15%). In Africa the share of females is substantially lower (3.1% in the whole of Africa). The European average of 5.3% is close to the global average of 5.1%. The highest shares in Western Europe are found in the Netherlands (8.7%), Spain (8%) and Finland (7.0%). Upon closer analysis, the share of female prisoners seems to be unrelated to the overall number of prisoners as well as to the occupancy rate.

Figure III.3. Comparisons with the share of pre-trial prisoners

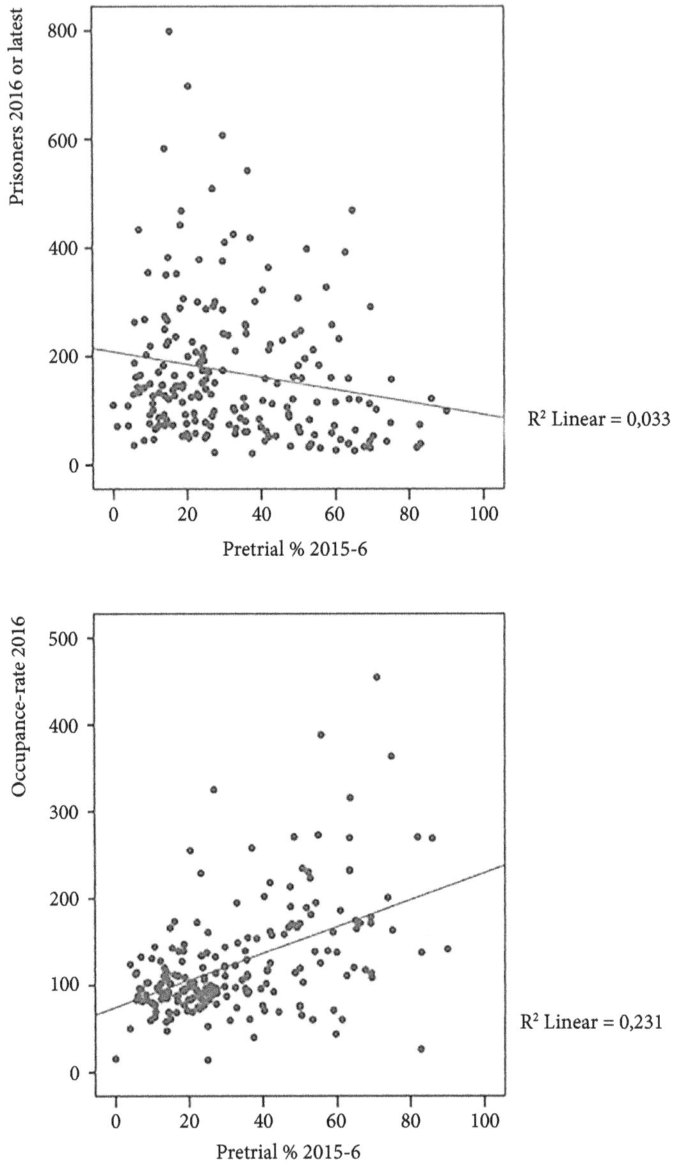

III.3. FOREIGN PRISONERS

Figures III.6 and III.7 display the share of foreign prisoners of the whole prison population by countries and by regions.

There are equally extensive differences at country level in the share of foreign prisoners. Isolated small countries exceed the level of 80%, while the overall

Figure III.4. Female prisoners by regions and continents 2015/2016

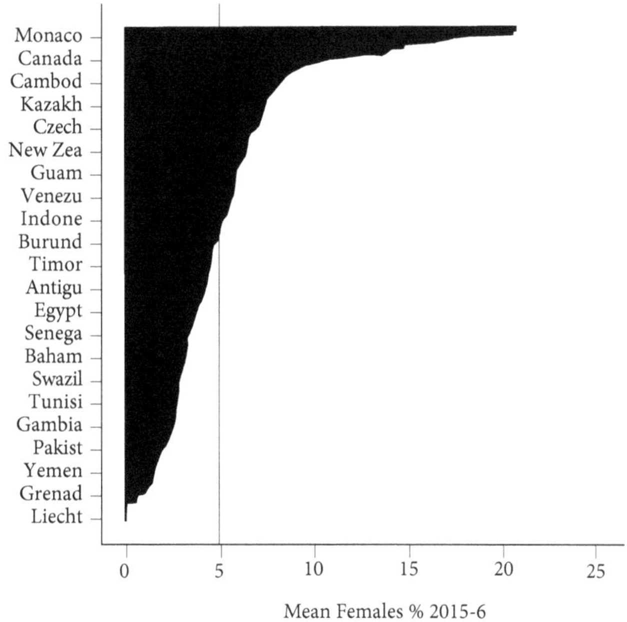

Figure III.5. Female prisoners (%) by continents and regions 2015-6 (Unweighted, pop > 100,000)

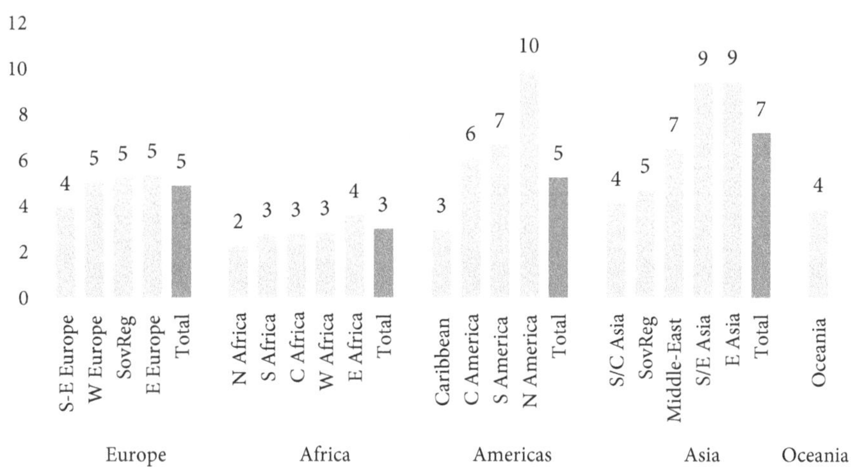

average is around 14%. The highest share of foreigners is found in Western Europe and the Middle East. The share of foreigners is lowest in Africa and former socialist countries, the former Soviet region and Oceania.

Figure III.6. Foreign prisoners by regions and continents 2015/2016

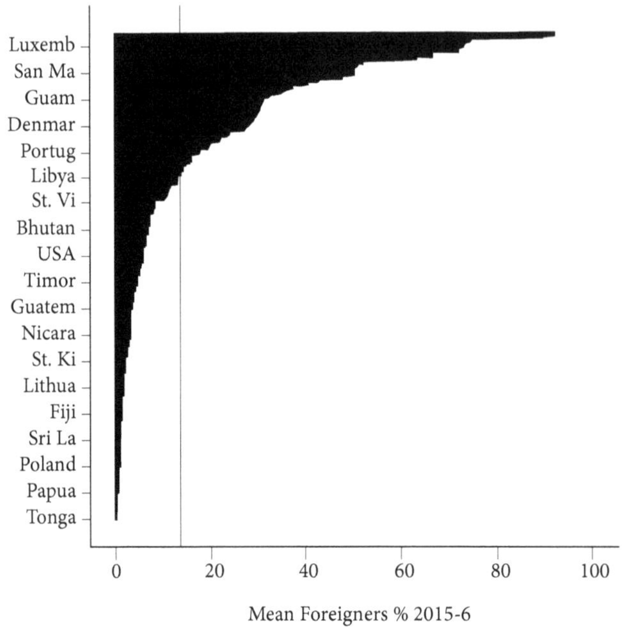

Figure III.7. Foreign prisoners (%) by continents and regions 2015-6 (Unweighted, pop > 100,000)

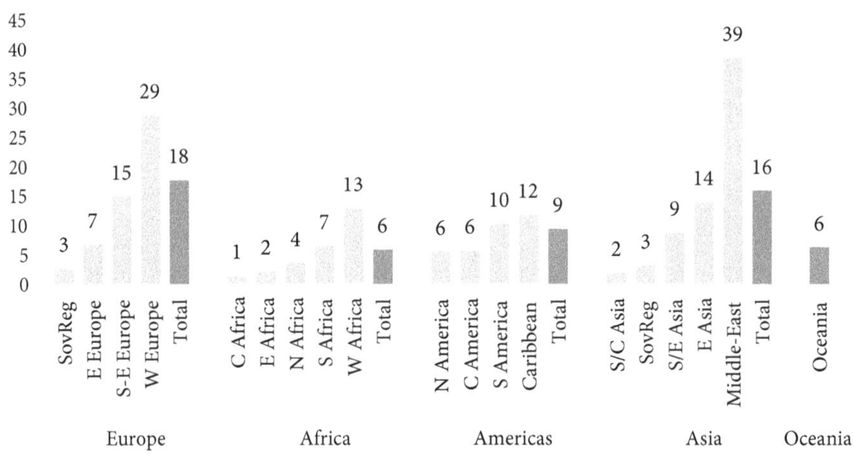

Figure III.8 illustrates the correlation between foreign prisoners, the overall prisoner rates and occupancy rate.

Figure III.8. Foreign prisoners (%) compared to total rate and occupancy rate

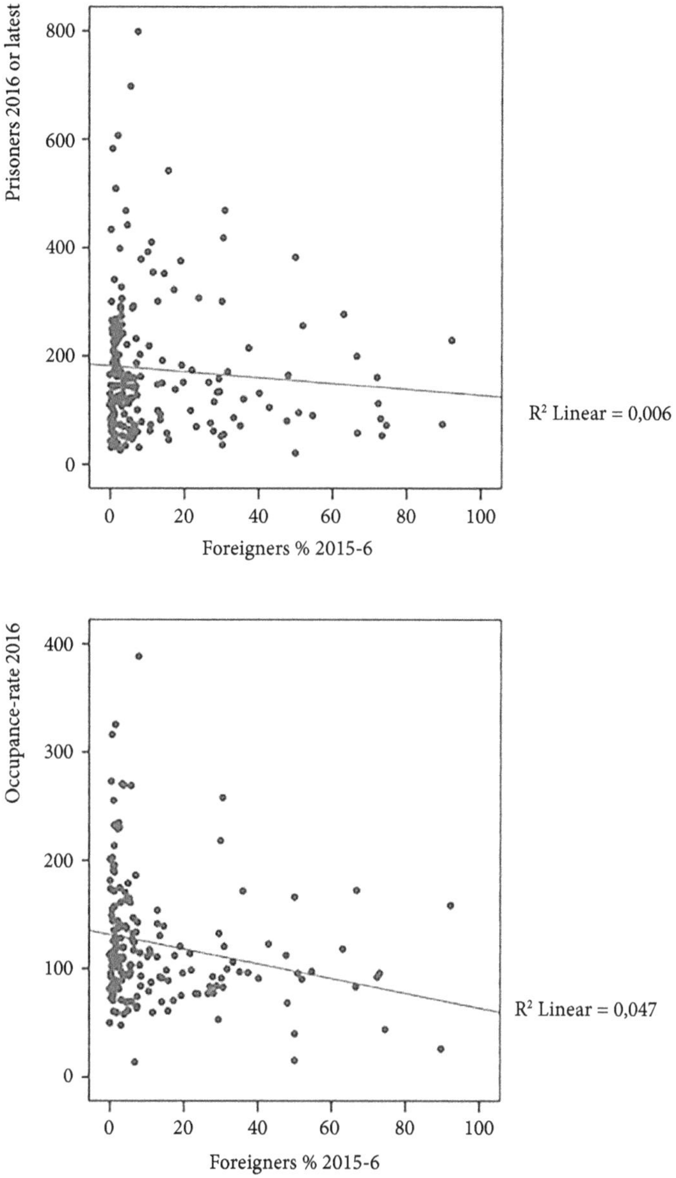

The share of foreign prisoners is unrelated to the overall prisoner rate, as well as to the occupancy rate. In fact, the higher the share of foreign prisoners, the lower the occupancy rate. In other words, the share of foreign prisoners cannot be used as a *general explanation* for overcrowding – or for high imprisonment rates, for that matter.

IV. TRENDS AND CHANGES

This chapter will examine both short-term (2004/5-2016) and longer-term trends (1960/90-2016) by continents, regions and individual countries. Regional analyses consist of three elements. (1) A table-format presentation of sub-regional means of general prisoner rates, as well as information of pre-trial, female and foreign prisoners. The table includes also information about occupancy rates, rate-based and percentual changes, and the total absolute number of prisoners in the region. (2) Aggregated regional information is complemented country-level graphic presentations of changes in 2004/5-2016. (3) After that follows longer term trends of selected countries from the 1960s onwards.

IV.1. OVERVIEW

Figure IV.1 displays percentage changes from 2004 to 2016 (or latest available) by country. Again, only countries with populations of over 100,000 inhabitants are included.

In 2004-2016 about 40% of the countries increased their prisoner rates by at least 10%. But almost as many (about 30%) decreased their rates by at least 10%. The growth of imprisonment has slowed down compared to the situation ten years earlier. In 1992/5 – 2007/8 the corresponding figures were 63% countries increasing and 19% decreasing their incarceration rates.

Figure IV.1. Changes by countries 2004-2016 (% changes)

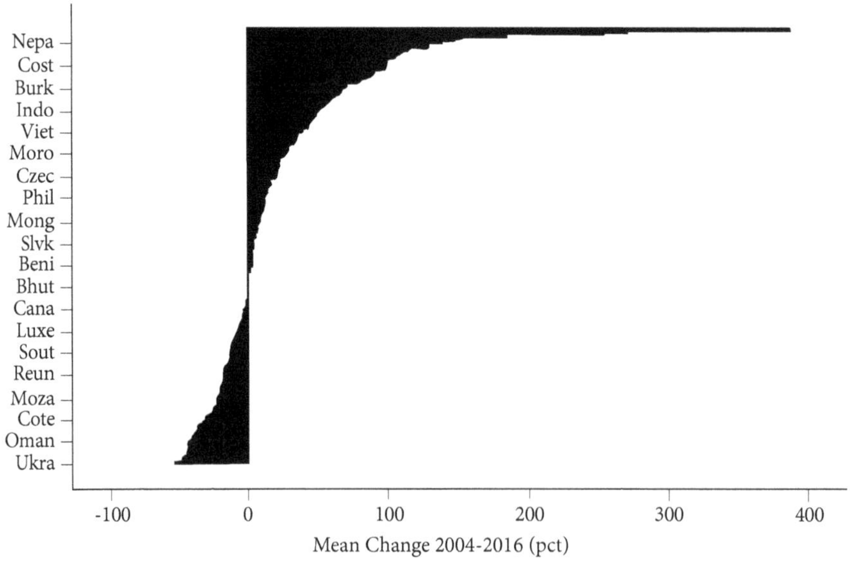

Figure IV.2. Changes by continent 2004-2016 by rates: Unweighted and weighted values

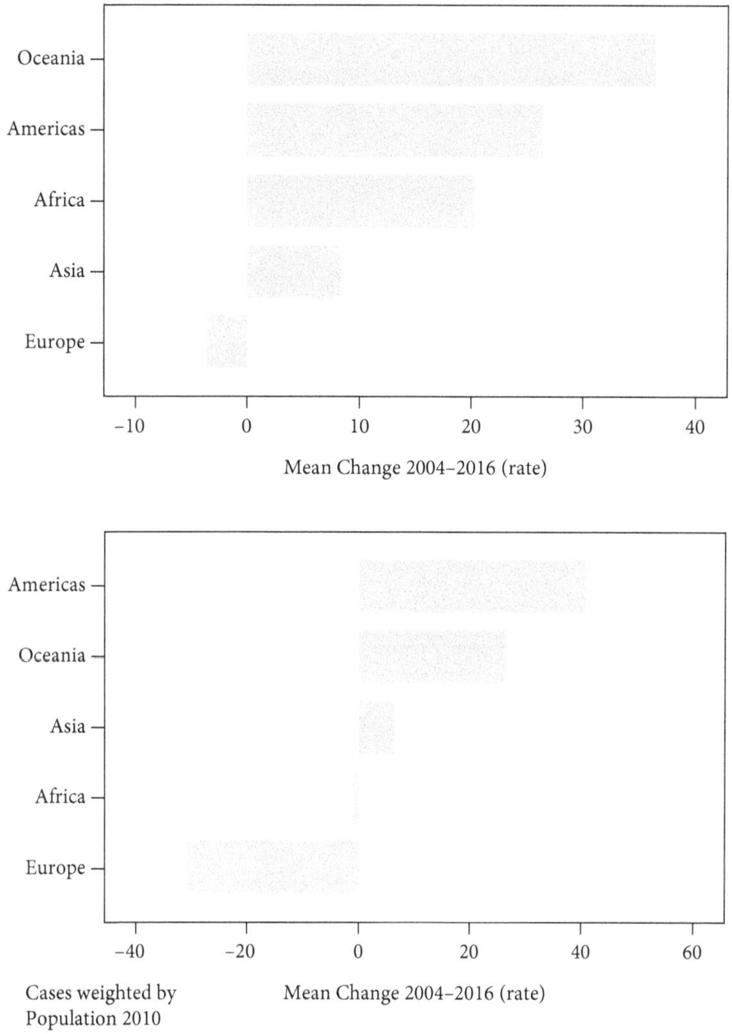

Changes can be measured also by counting unweighted global means among the same countries in different point of time. This data is available from 1992 to 2015 from 186 countries. In the early 1990s, the mean rate was 142, in the mid-2000s 168, and in 2015 182. This corresponds to an increase of about 18% in 1992-2005, and an increase of 8% in 2005-2015. The total mean percentage increase in 186 countries from the early 1990s to the mid-2010s was 28%. Imprisonment rates have still been increasing, even though the phase has slowed down.

Figure IV.3. Changes by continent 2004-2016 by %. Unweighted and weighted values

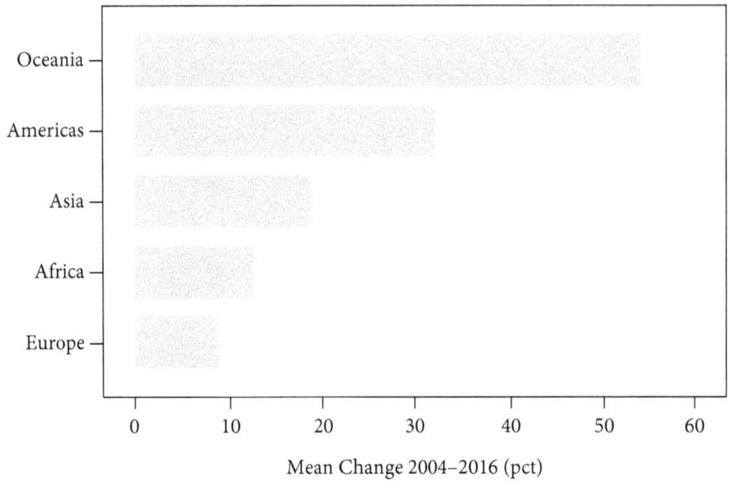

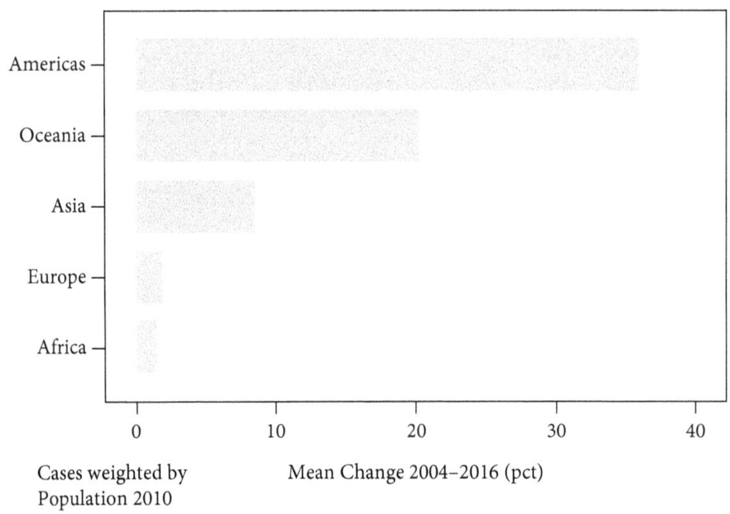

Changes by continents by rates (unweighted and weighted values) are displayed in Figure IV.2.

Imprisonment rates have increased in all continents with the exception of Europe. Rate-based changes point downwards in Europe mainly due to the decline of prison populations in Russia and countries in Former Soviet Region. The impact of Russia in the overall picture becomes visible when changes are weighted against population size. Percentual changes are displayed in Figure IV.3.

Percentual changes point upwards in all regions. This applies both to unweighted and weighted values. Opposite results in Europe between rate-based and percentual changes follows from the fact that when prisoner-rates range in the level from 300 to 600 (as in the Baltic countries and Russia) an average rate based drop of 30 prisoners/pop (weighted and only 4 prisoners unweighted) does not make much difference in terms of percentual changes.

The rest of this chapter will examine both short-term (2004/5-2016) and longer-term trends (1960/90-2016) by continent, regions and individual countries. The analyses proceeds from one continent to another starting from regions which has most complete data.

IV.2. EUROPE

Overview. Europe can be divided either roughly into Western and Eastern Europe, but we may use also more refined groupings. Most detailed one divides Western Europe into 6 blocks: Scandinavia[7], France/Benelux[8], German-speaking Europe[9], the British Isles[10], Southwest Europe[11], and Southeast Europe.[12] Eastern Europe is divided into three sub-regions: Baltic (Estonia, Latvia, Lithuania), Former socialist Europe[13], and Former Soviet Region/Europe (Armenia, Azerbaijan, Belarus, Georgia, Moldova, Russian Federation, Ukraine). The following uses different groupings depending on the analyses at hand. Basic profiles by detailed grouping are displayed in Table IV.1.

The total number of prisoners in Europe ranges around 1.6 million, of which half originate from the former Soviet region (mostly from Russia). Southeast Europe holds around 220,000 prisoners, of which well over 80% are in Turkey. In all, half of all European prisoners are either in Russian or Turkish prisons.

The Nordic countries (Scandinavia) display the lowest and decreasing rates, followed by the German speaking countries with similar trends. Steepest overall decrease has taken place in the Baltic countries and in the Former Soviet Region, however, on a fairly high level. These downward changes are, in addition, largely percentual and appear together with only modest rate-based declines (in fact, they are heavily affected by exceptional changes in few individual countries). In order to obtain a more accurate picture of recent trends, one needs to examine country-level changes.

In both Western and Eastern Europe half of the countries have increased and half of the countries have decreased their imprisonment rates since the mid-2000s; for this and the following, see Figure IV.4. Compared to this, trend in

---

7 Denmark, Finland, Iceland, Norway, Sweden.

8 Belgium, France, Luxembourg, Netherlands.

9 Austria, Germany, Switzerland.

10 Ireland, England & Wales, Northern Ireland, Scotland.

11 Italy, Malta, Portugal, Slovenia, Spain.

12 Albania, Bosnia and Herzegovina, Croatia, Cyprus, Greece, Kosovo, Macedonia (former Yugoslav Republic of), Montenegro, Northern Cyprus, Serbia, Turkey.

13 Bulgaria, Czech Republic, Hungary, Poland, Romania, Slovakia.

Table IV.1. Imprisonment profiles by sub-regions in Europe 2016 (or latest available data). Only countries with total population over 100,000

Sub-region	Prisoners / pop	Pre-trial %	Females %	Foreigners %	Occupancy rate	Prisoners (N, 1000s)	Change 2004-16 (rate)	Change 2004-16 (%)
Scandinavia	58	23.1	5.2	25.0	92.0	16	-6.4	-6.8
France/ Benelux	96	35.6	4.3	40.0	101.5	91	-9.8	-6.1
German speaking Europe	85	27.0	5.5	50.3	91.6	77	-11.3	-10.8
British Isles	113	17.9	4.2	9.6	97.3	99	5.3	5.0
Southwest Europe	112	19.9	5.9	26.2	101.5	132	15.8	24.3
Southeast Europe	131	26.2	3.9	15.0	103.4	217	43.6	43.5
Baltic	241	21.3	5.3	13.6	79.6	15	-68.0	-18.1
Former socialist Europe	172	13.6	5.4	3.4	99.5	159	0.2	0.7
Former Soviet Reg	258	19.9	5.2	2.7	90.4	790	-60.7	-1.2
Total	145	22.5	4.9	17.8	96.6	1.6 m	-4.2	9.8

South East Europe has been much more systematic: all countries have experienced increased rates, usually by 40% of more. In Former Soviet Region one finds several countries with strong percentual decreases, but also countries with substantial relative drops in their prison populations. Figure IV.5 shows the actual imprisonment rates in 2016 (pillars), as compared to 2004/5 (dots).

Trends in Western Europe. Imprisonment rates in six western European countries in 1960-2016 are displayed in Figure IV.6.

Within the Nordic cluster, imprisonment rates in Denmark, Sweden, and Norway have remained both low and relatively stable since 1960, with rates bounded by 40 to 70 per 100,000. Finland has followed a different course. From the early 1960s Finland reduced its prison rate from 160 per 100,000 to a little over 60 in the early 1990s. The background for these changes is discussed elsewhere in this volume.[14] Since the early 2000s, all four Nordic countries have experienced a short upward spurt in imprisonment rates, followed by a smooth drop. Patterns of regional alignment can also be seen in Germany, Austria, and

14 See the national report of Finland.

Figure IV.4. Rate-based changes by sub-regions and countries 2004-2016: Europe

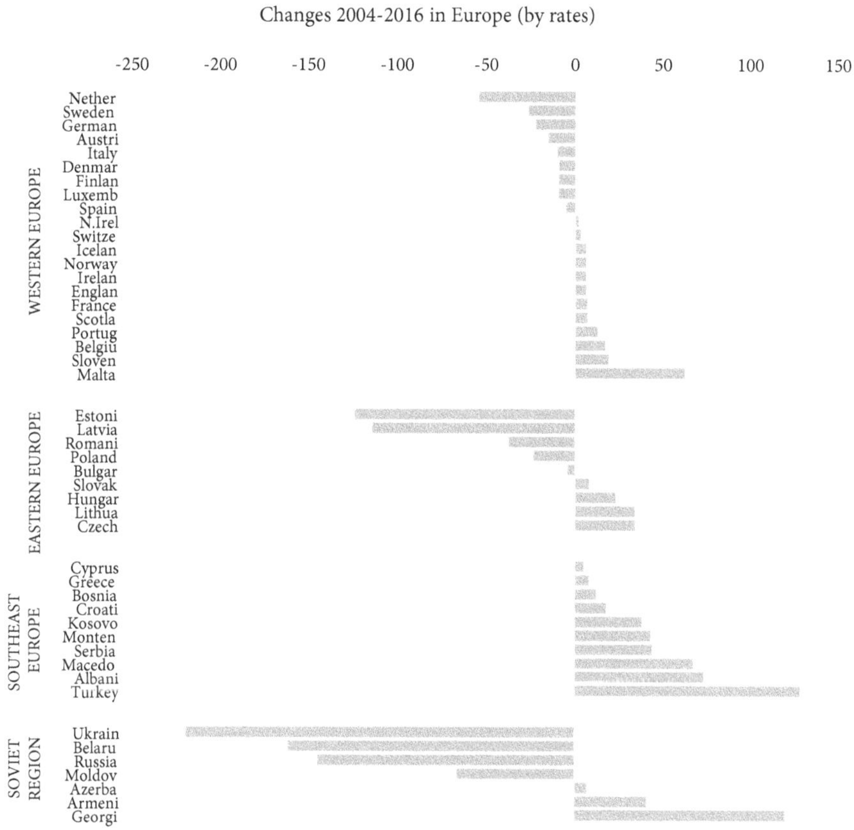

Switzerland. These three German-speaking countries all have roughly comparable prison rates, with a bandwidth of 75 to 100 per 100,000. Imprisonment rates have also remained fairly stable. Germany started from a rate of around 100 per 100,000 in 1962, but experienced two short-term declines. The first decline, in the late 1960s, was mainly due to the replacement of short-term prison sentences with the then newly adopted day-fines. The second drop, in the early 1980s, resulted mainly from the reduced use of pre-trial detention, the expansion of suspended sentences and youth justice reforms (see Dünkel & Morgenstern 2010). Both periods of decline were followed by a nearly equivalent period of growth. Despite such peaks, Germany had about the same incarceration rate in 1971, 1992, and 2013.

Over the last 50 years, Belgium, France, and the Netherlands have seen a substantial increase in incarceration, although their paths have been somewhat different. France and Belgium witnessed a slow but steady increase from around 60 to 90 or 100 in a period of 50 years. The latest period of increase in France

Figure IV.5. Changes and rates by sub-regions and countries 2004-2016: Europe

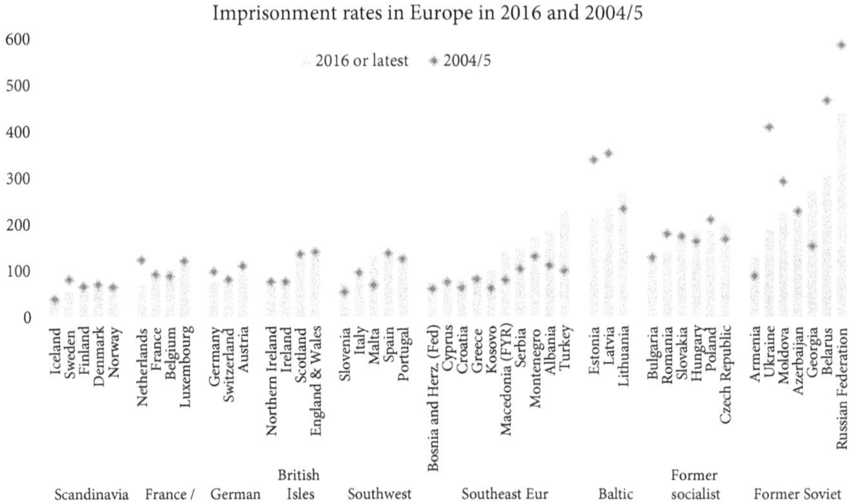

Figure IV.6. Imprisonment rates by sub-regions and countries 1960-2015: Western Europe

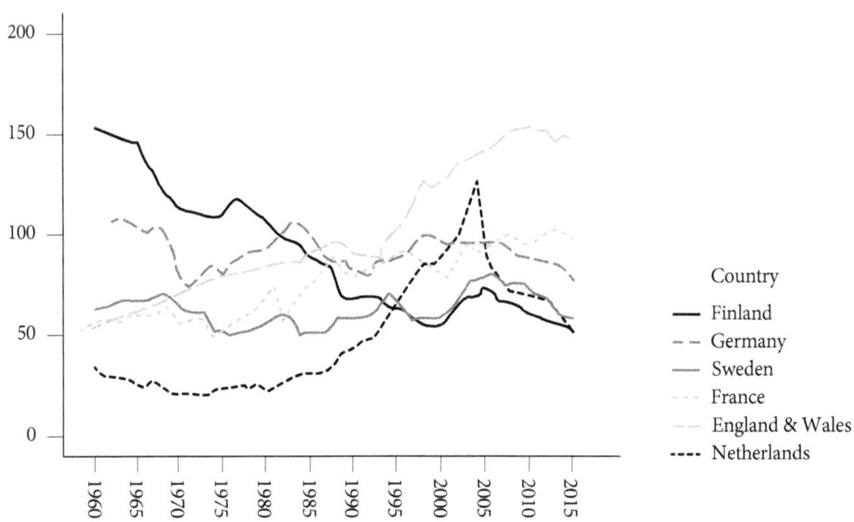

took off after the 2002 presidential campaigns focused on security and zero-tolerance, and under the influence of Nicolas Sarkozy, first as minister of the interior (2002-2007) and then as president of the Republic (2007-2012). This period is characterized by new criminalizations, the introduction of minimum sentences, formerly unknown to the French system, as well as the possibility of additional supervision of offenders on medical ground after completion of the sentence. In 2000 and 2014 the total number of prisoners rose from 51,000 (85/pop) to 67,000 (102/pop). For a lengthy period, French imprisonment rates were regulated partly by mass pardons, which took traditionally place every year on Bastille Day. This practice was ended through a constitutional reform in 2007. The most recent figures indicate a downward trend, possibly influenced by a reform in 2014 intended to take back some of the changes made during the Sarkozy period.[15]

The most radical swings in prison policy have taken place in the Netherlands. After a relatively long period of very low rates (around 20 to 30 prisoners per 100,000 up to the 1970s), the Netherlands saw an accelerating pace of growth starting in the 1980s to the early 2000s, peaking at a rate around 110, followed by an equally sharp decrease back to the level of around 60.[16] The increase was mainly a result of stiffer sentencing practices and the changed mood of penal policy. The mid-1980s were the turning point, when the ministry of justice published a policy document in response to public and political concern about rising crime and the ineffectiveness of the Dutch criminal justice system. Stiffer actions, more control and less discretion for the administration of criminal justice was promised. In 1985-1995 the length of prison sentences increased by 50% and the total amount of sentenced prison years doubled (Boone & Moerings, 2010, and in more detail Downes & Swaaningen, 2007). Even after the crime rate in the Netherlands started to level off, the use of imprisonment continued to rise. The political focus remained on crime and security, on both the left and the right. Crime and criminal policy became standard parts of electoral manifestos. Incidents such as the murder of populist political leader Pim Fortuyn in 2002 and the film-director Theo van Gogh in 2004 contributed to what commentators call a "social climate of fear and rancor" (Boone & Swaaningen 2013 p. 11). Dutch drug policy also shifted towards tougher enforcement. The next turning point occurred in the mid-2000s. By 2016 imprisonment rates have fallen by over 50% (from around 120 to 60). This decrease has been attributed to the general decline in crime (decrease in the number of convicted offenders) and new prosecution guidelines promoting the use of community service in place of short prison sentences (Boone & Swaaningen 2013). Whether this decline can also be interpreted as a sign of a new, more tolerant penal climate, however, is disputed. Critical commentators point out examples of more punitive orientation in other fields of crime policy, the scope of criminalization and in the enforcement of sanctions that are targeted especially at outsiders, including Muslims, irregular migrants and possible terrorists, while reformative and inclusive policies are reserved for a "relatively successful, harmless group of white offenders", while

15 For the French development, see in more detail Hodgson & Soubise 2016.

16 Counting rules for the Dutch prisoner rates have undergone changes that complicate comparisons over time. For discussion, see Lappi-Seppälä 2017.

those that would probably profit most are not qualified for them (Boone & Swaaningen 2013 p. 28-29).

The British Isles have seen constant and ongoing increases in prison populations. Over the full 50-year history, there is visible similarity in trends among England and Wales, Scotland and Ireland (see Lappi-Seppälä 2013). The growth in England and Wales and in Scotland is clearly the result of increasingly punitive governmental strategies that have expanded not only the use of custodial sanctions, but also the introduction of ever more demanding community measures and non-criminal interventions (such as Anti-Social Behaviour Orders in England and Wales). England & Wales and Scotland have tripled their rates from around 50 in the early 1960s to 150 (Dignan & Cavadino, 2010).

Trends in Southern Europe. Figures for seven South- and South-Eastern European countries are displayed in Figure IV.7.

Figure IV.7. Imprisonment rates by sub-regions and countries 1990-2015: Southern and South-Eastern Europe

Most countries report increasing trends. The steepest increases have taken place at the borders of South East Europe. The changes have been most radical in Turkey, where the rates have grown from the level of 73 in 2000 to the present 285 (2017). This change has been a direct result of increasingly punitive policies with prolonged prison terms, restriction of parole and prolonged remand periods (Coyle et al., 2016 p. 54). But that is not all. Prisons are also being used increasingly for political purposes, as the attempted coup in 2016 prompted a massive government crackdown against civil servants and civil society. Over 40,000 people were remanded in pre-trial detention during six months of emergency rule.[17] In three years' time the total number of prisoners increased from 158,837 (2014) to 229,790 (2017, 45% increase). Along with Turkey, countries in Western Balkans have also seen an increase in prison populations. This applies especially to Albania, Serbia, Macedonia and Croatia. These countries have at least doubled or tripled their imprisonment rates. Increases have been much more modest in two outliers, Slovenia and Bosnia & Herzegovina.[18]

In Southwestern Europe, Spain has more than tripled its prison population rates from a little below 50 in the early 1980s to 160 in 2010. The changes in the 1980s have been attributed mainly to an increase in crime (and due to the lack of alternatives to custodial sanctions, see Cid & Larrauri, 2010). Another upswing took place after a short stable period in the mid-1995. This change has been connected to a criminal law reform that restricted the use of early release (good time reduction) and increased minimum penalties for several basic offenses (Cid & Larrauri 2010). Portugal doubled its incarceration rates in the 1990s, but in the 2000s there has been a clear downward trend. This decline has been attributed to a change in the national drug policy. In 2001 the possession and use of all drugs was decriminalized and criminal sanctions replaced with public health interventions. This resulted in a major decrease in imposed prison sentences, also visible in incarceration statistics.

Shifts in Italy are deeper and more sudden than elsewhere in the region. The trends have pointed upwards, but have been interrupted by sharp declines caused by amnesties, the major device used by the government to ease the pressures created by increasing prisoner rates. By the early 2000s, law and order campaigns had become a standard part of elections and penal policies became increasingly punitive. The following increase in national prisoner rates was tempered by a massive amnesty and collective pardon in 2006, with only temporary results. However, since 2010 the rates have been declining. This decline has been attributed to responses to condemnatory verdicts from the ECtHR from 2009 and 2013. The use of early release has been expanded and overreliance on pre-trial detention curbed. Sentences for soft drugs have been reduced and opportunities to enforce custodial sentences outside prison have been improved (see Corda 2016 p. 111-112).

Trends in Eastern Europe and Former Soviet Region. Eastern Europe is divided into two regions: the Baltic countries and former socialist countries in Central Europe, and countries that were Soviet Socialist Republics in the Soviet Union; see Figures IV.8 and IV.9.

17 https://www.amnesty.org/en/countries/europe-and-central-asia/turkey/report-turkey/
18 But most probably, for different reasons. For Slovenian trends, see Dunkel 2017 with references.

Figure IV.8. Imprisonment rates by sub-regions and countries 1990-2015: Eastern Europe

The Baltic countries were also part of the Soviet Union, which is also visible in the graph. Starting rates in these countries were markedly higher compared to the old socialist countries in Eastern Europe. During the first years of independence, Estonia, Latvia and Lithuania all increased their imprisonment rates. This was mainly attributable to a radical increase in crime: in Lithuania robberies rose ten-fold and the rates of most violent and property offences increased rapidly. However, both countries managed to reduce their prison populations during the 2000s, partly by introducing new alternatives to imprisonment and by extending the use of early release (for Estonia, see Markina & Sootak, 2010 and for Lithuania Dobryianis & Sakalauskas, 2011). The decline was especially deep in Lithuania, associated with a penal reform in 2003. However, since 2009 policies have taken another turn. The very recent trend in these countries is, again, pointing downwards.

In the rest of Eastern Europe trends have been fairly stable since 1990s (but fluctuated greatly before that, see Lappi-Seppälä 2013). In Poland a major increase took place in the early 2000s. This was mostly a result of stiffening social and political pressures for tougher punishments, as the political atmosphere switched from "liberal optimism" to the "tough-on-crime" rhetoric of the 2000s (Krajewski 2016 p. 178). The new penal code of 1997, which aimed to reduce sentences, was attacked in the media and by politicians for its excessive leniency and became the target of several changes in the 2000s. Details in the sentencing system, such as rigid revocation rules for community sanctions, have also played an important role (Stando-Kawecka & Krajewski 2010, Krajewski 2016). Subsequent changes in Hungary from the mid-1990s onwards follow much the same path. An increase from the levels of 120 to 180 coincides with high fear of crime by European standards, as well as by increasingly punitive political

Figure IV.9. Imprisonment rates by sub-regions and countries 1992-2015: Former Soviet Region

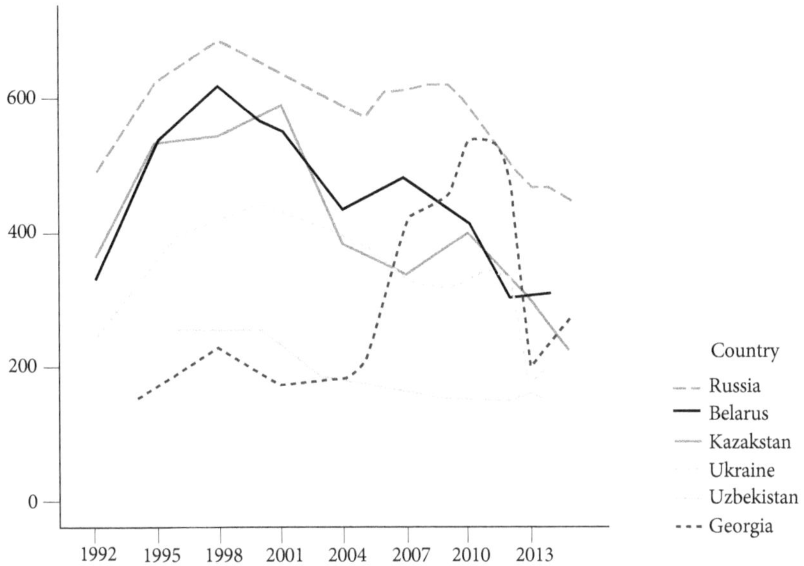

discourse, marked by racial stereotyping of Hungary's Roma and Gypsy communities in the media and the political rhetoric of the radical right-wing Jobbik party. The 2010 elections were won by the Centre-right Fidez party with a tough-on-crime program, and the reforms that followed included mandatory life sentences for habitual offenders committing serious violent crimes, a reduction in the age of criminal responsibility from 14 to 12 years for certain more serious crimes and the expansion of imprisonment for fine default (Nagy 2010; Jacobson et al 2017 p. 19-20).

Of the countries in the region, Bulgaria has kept its rates relatively stable, whereas Romania has experienced a steep decrease of around 50% in 2002-2010. Part of this decrease may be attributed to the EU accession process, and the requirements related to prison services and the treatment of prisoners.

The *Former Soviet Region* includes Russia and former socialist republics of the Soviet Union (Belarus, Ukraine, Armenia, Azerbaijan, Kazakhstan, Kyrgyzstan, Tajikistan, Turkmenistan, and Uzbekistan). Part of these countries belong to Europe (Armenia, Azerbaijan, Belarus, Georgia, Moldova, and Ukraine), part of them are defined as being part of Asia (Afghanistan, Kazakhstan, Kyrgyzstan, Tajikistan, Turkmenistan and Uzbekistan).

Regime changes in all these countries in the early 1990s led to drastic increases in imprisonment rates (as well as homicide rates, see Lappi-Seppälä & Lehti 2014). Since the late 1990s, rates have generally been decreasing. The downward trend is most visible in Russia, Belarus, Kazakhstan and Kyrgyzstan. All these countries also experienced declines in homicide of about 50-70% in 2000-2015 (see Lappi-Seppälä & Lehti 2014). The number of all convicted offenders fell in Russia from 1.2 million in 2000 to about 720,000 in 2014. The fall of the Russian prison population resulted from a decline in the number of convictions, not because of a real change of policy. One additional factor, according to Dünkel (2017 p. 640), influencing the trends in the 2010 is the militarisation of Russia at the time of the war with Ukraine and in general since the conflict with NATO. This has resulted in massive drafting of young men into the army. Further explanations include pressures from the Council of Europe and the decisions of ECtHR (130-140 convictions/year). Much the same applies to Belarus and Ukraine (ibid p. 640-641).

Georgia displays sharp increases and declines. The country almost tripled its imprisonment rates from 2005 to 2010 to the same levels with Russia. The increase took off after the regime change in 2004 (the Rose revolution). The country suffered first from internal conflicts in 2004, and later got into a war with Russia in 2008. Both episodes may have had some impact on imprisonment rates. Still, the main reason for this increase was the authoritarian regime and tough anti-crime and anti-corruption policy of Mikheil Saakashvili (the elected president after the Rose revolution). The steep decline of over 50% in 2013 resulted from several amnesties. These amnesties were preceded by an exceptional prison scandal caused by videos released in social media and later in national TV channels of brutal rapes of prisoners in Glandi prison. The prison director was removed from his office and the ministry of justice resigned from his post. The ensuing protests and public outcry presumably also resulted in Saakashvili's party losing power in the next elections.

IV.3. AMERICAS AND THE CARIBBEAN

The American continent is divided into three main blocks: North America[19], Central America[20], and South America.[21] In addition, the region includes the Caribbean islands, consisting of x small Island states in all, of which 16 hold a population of over 100,000 inhabitants.[22] Regional data is provided in Table IV.2.

The region has the highest overall regional mean incarceration rates. The region is also troubled by serious overcrowding with regional mean occupancy

19 Canada, United States of America.

20 Belize, Costa Rica, El Salvador, Guatemala, Honduras, Mexico, Nicaragua, Panama.

21 Argentina, Bolivia, Brazil, Chile, Colombia, Ecuador, Guyane (France), Guyana, Paraguay, Peru, Suriname, Uruguay, Venezuela.

22 Aruba (Netherlands), Bahamas, Barbados, Cuba, Dominican Republic, Grenada, Guadeloupe, Haiti, Jamaica, Martinique, Puerto Rico (USA), St Lucia, St Vincent and the Grenadines, Trinidad and Tobago, Virgin Islands (United Kingdom), Virgin Islands (USA).

Table IV.2. Imprisonment profiles by sub-regions in the Americas 2016 (or latest available data). Only countries with total population over 100,000

Sub-region	Prisoners / pop	Pre-trial %	Females %	Foreigners %	Occupancy rate	Prisoners (N, 1000s)	Change 2004-16 (rate)	Change 2004-16 (%)
North America	402	27.8	10.0	5.5	99.6	2.3 m	-13.5	-2.7
Central America	295	36.4	6.1	5.7	172.1	353	78.3	58.7
South America	216	52.8	6.7	10.3	154.3	1.0 m	61.2	55.0
Caribbean	310	40.9	3.0	11.8	140.9	121	-0.9	25.2
Total	280	43.1	5.3	9.4	149.9	3.8 m	35.4	40.6

rates ranging between 140-170%, with the exception of North America. Those sub-regions with worst overcrowding have also experience steep percentual and rate-based increases. Country level date is provided in Figure IV.10.

Trends in North America. North America is the home of two outlier nations of very different natures. While the U.S. curve shares a consistent upward slope since late 1970s unparalleled on an absolute scale with any western nation, Canada, in contrast, is an outlier for its *nonparticipation* in the thrust toward punitive expansionism in the Anglophone countries. See Figure IV.11.

The US incarceration rates and penal change has been a widely analysed topic in criminological literature from the mid-1980s onwards. Explanations for the "American exceptionalism" vary from technical descriptions to historical, sociological, cultural and political analyses. In a technical sense the growth of the US prison population is a result of policy decisions and changes in judicial practices towards increased use of prison and longer sentences. This has the form of new mandatory minimum sentences (including the "three strikes laws"), by stricter guidance of sentencing through guidelines, and through more restricted use of parole and early release. The US was the first country to place crime and crime control on the highest political platforms in the 1960s, when President Johnson declared the "War on Crime", with the "War on Drugs" (Reagan) and the "War on Terror" (George W. Bush) following. Explanations for the salience of crime and crime control in the US politics have thereafter been sought in the specifics of American democratic processes (high polarization, but at the same time high localism and large number of elected officials in public offices), historical and cultural traditions, increase of mass criminality and socio-

Figure IV.10. Changes and rates by sub-regions and countries 2004-2016: Americas

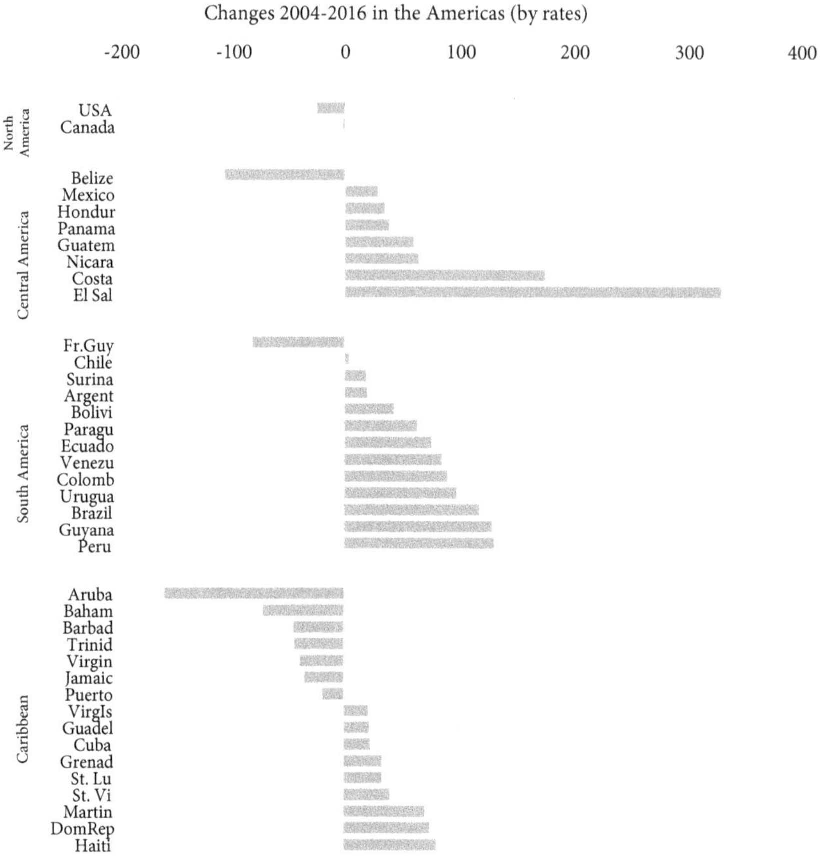

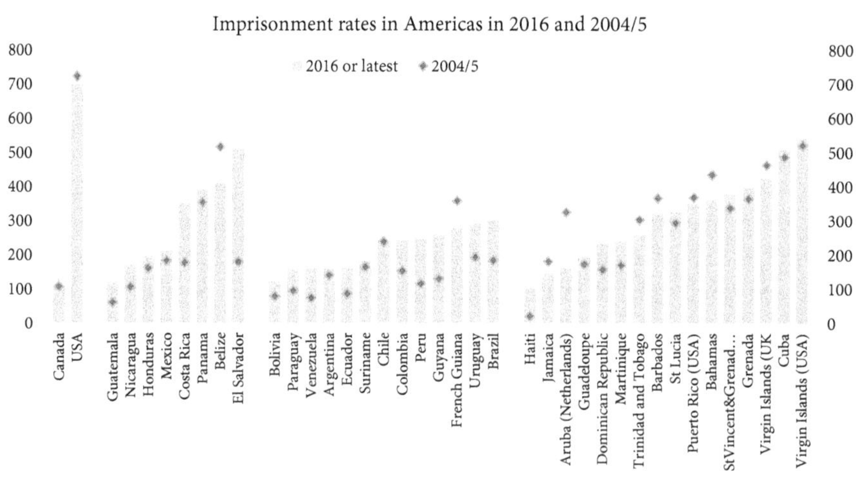

Figure IV.11. Imprisonment rates by countries 1960-2015: North America (USA and Canada)

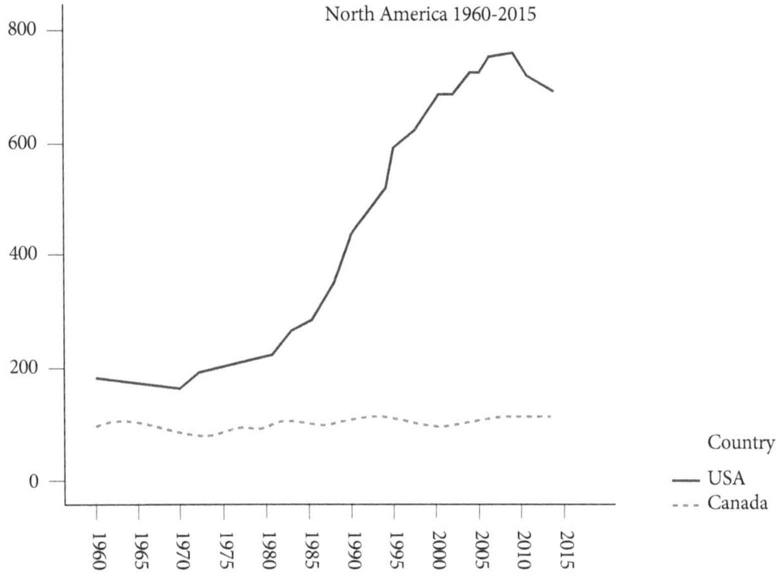

economic structures and insecurities.[23] This expansion seems to have reached its peak in 2010. Since then rates have been declining, most probably due to fiscal pressures and declining crime rather than humanitarian arguments.

As a stark contrast to the US, the closest neighbour, Canada, has maintained incarceration rates at a stable level of around 100 per 100,000 across the entire period. This "Canadian exceptionalism", in turn, has been attributed to the lack of many of the above-mentioned features in the US, as well as its strong European ties and traditions, different value-structures, and different ideological and mental attitudes as regards issues related to crime and the treatment of criminals.[24]

Trends in Central America. The eight Central American countries in Figure IV.12 have all increased their imprisonment rates. The average increase since the early 1990s in the region has been about 130%. The most drastic changes have taken place in El Salvador and Costa Rica. The largest country in the region, Mexico, has also doubled its incarceration rates.

23 Classic work in the field is Garland 2001. See also Wacquant 2010, Hinton 2016, and for a recent collection of works see Reitz 2017.

24 For a comparison of incarceration history in Canada and the US with stress on mental and ideological differences, see Webster and Doob (2017). For explanations stressing also structural and political arguments, see Webster & Doob 2007.

Figure IV.12. Imprisonment rates by countries 1992-2016: South and Central America

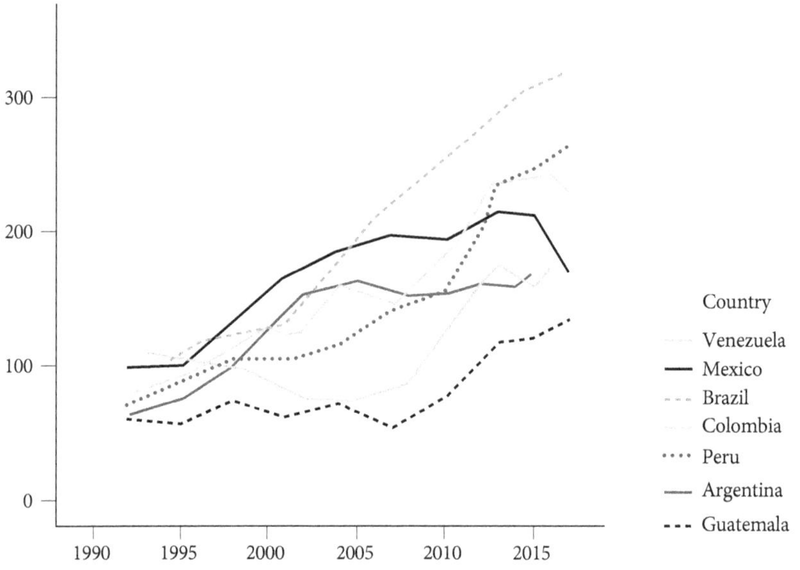

Trends in South America. The picture is pretty much the same in South America. All countries in the region have either doubled or tripled their prisoner rates since the early 1990s. The steepest increases have taken place in Brazil, Paraguay, Venezuela, Ecuador, Peru and Colombia. At the moment Chile is the only country in the region showing downward tendencies.

Brazil currently has the fourth largest total prison population (over 600,000 people) in the world and a prison population rate of 301. Brazilian imprisonment rates have tripled since the mid-1990s. The conditions in Brazilian prisons have been characterized as a 'human rights disaster' (Human Rights Watch 2015), with a history of serious outbreaks of violence and riots with several victims (during a riot in 1992 111 prisoners were killed and in the most recent massacre in 2017 there were 56 victims, see Jacobson et al 2017 p. 8-9). Prisons are largely run by the prisoners themselves, in a complex form of "inmate self-governance", which includes even the organizing of drug trafficking, extortion and prostitution operations across large swathes of the country (Miraglia, 2015). High incarceration rates coincide with high homicide rates (around 25 victims / 100,000 population, compared to around 1/pop Western Europe). Much of the recent increase in incarceration has followed new drug laws (in 2006) that led to a wide-scale imprisonment of first-time offenders for relatively low-level drugs offences. This has led to a rise in the number of people incarcerated for drug trafficking from 33,000 in 2005 to 138,000 in 2013. Another factor contributing to this increase was a high proportion of pre-trial prisoners (around 40%), brought about by inefficient judicial processes, lack of legal representation and the denial

Figure IV.13. Imprisonment rates by countries 1992-2016: The Caribbean

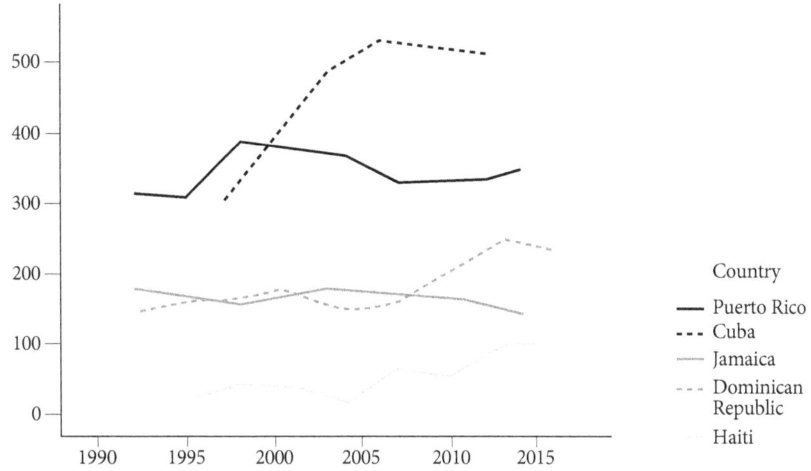

of bail in drug-related offences, as well as discriminatory judicial practices (see Jacobson et al 2017 p. 9-10 with references).

Caribbean. The Caribbean states in Figure IV.13 consist of both small, wealthy tourist regions (such as Bahamas and Barbados) and of poor countries like Haiti and Jamaica. The region is much burdened by the illicit drug industry, political unrest and high levels of lethal violence (as is also the case in parts of Latin America more generally). Imprisonment rates also range in the region from the low level of below 100 in Haiti to over 500 in the Barbados. In most cases the trend has been upwards, with the exception of stable and declining trends in the Bahamas and Jamaica.

IV.4. ASIA AND MIDDLE EAST

The joint region of Asia and the Middle East (which extends partly to North Africa) covers a huge geographical area, starting from the borders of Europe and reaching all the way to the Oceanian Islands. Countries also vary in terms of their size (China, India) and economic development (Hong Kong, Singapore). In terms of political development during the last half century, the countries include both stable countries (Japan, Hong Kong, Singapore), as well as crisis-ridden countries (for example Thailand, Sri Lanka, Myanmar, Iran). In the following the region is

Table IV.3. Imprisonment profiles by sub-regions in Asia and Middle East 2016 (or latest available data). Only countries with total population over 100,000

Sub-region	Prisoners / pop	Pre-trial %	Females %	Foreigners %	Occupancy rate	Prisoners (N, 1000s)	Change 2004-16 (rate)	Change 2004-16 (%)
Former Soviet Reg/ Asia	219	17.6	4.7	3.2	73.0	160	-6.5	40.3
Middle East	136	41.2	6.5	38.5	114.6	172	16.6	22.0
South-central Asia	128	57.0	4.1	1.9	162.7	831	12.1	19.3
East Asia	158	17.7	9.4	14.0	92.9	1.8 m	-8.7	-6.2
Southeast Asia	152	25.6	9.4	8.8	152.9	893	16.1	24.3
Total	154	32.4	7.2	15.9	124.4	3.9 m	8.2	18.9

divided into two blocks. One consists of the Middle East[25] and South-central Asia[26], and the other covers East Asia[27] and Southeast Asia.[28] Oceania, while being part of the same geographical area in south, is discussed separately together with Africa (below section IV.5).

Sub-regional profiles differ, as Table IV.3 shows. The Former Soviet Region has the highest overall incarceration rate, but lowest occupation rate (for explanations, see above) and inconsistent trends (increase by percentages by decrease by rates). Much of these findings are explainable by the instability of the region, which is visible in the short-term radical shifts in the number of prison populations (see below for comments). With the exception of East Asia, other regions have experienced both percentual and rate based increases. For details, see Figure IV.14.

Trends in East Asia and Southeast Asia. Southeast Asian figures (Figure IV.15) are dominated by high and increasing incarceration rates in Thailand from 1992 to 2001 and again since 2007. The latter increase started after a steep drop from 2000 to 2003. These changes are related to drug policy and the use of royal pardons. The increase from 1992 to 2001 resulted from stiffer penalties for

25 Bahrain, Iraq, Israel, Jordan, Kuwait, Lebanon, Oman, Qatar, Saudi Arabia, Syria, United Arab Emirates, Yemen.

26 Bangladesh, India, Iran, Maldives, Nepal, Pakistan, Sri Lanka.

27 Bhutan, China, Hong Kong, Japan, Macau, Mongolia, North Korea, Republic of (South) Korea, Taiwan.

28 Brunei Darussalam, Cambodia, Indonesia, Laos, Malaysia, Myanmar, Philippines, Singapore, Thailand, Timor-Leste, Vietnam.

methamphetamine users, the following decline by the replacement of prison sentences for drug addicts with treatment orders in 2002 and two sets of pardons in 2004 and 2006. The new increase from 2006 was a result of a new "Drug War Policy" instigated by the Thai government in 2003. By the beginning of the 2010s, well over half of the prisoners (over 70% according to some sources) were serving sentences for drug-related offenses.[29] The last decline was a result of a massive pardon by the new King in December 2016, involving 100,000 prisoners of whom 30,000 were released and 70,000 had their sentences reduced.[30] Female prisoners are over-represented in Thailand (14% against the global mean of 5%), and four out of five of them have been sentenced for drug offenses.

Other countries in the region show much more moderate policies, both in terms of levels and trends. Singapore has been able to reduce its imprisonment rates after a steep period of increasing imprisonment rates during the 1990s – from the level of 400 in 2005 to around 220. Even so, according to the statistics by the Singapore Prison Service, drug offenders constituted 70% of the total prison population in 2016.[31]

East Asia. East Asian countries (Figure IV.15) range from the low figures in Japan of around 50 to over 250 in Taiwan and Mongolia. Both Japan and China display relative stable trends (figures for China, however, do not include persons held in labour camps). Both Hong Kong and South Korea have been able to reduce prison figures over the last 20 years, whereas Taiwan and Macao have gone in the opposite direction.

South-central Asia. The second most populated country in the world, India (Figure IV.16), has over 400,000 prisoners (5th in world order), but rates relative to population (over 1.2 billion) are low and stable. The prison profile in India, however is both peculiar and problematic. Almost 70% of prisoners are waiting for trial in remand. On the other hand, over half of prisoners serving a sentence have been sentenced to life imprisonment and almost 30% are serving terms of

29 The impact of the new policy was first stalled by pardons (in 2007, 30,000 prisoners were pardoned), but as the pardons ceased, the rates rapidly increased. The drug crackdown launched by former Prime Minister Thaksin Shinawatra in 2003 also resulted in over 2,800 extrajudicial killings, according to Human Right Watch, 2 Human Rights Watch, Not Enough Graves: The War on Drugs, HIV/AIDS, and Violations of Human Rights, Vol. 16, no. 8(C), June 2004, www.hrw.org/reports/2004/thailand0704/thailand0704.pdf. See also see Jon Fernquest, Soaring prison population: Drug war rethink, Bangkok Post 18 July 2016, https://www.bangkokpost.com/learning/advanced/1038534/soaring-prison-population-drug-war-rethink and Nathee Chitsawang, Prisons Statistics. Thailand, Criminology and Corrections. http://thaicriminology.com/statistics-3.html

30 See https://www.yenisafak.com/en/world/massive-royal-pardon-by-new-thai-king-2579316.

31 www.sps.gov.sg/docs/default-source/in-the-news-(news-release)/sps-annual-stats-release-for-2016-(14-feb-2017)_for-upload.pdf?sfvrsn=2.

Figure IV.14. Changes and rates by sub-regions and countries 2004-2016: Asia

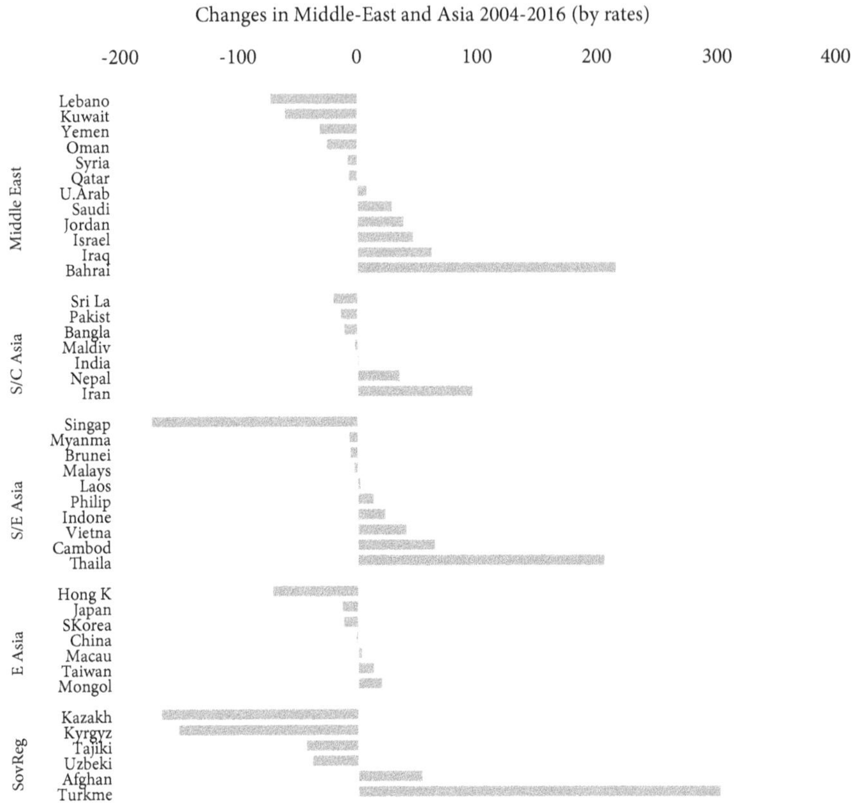

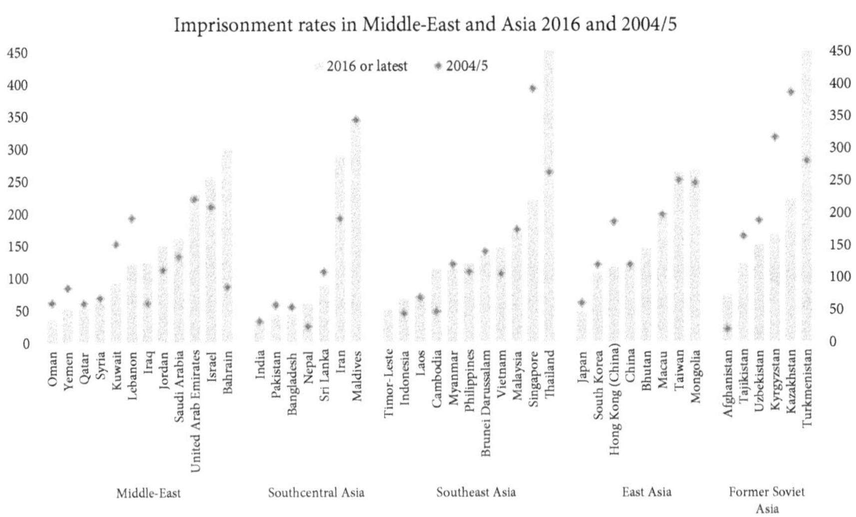

Figure IV.15. Imprisonment rates by countries 1992-2016: East Asia and Southeast Asia

Figure IV.16. Imprisonment rates by countries 1992-2015: Southcentral Asia and Middle East

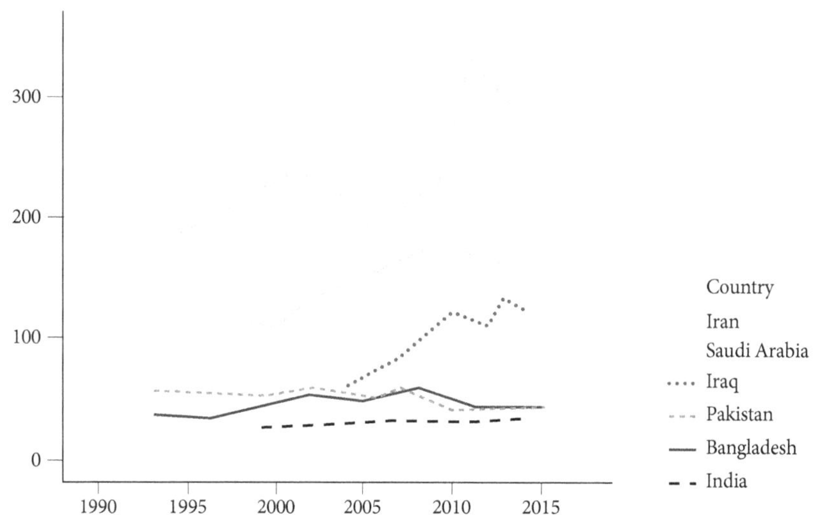

five years or more (Jacobson et al 2017 p. 14). This all gives a picture of an ineffective, and at the same time a very harsh, criminal justice system.

The Middle East. The Middle East forms a mixed set of countries, many of them troubled by political tensions and conflicts. Israel displays a rising trend from early 2000s, peaking in 2008. The increase starts after the Second Intifada (2000), and particularly after Operation Defensive Shield (2002), and consists mainly of incarcerated Palestinians.[32] The other rapidly increasing trend in the Middle East (Bahrain) also seems to have a political background. Incarceration rates in Bahrain have more than tripled since the late 2000s. While exact information on the composition of prisoners is not available, International Human rights agencies report widespread confinement of political opposition and human rights abuses, especially after the government's suppression of pro-democracy demonstrations in February 2011. An independent enquiry reported hundreds of convictions based on political charges relating to the exercise of the rights to free expression and peaceful assembly.[33]

IV.5. AFRICA AND OCEANIA

Africa. African continent is divided into North[34], Central[35], East[36], West[37], and South Africa (see Table IV.4).[38] With the exception of South Africa, all regions suffer from serious prison overcrowding. Most regions have also experienced increasing incarceration rates, albeit with considerable internal differences.[39]

With the exception of South Africa, all regions are suffering of serious overcrowding; see Figures IV.17 and IV.18. Most regions have experienced both rate based and relative increase. In parts of Africa the share of pre-trial prisoners forms over half of prison populations, as Table IV.4 shows.

32 By March 2008, more than 8,400 Palestinians were held by Israeli civilian and military authorities, of whom 5,148 were serving sentences, 2,167 were facing legal proceedings and 790 were under administrative detention. See https://en.wikipedia.org/wiki/Palestinian_prisoners_of_Israel.

33 Human Rights Watch 2014. Criminalizing Dissent, Entrenching Impunity. Persistent Failures of the Bahraini Justice System Since the BICI Report. https://www.hrw.org/report/2014/05/28/criminalizing-dissent-entrenching-impunity/persistent-failures-bahraini-justice.

34 Algeria, Egypt, Eritrea, Libya, Morocco, Palestine, Sudan, Tunisia.

35 Angola, Cameroon, Central African Republic, Chad, Congo (Brazzaville), Democratic Republic of Congo (formerly Zaire), Gabon, Sao Tome e Principe.

36 Burundi, Comoros, Djibouti, Ethiopia, Kenya, Madagascar, Malawi, Mauritius, Mayotte, Mozambique, Reunion (France), Rwanda, Tanzania, Uganda, Zambia, Zimbabwe,.

37 Benin, Burkina Faso, Capo Verde, Cote D'Ivoire, Equatorial Guinea, Gambia, Ghana, Guinea Bissau, Liberia, Mali, Mauritania, Niger, Nigeria, Republic of Guinea, Senegal, Sierra Leone, Togo.

38 Botswana, Lesotho, Namibia, South Africa, Swaziland.

39 In Africa, Rwanda forms a special case with huge number of prisoners convicted for the participation on the 1994 genocide. Adding these prisoners to national imprisonment rates, the rates show a radical decline from around 2000/pop in 1998 to around 400/pop in 2015 (see Coyle et al 2016 p. 42-43). Given the strong impact of these figures on the overall means, figures for Africa are counted without data from Rwanda.

Table IV.4. Imprisonment profiles by sub-regions in Africa 2016 (or latest available data). Only countries with total population over 100,000

Sub-region	Prisoners / pop	Pre-trial %	Females %	Foreigners %	Occupancy rate	Prisoners (N, 1000s)	Change 2004-16 (rate)	Change 2004-16 (%)
North Africa	137	37.2	2.3	3.6	156.3	247	−9.8	-0.4
Central Africa	84	52.5	2.8	1.5	186.2	81	7.6	20.4
East Africa	118	36.0	3.6	2.1	177.5	397	9.9	7.5
West Africa	69	50.7	2.9	12.9	161.6	135	35.4	11.9
South Africa	202	19.2	2.8	6.6	103.7	173	−55.2	-22.3
Total	107	41.7	3.0	5.9	163.1	1.0 m	9.3	6.9

Rates in *Northern Africa* have been either moderately increasing (Algeria, Morocco. Egypt) or declining (Tunisia). The radical drop in Libya in 2011-2012 was a result of civil war and the fall of the Gaddafi regime in 2011. The new regime released political prisoners after the regime change. However, the drop was mainly a result of the collapse of the prison system during the uprising. Hundreds of prison guards had left their posts to help maintain order in the streets, and others simply fled. The doors of unguarded prisons were opened in order to avoid further riots. While prisoners were also released in the hope that they would join the government forces, most of them joined the rebels or simply disappeared.[40] Since the change of regime, Libya has been torn among numerous rival, armed militias affiliated with distinct regions, cities and tribes, while the central government has been weak and unable to effectively exert its authority over the country.

Central African countries are among the poorest in the world. The only country in the region with a recovering economy is Angola, which has in recent years moved on from the disarray caused by a quarter-century of civil war to become the fastest-growing economy in Africa and one of the fastest-growing in the world. Over the period 2001–10, Angola had the world's highest annual average

40 According to some source in order to create more chaos in the streets and to https://www.pri.org/stories/2012-03-27/libyas-missing-prisoners-after-revolution, www.telegraph.co.uk/news/worldnews/africaandindianocean/libya/8718861/Libya-prisoners-released-or-escape-in-their-hundreds.html.

Figure IV.17. Changes and rates by sub-regions and countries 2004-2016: Africa

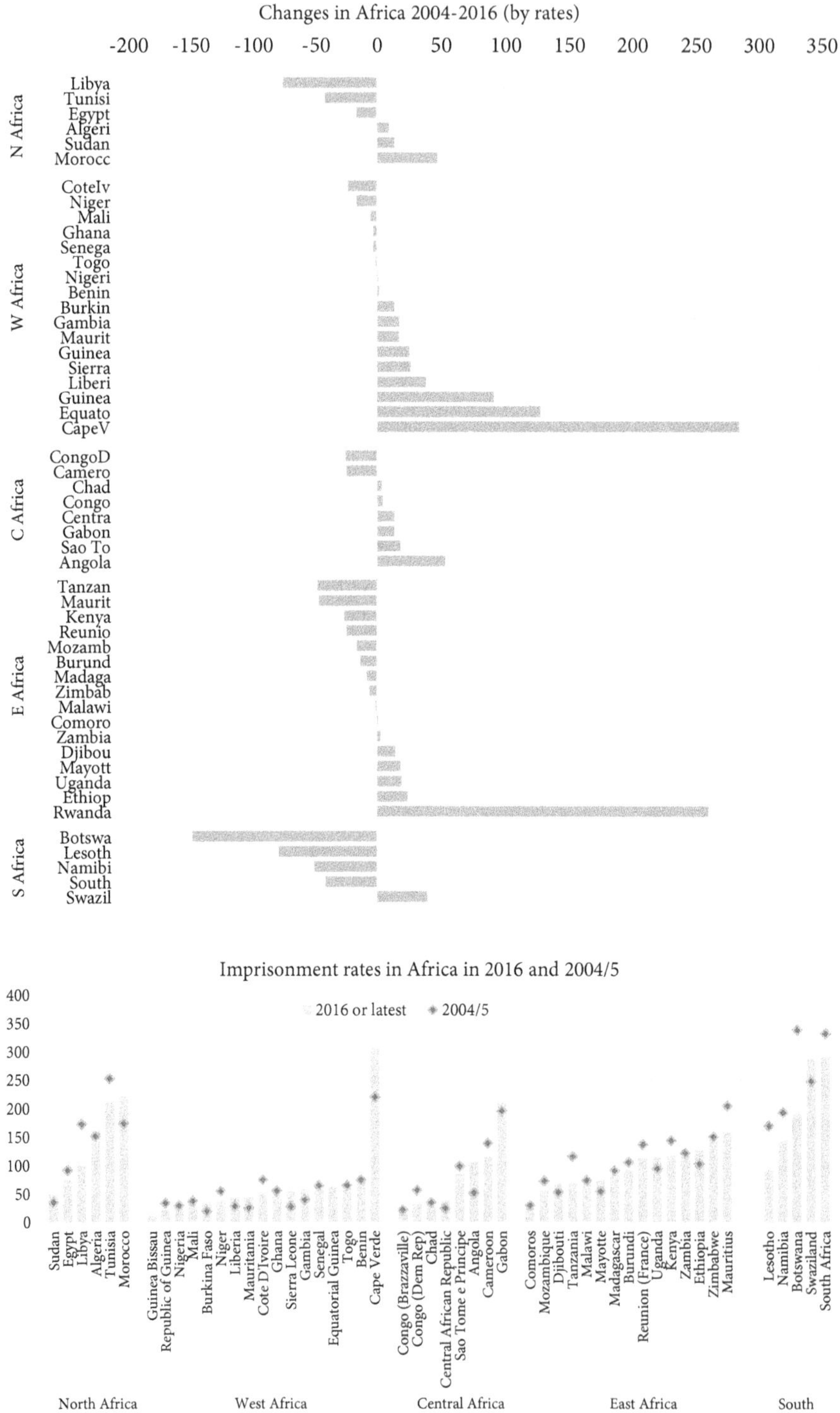

Figure IV.18. Imprisonment rates by countries 1992-2016: Africa

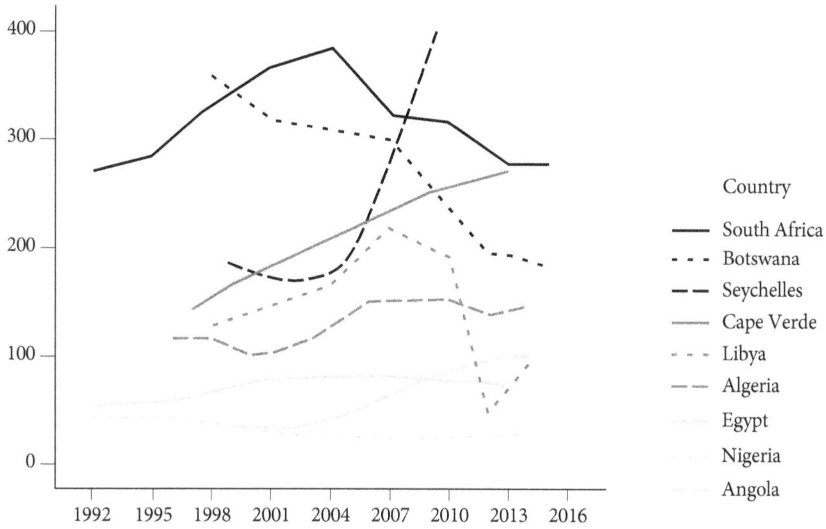

GDP growth, at 11.1%.[41] As is visible in the figure, this economic recovery coincides well with a rapid increase in the number of prisoners. The increase in Cape Verde is related, in turn, to increased crime, related both the country's position as a touristic resort and also as a major stop in the drug-trade route to Europe.

East African figures are dominated by a steep increase in the small island (around 100,000 inhabitants) of Seychelles, jumping out from the figure due to scale differences. The country exceeded in the early 2010s the rates of the long-standing world leader the United States with imprisonment rates peaking over 800/pop. This rise coincides with the worsening of drug situation in the island and the use of custodial sentences for drug users. According to the Seychelles Ministry of Health, heroin was used in injection form by some 1,000 heroin users in a country with a total population of 90,000 in 2011. This means the Seychelles has one of the highest proportions of intravenous drug users worldwide.[42] Drugs laws were revised in 2016 with the intent to replace prison sentences with treatment orders. As part of the implementation of new provisions, 150 drug offenders were released in 2016.[43] The deviant position of Cape Verde in the

41 See https://en.wikipedia.org/wiki/Angola.

42 See, World Drug Report 2013. UNODC 2013. https://www.unodc.org/unodc/secured/wdr/wdr2013/World_Drug_Report_2013.pdf.

43 As is also visible in the figure above. See www.seychellesnewsagency.com/articles/6286/Seychelles+judiciary+releases++drug+offenders+as+new+law+comes+into+effect.

Table IV.5. Imprisonment profiles in Oceania 2016 (or latest available data). Only countries with total population over 100,000

	Prisoners / pop	Pre-trial %	Females %	Foreigners %	Occupancy rate	Prisoners (N, 1000s)	Change 2004-16 (rate)	Change 2004-16 (%)
Oceania	172	28,8	3,9	6,3	97,4	55	57,6	42,8

"Western block" is explainable by similar reasons. Drugs play an important role, and Cape Verde is one of the key transit points for drug trafficking between Latin America and the African continent. As a country with substantial income from tourism, it has also been able to invest in police forces and law enforcement more than the other countries in the region. This is all visible in the increasing number of offenders sentenced to and placed in prison.

The sub-region of *South Africa* consists of relative wealthy countries in African terms, most of them displaying declining trends during the last 10 years. The Republic of South Africa is by far the largest of these countries, with the highest absolute number of prisoners as well (around 160,000 prisoners, corresponding 92% of the total prison population in the region). South African imprisonment rates increased in 1992-2005 from below 300 to over 400/pop. The increase was mainly a result of the introduction of mandatory sentences for a range of violent and sex offenses, a substantial increase in the use of life imprisonment and a general toughening of sentencing practices (van Zyl Smit 2000). Since then the rates have declined back to around 290/pop. This has been attributed mainly to decreasing crime rates in the region (Jacobson et al 2017 p. 7). Even after this decline, imprisonment rates in South Africa are among the highest in large countries in the world.

Oceania. The continent of Oceania (Figures IV.19 and IV.20) consists of three larger states – Australia, New Zealand and Papua New Guinea – and 14 smaller Island nations, with 9 having more than 100,000 inhabitants.[44] Over the last 10 years the number of prisoners in the region has grown by a little over 50%. The regional average rate among 12 states with populations over 100,000 is 172/pop, the highest in the world; see Table IV.5. Figures IV.19 and IV.20 display trends separately for the three largest countries and the other 9 with population over 100,000.

44 Fiji, French Polynesia, Guam, Micronesia, New Caledonia, Samoa, Solomon Islands, Tonga and Vanuatu.

Figure IV.19. Changes and rates by sub-regions and countries 2004-2016: Oceania

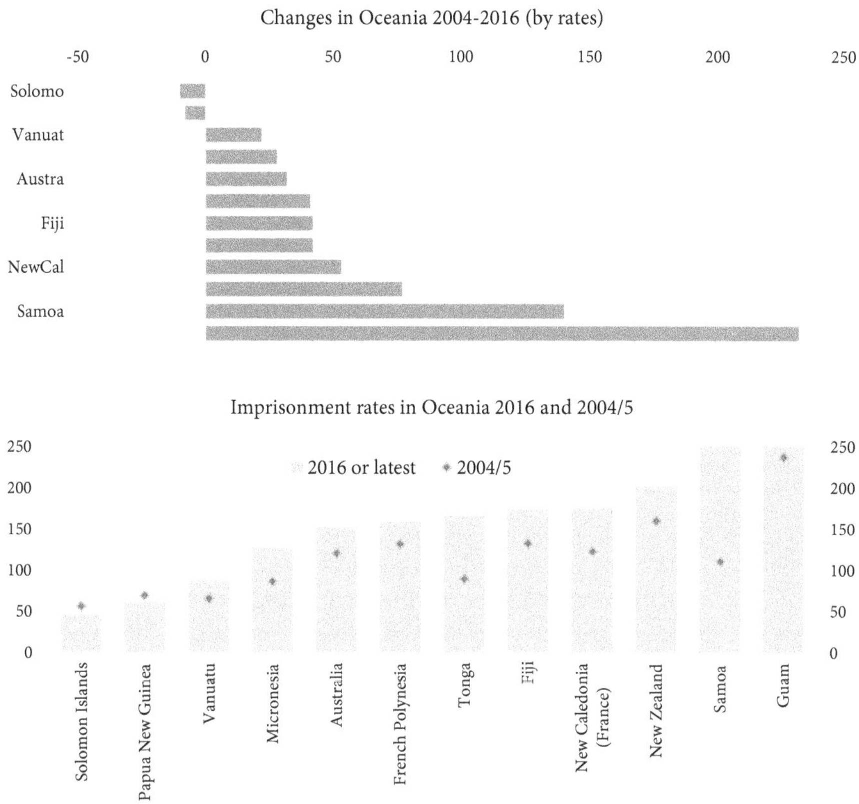

New Zealand and Australia have more than doubled their incarceration rates from the early 1980s. Long-term consistent prison population growth in Australia (an increase from 11,000 prisoners in 1984 to 36,000 prisoners in 2015) has been attributed first and foremost to the politicization of criminal justice and sentencing with the increasing influence of populist media (Freiberg 2016 p. 451). The change has taken place without dramatic single events, but as an accumulation of incremental minor changes in the criminal justice system, including denial of bail, gradual abolition of remissions, restriction of parole, increase in sentence lengths, mandatory and presumptive sentences and new risk-based security measures (Freiberg 2016 p. 448-449, see also Jacobson et al 2017 p. 23-24, Coyle et al 2016 p. 58).

The turning points in New Zealand have been more visible. Major changes in political discourse took place over the turn of the millennium and after a Citizens Initiated Referendum in which 92% of the population "voted" in favour of stricter

Figure IV.20. Imprisonment rates by sub-regions and countries 1980-2015: Oceania

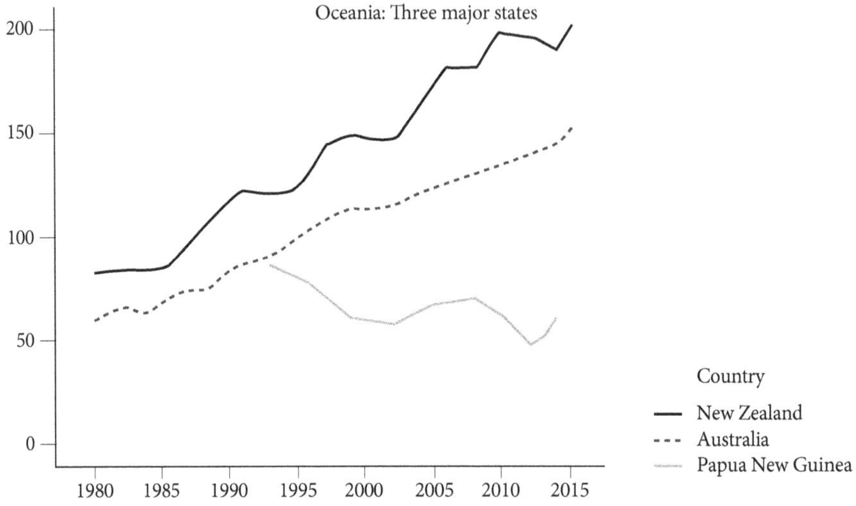

punishments.[45] The result was treated as a political mandate for a tougher penal reform. This was accomplished by a new Sentencing Act in 2002, which significantly increased penalties for serious violent and sexual offences and mandated judges to make greater use of maximum penalties. Parole opportunities were also restricted. In all, criminal political debate and law drafting was heavily influenced by both the media and extra-parliamentary forces including various victims' rights and citizens-based lobby groups demanding more effective protection against crime.[46]

The third country in the comparison, Papua New Guinea, has among the lowest number of prisoners in the region. For the last 20 years, the trend has been predominantly of decline. These changes, however, have much less to do with moderate or reductionist prison policy than a simple lack of resources and the ineffectiveness of the criminal justice system. As reported by Coyle et al (2016 p. 59), over 20,000 prisoners escaped from the prisons in 1995-2013. This gives on average about 1000 escapes each year, in a country with a daily average of around 5000 prisoners, meaning that one out of every five inmates escapes prison.

45 The question itself was both provocative and suggestive: 'Should there be a reform of our justice system placing greater emphasis on the needs of victims, providing restitution, and compensation for them and imposing minimum sentences and hard labour for all serious violent offences?' For critics, see Pratt & Clarke 2005.

46 About the socio-economic background of these anxieties and feelings of insecurities, see Pratt 2005 p. 307-310.

V. DISCUSSION

The focus of this presentation has been in description. Possible explanations are discussed only in the level of political and legislative changes and for selected countries. Even these notions, together with the detected gross differences make it clear that there is no easy way to explain these variations and trends. The most obvious explanation for changes in imprisonment – not discussed systematically - rates would be changes in crime rates. Crime could influence incarceration rates directly, as a function of volume when higher crime rates translate into rising numbers of arrests, convictions, and sentences ("volume effect"). But increase in crime – or even just single high-profile individual offenses - may lead to greater fear of crime in the community, for example, or an increase in the political salience of crime and punishment. If such dynamics drive the adoption of tough war-on-crime policies, there is a "policy effect".

However, statistical comparisons – which mainly study the "volume effect" – generally point towards the conclusion that neither reported crime nor victimization is systematically reflected in levels of incarceration. Trends in the use of imprisonment and trends in crime may differ without an apparently consistent pattern. Thus, in global comparisons the correlation between lethal violence and incarceration is close to zero. The same applies to imprisonment rates and victimization in industrialized countries (see Lappi-Seppälä 2011, 2017). Having said this, the absence of systematic positive correlation between crime and incarceration does not preclude the possibility that under some conditions and in certain regions penal policies may well be influenced by the salience of different forms of serious crime. High-profile murder cases, in turn, have had notable policy effects in national policy in England and Wales in the 1990s. In some countries drugs and drug-related criminality may play such an extraordinary role that it gives a specific profile for that country's prison problem just by numbers. Examples in that direction are found, for example, in several Asian countries.

Crime is certainly not irrelevant, but it does not seem to explain the overall use of imprisonment. The statistical fact remains that sometimes crime trends and prison trends follow each other, sometimes not. This leaves us with the conclusion that incarceration rates, in the end, are very much a result of political choices: "political constructs", as expressed by Hanns von Hofer (2003). Increased (and sometimes decreased) incarceration rates result from changed policies, either through new laws or altered practices, or both. This, of course, is merely a technical explanation. It leads us to ask after the factors that have influenced these policy choices. And these factors should also be able to explain why some systems respond to increased crime with stiffer legislation, while others may maintain their policies intact. This inquiry would lead us to compare general criminal political priorities, the prevailing political culture, social values and the surrounding socio-economic conditions, as well as historical traditions. Analyses that confine themselves mostly with affluent democracies indicate that the overall use of imprisonment is conditioned by social, political, economic and cultural factors, as well as prevailing social and moral sensibilities and values. There is a connection between welfare orientation and penal culture. A 'War on Poverty' leads to a different penal policy than a 'War on Crime'. Thus, income inequality (as a measure of social equality and welfare differences) as well as investments in social welfare (as a measure of social security and the strength of the welfare state) correlate strongly with imprisonment among European countries. The same applies to social sentiments such as fear of crime, subjective punitivity and social and institutional trust. Some political structures seem to be more prone to resorting to more repressive policies than others. Bi-polar competitive majoritarian democracies seem to associate with higher prisoner rates, while consensual and corporatist democracies go together with more moderate penal systems.[47]

On the other hand, the preceding analyses have also shown that conditions hugely vary across countries, and a combination of factors that seems explain penal variation in one part of the world may not work elsewhere. Most radical changes in incarceration have been related to political crises and misuse of criminal law for political purposes under conditions that would fall outside the framework of any analyses conducted among developed democratic countries. In addition, countries in different stages of social-economic or political development may react differently to changes in these factors. The relation between GDP and incarceration is exemplified in Figure V.1.

The growth of a country's economy is first associated with increasing imprisonment rates (higher GDP, more prisoners), but changes its course after a while (higher GDP, less prisoners). Two outliers disturb the picture. The USA has the highest imprisonment rate and highest GDP in the world. Rwanda has a much higher imprisonment rate than other countries at the same level of GDP.[48] This indicates that among the poorest countries economic restraints temper the overall use of imprisonment, but once the economic situation improves, money will also be spent building prisons. The relevance of GDP for penal policy is thus context-related. Under one set of conditions, the growth of economic resources allows a country to invest more in social services and produce greater social

---

47 Thus, for example, the explanations for "Nordic exceptionalism" in terms of penal moderation rest on a multi-level combination of inter-related factors, including a consensual negotiating political culture and highly organized labour markets, a strong universalistic welfare state with high social and economic security and low welfare differences, high social and institutional trust, low levels of fear and public punitivity, (fairly) reasonable media, strong civil servants, and a highly professional judiciary (see for details Lappi-Seppälä 2011 and 2017).

48 High figures in Rwanda follow from prisoners serving sentences for the participation in the genocide. The outlier position of the US has been studied in the rich and growing literature about "American exceptionalism" (most recently Reitz 2017).

Figure V.1. Imprisonment rates and GDP by countries and continents (logged scales)

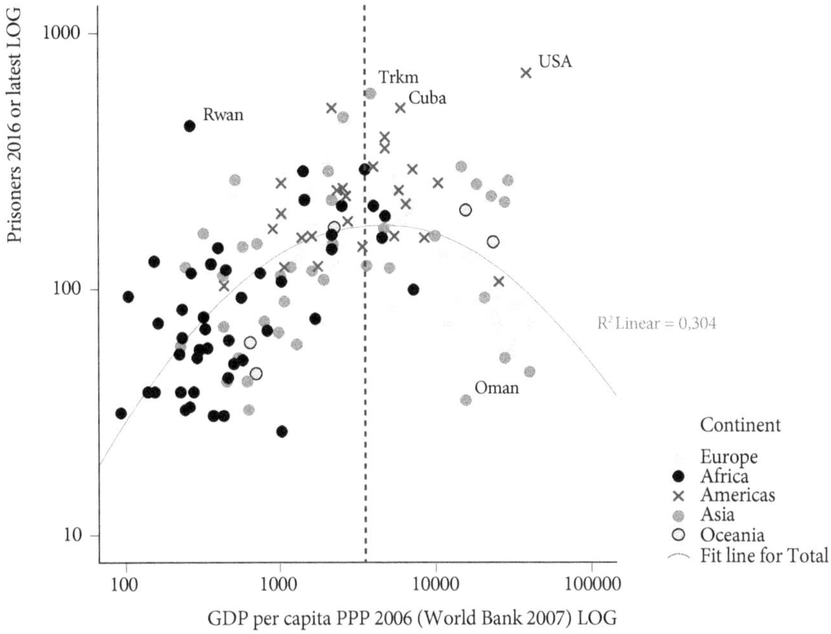

security and equality (and fewer prisoners); under another set of conditions, the growth of economic wealth allows more investment in police forces and the building of more prisons. Similarly, higher levels of democracy usually result in fewer prisoners (again with the exception of the US). However, the very first steps in the democratization process seem to increase the rate of imprisonment, while further progress then starts to reduce their numbers.

Given the facts that the meaning and relevance of different factors is context-related, that the correlations may also be curvilinear, and that major changes in the use of imprisonment may be caused by exceptional crises that are not easy to fit in to any statistical model, simple global explanations for penal variation are unlikely to appear. But to counteract the overuse of imprisonment in any country does not require such knowledge. Perhaps the most important finding from global comparisons is that imprisonment rates are not determined and they are not simply the mechanical results of changing crime rates. As summarized in the United Nations Handbook on Strategies to Reduce Overcrowding in Prisons[49]:

49 *Handbook on Strategies to Reduce Overcrowding in Prisons.* United Nations Office On Drugs And Crime. Vienna 2016. www.unodc.org/documents/middleeastandnorthafrica//criminal_justice/Overcrowding_in_prisons_Ebook.pdf.

"Thus, the answer to the question of why an increasing proportion of people are being deprived of their liberty worldwide is complex. The reasons are multiple, varying from region to region and country to country. Those who wish to embark on a process to reduce overcrowding in their country's prison system need to begin with a thorough assessment to identify the precise reasons for prison overcrowding in their particular jurisdiction, including an assessment of the entire criminal justice system, in order to develop policies and programmes that are relevant and effective." (UNODC 2016)

VI. BIBLIOGRAPHY

Aebi M, Tiago M and Burkhardt C (2015). SPACE I - *Council of Europe Annual Penal Statistics: Survey 2014*. Strasbourg: Council of Europe. Cited as Space I.

Boone M and Moerings M (2010) Niederlande. In: Dünkel F, Lappi-Seppälä T, Morgenstern C, and van Zyl Smit D (eds) *Kriminalität, Kriminalpolitik, strafrechliche Sanktionspraxis und Gefangenenraten im europäischen Vergleich. Schriften zum Strafvollzug, Jugendstrafrecht und zur Kriminologie.* Godenburg: Band 37.

Boone M and Swaaningen R (2013) Regression to the Mean: Punishment in the Netherlands. In V. Ruggiero & Ryan M (2013). *Punishment in Europe. A Critical Anatomy of Penal Systems.* Palgrave MacMillan.

Cavadino M and Dignan J (2006) *Penal Systems. A Comparative Approach.* London: Sage Publications.

Cid J and Larrauri E (2010) Spanien. In: Dünkel F, Lappi-Seppälä T, Morgenstern C, and van Zyl Smit D (eds) *Kriminalität, Kriminalpolitik, strafrechliche Sanktionspraxis und Gefangenenraten im europäischen Vergleich. Schriften zum Strafvollzug, Jugendstrafrecht und zur Kriminologie.* Godenburg: Band 37.

Corda A (2016) Sentencing and Penal Policy in Italy, 1985-2015: The Tale of a troubled Country. In M. Tonry (ed) *Crime and Justice*, Volume 45: Sentencing Policies and Practices in Western Countries: Comparative and Cross-National Perspectives by The University of Chicago Press

Coyle A, Fair H, Jacobson J and Walmsley R (2016) *Imprisonment Worldwide. The Current Situation and an Alternative Future.* Policy Press. Bristol.

Dignan, J and Cavadino M (2010) England/Wales In: Dünkel F, Lappi-Seppälä T, Morgenstern C, and van Zyl Smit D (eds) *Kriminalität, Kriminalpolitik, strafrechliche Sanktionspraxis und Gefangenenraten im europäischen Vergleich. Schriften zum Strafvollzug, Jugendstrafrecht und zur Kriminologie.* Godenburg: Band 37.

Dobryianins A and Sakalauskas G (2011) Crime, Criminology and Criminal Justice in Lithuania. *European Journal of Criminology* Vol. 8, iss. 5, 421-434.

Downes D and Swaaningen R (2007) The Road to Dystopia? Changes in the Penal Climate of the Netherlands. In: Tonry M (ed.) Vol. 35 of *Crime and Justice: A Review of Research.* Chicago: The University of Chicago Press, 31–72.

Dünkel F (2017) European penology: The Rise and fall of prison population rates in Europe in times of migrant crises and terrorism. *European Journal of Criminology* vol 14 nr 6 2017 p. 629-653.

Dünkel F and Morgenstern C (2010) Germany. In: Dünkel F, Lappi-Seppälä T, Morgenstern C, and van Zyl Smit D (eds) *Kriminalität, Kriminalpolitik, strafrechliche Sanktionspraxis und Gefangenenraten im europäischen Vergleich. Schriften zum Strafvollzug, Jugendstrafrecht und zur Kriminologie.* Godenburg: Band 37.

Freiberg A (2016) The Road Well Traveled in Australia: Ignoring the Past, Condemning the Futute. In M. Tonry (ed) *Crime and Justice*, Volume 45: Sentencing Policies and Practices in Western Countries: Comparative and Cross-National Perspectives by The University of Chicago Press

Garland D (2001) *The Culture of Control. Crime and Social Order in Contemporary Society.* The University of Chicago Press.

Hinton E (2016) *From the War on Poverty to the War on Crime. The Making of Mass Incarceration in America.* Harvard University. 2016.

Hodgson J. and Soubise L. (2016). Understanding the Sentencing Process in France. . In M. Tonry (ed) *Crime and Justice*, Volume 45: Sentencing Policies and Practices in Western Countries: Comparative and Cross-National Perspectives by The University of Chicago Press

Hofer H von (2003) Prison populations as Political Constructs: The Case of Finland, Holland and Sweden. *Journal of Scandinavian Studies in Criminology and Crime Prevention* 4: 21–38.

Jacobson J, Heard C and Fair H (2017). *Prison. Evidence of its use and over-use from around the world.* Institute for Criminal Policy Research, Birkbeck, University of London. www.prisonstudies.org/sites/default/files/resources/downloads/global_imprisonment_web2c.pdf.

Karstedt S (2010) Freiheit, Gleicheit und (Straf)recht: Weste und Strafen in demokratischen Gesellsften. In: Dünkel F, Lappi-Seppälä T, Morgenstern C, and van Zyl Smit D (eds) *Kriminalität, Kriminalpolitik, strafrechliche Sanktionspraxis und Gefangenenraten im europäischen Vergleich. Schriften zum Strafvollzug, Jugendstrafrecht und zur Kriminologie.* Godenburg: Band 37.

Krajewski K (2016) sentencing in Poland: Failed Attempts to reduce Punitiviness. In M. Tonry (ed) *Crime and Justice*, Volume 45: Sentencing Policies and Practices in Western Countries: Comparative and Cross-National Perspectives by The University of Chicago Press

Lacey N (2008) *The Prisoners' Dilemma. Political Economy and Punishment in Contemporary Democracies.* The Hamlyn Lectures 2007. Cambridge University Press.

Lappi-Seppälä T (2007) Penal Policy in Scandinavia. In: Tonry M (ed) Vol. 36 of *Crime and Justice: A Review of Research.* Chicago: The University of Chicago Press, 217–295.

Lappi-Seppälä T (2008) Trust, Welfare, and Political Culture: Explaining Difference in National Penal Policies. In: Tonry M (ed) Vol. 37 of *Crime and Justice: A Review of Research.* Chicago: The University of Chicago Press, 313–387.

Lappi-Seppälä T (2011) Explaining Imprisonment in Europe. *European Journal of Criminology* 8(4) 303-328.

Lappi-Seppälä T (2017) *American Exceptionalism in Comparative Perspective: Explaining Trends and Variation in the Use of Incarceration.* In Reitz 2017.

Lappi-Seppälä T and Lehti M (2014) Cross-Comparative Perspectives on Global Homicide Trends. In M. Tonry (ed) *Why Crime Rates Fall and Why They Don't. Crime and Justice*, vol 43. Chicago University Press.

Markina A and Sootak J (2010) Estland. In: Dünkel F, Lappi-Seppälä T, Morgenstern C, and van Zyl Smit D (eds) *Kriminalität, Kriminalpolitik, strafrechliche Sanktionspraxis und Gefangenenraten im europäischen Vergleich. Schriften zum Strafvollzug, Jugendstrafrecht und zur Kriminologie.* Godenburg: Band 37.

Miraglia P (2015) *Drugs and drug trafficking in Brazil: Trends and policies*, Washington DC: Brookings Latin America Initiative https://www.brookings.edu/wp content/uploads/ 2016/07/Miraglia-Brazil-final.pdf

Nagy F (2010) Ungarn In: Dünkel F, Lappi-Seppälä T, Morgenstern C, and van Zyl Smit D (eds) *Kriminalität, Kriminalpolitik, strafrechliche Sanktionspraxis und Gefangenenraten im europäischen Vergleich. Schriften zum Strafvollzug, Jugendstrafrecht und zur Kriminologie.* Godenburg: Band 37.

Pratt J, Clark M (2005) Penal populism in New Zealand. *Punishment & Society. The International Journal of Penology* 07(3): 303–322.

Reitz K (2017) *American Exceptionalism in Crime and Punishment.* Oxford University Press. New- York.

Stando-Kawecka B and Krajewski (2010) Polen. In: Dünkel F, Lappi-Seppälä T, Morgenstern C, and van Zyl Smit D (eds) *Kriminalität, Kriminalpolitik, strafrechliche Sanktionspraxis und Gefangenenraten im europäischen Vergleich. Schriften zum Strafvollzug, Jugendstrafrecht und zur Kriminologie.* Godenburg: Band 37.

UNODC 2016. *Handbook on Strategies to Reduce Overcrowding in Prisons.* United Nations Office on Drugs And Crime. Vienna 2016. www.unodc.org/documents/ middleeastandnorthafrica//criminal_justice/Overcrowding_in_prisons_Ebook.pdf.

Wacquant L (2010) *Punishing the Poor.* London: Duke University Press.

van Zyl Smit, D. (2000) 'Mandatory sentences: A conundrum for the new South Africa?, *Punishment & Society*, 2 (2), 197-212.

Webster C-M and Doob A (2007) Punitive Trends and Stable Imprisonment Rates in Canada. M. Tonry (ed) *Crime, Punishment, and Politics in a Comparative Perspective. Crime and Justice*, Vol. 36. University of Chicago Press.

Webster C-M amd Doob A (2017) *Penal Optimism: Understanding American Mass Imprisonment from a Canadian Perspective.* In Reitz 2017.

MINIMISING PRISONISATION AND THE HARMS OF CUSTODY

Mary ROGAN*

I. INTRODUCTION

This chapter will explore two central themes: first, efforts to minimise the harmful effects of incarceration; and second, the regulation of the use of imprisonment through release and other back door strategies. The chapter will examine ways to reduce the harms of prison by examining the issues of contact with the family and the outside world, and material conditions in prison. The chapter then moves to address an area which, it is submitted, has been given insufficient attention within the literature, policy, and the international human rights standards: the question of accountability within the prison system. The chapter argues that fairness within the prison environment is an important facet of legitimacy and, by extension, an environment which promotes the possibility of reintegration. The chapter then moves to give an overview of backdoor strategies to reduce the prison population.

II. THE HARMFUL EFFECTS OF INCARCERATION

In 2008, Andrew McLellan, then Chief Inspector of Prisons for Scotland, gave evidence to the Scottish Prisons Commission. McLellan stated: "prison may sometimes do good, but it always does harm".[1] There is a considerable literature

* Associate Professor, School of Law, Trinity College Dublin. E: mary.rogan@tcd.ie. I wish to thank all the participants at the International Penal and Penitentiary Foundations' Colloquium in Helsinki, June 2016 for their questions and comments which shaped much of the thinking behind this chapter.

1 Transcription of Interview, SPC Evidence Session, 5 February 2008, p. 2.

indicating the damaging effects of imprisonment. Prison interferes with family relationships. Prison has a major effect on the children of prisoners.[2] Prison negatively affects a person's chance of future employment.[3] Prison can harm a person's mental health.[4] Prison is very expensive and drains resources from other public services.[5]

It is not possible to divorce the subject of the harms of custody from the overuse of prison, overcriminalisation and the overuse of prosecution. Indeed, this is something recognised by the European Court of Human Rights and the European Committee for the Prevention of Torture. The Court does not confine its views on overcrowding to the need to address its effects on the material and physical conditions in prisons, but, rather, states clearly that alternatives to custody must also be used to address this problem. This is evident from cases concerning overcrowding in Bulgaria[6], Italy[7] and Hungary.[8] The Council of

2 See, for example, Scharff Smith, *When the innocent are punished: the children of imprisoned parents* (Basingstoke, Palgrave Macmillan, 2014); Arditti and Savla, "Parental Incarceration and Child Trauma Symptoms in Single Caregiver Homes" (2015) 24 *Journal of Child and Family Studies* 551-561: Manby, Jones, Foca, Bieganski, and Starke, "Children of prisoners: exploring the impact of families' reappraisal of the role and status of the imprisoned parent on children's coping strategies" (2015) 18(2) *European Journal of Social Work* 228-245; Dallaire, Zeman, Thrash and Todd, (2015) 44(1) "Children's Experiences of Maternal Incarceration – Specific Risks: Predictions to Psychological Maladaptation" *Journal of Clinical Child and Adolescent Psychology* 109-122; Scotland's Commissioner for Children and Young People, *Not seen: not heard: not guilty: the rights and status of the children of prisoners in Scotland* (Scotland's Commissioner for Children and Young People, 2008); Irish Penal Reform Trust, *Picking up the pieces: the rights and needs of children and families of prisoners* (Dublin, Irish Penal Reform Trust, 2012).

3 Decker, Ortiz, Spohn and Hedberg, (2015) 43(2) "Criminal stigma, race and ethnicity: the consequences of imprisonment for employment" *Journal of Criminal Justice* 108-121; Alos, Jodar and Miguelez, "Effects of prison work programmes on the employability of ex-prisoners" (2015) 12(1) *European Journal of Criminology* 35-50; van der Geest, Bijleveld, Blokland, and Nagin, "The effects of incarceration on longitudinal trajectories of employment" (2016) 62(1) *Crime and Delinquency* 107-140.

4 See, for example, Gonçalves, Endrass, Rossegger, and Dirkzwager, (2016) 16(91) "A longitudinal study of mental health symptom in young prisoners: exploring the influence of personal factors and the correctional climate" *BMC Psychiatry* 1-11; Goomany and Dickinson, (2015) 22(6) "The influence of prison climate on the mental health of adult prisoners: a literature review" *Journal of Psychiatric and Mental Health Nursing* 413-422.

5 See, for example, Orrick and Vieraitis, (2015) 40(2) "The cost of incarceration in Texas: estimating the benefits of reducing the prison population" *American Journal of Criminal Justice* 399-415; Henrichson and Delaney, *The Price of Prisons: What Incarceration Costs Taxpayers* (The Vera Institute, 2012). The average spending in the EU28 countries on prisons is 0.2% of GDP. See: http://ec.europa.eu/eurostat/statistics-explained/index.php/Government_expenditure_on_public_order_and_safety#Database (last acccessed 5 August 2016).

6 *Neshkov v. Bulgaria*, application nos. 36925/10, 21487/12, 73196/12, 77718/12, 9717/13, 27 January 2015.

7 *Torreggiani v. Italy*, application nos. 43417/09, 46882/09, 55400/09, 57875/09, 61535/09, 35315/10 and 37818/10, 8 January 2013.

8 *Varga v. Hungary*, application nos. 14097/12, 43135/12, 73712/12, 34001/13, 44055/13 and 64586/13, 10 March 2015.

Europe's Committee of Ministers also made a recommendation to Member States in 1999 which specifically states that building new prisons alone cannot reduce the rates of imprisonment.[9]

There is a school of thought to the effect that talking about reducing the pains of imprisonment is entirely the wrong conversation, and that prison can never be a constructive or purposeful experience.[10] This chapter acknowledges the abolitionist perspective. It proceeds on the basis, however, that it is a fact that we do use prison, and in those circumstances, exploring ways in which we can minimise its harms is worthwhile. It is also the case that where prison is necessary, minimising its negative effects makes good economic and social sense. It is also a human rights obligation.

III. CONTACT WITH THE OUTSIDE WORLD

There is now a great deal of literature on the effects of imprisonment on the families of prisoners. That literature indicates that the imprisonment of a parent has a very negative effect on children.[11] On the other side of the prison walls, contact with one's family has also been shown to have positive effects on the prospects of a prisoner's reintegration back into the community.[12]

International human rights standards require contact with the family of a prisoner to be permitted. Rule 24.1 of the European Prison Rules[13] makes the possibility of communication by letter, telephone or other forms of communication with prisoners' families mandatory. This rule also provides an entitlement to receive visits from one's family. The rules recognise that there may be limitations on visits, but "such restrictions … shall nevertheless allow an acceptable minimum level of contact"[14], and that "the arrangements for visits shall be such as to allow prisoners to maintain and develop family relationships in as normal a manner as possible".[15]

The United Nations Standard Minimum Rules for the Treatment of Prisoners (the Mandela Rules) also state that "prisoners shall be allowed, under necessary

9 Recommendation 99(22) concerning prison overcrowding and prison population inflation.

10 For an overview, see Ryan and Ward, (2015) 41(3) "Prison abolition in the UK: They dare not speak its name" *Social Justice* 107-119.

11 See the material cited in footnote 3.

12 Mitchell, Spooner, Jia, and Zhang (2016) 47 "The effect of prison visitation on re-entry success: a meta-analysis" *Journal of Criminal Justice* 74-83.

13 Recommendation Rec(2006)2 of the Committee of Ministers to member states on the European Prison Rules.

14 Rule 24.2, Recommendation Rec(2006)2 of the Committee of Ministers to member states on the European Prison Rules.

15 Rule 24.4, Recommendation Rec(2006)2 of the Committee of Ministers to member states on the European Prison Rules.

supervision, to communicate with their family and friends at regular intervals, including now electronic and digital means, and by receiving visits".[16]

The Bangkok Rules[17] state that visits involving children shall take place in an environment that is conducive to a positive visiting experience, and such an experience should include positive staff attitudes, and open contact between mother and child.[18] Visits involving extended contact with children should be encouraged, where possible.[19]

The European Court of Human Rights has indicated clearly that states must provide the possibility for prisoners to have visits with members of their family in relatively unrestricted circumstances. It has also made clear that the use of barriers, screens, or the denial of visits can only be justified following a risk assessment specific to those involved, which points to the need for restrictions. The Court has also emphasised the need for a clear legal foundation for the use of any restrictions. Any law which provides the possibility for a restriction on visiting rights must indicate the extent of the discretion very clearly.[20]

Even if a restriction on visits has some basis in law, it must still pass the test of proportionality, and go no further than is necessary to pursue a legitimate interest. The Court has looked very closely at the official reasons given for the refusal of visits or the use of barriers or screens. In *Kuĉera v. Slovenia*[21] for example, the applicant's wife was a co-accused and visits between them were banned for 13 months; this was not justified because of the length of time and the fact that it was possible to utilise other security mechanisms if there were fears about collusion in any particular visit. In *Lavents v. Latvia*[22] a prisoner was barred from having visits for up to 19 months for similar reasons; this was also viewed as being unnecessary. The length of time for a restriction was also a reason for a breach of Article 8 in *Piechowicz v Poland*.[23] There, a child was also affected by the ban. The court stated that it was legitimate for the authorities to take account of the fact that the prisoner was viewed as dangerous and some restrictions, such as having another adult present during the visit, were inevitable, but a blanket ban on visits was not justified.

16 Rule 58, Recommendation Rec(2006)2 of the Committee of Ministers to member states on the European Prison Rules.

17 United Nations Rules for the Treatment of Women Prisons and Non-custodial Measures for Women Offenders (the Bangkok Rules).

18 Rule 28, United Nations Rules for the Treatment of Women Prisons and Non-custodial Measures for Women Offenders (the Bangkok Rules).

19 *Ibid.* Rule 43 also states that prison authorities shall encourage and, where possible, also facilitate visits to women prisoners as an important prerequisite to ensuring their mental well-being and social reintegration.

20 *Ciorap v. Moldova,* application no. 12066/02, 18 June 2007; *Moiseyev v. Russia*, application no. 62936/00, 9 October 2008.

21 17 July 2007, application no. 48666/99.

22 28 February 2003, application no. 58442/00. Translated from the French by the author.

23 Application no. 20071/07, 17 July 2012.

It is possible to impose a total ban in compliance with the Convention, but very strong reasons are required. This indicates that European human rights law is acutely aware of the need to reduce the harms of prison by ensuring visits between prisoners and their families are as unrestricted as possible.

Another factor here concerns the best interests of children. The denial of visits and the use of barriers can have a particular effect on children. The best interests of the child test from the United Nations Convention on the Rights of the Child has become well established in a variety of contexts, including extradition in the cases of *BH, KAS, HH, PH, F-K*[24], from the Supreme Court of the United Kingdom, but appears not to have been directly used in European Court of Human Rights prison law decisions to date. This test requires that the best interests of the child should be the primary consideration for any decision maker faced with a decision which affects a child; it is submitted that this test should also be deployed when making decisions about whether to allow visits, or how visits are regulated.

IV. CONDITIONS

The question of decent physical and material conditions is also directly related to the minimisation of the harms of imprisonment. Poor physical conditions have been linked to decreased prospects of rehabilitation and reintegration. Conditions can give rise to harm through, for example, the unnecessary use of restraints or the use of solitary confinement. This chapter focuses on overcrowding and the harms of prison, in light of the fact that it remains a matter of global concern.[25]

The Council of Europe's Committee for the Prevention of Torture (CPT) has stated:

24 [2012] UKSC 25.

25 On the position in the United States, see James, *The Federal Prison Population Build-up: Options for Congress* (Congressional Research Service, 2016), available at: https://www.fas.org/sgp/crs/misc/R42937.pdf (last accessed 5 August 2016). On the position in Council of Europe countries see: Council of Europe, *Annual Penal Statistics* (SPACE I), 2014, available at: http://wp.unil.ch/space/files/2016/05/SPACE-I-2014-Report_final.1.pdf (last accessed 5 August 2016). For the occupancy levels of prison systems worldwide, see Institute for Criminal Policy Research, *World Prison Brief*, available at: www.prisonstudies.org/highest-to-lowest/occupancy-level?field_region_taxonomy_tid=All (last accessed 5 August 2016). At the time of writing, the most overcrowded prison systems (based on official capacity levels) are found in Haiti, Benin, the Philippines, El Salvador and Guatemala.

> all the services and activities within a prison will be adversely affected if it is required to cater for more prisoners than it was designed to accommodate; the overall quality of life in the establishment will be lowered, perhaps significantly.[26]

The CPT's position on the living space per prisoner was most recently consolidated in a set of standards in 2015.[27] In short, the CPT's minimum standards for personal living space are as follows:

1. $6m^2$ of living space for a single-occupancy cell, not including an annex for a sanitary facility[28];
2. $4m^2$ of living space per prisoner in a multiple-occupancy cell, which must have a full-partitioned sanitary facility;
3. At least 2m between the walls of the cell; and
4. At least 2.5m between the floor and the ceiling of the cell.

The CPT has also, however, gone on to promote *desirable* standards regarding multi-occupancy cells of up to four inmates. These are:

1. 2 prisoners: at least 10m of living space + sanitary annexe;
2. 3 prisoners: at least 14m of living space + sanitary annexe;
3. 4 prisoners: at least 18m of living space + sanitary annexe.

The CPT further recognises that the question of space is a nuanced one, and that there is a qualitative difference between a double cell, and one which is designed for holding six or more people. The CPT's view is that large-scale dormitories are fundamentally objectionable.[29] Moreover, the regime offered to prisoners is a factor to be considered when examining the matter of cell size.

The CPT has shown itself to be somewhat uncomfortable with the notion that its standards could give, or have given, rise to the perception that space alone can constitute a breach of the European Convention on Human Rights. The CPT addressed this directly in 2015, when it noted that the Court has been asked to deal with more and more complaints from prisoners alleging a breach of the Convention on the basis of limited living space. The CPT has differentiated its role from that of the Court sharply, noting that it is a preventive monitoring body and not a court obliged to decide on whether the Convention has been violated in a particular situation, though it noted that it has declared certain egregious prison conditions to be inhuman and degrading treatment. The CPT stated that it

---

26 European Committee for the Prevention of Torture and Inhuman or Degrading Treatment or Punishment, 2nd general report, para 46.

27 European Committee for the Prevention of Torture and Inhuman or Degrading Treatment or Punishment, *Living space per prisoner in prison establishments: CPT standards*, CPT/Inf (2015) 44.

28 This annexe would usually be 1m to 2m, and should be excluded from the calculation of the living space in the cell.

29 CPT, 11th General Report, CPT/Inf (2001).

has "never considered that its cell-size standards should be regarded as absolute. In other words, it does not automatically hold the view that a minor deviation from its minimum standards may in itself be considered as amounting to inhuman and degrading treatment … as long as other, alleviating, factors can be found".[30] While that is so, the CPT still recommends that the minimum standard be adhered to.

The position of the CPT on cell size has therefore become quite clearly stated, perhaps as a result of a series of cases which has appeared to move the European Court of Human Rights towards the establishment of a minimum space requirement for prisoners.

Traditionally, conditions cases have involved the Court engaging in a consideration of a variety of factors and making an overall assessment of the totality of those conditions when deciding if Article 3 has been breached. Cases dealing more squarely with overcrowding have, however, suggested that the Court is willing to consider certain levels of overcrowding to be breaches of Article 3 on their own.

In *Ananyev v. Russia*[31] the Court reiterated that it must examine the cumulative effect of the conditions of detention, as well as the length of time during which the conditions have been endured. In assessing its previous case law, the Court found that: that each detainee must have an individual sleeping place in the cell; each detainee must have at least 3 sqm of floor space; and the overall surface area of the cell must be such as to allow detainees to move freely between items of furniture. In its pilot judgment[32], the Court held that the absence of any of these elements gives rise to a strong presumption that the conditions breach Article 3. The Court went on to make quite an explicit differentiation between this and circumstances where there is sufficient personal space. In the latter case, the Court suggests that "other aspects of physical conditions of detention as being relevant for the assessment of compliance [with Article 3]. In *Ananyev*, the Court seems content to lay down a norm whereby certain levels of overcrowding are *ipso facto* breaches of Article 3, but where there is more than this minimum level of space available to prisoners, it is then that other factors come into play in deciding if Article 3 has been breached.

In *Torreggiani v. Italy*[33] the Court also found a violation of Article 3 in circumstances of structural overcrowding within the Italian prison system. The

30 European Committee for the Prevention of Torture and Inhuman or Degrading Treatment or Punishment, *Living space per prisoner in prison establishments: CPT standards*, CPT/Inf (2015) 44, at para 21.

31 Application nos. 42525/07 and 60800/08, January 10 2012. Hereinafter, *Ananyev*.

32 This involves the state being placed under a legal obligation to implement, under the supervision of the Committee of Ministers, appropriate general and/or individual measures to secure the right of the applicant which has been found to be violated.

33 Application nos. 43417/09, 46882/09, 55400/09, 57875/09, 61535/09, 35315/10 et 37818/10, 8 January 2013.

prisoners involved were sharing what were found to be 9 sqm cells with two others. This was below the standards expected by the Court, being below the CPT standard of 4 sqm in particular. This shortage of space was compounded by the lack of hot water over long periods, and inadequate heating and ventilation. These were characterised as additional suffering. In this case, the Court also noted the CPT minimum standards. The Court considered that the living space provided did not meet the criterion laid down as acceptable in its case law. This further suggests that overcrowding can be a standalone breach of Article 3, when it is particularly severe.[34]

However, a different emphasis became apparent in *Varga v. Hungary*.[35] The Court referred to the *Ananyev* case and its principles concerning overcrowding, as well as cases where a finding of a violation of Article 3 was found on the basis of severe overcrowding on its own. The Court chose to respond to these developments in the following terms:

> The Court has so far refrained from determining how much space should be allocated to a detainee in terms of the Convention, having considered that a number of other relevant factors, such as the duration of detention, the possibilities for outdoor exercise, the physical and mental condition of the detainee and so further, play an important part in deciding whether the detention conditions complied with [art. 3]".[36]

The *Varga* decision, and in particular its efforts to suggest that the circumstances in which overcrowding alone will be a breach of Article 3 are limited, indicates that the European Court of Human Rights shares the concern of the CPT about a wide reading of Article 3 in this field.

However, in the *Varga* case itself, it is of note that one of the applicants, Mr Pesti, was not in the smallest living space of all the applicants, but the Court did not find other factors, such as poor ventilation, were present. It is clear, therefore, that severe overcrowding on its own, though for a sustained period of uncertain duration, but, following *Varga*, for a period of three years, will still be a standalone breach of Article 3. While the CPT and the Court may be uncomfortable with overcrowding as a standalone breach, it is clear the Court will nonetheless find one if it the level of space is below 2.86sqm, for a period of three years.

34 Italy has since reduced its prison population and created more prison places, and the Court has refused to hear further cases concerning overcrowding, finding that Italy has now put in sufficient remedies for breaches of article 3, for example in *Stella v Italy* (application no. 49169/09, 25 September 2014).

35 Application nos. 14097/12, 43135/12, 73712/12, 34001/13,44055/13 and 64586/13, 10 March 2015. Hereinafter, *Varga*.

36 At para 76.

While the exact detail of the circumstances in which it will amount to a breach of Article 3 may not clear, it is evident that the European Court of Human Rights and the CPT consider overcrowding to be a very serious harm of imprisonment.

This concern is ongoing, Belgium has also been told by the European Court of Human Rights in *Vasilescu v. Belgium*[37] that the levels of overcrowding in Belgian prisons, when coupled with unhygienic and dilapidated prison institutions were in breach of article 3, and a pilot judgment was issued.[38]

Increasing pressure from the European Union on overcrowding and prison conditions?

A recent case from the Court of Justice of the European Union on the issue of prison conditions is likely to prove quite consequential, not least because it represents the growing interest and muscle of the European Union in the realm of penal affairs. In April 2016 the Court of Justice of the European Union heard a preliminary reference[39], from a court in Bremen, Germany. The case concerned the issue of a European Arrest Warrant[40] by authorities in Hungary and Romania concerning two individuals, Mr Aranyosi and Mr Caldararu.[41] The Bremen court asked a very fundamental question of the Court of Justice; essentially it was this: when a request to send a person back to a state where there are strong indications that the detention conditions in the issuing Member State infringe the fundamental rights of the person concerned and the fundamental legal principles as enshrined in Article 6 of the Treaty of the European Union, may the state refuse to transfer the person, or must assurances be sought about the conditions in which the person is likely to be held? The countries at issue, Hungary and Romania, have major overcrowding problems, and were found by the ECtHR to breach Article 3 as a result. The Court of Justice of the European Union found that a refusal to transfer the person is not required, but the court considering the request must assess whether there is a real risk of a breach of rights in the particular case, based on up to date and specific information. The executing state can postpone execution of the warrant until that information is received.

---

37 Application no 64682/12, 25 November 2014.

38 In its report of its visit to Belgium published in March 2016, the CPT recommended that Belgium provide at least 4 square metres of living space for each prisoner and to improve detention conditions. CPT, Report to the Government of Belgium, (2016), available at: www.cpt.coe.int/documents/bel/2016-13-inf-fra.pdf (last accessed 5 August 2016).

39 A preliminary reference is a question of European Union law referred by a domestic court to the Court of Justice of the European Union, which seeks an answer clarifying or resolving a matter.

40 The European Arrest Warrant is an instrument which permits the transfer prisoners who are facing trial or sentence in one EU country from another EU country. 2002/584/JHA: Council Framework Decision of 13 June 2002.

41 C-404/15, *Aranyosi*, C-659/15, *Caldararu*.

This case is particularly interesting because it is an example of the European Union's engagement with the question of the harms of prison, though progress has been much slower and more haphazard than might be hoped. In 2011 the European Commission and the Parliament expressed concern[42] that poor detention conditions had the potential to undermine the mutual trust and confidence which Member States must have in each other's criminal justice systems, and affect the operation of the EU's criminal justice instruments, including the Transfer of Prisoners Framework Decision.[43] As well as showing that the European Union recognises that poor prison conditions are a harm of prisonisation as they infringe a person's dignity, it is clear that the Union considers that poor conditions are a harm of prison in ways that, before the concept of mutual trust and recognition, may not previously have been conceived. Poor prison conditions can, and clearly do, impact negatively on the mutual trust which member states of the European Union need to have in each other's systems for them to work properly.

The United States Supreme Court has also shown its willingness to identify severe overcrowding as a harm of imprisonment. In *Plata v. California* the Supreme Court of the United States was faced with the Californian prison system which was then running at 200% capacity. In the view of the majority:

> Overcrowding has overtaken the limited resources of prison staff; imposed demands well beyond the capacity of medical and mental health facilities; and created unsanitary and unsafe conditions that make progress in the provision of care difficult or impossible to achieve.[44]

Such a prison is, in the majority's view, incompatible with the concept of human dignity and "has no place in civilized society".[45] The strong statements from the European Court of Human Rights in *Ananyev* and the Supreme Court of the United States in *Plata* suggests that judicial action may become a key source of resistance to poor prison conditions.[46]

---

42 European Commission, Green Paper: Strengthening mutual trust in the European judicial area – A Green Paper on the application of EU criminal justice legislation in the field of detention, COM(2011) 327. European Parliament resolution of 15 December 2011 on detention conditions in the EU (2011/2897(RSP)) (2013/C 168 E/11).

43 Framework Decision 2008/909/JHA, 27 November 2008.

44 563 US 493 (2011), hereinafter *Plata*, at p. 3.

45 *Plata*, at p. 13.

46 On *Plata* see Simon, (2013) 48(1) "The Return of the Medical Model: Disease and the Meaning of Imprisonment from John Howard to Brown v. Plata" *Harvard Civil Rights- Civil Liberties Law Review* 217-256; Simon, *Mass incarceration on trial: a remarkable court decision and the future of prisons in America* (New York, The New Press, 2014), Schlanger, (2013) 48(1) "Plata v. Brown and Realignment: Jails, Prisons, Courts, and Politics" *Harvard Civil Rights-Civil Liberties Law Review* 165-216.

V. THE HARMS OF UNFAIRNESS AND A LACK OF ACCOUNTABILITY

There is now a good deal of literature on the importance of the legitimacy of penal power. As Liebling and Crewe have noted, empirical research has converged with "some of the most significant penological insight of the twentieth century: the prison is a *sui generis* institution, uniquely liable to abuses and distortion of power".[47] Drawing on policing work, in the prison context, legitimacy has traditionally been linked to procedural fairness. This is an insight which applies across all of the criminal justice system, but the particular power differentials and special, closed, nature of prison means that the harm of feeling that one has been treated unfairly is both particularly likely, and particularly serious. Treating people unfairly is itself obviously a harm, but it can lead to other harms, including resentment and potentially disorder. Riots in the UK and elsewhere have been linked with a lack of legitimacy in prison regimes.[48] Liebling further suggests that, as prisons usually aim at rehabilitation, the values inherent in the idea of legitimacy are important to address in order to support prisoners to reconnect to social values.[49]

Research has found feelings of frustration and hopelessness amongst prisoners when asked to discuss the possibilities for challenging decisions or seeking redress in prisons. Calavita and Jenness, in their study of the grievance procedure in Californian prisons, found a complex picture, but also many examples of deep cynicism about the fairness of the procedure.[50] In the UK, Ben Crewe has found a distinct lack of trust or faith in visiting committees by prisoners in an English prison[51] and the Ombudsman for Children's Office has noted similar issues amongst young prisoners in Ireland.[52]

International human rights law has only fairly recently began to lay down some detailed principles concerning how inspections and complaints mechanisms should operate. It is instructive to contrast the by now fairly well-developed principles on, for example, overcrowding and cell size, and family contact, with those around the kinds of accountability structures which should

47 Liebing and Crewe "Prisons beyond the new penology: the shifting moral foundations of prison management" in Sparks and Simon (eds.), *The Sage Handbook of Punishment and Society* (Sage Publications, London, 2013) 283-307.

48 Woolf, *Prison Disturbances 1990*, Cmnd 1456 (HMSO 1991).

49 Liebling and Arnold, *Prisons and Their Moral Performance: A Study of Values, Quality, and Prison Life* (Oxford, Oxford University Press 2004).

50 Calavita and Jenness *Appealing to Justice: Prisoner Grievances, Rights, and Carceral Logic* (Oakland, University of California Press 2014).

51 Crewe, *The Prisoner Society* (Oxford, Oxford University Press, 2009).

52 Ombudsman for Children, 'Young People in St Patrick's Institution' www.oco.ie/wp-content/uploads/2014/03/St-Pats-Report.pdf (last accessed 5 August 2016).

exist for our prisons. However, the Mandela Rules[53] and the European Prison Rules[54] do contain requirements for inspection by independent monitoring bodies. These rules make it clear that internal and independent inspections are required in order to ensure compliance with national and international law. The Optional Protocol to the United Nations Convention against Torture (OPCAT) represents the high point in international human rights law concerning inspection of places of detention, and its introduction represents a very important turn towards independent inspection and monitoring within the international legal order.

The European Court of Human Rights has also repeatedly emphasised the need for effective compensatory and preventive remedies concerning inhuman and degrading treatment. This issue has been examined primarily in the context of whether an applicant has exhausted the domestic remedies in the state, or whether there is an effective domestic remedy in place. In the case of *Neshkov and others v. Bulgaria*[55] the court held that effective remedies to prevent inhuman and degrading treatment must:

(a) be independent of the authorities in charge of the penitentiary system;
(b) secure the inmates' effective participation in the examination of their grievances;
(c) ensure the speedy and diligent handling of the inmates' complaints;
(d) have at its disposal a wide range of legal tools for eradicating the problems that underlie these complaints; and
(e) be capable of rendering binding and enforceable decisions. Any such remedy must also be capable of providing relief in reasonably short time-limits.

The adequacy of complaints mechanisms has also pronounced upon by the US Supreme Court in the case of *Ross v. Blake*.[56] This case concerned the requirement under US law, in the infamous Prison Litigation Reform Act of 1995, that prisoners exhaust the administrative remedies which are available before bring a court case to challenge prison conditions. The Supreme Court held that whether a remedy was available required consideration of whether in reality it is a dead end, because officers are unable or consistently unwilling to provide any relief. A remedy might be incapable of use in practical terms because it is so opaque that no ordinary prisoner can navigate it. A complaints procedure might also be unavailable because prison administrators thwart inmates from taking advantage of it through misrepresentation or intimidation. There was evidence in the case that wardens routinely dismissed grievances when investigations into staff

53 Rule 56.
54 Rule 9, part VI, rule 70.
55 *Neshkov v. Bulgaria*, application nos. 36925/10, 21487/12, 73196/12, 77718/12, 9717/13, 27 January 2015.
56 578 U.S. ___ (2016).

misconduct were underway. Further consideration of whether the remedies were available in practice was therefore, according to the Supreme Court, required by the lower court.

It is submitted that we need to develop minimum standards for accountability in prison to minimise the harms associated with a lack of redress, a lack of independent monitoring and a lack of feelings of being treated fairly. The international human rights standards currently do not contain sufficient detail to address this emerging harm of imprisonment.

VI. RELEASE FROM PRISON

The judicious use of release from prison can be a key factor in minimising the harms of imprisonment and reducing the size of the prison population. This part of the chapter will give two examples of downsizing of the prison population through release, one massive and one modest. Human rights standards around release will also be considered.

California

As Joan Petersilia has said: "California has embarked on a prison downsizing experiment of historical significance". Following the *Plata* decision, the then Governor of California, Jerry Brown, enacted the Public Safety Realignment Act. This planned to reduce prison overcrowding by transferring lower-level offenders from state facilities to county systems (and in some cases to out of state institutions), and also through liberalising release regimes. The realignment has involved the use of mental health and other collaborative courts to divert people from incarceration, and, at least in theory, moving offenders closer to their families and community services, and prohibiting the return of most probationers and parolees to prison for technical violations of the conditions of their release. All in all, the largest reduction in prison admissions ever undertaken in the United States has occurred in California. Petersilia has found, following interviews with 125 officials in 21 counties of California, that there are mixed views of the impact of the realignment. There was a consensus, however, that Realignment was there to stay, and there was some evidence of success in terms of better interagency working and the encouragement of a more holistic view of offender needs.[57]

57 Petersilia, (2014) 8(2) "California Prison Downsizing and Its Impact on Local Criminal Justice Systems" *Harvard Law and Policy Review* 327-357.

On a much more modest scale we have an example from Ireland. Ireland's prison population was increasing quite dramatically during the mid and late 2000s.[58] Following a change of government in 2011, a review of an earlier decision to build a very large prison was instigated.[59] As part of this review, a group of experts recommended the introduction of a back door strategy to reduce the prison population. This eventually became an initiative called 'community return'. It involves prisoners serving up to 8 years becoming eligible for consideration for supervised release at the half-way point of their sentence. Remission of a sentence is automatic in Ireland after three quarters of the sentence. Under community return, the prisoner is assessed and released into the supervision of the probation service to do community work. Reviews suggest it has been successful, with a completion rate of 89%[60] and it has reduced the prison population by about 300 annually, which is significant in a daily average prison population of about 3,500. Further analysis is needed examining suitability for this sanction and outcome measures in the longer term.

Amending the conditions under which a person can obtain parole is also another mechanism for reducing prison populations, which has been tried in several states recently in the United States. The Vera Institute published a review of legislative changes in US states which shows, for example, that in 2015 Illinois increased the amount of sentenced credits one could earn for completion of a GED[61] in custody, while Kansas now permits good time credit for those imprisoned for serious drug offences, and in 2014 Louisiana reduced the possibility of automatic denial of parole eligibility for those who have committed a major disciplinary offence.[62] The Council of Europe's recommendation on conditional release or parole in 2003 has also stated: "it is desirable to reduce the length of prison sentences as much as possible and that conditional release before the full sentence has been served is an important means to that end".[63]

58 See further, Rogan, *Prison Policy in Ireland: Politics, Penal-Welfarism and Political Imprisonment* (Abingdon, Routledge, 2011).

59 Thornton Hall Project Review Group, *Report of the Thornton Hall Project Review Group* (2011), available at: www.justice.ie/en/JELR/ThorntonReviewReportRedacted.pdf/Files/Thornton ReviewReportRedacted.pdf (last accessed 5 August 2016).

60 Irish Prison Service and Probation Service, *Community Return: A unique opportunity* (Irish Prison Service and Probation Service, 2014), available at: www.probation.ie/website/probationservice/websitepublishingdec09.nsf/AttachmentsByTitle/Community+Return+Study+Report+(November+2014)/$FILE/Community+Return+Study+Report+(November+2014).pdf (last accessed 5 August 2016).

61 General Educational Development Test.

62 Silber, Subramanian, and Spotts, *Justice in Review: New Trends in State Sentencing and Corrections 2014-2015* (Vera Institute of Justice, 2016).

63 Recommendation Rec(2003)22 of the Committee of Ministers to members states on conditional release (parole).

It is clear that the European Convention on Human Rights requires the possibility of release for an individual, no matter how long the sentence. The case of *Vinter v. United Kingdom*[64] concerned whole life sentences. The UK is a rare example in Europe of a jurisdiction which uses whole life orders, from which release is virtually impossible, being allowed only on compassionate grounds. Life without parole or LWOP is of course, a well-known feature of the US system, though there it is also coming under pressure from the US Supreme Court in the context of juveniles.[65] The European Court of Human Rights' Grand Chamber concluded that a whole life order must give rise to the possibility of a review of the sentence, and suggested that such a review must take place no later than the 25 year point. Release is not mandatory, but there must be an assessment of whether it is possible. A subsequent case, however, that of *Hutchinson v. United Kingdom*[66] shows the Court more deferential to the United Kingdom. Subsequently, the Court revisited the question of release in *Murray v. Netherlands*.[67] There, the applicant was serving a life sentence. He argued that he had *de facto* no hope of release as he had never been provided with any psychiatric treatment, and his risk of recidivism was deemed too high to be eligible for release. In the view of the Grand Chamber, there was no 'right' to rehabilitation as such, but its prior case law presupposes that convicted persons should be allowed to rehabilitate themselves, and it is a duty on states to make this possible. Article 3, further, requires states to ensure that the health and well-being of prisoners are adequately secured, and the vulnerability of those with mental illnesses must be considered. All in all, in the case of life sentenced prisoners with mental disabilities and/or mental health problems, for states to comply with Article 3, they must make an assessment of the prisoners' needs concerning treatment and provide prisoners with a real opportunity to undergo rehabilitation. It is for states to decide how this should be dealt with in practice, but a failure to provide a life sentenced prisoner with such an opportunity may render a life sentence *de facto* irreducible, and therefore in breach of Article 3. This important statement of principle is a further example of the European Court of Human Rights' focus on the need to provide access to rehabilitation, and by extension release.[68]

---

64 Application nos 66069/09, 130/10 and 3896/10, July 9 2013. Hereinafter, *Vinter*.

65 *Miller v Alabama* 567 U.S. ___ (2012); *Graham v Florida* 560 U.S. 48 (2010).

66 Application no 57592/08, 3 February 2015.

67 Application no 10511/10, 26 April 2016.

68 *James, Wells and Lee v United Kingdom*, application nos 25119/09, 57715/09, 57877/09, 18 September 2012.

VII. CONCLUSION

It is impossible to unravel the overuse of prison from overcriminalisation, and the overuse of prosecution. While that is so, it is clear from the literature, policy and law examined in this chapter that the harms of imprisonment must be mitigated by promoting access to family contact, reducing overcrowding, robust systems of oversight, accountability and procedural fairness, and in making judicious use of release.

CRIMINAL POLICY AND IMPRISONMENT

The Case of Lithuania: Open Prisons, Prison Leave and Release on Parole

Gintautas Sakalauskas*

I. INTRODUCTION: VIEW TO THE PRESENT THROUGH THE PAST

Lithuania is a small and the southernmost Baltic country with just about 3 million inhabitants. On 11 March 1990, Lithuania proclaimed its independence after Soviet occupation, which lasted for almost 50 years. Lithuania is a member of NATO and of the European Union since 2004.

From criminological research and analysis we know that historical and cultural contingencies, structural features of countries' legal and social systems and distinctive cultural and historical characteristics have a powerful influence on the reality of criminal policy.[1] After almost 30 years of independent legislation and the creation of a separate criminal justice system the influence of a long punishment culture and tradition is still appreciable.

The modern independent Republic of Lithuania was established in 1918, following the end of the First World War and the collapse of the Russian Empire. Lithuania had become a part of the Empire at the end of the 18th century, after almost 500 years of statehood, the Grand Duchy of Lithuania (the largest country in Europe) and a voluntary two-state union, the Polish-Lithuanian Commonwealth. In 1918, when the independence of Lithuania was restored, the Russian Criminal Statute of 1903 was proclaimed as coming into force (in its

* G. Sakalauskas is associated Professor at Vilnius University, Law Faculty, Department for Criminal Justice.

1 Tonry, M. (2014) 'Thinking about Punishment across Space and Time', *1 Kriminologijos studijos 1*, p. 7.

entirety)[2] in Lithuania, with some changes.[3] The practise of punishment was relatively harsh, and the Republic of Lithuania had one of the highest levels of imprisonment rates in Europe.[4]

The Soviet ideology in place since 1944 brought a new totalitarian thinking. Crime, according to Soviet ideology, was a phenomenon that could not take root in a socialist society and that must inevitably die out there.[5] The crimes that still existed were explained as being caused by remnants of capitalism in the consciousness of individual Soviet citizens and foreign influences.[6] This meant a corresponding approach to deal with people who (still) committed crimes. They had to be either "corrected" or "re-educated" and exploited as a cheap labour force.[7] In order to implement this ideology the Criminal Code and the Criminal Enforcement Code, and the infrastructure of penal institutions and education of staff was developed. Imprisonment was often used, and sentences were usually long, especially for repeated crimes. The recidivism (repeated criminal behaviour) was "an indication" of incomplete correction or re-education and by subsequent sentencing, recidivists were automatically punished with much longer imprisonment sentences.

Since the proclamation of independence, a lot of new tendencies and social phenomena have emerged in Lithuania. The number of criminal offences recorded by police for the period 1989-2000 increased from 31,238 to 82,370 (from approximately 1,000 per 100,000 of inhabitants to 2,400).[8] Possible causes of this increase were the following: a) failures and delays in the creation of a democratic system of formal and informal social control after the transition from a totalitarian to a democratic system of state and b) increased opportunities to commit criminal offences (especially those related to property).[9] However, the new tendencies which emerged were not just limited to the dramatic increase in

2 In the Russian Empire, just a few sections of this law came in to force.

3 Švedas, G. (2000) *Criminal Justice Systems in Europe and North America: Lithuania.* Helsinki: HEUNI, p. 6.

4 von Hofer, H. (2010) 'Anmerkungen zum Forschung bzgl. Der Erklärung von Gefangenenraten', in: F. Dünkel, T. Lappi-Sepälä, C. Morgenstern & D. van Zyl Smit (Hrsg.), *Kriminalität, Kriminalpolitik, strafrechtliche Sanktionspraxis und Gefangenenraten im europäischen Vergleich*, Band 37/2, Mönchengladbach: Forum Verlag Godesberg, p. 36.

5 Feldbrugge, F. J. (1963) 'Soviet Criminal Law – The Last Six Years', *54 Journal of Criminal Law, Criminology & Police Science 3*, p. 263. See also Dobryninas, A. (2018) 'Criminology in Lithuania: Restoring Paradigms', in: R.A. Triplett (ed.), *The Handbook of the History and Philosophy of Criminology*, Oxford: Wiley Blackwell, p. 410-414.

6 *Idem.*

7 In 1941 and 1945–1952 at least 130,000 people from Lithuania were forcibly transported to labour camps and other forced settlements in Siberia. Approximately 150, 000 Lithuanian partisans and political prisoners were deported to Gulags (prison camps).

8 See also Dobryninas, A. & G. Sakalauskas (2011) 'Country survey: Criminology, crime and criminal justice in Lithuania', *8 European Journal of Criminology 5*, p. 423-424.

9 Čepas, A. & G. Sakalauskas (2010) 'Lithuania', in: R. G. Newman, M. F. Aebi & V. Jaquier (eds), *Crime and punishment around the world. Europe*, Vol. 4. Santa Barbara: ABC-CLIO, p. 201.

the numbers of registered crimes. Free media showed the true picture of crime prevalence with additional dramatisation. Organised crime was on the rise with spectacular murders, explosions and extortion broadcast through the media. Citizens were confronted with the true reality of crime rates and a poorly performing police force seemed to have lost control of it.

After the restoration of the independent state of Lithuania, the (Soviet) Criminal Code of 1961 was retained. However, during the period of independence it has undergone several fundamental reforms (in 1992, 1994, 1996 and 1997–1998), as a consequence of which 90% of the Articles have been amended.[10] The growth of punitiveness during the 1990s and early 2000s was understood as a "necessary" and "matter-of-course" reaction to the increasing crime rate. One important example, capital punishment was only abolished in Lithuania by law on 21 December 1998 (very late in comparison to other countries in Europe!) when the Constitutional Court of the Republic of Lithuania ruled that this punishment was unconstitutional. Between 1991 and 2002 the proportion of custodial sentences in the annual total of court-imposed punishments nearly doubled, rising from 27% to 47%.[11] As a result, by 1999, the prison population in Lithuania reached 410 per 100,000 population, up from 248 in 1991.[12]

The year 2000 saw the Lithuanian state granting the sixth but largest amnesty since 1990, which helped reduce the prison population at the time.[13] However, the pressure to reduce the prison population and to balance criminal policy came from outside; it was not an inward political or social conviction regarding the need for more responsible criminal policy.[14] Lithuania sought EU and NATO membership; many reforms were resulted from this desire. International standards of human rights were immediately embraced, but in practice change came slowly.[15]

On 1 May 2003 the first national Criminal Code of the Republic of Lithuania came into force along with the Code of Criminal Procedure and the Code of Execution of Penalties. Significant changes included additions of new types of penalties and their application, limitations on the use of prison, the availability of

10 Švedas, G. (2000) *Criminal Justice Systems in Europe and North America: Lithuania.* Helsinki: HEUNI, p. 7.

11 Dobryninas, A. & G. Sakalauskas (2011) 'Country survey: Criminology, crime and criminal justice in Lithuania', *8 European Journal of Criminology 5*, p. 424.

12 Idem, p. 425, 427.

13 Idem, p. 425.

14 See, for example, *Prison Populations and Penal Policy in Estonia, Latvia and Lithuania.* Council of Europe Conference. Stockholm 22-24 October 1997. Documentation.

15 Čepas, A. & G. Sakalauskas (2010) 'Lithuania', in: R. G. Newman, M. F. Aebi & V. Jaquier (eds.), *Crime and punishment around the world. Europe*, Vol. 4. Santa Barbara: ABC-CLIO, p. 198.

reconciliation,[16] and separate treatment for minors, including alternatives to imprisonment.[17] As a result, the share of custodial sentences in the annual total of court-imposed punishments fell to an average of 30% during the period 2004-2011 (penalty of arrest (i.e. short-term imprisonment) accounted for approximately of 40% of the decrease). The use of fines underwent a considerable increase at this time (it had risen to approximately 30% of the total of penalties in recent years). The corresponding proportions of limitation of liberty ("house arrest") and suspension of imprisonment in the form of probation together averaged 30%.[18] The prison population was reduced; nevertheless it was still one the highest in the EU (240 per 100,000 inhabitants). The prison population started growing again in 2009 and began to fall in 2011 (330). At the end of 2018 there were 235 imprisoned per 100,000 of inhabitants of Lithuania. Even after the decrease in the number of prisoners, Lithuania together with Latvia and Estonia (both 195 in 2018) remained in the top of the list of EU countries where the number of prisoners is the biggest.

For a generalisation on this "past tradition" and its influence for the present, remarks of famous criminologists are very helpful. Firstly, the words of K. Krajewski should be noted: he asserts that "most important causal factors are the region's communist past and the persisting influence of Soviet-imposed thinking about crime and punishment. This thinking was permeated by rigorist and punitive attitudes, with the deeply rooted belief that harsh sanctions constitute a panacea for all social problems, and that imprisonment is the most important and effective sanction."[19] And the attitudes towards criminals and (ex-)prisoners in the Baltic countries were rightly described by M. Tonry: "the former Soviet view of prisoners as class enemies is likely for a good while yet to engender a fundamental lack of sympathy with the interests and experiences of prisoners."[20] This insight is very important for the subhead of this article and the rare use of open prisons, prison leave and release on parole in Lithuania.

16 See also Bikelis, S. & G. Sakalauskas (2015) 'Lithuania', in: F. Dünkel, J. Grzywa-Holten & P. Horsfield (eds.), *Restorative Justice and Mediation in Penal Matters*, Mönchengladbach: Forum Verlag Godesberg, p. 477-500.

17 See also Čepas, A. & G. Sakalauskas (2010) 'Lithuania', in: R. G. Newman, M. F. Aebi & V. Jaquier (eds), *Crime and punishment around the world. Europe*, Vol. 4. Santa Barbara: ABC-CLIO, p. 197-198.

18 Dobryninas, A. & G. Sakalauskas (2011) 'Country survey: Criminology, crime and criminal justice in Lithuania', *8 European Journal of Criminology 5*, p. 425-426.

19 Krajewski, K. (2014) 'Different penal climates in Europe', *1 Kriminologijos studijos 1*, p. 109.

20 Tonry, M. (2014) 'Thinking about Punishment across Space and Time', *1 Kriminologijos studijos 1*, p. 23.

II. OVERUSE OF IMPRISONMENT

The research of T. Lappi-Seppälä shows that moderate penal policies have their roots in a consensual and corporatist political culture, in a high level of social trust and political legitimacy, and in a strong welfare state.[21] These factors have both indirect and direct influence on the contents of penal policy, and of course on the imprisonment rates. The lack of all the aforementioned factors[22] is extremely adverse to the creation of a moderate penal policy in Lithuania.

Figure 1 shows the stabilisation of numbers of imprisoned persons per 100,000 of the population in Lithuania from 2003 to 2007 (237–245), but the prison population rate started growing again in 2008–2009. There were 6,599 persons incarcerated in Lithuanian prisons, including 611 remand prisoners on 31 December 2017. Thus, the prisoner rate was 235 prisoners per 100,000 of the population and was the highest in the EU, despite the significant decrease since 2011 (from 330).

An important question is what the reasons were for the increase of imprisonment in 2008–2011 and the decrease in 2012–2017. What trends can be expected in the future?

The reasons for the increase of the number of imprisoned persons in 2008–2011 were:

- The economical / financial crisis → more punitiveness;
- the tightening of criminal law; and
- more restrictive praxis of release on parole.

The economy in Lithuania experienced a dramatic change by the end of 2008. Lithuania had been hit considerably by the economic crisis. There was a minimal rise of 2.9% in GDP in 2008 and a decline in GDP of 14.8% in 2009. The official unemployment rate was 13.7%. In 2010, GDP rose again by 1.5% and in 2011 by 5.9%, and the unemployment rates were 17.8% and 15.3%, respectively.[23] It is often believed that bad economic times must cause an increase in crime, but there is no simple or linear relationship between financial crisis and crime.[24] Nonetheless, the worry of a purported increase in crime caused harsher actions

---

21 Lappi-Seppälä, T. (2011) 'Explaining imprisonment in Europe', *8 European Journal of Criminology 4*, p. 321.

22 See also DeMichele, M. (2013) 'Using Weber's Rechtssoziologie to Explain Western Punishment: A Typological Framework', *21 European Journal of Crime, Criminal Law and Criminal Justice 1*, p. 85-109; Sakalauskas, G. & F. Dünkel (2017) 'Kriminalpolitik und Sanktionspraxis in Litauen im europäischen Vergleich', *Monatsschrift für Kriminologie und Strafrechtsreform, 100. Jahrgang, Heft 2*, p. 103–122.

23 See also Sakalauskas, G. (2014) 'Lithuania', in: K. Drenkhahn, M. Dudeck & F. Dünkel (eds), *Long-Term Imprisonment and Human Rights*, Abingdon: Routledge, p. 198.

24 Aromaa, K. (2014) 'Responsible criminal policy / Crime and criminal policy', *1 Kriminologijos studijos 1*, p. 81-82.

Figure 1. Imprisoned persons in Lithuania, 2003–2017 (one-day snapshots at the end of every year)

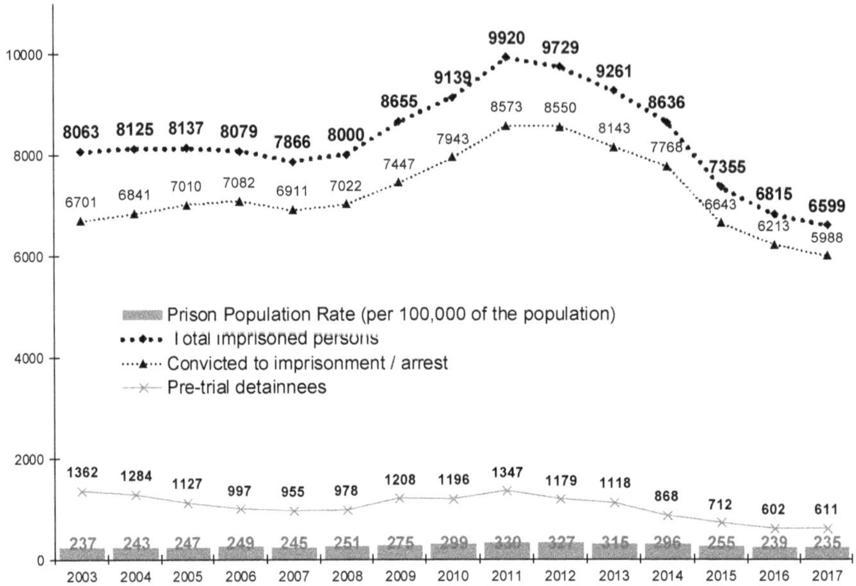

to be taken against criminals. During this period, the number of crimes in Lithuania remained unchanged, while the most serious and grave violent crimes (homicide, serious bodily injury, rape, robbery) were declining continuously. The intensified criminal prosecution of those found guilty of domestic violence has increased the total number of convicted persons by about 20%, but it is not an essential reason for the growth of the prison population.

Figure 2 shows the crime rate (per 100,000 of the population) and imprisonment rate (per 1 Mio of the population).[25] The gap began to grow wider in 2009 and continued this wan until 2011, when in 2012 it began to narrow.

Figure 3 shows the imprisonment rate and the rate of significant serious and grave violent crimes in Lithuania. The number of significant serious and grave violent crimes (intentional homicide, serious bodily injury, rape, sex abuse and robbery) recorded by police for the period 2004 to 2017 decreased continually from 6,459 to 1,602.

It is worth noting that the level of recorded criminal offences in Lithuania is several times lower compared to many Western and Central European countries.[26] For example, in 2015 there were 2,490 registered criminal offences

25 There are different numbers of population (crime rates per 100,000 and prison rates per 1 million of the population).

26 There are a lot of reasons for this, but two main reasons can be mentioned: less criminalisation (for example, decriminalisation of small thefts or drunk driving) and a lack of trust in criminal

Figure 2. Crime rates and prison population rates in Lithuania, 2004–2017

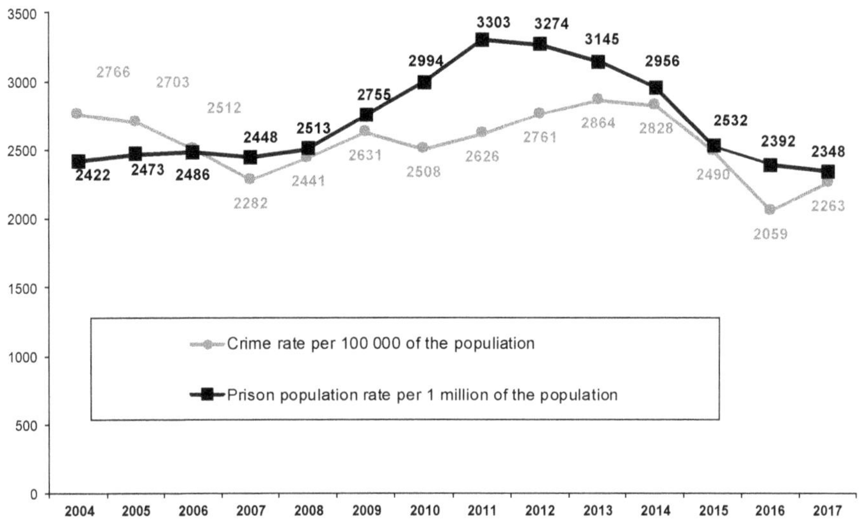

per 100,000 of population in comparison with 7,169 in the Netherlands, 7,328 in Germany, 8,525 in Finland or 15,042 in Sweden (all in 2011).[27] However, Lithuania, like many other post-Communist countries, demonstrates substantially higher rates of violent offences. In 2017 129 intentional homicides were recorded in Lithuania, making up 4.5 of recorded intentional homicides per 100,000 of the population. It was the year when the number of recorded intentional homicides was the lowest in Lithuania since 1991 (the biggest number of intentional homicides was recorded in 1994 – 523, 14.3 (!) per 100,000 of population). According to EUROSTAT, this indicator was the highest in the Baltic countries in 2016, as compared to all other European countries, for example 5.64 in Latvia, 2.51 in Estonia, 1.42 in Finland, 1.22 in England and Wales, 0.91 in Germany, 0.67 in Italy and in Poland. Riga (capital city of Latvia) was demonstrating the highest rates compared to all other European capitals (7.19) together with Vilnius (3.31) and Tallinn (2.36). In absolute terms, 21 intentional homicides were recorded in Vilnius (approx. 0.5 million population) in 2016; this number was just 2.2 times lower as in Berlin – 47 (with 3.5 million population). Domestic murders, often involving alcohol intoxication as an important factor, account for the majority of intentional homicides.

justice, which results in less frequent reporting of crimes to the police in comparison with Western countries.

27 Aebi, M.F., G. Akdeniz & G. Barclay (et al.) (2014) *European sourcebook of crime and criminal justice statistics* 2014, Fifth edition, Helsinki: Heuni, p. 32.

Figure 3. Imprisonment flow and serious/grave violent crimes in Lithuania, 2004–2017

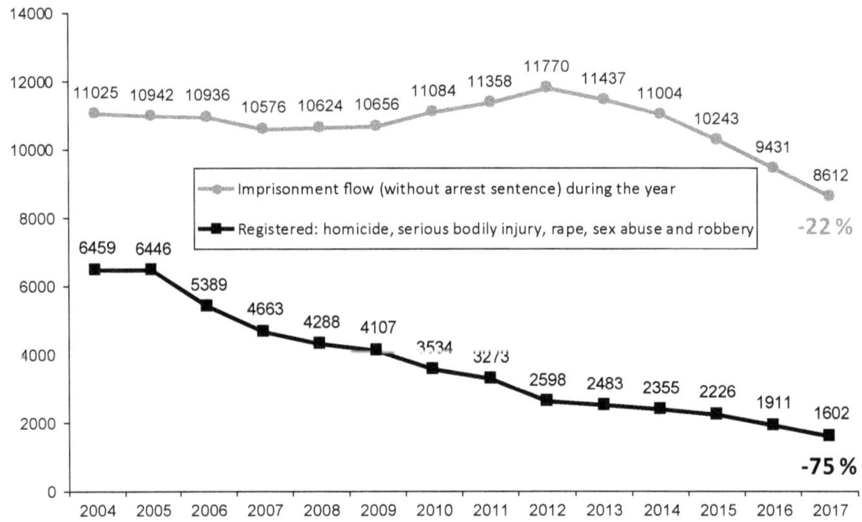

Robberies account for about 70–80% of registered serious and grave violent crimes shown in Figure 3. The number of robberies recorded by police for the period 2004 to 2017 decreased continually from 5,323 to 1,088. It is worth paying attention to the fact that more than 50% of the prisoners serve their sentences for one of the five crimes presented in Figure 3. In 2004, the most serious and grave crimes for which prisoners served their sentences were the ones mentioned in Figure 3:[28] robbery (24.5%), intentional homicide (20.7%), followed by rape (5.1%) and serious bodily injury (4.0%). In 2017 the corresponding crimes were intentional homicide (25.8%), robbery (10.5%), rape (5.7%) and serious bodily injury (4.2%).[29] Therefore, a decrease (75%) in the numbers of these crimes should also have a positive influence (decreasing) on imprisonment rates, but this was not the case. The punishment was harsher for aforementioned crimes and also for other crimes.

The problem of the high prisoner rate is caused by sentences for long-term imprisonment. The average length of sentences imposed by courts stood at 80 months at the end of 2017 and it was the largest number in this period (Figure 4).

28 In first place was theft, with 25.5% of all prisoners being convicted of this, and 4.4% of all prisoners were convicted of drug offences.

29 In 2017, the proportion of prisoners convicted for thefts decreased to 13.1% of all prisoners, those convicted of drug offences increased to 12.2% and for swindling, the proportion increased to 5.8% of all prisoners.

Figure 4. Average length of sentences of imprisonment imposed by courts for prisoners and average length of stay in prison, 1998–2017 (prisoner one-day snapshots at the end of every year)

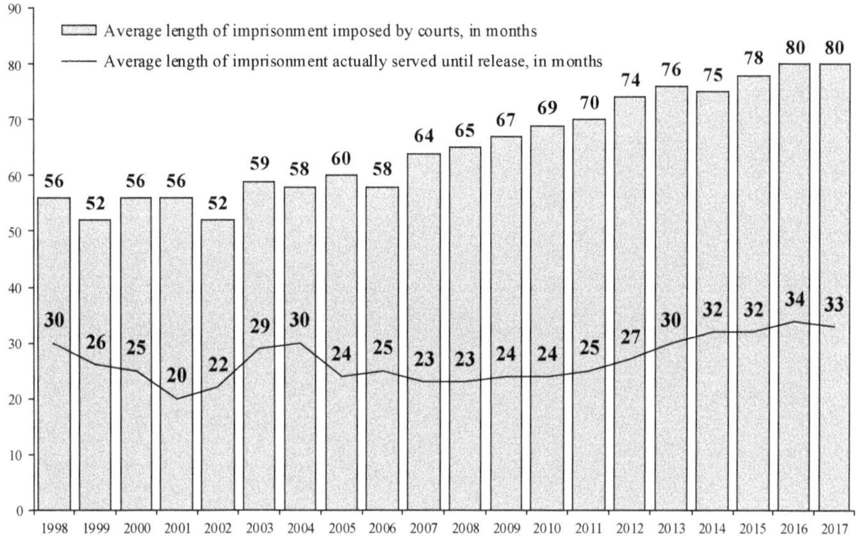

The average length of imprisonment sentences actually served before release from prison, however, was less than half as long, 33 months, but was also in the last two years the longest in this period.

Figure 5 shows that almost 50% of sentenced prisoners were facing a term of more than five years at the end of 2017. Almost 1/5 of the prisoners had to serve a sentence of three to five years. A look at the developments since 2003 shows that the proportion of prisoners serving a longer term of imprisonment slightly increased. The proportion of prisoners sentenced from 10 to 15 years has increased the most – from 612 to 1,142 (from 9.1% to 19.1% of all prisoners).[30]

This indicates the prevalence of quite a repressive penal policy and culture in Lithuania, as the rates of recorded criminal offences and convicted persons do not differ significantly in Lithuania as compared to other countries. On the contrary, the aforementioned indicators are up to several times lower in Lithuania. One of the main reasons lies in the long terms of imprisonment, the relatively frequent imposition of pre-trial detention and the very restrictive praxis of parole. In Lithuania, one of the peculiarities of life imprisonment is the

30 See also Sakalauskas, G. (2014) 'Lithuania', in: K. Drenkhahn, M. Dudeck & F. Dünkel (eds), *Long-Term Imprisonment and Human Rights*, Abingdon: Routledge, p. 200–202.

Figure 5. Number of prisoners according to length of imprisonment, 1997–2017 (one-day snapshots at the end of every year)

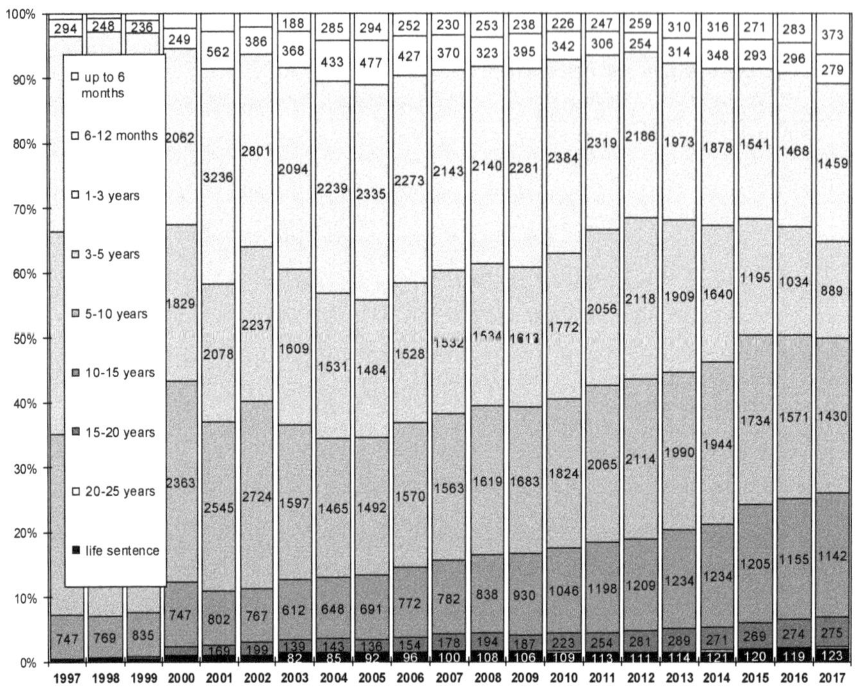

absence of a parole option set forth in legislation.[31] At the beginning of 2018, there were 123 convicted persons serving life imprisonment.

The next important question is: what are the reasons for the decrease in imprisonment since 2011, in particular in 2015 (see Figure 1)? Can it be an indication of a more moderate "penal climate" in Lithuanian penal practice? Partially yes, but these tendencies are also caused by natural trends of recorded crimes, crime investigation processes and the consequences of restricted practice of release on parole since 2011.

Figure 6 shows the differences between numbers of newly imprisoned persons and released persons. The number of released persons for the period 2011 to 2015 increased from 2,839 to 3,492. In recent years, more prisoners were released after a fully served sentence, because they had not been released for parole earlier (see also Figure 9). The number of released persons after fully served prison sentences increased from 1,676 in 2011 to 2,288 in 2015 (36.5%).

31 On 23 May 2017, in the case of *Matiošaitis and Others v. Lithuania*, the European Court of Human Rights found a violation of Article 3 ECHR, which prohibits torture, because Lithuanian law does not provide prisoners serving a life sentence with a realistic possibility to apply for a commutation of their sentence.

Figure 6. Relation between new entries and release from imprisonment, 1998–2017

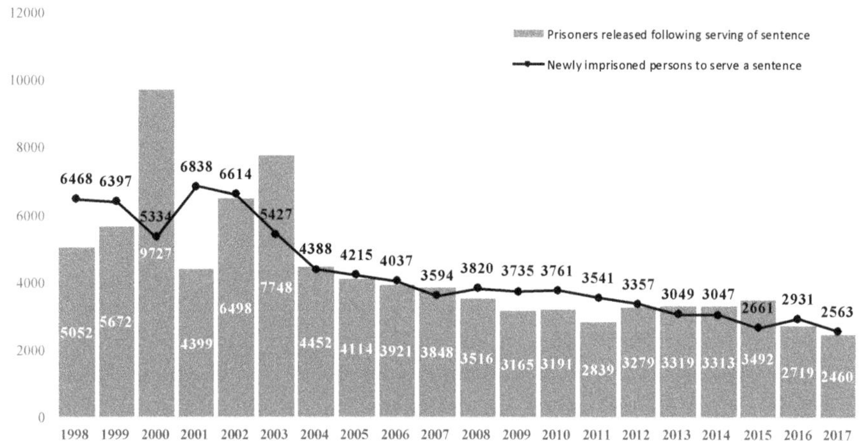

Therefore, a significant reason for the decrease of imprisonment rates is the prisoners' "jam". This jam developed because fewer prisoners were released on parole, but it was later dissolved because many prisoners reached the end of their prison sentences while at the same time the restricted use of parole came to an end.

The first reason for the decrease in imprisonment rates is the decrease of recorded serious and grave crimes and the number of persons accused of these crimes:[32] the number of crimes decreased from 4,634 in 2012 to 3,778 in 2015 and 2,835 in 2017; and the number of the accused decreased from 2,713 in 2010 to 1,782 in 2016. The decrease in the number of accused persons (27.6%) was the largest in 2016, from 2,461 in 2014. The decrease in recorded serious and grave crimes in 2016 was 18.4% (from 4,063 to 3,315). Both these reasons (released prisoners' "jam" and decrease in serious and grave crimes including decrease in numbers of persons accused of these crimes) are the most significant reasons explaining the decrease in imprisonment rate in 2012–2014 and in particular in 2015–2016.

32 According to Article 11 of the Criminal Code of the Republic of Lithuania, crimes can be committed with intent and through negligence. Intentional crimes are divided into minor, less serious, serious and grave crimes. A minor crime is an intentional crime punishable, under the criminal law, by a custodial sentence of a maximum duration of three years. A less serious crime is an intentional crime punishable, under the criminal law, by a custodial sentence of a maximum duration in excess of three years, but not exceeding six years' imprisonment. A serious crime is an intentional crime punishable, under the criminal law, by a custodial sentence of a duration in excess of three years, but not exceeding ten years' imprisonment. A grave crime is an intentional crime punishable, under the criminal law, by a custodial sentence of a maximum duration in excess of ten years.

There were a couple of legal changes that influenced the decrease. At the end of 2014 a new provision of the Criminal Code of the Republic of Lithuania came into force, establishing that small thefts up to the value of 114 Euros (instead of up to 38 Euros before) were decriminalised (they became administrative infringements only).[33] In 2015 the number of registered thefts decreased by 17.5%. Therefore, some people were not convicted of theft.[34] Furthermore, according to Article 3, Paragraph 2 of the Criminal Code of the Republic of Lithuania, a criminal law nullifying the criminality of an act, commuting a penalty or otherwise mitigating legal circumstances of the person who committed the criminal act shall have a retroactive effect, i.e., shall apply to the persons who have committed criminal acts prior to the coming into force of the law, and also to persons serving a sentence and those with previous convictions. In 2015, 113 prisoners were released from prison because of replacement of the sentence (see last Figure 9), and most of the cases related to the decriminalisation of minor theft.

The changes that took place in the criminal law in 2015 were more significant as regards the imposition of a penalty and less significant in relation to the imprisonment rate. Since 23 March 2015 imprisonment is no longer an "ordinary penalty" for a repeat offender (recidivist).[35] Before the aforementioned change took place Article 56, Paragraph 1 of the Criminal Code of the Republic of Lithuania stated that "as a rule a court shall impose a custodial sentence upon a repeat offender for the commission of an intentional crime." This provision was abolished. Currently it is difficult to say what impact this change has had and will have in the future in practice. Looking at the practice of Lithuanian courts, though, it could be guessed that this new regulation could save a few hundred convicted persons from custodial sanctions every year.

The next important change was a new possibility for suspended imprisonment (probation) to be imposed in cases of serious crimes. According to Article 75, Paragraph 1 of the Criminal Code of the Republic of Lithuania, when a person is sentenced to imprisonment for a term not exceeding three years for the commission of one or several minor, less serious or serious intentional crimes, or a term not exceeding six years for crimes committed through negligence, a court may suspend the imposed sentence for a period ranging from one to three years. The sentence may be suspended when the court rules that

33 Since 1 January 2018 this value is 150 euros.

34 Sure, one small theft does not always result in imprisonment, but this decriminalisation can be important in case of reoffending.

35 According to Article 27 of the Criminal Code of the Republic of Lithuania, repeat offence is a situation when an adult person already convicted for the commission of an intentional crime, where his prior conviction has not expired yet or has not been expunged in accordance with the procedure laid down by laws, repeatedly commits one or several intentional crimes. Such a person shall be considered a repeat offender.

there is a sufficient basis for believing that the purpose of the penalty will be achieved without the sentence actually being served. In 2015 there were 1,683 persons accused of serious crimes – the lowest number since 2008; in 2009–2014 there were approximately 2,000 persons accused of serious crimes each year. It is also difficult to say what number of sentenced persons will benefit from this legal change and will evade real imprisonment. However, the number could be a few hundred convicted persons every year. Unfortunately, the possibility to suspend imprisonment for serious crimes was abolished in October 2017.

In summary it can be said that imprisonment retains a very important role in Lithuanian criminal policy. Despite some changes in the Criminal Code of the Republic of Lithuania, there were 235 prisoners per 100,000 of population in 2017 and Lithuania ranked highest in the EU in terms of incarceration rate. For a further decline of the prison population there must be foremost a significant change in penal culture. One view on the purpose of the penalty and the nature of imprisonment is also a very restrictive use of prison leave, open prisons and a very rare application of conditional release from prison.

III. OPEN PRISONS, PRISON LEAVE AND RELEASE ON PAROLE

The possibilities for prison leave, the presence of open prisons and general conditions for release on parole are excellent indicators of a humane and inclusion-orientated prison system. According to the European Prison Rules (2006), restrictions placed on persons deprived of their liberty shall be the minimum necessary and shall be proportionate to the legitimate objective for which they are imposed (Article 3); life in prison shall approximate as closely as possible the positive aspects of life in the community (Article 5); all detention shall be managed so as to facilitate the reintegration into the free society of persons who have been deprived of their liberty (Article 6); the security measures applied to individual prisoners shall be the minimum necessary to achieve their secure custody (Article 51.1); there shall be a system of prison leave as an integral part of the overall regime for sentenced prisoners (Article 103.6); sentenced prisoners shall be assisted in good time prior to release by procedures and special programmes enabling them to make the transition from life in prison to a law-abiding life in the community (Article 107.1).

A modern prison system is orientated not to "do bird" in maximum closed conditions, but to ensure the possible reintegration of prisoners and minimisation of incarceration damage. The maximum possible "opening" of prison institutions will also serve to lower the tension inherent in any prison environment and by the same token significantly reduce the likelihood of violent incidents and associated ill-treatment.[36] The Soviet imprisonment system was created to exploit and to repress "social enemies" under maximum closed conditions. Unfortunately, this thinking goes into decline very slowly.

The open prisons (named "open colonies") are designed for adults who have been sentenced for offences of negligence and minor intentional offences and for whom the court has ordered the sentence to be served in an open prison (Article 90, Paragraph 1 of the Code of the Execution of Penalties of the Republic of Lithuania).[37] The prisoners in open colonies have significantly more rights than prisoners in closed prisons. There are no physical precautions against escapes, but prisoners are supervised. They are allowed to move freely within a certain area during the day, to possess money and valuables and they may dispose of their money without restrictions. Moreover, they are allowed to receive visitors, parcels and print media, to receive and send letters, and to make long-distance calls without restrictions. They are allowed to leave the open prison without supervision on permission of the administration. Until the middle of 2012, the law did not provide for a possibility to transfer prisoners from closed prisons ("houses of correction") to an open prison. Since 1 July 2012, prisoners with a remaining term of up to one year may be transferred from a closed prison to an open prison by way of a court decision.[38] There is (and always has been) only one open prison in Lithuania and there are very few prisoners serving their sentence in the open prison: only 60-80 persons at any given time, just in 2017 the number increased up to 121 persons (Table 1), but nevertheless it makes up just 2% of all prisoners.

---

36 CPT reports on visits in Lithuania show the situation in prisons very well and it is not good. Available at: www.cpt.coe.int/en/states/ltu.htm.

37 The Code of the Execution of Penalties of the Republic of Lithuania came in to force on 1 May 2003 together with the Criminal Code and the Criminal Procedure Code; it regulates the enforcement of all sanctions provided by the Criminal Code. Thus, there is no separate prison act. See also Sakalauskas, G. (2005) 'The rights of the persons with restricted freedom', in: A. Čepas (ed.), *Human Rights in Lithuania*, Vilnius: Naujos sistemos, p. 315-316; Sakalauskas, G. (2006) *Strafvollzug in Litauen. Kriminalpolitische Hintergründe, rechtliche Regelungen, Reformen, Praxis und Perspektiven*. Mönchengladbach: Forum Verlag Godesberg, 2006; Sakalauskas, G. (2014) 'Lithuania', in: K. Drenkhahn, M. Dudeck & F. Dünkel (eds.), *Long-Term Imprisonment and Human Rights*, Abingdon: Routledge, p. 204; Sakalauskas, G. (2015) 'Strafvollzug in Litauen: Blick zurück oder nach vorne?', *27 Neue Kriminalpolitik 2*, p. 190-201; Sakalauskas, G. (2019) 'Prisoner resettlement in Lithuania – Between Soviet tradition and challenges of modern society', in: F. Dünkel, I. Pruin, A. Storgaard & J. Weber (ed.), *Prisoner Resettlement in Europe*, Routledge Frontiers of Criminal Justice, Abingdon: Routledge, p. 219-239.

38 Sakalauskas, G. (2014) 'Lithuania', in: K. Drenkhahn, M. Dudeck & F. Dünkel (eds.), *Long-Term Imprisonment and Human Rights*, Abingdon: Routledge, p. 206.

Table 1. Prisoners in the open prison in Lithuania 1998-2017 (one-day snapshots at the end of every year)

Year	1998	1999	2000	2001	2002	2003	2004	2005	2006	2007
Total prisoners	11983	12205	7601	9755	9414	6701	6841	7010	7082	6911
Of whom are in an open prison	99	130	165	73	82	58	41	47	48	55
%	0.8	1.1	2.2	0.7	0.9	0.9	0.6	0.7	0.8	0.8

Year	2008	2009	2010	2011	2012	2013	2014	2015	2016	2017
Total prisoners	7022	7447	7943	8573	8550	8143	7768	6643	6213	5988
Of whom are in an open prison	59	78	82	97	92	80	62	66	94	121
%	0.8	1.0	1.0	1.1	1.1	1.0	0.8	1.0	1.5	2.0

Closed prison leave is being allowed very rarely in Lithuanian imprisonment practice. There are a few grounds for prison leave:

1) prison leave for work, education and rehabilitation; this right can be granted to prisoners who are serving a sentence in a light discipline group or in a common discipline group after serving one-third of the sentence imposed (Article 154, Paragraph 1 of the Code of the Execution of Penalties of the Republic of Lithuania);[39]
2) short-term prison leave home for three days per three-month period; this leave can be granted to prisoners who are serving a sentence in a light discipline group or in a common discipline group after serving half of the sentence imposed (for juveniles after serving one-third of the sentence imposed) (Article 104 of the Code of the Execution of Penalties of the Republic of Lithuania);
3) prison leave for up to ten days in case of a crisis at home (Article 105 of the Code of the Execution of Penalties of the Republic of Lithuania); and
4) prison leave for 14 days per year as a kind of holiday for working prisoners (Article 130 of the Code of the Execution of Penalties of the Republic of Lithuania).

Figure 7 demonstrates that at the beginning of 2018 only 305 out of 5,798 (5.3%) prisoners had the right to leave prison for work, education or rehabilitation. This rate is calculated as one-day snapshots at the beginning of the year, because some

39 For juveniles it is possible after three months of the sentence imposed. Nevertheless, there are many restriction exceptions for adults, for example, when a sentence is longer than ten years, the prisoner is a dangerous recidivist etc.

prisoners have been granted this right and can use it until this right will be taken away. However, the continual increase in this number since 2010 is positive.

Figure 7. Prison leave for work, education and rehabilitation, 2000–2017

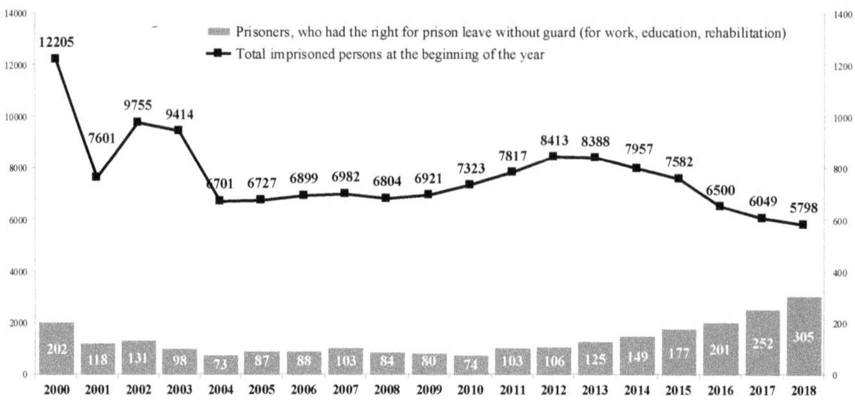

Figure 8 shows other possibilities for prison leave. These rates are calculated as an annual sum (number of cases per year); therefore it is demonstrated in relation to annual prison flow. In 2014-2017 there was an increase in the number of short-term prison leave home, nonetheless 347 cases in 2017 only amounted to 4.0% of all prisoners. The numbers of cases of prison leave because of a crisis at home[40] and as a kind of holiday for working prisoners are even less.

The numbers presented in Figure 7 and Figure 8 indicate a very closed nature in the Lithuanian prison system, inherited from the Soviet era, and which is changing very slowly despite new legislation.

According to Article 157, Paragraph 1 of the Code of the Execution of Penalties of the Republic of Lithuania, prisoners may be granted release on parole if they implement the measures provided for in the individual plan of social rehabilitation and have applied to the commission for release on parole. Furthermore, they can be released only if their risk of recidivism is low and (or) their progress in reducing of risk of recidivism justifies an assumption that they will behave in a law-abiding manner and will not commit any crimes in future. Prisoners who have actually served the following minimum parts of their sentences may be granted release on parole:

1) prisoners sentenced for offences of negligence if the sentence imposed does not exceed six years, other inmates if the sentence imposed does not exceed three years, as well as juveniles after serving one-third of the sentence imposed, but not earlier than after having served four months;

40 This right cannot be granted to persons sentenced to life imprisonment.

2) inmates sentenced for offences of negligence if the sentence imposed exceeds six years and other inmates with a sentence of more than three years and less than ten years after serving half of the sentence imposed;
3) inmates sentenced to more than ten years but less than fifteen years of imprisonment after serving two-thirds of the sentence imposed;
4) inmates sentenced to more than fifteen years but less than to twenty-five years of imprisonment after serving three-quarters of the sentence imposed (Article 157, Paragraph 2 of the Code of the Execution of Penalties of the Republic of Lithuania).

Figure 8. Prison leave on other grounds, 2004–2017

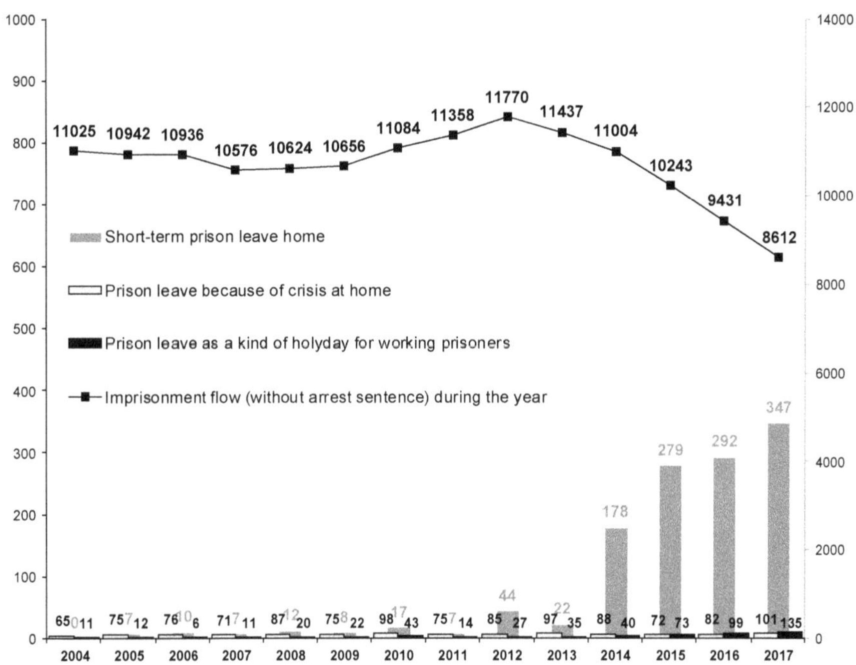

The Probation Act of 2011 provides for, among other things, electronic monitoring. If the inmate consents to electronic monitoring, he or she may be granted release on parole six months earlier than the date set in Article 157, Paragraph 2 of the Code of the Execution of Penalties of the Republic of Lithuania.

The decision on release on parole falls within the remit of a commission of release on parole, which is established in each institution (there are even multiple commissions within some institutions). However, this decision has to be confirmed by a district court. The commissions consist of representatives of municipal councils, communities, associations and educational institutions as well as volunteers.[41]

Figure 9. Grounds for release from prison, 1998–2017

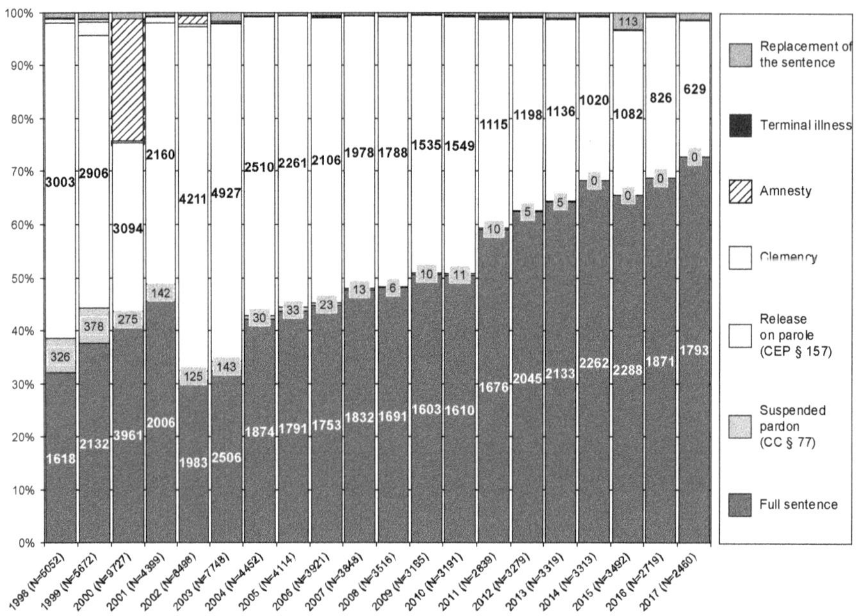

If the commission refuses the inmate's application, it cannot be addressed again for the next six months. The practice of release on parole has been very limited in recent years. As Figure 9 demonstrates, the absolute annual number of total released prisoners decreased rapidly in 2011; whereas 7,748 prisoners were released in 2003, only 2,839 were released in 2011 (see also Figure 6). In addition, the proportion of prisoners discharged after having served their full sentence increased from around 30% in 2003 to 65-75% in 2015-2017. Conversely, the proportion of prisoners released early on parole fell from two-thirds of total release in 2002 to a mere 25-30% in 2014–2017.

It can be assumed that the practice of release on parole has become more limited because of the new regulation from 2012 and the establishment of commissions. An interesting negative side effect has been that the courts deny half of commissions' the positive decisions. Prisoners are more likely to be assessed with groundless mistrust. This was influenced by a false "message" to the

41 See also Sakalauskas, G. (2014) 'Lithuania', in: K. Drenkhahn, M. Dudeck & F. Dünkel (eds), *Long-Term Imprisonment and Human Rights*, Abingdon: Routledge, p. 214; Sakalauskas, G. (2015).'Strafvollzug in Litauen: Blick zurück oder nach vorne?', *27 Neue Kriminalpolitik 2*, p. 197-199.

courts from the legislation, some spectacular crimes committed by released prisoners and of course by the general increase in punitiveness mentioned in Chapter 2 of this article. It is necessary to mention that some groups of prisoners are excluded from release on parole, for example, persons sentenced for sexual offences against minors (new since 2013), persons who are sentenced to life imprisonment, persons who are sentenced for intentional crimes committed in prisons, and persons have less than three months to serve of their sentence. It should be noted that the number of repeated crimes committed by released prisoners has not changed significantly and amount to just 2-3% of the total registered crimes.

IV. CONCLUSION

In summary, Lithuania is not yet a good example in the area of imprisonment, the use of open prisons, prison leave and conditional release. Long years of totalitarianism have left a deep scar as regards the nature of dealing with criminals and prisoners. In the penal system, especially in prisons, changes come at the latest. Nevertheless, the present situation shows a significant influence of common political, economic, social and cultural factors, which are difficult to change quickly. It can be assumed that the attitudes to intensity and substance of punishment, and in particular imprisonment, will change together with the aforementioned factors. From our experience in changing something, the importance of good examples in Western Europe, the region of which we want to be a part, is noted, also in the area of dealing with criminals. The tendencies in the future will depend on the political will to change the situation in the Lithuanian prison system, and also from the media, which paints the prisoners mostly in a negative light and is orientated towards sensational and unusual events. The researchers face a challenge in showing the real situation to politicians and the media, and also to practitioners and students who will change this system in the future.

V. BIBLIOGRAPHY

Aebi, M.F., G. Akdeniz & G. Barclay (et al.) (2014) *European sourcebook of crime and criminal justice statistics* 2014, Fifth edition, Helsinki: Heuni.

Aebi, M.F., N. Delgrande & Y. Marguet Y. (2015) 'Have community sanctions and measures widened the net of the European criminal justice systems?', *17 Punishment & Society 5*, 2015, p. 575-597.

Aromaa, K. (2014) 'Responsible criminal policy / Crime and criminal policy', *1 Kriminologijos studijos 1*, p. 77-85.

Bikelis, S. & G. Sakalauskas (2015) 'Lithuania', in: F. Dünkel, J. Grzywa-Holten & P. Horsfield (eds.), *Restorative Justice and Mediation in Penal Matters*, Mönchengladbach: Forum Verlag Godesberg, p. 477-500.

Čepas, A. & G. Sakalauskas (2010).'Lithuania', in: R. G. Newman, M. F. Aebi & V.Jaquier (eds.), *Crime and punishment around the world. Europe*, Vol. 4. Santa Barbara: ABC-CLIO, p. 197-207.

DeMichele, M. (2013) 'Using Weber's Rechtssoziologie to Explain Western Punishment: A Typological Framework', *21 European Journal of Crime, Criminal Law and Criminal Justice 1*, p. 85-109.

Dobryninas, A. (2018) 'Criminology in Lithuania: Restoring Paradigms', in: R.A. Triplett (ed.), *The Handbook of the History and Philosophy of Criminology*, Oxford: Wiley Blackwell, p. 406-421.

Dobryninas, A. & G. Sakalauskas (2011) 'Country survey: Criminology, crime and criminal justice in Lithuania', *8 European Journal of Criminology 5*, p. 421-434.

Feldbrugge, F. J. (1963) 'Soviet Criminal Law – The Last Six Years', *54 Journal of Criminal Law, Criminology & Police Science 3*, p. 249-266.

Krajewski, K. (2014) 'Different penal climates in Europe', *1 Kriminologijos studijos 1*, p. 86-111.

Lappi-Seppälä, T. (2011) 'Explaining imprisonment in Europe', *8 European Journal of Criminology 4*, p. 303-328.

Prison Populations and Penal Policy in Estonia, Latvia and Lithuania. Council of Europe Conference. Stockholm 22-24 October 1997. Documentation.

Sakalauskas, G. (2005) 'The rights of the persons with restricted freedom', in: A. Čepas (ed.), *Human Rights in Lithuania*, Vilnius: Naujos sistemos, p. 304-331.

Sakalauskas, G. (2006) *Strafvollzug in Litauen. Kriminalpolitische Hintergründe, rechtliche Regelungen, Reformen, Praxis und Perspektiven*. Mönchengladbach: Forum Verlag Godesberg, 2006.

Sakalauskas, G. (2010) 'Litauen', in: F. Dünkel, T. Lappi-Sepälä, C. Morgenstern & D. van Zyl Smit (Hrsg.), *Kriminalität, Kriminalpolitik, strafrechtliche Sanktionspraxis und Gefangenenraten im europäischen Vergleich*, Band 37/2, Mönchengladbach: Forum Verlag Godesberg, p. 561-620.

Sakalauskas, G. (2014) 'Lithuania', in: K. Drenkhahn, M. Dudeck & F. Dünkel (eds.), *Long-Term Imprisonment and Human Rights*, Abingdon: Routledge, p. 198-217.

Sakalauskas, G. (2015) 'Strafvollzug in Litauen: Blick zurück oder nach vorne?', *27 Neue Kriminalpolitik 2*, p. 190-201.

Sakalauskas, G. (2019) 'Prisoner resettlement in Lithuania – Between Soviet tradition and challenges of modern society', in: F. Dünkel, I. Pruin, A. Storgaard & J. Weber (eds.), *Prisoner Resettlement in Europe*, Routledge Frontiers of Criminal Justice, Abingdon: Routledge, p. 219-239.

Sakalauskas, G. & F. Dünkel (2017) 'Kriminalpolitik und Sanktionspraxis in Litauen im europäischen Vergleich', *Monatsschrift für Kriminologie und Strafrechtsreform, 100. Jahrgang, Heft 2*, p. 103–122.

Švedas, G. (2000) *Criminal Justice Systems in Europe and North America: Lithuania*. Helsinki: HEUNI.

Tonry, M. (2014) 'Thinking about Punishment across Space and Time', *1 Kriminologijos studijos 1*, p. 5-30.

von Hofer, H. (2010) 'Anmerkungen zum Forschung bzgl. Der Erklärung von Gefangenenraten', in: F. Dünkel, T. Lappi-Sepälä, C. Morgenstern & D. van Zyl Smit (Hrsg.), *Kriminalität, Kriminalpolitik, strafrechtliche Sanktionspraxis und Gefangenenraten im europäischen Vergleich*, Band 37/2, Mönchengladbach: Forum Verlag Godesberg, p. 25-50.

PART III
NATIONAL REPORTS

3ème PARTIE
RAPPORTS NATIONAUX

OVERUSE IN THE CRIMINAL JUSTICE SYSTEM IN ARGENTINA*

Roberto P. Ortenzi & Alejo García Basalo**

I. INTRODUCTION

As an introductory note to the topic of this chapter, we would like to refer to the comments presented in the introduction of our work on the various forms of deprivation of liberty prior to the final judgment in the Argentine Republic.[1] Given the federal, republican and representative system of government adopted under Section 1 of the Argentine Federal Constitution, the enactment of the civil, commercial, criminal, mining, and labour and social security codes, as well as of general laws applicable throughout country, lies within the powers of the Federal Congress only (Section 75(12)), which means that these bodies of regulations apply to the whole territory of the country. On the other hand, the enactment of procedural rules lies within the powers of the provinces, which, in exercising such power, are entitled to pass their own codes of procedure, including the code of criminal procedure, which is the one we will be dealing with in this work. Based on time, extension, and specificity reasons, this work will only focus on the federal jurisdiction and the jurisdiction of the city of Buenos Aires; however, it should be noted that there are no significant differences in the regulation of coercive measures (involving deprivation of liberty) within those jurisdictions

---

* Translated from Spanish by María Natalia Rezzonico.

** Roberto P. Ortenzi is the former Head of the Criminology Institute of the Argentine Federal Penitentiary Service, a former Judge at the Court of Criminal Appeals and Guarantees (Judicial Department of Zarate-Campana, Argentina). Alejo García Basalo is an architect as well as a professor at John F. Kennedy University, Argentina.

1 Julio Enrique Aparicio & Roberto Patricio Ortenzi, 'Pre-trial detention in the Argentine Republic', in P.H.P.H.M.C. van Kempen (ed.), *Pre-trial detention. Human rights, criminal procedural law and penitentiary law, comparative law/Détention avant jugement. Droits de l'homme, droit de la procédure pénale et droit pénitentiaire, droit comparé*, Cambridge/Antwerp/Portland: Intersentia 2012, p. 225-239.

and the jurisdictions of the rest of the provinces.[2] This chapter will only refer to individuals over 18 years of age.

II. OVERUSE OF CRIMINALIZATION

Under the Argentine legal system, both substantive law – such as the CC – and procedural law – such as the FCCP and similar codes of the provinces and City of Buenos Aires – as well as any other law, must be in line with the provisions of the FC, which is our fundamental law, and international treaties of constitutional rank (as per Sections 5 and 31 of the FC).

Under Section 75(22) of the FC, "*... Treaties and concordats rank higher than laws.* The American Declaration of the Rights and Duties of Man[3]; the Universal Declaration of Human Rights[4]; the American Convention on Human Rights[5]; the International Covenant on Economic, Social and Cultural Rights[6]; the International Covenant on Civil and Political Rights and the Optional Protocol thereto[7]; the Convention on the Prevention and Punishment of the Crime of Genocide[8]; the International Convention on the Elimination of all Forms of Racial Discrimination[9]; the Convention on the Elimination of all Forms of

2 In this chapter, the Argentine Supreme Court of Justice—the highest court in the country—will be referred to as "CSJN" (for its Spanish acronym); the Argentine Federal Constitution will be referred to as "FC"; the Argentine Criminal Code will be referred to as "CC"; the Argentine Federal Code of Criminal Procedure, which applies to the federal jurisdiction and the jurisdiction of the City of Buenos Aires, will be referred to as "FCCP"; and the Argentine Official Gazette will be referred to as "BO" (for its Spanish acronym). Furthermore, all references are to the FCCP in force at the moment of concluding this chapter in 2016, as approved by Law No. 23984 and its amendments, since the Code of Criminal Procedure passed by Law No. 27063 has not become effective yet.

3 Organization of American States, American Declaration of the Rights and Duties of Man, adopted by the Ninth International Conference of American States, Bogota, Colombia, 1948.

4 United Nations, Universal Declaration of Human Rights, proclaimed by the United Nations General Assembly, Paris, 10 December 1948.

5 Organization of American States, American Convention on Human Rights – "Pact of San Jose, Costa Rica", San José, Costa Rica, 22 November 1969.

6 United Nations, International Covenant on Economic, Social and Cultural Rights, adopted and opened for signature, ratification and accession by General Assembly resolution 2200A (XXI) of 16 December 1966.

7 United Nations, International Covenant on Civil and Political Rights and Optional Protocol thereto, adopted and opened for signature, ratification and accession by General Assembly resolution 2200A (XXI) of 16 December 1966.

8 United Nations, Convention on the Prevention and Punishment of the Crime of Genocide, adopted by the United Nations General Assembly on 9 December 1948.

9 United Nations, International Convention on the Elimination of All Forms of Racial Discrimination, adopted and opened for signature and ratification by General Assembly resolution 2106 (XX) of 21 December 1965.

Discrimination against Women[10]; the Convention against Torture and Other Cruel, Inhuman or Degrading Treatment or Punishment[11]; the Convention on the Rights of the Child[12]; as they may be in effect from time to time, have constitutional rank, do not repeal any section of the First Part of this Constitution and are to be understood as complementing the rights and guarantees recognised herein... In order to enjoy constitutional status, all other treaties and conventions on human rights shall require the vote of two-thirds of all the members of each House after their approval by Congress" (emphasis added).

The CC is structured into two books, entitled "General Provisions" and "Crimes", respectively, and each of them, in turn, is made up of 13 titles divided into several chapters.

Book I (General Provisions) includes the following titles: Application of Criminal Law, Penalties, Suspended Sentence, Restitution and Compensation, Attribution of Guilt, Attempt, Participation in Crimes, Recidivism, Joinder of Crimes, Termination of the Right to Bring a Criminal Action and Termination of Criminal Liability, Prosecution, Deferred Prosecution, and Guidelines for the Interpretation of the Code.

In turn, Book II (Provisions on Crimes) deals with specific crimes and includes the following titles: Crimes against the Person, Crimes against a Person's Good Name or Reputation, Sex Crimes, Crimes against Marital Status and Identity, Crimes against a Person's Freedom, Crimes against Property, Crimes against Public Welfare, Crimes against Law and Order, Crimes against National Security, Crimes against the Branches of Government and the Constitutional Order, Crimes against the Government, Crimes Involving Public Instruments, and Crimes against the Economic and Financial Order. All these titles correspond, in order of importance, to various legally protected interests understood as social interests worthy of protection. For crimes punished with confinement or imprisonment – except for life imprisonment – there are maximum and minimum limits, within which the courts, in compliance with the rules of the CC, may determine the severity of the prison sentence to be applied to the case, as will be explained further on.

Finally, there are the Supplementary Provisions.

After this brief introduction to the topic, we should go into the question of whether there is an excessive and unnecessary set of conducts defined as crimes in the CC. Though we will discuss this further, we would like to mention now

10 United Nations, Convention on the Elimination of All Forms of Discrimination against Women, adopted by the UN General Assembly in 1979.

11 United Nations, Convention against Torture and Other Cruel, Inhuman or Degrading Treatment or Punishment, adopted and opened for signature, ratification and accession by General Assembly resolution 39/46 of 10 December 1984.

12 United Nations, Convention on the Rights of the Child, adopted and opened for signature, ratification and accession by General Assembly resolution 44/25 of 20 November 1989.

that our view is that this is not the case. Even though it is true that a reading of Book II of the CC shows that a large number of conducts are considered and specifically described as crimes, it is also true that this operates as a guarantee for citizens, since in order for a conduct to be considered a crime, and thus, to be punishable, it must necessarily meet several requirements that turn it into a crime. These requirements are established in the rules included in both the General Provisions and the Provisions on Crimes of the CC, and according to the theory of crime they are the following: the conduct must be previously defined by law and fit that definition, it must be unlawful, and it must be attributable to the offender.

It should be pointed out that the *statutory definition of a crime* is the description in the law of an action that is contrary to a rule, while *fit between the conduct and the statutory definition of the crime* consists in an action actually performed fitting the definition of the crime.

As explained by Carlos Creus, the statutory definition of a crime, as a description of the crime, and the consequence thereof – the fit between the conduct and the statutory definition – operate as limits to the extent of punitive power, since conducts which do not fit the definition of the crime may not be punished. Therefore, the definition of the crime operates as a guarantee for individuals. From a constitutional perspective, this limiting and safeguarding function relates to the principle of legality, enshrined in Section 18 of the FC, and supplemented by the principle under which anything which is not forbidden is allowed, enshrined in Section 19 of the FC, "both of which make our criminal law system a lawful system".[13]

Within this framework of description of criminal conducts, case law, which results from the overall interpretation of the rules made by the courts when applying the law, operates as a remedy to counteract any excess in the criminalization of conducts defined as crimes. This is the case, e.g., when the crime is committed under necessity, as regulated under Section 34(3) of the CC (Book I), when deemed to be a justification defence, or in cases of self-defence or defence of others or other's rights, as long as the circumstances required under the law are met (Section 34(6)(7) of the CC).

And the same applies to crimes, the criminalization of which is deemed to be unconstitutional, such as the conduct regulated under Section 14(2) of Law No. 23737 on Narcotic Drugs and Psychotropic Substances[14], which provides for a sentence of one month to two years in prison "when the small amount and other surrounding circumstances suggest beyond a reasonable doubt that the possession is for personal use". In this regard, in the CSJN decision in *Arriola,*

13 Carlos Creus, *Derecho penal. Parte general*, Buenos Aires: Astrea, 2011, p. 187.
14 Law No. 23737, passed on 21 September 1989 and published in BO No. 26737 of 11 October 1989.

Sebastián et al.[15] of 25 August 2009, the Court, based on the elements and grounds explained therein, deemed this crime to be unconstitutional in this particular case, with the understanding that this conduct should be exclusively left to the private sphere of individuals, protected under Section 19 of the FC.

Also, Sections 76 bis, 76 ter, and 76 quater, Title XII, Book II (General Provisions) of the CC regulate the device of deferred prosecution, applicable in certain cases of crimes punished with confinement or imprisonment of a maximum of three years. The following requirements must be met under this device: during a term of one to three years, depending on the severity of the crime, the accused must (i) respect certain behavioural rules, (ii) refrain from committing new crimes, and (iii) repair the damage caused as agreed upon. Then, the charges will be dismissed.

Furthermore, Book II of the CC includes provisions which operate as measuring devices for the courts to determine in a balanced manner the length of the penalty to be imposed in a particular case based on the punitive system of the CC, which provides minimum and maximum penalties for the various criminal offenses regulated therein (e.g., for voluntary manslaughter, Section 79 of the CC establishes a penalty of 8 to 25 years of confinement or imprisonment). Section 40 of the CC establishes that "in the case of crimes for which a range of time or amount is provided for the penalty to be imposed, the courts shall set the sentence pursuant to the specific extenuating or aggravating circumstances of the case and pursuant to the rules set forth in the following section". Under Section 41 of the CC, the following circumstances must be taken into account: the nature of the act and of the means used to perform it; the extent of the damage and danger caused; the age, education, habits and previous behaviour of the individual; the reasons which led the individual to commit the crime, in particular, poverty or difficulty to earn a living for him/herself and his/her family; the extent of his/her participation in the events; his/her recidivism; and any other criminal record and background; "as well as his/her personal ties, his/her characteristics, and the circumstances of time, place, method and occasion showing his/her greater or lesser dangerousness. The judge shall take personal cognizance of the accused, the victim, and the factual circumstances, as required in each case".

As we can see, in addition to all the items to be analysed, the courts must necessarily have personal contact with the accused before sentencing him or her. This is aimed at contributing towards the determination of a fair sentence relative to the specific case.

Furthermore, some mitigating factors for punishment and exculpatory circumstances have been set forth for some specific crimes and under certain circumstances:

15 CSJN, Judgment of 25 August 2009, *Arriola, Sebastián et al.*, Case No. 9080.

(a) Section 29 *bis*, last paragraph, of Law No. 23737 on Narcotic Drugs and Psychotropic Substances establishes, for cases of conspiracy between two or more individuals to commit any of the crimes regulated in Sections 5, 6, 7, 8, 10 and 25 of the Law and Section 866 of the Customs Code[16], that "any person revealing the conspiracy to the authorities before the commission of the crime has commenced as well as any person preventing on his or her own initiative the perpetration of the scheme shall be released from prison". In turn, Section 29 *ter* of the above-mentioned Law establishes that "any person committing any of the crimes provided for under this Law and under Section 866 of the Customs Code may have his or her penalty reduced by the courts up to half the minimum or the maximum, or may even be exempted from punishment altogether, if during the course of or prior to the commencement of the proceeding any of the following circumstances took place: (i) the individual revealed the identity of the joint perpetrators or accessories in the commission or concealment of the events under investigation or other related events, by providing sufficient data making it possible to file an action against them or allowing for substantial progress in the investigation; or (ii) the individual provided information making it possible to seize substances, raw materials, chemical precursors, means of transport, valuables, goods, moneys, or any other important assets related to the crimes provided for under this Law. In ordering an exemption from punishment, special attention shall be paid to any information allowing the dismantling of an organization engaged in narcotic drugs production, trading, or trafficking. Mitigation of punishment or exculpatory circumstances shall not apply in connection with the punishment of disqualification from holding public office or practising a profession".
(b) For the crime of kidnapping for ransom, regulated in the last paragraph of Section 170 of the CC (Book II, Title VI, Chapter III), a mitigation of punishment is set forth in the following terms: "any person participating in the crime who, dissociating him or herself from the others, made an effort for the victim to recover his or her freedom, without receiving payment of any price, shall have his or her punishment reduced from a third to a half".

As regards criminal statistics, it should be first mentioned that information on this issue is dispersed, since it is produced by various government bodies, both at the federal and provincial levels: the Federal Judiciary provides information on judicial cases, the Ministry of Justice and Human Rights compiles statistical information about penitentiary systems, and the Recidivism Registry also gathers its own information. In addition, this information is not produced at periodical intervals and is released with delay. All of this makes it difficult to have proper access to the data.

As a consequence, research, academic and scientific reports tend to provide arguments and analyses based on legal, philosophical or political matters, but rarely on "hard data" resulting from consistent and comprehensive statistical

16 Argentine Customs Code, Law No. 22415, passed on 2 March 1981.

series of the criminal justice system in Argentina. Unfortunately, this chapter will be no exception.

As for the number of crimes committed per year, according to the information provided by the Federal Ministry of Security, 1,597,052 crimes have been reported in the country in 2015, which means a rate of 3,749.7 per 100,000 inhabitants; see Table 1. This rate shows a 3% reduction compared to the rate for 2014, but is 10% higher than the rate for 2008.

Table 1. Number of crimes and rate per 100,000 inhabitants

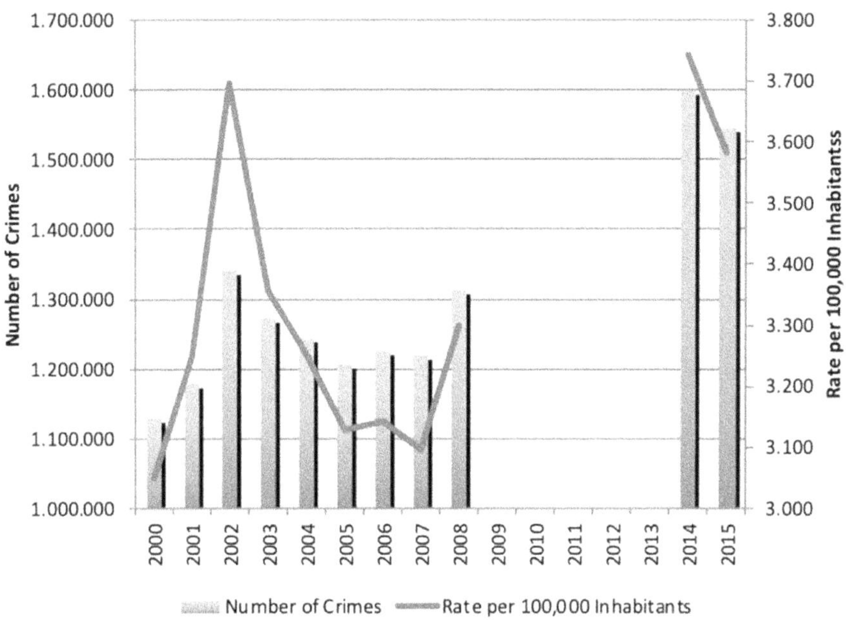

Source: National System of Criminal Information (SNIC, for its Spanish acronym); Ministry of Justice and Human Rights (2000-2008); Ministry of Security (2014-2015). There are no official data available for 2009-2012.

As Table 2 shows, crimes against property are at the top. Among them, robbery and theft amount to 53% of the total, followed by threats and criminal battery, in a lower proportion. There were 2,837 cases of voluntary manslaughter in 2015, with a rate of 6.6 per 100,000 inhabitants, which shows a reduction of 13% compared to the previous year, but an increase of 10% compared to 2008. If compared with other South American countries, the voluntary manslaughter rate is a bit lower than those of neighbouring countries, but higher than that of Chile.

Table 2. More preponderant crimes

	Crimes	2014	%	2015	%
1	Robbery	459,289	29%	433,617	28%
2	Theft	287,063	18%	271,921	18%
3	Threats	190,941	12%	193,944	13%
4	Criminal battery	178,611	11%	181,321	12%
5	Other crimes against property	108,320	7%	107,586	7%
Total number of crimes		1,597,052		1,545,375	

Source: National System of Criminal Information (SNIC); Ministry of Security.

Concerning the trend towards the decriminalization of certain conducts currently considered as crimes, in order not to exceed the limits of this chapter, we will only make reference to the case of narcotic drugs and psychotropic substances.

Before the already-mentioned judgment in *Arriola*, the CSJN had rendered different decisions on the topic. In *Colavini*[17], in 1978, the CSJN endorsed the constitutionality of the criminalization of the possession of drugs for personal use. Later on, in *Bazterrica*[18] and *Capalbo*[19], in 1986, it departed from that precedent and decided in favour of the unconstitutionality of the crime, punished by Law No. 20771 in force by then, which in Section 6 imposed a penalty of one month to two years in prison on any person having drugs in his or her possession when based on the scarce amount and other circumstances it was clear that they were for personal use (Section 6). Then, in *Montalvo*[20] (1990) the CSJN went back to the stance adopted in *Colavini*. Finally, in *Arriola* (2009) it reinstated the precedent of *Bazterrica* and *Capalbo*, and declared Section 14(2) of Law No. 23737 to be unconstitutional in the case of possession of drugs for personal use in conditions not entailing a specific danger or damage to third parties' rights or property, with the understanding that otherwise Section 19 of the FC would be infringed by the courts' interference in the personal sphere of individuals which is to remain out of their jurisdiction.[21]

After *Arriola*, there were some legislative attempts to decriminalize the possession of drugs for personal use which were reflected in bills prepared between 2011 and 2013, including, without limitation, those drafted by Diana

17 CSJN, Judgment of 1978, Colavini, Fallos 300:254.
18 CSJN, Judgment of 1986, Bazterrica, Fallos 308:1392.
19 CSJN, Judgment of 1986, Capalbo, Fallos 308:1468.
20 CSJN, Judgment of 1990, Montalvo, Fallos: 313:1333.
21 Mauro A. Divito & Santiago Vismara (eds), *Corte Suprema de Justicia de la Nación. Máximos Precedentes. Derecho Penal. Parte General*, Volume I, Buenos Aires: La Ley, 2013.

Conti; Victoria Pérez; Adriana Puigrós, Adela Segarram and María del Carmen Bianchi; Ricardo Gil Lavedra and Manuel Garrido; and Fabián Peralta, Gerardo Milman, María Linares, Omar Duclos and Margarita Stolbizer.[22]

It should be borne in mind that judgments rendered both by the CSJN and by lower courts refer to the specific case at hand, and they do not repeal any laws in force; also, the precedents resulting from such cases needs not be followed by other judges or courts in other similar cases.

III. OVERUSE OF PROSECUTION

As it results from the interpretation of Section 72 of the FCCP, an individual becomes an accused in a criminal proceeding with the mere statement that he or she has in any way been a participant in a crime. However, a mere report or private criminal complaint shall not suffice, but rather a judicial order must be duly issued for a criminal investigation to be considered to have been validly opened, whether at the request of the police or of the Office of the Prosecutor General by means of an information.[23] Nevertheless, this is not an undisputed interpretation among legal scholars.

The formal accusation (which is an essential requirement for ordering pre-trial detention) shall be issued by the judge within ten days following the accused's formal statement at the initial appearance (when the accused is heard and is entitled to raise his or her defence or to refuse to make any statement, which shall entail no presumption at all to his or her detriment), provided that there are reasonable grounds to deem that there has been a crime and that the accused may have been involved in the perpetration thereof (Section 306 of the FCCP).

Under procedural regulations, accused persons must not be held in pre-trial detention (Section 310 of the FCCP) if the case fails to meet the requirements provided for under Section 312 of the FCCP for ordering pre-trial detention. This means that the individual is still involved in the criminal proceeding as an accused, but he or she is entitled to pre-trial release and to make use of, for example, the device of deferred prosecution. Pre-trial release may be restricted by specific limits, which may be imposed in the order to prosecute or afterwards, and in both cases such limits must be well-founded.

---

22 Argentine House of Representatives, Bill to Amend Law No. 23737 on Drugs: Amendment of Section 5 on the Criminalization of the Possession of Drugs for Trading, Distribution, Storage, and Transport Purposes, submitted on 11 May 2012.

23 Guillermo Rafael Navarro & Roberto Raúl Daray, *Código Procesal Penal de la Nación. Análisis doctrinal y jurisprudencial*, Volume 1, Buenos Aires: Hammurabi, p. 258.

Table 3. Crimes and convictions

Year	Inhabitants	Crimes		Convictions	
		Number	Rate per 100,000 inhabitants	Number	%
2000	36,784,000	1,129,900	3,051	18,337	1.62%
2001	37,156,000	1,178,530	3,250	23,044	1.96%
2002	37,516,000	1,340,529	3,697	25,538	1.91%
2004	38,226,000	1,234,827	3,254	33,940	2.73%
2007	39,356,000	1,218,243	3,095	29,804	2.45%
2008	39,746,000	1,310,997	3,298	30,151	2.30%
2014	42,669,500	1,597,052	3,743	33,688	2.11%

Source: Argentine Institute of Statistics and Census (INDEC, for its Spanish acronym); National System of Judicial Statistics (SNEJ, for its Spanish acronym); Ministry of Justice and Human Rights.

The case when the formal accusation includes a pre-trial detention order will be analysed more deeply in the following section.

Our legal system provides alternative solutions preventing the overuse of prosecution. These include deferred prosecution, which is regulated in Sections 76 *bis*, 76 *ter* and 76 *quater* of the CC (mentioned in Section II, paragraph 2 hereof), and governed by Sections 293 and 515 of the FCCP as regards its application in the City of Buenos Aires and at the federal level. Deferred prosecution may result in the reduction of the prosecution length.

We should also consider the device of summary proceeding, which eliminates the court trial and therefore all the acts required before it, such as the summons and the production of evidence, among others, if both of the parties involved accept the evidence produced at the investigation stage. This device allows for a faster resolution of the large number of cases filed with criminal courts. This special device is regulated under Section 431 *bis* of the FCCP, which sets forth the requirements to be met for it to apply and the procedures to be followed.

The small number of convictions shows that the punitive activity of the police and judicial system is scarce; see Table 3. Though an upward trend is observed by the middle of last decade, this trend then goes gradually downwards again. These percentages are way too far from those reported by other countries, where the percentage of effectiveness is around 50%.[24]

24 Julio Enrique Aparicio, *Delito y sociedad. El fenómeno delictivo contemporáneo*, Buenos Aires: Lumen-Humanitas, 2013, p. 27-46.

Table 4. Number of convictions per type of crime in 2012

Convictions		Number	% of Total
1	Robbery	15,521	52%
2	Crimes against the Person	4,979	17%
3	Other Crimes against Property	3,996	13%
4	Crimes against Public Welfare	2,872	10%
5	Crimes against the Government	2,542	9%
Total Number of Convictions		29,773	

Source: Ministry of Justice and Human Rights, 2012 Report; National System of Judicial Statistics (SNEJ).

Table 5. Percentage of convictions per type of crime in 2008

Type of crime	Crimes	Convictions	%
Crimes against public welfare	5,992	2,875	47.98%
Voluntary manslaughter	2,305	1,094	47.46%
Crimes against the government	16,101	2,179	13.53%
Sex crimes	10,360	1,381	13.33%
Crimes involving public instruments	3,567	427	11.97%
Robbery	398,361	15,877	3.99%

Source: Ministry of Justice and Human Rights, 2008 Report; National System of Criminal Information (SNIC).

As regards the distribution of convictions in 2012, according to Table 4 most of them were imposed on crimes against property – 65% of the cases – followed by crimes against the person (17%).

As regards the effectiveness of convictions, as follows from Table 5 the highest percentages may be found in crimes involving flagrancy, notorious evidence, or easily-obtained testimonies leading to the clarification of the crime and later conviction of their perpetrators, while crimes demanding a deeper investigation due to lack of the above-mentioned elements usually remain unsolved.

Regarding the duration of the proceedings resulting in convictions (see Table 6), it should be pointed out that statistics are rather weak, since there are no data available about the duration of the proceeding for 60% of the cases. Nevertheless, as we will see further on when analysing penitentiary statistics, and despite remarkable differences from jurisdiction to jurisdiction, it is noticed that proceedings last longer than reasonable.

Table 6. Convictions according to the duration of the proceedings in 2012

Duration of the proceedings	Convictions	
	Number	%
Up to 1 year	4,351	15%
Up to 2 years	3,396	11%
Up to 3 years	1,930	6%
Over 3 years	2,315	8%
Not available	17,781	60%
Total	29,773	100%

Source: Ministry of Justice and Human Rights, 2012 Report; National System of Judicial Statistics (SNEJ).

Table 7. Duration of custodial sentences

Custodial sentences imposed in 2012		
Duration	**Number**	**%**
Life imprisonment (20 years)	104	0.35%
Over 5 years imprisonment	5,458	18.50%
From 3 to 5 years imprisonment	5,864	19.87%
Up to 3 years imprisonment	18,084	61.28%
Total	29,510	100.0%

Source: Ministry of Justice and Human Rights, 2012 Report; National System of Judicial Statistics (SNEJ).

As Table 7 shows, custodial sentences of up to three years amounted to 61.28% of all custodial sentences in 2012. However, Section 26 of the CC empowers the courts to stay the enforcement of the conviction under certain conditions (suspended sentence), so a large number of the individuals included in the above-mentioned percentage are not actually in prison. In 2012, people deprived of liberty with custodial sentences of up to three years amounted to 8% of the criminal population, though over 60% of the convictions were for that term. On the other hand, as pointed out in section III hereof, the CC provides for the use of deferred prosecution in cases of penalties not exceeding three years (Section 76 bis, ter and quater of the CC). This means that the data are affected by this device, though we cannot assert to what extent.

IV. OVERUSE OF IMPRISONMENT

Though it is true that in the federal jurisdiction and in the jurisdiction of the City of Buenos Aires there are cases of pre-trial detention that take long periods of time due to different reasons, there are legal provisions aimed at limiting both the application and the duration of this coercive measure. In the following paragraphs we will deal with some of them.

The Universal Declaration of Human Rights (Section 11(1)), the International Covenant on Civil and Political Rights (Section 14(2)), the American Declaration of the Rights and Duties of Man (Section XXVI) and the American Convention (Section 8(2)) expressly acknowledge without limits the fundamental judicial guarantee of the presumption of innocence, enshrined in Section 18 of the FC, which reads: "No inhabitant of the Nation may be punished without a trial based on a law passed before the occurrence of the offense..." and that "... No one may be... arrested without a written warrant issued by a competent authority...".

Along these lines, Section 1 of the FCCP states that "no one may be... found guilty in the absence of a final judgment which rebuts the presumption of innocence enjoyed by all the accused persons, or criminally prosecuted more than once based on the same offense". This has been replicated in the procedural codes of the rest of the country.

Abiding by this presumption entails specific consequences. One of them is that the accused must be free during the proceeding, which turns pre-trial detention into an exceptional measure that needs to be grounded on specific and legitimate requirements warranting it, pursuant to the principle of the last-resort nature of pre-trial detention recognised at the international level in the International Covenant on Civil and Political Rights (Section 9(3))[25], the United Nations Standard Minimum Rules for Non-custodial Measures (the "Tokyo Rules") (Section 6)[26], the Body of Principles for the Protection of All Persons under Any Form of Detention or Imprisonment (Sections 36(2) and 39), and by the Inter-American Court of Human Rights and the Inter-American Commission on Human Rights.

Thus, pre-trial detention is to be interpreted on a restrictive basis by virtue of the *pro homine* principle, and therefore, the State, in exercising its punitive power, is responsible for setting the limits thereto.

---

25 International Covenant on Civil and Political Rights, adopted and opened for signature, ratification and accession by General Assembly Resolution No. 2200A (XXI) of 16 December 1966.

26 United Nations Standard Minimum Rules for Non-custodial Measures (the "Tokyo Rules"), G.A. res. 45/110, annex, 45 U.N. GAOR Supp. (No. 49A), p. 197, U.N. Doc. A/45/49 (1990).

Along these lines, Section 280 of the FCCP sets forth that "personal freedom may only be restricted in accordance with the provisions of this Code in so far as absolutely indispensable to ensure the discovery of the truth and the application of the law", and at the same time, Section 312 establishes that a judge will order the accused's pre-trial detention when issuing the formal accusation where:

> (a) The crime – or joinder of crimes – in question carries a penalty of imprisonment and prima facie the judge deems that suspended sentence may not apply.
> (b) In spite of suspended sentence being applicable, release from prison is not deemed to be appropriate on the basis of a reasonable presumption that the accused may fail to appear in court for trial or may act so as to hinder the investigation into the crime. Such presumption shall derive from an objective and provisional assessment of the characteristics of the crime, the chances of recidivism, the personal characteristics of the accused, or the fact of him or her having been released from prison in prior proceedings (Section 319 of the FCCP).

Pre-trial detention shall be ordered by the judge, except if pre-trial release already granted was confirmed. Thus, pre-trial detention functions as a precautionary measure to ensure the completion of the investigation and to prevent a possible custodial sentence from becoming futile. Given that the restriction of personal freedom is more sensitive in this case, the burden of ensuring the lesser harm possible is increased, especially as regards duration, in accordance with the presumption of innocence which applies throughout the criminal proceeding and up to the final judgment.

Section 316 of the FCCP provides for exemption from imprisonment for an accused who, pursuant to the determination of the specific crime(s) made by the judge, may be faced with a sentence of no more than eight years in prison. The judge may also order an exemption from imprisonment if he or she deems *prima facie* that a suspended sentence will apply, except if the individual is being accused of any of the crimes provided for under Sections 139, 139 bis and 146 of the CC. Section 139 of the CC penalizes any woman "who faked to be pregnant or to have given birth to a baby in order to make her alleged child entitled to rights which do not correspond to the child" and "any person who, through any action, modified or suppressed the identity of a child below 10 years of age, and any person withholding or hiding a child". Section 139 bis punishes "any person facilitating, promoting, or being an intermediary in any way in the perpetration of the crimes regulated under this Chapter, whether there was a promise for reward or not, a threat or abuse of authority", and "any public officer or healthcare professional engaging in any of the conducts provided for under this Chapter", who are also punished with disqualification from holding public office or practising a profession. The chapter referred to is Chapter II of Title IV of the CC, which deals with the "suppression and simulation of marital status and identity". Section 146, included in Chapter I on "Crimes against a Person's Freedom", under

Title V of the CC, punishes any person "taking a minor below 10 years of age away from his/her parents, guardian or the person in charge of him/her, as well as any person retaining or concealing the minor". All these sections, including Section 316 of the FCCP have been approved by Law No. 24410 (BO 2/1/1995).

Through the device of *release from prison,* an accused held in pre-trial detention may be released from prison, as per the provisions of Section 317 of the FCCP, under which: "Release from prison may be granted when: (1) exemption from imprisonment applies; (2) the accused has been in prison or held in pre-trial detention for the maximum of the penalty provided for under the Criminal Code for the crime(s) attributed to him or her; (3) the accused has been in prison or held in pre-trial detention for the same length of time as the penalty requested by the prosecutor, which at first sight looks appropriate; (4) the accused has served the sentence imposed by a final appealable judgment; (5) the accused has been in prison or held in pre-trial detention for a length of time which, had there been a final sentence, would have entitled him or her to conditional release, had prison rules been complied with".

Exemption from prison may be granted at any stage of the proceeding, as per Section 318 of the FCCP. Both exemption from prison and release from prison will be granted, depending on the specific case, on the accused's own recognizance, bail bond or secured bail bond (Sections 320, 321, 322, 323, 324 and 325 of the FCCP).

Pre-trial detention may also be served at the accused's address (house arrest), if the accused meets the specific conditions set forth in the CC for house arrest to apply (Section 314 of the FCCP and Section 10 of the CC). In the event of death or serious illness of a close relative of an accused held in pre-trial detention, the judge may allow the latter, by means of a well-founded decision, to leave the prison facilities guarded by police officers and for the term deemed convenient, so that he or she may fulfil his moral duties (Section 313 of the FCCP).

Federal Law No. 24660 on the Execution of Custodial Sentences[27] regulates home detention in Section 33 for the people falling within Section 32, that is, "(a) a sick convict, when deprivation of liberty at prison facilities prevents him or her from recovering or duly treating his or her disease and hospitalization is not applicable; (b) a convict suffering an incurable disease at the terminal stage; (c) a handicapped convict when deprivation of liberty at the prison facilities is inappropriate due to his or her condition and entails a degrading, inhuman, or cruel treatment; (d) a convict of over 70 years of age; (e) a convict that is pregnant; and (f) a convict that is the mother of a child younger than five years of age or of a handicapped person under her charge".

---

27 Law No. 24660 on the Execution of Custodial Sentences, passed on 19 June 1996, published in BO No. 28436 of 16 July 1996.

In turn, Section 11 establishes that, except in cases falling within Section 7, home detention "applies to accused persons as long as its rules are not against the presumption of innocence and are more favourable and useful for him or her", therefore, the accused must go through the various stages of the period of treatment without exceptionally being promoted to any stage of the period, as happens with sentenced people who meet the conditions set forth in the same section. Accused persons held in pre-trial detention stay, both in the federal jurisdiction and in the jurisdiction of the City of Buenos Aires, in the facilities of the Federal Penitentiary Service.

As regards the duration of pre-trial detention, Section 1 of Law No. 25430[28] sets forth that "pre-trial detention may not last longer than two years without a judgment. Nevertheless, when the number of crimes attributed to the accused or the notorious complexity of the case have made it impossible to render a judgment within the term set, the latter may be extended for one more year, based on a well-grounded order. This must be immediately communicated to the applicable higher court, for control purposes". In turn, Section 2 of the same Law establishes that "the terms provided for in the preceding section shall not be counted for the purposes of this Law when they are reached after a judgment of conviction has been rendered, even if the latter was appealable". Therefore, an interpretation of both sections reveals that Section 1 refers to cases in which no conviction has been ordered yet. This is so because, if there is an appealable judgment, the suspicion and procedural danger that led the accused to be held in pre-trial detention become more relevant.

According to the latest official numbers available (see Table 8), criminal population in the Argentine Republic amounted to 68,407 individuals by 31 December 2014, out of which 34,613 (51%) were at the trial stage. As already said, Argentina is a federal country comprising one federal jurisdiction and 24 local jurisdictions, each of which has its own judicial and penitentiary systems.

The numbers in Table 8 do not include people under arrest by federal law enforcement authorities and those arrested at police stations, so both the number of people in prison and people in trial could be higher.

Most of the criminal population with a conviction has been sentenced for crimes against property, which amount to 47% of the total, followed by voluntary manslaughter and rape, while 6% of the people deprived of liberty for drug-related crimes were sentenced (see Table 9).

Table 10 shows the number of prisoners by year of arrest. The chart indicates that in the last two years, the number of accused persons exceeded the number of convicted prisoners. Only in 2012 there were more convicted prisoners than

28 Law No. 25430 on Pre-trial Detention Terms, passed on 9 May 2001, published in BO No. 29660 of 1 June 2001.

Table 8. Criminal population by 31 December 2014

Jurisdiction	Criminal population				
		With a conviction		In trial	
	Total	Subtotal	%	Subtotal	%
Federal	5,584	1,436	26%	4,142	74%
Provincial	56,796	28,825	51%	27,334	49%
City of Buenos Aires	5,817	2,679	46%	3,137	54%
Country total	68,407	32,940	49%	34,613	51%

Source: Ministry of Justice and Human Rights, 2014 Argentina Report of the National System of Statistics of Execution of Sentences (SNEEP, for its Spanish acronym) (at: (at: www.jus.gob.ar/areas-tematicas/estadisticas-de-politica-criminal/mapa.aspx) (last visited: 11 December 2016).

Table 9. Convicted people. Most mentioned crimes in 2014

Most Mentioned Crimes	With a Conviction	%
Robbery and attempted robbery	11,847	36%
Voluntary manslaughter	4,556	14%
Rape	3,004	9%
Theft and attempted theft	2,134	6%
Drug-related crimes	2,024	6%
Other crimes against property	1,564	5%
Crimes against the person	1,445	4%

Source: Ministry of Justice and Human Rights, 2014 Argentina Report of the National System of Statistics of Execution of Sentences (SNEEP, for its Spanish acronym) (at: (at: www.jus.gob.ar/areas-tematicas/estadisticas-de-politica-criminal/mapa.aspx) (last visited: 11 December 2016).

accused persons, but all the same in the preceding years there were accused persons who remained as such.

This reflects that the high proportion of accused persons relative to the total number of people under arrest (51%) is related to the duration of the proceedings, though the lack of effectiveness in the application of pre-trial detention, the large number of investigations, the reduced number of courts, and the delay in appointing judges – which forces those already appointed to act at the vacant courts – are also factors which have an impact at the federal level.

Given the large number of jurisdictions, there is a wide range in the percentage of total inmates which goes from 74% in the federal jurisdiction to 17% in the Province of Entre Ríos.

As for Table 11, if we consider the inmates put in jail, e.g., in 2010 in the federal jurisdiction, we can see that out of the total of individuals put in jail, 1,366

Table 10. Accused and convicted persons by year of arrest

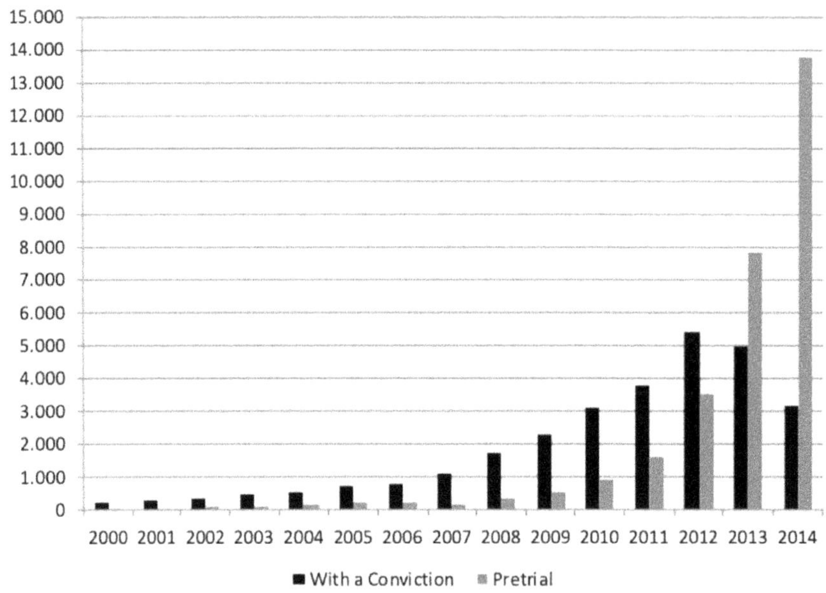

Source: Ministry of Justice and Human Rights, 2014 Argentina Report of the National System of Statistics of Execution of Sentences (SNEEP, for its Spanish acronym) (at: (at: www.jus.gob.ar/areas-tematicas/estadisticas-de-politica-criminal/mapa.aspx) (last visited: 11 December 2016).

Table 11. Accused persons put in jail in 2010 in the Federal jurisdiction*

Federal jurisdiction							
Year	**2010**	**2011**	**2012**	**2013**	**2014**	**Total**	**%**
In trial	1366	770	336	140	79	79	6%
With a conviction	100	190	104	47	9	450	31%
Left prison		406	330	149	52	937	64%
Total	1466	1366	770	336	140	2612	100%

* Prepared by us based on data provided by the Ministry of Justice and Human Rights, Report of the National System of Statistics of Execution of Sentences (SNEEP).

were still in prison by the end of the period while the trial was pending, and only 100 of those who were imprisoned in the period were sentenced (7%). In the following year, 770 individuals were still criminal defendants and 190 were sentenced (13%); in 2012, 104 individuals were sentenced (7%); 47 in 2013 (3%); and 9 in 2014 (1%), and there were still 79 individuals without a conviction. This means that in five years, only 31% of those put in jail were sentenced, while a total of 937 individuals (64%) left the system based on various reasons without

Table 12. Accused persons put in jail in 2010 in the Province of Entre Ríos

Jurisdiction of the Province of Entre Ríos							
Year	**2010**	**2011**	**2012**	**2013**	**2014**	**Total**	**%**
In Trial	67	20	5	2	1	1	1%
With a Conviction	31	28	13	3	1	76	78%
Left Prison		19	2	0	0	21	21%
Total	98	67	20	5	2	94	100%

serving a conviction resulting from a final non-appealable judgment. This entailed the use of 342,000 days/bed in housing accused individuals who were finally not convicted to a prison sentence and represented a cost of over 20 million euros for the criminal jurisdiction, plus other 2.5 million euros in days/bed for individuals sentenced out of term.[29] This represents a surcharge per inmate of 15,700 euros in 2010.

In the Province of Entre Ríos (see Table 12), the situation is very different. Out of those put in jail in 2010, 32% were sentenced during that year, 29% in the following year, and 13% in 2012; that is, in the first three years, 73% of the individuals were sentenced and only 21 individuals left the system, 19 of them after one year. As regards surcharges in days/bed during the proceeding, these amounted to 7,500 euros per inmate in 2010, that is, 50% of the cost borne at the federal jurisdiction.

Procedural codes are currently being updated, and it is expected that this will contribute towards the reduction of accused persons in prison. For example, in the Provinces of Chubut and Entre Ríos, procedural codes were updated in 2006[30] and an important improvement in the resolution of proceedings was achieved, which contributed towards the reduction of individuals' terms in prison, with the resulting reduction in the proportion of accused persons imprisoned.

V. CONCLUSION

As may be seen from the discussion of the topics dealt with in this chapter, the Argentine criminal legal system is organised within the framework of the principles of legality, freedom, principle under which anything which is not forbidden is allowed, prosecutorial discretion and *pro homine*, in line with the provisions of the FC and international treaties.

29 The daily cost per inmate at the Federal Penitentiary Service for this year is ARS 1,065, that is, around 60 euros, see Federal Penitentiary Service, Annual Report, 2015.

30 Code of Criminal Procedure of Chubut, Law No. XV-9, 2006.

There is not an excessive and unnecessary variety of criminalized conducts, since their detailed description operates as a limit to the State's punishing powers, the duration of pre-trial detention is established based on the case, and there are alternative devices thereto and mitigations thereof.

Nevertheless, it may be observed that all the same there is a high number of individuals held in pre-trial detention, which makes it imperative to decompress the accumulation of cases pending before the various judicial bodies, by creating new bodies in order to accelerate the trying of cases, activating the appointment of judges in vacant positions and implementing public policies oriented towards modifying the causes which create a favourable environment for engaging in criminal activities.

The causes of the high number of accused persons do not result from an excess of punishable conducts in the legislation. Rather, these causes are related to the provisions of the procedural codes and the administrative inadequacies of the Judiciary, whether due to lack of staff or operational difficulties in the courts.

Nevertheless, efforts are being made to implement solutions to these issues, which makes it possible to predict a gradual reduction in the number of individuals in jail while their proceedings are pending, provided that these measures turn out to be successful.

VI. BIBLIOGRAPHY

Several authors, 'Prisión Preventiva', in: *Sistemas Judiciales*, Centro de Estudios de Justicia de las Américas, Year 7, No. 14.

Report of the Inter-American Commission on Human Rights, OEA/Ser.L/V/II. Doc. 46/13, *Report on the Use of Pretrial Detention in the Americas,* 30 December 2013.

Report of the Argentine Penitentiary Office, Alcira Daroqui (ed.), *Statistical Report. November 2014*, 2014.

Diego García Yomha (ed.), *El estado de la prisión preventiva en la Argentina. Situación actual y propuestas de cambio*, Buenos Aires: Instituto de Estudios Comparados en Ciencias Penales y Sociales, 2012.

Tatiana Gos, 'La persecución penal en los nuevos códigos procesales penales provinciales', *Lecciones y Ensayos* 85 (2008).

Federal Board of High Courts and Tribunals of the Argentine Provinces and City of Buenos Aires, *Statistics of the Judicial Branches of the Argentine Provinces and City of Buenos Aires for 2012-2013*, No. 4, Buenos Aires, 2016 (at: www.jufejus.org.ar/).

Santiago Martínez, *El dictado de la prisión preventiva en Argentina*, Experts Meeting on Pretrial Detention, Inter-American Convention on Human Rights, Organization of American States, 9-10 May 2013.

Anabella Museri & Paula Litvachky, "El uso de la información estadística y la forma de definir el problema de la prisión preventiva", Buenos Aires: CELS, September 2010.

Argentine Judiciary. Office of Statistics (at: www.pjn.gov.ar/07_estadisticas/index.htm).

Report of the United Nations Development Programme, *Regional Human Development Report 2013-2014. Citizen Security with a Human Face: Evidence and proposals for Latin America*, Panama, 2013.

Luis A. Schiappa Pietra, 'Prisión preventiva y reforma procesal penal en Argentina', in: *Prisión Preventiva y Reforma Procesal Penal en América Latina: Evaluación y Perspectivas,* Volume 2, Santiago de Chile: Centro de Estudios de Justicia de las Américas, 2011.

LE RECOURS AU SYSTÈME DE JUSTICE PÉNALE EN BELGIQUE : ÉTAT DES LIEUX ET PERSPECTIVES

Christian De Valkeneer*, Marc Dizier** & Vincent Seron***

I. INTRODUCTION

Cette contribution à trois voix a pour objectif d'apporter un éclairage sur les grandes tendances du recours au système de justice pénale en Belgique. Après avoir traité du recours aux sanctions pénales, principalement au regard de l'interprétation des statistiques policières de criminalité (II), nous nous attacherons à dresser un état des lieux – tant s'agissant des aspects quantitatifs que qualitatifs –, du recours aux poursuites pénales et à mettre en exergue les alternatives actuellement mobilisées dans ce domaine (III). Le dernier volet de ce triptyque abordera quant à lui l'évolution du recours à la détention et les perspectives qui y sont liées (IV).

II. LE RECOURS EXCESSIF AUX SANCTIONS PÉNALES

II.1. REMARQUE MÉTHODOLOGIQUE

Les données présentées dans cette section proviennent exclusivement des statistiques des infractions relevées par les services de police, tant locaux que fédéraux. Sont ici comptabilisées les infractions pénales (infractions au Code pénal, aux lois

* Ph. D., Procureur général près la Cour d'appel de Liège, Professeur extraordinaire à l'Université Catholique de Louvain, Belgique.
** M. Sc., Directeur de la prison d'Andenne, Collaborateur au Département de criminologie de l'Université de Liège, Belgique.
*** Ph. D., Maître de conférences au Département de criminologie de l'Université de Liège, Belgique.

spéciales et aux règlements de police locaux) enregistrées par lesdits services et qui ont fait l'objet d'un procès-verbal initial transmis au ministère public.

Précisons que ces données intègrent à la fois les faits accomplis et les tentatives. Sont par contre exclus les faits commis par des Belges à l'étranger, les infractions au Code de la route[1] ainsi que celles enregistrées par les services d'inspection particuliers.[2]

En dépit de leur vision parcellaire de la délinquance, les statistiques policières constituent, à l'heure actuelle, le seul indicateur de la criminalité en Belgique. Pour des raisons budgétaires, il n'existe en effet plus, depuis 2009, d'enquête nationale de victimisation.[3] La quasi-absence d'autres compteurs de la délinquance ne permet par conséquent pas une confrontation des données.[4]

II.2. APERÇU DE LA CRIMINALITÉ EN BELGIQUE

a. Criminalité totale enregistrée

S'agissant de la criminalité commise au niveau national, en 2015, les services de police belges ont enregistré 898.826 infractions[5] – ce qui représente le chiffre le plus bas affiché depuis 2000 – pour une population de 11.209.044 habitants[6], soit un taux de criminalité s'élevant à 80.19 délits pour 1000 habitants. En 2000, la criminalité enregistrée au niveau national était quant à elle de 1.002.022 infractions pour une population de 10.239.085 habitants[7], soit un taux de criminalité de 97.86 délits pour 1.000 habitants.[8] Voir Graphique 1.

1 Il existe par ailleurs une banque de données qui recense les infractions à la loi relative à la police de la circulation routière ainsi qu'aux lois spéciales, dénommée « banque d'infractions routières ».

2 Inspection des lois sociales, de l'environnement, etc. Bien que disposant de compétences de police, ces services ne sont toutefois pas considérés comme des services de police au sens strict du terme.

3 De 1997 à 2009, il existait en Belgique une enquête téléphonique relative à la sécurité des citoyens et au fonctionnement des services de police, dénommée *Moniteur de sécurité*. À la suite de l'abandon de cet instrument, des *enquêtes locales de sécurité* comportant un volet victimisation ont vu le jour mais ces dernières ne sont cependant pas mises en place par tous les pouvoirs locaux.

4 Au-delà de leur faible ampleur en Belgique, les enquêtes de délinquance auto-révélée sont presque toujours réalisées, pour des raisons pratiques et idéologiques, auprès d'adolescents scolarisés.

5 Police Fédérale - DGR/DRI, *Statistiques de criminalité*, 2000-2015.

6 SPF Économie, Direction Générale Statistique, *Chiffres clés – Aperçu statistique de la Belgique*, 2015, www.statbel.fgov.be.

7 SPF Économie, Direction Générale Statistique, *Population résidente totale au 1er janvier, par année (1990-2008), par groupe et classe d'âges et par sexe, Belgique*, www.statbel.fgov.be.

8 N.B.: Les données pour les années 2001 jusqu'à 2005 ne sont plus publiées.

Graphique 1.

Nous tenons à préciser que l'évolution de cette criminalité totale enregistrée par la police est à relativiser et à interpréter avec précaution dans la mesure où elle intègre tant les infractions graves que celles de moindre gravité. À titre d'exemple, statistiquement parlant, un homicide sera comptabilisé sur un même pied d'égalité qu'un fait de vandalisme. Une analyse plus précise doit donc être effectuée au regard de chaque catégorie d'infraction.

Cela étant, mise en relation avec l'évolution de la population pénitentiaire que nous détaillerons au point IV, la lecture de ces données permet notamment de rompre avec certaines idées préconçues, dont celle que l'un des facteurs explicatifs de la surpopulation carcérale est indubitablement constitué par une augmentation de la criminalité.[9]

Entre 2000 et 2015, le nombre de condamnés séjournant dans les prisons a en effet connu une augmentation très importante nonobstant une stabilité - voire une diminution, à partir de 2012 - de la criminalité enregistrée au cours de la même période comme l'indique le Graphique 2.

b. Top 5 des infractions

Les cinq catégories d'infractions les plus enregistrées en 2015 par les différents services policiers sont, par ordre décroissant, le vol et extorsion (355.414 faits), la

9 E. Maes, 'Evoluties in punitiviteit: lessen uit de justitiële statistieken', *in* I. Aertsen, K. Beyens, T. Daems & E. Maes (eds), *Hoe punitief is België?*, Antwerpen/Apeldoorn: Maklu, 2010, p. 43-83.

Graphique 2. Evolution comparée du nombre de condamnés emprisonnés et la criminalité enregistrée

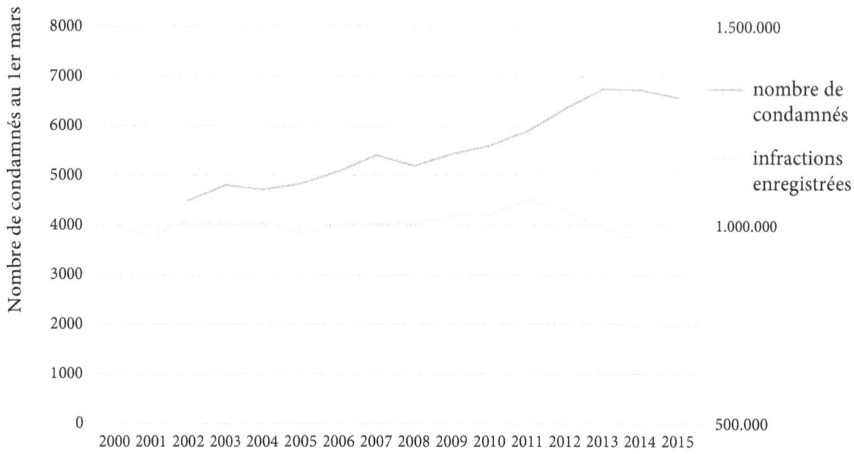

dégradation de la propriété (88.765), les infractions contre l'intégrité physique (77.439), les crimes et délits liés à la drogue (51.292) et la fraude (40.921).[10] Voir Graphique 3.

Comme nous le verrons dans la section consacrée au recours aux poursuites (III), les trois catégories que sont le vol, les atteintes à l'intégrité physique et les fraudes font également partie des contentieux les plus représentés au niveau du parquet.

L'histogramme ci-dessous donne un aperçu de l'évolution de ces catégories d'infraction depuis 2000.

Bien que le constat ne soit pas propre à la Belgique, il nous paraît important d'à nouveau rappeler que ces statistiques sont un reflet de l'activité des services de police et non de la délinquance en elle-même.

Dès lors, si les variations des chiffres de la criminalité enregistrée peuvent représenter une réelle hausse ou une baisse de la délinquance, ce n'est pas nécessairement toujours le cas. D'autres éléments peuvent en effet jouer un rôle à cet égard. Il en va notamment ainsi des modifications du champ législatif, des changements de politique criminelle, de la proactivité des services de police, ou de la propension des victimes à (ne pas) porter plainte.[11] Il convient par conséquent d'être extrêmement prudent quant à la lecture de ces données, notamment eu

10 Police Fédérale - DGR/DRI, *Statistiques de criminalité*, 2000-2015.

11 Pour la Belgique, voy. notamment F. Vesentini (ed.), *Les chiffres du crime en débat. Regards croisés sur la statistique pénale en Belgique (1830-2005)*, Louvain-la-Neuve: Bruylant-Academia, 2005.

Graphique 3. Top 5 des infractions – Evolution 2000-2015

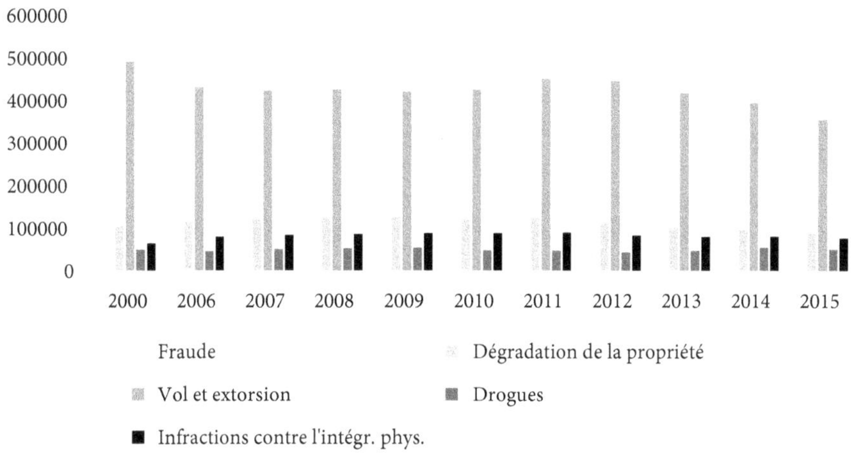

égard aux chiffres noir et gris de la criminalité qui peuvent s'avérer plus ou moins importants en fonction des types d'infraction.

II.3. DÉPÉNALISATION ET TOLÉRANCE AU TRAVERS DE L'ILLUSTRATION DE LA POLITIQUE EN MATIÈRE DE DROGUES

Hormis quelques comportements inciviques (jets de détritus sur la voie publique, souillures, animaux agressifs, jets de pierre contre des édifices,...) qui ont, par le passé, fait l'objet d'une dépénalisation en vue d'être sanctionnés administrativement[12], la tendance actuelle en Belgique n'est pas à la décriminalisation. Il n'en reste pas moins, qu'en la matière, une série d'infractions sont toutefois davantage sujettes à débats.

Il en va par exemple ainsi de la criminalité liée à la drogue, illustrative des dissensions que l'on peut relever concernant la tolérance, voire la dépénalisation de certaines catégories de comportements.

Après avoir instauré, pendant moult décennies, un régime pénal identique pour toutes les drogues, la législateur belge a en effet opté au début des années 2000 pour une approche différenciée concernant la détention de cannabis. Dans ce contexte, depuis 2003, si le fait de détenir ou cultiver du cannabis demeure toujours une infraction punissable d'une amende ou d'une peine d'emprisonne-

12 Depuis la loi du 13 mai 1999, profondément modifiée en 2013, les communes ont la possibilité de recourir à des sanctions et amendes administratives dans le cadre du non-respect de leurs règlements communaux. Avant l'apparition de ces sanctions administratives communales (SAC), ces comportements ne pouvaient être sanctionnés que par le biais de la voie pénale.

ment, la détention, par une personne majeure[13], d'une quantité de cannabis à des fins d'usage personnel, est désormais considérée – sauf si celle-ci est accompagnée de circonstances aggravantes ou d'un trouble à l'ordre public – comme relevant du degré de priorité le plus bas de la politique des poursuites.[14]

L'hypothèse d'une inversion de cette tendance à la tolérance n'est néanmoins pas à exclure: l'accord de l'actuel gouvernement prévoit en effet une tolérance zéro en matière de détention de drogues[15] – allant ainsi à l'encontre du courant prôné par les professionnels œuvrant dans le secteur de la toxicomanie.[16] Dans l'attente de ce revirement potentiel, force est toutefois de constater qu'à l' heure actuelle, « malgré la diversité des processus qui s'offrent aux États pour opérer la dépénalisation voire la décriminalisation de comportements incriminés et malgré l'éventail des systèmes de remplacement, le « compromis pénal » adopté en matière de drogues se maintient et si sa légitimité est questionnée à différentes reprises, cela ne suffit pas à le faire vaciller ».[17]

III. LE RECOURS EXCESSIF AUX POURSUITES PÉNALES

III.1. NOTE MÉTHODOLOGIQUE

Les chiffres présentés dans cette partie du rapport sont extraits de la banque de données du collège des procureurs généraux.[18] Celle-ci contient des informations relatives à l'input et l'output des parquets correctionnels. Ceux-ci connaissent de toutes les affaires pénales, à l'exception des matières du roulage, des contraventions (infractions punissables d'une peine de moins de sept jours d'emprisonnement et d'une amende inférieure à 25 € multiplié par un coefficient variable actuellement de 5,5) et des causes concernant les mineurs. La banque de données relative aux mineurs ne contient pas d'informations sur les suites données aux affaires. Celle relative aux affaires de roulage est en cours de développement.

---

13 Au contraire des mineurs d'âge pour lesquels la tolérance zéro est d'application, tant en ce qui concerne la détention que la consommation de cannabis.

14 Directive commune du 5 janvier 2005 de la Ministre de la Justice et du Collège des procureurs généraux relative à la constatation, l'enregistrement et la poursuite des infractions en matière de détention de cannabis. Voy. également C. Guillain, 'La politique pénale du gouvernement arc-en-ciel en matière de drogues', *Courrier hebdomadaire du CRISP*, n° 1796, 2003/11.

15 *Accord de Gouvernement*, 10 octobre 2014, p. 133.

16 A cet égard, voy. notamment M. Hautefeuille & E. Wieviorka, 'La légalisation des drogues: une mesure de salut public. Inévitable, utopique, dangereuse?', *Mouvements*, n° 86, 2016/2, p. 44-51.

17 C. Guillain, Dépénalisation et décriminalisation de l'usage de drogues: tenants et aboutissants, *Le Courrier des Addictions*, Vol. 15, 2013, p. 22-24.

18 www.om-mp.be/stat/corr/start/f/home.html.

Nous ne présenterons, donc, ici que les chiffres relatifs aux parquets correctionnels.

Ajoutons que l'input des parquets correctionnels belges ne s'identifie pas avec l'ensemble des crimes et délits enregistrés par les services de police ou les autres services d'inspection. En effet, un certain nombre de procès-verbaux dits simplifiés ne sont pas transmis aux parquets du procureur du Roi. Ceux-ci concernent une liste limitative d'infractions arrêtée par le collège des procureurs généraux et pour lesquels on sait au moment de l'enregistrement des faits qu'elles ne seront jamais élucidées à défaut du moindre indice disponible.

Enfin, à côté des parquets du procureur du Roi, il existe en Belgique un organe du ministère public dénommé l'auditorat du travail qui est, notamment, compétent pour exercer l'action publique pour les affaires de droit pénal social. Il n'existe pas, actuellement, de données complètes concernant les activités de cette branche du ministère public.

III.2. DIRECTION DONNÉE AUX AFFAIRES CORRECTIONNELLES ENTRÉES DANS LES PARQUETS BELGES ENTRE 2003 ET 2015

Graphique 4. Evolution des directions données aux affaires

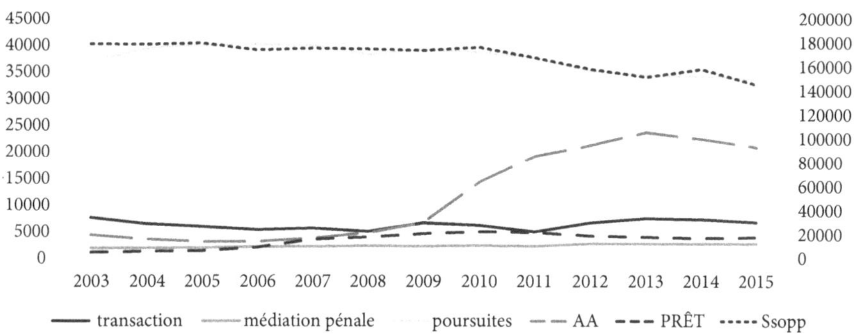

Le Graphique 4 et le Tableau 1 donnent un aperçu des directions données aux affaires poursuivables par les parquets correctionnels belges entre 2003 et 2015. Préalablement à l'analyse de ces données, un certain nombre de précisions s'imposent.

Premièrement, ces données ne portent que sur les affaires poursuivables. En effet, la Belgique connait le système du classement sans suite qui se décline en un classement technique lorsqu'il n'y a pas d'élément suffisant pour engager les poursuites ou lorsque l'auteur est resté inconnu, et un classement sans suite d'opportunité lorsque malgré l'existence de charges pour mettre en mouvement l'action

Tableau 1.

	2003	2004	2005	2006	2007	2008	2009	2010	2011	2012	2013	2014	2015
Transaction	7663	6441	5998	5380	5683	5075	6682	6210	4985	6677	7549	7363	6804
Médiation pénale	1939	1949	1998	2157	2226	2361	2324	2420	2304	2800	2800	2763	2808
Poursuites	37.039	39.421	40.045	40.163	40.004	38.286	39.248	38.683	37.638	35.210	34.448	34.307	33.607
Renvoi aux amendes administratives	4397	3575	3174	3158	3792	4810	6733	14349	19199	21265	23719	22495	20938
Probation prétorienne	1140	1322	1419	2062	3592	4017	4636	5014	4902	4233	4022	3836	3978
Sans suite opportunité	178928	178543	179684	173897	175364	174819	173602	176205	167533	158035	151480	158035	145127
Affaires poursuivables	231106	231251	232318	226817	230661	229368	233225	242881	236561	228220	224018	228799	213262
Taux de réaction pénale	23 %	23 %	23 %	23 %	24 %	24 %	26 %	27 %	29 %	31 %	32 %	31 %	32 %
Taux de poursuite	16 %	17 %	17 %	18 %	17 %	17 %	17 %	16 %	16 %	15 %	15 %	15 %	16 %
Taux de classement SS opport.	77 %	77 %	77 %	77 %	76 %	76 %	74 %	73 %	71 %	69 %	68 %	69 %	68 %

publique, le parquet estime, pour de multiples raisons, que les poursuites ne sont pas opportunes. Nous reviendrons sur cette distinction.

Afin de pouvoir correctement appréhender le taux de poursuites, il convient de ne prendre en considération que les affaires poursuivables et d'examiner combien parmi celles-ci font l'objet de poursuites ou plus généralement d'une réaction pénale. En effet, les dossiers classés sans suite pour raisons techniques sont neutres par rapport aux taux de poursuites puisqu'ils ne pourraient en faire l'objet.

Deuxièmement, il convient de distinguer le taux de poursuites et le taux de réaction pénale. Le premier renvoie à la saisine d'un juge en vue d'instruire l'affaire[19] ou de déclarer les préventions établies et de prononcer une peine. Le second inclut le taux de poursuite mais intègre, en outre, les différentes alternatives à celles-ci telles que la médiation pénale, la transaction, le renvoi aux amendes administratives ou la probation prétorienne. Ne reviendrons ultérieurement sur ces différentes figures.

Les chiffres ci-avant indiquent une très grande stabilité des taux de réaction, de poursuites et de classement sans suite d'opportunité. Celle-ci s'observe pour tous les types de direction hormis le renvoi aux amendes administratives qui a connu une augmentation importante depuis 2009 découlant de la mise en place d'un système communal de sanctions administratives pour les incivilités (dégradations, coups simples, propreté publique, etc.). Cet accroissement a eu pour effet de pousser vers le haut le taux de réaction et vers le bas les classements sans suite d'opportunité. Néanmoins, si l'on peut considérer que le renvoi aux amendes administratives constitue une forme de réaction, il n'en demeure pas moins que celle-ci est exogène au système pénal. Les réactions pénales endogènes sont, par contre, très stables en l'espace de treize années.

Par ailleurs, on relèvera les taux élevés de classement sans suite d'opportunité puisqu'ils avoisinent les 70%. Cela signifie que plus des deux-tiers des affaires poursuivables ne le sont pas pour des motifs d'opportunité. Ce constat indique que le recours aux poursuites est relativement faible en Belgique du moins pour ce qui est des affaires correctionnelles. Ce constat doit, bien entendu, être nuancé en fonction de la nature des faits. Il est évident qu'il n'y a pas de classement sans suite d'opportunité pour des meurtres ou des assassinats.

III.3. LES CONTENTIEUX NUMÉRIQUEMENT LES PLUS REPRÉSENTÉS

En 2015, pour les affaires qui avaient fait l'objet d'une décision d'orientation, les cinq contentieux les plus représentés étaient dans l'ordre (voir Graphique 5):

19 La mise à l'instruction d'une affaire met en mouvement l'action publique et le ministère public perd la faculté de classer le dossier sans suite. L'affaire pourra, le cas échéant, déboucher sur un non-lieu si l'instruction n'a pas permis de rassembler suffisamment de charges à l'égard d'un ou plusieurs inculpés.

1. Les vols (simples, qualifiés et avec violences),
2. Les atteintes à l'intégrité physique (meurtre, assassinat et coups et blessures volontaires),
3. Les atteintes à l'ordre public (rébellion, outrage, etc.)
4. Les fraudes (recel, blanchiment, escroquerie, informatique),
5. Les mœurs et l'atteinte à l'ordre des familles (viol, attentat à la pudeur, outrage aux mœurs, non présentation d'enfant, non-paiement de pension alimentaire).

Graphique 5. Contentieux les plus représentés

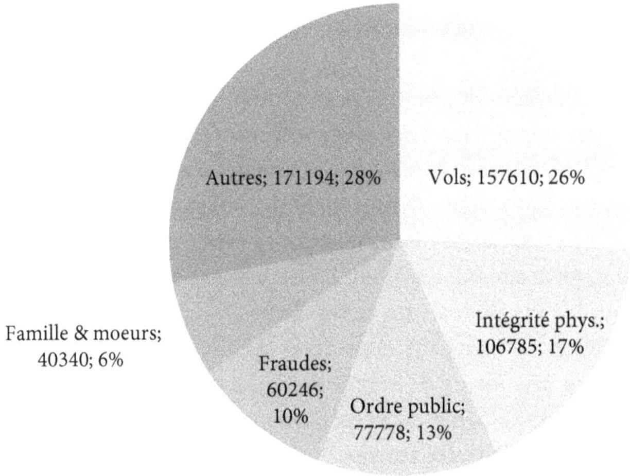

Précisons qu'il n'y a pas nécessairement de corrélation entre le volume d'un contentieux et la charge de travail qu'il génère. Ainsi, en matière d'affaires financières ou fiscales, l'input est relativement modeste mais la charge de travail qui en découle est importante.

III.4. LES RÈGLES LÉGALES EN MATIÈRE DE POURSUITES EN BELGIQUE

La Belgique connait le principe de l'opportunité des poursuites qui permet aux magistrats du ministère public de ne pas engager l'action publique nonobstant le fait qu'il existe suffisamment de charges pour le faire. Cette décision peut découler de différents motifs:

- Les répercussions sociales limitées,
- La régularisation de la situation,
- Le préjudice peu important,
- Le dépassement du délai raisonnable,
- L'absence d'antécédents dans le chef de l'auteur présumé,

- La jeunesse de l'auteur,
- Les conséquences disproportionnées liées aux poursuites,
- Le comportement de la victime,
- L'indemnisation de la victime,
- La priorité à la voie disciplinaire.

Le principe de l'opportunité des poursuites connait différents tempéraments:

a. La possibilité pour la victime de mettre en mouvement l'action publique en se constituant partie civile devant le juge d'instruction ou en citant directement devant le tribunal l'auteur présumé des faits,
b. Les injonctions positives du Ministre de la justice ou du Procureur général qui peuvent donner l'ordre d'engager des poursuites,
c. Les directives de politique criminelle émanant du Ministre de la justice ou du collège des procureurs généraux qui fixent des orientations en termes de réponses pénales et qui imposent aux magistrats du ministère public de s'y conformer dans le cadre de leur prise de décision.

III.5. LES ALTERNATIVES AUX POURSUITES PÉNALES ET LA JUSTICE NÉGOCIÉE

Il existe différents types d'alternatives aux poursuites en droit belge qui peuvent être classées en deux grandes catégories:

- Les alternatives endogènes au système judiciaire c'est-à-dire celles qui sont mises en œuvre au sein même de celui-ci,
- Les alternatives exogènes qui consistent pour le système judiciaire à se défaire du dossier et le renvoyer à une instance administrative.

Les alternatives exogènes se sont fortement développées ces dernières années dans différents secteurs du droit pénal. Ainsi, comme nous l'avons mentionné précédemment, les communes se sont vues octroyer la possibilité de *sanctionner administrativement* un nombre important de délits mineurs et d'incivilités. Les parquets, comme nous l'avons déjà indiqué, ont fait un usage substantiel de cette nouvelle voie en se dessaisissant d'un nombre important de dossiers. Récemment, les communes se sont vues accordées la possibilité de proposer des amendes administratives pour certaines infractions de roulage.

Le recours aux amendes administratives existe, également, de manière assez abondante en droit pénal réglementaire (environnement, santé publique, affaires économiques, droit pénal social, etc.).

Le renvoi aux amendes administratives empêche le ministère public d'encore intenter des poursuites.

À côté des alternatives exogènes, existent différentes alternatives endogènes.

La *transaction pénale* (art. 216*bis* du Code d'instruction criminelle) qui permet l'extinction de l'action publique moyennant paiement d'une somme d'argent. Cette formule est largement utilisée en matière de circulation routière mais également en matière correctionnelle mais de manière plus modeste. En 2011, le législateur a donné la possibilité au ministère public de mettre fin aux poursuites déjà engagées moyennant paiement d'une somme d'argent par le prévenu ou l'inculpé. Cette possibilité, du moins dans sa forme actuelle c'est-à-dire sans contrôle de la part d'un juge, a été récemment sanctionnée par la Cour constitutionnelle.[20] Le gouvernement s'attache à modifier le système en prévoyant un contrôle par un juge, de la transaction intervenue après mise en mouvement de l'action publique. Celui-ci serait, notamment appelé à vérifier la proportionnalité de la somme proposée par rapport à la gravité des faits. Notons que la transaction éteint l'action publique pour autant qu'il y ait paiement de la somme d'argent proposée et indemnisation de la victime éventuelle.

La *médiation pénale* (art. 216*ter* du Code d'instruction criminelle) constitue une forme de transaction en nature qui produit les mêmes effets que celle-ci. Il est proposé à l'auteur présumé des faits différents types de prestation: suivi d'une formation, thérapie, prestations d'intérêt général. Le cas échéant, l'indemnisation de la victime sera la seule prestation qui lui sera proposée. En tout état de cause l'indemnisation sera toujours une condition nécessaire de la réussite de la médiation pénale. La médiation pénale vise, également, à ce que l'auteur présumé et la victime puissent se rencontrer et qu'une forme de réparation symbolique puisse intervenir.

Enfin, la *probation prétorienne* est une mesure non organisée par la loi mais appliquée par le ministère public. Elle consiste principalement en un rappel de la norme à l'auteur présumé de l'infraction et d'une mise en garde par rapport à toute nouvelle réitération des faits.

Récemment le législateur belge a introduit un nouveau dispositif de règlement du contentieux pénal dénommé la « *déclaration préalable de culpabilité* » (art. 216 du Code d'instruction criminelle). Il s'agit d'une forme de justice négociée qui peut se résumer synthétiquement comme suit:

- La conclusion d'une convention entre le ministère public et le suspect/prévenu contenant une reconnaissance de culpabilité et un accord sur la peine,
- La victime n'est pas associée à la convention,
- La peine peut être réduite en échange de la reconnaissance de culpabilité,
- L'accord doit être homologué par le tribunal qui vérifie la légalité de la procédure, la sincérité de la reconnaissance de culpabilité et la proportionnalité de la peine,
- Le tribunal homologue ou rejette l'homologation

20 Cour const., Arrêt n° 83/2016 du 2 juin 2016.

- Le tribunal peut recevoir la constitution de partie civile de la victime,
- Le jugement (homologation ou rejet) n'est pas susceptible d'appel sauf sur les intérêts civils.[21]

III.6. LA DIRECTION DONNÉE AUX AFFAIRES CORRECTIONNELLES EN FONCTION DU TYPE DE MATIÈRE

Graphique 6. L'orientation des affaires en fonction de leur nature – 2015

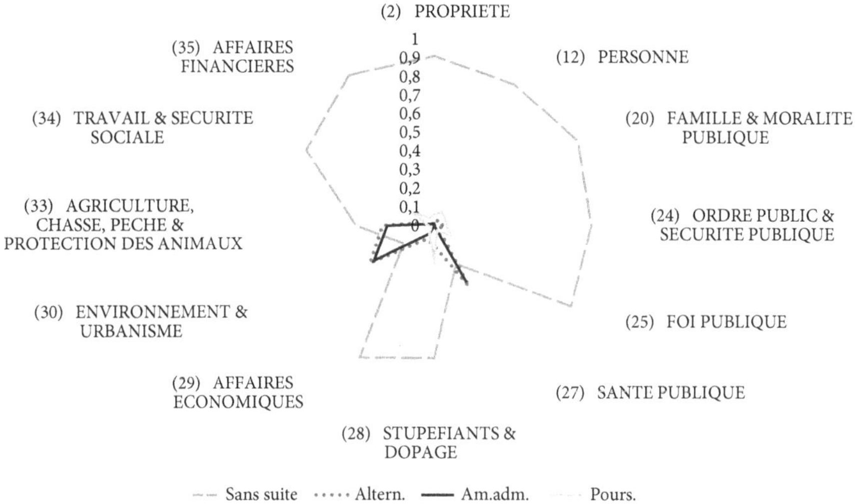

Le Graphique 6 livre un aperçu très schématique des grandes orientations données aux dossiers en fonction de leur nature. Trois directions ont été retenues: le classement sans suite (technique et d'opportunité)[22], les poursuites et les alternatives aux poursuites que nous avons déjà eu l'occasion de détailler précédemment.

Ce graphique confirme les constatations opérées sur base des données globales à savoir une dominance des classements sans suite dans toutes les grandes catégories de contentieux. On notera toutefois un recours plus important aux alternatives dans les matières à caractère davantage réglementaire (santé publique, environnement, les lois spéciales, l'agriculture, la chasse et la pêche).

---

21 À cet égard, voy. Ch. De Valkeneer, 'La reconnaissance préalable de culpabilité', *in* M. Cadelli & Th. Moreau (eds), *La loi pot-pourri II: un recul de civilisation?*, Limal: Anthemis, 2016, p. 111-126.

22 Les données disponibles croisant la direction des affaires et leur nature n'opèrent pas la distinction entre les deux types de classement.

Elles prennent alors, massivement, la forme d'un renvoi aux amendes administratives.

III.7. PERSPECTIVES

De cette brève présentation de l'activité des parquets correctionnels belges ressort plusieurs constats:

- Les taux de classement sans suite d'opportunité sont relativement élevés comparés notamment à la France et aux Pays-Bas[23],
- Les chiffres des différentes directions sont très stables sur les treize années examinées,
- Si l'on excepte le renvoi aux amendes administratives, la réaction pénale est majoritairement constituée par la mise en mouvement de l'action publique. Seules une affaire sur quatre pour laquelle il y a réaction, fait l'objet d'une alternative.
- Nous pouvons formuler l'hypothèse que le système belge, du moins en matière correctionnelle, se caractérise par un degré assez élevé de sévérité mais par une faible certitude d'être sanctionné puisque les taux de classement sans suite d'opportunité sont élevés. Or, l'état actuel de la recherche criminologique tend à montrer que ce n'est pas tant la sévérité qui génère un effet dissuasif que la certitude d'être sanctionné.[24] Cette augmentation présumée de la sévérité ne semble pas avoir produit d'effet sur la criminalité enregistrée.

IV. LE RECOURS EXCESSIF À LA DÉTENTION[25]

Une lecture instantanée de la statistique pénitentiaire belge permet d'avancer le chiffre suivant: à la date du 30 août 2016, pour une population globale de 11 millions d'habitants, nos établissements renfermaient 10.266 détenus. Parmi ces hommes et femmes de 130 nationalités, 32% l'étaient sous les liens du mandat d'arrêt, 58% subissaient des peines définitives de privation de liberté et près de 10% d'internés tombaient sous le coup de la loi de défense sociale.[26]

---

23 En 2015, le taux de classement sans suite d'opportunité aux Pays-Bas était de moins de 10 % (https://www.om.nl/actueel/jaarberichten-0/@94575/jaarbericht-2015/) et de 11,3 % en France en 2015 (www.justice.gouv.fr/publication/chiffres_cles_20151005.pdf).

24 Voy. à ce sujet Ch. De Valkeneer, 'Vers un « sanction shift »? Réflexions sur la dissuasion pénale', Les @nalyses du CRISP en ligne, 4 décembre 2015 (www.crisp.be/2015/12/vers-un-sanction-shift-reflexions-sur-la-dissuasion-penale/).

25 Les données présentées dans cette section font notamment référence aux rapports annuels de la Direction générale des Établissements pénitentiaires (2012, 2013, 2014 et 2015), publiés par le Service public fédéral Justice.

26 Population – Date 30.08.2016, Statistique journalière interne non publiée de la DGEPI, SPF Justice, Bruxelles, 30 août 2016.

Dans le contexte du recours à l'incarcération, précisons que ce chiffre de population journalière présente une diminution, significative, de plus de 1.000 unités par rapport à la même date de l'année 2012.

Faut-il pour autant crier victoire?

Certes, la volonté déclarée du Ministre K. Geens dès son arrivée à la Justice fin 2014 était-elle de réduire drastiquement la population pénitentiaire via un certain nombre de mesures, législatives et administratives, nécessitant un délai de préparation et de mise en œuvre préalables à l'obtention de premiers résultats.

L'examen objectif de l'ensemble des données disponibles pour la période 2012-2016 conduit en réalité au constat, paradoxal, d'une augmentation significative du nombre d'écrous de plus de 1.000 unités (17.700 à 18.700).

Ce différentiel de 2.000 unités dans le rapport flux/stock nécessite par conséquent une analyse des processus tant de mise en détention que d'aménagement des peines, en particulier de la libération.

En matière de détention préventive, il s'avère que l'écrou de personnes retenues sous les liens du mandat d'arrêt est en diminution de 400 unités. Par contre, lorsque mandat d'arrêt a été décerné, les juridictions d'instruction libèrent moins aujourd'hui qu'en 2012 de sorte que le chiffre de stock demeure constant. Les alternatives au mandat d'arrêt, aujourd'hui à la disposition des magistrats instructeurs, sont toujours sans effet sur la réduction de la population pénitentiaire.

Entre 2012 et 2016, l'écrou annuel de condamnés a augmenté de 1.200 unités. Or, les chiffres relatifs aux différentes modalités d'élargissement anticipé demeurent stables et le nombre de détenus choisissant ou étant contraints de subir la totalité de leurs peines est en augmentation constante.

La libération conditionnelle, transférée au pouvoir judiciaire depuis la promulgation des lois sur le statut juridique externe des personnes condamnées à une peine privative de liberté[27] et sur le tribunal de l'application des peines (TAP)[28] emporte moins de 300 décisions annuelles d'octroi. Modalité d'aménagement de la peine, ancienne, hautement symbolique, à l'organisation coûteuse, elle n'en demeure pas moins extrêmement marginale pour les 7.000 condamnés à des peines d'un total cumulé de plus de 3 ans qu'elle concerne exclusivement. Elle est donc quasiment sans impact sur le stock de population pénitentiaire.[29]

27 Loi du 17 mai 2006 relative au statut juridique externe des personnes condamnées à une peine privative de liberté et aux droits reconnus à la victime dans le cadre des modalités d'exécution de la peine.

28 Loi du 17 mai 2006 instaurant des tribunaux de l'application des peines.

29 A cet égard, voy. aussi E. Maes & C. Tange, 'Chronique de criminologie. La libération conditionnelle sous le régime des tribunaux de l'application des peines. Bilan et enjeux émergeant d'une première année de fonctionnement (2007)', *Rev. dr. pén.*, 2011, p. 929-964.

Un constat semblable vaut pour cette autre modalité d'aménagement des peines qu'est la détention limitée[30] (nouvelle mouture de la semi-liberté) ou encore pour la libération anticipée des détenus étrangers en vue de leur éloignement du territoire.[31]

L'explication d'un rapport flux/stock bénéficiaire à la réduction de la population pénitentiaire journalière réside dans l'exécution de la peine sous le régime de la surveillance électronique. En Belgique, l'octroi de cette mesure dépend d'une décision de l'autorité administrative[32] pour certains cas, du TAP pour d'autres.[33]

À quelques exceptions près, concernant essentiellement les délinquants sexuels sur mineurs qui ne peuvent espérer en bénéficier, les condamnés à un total de peines ne dépassant pas trois ans sont écroués mais automatiquement et immédiatement libérés à titre provisoire et exécutent leur(s) peine(s) sous le régime de la surveillance électronique. Il s'agit pour ces cas d'une décision de l'administration des établissements pénitentiaires. Outil de gestion de la surpopulation pénitentiaire avant tout, cette mesure présente aussi le bénéfice secondaire de maintenir le condamné dans son environnement familial, social et, parfois, professionnel, permettant à tout le moins d'éviter les effets préjudiciables de la détention. En cas de non-respect des conditions contractuellement définies dans le plan de surveillance électronique, la poursuite de la peine s'exécute par le retour en prison.

La mesure est également accessible aux condamnés subissant un total de peines supérieur à trois ans. Elle ne présente alors plus ces caractères d'automaticité et d'immédiateté valables pour les courtes peines mais s'inscrit dans une démarche progressive de retour à la liberté. Dans le prolongement des permissions de sorties, des congés pénitentiaires voire de la détention limitée, la surveillance électronique constitue le plus souvent une ultime étape demandée par le condamné et décidée par le TAP avant l'octroi d'une libération conditionnelle.

Accordée par l'administration ou par le TAP, la mise en place et le contrôle de l'exécution de la mesure passent aux mains d'une Maison de Justice quand bien

---

30 La détention limitée est un mode d'exécution de la peine privative de liberté qui permet au détenu condamné à un total de peines supérieur à 3 ans d'emprisonnement de quitter, de manière régulière, l'établissement pénitentiaire pour une durée de 16 heures par jour. Elle peut être accordée par le TAP au condamné afin de défendre des intérêts professionnels, de formation ou familiaux qui requièrent sa présence hors de la prison.

31 La mise en liberté provisoire en vue de l'éloignement du territoire est un mode d'exécution de la peine privative de liberté par lequel le condamné, pour qui il ressort d'un avis de l'Office des étrangers qu'il n'est pas autorisé ou habilité à séjourner dans le Royaume, subit sa peine en dehors de la prison dans un autre pays que la Belgique.

32 Circulaire n° ET/SE-2 du 17 juillet 2013, amendée par la circulaire ET/SE-2*bis* du 26 novembre 2015 (détenus subissant une ou plusieurs peines d'emprisonnement dont la partie exécutoire n'excède pas 3 ans).

33 Loi du 17 mai 2006 relative au statut juridique externe, précitée (condamnés subissant une ou plusieurs peines d'emprisonnement dont la partie à exécuter est supérieure à 3 ans).

même le dossier papier demeure actif au sein de l'établissement où l'individu avait été écroué.

L'octroi de la surveillance électronique explique quasi à lui seul le différentiel de 2.000 unités constaté entre la progression du nombre d'écrous et la diminution de la population journalière de condamnés au sein des établissements pénitentiaires belges. En chiffres bruts, 2.666 surveillances électroniques ont été accordées en 2012 pour 4.878 en 2016. La plus grande partie d'entre elles l'ayant été pour des condamnés à un total de peines ne dépassant pas trois ans.

Le paradoxe est là: le nombre de personnes annuellement incarcérées en Belgique augmente mais, dans le même temps, la population pénitentiaire recule de manière significative.

L'explication réside dans l'octroi par l'administration pénitentiaire, sous l'autorité du Ministre de la Justice, de la surveillance électronique à la majeure partie des personnes condamnées à un total de peines n'excédant pas trois ans.

Il s'agit là, pour l'heure, de la seule alternative effective à la détention dans notre pays.

Le législateur l'a compris, qui a ajouté la surveillance électronique comme peine principale autonome à l'éventail des peines, au même titre que la peine de travail et la probation.

V. CONCLUSIONS

À l'issue de cette présentation synthétique de la situation de la Belgique quant au recours au système de justice pénale, nous sommes d'avis, qu'au cours des prochaines années, la politique criminelle devrait s'orienter vers:

- Une réduction importante des taux de classement sans suite d'opportunité,
- Une augmentation conséquente du recours aux alternatives aux poursuites, notamment endogènes (médiation et transaction pénales),
- Une réduction du recours à l'emprisonnement comme peine en privilégiant les amendes, les peines autonomes de travail, de probation et de surveillance électronique.

On peut postuler que cette approche pourrait générer deux types d'effets:

- L'accentuation d'une courbe descendante de la population pénitentiaire, indispensable compte tenu de la surpopulation existante,
- Une augmentation de l'effet dissuasif de la réaction pénale. On sait, en effet, que la prison produit un taux élevé de récidive mais que, par contre, une intervention dirigée vers des primo-délinquants au travers de mesures alternatives peut produire un effet positif en termes de futurs passages à l'acte.[34]

---

34 Ch. De Valkeneer, 'Vers un « sanction shift » ? Réflexions sur la dissuasion pénale', *op. cit.*

OVERUSE OF CRIMINAL LAW IN FINLAND

Tapio Lappi-Seppälä*

I. INTRODUCTION

Finland is a small Nordic country with a population of 5.4 million. The Finnish juridical system is manifestly rooted in western, continental legal culture with strong influence from neighbouring Nordic Countries. Today Finland profiles itself – together with the other Nordic countries Denmark, Iceland, Norway and Sweden – as a county with internationally high level of social security and equality, high levels of social trust and political legitimacy, and low levels of penal repression. However, this has not always been the case. During the last Century, Finland has experienced three wars (the 1918 Civil War and the two wars against Soviet Union between 1939 and 1944). These crises have left their marks in the Finnish society and its criminal policy. The trends in prison rates have been more turbulent than presumably in any other Westerns European country, leading to a gross overuse of imprisonment in connection with the societal crisis during the first half of the 1990s. At times imprisonment rates reached the levels of 250-300 / 100,000 inhabitants, five to six times higher than those in Denmark, Sweden and Norway. Figure 1 displays trends in imprisonment rates in four Nordic countries in 1900-2014.

* Dr. Tapio Lappi-Seppälä (PhD) is the Director General of the National Research Institute of Legal Policy in Finland. Alongside his current position, he has been acting as a part-time professor in criminology and sociology of law at the University of Helsinki.

Figure 1. Imprisonment rates in Four Nordic countries 1900–2014 (annual averages)

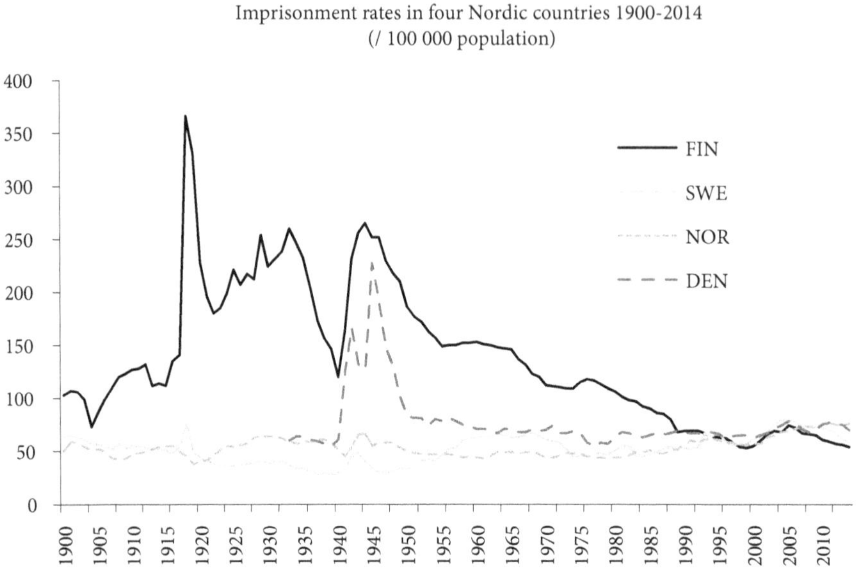

Source: Lappi-Seppälä (forthcoming).

Three "imprisonment peaks" may be detected during the first half of the last century. In the aftermath of the civil war in 1918 and 1919, Finnish prisons were filled with political prisoners. During the prohibition period in the shift of the 1920/30s and followed by the recession in the 1930s, prohibition-related crime and property offences increased, resulting in severe overcrowding in the Finnish prisons. The third peak appeared in the aftermath of the Second World War, partly consisting of war-time offences, partly of the post war crime wave.

In the 1950s, a period of normalization, known as the "age of reconstruction", began in Finland. The country was recovering from the damages of the two World Wars and the burden of paying war compensation to the Soviet Union, while at the same time establishing the industrial infrastructure which formed the foundations of the forthcoming welfare state. Finland was catching up with her Nordic neighbours that had survived the first half of the 20th century with significantly smaller damages. Crime rates remained fairly stable, and the courts were also slowly adopting more liberal sentencing practices. These changes are reflected in the rapidly declining incarceration rates from the level of 250/100,000 pop in the mid-1940s to 150/100,000 pop, when reaching the 1960s. But, compared to our Nordic neighbours, the Finnish criminal justice system of the 1960s was still less resourceful, less flexible and more repressive than that of its neighbours. Finland had three times more prisoners compared to Denmark, Norway and Sweden. This was also the background of the reform-movement that started in Finland in the late 1960s.

II. REDUCING PRISON POPULATIONS IN FINLAND IN 1960-1990

In the 1960s, the Nordic countries experienced heated social debate on the results and justifications of involuntary treatment in institutions, both penal and otherwise (such as in health care and in the treatment of alcoholics). In Finland the criticism of the treatment ideology was merged with another reform ideology that was directed against the overly severe Criminal Code and the excessive use of custodial sentences. The resulting criminal political ideology was labelled as "humane neo-classicism". It stressed both legal safeguards against coercive care and the goal of less repressive measures in general.[1]

II.1. THE FALL OF THE FINNISH PRISON POPULATION

Systematic legislative reforms started during the mid-1960s, and continued until the mid-1990s. They dealt with the general sanction system as well as specific offences. The major law reforms affecting the number of prisoners are summarized and commented on briefly below.[2]

In 1977 the law on drunk driving was changed in order to replace unconditional prison sentences with conditional sentences and fines. In a short period of time the proportion of prison sentences dropped from 90% to 20%. The introduction of community service in the mid-1990s brought another drop in the use of imprisonment to around 10%.

Besides drunk drivers, Finnish prisons in the 1950-1970s were also crowded with property offenders, especially with people convicted for theft. Penalties for theft were reduced both in 1972 and 1991. These reforms decreased the share of unconditional imprisonment from 50% to 25%, while the share of fines increased from 20% to 50% (Figure 2). This de-penalization of drunk-driving and property offences was reflected also in the prison statistics. In the mid-1970s two out of

1 The reform ideology and its criminological foundations are presented in numerous articles by the two leading architects of the reform movement of the 1960/70s, Inkeri Anttila and Patrik Törnudd. See Inkeri Anttila, *Ad Ius Criminale Humanius. Essays in Criminology, Criminal Justice and Criminal Policy,* Helsinki: Finnish Lawyers' Association, 2001; Patrik Törnudd, *Facts, Values and Visions, Essays in Criminology and Crime Policy,* Volume 138, Helsinki: National Research Institute of Legal Policy, 1996.

2 The effects of individual reforms are analysed in more detail in Tapio Lappi-Seppälä, 'Imprisonment and Penal Policy in Finland', in: Peter Wahlgren (ed), *Scandinavian Studies in Law,* vol. 54, Stockholm: Stockholm Institute for Scandinavian Law, 2009, p. 333-378; Tapio Lappi-Seppälä, 'Changes in Penal Policy in Finland', in: Helmuth Kury & Evelyn Shea (eds), *Punitivity. International Developments. Vol. 1: Punitiveness - a global Phenomenon?* Bochum: Universitätsverlag Dr. Brockmeyer, 2011; Patrik Törnudd, *Fifteen years decreasing prisoner rates in Finland,* Research Communication 8, Helsinki: National Research Institute of Legal Policy, 1993.

Figure 2. Prison rates and policy reforms in Finland 1960–2010

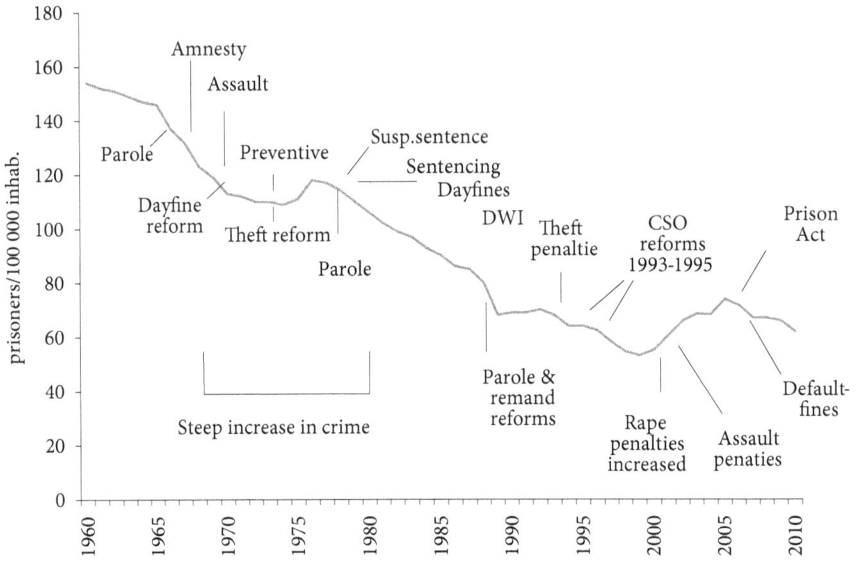

three prisoners were convicted either for drunk driving of theft. Today the relative share of these offences has dropped to about one third. In 1975 there were 1,800 prisoners serving a sentence for theft, today their number is around 450. For drunk driving the corresponding figures are 1,000 and 300.

The use of default imprisonment for unpaid fines was restricted in 1969 and the major source for these fines was removed by decriminalizing public drunkenness. The daily number of fine-defaulters fell from over 1,000 to less than 50. In 1971 the use of preventive detention was restricted only to serious violent recidivists, and the number of people held in preventive detention fell overnight from 250 to less than 10.

During the 1970s the courts took a more critical view on the use on imprisonment for young offenders. Two law reforms contributed to this change in the shift of the 1990s. The Conditional Sentence Act was amended in 1989 by including a provision which allows the use of unconditional sentences for young offenders only if there are extraordinary reasons calling for this. Also the rules of non-prosecution were relaxed in order to divert minor offences from the criminal justice process. In 1975 the courts had imposed over 2000 prison sentences for young adults (18-20 years) and more than 700 sentences for juveniles/15-17 years). In 2010 the corresponding figures were 500 and 50 and in 2015 300 and 30. In 2010 there were about 70 prisoners between the ages of 18 and 20 and 5 in the 15-17 age group. In the mid-1970s the numbers were five to ten times higher.

The system of parole and early release has also proven to be a very powerful tool in controlling prisoner rates. In Finland practically all prisoners are released on parole on a routine basis. Adult prisoners are released on parole after serving half or two-thirds of their sentences and juveniles after serving either a third or half. The minimum time to be served before the prisoner is eligible for parole is 14 days. A series of reforms have brought it down to this. During the mid-1960s this period was shortened from six to four months, during the mid-1970s from four to three months, and finally in the late 1980s from three months to 14 days. Also the criteria for early release were relaxed and the conditions for the revocations of parole were made stricter. All this had a substantial effect on the overall scope of parole and early release. In the early 1960s, less than 40% of annually released prisoners were released on parole. In the late 1960s their share increased to 50% and during the 1970s to 75%. After the 1989 parole reform practically all prisoners are released on parole.

In the 1990s the major reform to counteract the overuse of imprisonment was the introduction of community service in 1992. In order to ensure that community service will really be used in lieu of unconditional sentences of imprisonment (and not instead of other more lenient penalties), a specific two-step procedure was adopted. First the court is supposed to make its sentencing decision without considering the possibility of community service. If the result is unconditional imprisonment, then the court may commute the sentence into community service under certain conditions prescribed in the law. The duration of community service varies between 20 and 200 hours. In commuting imprisonment into community service, one day in prison equals one hour of community service. The number of prison sentences fell together with the increase in the number of community service orders in 1992–1997. Within a short period of time, community service proved to be an important alternative to imprisonment. Today community service replaces around 35% of short-term (max 8 months) prison sentences.

Imprisonment rates showed a short upward trend in the shift of the millennium. This was partly due to increased penalties for violent offences, partly due to an increased number of drug-offences and foreigners. The number of prisoner increased from the level of 2800 in late 1990s to 4000 in mid-2000. This peak turned out to be a short one, as in 2015 the number of prisoners returned to the level of 3000. The decline was partly a result of declining crime rates, partly due to the restrictions in the use of default imprisonment for fines and the extension of early release programs since 2006 (see below).[3]

---

3 The post 1990s development both in Finland and in the other Nordic countries is analysed in more detail by the author in "Penal policies in the Nordic countries 1960–2010," *Journal of Scandinavian studies in criminology and crime prevention* 13(supplement 1) 2012 and in "Nordic Sentencing", in Michael Tonry (ed.),*Crime and Justice: A Review of Research,* vol. 45. Chicago: University of Chicago Press. 2016.

An updated list of major law reforms and their impact in the use of criminal law (aggravating/mitigating) is attached in the appendix.[4]

II.2. CRIME RATES AND PRISON RATES

A substantial change in the use of imprisonment raises the question about the effects on crime rates. Nordic statistics provide an opportunity to compare countries with strong social and structural similarities but different history in the use of imprisonment. These form a kind of natural experiment to test experiences how a decrease in the use of imprisonment in one country is reflected in the crime rates, as compared to countries which have kept their penal system more or less stable. Figure 3 and Figure 4 provide information on prisoner rates and reported crime in Finland, Sweden, Denmark and Norway from 1950 to 2000.

Figure 3. Prison rates 1950–2010

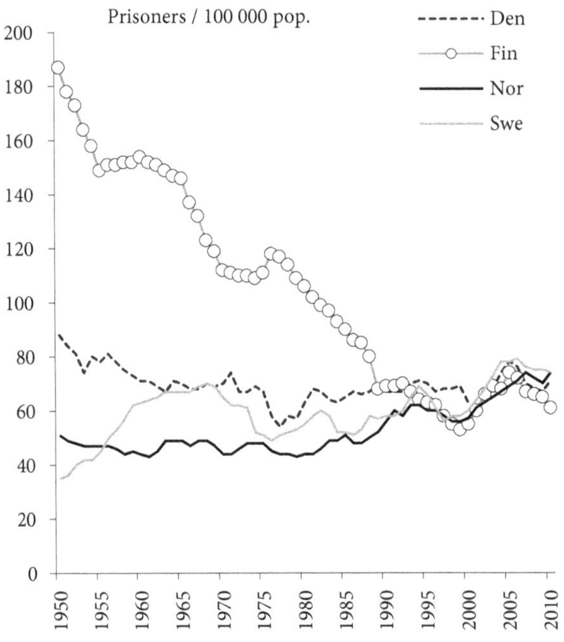

A simple comparison between the Nordic countries reveals a striking difference in the use of imprisonment, as well as a striking similarity in the trends in recorded criminality. Crime has been increasing, as it has been increasing in all developed industrialized countries, in a similar fashion. This can be attributed to

4 For a similar list for other Nordic countries, see Lappi-Seppälä 2016 supra note 3 with further comments..

Figure 4. Crime rates 1950-2010

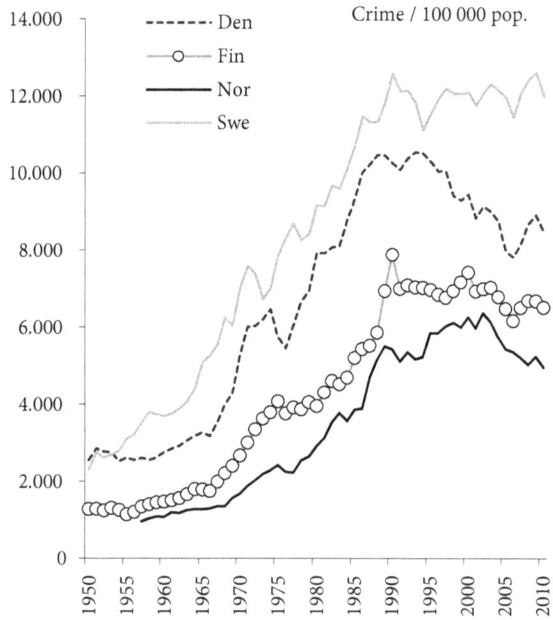

Source: Compiled from von Hofer et al 2012.

the socio-economic development and to the changed crime opportunity structures.[5] The figures support the general criminological conclusion that crime rates rise and fall according to laws and dynamics of their own, and sentencing policies in turn develop and change according to dynamics of their own; these two systems are fairly independent of one another. The grand-scale factors explaining the level of criminality override any effects that might be obtainable by using of criminal sanctions. As for Finland, this means that it was possible to decrease the use of imprisonment into one third without disturbing the symmetry of Nordic crime trends.

III. CRIME AND CRIMINALIZATION PROCESSES 1990-2015

In general, recorded crime increased in Finland from the mid-1960s to the beginning of the 1990s. Factors that contributed to this development were the

5 For global comparisons see Jan van Dijk, *The World of Crime: Breaking the Silence on Problems of Security, Justice and Development Across the World, Sage* Publications Inc., 2008.

rapid urbanization of the country, economic development and the fact that large post-war age cohorts reached a crime-intensive age in the 1960s and 1970s. The liberalization of alcohol legislation in 1969 doubled the consumption of alcohol in a short period, increasing especially violent crime and drunk driving. Part of the subsequent increase in recorded crime is also due to changes in the recording system of crimes, increased detection rate and increased propensity to report crimes to the police. In the early 1990s, together with the economic recession, major property crime categories stabilized and thefts rates, for instance, even began to decrease. In the 2000s the decreasing trend in theft, especially in car thefts and burglaries has continued. Since the 1960s there has been a rather constant increase in police recorded assaults. This trend has obviously been partly caused by increased reporting, as crime victimization surveys show no corresponding increase. Recently, also the number of recorded assaults seems to have levelled off. Homicide shows a clear downward trend in the last decades. All these developments are strikingly similar to that in other Scandinavian countries, indicating that there are similar factors affecting the development (as noted above). In international comparison, based on crime victim surveys, Finland is considered to be a country with low levels of property crime, but high levels of homicide, when compared to Western Europe and the Nordic countries.

Statistically, crime is inherently a "domestic" problem, even if the number of convicted foreigners has increased from the early 1990s onwards. In 2015, about 12,850 foreigners who resided in Finland (immigrants), were suspected of having committed some offence (excluding drunk driving and other traffic offences). This rate was 5.9% out of all persons suspected of offences known to the police in Finland. In 2015, about 230,000 foreigners (4.2% of the whole population) had residence in Finland. In addition, about 14,400 foreigners not residing in Finland, tourists and other visitors were suspected of having committed offences in 2015. In total, 27,260 foreigners were suspected of crimes in (12.5% of all suspects) in 2015. In addition about 26,600 foreigners were suspected of having committed traffic offences in 2015.

The following takes brief look on major legislative changes in individual offences and crime trends in 1990-2015.[6]

6 More information about crime trends is available at Rikollisuustilanne 2015, Institute of Criminology and Legal Policy, Katsauksia, 2016 (at: www.helsinki.fi/kriminologian-ja-oikeuspolitiikan-instituutti/tutkimus/rikollisuustilanne.html) (last visited: 13 January 2017).

III.1. VIOLENT CRIME

a. Legislation

Definitions of violent crimes underwent a profound change in 1969 by the adoption of culpability and endangerment principles and by rejecting liability of unforeseen consequences. The only consequences that were covered either by intent (in intentional crimes) or by negligence (in crimes of negligence) should be taken in account. This narrowed the scope of criminal liability. However, at the same time also behaviour that increased the risk of harm (without actual consequences) became criminalized more extensively than before.

From the mid-1970s criminalization of violent crime has pointed towards more extensive and severe sanctions. The definition of assault has expanded to cover also the violation of "health", including mental wellbeing (in 1975 and 1994). Assault reform in 1995 placed domestic violence (and other assault offences committed in private locations) under public prosecution. After the change, police-house calls doubled and the number of court-imposed penalties increased substantially. In 2000 the minimum penalty for aggravated assault was doubled from 6 months to one year. The average length of prison terms for aggravated assault also increased by 6 months. The penalties for normal assault also became more severe.

The law on homicide has undergone only technical changes since 1969. However, sentence severity has increased from the 1990s onwards. This is mainly due to changes in psychiatric interpretations and more narrow application of the category of diminished responsibility in sentencing. This has resulted in an increased number of life sentences and longer prison terms (see below V.4.).

b. Homicide

Homicide has declined almost by 50% in 1990–2015 (see Figure 5). This development follows global changes in lethal violence, which has puzzled the criminologists during recent years. In 2015, 84 homicides (excl. attempts) were reported to the police. In 2015, the annual homicide rate per 100,000 inhabitants was 1.5. In Finland, homicides are most often committed by middle-aged, unemployed, alcoholic men from the lowest social stratum. The typical conflict type leading to lethal outcome is a drinking group quarrel between friends or acquaintances. The economically deprived provinces of eastern and northern Finland are also overrepresented in the homicide statistics.

Figure 5. Recorded homicide and assault crimes in Finland 1990-2015

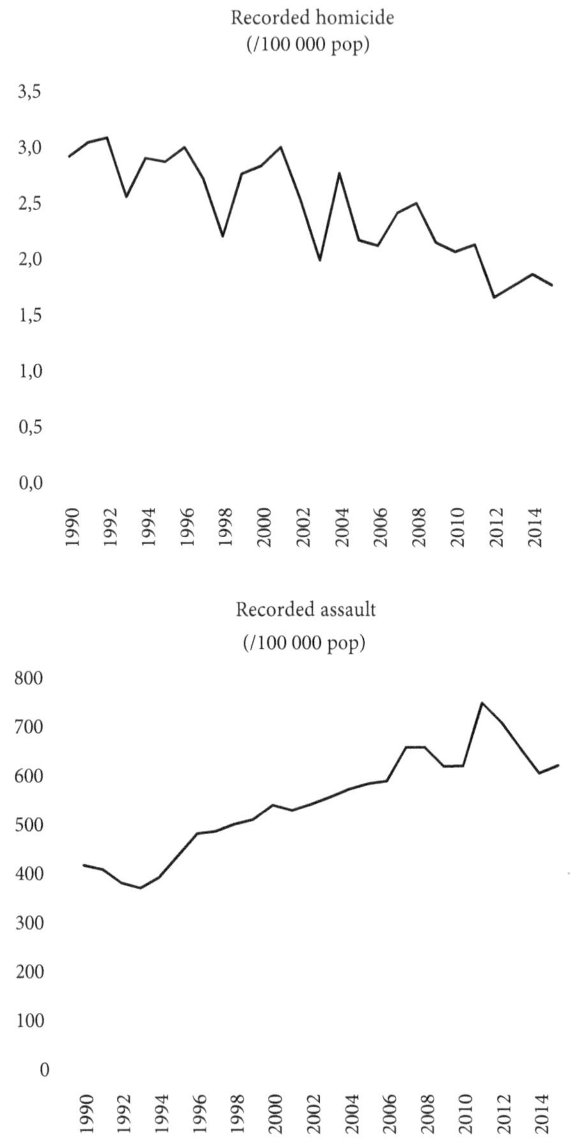

Source: Complied from Statistics Finland.

c. *Assault and robbery*

In 2015, altogether 33,874 assault offences were reported to police (around 600 / 100 000). The annual number of assault offences increased 3% in comparison to the year before. Since the end of the 1980s, the annual number of recorded non-fatal assault offences has increased over 90%. This increase has been partly due to technical factors and an increasing reporting rate; the national victimization surveys indicate that the annual percentage of adults who have experienced violence resulting in physical injury has been stable (about 2%) during the last twenty years. In 2011, the number of assault offences increased over 20% in one year, due to changes in legislation and a police campaign against domestic violence. There is no sign that the increase of sentence length for assault offences in 2000 would have had an effect on the level of criminality.

The annual number of recorded robberies (see Figure 6) increased significantly at the end of the 1980s and in the early 1990s. In the mid-1990s, the number dropped back to an annual level of about 2,000 offences. In 2015, the number of recorded robberies was 1,550. Recorded rates of robberies are highest in the largest cities.

Recorded rates of assault offences and robberies are highest in the most urbanized regions. This is true also of violence measured by victimization surveys. Apart from definition and control action influences, the annual number of assaults and robberies has been roughly paralleled by changes in alcohol consumption and economic affluence.

III.2. SEXUAL AND MORAL OFFENCES

a. *Legislation*

Criminalization of sexual offences intensified from the late 1990s onwards. In 1999 the penalties for rape were increased by dividing rape offences in three categories of gravity, by increasing the minimum penalty for basic crime from 6 months to one year and by defining rape in all circumstances as an offence under public prosecution irrespective of the view of the victims. As a result, also the length of prison sentences increased in average by 6 months and the number of cases processed increased substantially. In 2011 the definition of rape was expanded by defining sexual intercourse with an unconscious victim as rape. In 2013 rape under "mitigating circumstance" (forced sexual intercourse) was abolished from the law. Penal latitudes and offence categories in sexual abuse of children also increased in 2011 and the child welfare and health authorities were obliged to report all susceptible findings to the police. The same trend also concerns other related moral offences. In 2004 the penalties for human trafficking, procuring and child-pornography were increased. In addition, some extensions were made in the scope of criminalization. In 2006 a prohibition for purchasing prostitution services entered in force. The scope of criminalization was restricted only to cases where the services are offered in connection with human trafficking or organized procuration.

Figure 6. Recorded robberies and rapes in Finland 1990-2015

Source: Complied from Statistics Finland.

b. *Offences*

Reported forcible rapes display an increasing trend from mid-1990s, likely to reflect increasing reporting (see Figure 6). National victimization studies indicate that the level of criminality has been either stable or decreasing. The number of forcible rapes was 1,052 in 2014, and it increased 4% compared with the foregoing year.

Recorded numbers of sexual offences against children and minors fluctuate annually relatively much, reflecting the probably very large proportion of hidden crime in this event type and changeable recording practices of serial crimes. Over time, the tendency to report these offences is likely to have increased. Surveys conducted at schools for 12- and 15-year-old pupils indicate either a stable, or more probable, declining trend in sexual abuse against children in 2008 and 2013, compared to the situation in 1990.

III.3. PROPERTY OFFENCES

a. *Legislation*

Penalties for theft were reduced in 1972 and 1991, with considerable effects on sentencing practices. Since these reforms very little has changed. Crimes against cars, however, have occasionally become an issue of public concern. In 2002 the penalties for unauthorized use of motor vehicles (= "car-thefts") were increased as a result of individual initiatives by parliament members. The proposal was motivated by a "dramatic increase in crime" and by "more professional and organized" offenders. The reform stood on feeble ground, in terms of empirical facts, since crime had been in a steep decrease for several years.[7] However, the factual effects of this reform have remained fairly small, leading to an annual increase of some 60 new prison sentences.

b. *Theft*

The long-time increase in recorded thefts has levelled off in the early 1990s and in the 2000s there has been a downward trend in the number of thefts (see Figure 7). National victimization surveys also indicate a decrease in thefts after the mid-1990s.

In 2015 the police recorded in total 138,000 crimes of theft or 2,600 crimes per 100,000 in population. The number of crimes was three % lower compared to the year before.

In the long run, changes in the level of theft offences appear to have been connected with the economic development. Periods of economic upswings have often been followed by an above-average increase in recorded theft. The recent economic crisis, however, has not resulted in increased numbers of thefts.

---

7 See for a critique Tapio Lappi-Seppälä, 'Politics or Policy – Fluctuations in the Finnish Penal Policy', in: Ikke kun straf… Festskrift til Vagn Greve, Copenhagen: Juris- og Ökonomiforbundets Forlag, 2008, p. 333-357.

Figure 7. Recorded thefts and credit card offences in Finland 1990-2015

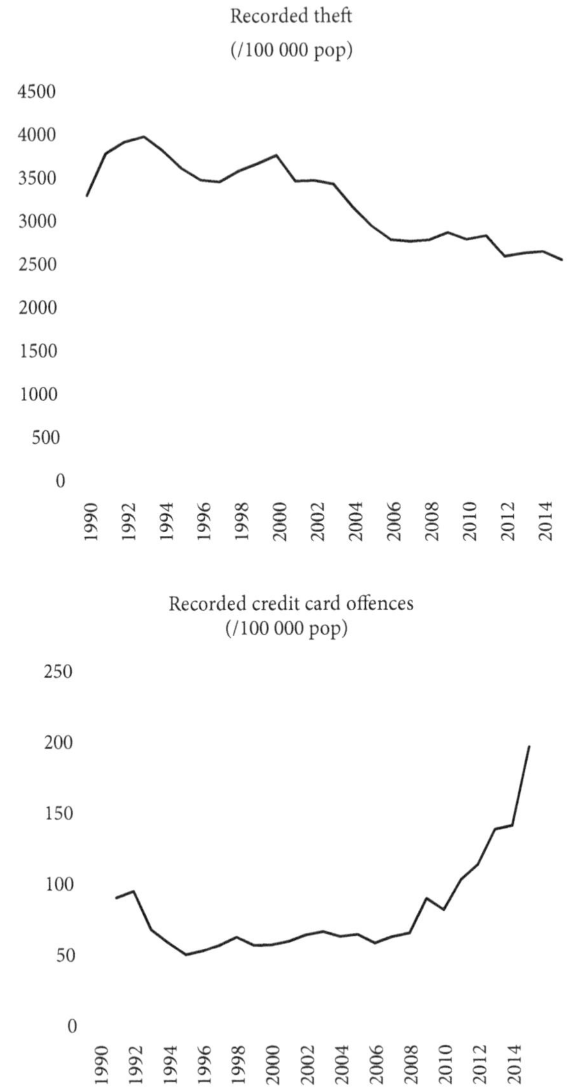

Source: Complied from Statistics Finland.

c. *Thefts of motor vehicles*

The number of recorded thefts of motor vehicles, the majority of which are car thefts, has more than halved in the last ten years. Improved security measures are probably the most important factor behind the downward trend in crime figures. At the same time there appears a shift in these crimes from joyriding to more planned and profit seeking type of thefts. In 2015 the police recorded 7,500 such thefts, or 136 crimes per 100,000 in population. There was a 4% decrease in the number of crimes from the previous year. According to the International Crime Victim Surveys, Finland scores below the European average in the frequency of car thefts.

d. Fraud

Recorded frauds increased steeply during the 1980s following the rapid introduction of credit cards. During the early 1990s, presumably because of the tightened controls in the granting of credit and credit cards, the number of recorded frauds decreased considerably (see Figure 7). Part of the decrease is also due to the new counting rule of serial frauds, the same applied for embezzlement. In the late 1990s and in the 2000s the number of recorded credit card frauds has been quite stable. However, in recent years in both credit card and other frauds increased again, the latter reflecting new forms of fraud connected with the use of the Internet.

In 2015 the police recorded 199 credit card frauds and 475 other frauds per 100,000 in population (absolute figures 10,913 and 26,091), both showing substantial increases when compared to previous years. The rates of fraud by the population size of the region follow the same pattern as the rates of theft and embezzlement. They are clearly higher in big cities than in rural regions.

III.4. DRUNK DRIVING

The major reform of the criminalization of drunk driving took place in 1977, when Finland adopted the system of fixed promille-limits by basing the criminalization on the level of blood alcohol concentration (BAC 0.5‰ indicating drunken driving and 1.5‰ indicating aggravated drunken driving) and prison sentences were largely replaced by fines or conditional sentences. Thereafter, reforms have pointed towards intensified penal control. In 1994 the limit of aggravated drunken driving was reduced from 1.5‰ to 1.2‰. In 2003, the zero-limit policy with drugs in traffic was adopted. Prior to that, the effects of drugs were evaluated on individual bases. Now all that is needed is a positive test on drugs for anyone driving a motor vehicle. Since the adoption of Zero-limit for drugs the amount of registered "drug-drivers" more than doubled from 2002-2006 (from 1,500 to 3,500 cases).

Recorded drunk driving (see Figure 8) is highly influenced by the resources and priorities of traffic control, and estimations of crime trends need to be complemented with other sources. Long-term follow up based on road traffic routine controls indicates that drunk driving was reduced by about 50% in the late 1970s. After that the trend has been either stable or declining. Recorded crime displays a downward trend in the early 1990s and post 2008. In 2015 there

Figure 8. Recorded drunk driving and drug offences in Finland 1990-2015

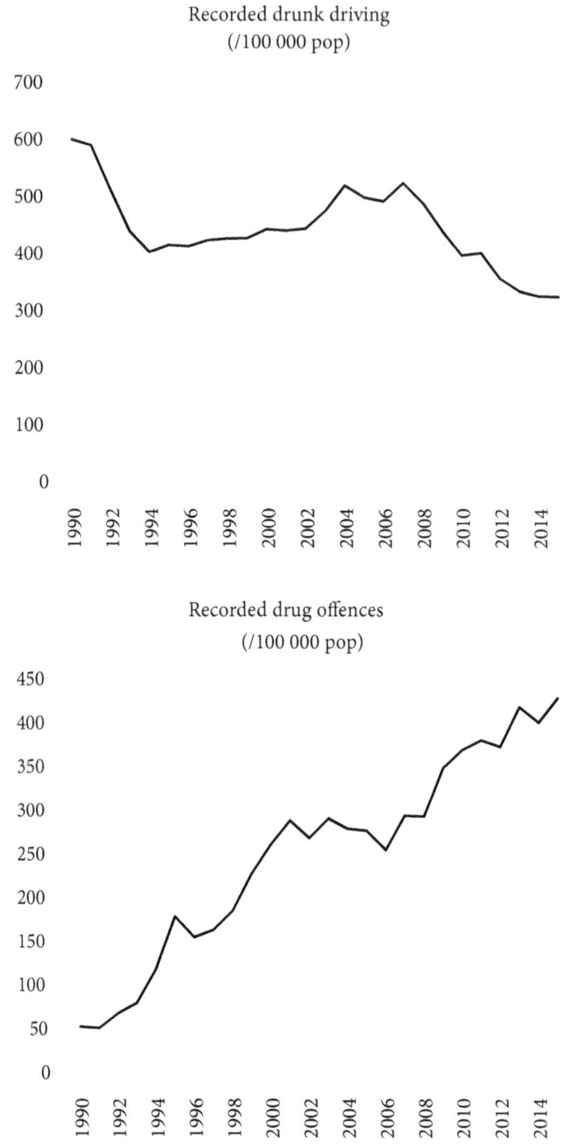

Source: Complied from Statistics Finland.

were about 40% less recorded offences than 25 years ago. The increase in 2003–2008 was mostly caused by the adoption zero limit for drug driving. In the measurements of random roadside checks, the proportion of drivers with a blood alcohol content of 0.05% or higher has been about 0.2% in the last ten years. In international perspectives these rates are very low.

III.5. DRUG OFFENCES

Use and possession of drugs for personal use are considered to be crimes in Finland. Separate legislation for offences was enacted in 1972 based on total prohibition (including consumption of drugs) with increased penal latitude, compared to previous scatter legislation. The provisions were revised in 1993 and in 2001 in order to meet the requirements of international obligations. In 2001, control was increased by introducing the possibility of writing summary fines for drug-users. In practice the reform replaced previous cases of non-prosecution by summary fines. In 2001-2005 the number of cases dealt by non-prosecution decreased from 1,400 to 400 and the number of fines increased from 5,500 to 8,000. Drug crimes are punished quite severely in Finland, compared to other offences. Punishments imposed in serious cases approach the penalty levels of lethal violence, which has raised critical comments among legal professionals.

Recorded drug offences show (see Figure 8) a constant increase from the 1990s. However, the offence is quite sensitive to statistical recording changes, and other sources need to be looked at also, including population surveys and confiscation statistics. Both point at the same direction. The results of recent drug surveys show that the prevalence of drug use has increased steadily. In recent years there has been a slight increase in the home growing of cannabis. The principal drugs in Finland are cannabis and amphetamine.

IV. PROSECUTION

In numbers, the main workload of the prosecutor consists of classical property offences, drunk driving and assault. However, in terms of invested time, economic crimes and complicated drug offences are the most demanding. Exact statistical descriptions about the evolvement of the workload are, however, difficult to establish due to the unreliability of prosecutorial statistics. The statistical units used in these statistics vary and where sometimes one observation refers to one single case with one offender, at other times it may refer to a complex series of crime with several offenders.

Recent law reforms have aimed to simplify the processing of mass infractions. Efforts have also been made to speed up the processing of complicated and more time consuming cases. All in all, the role of the prosecutor has grown stronger during the last decades. The prosecutor has been given more responsibilities in moving cases through the process, more power to decide which cases should be handled by the court, and more independent power to decide on the final disposition. The following will briefly discuss three separate arrangements.[8]

IV.1. NON-PROSECUTION

Finland follows the *principle of legality* with respect to the prosecution of crimes. The prosecutor is obliged to pursue charges if there is probable cause. However, the strict requirements of the legality principle are softened by extensive rules of non-prosecution. The grounds for non-prosecution are defined in the law in detail. These rule give the prosecutor a fairly wide discretion in four types of cases: minor offences, young offenders, where the offender is suspected for several offences (concurrence), and for extraordinary reasons of equity and criminal political expediency. In Finland, the prosecutor may drop charges "when trial and punishment are deemed unreasonable or pointless considering the reconciliation between the offender and the complainant or other action taken by the offender to prevent or remove the effects of his offence, his personal circumstances, other consequences of the offence to him, actions by the social security and health authorities, or other circumstances".[9]

In addition to non-prosecution, the prosecutor has the power to close investigations regarding minor offences, for reasons of procedural expediency. However, this option is reserved only for cases that would result in waiver of prosecution and if dropping the investigations does not breach any important private or public interest.

The scope of non-prosecution has varied over time. Finland followed very strict and legalistic policies until the early 1990s, but then loosened the conditions.[10] However, in 1991 the scope of non-prosecution was extended through a law reform, which increased the number of offences diverted from the court proceedings due to non-prosecution from around 3,000 cases to 8,000. Current levels are around 6000-7000 cases, corresponding little over 10% of the number of sentenced offenders each year.

---

8 An overview of the role of prosecutor is provided in Tapio Lappi-Seppälä, 'The Finnish Prosecution Service', in: Peter Tak (ed), *Tasks and Powers of the Prosecution Services in the EU member States*, Nijmegen: Wolf Legal Publishers, 2004. For a more detailed account on the subject, see Petri Jääskeläinen, *Syyttäjä tuomarina* (The prosecutor as a judge), Vammala: Suomalainen lakimiesyhdistys (Finnish Lawyers' Association), 1997.

9 Tapio Lappi-Seppälä, 'The Finnish Prosecution Service', in: Peter Tak (ed), *Tasks and Powers of the Prosecution Services in the EU member States*, Nijmegen: Wolf Legal Publishers, 2004.

10 For reasons of conceptual clarity it is necessary to make a clear distinction between two-types of non-prosecution: decisions based on procedural circumstances such as lack of evidence and statutes of limitations where there are legal obstacles to prosecution ("procedural" non-prosecution) and when there is enough evidence to support prosecution, but the prosecutor chooses to drop the charge for other reasons, often related to the petty nature of the offence or the young age of the offender ("diversionary" non-prosecution).

IV.2. SUMMARY FINES

The prosecutor's right to impose penalties in summary processes has also gradually extended and the prosecutor has received more independent power to act. In Finland, summary fines were confirmed by a judge at the request of the prosecutor until 1994. Since then, the prosecutor decides on the request of the police. The right to impose summary sanctions includes also forfeiture and the revocation of driving licenses.

In practice, prosecutorial fines (penalty orders, summary fines) occupy a central position, as it is the standard sanction for minor offences. This includes mid-rank traffic offences (trivial ones are handled by the police and more serious ones by the courts) and petty property offences. In Finland, the police imposes around 240,000 fixed ticket fines and prosecutors issue around 180,000 penalty orders (summary day fines). Little over 50,000 offenders are sentenced by the courts, of whom 35,000 receive day fines, 14,000 receive suspended sentences, 5,000 receive unconditional prison sentence, and 2,000 receive community service orders. Police and prosecutors play the central roles in the imposition of criminal sanctions in numbers. Any decisions that concern loss of liberty, however, must be made by the criminal court.

IV.3. "PLEA-BARGAINING" AND SENTENCE NEGOTIATIONS AS A MEANS TO EASE THE WORKLOAD OF THE PROSECUTOR?

The Finnish criminal justice system allows limited mitigation based on the co-operation of the offender and his/her post-act behaviour and contributions in clearing up his/her offence. However, this reduction applies only to the offender's own offences. Finnish law does not recognize the system of a "Crown witness", where one participant may receive mitigation by giving information about his/her accomplices. The plea-bargaining system, familiar to the Common-law countries, has traditionally not been a part of the Finnish or the other Nordic criminal justice systems. However, in 2015, Finland introduced (after critical discussions) a limited form of plea-bargaining, mainly in order to speed up the pre-trial phase and court proceedings especially in economic crimes. The European Court of Human rights has criticized Finland several times about overly long criminal proceedings, especially for economic crimes. Plea-bargaining was introduced – as an alternative measure - to speed up the pre-trial phase and court proceedings and to allocate scarce criminal justice resources more effectively.

This option is restricted and its use is strictly defined. The prosecutor may propose the procedure either on his or her own initiative or at the injured party´s initiative. If the offender agrees to plead guilty, the prosecutor agrees to propose sentencing from the mitigated penal scale, which would bring about a 1/3 reduction to the sentence, under a set of specific requirements. The maximum authorized penalty may not exceed 6 years (this rules out crimes such as homicide, aggravated assaults, and aggravated drug offences). Offences directed against the personal integrity of the victims are also excluded (covering almost all sexual offences and most violent crime). And the victim must agree with the use of this procedure. These restrictions will effectively confine plea-bargaining mostly to economic, and tax, and property offences (as was intended). Up until now, the practical relevance of the process has been quite limited.[11]

V. SANCTIONS AND SENTENCING

Finnish sanction system consists of seven basic options: Formal warnings in the form of non-prosecution and waiver of sentence, summary fines, court-imposed day fines, conditional imprisonment, community sanctions, electronic monitoring and imprisonment. In addition, there are some special arrangements for juveniles. The following gives a brief overview of the contents and implementation of these alternatives.[12]

V.1. SANCTIONS

a. Fines

Fines are the most commonly used penalty. Finland adopted day fine systems in 1922. Their aim is to ensure comparable severity for offenders of different incomes and wealth. The number of day fines is based on the seriousness of the offence and the amount of a single day fine depends on the financial situation of the offender.

A fine may be imposed in an ordinary trial or, for petty offences, by the prosecutor or the police, using summary proceedings. Summary fines by the prosecutor are imposed as day fines and summary fines by the police as fixed

11 The government must monitor implementation and report to the parliament in 2017. First experiences indicate restricted implementation (after first 9 months about 20 cases, with sentence reductions of about one third).

12 On sentencing and sanctions, see in more detail Tapio Lappi-Seppälä, 'Sentencing and Punishment in Finland: The Decline of the Repressive Ideal', in: Michael Tonry & Richard Frase (eds), *Punishment and Penal Systems in Western Countries*, New York: Oxford University Press, 2001, p. 92-150; Tapio Lappi-Seppälä, 'Proportionality and other values in the Finnish sentencing system,' in: P. Asp, C.E. Herlitz & L. Holmqvist (eds), *Flores Juris et Legum: Festskrift till Nils Jareborg*, Uppsala: Iustus Förlag, p. 401-428; Tapio Lappi- Seppälä, 'Nordic Sentencing', in: Michael Tonry, *Crime and Justice: A Review of Research* vol. 45, Chicago: University of Chicago Press, 2016, p. 17-82.

fines. Police authority is limited to traffic offences. The majority of prosecutors' fines are also imposed for traffic offences. However, a substantial number of other types of minor criminal offences also can be sanctioned by prosecutorial fines. In all, the vast majority of fines are ordered in a summary process.

b. Conditional imprisonment

The lower end of community punishments consists of conditional imprisonment. In Finland the court imposes a sentence, but postpones the enforcement of the sentence. Sentences of imprisonment up to two years may be imposed conditionally. Conditional imprisonment can be combined with supervision (for juveniles) or fines. In addition, conditional prison sentences over 1 year may be combined with a 20-60 hour community service order. A person sentenced to conditional imprisonment may be ordered to serve the prison sentence if a new offence is committed during the suspension period. Revocation, however, is possible only if the court imposes a sentence of imprisonment for the new offence. A behavioural infraction alone is not enough to trigger the enforcement of a conditional prison sentence.

c. Community service

Community service appears as a sanction on its own in Finland (not as a condition attached to other penalties, with the abovementioned exception of conditional imprisonment over one year). Community service can be used only instead of imprisonment. This is secured by a specific process under which the possibility of reconsidering the use of community service comes into play only after the court has first passed a prison term. If the sentence does not exceed 8 months, the court may convert the sentence into community service, provided that the conditions stipulated in the law are present. The maximum number of hours of community service which may be imposed is 240, with a minimum of 20 hours.

d. Electronic monitoring (EM)

Finland adopted a back-door version of Electronic monitoring (EM) as a form of a specific early-release program in 2006. In 2011, a front-door version was attached to the criminal code by the enactment of a new supervision order. This order is to be imposed by the court. It is designed for offenders who would not qualify for community service and are at risk of being sentenced to prison. Like the community service, EM was also designed particularly with the view of replacing short prison sentences. Where short prison sentences are used only for offenders without a criminal history, a clean criminal record is not a prerequisite for EM. However, too heavy recidivism may be an obstacle for imposing this sentence. Certain offences are also excluded, especially violent offences in close relationships or against children in cases where the offender and the victim are living in the same dwelling. The sentence requires that persons living in the same place consent to it. The offender must also have a dwelling suitable for the enforcement of the sentence and he/she must be able to carry out the sentence without a "considerable risk" that the sentence is converted into prison terms.

Offenders sentenced to electronic monitoring are obliged to work or attend to some other activities which are determined in each offender's individual sentence plan. Offenders can i.a. take part in supervision meetings, work, study, attend rehabilitation programs, and other activities that maintain or improve the offender's social capacity.

e. Imprisonment

Finland has abolished the death penalty. The most severe sentence that may be imposed for a single offence is life imprisonment, which in practice means imprisonment for a term of 15–18 years. This option is used only for murder.

Imprisonment for a determinate period varies from fourteen days and to twelve years for a single offence (and fifteen years for several offences). The applicable penal latitude for each offence is defined separately in the law.

The majority of prison sentences are short, usually 2–6 months. In 2010 three out four prison sentences were less than one year and 60% less than 6 months. Of all imposed prison sentences (240 out of 6,296), 4% were four years or more, and 1.5% eight years or more (see Table 1).

Table 1. The length of court imposed unconditional prison sentences in 2010

Courts 2010	N	%
< 1 year	4834	76.8
1 < 2 years	717	11.4
2 < 4 years	505	8.0
4 < 8 years	156	2.5
8–12 years	55	0.1
over 12 years	4	0.9
Life	25	0.4
All	6296	100

Source: Compiled from Statistics Finland

f. Sanctions for young offenders

Youth justice takes a distinctive form in Finland and the other Nordic countries. Offenders under the age of 15 are dealt with by the child welfare authorities. Offenders aged 15 to 17 years fall under the jurisdiction of both the child welfare and criminal justice systems. Young adults aged 18 to 20 years are dealt with by the criminal justice authorities (and to some extent the child welfare system by providing after-care).[13] Major differences in the implementation of criminal sanctions for juveniles are listed below:

1. The use of imprisonment is heavily restricted for young offenders. Offenders aged 15 to 17 years can be sentenced to unconditional imprisonment only for exceptional reasons. In practice this means that the number of prisoners under the age of 18 held in penal institutions has varied in recent years between 5 and 10 individuals.
2. All offenders below 18 years at the time of the offence receive a general mitigation in sentencing. The court may go below the prescribed minimum sentence and the applicable maximum sentence is reduced by one third. The use of the life sentence is also excluded for this age group (and replaced by a prison term of 12 years).
3. Juvenile cases are diverted more effectively from the criminal justice process, whenever there are social reasons for doing so. The prosecutor has wider powers not to prosecute juvenile cases. Extra-judicial mediation schemes are also used in juvenile cases more frequently (see below).
4. The contents of specific sanctions vary with juvenile-specific features. Juveniles sentenced to conditional imprisonment are usually placed under supervision. Juveniles with more serious problems can also be sentenced to a specific, socially oriented non-residential juvenile punishment order.
5. As regards to the prison system, offenders below 21 at the time of the offence are released on parole either after serving either 1/3 or ½ of the sentence (instead of the regular ½ or 2/3, see above). Sentence enforcement, including program work and education, is also tailored individually according to the juvenile's specific needs.

In Finland, about 85% of the penalties imposed on juvenile offenders are issued outside the court through lighter procedure. Non-prosecution has received the

---

13 For a more detailed description of the Finnish juvenile justice system see Tapio Lappi-Seppälä, 'Nordic Youth Justice: Juvenile Sanctions in Four Nordic Countries', in: Michael Tonry & Tapio Lappi-Seppälä (eds), *Crime and Justice: A Review of Research*, vol. 40, Chicago: University of Chicago Press, 2011, p. 199-264; Tapio Lappi-Seppälä, 'Juvenile Justice without a Juvenile Court: a Note on Scandinavian Exceptionalism', in: Franklin E. Zimring, Maximo Langer & David S. Tanenhaus (eds), *Juvenile Justice in Global Perspective*, New York: New York University Press, 2015, p. 63-117.

widest application among juveniles. In the age group 15–17 years, the share of non-prosecution varies around 29% of all courts disposal and 7% of all disposals (fines included). Unlike general criminal justice in Finland and many other countries, sentencing practice of juveniles has not become harsher. The vast majority of penalties imposed by courts for all age groups consist of fines. The younger the offender, the higher the share of fines (78% in age group 15–17, 67% in 18–20 and 59% for offenders over 20 years). Second in the list is conditional imprisonment, which to large extent has a fairly formal character as well (16% in the age-group 15–17 and 25% in the age group 18–20). In about 30–50% of conditional sentences the young offender is given a supervision order.

V.2. MEDIATION AND RESTORATIVE JUSTICE

Mediation has gained a substantial role in the handling of criminal cases in Finland. However, this has taken place outside the field of criminal law. Mediation does not constitute a part of the criminal justice system but it has frequent interrelations with that system as far as referral of cases and their further processing is concerned. The criminal code mentions an agreement or settlement between the offender and the victim as a possible ground for the waiving of charges by the prosecutor, or waiving of punishment by the court and as a ground of mitigating the sentence.[14]

The first mediation experiment in Finland started in 1983, expanded in the 1990s and was institutionalized in 2006 by passing a national law on mediation. Provincial governments are obliged to arrange mediation service in their region, either in co-operation with municipal authorities or with other public or private partners. Participation in mediation is, in turn, always voluntary for all parties.

Mediation can start at any time between the commission of the offence and execution of the sentence and by any of the possible parties. Once a case has been referred to the mediation office, the office contacts the parties in order to query their willingness to participate in mediation. Where this is successful, a first meeting is arranged. The initiative for submitting cases to mediation comes, as a rule, from the police or from the prosecutor. The consent of all parties is required before going into reconciliation. The mediator's principal role is only to mediate and act on a neutral basis. Once the process has started it normally leads to a written contract.

In complainant offences, successful mediation automatically means that the prosecutor drops the case. In non-complainant offences it is under the discretion

14 On the role of mediation in Finland, see Tapio Lappi-Seppälä, 'Mediation in Finland', in: Frieder Dünkel, Joanna Grzywa-Holten & Philip Horshfeld (eds), *Restorative justice and Mediation in Penal Matters*, Schriften zum Strafvollzug, Jugendstrafrecht und zur Kriminologie, Godesberg: MG Forum Verlag, 2015, p. 246-267.

of the prosecutor whether he/she is willing to drop the charge. This would be possible according to the law if prosecution seemed "either unreasonable or pointless" due to successful reconciliation, and if non-prosecution did not violate "an important public or private interest".

The annual number of cases referred to mediation exceeds 10,000, of which around 60% lead to completed mediation. The clear majority of cases involve either minor property offences or minor forms of assault and battery (around 40% in both cases).

The number of criminal cases referred to mediation was about 11,000 offences in 2014. From 2007 on, the number of these cases increased by altogether 15%. Out of all the criminal cases referred to mediation in 2014, about a half (52%) were violent offences. Domestic violence cases accounted for about one third of the violent offences (32%). The corresponding percentage was 19% in 2010. The growth in the number and the proportion of domestic violence cases can be explained by an amendment of the Criminal Code, which defines petty domestic violence cases as offences under public prosecution.

Criminal cases referred to mediation accounted for about 10% of eligible criminal cases for mediation. Of the violent offences solved by the police about one fourth were referred to mediation in 2014. Agreement was reached in 80% of all mediated criminal cases. The corresponding percentage of cases referred to mediation was 57%. The mediation process was not initiated or discontinued altogether in 43% of cases referred to mediation. Monetary compensations accounted for 36% and work compensations for 4% of all mediation agreements in 2014. The signification of mediation is important in cases that are especially eligible for mediation. To such recommended cases belong offences where suspects are young offenders and children under 15 years or first-time offenders.

V.3. SENTENCING NORMS

a. *Regulating sentencing decisions*

Standards governing sentencing are set out in legislation. This guidance is expressed in penalty scales, classification of offences, and statutory sentencing criteria. The criminal code defines offences and indicates punishment severity by providing a minimum and maximum for each. Most offences are graded into three subcategories according to their internal seriousness (typically petty, standard, aggravated), each with a specific minimum and maximum penalty. The ranges are fairly broad. Upper limits are binding and with minor exceptions may not be exceeded. Minimums are also fairly low (a few months for many aggravated offences) and seldom compel courts to impose more severe penalties than they otherwise would. Moreover, the minimums are only presumptive. In practice, imposed penalties tend to be closer to the minimum, usually in the lower quarter or third of the authorized range.

b. Sentencing principles and criteria

Finnish sentencing theory formulated in the 1970s and 1980s stresses principles of proportionality, predictability, and equality. Section 6.4 of the Finnish Penal Code, for example, states: "The sentence shall be determined so that it is in just proportion to the harmfulness and dangerousness of the offence, the motives for the act, and the other culpability of the offender manifested in the offence." Consistency in sentencing and the avoidance of unwarranted disparities is also a value. The law explicitly states that the need to pay "specific attention to the uniformity sentencing practice."

Along with proportionality, consistency, and predictability, other aims and values need to be acknowledged. Finnish sentencing provisions contain specific mitigating provisions that are based on the values of humaneness, equity, and mercy. Thus circumstances related to post-act behaviour, personal conditions, and the accumulation of sanctions justify downward deviations from the "normal punishments". As regards the use of community alternatives, rehabilitative aims and needs have gained more footing in the application of sanctions during the last years. However, there are no code provisions that would justify the imposition of sanctions for reasons related to deterrence or the need to provide exemplary sentences. Such decisions would violate the requirements of both proportionality and equality. However, the law does contain a list of separate aggravating and mitigating circumstances which the courts needs to pay attention to.

c. The choice of sanction following the "ladder model": Imprisonment as a last resort

The proportionality principle requires not only that crimes be graded according to their internal seriousness and blameworthiness, but also that penalties be graded according to their internal severity. The three principal punishments have been the fine, the conditional sentence and imprisonment. "Withdrawal of sentence" and "non-prosecution" are also usually classified as criminal sanctions in their mildest form (because they both include assignment of guilt). These penalties can fairly easily be graded according to their severity in a kind of "ladder model", where different types of sanctions represent different levels of severity (non-prosecution → waiver of sentence → fine → conditional imprisonment → unconditional imprisonment). This also indicates that imprisonment is the last option to be considered, only after other alternatives were found ineffective. In the choice between unconditional and conditional imprisonment, the presumption is in favour of conditional sentences. For borderline-cases the legislator has created combinations that would still "keep" the case in the side of non-custodial penalties, by combining conditional imprisonment either with fines of short community service order.

Adding new community sanctions (community service and electronic monitoring) in this system complicates the straightforward severity based ladder-model by adding a "third dimension" with emphasis on rehabilitative aims and arguments.[15] These options are placed on the same severity level with imprisonment in the sense that community service is used as a conversion of unconditional prison sentences under the specific preconditions stipulated in the law, and electronic monitoring is used as a conversion of community service in cases where the offender is unable to pass the suitability test. The law creates a clear presumption in favour of community service over unconditional imprisonment. All offenders sentenced to an unconditional prison term of maximum eight months and who give their consent to community service and are considered able to carry out the service, should be sentenced to community service. This presumption may, however, be overturned by the offender's previous criminality, especially by his or her previous community service orders. The same logic applies when decisions are made between electronic monitoring and unconditional imprisonment. The decision process under this model starts with arguments related to proportionality-oriented criteria in steps, as follows (see Figure 9).

Figure 9. The "ladder model" of sanctions in Finland

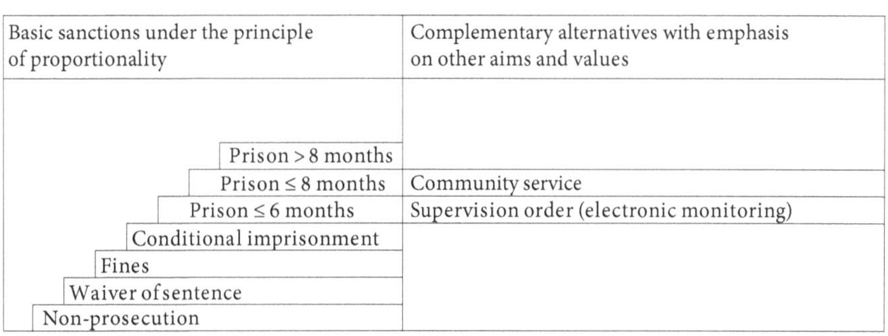

The choice between fine and imprisonment, as well as the decision between conditional and unconditional imprisonment, is primarily based on the seriousness of the offence (the harm and the risk of harm), the culpability and the previous convictions of the offender, and on other factors described in chapter 6, sections 5–6 of the Criminal Code. To a large extent these same arguments guide

15 Of the construction of the model, see sources in *supra* note 11.

the use of non-prosecution and waiver of sentence as well. The age of the offender is also of importance. If the court decides on a sentence of unconditional imprisonment of eight months or less, community service should be imposed instead of imprisonment if the offender is deemed to be suitable for community service, and previous sentence are not a bar to this. If the offender does not fulfil the criteria of community service, the court needs to consider electronic monitoring.

On top of the arguments related to proportionality and rehabilitation (in community sanctions), there are also arguments that justify a downward-deviation from the requirements of proportionality. Meritorious conduct of the offender after the act, repairing the damages, taking part in mediation or co-operating with the police may mitigate the sentence on more or less pragmatic grounds. Mitigation on the grounds of reasonableness and equity may enter the question if the offender is of an advanced age, there has been an accumulation of sanctions, or there is another serious reason for this. These factors may justify the use of a more lenient type of sentence, other mitigation in the sentence, or they may also justify a waiver of the sentence.

V.4. SENTENCING PRACTICE

The use of different sentencing alternatives in 2015 is displayed in Table 2.

All in all, the Finnish authorities impose around 470,000 sanctions each year. Almost 90% are imposed as fines through summary proceedings. Half of all sanctions (240,000) are police-fines and 38% (180,000) prosecutors-fines imposed mainly for traffic offences. Courts impose 53,000 sentences. In 2015 prison sentences (5,000) cover 10% of all court-imposed sanctions and 1% of all penalties imposed either by the police, prosecutor or the courts. Community sanctions cover 29% (community service is used in 3.5% conditional imprisonment in 25% of court cases). Fines cover 61% of all court dispositions. The number of successful mediations (6,254) represents over 10% the total number of court ordered penalties (and 1.3% of all penalties, including traffic fines).[16]

16 The available figures of the "total flow" of cases for 2014 is as follows: The total number of recorded offences was 828,296. The number of cleared offences in that year was 575,639. Out of these 261,457 received a ticket fines and 164 431 received a penalty order from the prosecutor. 6,520 charges were dropped for policy reasons (non-prosecution) and 19,403 for procedural reasons (mainly lack of evidence). The number of offenders prosecuted before the court was 60,611. The charge was dismissed in 3139 cases were. In all 56,282 offenders were sentenced of 121,830 offences. The number of offender discharged due to the lack of criminal responsibility was 35. Sanctions were distributed as follows: waiver (warning) 528, fines 33,604, conditional imprisonment 13,580, community service 1,926, electronic monitoring 222 and imprisonment 5,273 (see for details Seuraamusjärjestelmä 2015 p. 8).

Table 2. The use of different sanction options in 2015

SENTENCING STATISTICS 2015	N	% of court ordered penalties	% of all penalties
I. COURT IMPOSED PENALTIES			
PRISON	5 082	9.6	1.1
COMMUNITY SANCTIONS, Of which…	15 289	29.0	3.2
Electronic monitoring	*236*	*0.4*	*0.1*
Community service	*1 820*	*3.5*	*0.4*
Conditional imprisonment with community service	*281*	*0.5*	*0.1*
Conditional imprisonment with a fine	*5 584*	*10.6*	*1.2*
Conditional imprisonment alone	*7 363*	*14.0*	*1. 6*
Juvenile penalty	*5*	*0.0*	*0.0*
COURT FINE	32 329	61.3	6.9
ALL COURT IMPOSED PENALTIES	52 700	100.0	11.2
II. SUMMARTY PENALTIES			
Prosecutors fines	178 550		37.8
Police fines (fixed ticket fines)	240 700		51.0
All summary penalties	419 250		88.8
III. ALL PENALTIES	471 950		100.0
IV. NON PROSECUTION	6 328	12.0	1.3
V. MEDIATION			
Cases referred to mediation	10 997	20.9	2.3
Contract signed	6 254	11.9	1.3

Note: The population of Finland is 5.4 million.

Source: Compiled from Statistics Finland, *Crime and Criminal Justice in Finland* (Institute of Criminology and Legal Policy, Reviews 11/2016).

More detailed figures on the use of different sentencing options and the average length of prison term by offence-type in 2012 is displayed in the appendix. Only cases dealt by the courts are included. Results can summarized as followed:

- Completed homicide is punished by a little below a 10-year prison term (in addition some 10-15 murder cases receive a life sentence).
- Basic form of rape is punished with about 2-year prison term (around 60%) and aggravated rape by 4-5 years prison term.

- Basic assault leads to fines in around 65% cases, while aggravated assault is punished either by two years unconditional prisons (little below 60%) or by 1-2 years conditional prison.
- Basic theft is punished by fines (little over 50%) or 2-3 months unconditional or conditional prison term. Aggravated theft leads to around one year unconditional (50%) prison term or to a little shorter conditional prison term (40%). One out of ten offenders are sentenced to community service.
- Penalties for basic robbery are very much on the same level with aggravated theft. Aggravated robbery, in turn, leads to an unconditional (90%) prison term of around 2-3 years.
- Drunk drivers receive fines when their BAC is below 1.2‰. If the level of alcohol in ones blood exceed 1.2‰ the penalty is either conditional prison term (15-45 days), or, for repeat offenders, community service or an unconditional prison term (2-4 months).
- The consumption of drugs in punished in Finland by a fine (20 day fines, same as for petty theft). Distributing and trafficking smaller amounts is punished either by fines (66%) or short conditional (20%) or a 2-6 months unconditional prison term. Larger quantities are sanctioned as aggravated drug offences with unconditional prison terms starting from 2 up to 10 years (mean 3.5 years and 50% of cases falling between 22 and 60 months).

VI. THE PRISON SYSTEM

VI.1. ENFORCEMENT PRINCIPLES

Sentence enforcement is regulated in the prison law.[17] The general aim of rehabilitation is spelled out in the opening paragraph of the Finnish prison law (paragraph 1:2 PL): "The goal of the enforcement of imprisonment is to increase the ability of a prisoner to a crime free life by promoting the prisoner's potential to cope and his adjustment to society….". Alongside the general aim of rehabilitation and reintegration, the law stresses the principle of normalization, "The conditions in a prison shall be arranged, to the extent possible, so that they correspond to the living conditions prevailing in society" (paragraph 1:3 PL) and the aim of harm-minimization, "The possibilities of a prisoner to maintain his health and functional ability shall be supported. The goal is to prevent any detriment resulting from the loss of liberty." (paragraph 1:3 PL). Enforcement is constructed according to a step-by-step model towards a more open regime and more rights for detainees.

17 General information about the prison systems and prison law is provided in source supra note 2.

All prisoners are provided with a sentence plan drafted on a base of structured risk and needs assessment. The plan includes also plans and preparations for the release. The plan is updated and completed during the prison process. Several prisons arrange Cognitive Skills courses, which develop problem solving and social skills, the STOP Program is for convicted sex offenders whereas Anger Management Courses and the Cognitive Self Change Program are for prisoners convicted of violent offences. Still, the major part of the rehabilitative activity in Finnish prisons is about substance rehabilitation, as a clear majority of the prisoners has a problem with substance abuse. Substance rehabilitation is arranged in almost all institutions.[18]

VI.2. PRISONS

All prisons in Finland are state funded and run by the state officials. There are no private prisons in Finland, nor are there any plans in that direction. Private prisons would not meet the demands of the Finnish constitution's paragraph 124, stating that any "task involving significant exercise of public powers can only be delegated to public authorities."

Sentences of imprisonment are enforced either in closed prisons or in open institutions. The actual serving of the sentence starts, more often than not, in a closed prison. Usually the prisoner will later on be transferred to an open regime. Open institutions hold around 25% of the current prison population. Open institutions are in practice prisons without walls: the prisoner is obliged to stay in the prison area, but there are no guards or fences. There are 18 open prisons and 13 closed prisons. These prisons are fairly small in their size. The largest closed units carry over 300 prisoners, while the smallest have a size of 40-50 prisoners. The norm is 50 to 100 prison places.

VI.3. RELEASE FROM PRISON

a. Basic rules

In Finland, all prisoners are released conditionally before having served the full sentence, and the release on parole is based on the decision of the director of the prison. Release practices are quite fixed. Recidivists are released after they have served two-thirds of their sentence, and first-time prisoners are released after they have served one-half of their sentences. Offenders from 15 to 20 are released

18 More information about the enforcement of prison sentences in Finland is available from the Finnish Criminal Sanction Agency's (RISE) web page (at: www.rikosseuraamus.fi/en/index/enforcement.html) (last visited: 13 January 2017).

either after 1/3 (first offenders) or after ½ (recidivists). In all cases, a further condition is that the prisoner has served at least fourteen days.

The duration of parole reflects the amount of time remaining in the sentence, however, at least three months and at most three years. About one fifth of those released on parole are placed under supervision. Supervision is used if the probationary period is more than one year or the offence was committed when under 21 years of age. Prisoners may also request supervision by themselves. The supervisor may be the Probation Service or a private individual appointed by the Service. In principle, the supervision involves both control and support.

The court decides on the revocation of parole if the offender commits an offence during the period of his/her parole and on the grounds of a behavioural infraction. Practically all parole revocations are based on new offences, and only such an offence that would normally lead to a prison sentence may serve as a reason to revoke the parole order. Behavioural infractions may also justify a short-term – maximum 14 days – revocation, but this option is used quite seldom (10-20 times per year).

There are three exceptions from these basic rules: One concerning a specific supervised pre-release program, and another for high-risk violent recidivists. The third exception deals with the release from a life-sentence.

b. "Probationary liberty under supervision"

The Prison Law 2006 introduced a new type of pre-release program called 'probationary liberty under supervision'. It is designed especially for long-term prisoners who need more support and more intensive program-work. It provides an opportunity for earlier than usual release, but on the condition that the prisoner agrees to submit him/herself under more intensive supervision. Probationary liberty is available, on application, at the earliest of six months prior to the normal conditional release.

Prisoners in this program are placed under electronic supervision. They also agree to refrain from the use of any sort illegal substances or alcohol. Enforcement of the program follows similar lines as described above in connection with electronic monitoring. The total number of prisoners released on parole is little over 3000 and out these little over 500 are pre-released to probationary liberty under supervision.

c. Release of high-risk violent recidivists

The second exception concerns the release of high-risk violent recidivists. Finland abolished preventive detention in 2006. However, a compensating scheme was introduced that authorizes the courts to order serious violent offenders to serve their sentences in full. This option is reserved for the same category of high-risk violent recidivists as were affected by preventive detention.

This arrangement is reserved only for repeat violent recidivists, and only under the conditions defined in law in detail and by the order of the court. It applies only to cases where the offender is sentenced to at least three years in prison for a violent offence. Furthermore it is required that the offender has been found guilty of a similar serious violent crime in the ten years preceding the offence. If the offender is deemed to be "particularly dangerous to the life, health or liberty of others" the district court may pronounce that the offender has to serve the full length of the imposed sentence. Should that be the case, the decision needs to be confirmed also by the court of appeal, once the normal release time approaches. Prisoners serving their sentences in full may be released only after a risk assessment (as is the case with life imprisonment, see below). However, in this case the prisoner also needs to be released under supervised probationary liberty, at the latest, three months before their term is completely served. The ratio for this provision is the fact that releasing high-risk prisoners in society without any form of supervision or support is impractical, inhumane and unwise.[19]

VI.4. LIFE IMPRISONMENT

Most severe offences – including murder, genocide and aggravated forms of espionage and treason - are punishable by life imprisonment. In practice, life imprisonment has been used in peace times only for murder. In Finland, life imprisonment is the mandatory penalty for murder, unless there are extenuating circumstances such as the young age of the offender, or diminished responsibility.[20] The use of life sentences has also been increasing during the last 20 years, due to a much more restricted application of the category of diminished responsibility in murder cases. Life imprisonment plays a substantial role in the Finnish prison system. At the moment there are about 200 prisoners serving a life sentence in Finland with the total number of 3,100 prisoners. This corresponds to around 7% of the total prison population.[21]

There is no "life without parole" in Finland. All prisoners sentenced to life imprisonment are released through a court order. Before the reform of the prison

19 See for a more detailed description of releases from prison Tapio Lappi-Seppälä, 'Finland', in: Nicola Padfield, Dirk Zyl van Smit & Frieder Dünkel (eds), *Release from prison: European policy and practice,* Portland: William Publishing, 2010, p. 135-168.

20 In addition, one life sentence has also been imposed for and offenders found guilty of genocide in Rwanda.

21 For the following see especially Tapio Lappi-Seppälä, 'Life Imprisonment and related institutions in the Nordic Countries', in: Dirk van Zyl Smit & Catherine Appleton, *Life Imprisonment and Human Rights*, Oxford/Portland, Oregon: Hart Publishing, 2016, p. 461-506.

law in 2006, the release took place through presidential pardon. According to the new rules, the release from a life sentence is decided by the Helsinki Court of Appeal, on the basis of the prisoner's application.[22] For adult prisoners, release on parole may take place after 12 years have been served, or 10 years if the offence was committed before the prisoner was aged 21. If the application for parole is rejected, the matter can be reconsidered after a year. The prisoner may also appeal to the Supreme Court under the general rules. Before persons sentenced to life imprisonment are released on parole in Finland, they may be pre-released on 'supervised probationary liberty' for a period of at most six months prior to the 'regular parole'.

The release from a life sentence is conditional. In Finland, all prisoners released from life imprisonment are placed under probation for a period of three years. Revocation of parole follows common general principles. The threshold for revocation is fairly high, and usually requires a new offence punishable by a prison term. A breach of license conditions seldom qualifies as grounds for revocation, and if it does, only for a short period of time (around ten days). If a parole license is revoked because of a new offence, the length of the maximum revocation period is three years, but in practice it may be shorter.

The actual length of life imprisonment before release has varied over time. Life sentences became shorter in the 1970s and 1980s. In the 1970s the average time served in Finland was 16.5 years, in the 1980-1990s it was around 11 years and in the 2010s 15 years. The longest time a released prisoner has served since 2006 has been 22 years and 6 months. The shortest terms for adults are around 12-13 years.

VI.5. PRISONERS AND OFFENCES

The increase of prisoner rates in Finland in 1998–2005 is a summary effect of five major factors, each affecting in slightly different times: (1) An increase in the number of foreign prisoners (mainly from Russia and the Baltic countries), (2) an increase in drug trafficking (often linked with the former groups), an increase in the number of (3) fine defaulters and (4) prisoners in remand, and (5) an increase in violent offenders (as a result of increased penalties for assault). The decrease in 2005-2015 took place predominantly among prisoners serving a sentence. As a group the number of foreigners almost tripled. This change is also reflected in the rising number of remand prisoners (see Table 3).

The change can be viewed also from the point of view of different offence categories. In 2000–2005 the number of prisoners increased by 32% (2402-3173). In 2005 to 2015 the figures returned close to the starting position (2,513).

22 However, the possibility of using a pardon still remains (e.g. when the personal circumstances or health conditions of the prisoner have radically changed during the sentence).

Violence, drunk driving and drug offences show the most rapid increase from 2000 to 2005 (57, 48 and 37%). Since 2005 major declines have taken place in drunk driving and property offences (54 and 29%). The only offence category showing increase in 2005–2015 is the group "other" (increase by 41%), including i.a. sexual offences.

Table 3. Prisoners in 2000, 2005 and 2015 by prisoner groups (annual averages) and by offences

Prisoners by groups	**2000**	**2005**	**2015**
All	2,855	3,888	3,068
- Serving a sentence	2,358	3,190	2,419
- Remand prisoners	376	519	597
- Fine defaulters	121	179	52
Foreigners	173	282	477

Prisoners by offences	**1.5.2000**	**1.5.2005**	**1.5.2015**
All serving a sentence	2,402	3,173	2,513
- Violence	801	1,254	1,036
- Drugs	375	512	489
- Property	782	864	610
- Drunken driving	277	409	189
- Other	167	134	189

Source: Criminal Sanctions Agency.

VII. DISCUSSION

The aim of using imprisonment only as a last resort is confirmed in several international documents and agreements. Despite these declarations, very little has been achieved in practice. Prison systems have expanded during the last two or three decades in most parts of the world. This trend may have halted in some western countries, but intensified especially among the less developed nations. Today, the total number of persons held in penal institutions worldwide exceeds 10 million, in Asia 3.9 million, in Americas 3.8 million, in Europe (including Russia) 1.6 million and in Africa 1 million.[23]

23 See for details Andrew Coyle, Helen Fair, Jessica Jacobson & Roy Walmsley, *Imprisonment Worldwide, The Current Situation and Alternative Future,* Bristol: Policy Press, 2016.

Against this background, the humanization of the Finnish criminal justice from the 1960s onwards and the spectacular decrease of the Finnish prisoner rates from the highest western European level in the early 1970s to the lowest in the 1990s can be regarded as an achievement to be proud of. This policy was based on the belief that imprisonment was overused and over-trusted as a criminal political measure, and that more durable and constructive results can be achieved by criminologically informed evidence-based crime prevention techniques, and by developing alternative community sanctions to be used instead on incarceration. And as it turned out, this result actually was also achieved without any notable effects in the Finnish crime rates, when compared to the situation in the other Nordic countries.

Finnish experiences demonstrate that change is possible, once there is the political will to do so.[24] They also point out some examples of concrete means towards this end, including the following[25]:

- Lowering the penalties of high volume offences such as drunk driving and property offences by using shorter sentences and by expanding the use of fines and conditional imprisonment major effects in the 1970s.
- When *new alternatives for imprisonment* were introduced, care was taken that they will be used instead of prison, and not instead or fines of other community sanctions. To achieve this clear statutory/legal criteria for the application of different alternatives were enacted in the law. Care was also taken in creating the infrastructure and the network of service places to enforce the community service orders.
- Flexibility in the *sentencing system* was increased downwards by adopting "asymmetric limitation" of sentencing discretion, not by providing exact barriers against deviations towards more severe sanctions, but by allowing more flexibility when it comes to deviations towards more lenient direction (for example going below the prescribed minimum sentence). The impact of re-offending in sentencing was scaled down abolishing mechanical recidivism rules. Special efforts have been made in order to restrict the use of imprisonment for younger age groups to its minimum.

24 The reasons explaining the long-term period of penal liberalization in Finland are a mix of factors related to socio-economic structures, political culture, and legal and cultural traditions. These factors have been discussed elsewhere.

25 A much wider list of possible strategies can be found in the handbooks provided by the United Nations Office on Drugs and Crime, see United Nations Office on Drugs and Crime, *Handbook on strategies to reduce overcrowding in prisons*, New York, 2013 (at: www.unodc.org/documents/justice-and-prison-reform/Overcrowding_in_prisons_Ebook.pdf) (last visited: 13 January 2017); United Nations Office on Drugs and C rime, *Handbook of basic principles and promising practices on Alternatives to Imprisonment*, New York, 2007 (at: www.unodc.org/pdf/criminal_justice/Handbook_of_Basic_Principles_and_Promising_Practices_on_Alternatives_to_Imprisonment.pdf) (last visited: 13 January 2017).

- The impact of *secondary imprisonment* in connection with community sanctions has been minimized by revoking the parole or community orders, as a rule, only due to new offence, not just because of a license breach.
- Expanding the use of early release programs has been one of the most influential ways in regulating the prison population. Early release was made a part of normal prisons process that concerns all prisoners. Also the minimum time before eligibility to parole was pressed to the minimum.

While the long-term view is characterized by liber-humanitarian trends, short-term fluctuations may point at different directions. This was also the case in Finland during the shift of the millennium when incarceration rates rose in a short period of time by 40%, but returned afterwards almost to their original level. Some of these developments were crime driven, but others were policy driven. During the 1990s penalties for sexual and violent offences have been increased in several occasions, and this trend most likely will be continuing. It can hardly be explained by worsening crime situation, while the available evidence is more likely pointing at the opposite direction. More likely this signifies changes in social valuations and changing sensibilities towards violence.

With regard to the use of criminal law and criminal political argumentation, some of the changes signify a shift away from a pragmatic and rational consequentialist forward looking argumentation towards populist demands for harsher treatment in the name of "general sense of justice". Should that be the case, something essential would be lost. In the past decades, pragmatic consequentialist justification of punishment that called for a careful assessment of costs and benefits of criminal justice interventions as compared to other alternative approaches, provided barriers against unfounded overuse of criminal law.[26] It was, for example, possible to provide research-based evidence showing that, from pragmatic crime preventive point of view, society would act wiser in investing its scarce resources in social and situational prevention, instead of imprisonment. If the consequentialist assumptions that justify the use of criminal law fail, we should also be ready to re-evaluate whether the use of all this penal power can actually be defended. Deontological justification derived from the general sense of justice puts an end to this type of argumentation. It runs the risk of a return to a punishment-centred approach, thus narrowing our view from the wider aims and means of criminal policy. Criminal justice needs to be seen as a part of social justice, and the aims of criminal policy need to be set in line with the more general aims of social development policy, Human Rights and the

26 See Inkeri Anttila, *Ad Ius Criminale Humanius. Essays in Criminology, Criminal Justice and Criminal Policy,* Helsinki: Finnish Lawyers' Association, 2001; Patrik Törnudd, *Facts, Values and Visions, Essays in Criminology and Crime Policy,* Volume 138, Helsinki: National Research Institute of Legal Policy, 1996.

requirements of decency and humanity. This all is well captured in the old phrase "Good social policy is the best criminal policy." None of this is to undermine or deny the role and importance of criminal law and punishment, but only to provide understanding of its proper role as one means among many, and to maintain a realistic view on what it can achieve (and with what price), and what it cannot.

Appendix: Major Finnish law reforms and their impact on the extent of the use of criminal law 1966-2014

Direction & impact	Reform	Main area	
		Sanctions	Offences
- -	1966 Parole reform: Minimum time from 6 to 4 months	x	
- -	1967 Amnesty (Independence 60 years)	x	
- -	1969 Decriminalization of public drunkenness		x
-	1969 Day-fine reform: the number of dayfines reduced	x	
-	1969 Assault reform: less emphasis on unintended harm		x
- -	1972 Reduced penalties for theft		x
- -	1973 Restricting the use of preventive detention	x	
-	1973 Discount rules for remand	x	
-	1976 Reform of the prison law: Min. time for parole 4 mths -> 3 mths	x	
-	1977 Conditional sentence expanded	x	
-	1977 Sentencing reform; the impact of recidivism reduced	x	
-	1977 Day-fine reform: heavier fines to replace imprisonment	x	
- -	1977 DWI reform: fines and condition sentence instead of prison		x
-	1989 Fine-default exchange rate reduced	x	
- -	1989 Minimum for parole 3 mths -> 14 days	x	
-	1989 The use of prison for juveniles restricted	x	
-	1989 The length of pre-trial detention reduced	x	
-	1991 Reduced penalties for theft		x
-	1991 Expanding the scope of non-prosecution	x	
- -	1992 Introduction of CSO	x	
+	1994 Aggravated DWI 1.5 -> 1.2‰		x
-	1994 Experiment on (non-residential) juvenile penalty	x	
+	1995 Domestic violence under public prosecution		x
++	1999 Increased penalties for assault		x
+	2000 Increased penalties for rape		x
+	2001 More fines for drug-users		x
+	2003 Zero-limits for drugs in traffic		x
-	2000/4 Combination sentence (conditional + CSO)	x	

Direction & impact	Reform	Main area	
		Sanctions	Offences
–	2006 New prison law, parole expanded	x	
– –	2006 Fine default abolished for prosecutors fines	x	
+	2006 Criminalization of purchasing prostitution services		x
+	2010 Increasing penalties for domestic violence		x
+	2010 Increasing penalties for sexual abuse of children		x
+ +	2011 Increasing penalties for rape		x
+	2013 Stalking criminalized		x
+	2014 Increasing penalties for rape		x

OVERUSE IN THE CRIMINAL JUSTICE SYSTEM IN GERMANY[1]

Rita HAVERKAMP, Gabriele CIRENER,
Axel BOETTICHER & Johannes FEEST

I. INTRODUCTION

In 2016, the case of the satirist Jan Böhmermann has opened a lively public controversy on criminalization, concerning the rarely used offence "defamation of organs and representatives of foreign states" according to section 103 German Criminal Code.[2] In his television broadcast Jan Böhmermann read a satirical poem under the title "abusive criticism" on the Turkish State president Recep Tayyip Erdoğan. The government of Turkey as well as the State president reported to the Criminal Investigation Department or to the Public Prosecution Office and the German Chancellor Angela Merkel gave authorization to the prosecution (sec. § 104a German Criminal Code).[3] Hence, the views on this subject have been divided, strong support has been shown for the abolition of this 'majesty' offence.[4] Even the German Chancellor announced a bill of the German

1 The Report from Germany this year is a not adapted co-production of the two old members of the IPPF Johannes Feest and Axel Boetticher and their designated successors Rita Haverkamp and Gabriele Cirener. The queried contents of the Questionnaire are controversial topics also in Germany, thus we left it open to publish a coherent result of the discussion.

2 Pro and contra regarding the abolition of this offence (at: www.mdr.de/nachrichten/abschaffung-paragraf-majestaetsbeleidigung-pro-contra-100.html) (last visited: 3 May 2016).

3 The authorization is a controversial issue, see Boehme-Neßler, Volker, "Ziegenficken" und Kunst: Böhmermann zwischen Strafrecht, Außenpolitik und Verfassung, *LTO Legal Tribune Online, 11 April 2016* (at: www.lto.de//recht/hintergruende/h/boehmermann-erdogan-gedicht-kunst-meinungsfreiheit-strafrecht-politik-verfassung/) (last visited: 3 May 2016); Kaiser, Roman, Wer ermächtigt zur Strafverfolgung? Eine staatsorganisationsrechtliche Frage zum Fall Böhmermann, *20 April 2016* (at: https://www.juwiss.de/35-2016/) (last visited: 3 May 2016).

4 *Zeit Online* of 20 April 2016 (at: www.zeit.de/gesellschaft/zeitgeschehen/2016-04/praesidentenbeleidigung-recep-tayyip-erdogan-jan-boehmermann-hamburg-paragraf-103-abschaffung) (last visited: 11 May 2016).

government to abolish section 103 German Criminal Code.[5] Despite this special offence and this special case, the overuse of criminalization appears more significant concerning minor volume offences, like shoplifting and non-payment of fare. Recently, violations of laws applying to foreigners also gain importance, because of the migration of refugees.

II. OVERUSE OF CRIMINALIZATION

Criminalization is often connected with principles and moral values that change over times. This applies, in particular, to offences against sexual self-determination. Nowadays, a liberal understanding of sexual morals dominates and experiences its limits in socially damaging cases in order to ensure sexual intercourse without force.[6] Well-known examples of this change in moral values are the decriminalization of the homosexual orientation of men at the age of 21 years[7] and the abolition of adultery in 1969.[8] In contrast to this, male exhibitionism is still punishable according to sec. 183, paragraph 1 German Criminal Code. Against the backdrop of empirical findings the threat posed by male exposure is questionable.[9]

Though prostitution usually is not criminalized, an exception is unlawful prostitution in section 184f[10] German Criminal Code. The offence refers to prostitutes who persistently contravene a prohibition enacted by ordinance against engaging in prostitution in particular places at all or during particular times of the day.[11] The Federal Constitutional Court rejected a violation against the principle of clarity in law according to Article 103, paragraph 2 German Basic Law and upheld the statute as constitutional.[12] With regard to the protection of legal interests, academics consider the prohibition as the most problematic

5 *Die Welt* of 15 April 2016 (at: www.welt.de/politik/deutschland/article154396485/Erst-bei-Paragraf-103-findet-Merkel-ihren-Rhythmus.html) (last visited: 11 May 2016).

6 Knut Amelung,'Über Freiheit und Freiwilligkeit auf der Opferseite der Strafnorm', 146 *Goltdammer's Archiv für Strafrecht* 4 (1999), p. 182-204.

7 Since 1994 homosexual and heterosexual intercourse have been equated pursuant to the penal law due to the removal of sec. 175 German Criminal Code.

8 Edward Schramm, *Ehe und Familie im Strafrecht*, Tübingen: Mohr Siebeck, 2011, p. 433.

9 Brigitte Sick, 'Zweierlei Recht für zweierlei Geschlecht: Wertungswidersprüche im Geschlechterverhältnis am Beispiel des Sexualstrafrechts', 103 *Zeitschrift für die gesamte Strafrechtswissenschaft* 1 (1991), p. 43-91.

10 Since 27 January 2015, before sec. 185e German Criminal Code.

11 Translation of the German Criminal Code provided by Prof. Dr. Michael Bohlander (at: https://www.gesetze-im-internet.de/englisch_stgb/englisch_stgb.html#p1682) (last visited: 9 may 2016).

12 BVerfG, Decision of 7 October 2008 – 2 BvR 1101/08, 28 *NVwZ* 4 (2009), p. 239; BVerfG, Decision of 28 April 2009 – 1 BvR 224/07, 28 *NVwZ* 14 (2009), p. 905.

offence in chapter 13 of the German Criminal Code.[13] In 2014, 210 persons were convicted, three of them to imprisonment.[14] The persistent violation of unlawful prostitution could be sanctioned as an administrative offence, like the simple violation of unlawful prostitution in section 120 Administrative Offences Act.[15] Apart from these and other rare offences[16], more relevance have different petty crimes, which will be presented in more detail by first focusing on statistical data on the development of crime and on selected offences.

II.1. STATISTICS ON CRIME

Police Crime Statistics (PCS) covers criminal offences dealt with by the police, including drug offences handled by the customs authorities.[17] The informational value of PCS is limited due to the extent of unreported crime that depends on the type of offence and on cultural changes over the course of time.[18] Statistical developments might be influenced by public willingness to report offences, the intensity of police crime detection efforts, changes in the collection of data, and amendments to criminal law. As a result, PCS do not give an accurate situation

---

13 Martin Heger, 'Zum Einfluss des Prostitutionsgesetzes auf das Strafrecht', 23 *StV* 6 (2003), p. 355; Tatjana Hörnle, '§ 184e Ausübung der verbotenen Prostitution', in: Wolfgang Joecks & Klaus Miebach (eds), *Münchener Kommentar zum StGB*, München: C.H. Beck, 2012, recital 2; Tatjana Hörnle, *Grob anstößiges Verhalten. Strafrechtlicher Schutz von Moral, Gefühlen und Tabus*, Frankfurt a. M.: Vittorio Klostermann, 2005, p. 464.

14 Statistisches Bundesamt, *2014 Rechtspflege Strafverfolgung, Fachserie 10, Reihe 3*, p. 100 (at: https://www.destatis.de/DE/Publikationen/Thematisch/Rechtspflege/StrafverfolgungVollzug/Strafverfolgung2100300147004.pdf?__blob=publicationFile) (last visited: 9 May 2016).

15 See also the program of the police trade union in North-Rhine-Westphalia Gewerkschaft der Polizei Landesbezirk Nordrhein-Westfalen, *Kriminalpolitisches Programm*, Nordrhein-Westfalen: Gewerkschaft der Polizei, 2015, p. 57.

16 E.g. incest between siblings according to sec. 173 para. 2 s. 2 German Criminal Code: The Federal Constitutional Court (BVerfG, Decision of 26 February 2008 – 2 BvR 392/07, 61 *NJW* 16 2008, p. 1137-1146) rejected a constitutional complaint in 2008 as well as the European Court of Human Rights (EGMR, Judgement of 12 April 2012 – 43547/08, 66 *NJW* 4 (2013), pp. 215-216); the decision ensued a debate, e.g. Gunnar Duttge, 'Strafbarkeit des Geschwisterinzests aufgrund "eugenischer Gesichtspunkte"?', Manfred Heinrich, Christian Jäger, Hans Achenbac, Knut Amelung, Wilfried Bottke, Bernhard Haffke, Bernd Schünemann & Jürgen Wolter (eds), *Festschrift für Claus Roxin zum 80. Geburtstag am 15. Mai 2011*, Berlin: De Gruyter, 2011, pp. 227-243; Tatjana Hörnle, 'Das Verbot des Geschwisterinzests – Verfassungsgerichtliche Bestätigung und verfassungsrechtliche Kritik', 61 *Neue Juristische Wochenschrift* 29 (2008), p. 2085-2088; Sandra Karst, *Die Entkriminalisieurng des § 173 StGB*, Frankfurt a. M: Peter Lang, 2009.

17 Bundeskriminalamt (ed.), *Polizeiliche Kriminalstatistik Bundesrepublik Deutschland Jahrbuch 2012*, Wiesbaden: Bundeskriminalamt, 2013, p. 7-8, excluding offences against state security, offences against the criminal laws of the German federal states, and breaches of regulations and road traffic offences, the offences in sec. 315, 315b German Criminal Code and in sec. 22a Road Traffic Act are not classified as road traffic offences according to the guidelines.

18 Bundeskriminalamt (ed), *Polizeiliche Kriminalstatistik Bundesrepublik Deutschland Jahrbuch 2012*, Wiesbaden: Bundeskriminalamt, 2013, p. 6.

report of crime, also because of the "dark field" that varies according to the respective offence. Table 1 contains the number on total crime, total offence rate and number of inhabitants in Germany from 2000 to 2015.

Table 1. Development of total crime, total offence rate and number of inhabitants in Germany per year 2000-2015

Year	Recorded cases*	Total offence rate**	Number of inhabitants as of 01.01.2014
2000	6,264,723	7,625	82,163,500
2001	6,363,865	7,736	82,259,500
2002	6,507,394	7,893	82,440,300
2003	6,572,135	7,963	82,536,700
2004	6,633,156	8,037	82,531,700
2005	6,391,715	7,747	82,501,000
2006	6,304,223	7,647	82,438,000
2007	6,284,661	7,635	82,314,900
2008	6,114,128	7,436	82,217,800
2009	6,054,330	7,383	82,002,400
2010	5,933,278	7,253	81,802,300
2011	5,990,679	7,328	81,751,602
2012	5,997,040	7,327	81,843,743
2013	5,961,662	7,404***	80,523,746
2014	6,082,064	7,530	80,767,463
2015	6,330,649	7,797	81,770,900

* without traffic offences and offences against state security
** number of cases per 100,000 inhabitants
*** due to the change in the population data basis following the 2011 Census a comparison with the previous years is not possible

Source: Bundeskriminalamt: PCS Report 2014 Tab. 3.1.1 – T01; PCS Report 2015 p. 6; https://www.destatis.de/DE/ZahlenFakten/GesellschaftStaat/Bevoelkerung/Bevoelkerungsstand/Tabellen/Zensus_Geschlecht_Staatsangehoerigkeit.html.

The figures of recorded cases as well as the total offence rate peaked in 2004. Until 2013 a nearly continuous decrease can be observed. The total number of recorded cases was below six million offences between 2010 and 2013. The rise in the total number of offences in 2014 is due to the large number of violations of laws applying to foreigners. The ongoing migration of refugees led to an increase of illegal entry and illegal residence in Germany that increased even more sharply in 2015.[19] These violations are known as 'status offences' and cause the wide

19 Bundeskriminalamt (ed), *PCS Report 2014*, Wiesbaden: Bundeskriminalamt, 2015, p. 8.

criminalization of refugees for minor offences. Table 2 relates to the most frequent and other relevant offences in 2014 regarding the overuse of criminalization.

Table 2. Most frequent and other relevant offences* registered by the police in 2015

Selected offences or offence categories	Recorded cases	Share in %
Theft without aggravating circumstances	1,348,955	21.3
*Including Shoplifting***	*369,465*	*5.8*
Theft under aggravating circumstances	1,134,739	17.9
Fraud	966,326	15.3
Including Fraudulent obtaining of services	*279,144*	*4.4*
Damage to property	577,017	9.1
General violation – involving cannabis and preparations thereof	132,745	2.1
Offences against the Residence Act, the Asylum Procedures Act and the Freedom of Movement Act E.U.	402,741	6.4

* Translations in Bundeskriminalamt, Catalogue of criminal offences 2014 (at: www.bka.de/nn_257310/SharedDocs/Downloads/EN/Publications/PoliceCrimeStatistics/2014/pks2014CatalogueOfCriminalOffences.html) (last visited: (9 May 2016).

** without 21,936 cases of shoplifting committed under aggravating circumstances.

Source: Bundeskriminalamt, PCS Report 2015; Tab. 2 – T01 part 1, 3.1.1 – T02, 3.2.4 – T01

The most important offence category is theft with a share of 39.2%, followed by fraud with 15.3% and damage to property with 9.1%. Shoplifting and fraudulent obtaining of services are accounting together for 10.2%. Both offences usually cause minor damages: 68.0% of registered cases of shoplifting as well as 91.6% of those of fraudulent obtaining of services have damages under 50 Euro.[20] According to section 248a German Criminal Code theft of minor value may only be prosecuted upon request or special public interest. This also applies to fraudulent obtaining of services (sec. 265a paragraph 3 in conjunction with sec. 248a German Criminal Code). In supplementary penal provisions general violations involving cannabis have a share of 2.1%. Due to the growing migration of refugees, violations of laws applying to foreigners heightened considerably: While the share was 2.6% in 2014, it raised to 6.4% in 2015. The two offences are classified as less serious and demand requests for legalization or decriminalization.[21]

20 Bundeskriminalamt (ed), *Polizeiliche Kriminalstatistik Bundesrepublik Deutschland 2015 – Table 07*, Wiesbaden: Bundeskriminalamt, 2016.

21 Concerning cannabis Jörg Kinzig, 'Auf dem Weg zu einer Entkriminalisierung des Umgangs mit geringen Mengen von Cannabis?', in: Peter-Alexis Albrecht, Stefan Kirsch, Ulfrid Neumann & Stefan Sinner (eds), *Festschrift für Walter Kargl zum 70. Geburtstag*, Berlin: Berliner

II.2. PETTY VOLUME OFFENCES

In the 21st century decriminalization of minor volume offences is no longer an issue of criminal policy, but rather a constant tendency to include new offences in order to close assumed gaps.[22] This observation is particularly applicable to shoplifting. Since the reform of the criminal justice system in 1975, shoplifting has been prosecuted as a theft offence (sec. 242 German Criminal Code), which shall be punishable by a term of imprisonment up to five years or a fine. Before 1975, shoplifting was criminalized as "petty larceny of food" (sec. 370, paragraph 1 no. 5 German Criminal Code [old version]). The punishment of this transgression was milder than theft that meant imprisonment up to six weeks or a fine up to 500 German Mark.[23] Instead retaining the transgression, the legislator chose a procedural law solution with the introduction of the already mentioned theft of minor value (sec. 248a German Criminal Code) and the non-prosecution of petty offences as well as provisional dispensing with court action or provisional termination of proceedings (sec. 153, 153a German Code of Criminal Procedure).[24] Especially during the 1970s a decriminalization of minor shoplifting was supported: The suggestions ranged from civil liability[25] and an administrative offence[26] to misconduct as a category of its own[27] or minor theft.[28] None of the proposals was translated into law, probably due to a decision of the

Wissenschafts-Verlag, 2015, p. 273-286; concerning refugees Deutscher Bundestag, Bundestagsdrucksache 18/6346 of 14 October 2015, Entwurf eines Gesetzes zur Entkriminalisierung von Menschen ohne Aufenthaltsstatus der Abgeordneten und der Fraktion Bündnis 90/Die Grünen (at: http://dipbt.bundestag.de/dip21/btd/18/063/1806346.pdf) (last visited: 9 May 2016).

22 Winfried Hassemer, *Freiheitliches Strafrecht*, Berlin: Philo Verl. Ges., 2001, p. 11-18; Rainer Prätorius, 'Entkriminalisierung und alternative Sanktionen', in: Hans-Jürgen Lange (ed), *Kriminalpolitik*, Wiesbaden: VS Verlag für Sozialwissenschaften, 2008, p. 333.

23 Also "theft due to need" (sec. 248a German Criminal Code [old version]); see Friedrich Hoffmann, 'Der Ladendiebstahl. Erscheinungsformen – Täter – Sanktionen', 47 *BewHi* 1, 2000, p. 9.

24 Original translation by Brian Duffett & Monika Eibinger, translation updated by Kathleen Müller-Rostin and Iyamide Mahdi (at: www.gesetze-im-internet.de/englisch_stpo/englisch_stpo.html#p0041) (last visited: 10 May 2016).

25 Gunther Arzt, Albin Eser, Gerald Grünwald, Armin Kaufmann, Ernst-Joachim Lampe, Theodor Lencker, Peter Noll, Wolfgang Schöne, Walter Stree & Klaus Tiedemann, *Entwurf eines Gesetzes gegen Ladendiebstahl (AE-GLD)*, Tübingen: Mohr Siebeck, 1974; Gunther Arzt, 'Zur Bekämpfung der Vermögensdelikte mit zivilrechtlichen Mitteln – Der Ladendiebstahl als Beispiel, 14 *Juristische Schulung* 11 (1974), p. 693-698.

26 Beate Kohl & Sebastian Scheerer, *Zur Entkriminalisierung der gewaltlosen Eigentums- und Vermögensdelikte. Im Auftrag der Bundestagsfraktion DIE GRÜNEN*, Aachen: Hubert Wetzlar, 1989, p. 217.

27 Dieter Rössner, *Bagatelldiebstahl und Verbrechenskontrolle. Ein exemplarischer Beitrag zur Entkriminalisierung durch quantitative Begrenzung des Strafrechts*, Frankfurt a. M.: Peter Lang, 1976, p. 225.

28 Udo Bergfelder, *Ladendiebstahl und strafrechtliche Kontrolle. Ein Beitrag zur kriminologischen, kriminalpolitischen und rechtsdogmatischen Problematik der Kleinkriminalität*, Köln: Walter

Federal Constitutional Court.[29] The Court regarded the criminalization of petty offences within the legislative scope. The majority of the literature supports the existing procedural solution.[30] A differentiating path might be reasonable: Whereas simple shoplifting could be sanctioned as an administrative offence, persistent shop thefts should be punished according to the penal provisions in the German Criminal Code.

In contrast to shoplifting, the prevailing view in the literature challenges the settled case law concerning non-payment of fare. However, all proposals to decriminalize non-payment of fare failed so far. These include a bill of the Federal Council[31] to introduce an administrative offence for one-time cases and to restrict punishment for repeated offenders or offenders who suspend control measures as well as a bill of the fraction Bündnis 90/Die Grünen[32] to create an administrative offence. Besides, a reform commission of penal law in Lower-Saxony pleaded for a removal of section 265a German Criminal Law without replacement and the Hessian commission "criminal policy" wanted to complement the criterion "deception of a control person" in non-payment of a fare.[33] The strong opponents of decriminalization are worried about an erosion of rights awareness associated with an increase of fare evasion.[34] Only in 2009, the Federal Court of Justice in accordance with a former decision of the Federal Constitutional Court[35] affirmed the punishment of an offender who used public

---

Kleikamp, 1981, p. 121. See the overview by Ursula von Friedrichs, *Alternative Möglichkeiten der strafrechtlichen Kontrolle der Bagatellkriminalität am Beispiel des Ladendiebstahls*, Berlin: Logos Verlag, 2003, p. 137-199.

29 BVerfG, Decision of 17 January 1979 – 2 BvL 12/77, 32 *NJW* 20 (1979), p. 1039-1040.

30 Eckart Lang, *Die Strafbarkeit des Ladendiebstahls*, Frankfurt a. M.: Peter Lang, 1994, p. 251; with modifications Michael Nugel, *Ladendiebstahl und Bagatellprinzip. Eine materiell-rechtliche Abgrenzung*, Berlin: Duncker & Humblot, 2004, p. 255, 271; critical Rainer Prätorius, 'Entkriminalisierung und alternative Sanktionen', in: Hans-Jürgen Lange (ed), *Kriminalpolitik*, Wiesbaden: VS Verlag für Sozialwissenschaften, 2008, p. 333 and Roland Schmitz, '§ 242 Diebstahl', in: Wolfgang Joecks & Klaus Miebach (eds), *Münchener Kommentar zum StGB*, München: C.H. Beck, 2012, recital 23.

31 Deutscher Bundestag, Bundestagsdrucksache 13/374 of 2 February 1995, Entwurf eines Gesetzes zur Änderung des Strafgesetzbuches und des Gesetzes über Ordnungswidrigkeiten des Bundesrates (at: http://dipbt.bundestag.de/doc/btd/13/003/1300374.pdf) (last visited: 11 May 2016).

32 Deutscher Bundestag, Bundestagsdrucksache 13/2005 of 13 November 1997, Entkriminalisierung des Ladendiebstahls, Schwarzfahrens und der Fahrerflucht bei Sachbeschädigung der Fraktion BÜNDNIS 90/DIE GRÜNEN, rejected in Deutscher Bundestag, Bundestagsdrucksache 13/9064 (at: http://dip21.bundestag.de/dip21/btd/13/090/1309064.asc) (last visited: 10 May 2016).

33 Peter Alexis Albrecht (ed), *Rechtsgüterschutz durch Entkriminalisierung: Vorschläge der Hessischen commission "Kriminalpolitik" zur Reform des Strafrechts*, Baden-Baden: Nomos, 1992, p. 33-34, 59-61.

34 Deutscher Bundestag, Bundestagsdrucksache 13/4064 of 12 March 1996, Antrag der Fraktionen CDU/CSU und FDP Strafrechtlicher Schutz des Eigentums und des Vermögens (at: http://dipbt.bundestag.de/doc/btd/13/040/1304064.pdf) (last visited: 11 May 2016).

35 BVerfG, Decision of 9 February 1998 – 2 BvR 1907-97, 51 *NJW* 16 (1998), p. 1135-1136.

transport without a ticket by appearing to fulfil the terms and conditions of the operator.[36]

In contrast to the jurisdiction, the predominant literature requires the circumvention of precautions due to the criterion "deception".[37] Opinions break up here: While some statements find the non-usage of a ticket validating machine or an entrance only for passengers with a valid ticket sufficient[38], others emphasize the need to overcome barriers like turnstiles.[39] The latter view is convincing because the fare evader does not commit a deception, but uses public transport undisturbed by control measures.[40] In these cases a prosecution as administrative offence would be adequate.[41]

II.3. THE CRIMINALIZATION OF SUPPLEMENTARY PENAL PROVISIONS

The controlled legalization of cannabis repeatedly finds itself on the agenda.[42] In 1994, the Federal Constitutional Court declared that the comprehensive prohibition of cannabis is constitutional, but stressed, in this regard, an assessment prerogative of the federal government.[43] As a consequence, the legislator might change the Federal Law on Narcotics as a whole or concerning certain substances.[44] The medically indicated use of cannabis should be exempt

36 BGH, Decision of 8 January 2009, 62 *NJW* 15 (2009), p. 1091-1093.

37 With further references Walter Perron, '§ 265a Erschleichen von Leistungen', in: *Schönke/Schröder Strafgesetzbuch Kommentar*, München: C.H.Beck, 2014, recital 11.

38 With further references Martin Heger, '§ 265 Erschleichen von Leistungen', in: *Lackner/Kühl Strafgesetzbuch Kommentar*, München: C.H.Beck, 2014, recital 6a.

39 With further references Wolfgang Wohlers & Tilo Mühlbacher, '§ 265a Erschleichen von Leistungen', in: Wolfgang Joecks & Klaus Miebach (eds), *Münchener Kommentar zum StGB*, München: C.H. Beck, 2012, recital 61.

40 Wolfgang Wohlers & Tilo Mühlbacher, '§ 265a Erschleichen von Leistungen', in: Wolfgang Joecks & Klaus Miebach (eds), *Münchener Kommentar zum StGB*, München: C.H. Beck, 2012, recital 64.

41 In favor of civil liability Hjalmar Mahn, *Paradigmenwechsel im Recht der Beförderungserschleichung § 265a Abs. 1, 3. alt. StGB – Die normativ gebotene Umsetzung einer Entkriminalisierung des "Schwarzfahrens"*, Bonn: Schwarz, 2005, p. 278; a combination of administrative offence and penal offence is supported by Annette Eyers, *Die Entkriminalisieurng des Schwarzfahrens in den sog. "Einmalfällen"*, Gießen, 1999, p. 276-277.

42 Concerning the conditions for decriminalization see Hans-Jörg Albrecht, 'Voraussetzungen und Konsequenzen einer Entkriminalisierung im Drogenbereich', in: Wolfgang de Boor (ed), *Entkriminalisierung im Drogenbereich?*, Köln: Wienand, 1991, p. 1-37.

43 BVerfG, Decision of 9 March 1994 – 2 BvL 43/92, 47 *NJW* 24 (1994), p. 1577.

44 Kai Ambos, Lorenz Böllinger & Dian Schefold, 'Entwurf eines Gesetzes zur Änderung des Betäubungsmittelgesetzes. Wissenschaftlich begleitete Versuchs-Projekte mit örtlich kontrollierter Cannabis-Abgabe', 81 *ZRP* 3 (2016), p. 81; several legislative changes were carried out: E.g. the third amendment on the Federal Law on Narcotics has allowed the setting-up of consumption rooms for addicts since 2000 and the Act on Substitution Treatment with Diamorphine the consumption of the substance under specific conditions since 2009.

from punishment and the intended Law on Medical Cannabis is currently going through the legislative procedure.[45] Already in March 2015, the fraction Bündnis90/Die Grünen introduced a bill on the control of cannabis[46] which was dealt with at a hearing by the health committee of the German Bundestag one year later.[47] The initiators want to legalize cannabis in a strictly controlled market. The aim of protecting youth should call for the prohibition of the sale to juveniles under the age of 18 years, a minimum distance from cannabis retailers to schools and youth clubs, an advertising ban, and access controls with proof of age. The bill implies standards of comprehensive consumer and health protection for risk reduction. The draft is worthwhile in two more respects: On the one hand, differences between the German states in the area of criminal prosecution would be removed[48] and on the other hand, the controlled legalization would reduce health hazards due to extenders.[49] In the current political climate, the prospects of this initiative are not yet certain. More far-reaching demands, like the controlled legalization of all drugs, would not find parliamentary majorities.[50]

During the past three years a huge immigration to Germany has, as is well known, taken place. The illegal entry and illegal residence brought violations of laws only applying to foreigners to the fore. The protective purpose of criminal law pertaining to foreigners aims at stabilizing the administrative systems of

45 *Idem*, p. 82; the bill was approved by the federal cabinet on 4 May 2016 (at: https://hanfverband.de/nachrichten/pressemitteilungen/hanfverband-begruesst-laengst-ueberfaelliges-gesetz-zu-cannabis-als-medizin) (last visited: 11 May 2016); already since May 2011 finished medicinal products with cannabis and medicinal cannabis flowers have been available on a small scale, see Jörg Kinzig, 'Auf dem Weg zu einer Entkriminalisierung des Umgangs mit geringen Mengen von Cannabis?', in: Peter-Alexis Albrecht, Stefan Kirsch, Ulfrid Neumann & Stefan Sinner (eds), *Festschrift für Walter Kargl zum 70. Geburtstag*, Berlin: Berliner Wissenschafts-Verlag, 2015, p. 282.

46 Deutscher Bundestag, Drucksache 18/4204 of 4 March 2015, Entwurf eines Cannabiskontrollgesetzes (CannKG) der Abgeordneten und der Fraktion Bündnis 90/Die Grünen (at: http://dip21.bundestag.de/dip21/btd/18/042/1804204.pdf) (last visited: 11 May 2016).

47 List of experts (at: https://www.bundestag.de/blob/410116/315c55e29c33c69113f6a182eb86d229/sachverstaendige-data.pdf) (last visited: 11 May 2016).

48 Jörg Kinzig, 'Auf dem Weg zu einer Entkriminalisierung des Umgangs mit geringen Mengen von Cannabis?', in: Peter-Alexis Albrecht, Stefan Kirsch, Ulfrid Neumann & Stefan Sinner (eds), *Festschrift für Walter Kargl zum 70. Geburtstag*, Berlin: Berliner Wissenschafts-Verlag, 2015, p. 280.

49 Nicole Krumdiek, 'Rechtliche Folgen der Prohibition', in: Ralf Gerlach & Heino Stöver (eds), *Entkriminalisierung von Drogenkonsumenten – Legalisierung von Drogen*, Frankfurt a. M.: Fachhochschulverlag, 2012, p. 52-53.

50 In favor of a controlled legalization or decriminalization Henning Schmidt-Semisch & Monika Urban, 'Von der Utopie zur Wirklichkeit oder: Über die (Un-)Möglichkeit, den utopischen Charakter der Legalisierung abzustreifen', in: Ralf Gerlach & Heino Stöver (eds), *Entkriminalisierung von Drogenkonsumenten – Legalisierung von Drogen*, Frankfurt a. M.: Fachhochschulverlag, 2012, p. 269-271; Günter Tondorf, 'Die Entkriminalisierung von DrogenkonsumentInnen', in: Frank Neubacher & Michael Kubink (eds), *Kriminologie – Jugendkriminalrecht – Strafvollzug. Gedächtnisschrift für Michael Walter*, p. 817-818.

orders of law concerning foreigners.[51] Hence, the question arises whether a criminalization is appropriate with regard to the protection of legal rights.[52] Also, the distinction between penal and administrative offences seems to be unclear and not in accordance with the constitutional law.[53] Furthermore, it is questionable whether the offences concerning foreigners infringe the principle of proportionality.[54] The request for decriminalization of the penal law concerning foreigners not only bothers academics, but also politicians[55], humanitarian agencies[56], and even parts of the police.[57] The opinions differ with regard to the consequences: Whereas some want to abolish all penal and administrative offences[58], others prefer to replace penal offences with administrative offences.[59] The latter solution is more reasonable in order to react to minor violations and to cases of disobedience against administrative provisions.

III. OVERUSE OF PROSECUTION

III.1. THE PROSECUTOR AS INVESTIGATIVE AUTHORITY

The groups of criminal offences, which in terms of numbers are the heaviest burden on the law enforcement authorities are, according to category of offence,

51 Jan Gericke, '§ 95 AufenthG', in: Wolfgang Joecks & Klaus Miebach (eds), *Münchener Kommentar zum StGB*, München: C.H. Beck, 2013, recital 1.

52 Peter Fahlbusch, 'Vorbemerkung zu § 95 AufenthG', in: Rainer M. Hofmann (ed), *Ausländerrecht*, Baden-Baden: Nomos, 2016, recital 1.

53 Katharina Aurnhammer, *Spezielles Ausländerstrafrecht. Die Straftatbestände des Ausländergesetztes und des Asylverfahrensgesetzes – eine vergleichende Untersuchung*, Heidelberg: Nomos-Universitätsschriften, 1996, p. 1, 5-7.

54 Ute Hohoff, '§ 95 AufenthG', in: *Beck-Onlinekommentar Ausländerrecht*, 2016, recital vor 1.

55 Deutscher Bundestag, Bundestagsdrucksache 18/6346 of 14 October 2015, Entwurf eines Gesetzes zur Entkriminalisierung von Menschen ohne Aufenthaltsstatus der Abgeordneten und der Fraktion Bündnis 90/Die Grünen (at: http://dipbt.bundestag.de/dip21/btd/18/063/1806346.pdf) (last visited: 9 May 2016).

56 E.g. professional associations for sexual services (at: http://berufsverband-sexarbeit.de/entkriminalisierung-legalisierung-legale-anerkennung-sexarbeit-und-gesetz/) (last visited: 12 May 2016).

57 Bund Deutscher Kriminalbeamten, Entkriminalisierung von Flüchtlingen of 28 August 2015 (https://www.bdk.de/lv/bka/entkriminalisierung-von-fluchtlinge) (last visited: 10 May 2016).

58 Deutscher Bundestag, Bundestagsdrucksache 18/6346 of 14 October 2015, Entwurf eines Gesetzes zur Entkriminalisierung von Menschen ohne Aufenthaltsstatus der Abgeordneten und der Fraktion Bündnis 90/Die Grünen (at: http://dipbt.bundestag.de/dip21/btd/18/063/1806346.pdf) (last visited: 9 May 2016).

59 Peter Fahlbusch, 'Vorbemerkung zu § 95 AufenthG', in: Rainer M. Hofmann (ed), *Ausländerrecht*, Baden-Baden: Nomos, 2016, recital 1; Helmut Rittstieg, 'Einwanderung von Aus- und Übersiedlern – Verdrängung von Inländern fremder Staatsangehörigkeit', 23 *ZRP* 4 (1990), p. 129, 132.

fraud and breach of trust with 980,370 offences, offences in road traffic with 821,395, theft and embezzlement with 648,237, premeditated bodily injury offences with 430,365 and narcotic drugs offences with 316,966 ruled on in 2014. Commercial and tax crimes and money laundering offences only make up 126,773 of cases dealt with, but take up the longest average duration of proceedings. This is because of the complexity of the proceedings with issues that are not easy to understand and often also international aspects with a difficult body of evidence, but also the complexity of the relevant criminal offences.

Criminal law is naturally imbued in a special way with constitutional principles. Nevertheless, it is fundamentally up to the legislator to provide a binding definition of the area of criminal offences. The legislator is fundamentally free to decide[60] as regards the decision whether a certain legally protected right, whose protection seems essential, is to be protected by the very means of criminal law, and how this is to be done, if appropriate. The legislator must, however - because of the social ethical condemnation of society given expression in the threatening, imposing and enforcing of punishment - pay particular attention to the principle of proportionality, which so requires that a criminal provision serves the protection of others or the general public.[61]

Germany has entered into numerous international commitments – in particular relating to the European Union, but also other multilateral contracts – according to which certain patterns of behaviour are to be made criminal offences. Of note here are concrete and detailed European legal specifications with regard to the form of criminal tax law.[62] A particularly close interlinking with European law can be ascertained in any case for the entire area of commercial criminal law. This has led, in addition to an extremely complex form of criminal provisions, which makes their handling more difficult, also to a considerable extension of punishable offences in business life. Just to mention some examples here are the criminal offences bribery and corruption in commercial practice.[63] However, it has to be established that the adaption of economic criminal provisions in a common economic area is also required to avoid competitive disadvantages.

Moreover, in international agreements Germany has committed itself to extending its penal power to crimes against legally protected rights, whose protection is in the common interest of the international community of states, to overcome prosecution deficits in the state where crimes have been committed and, in the interests of the international community of states, to guarantee an

60 Cf. BVerfGE 120, 244 (Decision of the German Constitutional Court); to the demarcation of criminal offence and administrative law BVerfGE 27, 18, 30; 80, 182, 186.

61 Cf. BVerfGE 90, 145, 172, 184.

62 Cf. BGH (Decision of the Federal Court of Justice), Enquiry to the European Court of Justice, 07.22.2015 – 1 StR 447/14 to tax law.

63 Cf. BGH, 08.29.2015 – 2 StR 587/07, BGHSt 52, 332, 339 to the interlinking with European law.

effective criminal law protection of these legally protected rights (so-called universal jurisdiction).[64] This also leads to an extension of punishability.

Reflecting on the "ultima ratio" of criminal law is the best starting point for preventing the alarming increase in punishability of socially undesired, but not per se punishable behaviour. Only when certain behaviour – beyond being prohibited – is in a particular way socially damaging and intolerable for people's orderly coexistence, and its prevention therefore an especially urgent necessity, should criminal law then be resorted to. Social grievances and negative developments are not always to be met with criminal law instruments. An example here is the anti-doping law[65], which the German legislator brought into force on 1 January 2016, by means of which the integrity of sport was to be protected. According to this, athletes who have taken drugs and take part in organized sports events are liable to prosecution. The legislators decided on this criminal law sanction after sports associations had only combated this abuse insufficiently and ineffectively. In my opinion, however, the means of other government action, in particular a greater commitment and supervision on the part of the associations who gain substantial income from sport, have not been exhausted.

III.2. A LIMITED FORM OF THE LEGALITY PRINCIPLE

Although German criminal procedure law basically does envisage legal prosecution by the public prosecutor, there are, however, various possibilities[66] of terminating the proceedings due to aspects of expediency, despite sufficient grounds for suspicion and prosecution. The legislator has insofar consciously decided in favour of a limited principle of legality[67] through appropriateness provisions. Possibilities for termination according to the principles of appropriateness can on the one hand be differentiated according to whether they are connected to detrimental legal consequences or not; on the other hand compartmentalizing can be exercised according to the reason for the consideration of aspects of appropriateness. Cases such as, for example the minor nature of the offence, the preponderance of other offences or other peculiarities can be taken into account, which permit state interest in prosecution to decrease.

In 2014 around 21% of all proceedings ended with a public suit in the broader sense. A termination of proceedings against conditions took place in approximately 4% of all completed investigation procedures, amongst these the greatest part was the payment of a sum of money to charitable institutions or to

64 Cf. BVerfG NJW 2001, 1848, 1852; *Böse* in NK-StGB, 4. Aufl. Vor § 3 marginal notes 21, 26.
65 Bundesgesetzblatt 2015 I, 2210.
66 Summary by *Beulke*, Strafprozessrecht, marginal notes 333.
67 Cf. *Kühne* in Löwe/Rosenberg, StPO, 26. Aufl., Einl. I marginal notes, p. 19.

the state treasury. The second most frequent condition was offender-victim mediation. A further 25% cases were terminated without conditions, for example due to the minor nature of the criminal offence. In around 28% of investigations the cases were terminated due to lack of suspicion or due to lack of culpability of the accused. The remaining 21% of all investigation proceedings were brought to a close by other means. This included amongst others the handing over of such cases as administrative offences to the administrative authorities responsible.

In Germany sufficient alternatives for executing criminal proceedings exist due to the continued extension of non-prosecution authorizations, which limit the principle of legality. These are made use of in legal practice to a considerable extent and with increasing tendency.[68] This results in a decriminalization adapted to the individual case and relieves the burden on the judicial system.[69] This system is recognized as justified and appropriate[70] throughout. As far as in the literature a systematic recording of the reasons for limiting of the obligation to prosecute is considered desirable, this does not affect the fundamental form.[71] According to this there is no need for modification.

III.3. OVERUSE IN THE EXECUTION OF PRISON SENTENCES AND PREVENTION MEASURES

In Germany the prosecutors do not only have the role of an investigative authority. According to sec. 451 German Procedure Law, they have also to execute the sentences and the measures of preventive detention where adult convicts are concerned. The applicable law for the execution of sentences and of preventive detention is the Criminal Enforcement Order from 1 August 2011. On the modalities how to execute of the other preventive measures e.g. the placement in a mental hospital there are 16 different laws for hospital treatment in the 16 German Länder. Nevertheless: the only basis of legitimacy for the deprivation of liberty is the final court judgment with the fixed sentence or the fixed preventive measure.

That also means that according to sec. 78a Judicature Act (Gerichtsverfassungsgesetz – GVG), the decisions over the continuation or the early release from the sanctions are assigned to special courts of execution of prison sentences (Strafvollstreckungskammern) at the district courts in the Länder. So only the judges have according to art. 104, paragraph 2 German Constitution (GG) the exclusive authority to issue these decisions. That is why all decisions concerning the early release after having served ½ or 2/3 of the

68 Cf. the statistics material to 1.

69 *Beulke* in Löwe/Rosenberg, StPO, 26. Aufl., § 152 marginal notes 46; *Erb*, Legalität und Opportunität, p. 186.

70 *Rieß*, NStZ 1981, 5; *Roxin*, Strafverfahrensrecht, § 14,2

71 *Beulke* aaO in Löwe/Rosenberg, StPO, 26. Aufl., § 152 marginal notes 59, 60.

sentence (sec. 57 Criminal Code (StGB), sec. 57a for the lifelong penalty und sec. 58 for the overall penalty) are reserved to these independent courts for the execution of prison sentences. The courts also have to decide, according to sec. 67d Criminal Code, about the release or the final delay of one of the prevention measures laid down in sec. 64 Criminal Code.

The courts for the execution of prison sentences decide, according to sec. 454, paragraph 1 German Procedure Law, without a main hearing, by written decision. According to sec. 463 German Procedure Law, the rules of the execution law are valid also for the execution of the preventive measures. At this stage of the proceeding, public prosecutors, the convicted persons and the penal institutions are only "to be heard" ("zu hören") after sec. 454, paragraph 1 and 2 German Procedure Law. In these cases the prosecutor has the role of an investigating authority, which means that prosecutors are obliged to submit concrete and certain applications when they have new information about new crimes and concrete risks of recidivism. Simply the belonging to the group of sex offenders for a longer stay in prison is against the sentence of the court and in several cases against the freedom rights guaranteed in the Basic Law.[72] The public prosecutors "only" have the right of immediate appeal against the suspension decision, according to sec. 454, paragraph 3 § 1 German Procedure Law. But this remedy automatically has suspensory effect, according to sec. 454, paragraph 3 and 2. That means that this effect is independent from the state of the appeal. Due to this legal structure prosecutors can prevent the suspension for a longer time only by lodging the appeal. They can follow up the appeal but can also withdraw without any justification. As a consequence, prosecutors have too much power against the courts decisions.[73]

From 1996 on, German politicians delegated further rights to the prosecutors and greater influence regarding the execution of sentences and prevention measures. Public prosecutors often regard themselves as "the most objective organ" of the administration of justice. Indeed they are an independent part of the executive powers. However, in contrast to judges, they are bound by instructions of their direct superior and of their Ministries of Justice. The aforementioned does not give the prosecution authorities the legitimation to enforce a complete political security program of the majority of the conservative parties in the National Assembly. Because of the fundamental changes of the traditional criminal policy, many prosecutors totally lost their independence. Like in the Netherlands they "embraced politics" and "turned their face to the concerned society" (Paul Mevis). They accepted that thousands of detainees suffered from a climate of uncertainty in German prisons and psychiatric

72 Löwe-Rosenberg- Graalmann-Scheerer, German procedure law section 454 para 16.
73 Critics come from Pollähne Recht und Psychiatrie (R&P) 2015, 198ff.

hospitals and had to stay longer in total institutions.[74] On the other hand there was only very little justification for such over-arching regulatory interference. New legislation and directives of the Ministries of Justice came into force, which gave the prosecutors the direct and indirect power to intervene in the internal procedures and arrangements of the penal system and consequently in the decision making of the judges and the courts on the execution of sentences.

In accordance with the Law to Combat Sexual Offences and Other Dangerous Criminal Acts (SexualdelBekG) from January 26, 1998[75] the minimum penalties have increased and the rules and the practice for early release from prison and psychiatric hospitals became more complicated. What was intended for the special group of violent and/or sex offenders was established very soon for all detainees. Because prosecutors have lost a part of their independence, through their role as receiver of instructions of political powers in cases of the Law from 2004 and the implementation of the post-sentence preventive detention, the Law from 2008 for adolescent detainees and the extension of the reserved preventive detention in the Law of 2010. Without carefully examining the compelling necessity and the principles of proportionality and equal treatment they had to apply at the end of the service of the full sentence the various measures of preventive detention. Boetticher and Feest presented in the report for Germany on the occasion of the IPPF meeting 2008 in Stavern and Norway the modifications of the German Penal Code.[76]

The results to this change of juridical policy-making can easily be verified by the increasing number of detainees in the institutions for the preventive measures. Since 1998 the number of "normal" prisoners has declined because of the aging of the offenders in general: 2461 detainees with a lifelong sentence in 2014 and 521 with preventive detention in 2015. However, the numbers are still consistently high. The number of patients in psychiatric hospitals have increased considerably up to 6.675 in the year 2014.[77] See Figure 1.

74 Thomas Galli, *Lockerungsbegutachtungen im Vollzug*, Berlin: Springer, 2012.

75 BGBl. I S. 160 (Federal Law Gazette 1998 page 160).

76 Axel Boetticher & Johannes Feest, 'German criminal and prison policy', in: P.J.P. Tak (ed), *Prison Policy and Prisoners Rights*, Nijmegen: Wolf Legal Publishers, 2008, p. 361–390; Johannes Feest, 'Sicherungsverwahrung in Germany', in: P.H.P.H.M.C. van Kempen & Warren Young, *Prevention of reoffending and the management of high risk offenders*, Cambridge: Intersentia, p. 317-322.

77 (at: http://de.statista.com/statistik/daten/studie/75829/umfrage/strafgefangene-nach-vollzugs dauer- and https://www.destatis.de/DE/Publikationen/Thematisch/Rechtspflege/) (last visited: 9 May 2016).

Figure 1. Prisoners in preventive detention (Unterbringung) and prisoners with lifelong sentences (lebenslange Freiheitsstrafe)

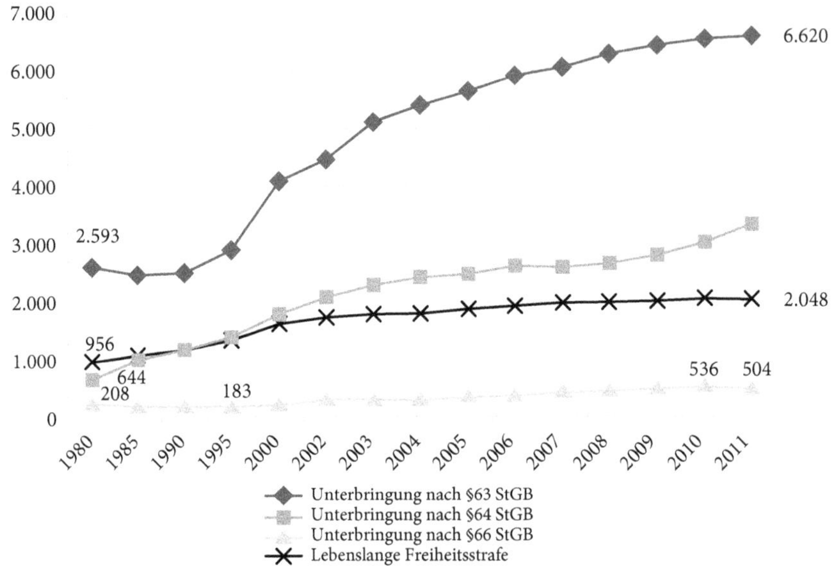

(Quelle: Strafvollzsta 2010, S. 12 und 32; Angaben für §§ 63, 64 StGB früheres Bundesgebiet; sonst ab 1995 für Gesamtdeutschland)

This increase of detainees has no reasonable basis nor a rational explanation. During that period the number of severe offences did not increase. Only a small number of bad sexual crimes put a high public pressure on the politicians to address this issue. So the "scandalization" in the media concerning single offences against children had the power to change the whole political climate. This new development might be reasonable for the politicians but it is not reasonable for independent prosecutors, who should be serving a high ethos of objectivity and independence. They knew the statistics of the constant number of severe offences. Nevertheless, the prosecutors also followed the new political mainstream.

Key examples for the overuse of the prosecution authorities concerning the execution of sentences and preventive measures can be pointed out in four areas:

- The reduction of the preparations for early release from prisons and psychiatric hospitals and the decrease of cases of early release on probation with the effect of more long stay detainees in total institutions,
- The increase of the nationwide implementation of the reserved and post-sentence preventive detention for the whole group of violent and sex offenders, without knowing whether this measure would be necessary for the whole group in respect to the principle of proportionality and their efficiency to protect the community. Thus, the prosecution authorities were willing helpers of the political mainstream without having an empirical legitimation

or being in accordance with the generally recognized psychological-psychiatric doctrines,
- The reduction of rehabilitation inside the prisons and the psychiatric hospitals and the displacement effects on the new "post-release supervision",
- The countermovement initiated by a number of judgments of the European Court of Human Rights and several scientific studies: the measures of the post-sentences were in reality penalties and only in second position instruments of rehabilitation. The measures were not as successful as the court sentences on probation and early release on probation from prisons or from psychiatric hospitals. The new instruments had not a higher level of protection for the public than the traditional instruments of rehabilitation. The main effect was that the prosecution authorities lost parts of their independence towards their Ministries of Justice.

a. The effect on the preparations for early release from prison

Since 1998 a change occurred in the penitentiary system – in addition to the changes in the penal code and the criminal procedure code – that was very much notable in the daily work inside the prison environment. It started in 1996, when the assembly of the Ministers of Justice decided on a bunch of administrative regulations. The boards of the prison authorities had to perform stricter reviews of the demands of relief, release on parole and preparation for early release. In many cases the prosecutors had to demand expert opinions or even psychiatric reports. Without the consent of the prosecution authorities nothing worked inside the prisons. These modifications produced an atmosphere of mistrust and fear, which was noticed in the entire prison sector. Feest & Lesting have recorded it exemplary with the decline of the various instruments to prepare prisoners for reintegration into society[78]:

The clearest reduction took place concerning the instrument of "home on parole" (Hafturlaub). Within only some years we could notice the reduction between 40 and 50% in all Länder. A differentiated view has to be done on the development at the "permission for the days' leave" (Ausgang). Hesse had the highest number (since 1998 we had a reduction 25.5%), the other Länder were more cautious.

Also the reduction of the "permission to work outside prison" (Freigang) had its highest level in the year 1999. The same applied for the very important instrument "open prison" (Offenen Vollzug). Also in this matter Hesse was on top. It has reduced the number of the detainees in the last years by 50%. Bremen and Hamburg followed Hesse, but today we see again a turnaround back to more open prisons in this Länder.

78 Feest/ Lesting, ZfStVollZ 2005, S. 76–82.

Unlike the prosecutors one-sided safety awareness, alternatives exist for the rehabilitation of detainees while incarcerated: in 1998 Germany acknowledged the right of a prisoner to join special social therapeutic units in prison, to improve the necessary rehabilitation of violent and sex offenders. After the second World War, social therapeutic facilities – which existed already in Denmark and in the Netherlands – should have constituted "the royal road" to correctional treatment in the German prison system, providing an integrated approach by means of cognitive-behavioural psychotherapy, vocational and job training, social work and leisure time therapy in a therapeutic community. Germany only has a very small version of this "royal road" in section 9 of the former Penal Code. The Centre of Criminological Research in Wiesbaden (KrimZ) publishes every year the new data[79]; we now have in 2015 69 social-therapeutic institutions with places for 2,429 prisoners. About 50% are offenders who were convicted for having committed sexual crimes.

Why did the prosecution authorities not demand more of these therapy units from their Ministries of Justice instead of more and more preventive detention: The therapy can follow immediately after the sentences in order to help the convicted person not to lose his motivation. In contrast to the mental hospitals, which have better legal possibilities for liberalization and release preparation with a rate between 60 and 70% temporary leave of absence. However, more than 75% of these prisoners do not receive any professional help to prepare them for early release, which is why many of the prisoners have to serve the full sentence. Another critical point is that, from 1997 to 2015, only 348 prisoners of all detainees in the German social-therapeutic facilities got professional aftercare. In the year 2015 at least 66 detainees took part in the various aftercare programs.[80] Nevertheless, we need more social therapy units in prisons.

b. *The effect on the post-sentence preventive detention*

Beginning in the year 2004, the prosecution authorities and the prison authorities were instructed to re-examine the sentences and the prison files of 6,000 detainees, in order to decide whether they had to make an application for a post-sentence detention, according to the new section 66b Penal Code. In Bavaria the prosecutors were directly instructed to lodge an appeal to the Bundesgerichtshof in those case where the District Courts had rejected the application. In these cases the Bavarian Ministry of Justice just wanted to have a landmark decision as an orientation for the following cases.

79

80 See p. 35 and 85 (at: www.krimz.de/fileadmin/dateiablage/E-Publikationen/bm-online4.pdf) (last visited: 9 May 2016).

The five Senates of the Federal High Court were not convinced of this new criminal provision preventive regulation (sec. 66b Criminal Code). They rejected most of the applications of the prosecution authorities, the majority coming from Bavaria. There was an agreement that this regulation was against the principles of the general liberty right rule of the detainees and the constitutional principle of proportionality.[81] Up to the year 2012 we had only 60 cases of post-sentence preventive detention at the Federal High Court out of a greater number of applications of the prosecution authorities of the Länder. Only 17 cases were successful. The majority of the detainees were released without post-sentence preventive detention. In most of the cases there were no bigger relapses. In the leading decision M. versus Germany, from 17 December 2009, the European Court of Human Rights (ECtHR) declared part of the new regulations as well as the practice of the execution of the preventive detention in the German prisons together with "normal" detainees incompatible with Article 7 of the European Convention on Human Rights (ECHR). After that decision the prosecutors hesitated to make new applications.

c. *The failure of the post-sentence preventive detention*

After a survey of criminologists from the University of Bochum, it became apparent that the demanded new measures were no more successful than when detainees are released in the regular way. The small number of cases did not increase the protection of the public. The criminologist Alex obtained the details of 77 cases and compared them with the dates of the Central Register of Conviction. Of 50 detainees released from prison till 31 December 2006 there was no new registration of recidivism. He also reviewed the execution files and the court files. Up to 30 June 2008 only 27 of the 77 released detainees were sentenced again after they were released from prison, in spite of a bad prognosis given by a psychiatrist and in spite of the application of the prosecutor to order a post-sentence detention. 10 of them only got a fine, 5 got a suspended sentence and 10 a sentence without probation. Among 10 subjects were 6 with smaller offences as theft or drug abuse. Only 3 released persons were again violent against persons in a way that they were sentenced again to imprisonment and preventive detention.[82]

81 Rissing-van Saan, 'Vorbehaltene und nachträgliche Anordnung der Sicherungsverwahrung als Bewährungsproben des Rechtsstaates' in: Rainer Griesbaum & Karlh Heinz Schnarr, *Festschrift für Kay Nehm zum 65. Geburtstag*, 2005, p. 191-204; Franz Streng *"Erkennbar gewordene Tatsachen" und rechtsstaatliche Anforderungen an die nachträgliche Sicherungsverwahrung*, StV 2006, p. 92.

82 Presseinformation der Ruhr-Universität Bochum vom 10.9.2009 (at: www.pm.ruhr-uni-bochum.de) (last visited: 9 May 2016); "Nachträgliche Sicherungsverwahrung – ein kriminalpolitischer Fehlschlag"; vgl. ausführlich Michael Alex, *Nachträgliche*

Alex repeated his survey in 2012 and received more details concerning the recidivism rate of 121 released detainees. He got information about a much longer observation period of 48 months on average after the release from prison between 1 January 2007 and 31 December 2009. Of the 121 released detainees, 63 or 52% were sentenced again, 16 of these subjects got a fine, 9 got a suspended sentence, 36 persons got a sentence without probation and 17 with additional preventive detention. The share of detainees with predicted danger of serious violent and sexual offences amounts with 15.7% as high as by regular release from prison. That means that for 84.3% of the 121 as dangerous predicted released detainees, the omnipresent fears of the public for serious crimes supported by the media have not come true.[83]

In a second academic research of a group of psychiatrists at the University of Göttingen in the year 2012, Müller and Stolpmann published a reoffending survey in which they came to similar results. They examined 32 cases that were decided by the Federal High Court. In these cases the post-sentence preventive detention was either rejected or the judgments of the district courts were set aside. They specifically looked into the psychiatric reports. The reoffending survey regarded a follow-up period of 24 months.[84] Despite the bad prognosis made up by the psychiatric reports, 34% of the subjects did not reoffend. A percentage of 37.5% were sentenced again because of smaller offences, 28.1% committed more serious crimes (imprisonment 1 year), 15.6% received a sentence with imprisonment over 1 year and 12.5% of the subjects committed severe crimes and therefore were sentenced to imprisonment again or they were sent to a mental hospital. Both surveys showed no significant imbalances to the later discussed first German "Systematic Recidivism Study" of the year 2013 by Prof. Jehle from the University of Göttingen and Prof. Albrecht of the Max Planck Institute for Foreign and International Criminal Law in Freiburg.

At least those surveys led to the famous decision of the German Constitutional Court of 5 May 2011 following the decision of the ECtHR of 17 December 2009. A major part of the regulations concerning the law of preventive detention and post-sentence preventive detention were declared unconstitutional. The Federal Legislator got the "order" to create a new form for the placement for subject under preventive detention apart from "normal" prisons, as well as to establish an individual therapeutic program to increase the chance for a release

Sicherungsverwahrung – ein rechtsstaatliches und kriminalpolitisches Debakel, Dissertation Bochum, Holzkirchen: Felix-Verlag, 2010, p. 91.

83 Michael Alex, 'Kriminalprognose und Legalbewährung,- Wie zuverlässig lässt sich Rückfallgefahr vorhersagen?', in: K. Höffler (ed), *Brauchen wir eine Reform der freiheitsentziehenden Sanktionen?*, Göttingen: Universitätsverlag Göttingen, p. 21-36.

84 J.L. Müller, G. Stolpmann, P. Fromberger, K.A. Haase & K. Jordan, 'Legalbewährung nach nicht angeordneter nachträglicher Sicherungsverwahrung', 84 *Der nervenarzt* 3 (2012), p. 1–9.

on probation. After the new 66c Penal Code[85], the clients shall receive therapy "a) which is individual and intensive and aimed at incentivizing and fostering the detainee's cooperation, particularly a psychiatric, psycho- or socio-therapeutical treatment tailored to the needs of the detainee, insofar as standardized offers do not appear promising, and b) whose aim is to minimize the detainee's dangerousness to the public to a degree that he may be conditionally released from the measure or the measure declared moot as soon as possible",

d. *The effect for a longer stay of the detainees in prison or in mental hospitals*

The overuse of influence by the Ministries of Justice and the prosecution authorities affected the development of the last years: a high number of detainees had to serve the complete sentence in prison. A correct number of those clients is not registered. But we know more about the length of stay in mental hospitals. After a survey of Kammeier – an expert of all the matters of mental hospitals – in the year 2006, the released subject had to serve in the psychiatric hospital an average time of 6.5 years. In the year 2013 this has extended to 7.2 years. Only in one of the bigger Länder, i.e. North Rhine-Westphalia, the number of persons who stayed over 10 years inside mental hospitals increased from 21.6% in the year 2006 up to 25.4% in the year 2009.[86]

These numbers are the result of a change in criminal policy over the last years and a systematic overuse of the activities of the more and more independent prosecutor authorities in the matters of the execution of sentences.

e. *The transfer of social rehabilitation in the new "post-release supervision"*

In order to ensure more safety for the public, the measure of "legal supervision" after the prisoners' release from prison or psychiatric hospital was revised and extended in the German Criminal Code in sec. 68, paragraph 1 and section 68b, paragraph 11 Criminal Code in 2007 to provide more "forensic aftercare". It was the will of the majority of the German Länder and their prosecution services to keep a tougher control of all prisoners who have served their complete sentences. Since then there is a growing number of people who will be supervised after release from prison or psychiatric hospital.

One positive aspect of this measure is that it makes it possible to avoid post-preventive detention. On the downside we notice the effect that now we have less suspension after 2/3 of the sentence, but more supervision orders combined with the order to join ambulant aftercare. Another problem is that people who have

85 BGBl. I S. 2425.

86 Heinz Kammeier, 'Reform of the measure after section 63 penal code', 21 *Forensische Psychiatrie und Psychotherapie* (2014), p. 8-16.

served their sentences are not as motivated to join the ambulant units. In several cases the prosecutor can request that the period of supervision shall last two but no more than five years section 68c, paragraph 1). After sec. 68c, paragraph 2 the prosecutor can request an indeterminate supervision.

We now have a comparable ambulant instrument of post-sentence preventive detention.

Figure 2. Comparison of post-sentence supervision cases (FA-Fälle) in German states

FA-Fälle	2008	2009	2010	2011	2012	2013	2014	2015
NRW	4.622	5.132	5.905	6.427	6.830	7.097	8.315	8.594
Bayern	6.496	6.732	7.100	7.362	7.623	7.847	8.005	8.058
Baden-Württemberg	1.665	2.060	2.358	2.499	2.612	2.708	2.758	2.461
Niedersachsen	1.656	2.001	2.233	2.462	2.588	2.731	2.751	2.887
Hessen	1.177	1.271	1.367	1.592	1.772	1.884	1.987	1.849
Sachsen	1.184	1.315	1.454	1.580	1.649	1.756	2251	2354
Rheinland-Pfalz	1.271	1.318	1.474	1.635	1.731	1.781	1.784	1.791
Berlin	2.164	2.306	2.289	2.360	2561	3.202	2.681	2.687
Schleswig-Holstein	572	576	637	656	706	739	771	808
Brandenburg	513	545	596	611	630	642	679	694
Sachsen-Anhalt	1.045	1.134	1.162	1.188	1.249	1.254	1.290	1.223
Thüringen	550	642	726	764	969	1.030	1.035	1.156
Hamburg	769	807	790	815	829	737	663	645
Mecklenburg-Vorp.	520	600	672	758	818	852	866	919
Saarland	369	378	438	469	477	506	502	492
Bremen	245	276	294	310	337	347	386	100
Total	24.818	27.093	29.495	31.488	33.381	35.113	36.724	37.018

Reckling from "The German Association for Social Work, Criminal and Criminal Policy" (DBH) has worked it out: We have a massive increase of post-sentence supervision cases.[87] The number of post-sentence supervision orders increased strongly from 2008 to 2015. See Figure 2.

A new branch of rehabilitation treatments was born, but with the same number of probation officers! In the end we have a new structure of treatments and proceedings in prison. In most cases, rehabilitation does not start while the

87 At: www.dbh-online.de/fa/FA-Zahlen-Bundeslaender-2015.pdf (last visited: 9 May 2016).

person concerned Is still incarcerated, but only after having served the complete sentence.

f. The first German "Systematic Reoffending Survey"

In order to demonstrate the extraordinary effect of probation, the main results of the first German "Systematic Reoffending Survey" by Prof. Jehle (University of Göttingen) and Prof. Albrecht (Max Planck Institute for Foreign and International Criminal Law) must be presented.[88] They published their study "Legal probation after criminal sanctions" in 2013. This survey, initiated by the German Ministry of Justice, represents a really profound statistical analysis of Criminal and Penal law in the German State and the 16 German Federal States (Bundesländer) who are responsible for the execution of sentences since 2006.

The study records data and information relative to reoffending for all sanctions in the whole of Germany, which are registered in the Central Register of Convictions.

The study records data for reoffending for the base years 2004 and 2007 with reference to the offence, the sanction, the sentence, the data of the beginning, the duration of the sentence and the release, the age of the sentenced person, the previous criminal sentences, gender and nationality.

The data of the Central Register of Convictions were recorded in three survey periods and they can now be used

- For the explanation and prediction of reoffending on the basis of the years 2004, 2007 und 2010 within an observation period of three years,
- Furthermore the data of the three survey waves are linked in a way that on the basis of the base year 2004 the observation period can successively be extended up to 9 years.

This study is indeed also the first quality evaluation of the work in prison and of the probation. The main results of the new study are:

- Out of 1,049,816 persons (adult and juvenal offenders) sanctioned or released from prison in the year 2007, 684,128 persons (65%) have not been registered again as convicted persons within 3 years of survey (page 36),
- In contrast to the traditional public opinion only every third person (34%) – sanctioned or released – is again convicted of a criminal offence within a risk period of three years: The highest risk of reoffending occurs within 69% of the juvenile sentences without probation, followed by juvenile detention, 65%, (Jugendarrest), the lowest figure being the fine, 29%.

88 At: www.bmjv.de/SharedDocs/Archiv/Downloads/Legalbwaehrung_nach_strafrechtlichen_ Sanktionen_2007_2010_u_2004_2010 (last visited: 9 May 2016).

But the study also shows that in most cases the criminal sentences did not lead again to a complete executed sentence but to milder sanctions: Only 4% of all persons sanctioned or released in 2007 were again sentenced to a sentence or juvenile sentence without probation, 7% were sentenced after reoffending to a sentence or juvenile sentence with probation, 15% got a fine and 5% got a decision of the juvenile court (conditional sentence or suspension under the supervision and guidance of probation officers. In 4% of all cases the procedure was closed without any conviction. As to the observation period of 3 years up to 6 years (2004-2010) the study underlines that the majority of the reoffenders are recommitted in the first three years. In half of the cases they reoffend in the first year after the sentence is completed or after being released from prison. Thus, the first year after one's release is the period in which such a person must be offered help and support in order to avoid reoffending (pp. 54–59).

In contrast to the prisoners who are released early from prison with a suspension of the rest of their sentence, prisoners who have served their complete sentence, commit more severe criminal offences after their release, get more severe and longer (juvenile) sentences and get more new sentences without suspension.

- early release: 38% new offences;
- complete service of the sentence: 52% new offences.

IV. OVERUSE OF IMPRISONMENT

Imprisonment has seen its ups and downs in Germany. Overuse of imprisonment was a big issue in the mid-1980s, when the West-German prison population had reached its highest point after Word War II. After many highly publicized protests by different organizations, among them the organization of German defence lawyers, the figures went down. They reached their lowest point in 1991 (with an imprisonment rate of 74/100,000), well after the German unification, when the prisons of the former German Democratic Republic had virtually been emptied. From then on, the imprisonment rate went continually up and reached an all-time high in 2004 (96), to decrease again steadily until the present day (2015:76).[89] The reasons for this up and down process have been discussed over and over. It appears that trends in criminal policy play a major role, not developments in crime nor demographic changes.[90]

89 Institute for Criminal Policy Research: International World Prison Brief (at: www.prisonstudies.org/country/germany) (last visited: 4 June 2016).

90 Johannes. Feest, 'Reducing the prison population: Lessons from the West German Experience', in: J. Muncie & R. Sparks (eds), *Imprisonment: European Perspectives*, Hemel Hempstead: Harvester Weathereaf, 1991; J. Feest & H.M. Weber, 'Germany: Ups and Downs in the Resort to Imprisonment – Strategic or Unplanned Outcomes?' in: R.P. Weis & N. South (eds), *Comparing*

While these figures places Germany in the middle to lower ranks on the scale of European nations with respect to imprisonment, one important aspect needs to be added: The German prison statistics include only those prisons run by the justice administration (remand prisons and serving prisons). In order to get the full picture, one has to add those prisons run by the Ministries of the Interior (police cells, facilities for immigration detention) and the Ministries of Health (hospitals for the criminally insane; alcohol and drug clinics. While Germany has, over the last 40 years not experienced an overall increase in the penitentiary population and even a decrease with respect to remand prisoners, the forensic prison population has seen a spectacular growth. Figures for forensic prisoners went up from 3,746 patients (in 1987) to 10,423 (in 2011). And all this, without data about the East Germany forensic prison population.[91]

IV.1. IMPORTANCE OF IMPRISONMENT

In Germany imprisonment was the dominant criminal sanction in the 19th century. In 1882, it amounted to three quarters of all sentences (with fines and a small number of death penalties making up the rest). Fines reached the same level as imprisonment in 1910 and became the dominant sanction by the mid-1920s.[92] In 2013, fines made up 74% of all sentences.[93]

While quantitatively reduced to second place, symbolically imprisonment has remained the most important sanction, the "gold standard" of sanctions. Since the introduction of the day-fine system (in the 1970s), even fines are measured in days of imprisonment and these days will have to be served in case of non-payment.

Table 3. Overview of adjudicated offences

	Prosecuted	Convicted	Prison sentences
2002	923.384	618.269	142.703
2014	811.523	676.688	121.818

Prison Systems. Toward a Comparative International Penology, Amsterdam: Gordon and Breach Publishers, 1998; A. Boetticher & J. Feest, 'German criminal and prison policy' in: P.J.P. Tak & M. Jendly (eds), *Prison Policy and Prisoners' Rights*, Nijmegen: Wolf Legal Publishers, 2008.

91 Johannes Feest, 'Abolition in the times of pre-crime. A view from Germany', in: Thomas Mathiesen, The Politics of Abolition Revisited, New York: Routledge, 2015.

92 Günther Kaiser, *Kriminologie: ein Lehrbuch*, Heidelberg: Müller, 1988, p. 902.

93 Statistisches Bundesamt, Press release, 2015 (at: https://www.destatis.de/DE/PresseService/Presse/Pressemitteilungen/2015/01/PD15_015_243.html) (last visited: 4 June 2016).

Table 4.

	Prosecuted	Convicted	Prison sentences
2014	811,523	676,688	121,818 (110,046 adult | 11,772 juvenile) = 15.0% / 18.0%
2002	923,384	618,269	142,703 (125,019 adult | 17,684 juvenile) = 15.5% / 23.1%

The figures in Tables 3 and 4 show that while the absolute number of prison sentences has decreased in the last twelve years, the percentage of prison sentences (with respect to prosecuted or adjudicated cases) has remained virtually constant. The decrease in prison sentences can be attributed to a similar decrease in prosecutions.

In Table 5 are listed the seven top categories of crimes people serve in German prisons (on 31 March 2014, with 54,515 persons serving a prison sentence):

Table 5. Prison-worthy crimes/offences

Theft	11,996 (22.0%)
Robbery	7,162 (13.1%)
Drug offences	7,144 (13.1%)
Assault and battery	6,996 (12.8%)
Fraud/embezzlement	6,271 (11.5%)
Murder, manslaughter	4,043 (7.4%)
Sexual offences	3,733 (6.8%)

Source: Statistisches Bundesamt: Fachserie. 10, Rechtspflege. 4, Strafvollzug. 1, Strafvollzug - Demographische und kriminologische Merkmale der Strafgefangenen zum Stichtag 31.3. 2014 (at: https://www.destatis.de/GPStatistik/receive/DEHeft_heft_00029274) (last visited: 4 June 2016).

In other words: non-violent property offences make up a third of the prison population. Another third stems from crimes of violence. Persons sentenced for drug offences constitute only 13% of the prison population, but drug dependence (drug related crime) is responsible for a much higher, but statistically not registered, percentage of the prison population. Of particular importance for filling German prisons, are long sentences, especially life sentences, the number of which is constantly increasing. Another important category, at the other end of the spectrum is imprisonment for fine default. On any given day almost 10% of all serving prisoners are fine defaulters, usually serving short sentences.

IV.2. OBLIGATIONS TO IMPOSE PRISON SENTENCES

The German criminal justice system uses sentencing frames, which are laid down for each crime in the criminal code. With most offences, the court has a choice between imposing a prison sentence or a fine. Imprisonment is, however, mandatory for a number of crimes, e.g. murder, manslaughter, severe forms of assault, burglary, robbery, rape, drug trafficking.

Within the sentencing frame (e.g. 1 to 15 years for robbery) the court has to determine the sentence on the basis of the guilt of the offender and a complex array of other factors spelled out in the criminal code. In theory, the court has only a very narrow margin of decision. In reality, the court is relatively free to make the decision, as long as both the defence and the prosecution do not appeal.

IV.3. NORMATIVE ALTERNATIVES TO IMPRISONMENT

As far as adult offenders are concerned, the German criminal law provides the courts with few alternatives to the prison sentence. The main alternative is the fine, if the law offers that sanction for the particular crime category. In case of a prison sentence of up to two years, the court can decide to suspend the sentence (§ 56 StGB) and impose certain obligations and instructions. In case of non-compliance, the offender will have to serve the sentence that was originally imposed. Community service does not exist as a criminal sanction. It was, however, introduced as a way to avoid serving prison sentences for fine default.

In juvenile court, a broad array of sentencing possibilities exist, alongside the prison sentence. Both with adults and with juveniles, the prosecution has been given broad powers to avoid a criminal trial (by dismissing the case, with or without imposing obligations on the offender). In the absence of sentencing alternatives, this has become the main road to avoid sentences of imprisonment.

IV.4. COURSES OF ACTION TO REDUCE IMPRISONMENT

A number of possibilities to further reduce imprisonment were under discussion in Germany.

- Decriminalization of minor offences and of "crimes without victims" (e.g. drug crimes)
- Broaden the possibilities to suspend prison sentences (raising the limit from 2 to 3 years)
- Broaden the possibilities for early release of prisoners (parole)
- Introduce community work as a sanction in its own right in adult criminal law

- Reduce or abolish fine default as a cause of imprisonment
- Early provision of lawyers in cases of remand imprisonment.

The criminologist Frieder Dünkel[94] has calculated that about 25,000 prison cells could be spared by introducing the above suggestions. So far, the legislation necessary to achieve these goals, has not been forthcoming. The last attempt in this direction was made by a "sanctions commission" convened by the Federal Justice Ministry. Their report from 2000 included the proposal to make community work a criminal sanction, as well as the proposal to broaden the possibilities for suspended sentences and parole.[95] However, a bill based on the commission's report did not find a majority. Presently new efforts are made to abolish imprisonment for fine default.[96] But also in this case, the chances of success are remote.

IV.5. SUMMARY ON THE OVERUSE OF IMPRISONMENT

Germany can, presently, not be seen as a clear example for the overuse of imprisonment. There are, however, at least four categories of offences/offenders that need consideration and law reform in this respect:
- Too many cases of life imprisonment (a reform of the legislation with respect to murder is underway);
- Drug offences & drug related offences (de-criminalization was put on the agenda by a petition of a large group of criminal law professors);
- Too many cases of people sentenced to indefinite detention in forensic hospitals;
  and, on the other end of the spectrum (legislation is underway to introduce proportionality limits)
- Far too many cases of imprisonment for fine default (a petition to abolish fine default as a reason for imprisonment was launched in January 2016).[97]

94 Frieder Dünkel, 'Wie die Gefängniskapazität in Deutschland um 25.000 Haftplätze reduziert werden könnte! Qualitätsverbesserung und Erfüllung verfassungsrechtlicher Vorgaben durch Reduzierung der Gefängnisbelegung' in: W. Pecher et al. (eds), '*...die im Dunkeln sieht man nicht', Perspektiven des Strafvollzugs. Festschrift für Georg Wagner*, Herbolzheim: Springer, 2005, 52-66.

95 Abschlussbericht der Kommission zur Reform des strafrechtlichern Sanktionssystems, presented in March 2000 (at: https://www.bib.uni-mannheim.de/fileadmin/pdf/fachinfo/jura/abschlussber-der-komm-strafreform.pdf) (last visited: 4 June 2016).

96 A proposal by the land of Brandenburg did not find the necessary majority among the Ministers of Justice at their bi-annual convention in Nauen on 2 June 016.

97 Johannes Feest, 'Weg mit der Ersatzfreiheitsstrafe. Eine Petition mit Fußnoten' in: Felix Herzog, Reinhold Schlothauer & Wolfgang Wohlers, *Gedächtnisschrift für Edda Weßlau*, Berlin: Duncker & Humblot, 2016.

V. CONCLUSION

What we need in Germany most is more pragmatism in dealing with juridical and penal matters accompanied by professional information to the public and resistance against scandalization by the media. More specifically, we need less criminalization, less detainees in prison who have not paid their fines, far more sentences with probation and far more early release from prison and mental hospitals well prepared by early professional risk management.

OVERUSE IN THE CRIMINAL JUSTICE SYSTEM IN GREECE

Effi LAMBROPOULOU & Olga TSOLKA*

I. INTRODUCTION

Overuse of criminal justice is a general but not significant characteristic of the Greek justice system as a whole. Looking at the analysis and the trend to carry criminal justice too far, we can see the picture is complicated. Overcriminalization is related to overregulation, which mainly pertains to the country's EU and international commitments.

The overuse of prosecution is a cause and effect of practical difficulties, vague legislation, the reluctance of prosecutors and inadequate support for them to use the few alternatives foreseen by law.

As for the (over)use of imprisonment we have to stress that during the last three decades a decreasing trend of those convicted have been sentenced to imprisonment, and from these sentences a small part cannot be paid off. Prison overcrowding is a result of longer sentences served on convicts due to the severity of their crimes, higher pre-trial detention rates due to the overload of cases to be judged and a higher number of foreigners for whom their unstable or illegal residence statuses hinders courts from granting an early conditional release or avoiding detention.

* Effi Lambropoulou, PhD, is Professor of Criminology at the Sociology Department of Panteion University of Social and Political Sciences, Athens – Greece. She is a member of various ad hoc reform-committees at the Ministries of Justice and Public Order. Member of Greek and European Scientific Societies, and Reviewer of International and European journals in the field.
Olga Tsolka, PhD, is Assistant Professor of Criminal Law at the Department of International, European and Area Studies of Panteion University, Athens-Greece. She is a member of various legislative-committees on the implementation of EU legislation at the Ministries of Justice and Public Order. Member of the Board of Directors of Hellenic Criminal Bar Association, and other Greek and European Scientific Societies and Journals in Criminal Law.
The references in this chapter with asterisk* are in Greek language and their titles are translated into English.

During the last 30 years, Greek governments without exception focused primarily on the prison situation and they have tried hopelessly to control prison overcrowding with successive changes in legislation that have proven ineffective in the long run. Curiously, they continue to insist on them, while criminal justice bureaucrats, law enforcement officials and academics have also proven unable to make sound suggestions and form strategic plans for the criminal justice system as a whole.

What is not taken into account is that these policies are financed by the taxpaying Greek citizens. These citizens also pay with their safety and the consequences of crime. One of these consequences is providing funds and capital for an ever-growing prison system, which sometimes violates human rights not because of choice, but because of its inability to deal with difficult situations or simply reacting to pressing conditions. In addition, delayed court dates make citizens unjustly suffer throughout their use of the criminal justice system, while the swelling legislation undermines security and rule of law.

II. OVERUSE OF CRIMINALIZATION

Overcriminalization is directly related to overregulation. The overproduction of law is a common feature of most EU countries, and Greece is no exception. The empirical examination of overregulation in Greece is limited and has been carried out mainly by jurists, who are mostly content with descriptive analyses. Other disciplines, such as sociology, political science and economics, have hardly researched the issue.

Anyway, the few Greek studies conducted have shown that the increasing number of laws is related to the emergence and growth of the welfare state, as confirmed by foreign research for other countries on the matter as well.[1]

The gradual increase of legislation which has been observed since 1990, is due not only to the national legislature, but mainly to the integration of the Greek legal and state system into the global regulatory environment. From 2001 to 2015 1,478 laws have passed in Greece, of which 749 (50.6%) were primary regulations

1 See more in Vassiliki Dalakou, *Long Term Development of the Regulatory Practice of the Greek Public Administration as Evidenced by the "Permanent Legislation Code"*, Presentation at the 1st Conference of public administration experts, School of Economics and Political Sciences, Faculty of Political Science and Public Administration, Athens, 2005 (at: www.pspa.uoa.gr/fileadmin/pspa.uoa.gr/uploads/Research/EDE/Conferences/SDE_2005/Proposals/Dalakou_Vasiliki.pdf) (last visited: 31 August 2016)*; Panagiotis Karkatsoulis, *Regulation, Deregulation, Reform: Changes to the Rule of Law in the Age of Globalization*, I. Sideris: Athens, 2011, p. 50-56.*

and 729 (49.3%) ratifications of conventions.[2] The 3,452 presidential and the 353 ministerial decrees necessary for the provisions to be enforced are not included in the total number. The vast amount of legislation produced by the international and the EU community has influenced Greek legislation in two ways: qualitatively and quantitatively. Qualitatively because the participation of the national legislature in the regulation of significant issues affecting social, political and economic development of the country is restricted, as such decisions are made by more powerful countries where small countries have very little power in decision making, and in particular when they don't have advanced corresponding policies.

Quantitatively, the growth of international legislation was accompanied by a sharp decline in national legislative production. This fact, associated with the shortage of measures that could improve the quality of legislation and rationalize its quantity, monitor their implementation and evaluate their impact, often results in an uncritical acceptance of these regulations and exacerbates the negative effects of the international and, in particular, the EU legislation.

The upward trend of ratified laws indicates that the "national" element that is necessary for a society to benefit from globalization, is in the Greek case either absent or it exists as an unfortunate further devaluation of the national laws and the national institutions based thereon, constituting ample evidence of a regulatory deficit.

It is not only that the Greek governments underestimated the globalized structures' impact on national laws, but also that the existence of weak parliamentary majorities or unstable political environments have contributed to the weakening of Parliament's regulatory role, which is mainly limited to a ratification mechanism. This is the case for example, of the period 1989-1991, and the current one, since 2010. In the three years from 1989 to 1991, 176 laws were passed (on the average 58.6 per year), of which 45% (80) were ratifications and only 55% (96) primary regulations. During the period 2010-2016, 591 laws have been passed (90.4 per year), of which 52.3% (309) were ratifications of international and European conventions, EU directives and decisions, as well as bilateral conventions, some of which related to EU commitments of the country. A percentage of 15.6% (49) of the ratifications were express legislation bypassing the regular law making process; 55.1% (27) of them are immediately connected with the three Economic Adjustment Programmes.[3] During the same period, 8.4% (50) of the laws that have been passed were of criminal interest, of which

2 Dimitris A. Sotiropoulos & Leonidas Christopoulos, *Overregulation, Bad Regulation and Bureaucracy in Greece. Analysis of Failures of the Past and Suggestions for Better Regulation*, DiaNEOsis: Athens, July 2016 (at: www.dianeosis.org/wp-content/uploads/2016/07/polynomia_new_final.pdf)((last visited: 31 August 2016), p. 6, 57: Table 4, 58: Table 5.*

3 National Printing Office Archive (at: www.et.gr) (last visited: 31 August 2016)*; European Council, Council of the European Union, *Greece: The Third Economic Adjustment Programme*,

24% (12) were ratifications of international and EU conventions and protocols, and 30% (15) directives and decisions.[4] The rest 46% (23) were primary laws, mostly amendments.

Furthermore it is significant that over the years apart from the Special primary laws which, by their nature, regulate specific issues in detail, the rate of presidential decrees and ministerial decisions (secondary legislation) in comparison with the primary legislation increase (46-65-90%), highlighting the strengthening of the executive power over the legislature (see above). This indicates that the Parliament is controlled by the executive and to a large extent, operates as a "purgatory" of political decisions taken, in order to serve party political interests or certain interest groups and not the common good. The previous situation explains that contemporary legislation in Greece is mainly fragmentary and circumstantial and therefore is not in line with the traditional doctrine of general and abstract rule of law.

If we had to indicate an area of excessive legislation and successive laws in Greece, this would be the tax and insurance legislation. From 1975 to 2015, 250 tax laws have been passed in total, making an average of six tax laws per year, while from 2002 to 2015, 36 tax laws along with 714 authorizations to ministers and the President of Democracy for completing the legislation in order to be enforced, as well as 238 relevant regulations dispersed among various laws.[5]

After 2010 and as a result of the debt crisis, several regulations have been issued to intensify the control of tax evasion and due debts toward the state. The last law of 2015 (4337/2015) increased prison sentences and fines foreseen by the previous Laws 4174/2013 and 2523/1997. The law violation above the amount of €150,000 has been for the first time characterized as a serious crime (felony) punishable with imprisonment over 5 years, as mentioned in Article 8. At the moment, it is too early for any conclusions to be made as no data has yet been published regarding convictions and sentences imposed.

Table 1 shows statistics on recorded crimes in Greece for the period between 2000 and 2013, which are divided into felonies, more serious crimes, and misdemeanours.

---

20 June 2016 (at: www.consilium.europa.eu/en/policies/financial-assistance-eurozone-members/greece-programme/) (last visited: 31 August 2016).

4 Ministry of Justice, *Legislation after 1990* (at: http://www.ministryofjustice.gr) (last visited: 31 August 2016)*.

5 Dimitris A. Sotiropoulos & Leonidas Christopoulos, *Overregulation, Bad Regulation and Bureaucracy in Greece. Analysis of Failures of the Past and Suggestions for Better Regulation*, DiaNEOsis: Athens, July 2016, p. 14 (at: www.dianeosis.org/wp-content/uploads/2016/07/polynomia_new_final.pdf)((last visited: 31 August 2016).

Table 1. Registered crimes and convictions in time series (1980-2013)

Year	Total number of registered crimes	per 100,000 inhabitants (over 7 y.o.)	Felonies*	per 100,000 inhabitants (over 7 y.o.)	Misde-meanours**	per 100,000 inhabitants (over 7 y.o.)	Convicted TOTAL (suspended sentences incl.)
1980	295353	3416	1043	12	294310	3404	118086
1985	291355	3242	2560	28	288795	3213	100896
1990	330803	3554	4692	51	326111	3504	103862
1995	329110	3385	8244	85	320866	3301	91966
1998	385681	3824	5340	53	380341	3771	63818
1999	373680	3686	4994	49	368686	3637	62663
2000	369137	3627	4444	44	364693	3583	58816
2001	439629	4305	4867	48	434762	4257	59262
2002	441138	4306	4695	46	436443	4260	66061
2003	441839	4299	5131	50	436708	4249	73161
2004	405627	3933	5350	52	400277	3881	74188
2005	455952	4405	5672	55	450280	4350	56923
2006	463750	4466	6276	60	457474	4406	70186
2007	423442	4067	6203	60	417239	4007	62346
2008	420059	4027	6979	67	413080	3960	65006
2009	386893	3748	8550	83	378343	3665	65048
2010	333988	3228	8817	85	325171	3143	61718
2011	194031	1874	9149	88	184882	1786	65006
2012	194244	1879	9024	87	185220	1792	65048
2013	199800	1943	14131	137	185669	1806	61718

Notes:

* Crime punishable by a prison sentence of 5–20 years or by a life sentence (GPC, Article 52).

** Crime punishable by a prison sentence of 10 days to 5 years (GPC, Article 53). Alternatively, some misdemeanours can incur a fine (specific reference in GPC).

Source: ELSTAT/Hellenic Statistical Authority (until 2010 NSSG/ESYE-National Statistical Service of Greece (For uniformity reasons, wherever possible, it was preferred the new acronym name instead of NSSG, even before 2010), *Criminal Justice Statistics* 1980-96: Table I; 1998, 2000, 2006-2013: Table 01F online (at: http://www.statistics.gr) (last visited: 31 August 2016)*; MPO/Ministry of Public Order, *1997 Statistical Bulletin of the Greek Police*, Athens, 18 June 1998*.

(All Tables and Figures contain data compiled by the author. Using the Statistical Service's recent online data, any deviations in the number of registered crimes or convictions in the author's previous publications will be updated.)

Overall, there has been a significant increase in the number of recorded crimes over a 30-year period ending in 2008, with a complex pattern of ups and downs over the intervening period, and the rate of recorded crime per head of population has increased significantly after 1998 (1990: 3,554, 1998: 3,934; 2005: 4,405; 2008: 4,027). In particular, between 2000 and 2008, the absolute number of recorded crimes rose from 369,137 to 420,059, while the rate per 100,000 per resident population rose from 3,627 in 2000 to 4,466 in 2006, then slightly declining until 2008 (4,027) ending up in a sharp drop in the following years (2013: 199,800/1,943 per head). Specifically, the total number of crimes from 386,893 (3,748 per head) in 2009 went down to 194,244 crimes (1,879 per head) in 2012, which is a decrease of 49.8%, while in relation to 2003 (441,839/4,293 per head) the decrease is 56%. In 2013, a slight increase of 2.8% (5,556 – 199,800) follows only in relation to the previous year, and rises to 1,943 per head (Table 1).

Trends for felonies were, nevertheless, entirely different from those for misdemeanours or for recorded crime in total. In terms of numbers, there were about 4,444 recorded felonies in 2000, compared with 5,672 in 2005, 8,817 in 2010 and 14,131 in 2013, which is the year with the highest number of recorded felonies ever, despite the official sharp decrease of the total number of crimes after 2011. In terms of the rate per 100,000 resident population, felonies increased about four times between 2000 and 2013 (45–137; Table 1), while in relation to the total number of registered crimes they increased almost sevenfold: 1.2% of all recorded crimes in 2000, 2.6% in 2010 and 7.07% in 2013 (Table 1).

The general decline of registered crimes and misdemeanours by the police from 2009/2010 until 2013 (when the last complete police data are available), as well as in the rate of recorded crimes per head of population cannot be easily explained. It seems at first to correspond with the decline of crime in Western Europe between 2003 and 2012 (–12% EU 28).[6] During this period, some misdemeanours turned to infractions involving only fines and not any prison time. The misdemeanours refer to prostitution, mendacity and market hygiene violations. However, the high drop still cannot be justified. The author's interviews for another study with local and state police, as well as the daily police press releases, and information from unofficial police officers' blogs, suggested that there was a surge in violence and property crimes at the start of the decade, keeping in mind that unreported crime cannot be estimated.[7] In addition, an extended report of young police officers about police, policing and crime control to the MPs in July 2015 describes a very different situation.

Recorded crimes that have substantially increased in number burden the police and, eventually, the prosecution service. Such crimes are thefts, robberies and homicides (murders and manslaughters), as well as serious and violent

6 Eurostat, *Statistics Explained – Crime Statistics,* 27 June 2015 (at: http://ec.europa.eu/eurostat/statistics-explained/index.php/Crime_statistics) (last visited: 31 August 2016).

7 See also the 2005 study of Jan M. van Dijk, et al., *The Burden of Crime in the EU. Research Report: A Comparative Analysis of the European Crime and Safety Survey (EU ICS),* 2005 (at: www.unicri.it/services/library_documentation/publications/icvs/publications/EUICS_-_The_Burden_of_Crime_in_the_EU.pdf) (last visited: 1 February 2018).

offences involving drugs, arms, and counterfeiting. These are followed by violations of building regulations, and of the labour welfare legislation (insurance and pension funds), forgery, mendacity (systematic begging), and crimes which are perpetrated against the security of the State and against political parties, absconding (or attempt) from prison and some public order offences (using explosives in demonstrations, plundering, harassment, alarm or distress etc...).

After all, the registered crimes referred to above, the most serious included as well, have nothing to do with overcriminalization on account of the fact that they constitute a part of the main core of the traditional criminal law not only in Greece, but in all countries. An exception might be the registered violations of building and labour welfare legislation wherein the criminal law has been extended during the last decade. The increase in arrests for public order crimes since 2010 can be associated with the social disorder, which is mainly due to the economic crisis.

In contrast with the general upward trend in recorded crimes until 2008, and especially for serious crimes (felonies), there has been a considerable downward trend in convictions, with substantial fluctuations from year to year. At the beginning of the period in 1980, there were 118,086 recorded convictions, which then dropped to 63,818 (–46%) by 1998, further down to 59,262 (–3.3%) in 2001, followed by a small increase (+4.1%) in the following years but with variations until 2010 (61,718). The highest number of convictions was reached in total and per head in 1980 (118,086/1,212), 1990 (103,862/1,012), 1995 (91,966/896) and 2004 (74,188/677). In general, the rate of convictions per head of population dropped dramatically in a period of 30 years, which along with the high rise of recorded crimes could be regarded as an inability of the justice system to protect society, to stabilize trust in the police, satisfy the victims' feelings and provide them with a sense of justice, since it is not connected with the crime decrease. In recent years, for which no official data has yet been made available, according to our information from the Ministry of Public Order the prosecution of several pending cases of assaults and other minor crimes has stopped in order to avoid overburdened court dockets; the same is repeated by a new Law which has been recently passed in August 2016 (Law 4411/2016).

After 1998, most convictions were those for violations of market regulations, labour welfare legislation (insurance and pension funds) and traffic law (Special Criminal Laws), ranging between 54.3% and 40.3% of the total number of crimes; see Table 2. Hereafter most convictions include violations of antidrug legislation – representing the highest proportion in the group, as well as dishonoured checks, illicit trade in antiquities, aliens smuggling, and other offences regulated, again, by Special Criminal Laws; they range from 23.8% to 36.7%. Three crime groups with more or less similar rates follow: crimes against the person (assaults, murders and manslaughters, rapes, abduction etc.), property offences, and offences against the public welfare ("common dangerous crimes", i.e. crimes

Table 2. Convicted according to crime (1998-2010)

Convictions in %	1998	1999	2000	2001	2002	2003	2004	2005	2006	2007	2008	2009	2010
TOTAL	100,0	100,0	100,0	100,0	100,0	100,0	100,0	100,0	100,0	100,0	100,0	100,0	100,0
Crimes against the person (e.g. homicide, assaults, rape, abduction etc)	7,0	6,9	7,0	6,4	6,0	6,2	6,4	6,6	6,1	6,1	5,8	6,3	6,0
Honour crimes (e.g. defamation/slander, abuse)	1,9	2,0	2,3	2,2	2,0	2,0	2,0	1,6	0,9	1,3	1,4	1,5	1,7
Property crimes	6,1	6,2	6,2	6,2	5,3	5,6	5,8	7,0	7,5	6,9	6,2	6,4	7,3
Common dangerous crimes (e.g.arson, environmental crimes)	7,5	6,5	6,4	5,6	5,0	4,6	4,9	6,0	8,3	6,7	4,5	3,4	2,7
Other offences of Penal Code	2,4	1,9	2,4	2,6	2,1	2,4	2,6	3,1	3,1	3,9	3,9	4,3	4,5
Violations of Market, Labour and Traffic Law	46,6	49,6	48,8	50,4	54,3	54,7	54,0	48,9	44,1	46,2	47,5	44,8	40,3
Violations of other Special Criminal Laws (e.g.drug crimes, alien smuggling, contraband)	27,6	26,1	25,6	25,9	24,5	23,9	23,8	26,2	29,0	27,8	30,0	32,6	36,7
Offences against the Military Penal Code	0,9	0,8	1,3	0,7	0,8	0,6	0,5	0,6	1,0	1,1	0,7	0,7	0,7

Source: ELSTAT 1998-2010: Table B4 available online.

against the security of traffic or violations of building regulations, arson), crimes against the public order and religious peace, such as using explosives in demonstrations, plundering, harassment, alarm and distress etc... Crimes against the person range between 5.8% and 7%, property offences between 5.3% and 7.3%, while the common dangerous crimes range between 7.5% and 2.7%.

Therefore, we see that the type of the most common registered crimes (thefts, robberies, homicides, violent offences) and the crimes for which the offenders have been convicted (Special Criminal Laws) have little association with each other.

Legal and societal opportunities for legalization and decriminalization of certain categories of conduct do exist, but as described, apart from drugs, they have little to do with the large number of arrests and convictions. In laws concerning environmental protection, consumer protection, government revenues and expenditures and urban planning, both administrative and criminal sanctions for the same violation have been laid down. Since this reaction violates the *ne bis in idem* principle (double jeopardy), it is absolutely necessary to decriminalize these violations.[8] Therefore, criminal behaviour must be distinguished from administrative violations, according to its seriousness, the offender's fault and its degree. Additionally, the preventive control i.e. control exercised before the publication and entry into force of the law should be strengthened (parliamentary control and presidential/Head of the state control). As far as the decriminalization of petty offences is concerned, the report of the committee for the reform of Penal Code is expected which has been working quite successfully for some years now.

As for drug crimes, governments and jurists are very sceptical about the effects, since drug use is only punishable when the person cannot prove that the narcotics quantity is for his or her own use and only if he or she is arrested twice for the same reason, which means that the violation was not occasional (Law 4139/2013, Articles 21, 29[1,2]). Drug abusers are not punished (Article 29, paragraph 1, 2) or are punished with mitigated sentences (Articles 21, paragraph 1b, 2, Article 22), in particular when they agree to participate in an integrated addiction treatment. Nevertheless, the legalization of cannabis possession, cultivation for one's own use, and its products are topics that have been, and continue to be, discussed in Greece over the last fifteen years.

III. OVERUSE OF PROSECUTION

In Greece the police and prosecution service apply the legality principle. The law explicitly requires the prosecutor (and the police) to investigate and prosecute every crime that has been committed. Thus, the prosecutor has no discretion

---

8 Ilias Anagnostopoulos, 'The End of Binary Sanctions?', 65 *Poinika Chronika* 8 (2015), p. 623-624*; Olga Tsolka, "Ne bis in idem' and the Binary Sanctions' System for the Same Law Violation', 65 *Poinika Chronika* 8 (2015), p. 625-638.*

whether or not to prosecute in the most serious cases. The opportunity (alias: expediency) principle is foreseen in very few cases (e.g. GPC, Article 187B, paragraph 3; GPPC/Greek Penal Procedure Code, Articles 45A, 309, paragraph 1, 310, paragraph 1, 311); on that account, alternatives to prosecution are limited.

Data regarding prosecution has only been available since 2015. Until then, the Ministry of Justice did not keep statistics at a central level, but each prosecution service (63) in the country collected data for its own use. Nevertheless, from earlier studies of the periods 1991–1993 and 1994-1998, solely at the prosecutorial service of Athens, the complaints that have been filed are on average 363 respectively 442 per day.[9] In detail, between 1991–1993, charges have been filed on average 132,433 annually, whilst between 1994-1998, 161,515 charges annually, which is an increase of 18% in relation to the previous period. From a recent study concerning the development of charges from 2001-2012, done by a prosecutor with respect to the prosecution service in Athens[10], there was a steady increase rate of submitted charges ranging from 5.3% in 2002 (209,062) to 53.5% in 2010 (304,810). The average complaints per year during this period were 238,236, corresponding to 653 per day, an increase of 47.5% compared with 1994-1998.

The national prosecution service is under such a heavy burden that it does not have enough time for a thorough preliminary examination. Thus, they either shelve the case and decline to file the charge (GPPC, Articles 43 and 47), or file the indictment, and send the case to court or to a judge for the main investigation. Since the courts are also overworked, a higher number of accused might have been acquitted by the courts during the last decade compared to previous decades, due to lack of evidence. Furthermore, since the vast majority of those convicted lodge an appeal, it is possible that a percentage is acquitted of the charges by the appellate courts. The previous tactic might explain the drop of convictions after 2007, which have been presented in section II (Table 1).

It is obvious that a comprehensive preliminary examination could help to lessen the workload of these busy courts. In 2003, the Law 3160 made preliminary examination obligatory for serious crimes in an effort to accelerate penal procedure and stop the prosecution before a thorough preliminary examination has taken place. With this legislation, the principle of legality has been made much more flexible and the public prosecutors obtained more discretion. Since then, an increasing rate of complainants have not been prosecuted, but instead their cases were shelved or dismissed, as is shown in the study of Zimianitis. The rate ranges from 16.4% to 50.5% of the cases that have

9 Effi Lambropoulou, *Sociology of Criminal Law and Institutions of Criminal Justice*, Athens: I. Sideris, 2013, p. 242.*

10 Dimitrios Zimianitis, 'The New Preliminary Examination. Critical Assessment of the First Decade', 16 *Poiniki Dikaiosini* 12 (2013), p. 1132 -1136.*

been ordered to undertake a preliminary examination. This also depicts a rising trend from 8.9-21.7% of the complaints filed in the prosecutorial service of Athens.[11]

According to several jurists, academics and practitioners, the main burden of the prosecution office during the last decade as regards to the number of cases are trafficking and possession of drugs, tax crimes, fraud and forgery, both against individuals' legal interests and against the public, honour crimes (e.g. slander), money laundering and crimes against justice (perjury, false accusation). The cases that are most labour insensitive for the prosecution, are those crimes that need an expert's report, namely fraud and breach of trust against the public interests, money laundering, tax crimes, stock exchange crimes (securities-, stock-, investment fraud), and environmental crimes.

As described in section II., a parallel administrative and criminal sanctioning system of the same law violation for certain crimes exists in our country. However, no study has been done on how to distinguish the criminal from the administrative violations, in order to decriminalize such crimes. What is more, under the present debt crisis, the government, in its effort to control tax violations, introduced the administrative procedure running parallel to criminal (Law 4174/2013 as amended by Law 4337/2015, Article 8). This causes delays in criminal courts, as well as administrative courts. It also violates the prohibition of double jeopardy, as already underlined, which is safeguarded by ECHR and the EU Charter of Fundamental Rights.

In 2010, the Law 3904 was passed in an attempt to ease the excessive workload of the judiciary with unsolved court cases, introducing restoration as an alternative to trial. It addresses only the offenders of property crimes, who will completely compensate the injured parties either before or during the preliminary examination or, for misdemeanours, at the end of an evidential procedure.[12] The compensation results either in barring prosecution, punishment, or a discharge plea (GPC Articles 384, 406A; Law 3904/2010, Article 6 [2]).

However, this alternative has not unburdened the court-dockets because the initiative for the compensation relies absolutely on the offender. In practice the offender and the victim wait until the first day of trial and appear in court to acknowledge their agreement, even though they may have conciliated before that date. Their main reason for appearing in court rather than following the out-of-court formal compensation procedure, is because the formal procedure does not

11 *Idem*; see also Haris Dalakouras, 'Preliminary Examination: Aspects of a Dynamic Institution after its Reform with the Law 3160/2003 and 3346/2005', *Nomika Chronika* online 44, July-August 2007 (at: https://www.nomikaxronika.gr/article.aspx?issue=44) (last visited: 31 August 2016).*

12 Christos Mylonopoulos, 'The 'Satisfaction of the Victim' and the Criminal Reconciliation regulated in Law 3904/2010', 14 *Poiniki Dikaiosini* 1 (2011), p. 53-58.*

end with acquittal, which is what the offender wants, but as previously mentioned with a barring prosecution or punishment. In general, according to academics and practitioners, the compensation as an alternative to the court has not been successful until now and its use in Greece is still limited, for one more reason, that the citizens and criminal defence lawyers are not familiar with the process of consensual negotiations to achieve the best possible outcomes.

The same Law (3904/2010) has introduced plea bargaining for serious property offences (Article 308B GPPC), namely embezzlement (Article 375), fraud (Article 386), computer fraud (Article 386 A), and usury (Article 404 GPC) after the commencement of prosecution and the filing of the indictment by the prosecutor. The provision does not apply when the relevant crimes have been committed against the public, public entities and local authorities (GPPC, Article 308B, paragraph 9, Law 3904/2010, Article 17, paragraph 1). However, in 2014, Law 4312 (Article 2, paragraph 4) was introduced for the mitigation of the sentence for the above crimes against the Greek public, the European Union, public entities and local authorities as well, foreseen of *full compensation*. The same applies for other crimes against property, tax crimes, corruption etc..., but the definition of "full satisfaction of the victim" causes serious practical problems, making the regulation impractical and unenforced.

In view of what is mentioned above and to deal with the enormous amount of work in criminal courts, the introduction of plea bargaining (corresponding to continental law tradition) for crimes concerning tax fraud, stock exchange and environmental crimes, money laundering, bribery, embezzlement and breach of trust in the public and private sector, is regarded by academics and practitioners as appropriate. It lessens the workload of the courts. The Anglo-Saxon form of plea bargaining cannot be used because of structural differences in criminal law and criminal procedure systems. In addition, plea bargaining could be applied to all crimes against property, regardless of whether the victim is a private or public entity, as well as for the crimes committed by civil servants (such as bribery, breach of trust or infidelity) and where a case could bring financial loss.[13]

In general, plea bargaining could be accompanied with a stepwise decriminalization of less serious economic crimes and violations of urban planning legislation, while the administrative sanctions, which are sufficient to protect society, will be maintained.

Furthermore, the diminishing of the prosecutions' number of cases could be achieved by applying reconciliation forms to the previously mentioned offences, firstly in the preliminary examination and then in the investigation stage. As a

13 Indicatively, see more in Adam Papadamakis, 'Thoughts Regarding Criminal Negotiation (Plea Bargaining) in Greek Criminal Procedure', *Enopion*. Bimonthly Journal of Thessaloniki's Bar Association, 72, January-March 2014, p. 31-33 (at: https://www.dsth.gr/enopion) (last visited: 31 August 2016)*; Aristomenis Janetis, The Plea Bargaining and the Principle of Seeking the Substantial Truth - Advocating for the New Institution, 66 *Poinika Chronika* 1 (2016), p. 14-24*.

result, the criminal system would not be as loaded, the harm of crime would be quickly repaired, real and personal property would not remain "frozen" for years until the issuance of an irrevocable criminal judgment, as usually happens, and justice would be restored.

The support of prosecutor offices with assistants, especially in the field of economic as well as the environmental crimes, and money laundering, would be also necessary so that a thorough preliminary examination could be carried out and criminal prosecution would not start without having adequately researched the case.

Nevertheless, the massive prosecution of defendants in courts, despite evidential weaknesses especially during the last years of debt crisis, depict a rather inadequate awareness of prosecutors regarding the function of the criminal trial. This applies to the majority of economic crimes, corruption cases included, whereby mass media and politicians promote the prosecution of cases in court as a social imperative, since the criminal law enforcement became a tool of politics; hence an enormous volume of case files and long-lasting procedures are generated, making citizens suffer undeserved delays throughout the criminal system and discredit justice, if the accused is acquitted in the end. The situation is also interrelated with the liability and accountability fear of prosecutors, investigators and judicial councils, who prefer to prosecute the case than to reject the charge.

Yet, the first attempts to introduce alternatives to prosecution in the Greek criminal law system were in 2003 and 2006. The Law 3189/2003 regarding the Reform of Juvenile Justice (Article 4, paragraph 2) and the Law 3500/2006 about Domestic violence and abuse (Article 11) introduced an alternative dispute resolution, regulating the possibility of the prosecutor to stop prosecution and start mediation.

The 2003 Law foresees reconciliation between the juvenile offender and the victim and the payment of restitution for harm caused, as well as participation in community service (Article 1, paragraph 3). The initiative lies with the prosecutor or the court after the offender confessed to the crime and stated his/her willingness to pay restitution, as well as with the cooperation of the victim (GPPC, Article 45A). Between 2010 and 2015, the juvenile court of Athens has imposed to 56 (11.6% in relation to the total number of restorative justice) cases mediation, to 377 (78.2%) restitution to the victim, and to 49 (10.1%) cases community service, which corresponds to 5.3% (482) of the 8,981 court decisions for these five years.[14] Despite many practical (overtaxed Juvenile Service) and

14 Dimitra Mouhimoglou, *The Implementation of Educational Measures to Juvenile Offenders in the Context of Restorative Justice*, Association of Greek Judges and Public Prosecutors, 3 April 2016 (at: http://eedd.gr/%... -%CF%83/) (last visited: 31 August 2016)*.

legislative problems, the alternatives to prosecution for juvenile offenders work and have many possibilities for improvements.

The 2006 law regulates mediation for misdemeanours of domestic violence. Either the prosecutor or the offender takes the initiative to start this procedure (Article 11). Mediation has become widely accepted by the police and the justice system, although we neither have a formal assessment nor statistics measuring the success of the institution. Nonetheless, mediation has been criticized for its institutional appropriateness for such crimes, transgender inequality, power imbalances, and inadequate training of mediators.[15]

IV. OVERUSE OF IMPRISONMENT

IV.1. OUTLINE OF LEGAL PROVISIONS AND PRISON POPULATION

Greek Criminal Law follows the trichotomy of criminal offences into petty offences, misdemeanours and felonies/very serious crimes (GPC, Article 18). A felony is a crime punishable by a prison sentence of 5–20 years or by a life sentence (GPC, Article 52). A misdemeanour is any offence punishable either with imprisonment from over 10 days to five years, or a fine or confinement in a juvenile correctional institution (Articles 18, 53, 54). The misdemeanours which can incur a fine are specifically referred to in the GPC. Petty offences are punished by one to thirty days' detention, or mainly with fines of €29-590. Therefore, the courts are free to decide on whether a prison sentence will be imposed and on its length, still in the limits the law foresees. The law also foresees the cases and conditions for cease or refrain from prosecution, referred to above in section III.

As described (section II, Table 1), there has been a significant increase in the number of recorded crimes over a 30-year period ending in 2008, and a sharp decrease in the following years. In contrast with the general upward trend in recorded crimes until 2008, and especially in serious crimes, there has been a considerable downward trend in convictions, with substantial fluctuations from year to year. It is also remarkable that the types of crimes of those arrested with those convicted do not particularly coincide (Table 2).

Over the period 1998–2010, the great majority of defendants found guilty received a prison sentence up to 12 months, which is automatically converted to a

15 Vassiliki Artinopoulou & Iro Michail, 'The Directive 2012/29/EU and Restorative Justice: A Step Forward for the Protection Of Crime Victims?', in: Margarita Gasparinatou (ed), *Essays in Honor of Prof. Dr. Nestor Courakis*, A.N. Sakkoulas: Athens: Komotini, 2016, p. 551-589 (at: www.ant-sakkoulas.gr/periexomena/15-2764-2.pdf) (last visited: 31 August 2016)*.

cash penalty at a specified daily rate (Table 3). Under the Greek Penal Code (GPC), short prison sentences are convertible to fines (GPC Article 82). Imprisonment of up to 12 months, as the sentence originally handed out accounted for a declining, although still very large, proportion: 83.7% in 1998 compared with 59.9% in 2010 (Table 3). In fact, since the middle of the 1990s, the length of a prison sentence which could be changed to a cash penalty or that could be suspended has been extended several times in order imprisonment to be avoided. In parallel, longer prison sentences of 1–5 years and of over 5 years (up to life) for "serious" crimes such as aggravated assault, murder, robbery, and serious drug-related offences have not changed substantially, although the absolute numbers for the second group are very low *(15-34)*. Regarding the first group, those sentenced to imprisonment from 1-5 years showed a rise in 2005 (6.73%), and again in 2010 (6.07%).

Educational and therapeutic measures (non-custodial) for juvenile offenders decreased significantly from 6.91% in 1998 to 2.4% in 2010, while the custodial (juvenile institution) moderately increased between 1998 and 2007 from 0.05 to 0.18% (Table 3).

Although until 1990 fines, as the sentence originally handed out, represented 10% of all sentences, this proportion has since decreased to about 5% of all sentences (5.7% in 1996). Since 1998 it started increasing again until 2003 (3.41-8.91%), and since 2005 declined rapidly from 7.3% to 0.83% in 2010 (Table 3).

Overall, there was a significant decrease in convictions to prison sentences during the examined period, from 89.1% in 1998, to 86.3% in 2003 and further down to 66.1% in 2010. It is an indication that despite the increasing severity of crimes (Table 1) imprisonment is used less, which implies that if it would be used more, then it would aggravate the existing prison overcrowding.

Criminal legislation involving harsh sentencing laws over the past fifteen years in the main concerns money laundering, fraud (e.g. stock market, customs fraud), organized crime (e.g. human trafficking, drug trafficking), terrorism and maritime smuggling (Laws 2331/1995, 2928/2001, 2943/2001) or other offences resulting from Greece's EU and international commitments. Furthermore, there has been a high level of activity in anticorruption legislation and the creation of special anticorruption authorities, as well as control bodies, independent agencies and special services.[16] In addition, criminal law has been extended in such areas as employment, urban planning and commercial law. Yet it seems that these

16 Effi Lambropoulou, 'Corruption Discourse as a Wild Card: Politics and Media in Greece and the 'Modern' Triumphalism of Anti-corruption', in: Dirk Tänzler, Konstantinos Maras & Angelos Giannakopoulos (eds), *Social Construction of Corruption in Europe*, Surrey: Ashgate, 2012, p. 265-296.

Table 3. Convicted according to imposed sentences (1998-2010)

Sentences/Year	**1998**	**1999**	**2000**	**2001**	**2002**	**2003**	**2004**	**2005**	**2006**	**2007**	**2008**	**2009**	**2010**
Total no. of Convicted	**63818**	**62663**	**58816**	**59262**	**66061**	**73161**	**74188**	**56923**	**70186**	**62346**	**65006**	**65048**	**61718**
in % in relation to the total No. of convictions	100	100	100	100	100	100	100	100	100	100	100	100	100
Fines	3,41	4,54	5,01	6,58	8,2	8,91	8,24	7,73	2,62	3,2	0,63	0,66	0,83
Imprisonment up to 12 months	83,2	83,77	83,7	81,07	81,21	81,3	80,96	78,4	57,27	58,56	61,17	59,91	59,96
1 -5 years	5,9	5,02	4,42	5,19	4,72	4,95	5,25	6,73	5,91	5,85	5,05	5,24	6,07
5-20 Years	0,42	0,47	0,47	0,62	0,34	0,46	0,57	0,81	0,82	1,06	1,06	0,94	0,87
Life sentence	0,05	0,02	0,03	0,04	0,03	0,02	0,03	0,05	0,05	0,05	0,04	0,03	0,03
Psychiatric confinement of offenders with mental disorders	0,02	0,01	0,14	0,05	0,01	0,02	0,02	0,02	0,02	0	0,04	0,01	0,01
Juvenile Institution	0,05	0,24	0,04	0,16	0,16	0,07	0,24	0,17	0,21	0,18	0,17	0,1	0,07
No information about the sentence	0,02	0,07	0,18	0,3	0,01	0,01	0,02	0,01	0	0	0	0	0
Educational or therapeutic meaures for Juveniles	6,91	5,86	6,01	6	5,33	4,26	4,67	6,09	4,57	3,16	2,8	2,48	2,04
Prison sentence in Total	89,16	89,03	88,16	86,41	86,08	86,33	86,45	85,3	63,39	64,59	66,39	65,25	66,11

Source: ELSTAT 1998-2010: Table 03F available online.

developments have not especially affected convictions, apart from labour welfare legislation and market regulations.

Contrary to the decrease of convictions to imprisonment, in Table 4 we see that the total prison population (pre-trial detainees included)[17] and convicted prisoners steadily increased over the years. The greatly increasing prison population is more than obvious, even comparing the rates per 100,000 resident population after 2000, and not only with the previous two decades (2000:70; 2005:90; 2010:102; 2013:120, Table 4). The decline in 2015 is due to the release measures of the government since April 2015 (Law 4322/2015). In July 2016, this figure decreased further to 10,122 persons.

Thus, comparing the growing prison population with that of convictions on the one hand, and the registered crimes on the other hand, the situation is indeed quite complicated. In order to explain this we examined the trend of registered felonies and misdemeanours with that of convictions and convicted prisoners (Figure 1).

The figure shows that the prison population follows a somewhat similar trend with that of registered felonies by the police and not with the convictions to imprisonment by the courts, while the number of registered crimes matches with the registered misdemeanours almost exactly, as well as the convictions to imprisonment match with the total number of convictions by the courts (Figure 1).

Moreover, it is remarkable that the percentage of prisoners calculated on the convicted persons to imprisonment grew from 7.7% in 1980 to 8.1% in 1990, further to 18.2% in 2000, to 26.7% in 2005 and to 35.3% in 2010, which means a fivefold increase during those three decades and a twofold increase after 2000.

Summing up, 12-40% of those arrested for registered crimes have been convicted, with a significant decrease between 2000-2010 (Table 1), 64-90% of offenders have been sentenced to imprisonment, with a decrease after 2006 (Table 3), whilst 6-23.7% of those convicted were finally incarcerated with an increasing trend after 2005[18], and 8-35% of those sentenced to imprisonment with an increasing trend after 2004.[19]

17 Pre-trial detention has the same meaning with remand in custody and remand in detention, but the latter refers also to when a convicted offender is serving his/her prison sentence imposed by the first instance court, and is waiting upon the decision of the appellate court. The rates of persons in detention per 100,000 inhabitants show a much moderate increase, which ranges from 16-31 persons; see more in Marcelo F. Aebi & Natalia Delgrande, *Council of Europe Annual Penal Statistics SPACE I: Survey 2013*, Strasbourg: Council of Europe, 2015, p. 99: Table 5.1 (at: www.coe.int/t/DGHL/STANDARDSETTING/PRISONS/PCCP%20documents%202015/SPACE-I-2013-English.pdf) (last visited: 31 August 2016).

18 *ELSTAT, Prison statistics* 1980-1995; 1998, 1999, 2001, 2005-2012 online, Table 03F (at: http://www.statistics.gr) (last visited: 31 August 2016)*.

19 *ELSTAT, Prison statistics* 1980-1995; 1998, 1999, 2001, 2005-2012 online, Table E24 (at: http://www.statistics.gr) (last visited: 31 August 2016)*.

Table 4. "Stock" and "Flow" prison population in time series (1980–2015)

YEAR	STOCK Total Prison population incl. Pretrial detainees ELSTAT	STOCK Convicted Prisoners at the end of the year ELSTAT	Per 100,000 resident population Convicted & Pretrial detainees - ELSTAT & WPB	FLOW Convicted prisoners during the whole year ELSTAT
1980	3135	2472	33	8186
1985	3383	2372	35	6198
1990	5133	3537	52	7588
1995	5811	3825	55	9377
1998	7006	4602	*64*	10130
1999	6145	4413	*56*	9910
2000	6003	3786	70	9519
2001	7971	6074	*73*	12687
2005	9871	6795	*90*	13082
2006	10280	7234	90	13170
2008	11165	8050	104	15074
2010	11187	7536	102	14598
2011	11576	7441	107	15007
2012	11942	8502	113	15128
2013	13147	10043	120	n.D.
2014*	12728	10002	117	n.D.
2015*	10726	n.D.	99	n.D.

Note: In regular font style are the rates per 100,000 resident population given by *ICPS/*WPB, and in *italics* are the author's calculations who has used the 2001 (10,964,020) and 2011 Census (10,815,197), all ages of the de facto population. According to population estimates 11,123,000 for 2012 of Eurostat (2013), in 2014, 114 prisoners correspond to 100,000 residents.

Source: *ELSTAT, Prison statistics* 1980-1995: Table G1; 1998, 1999, 2001, 2005-2012: Table G01A, G12 online (at: www.statistics.gr) (last visited: 31 August 2016)*; ICPS/International Centre for Prison Studies, *2012, 2013 World Prison Brief*, 2014, 2015 (at: www.prisonstudies.org/country/greece) (last visited: 31 August 2016); *Ministry of Justice, March 2014, May 2015 unpublished data; NSSG/ESYE-National Statistical Service of Greece, *Statistical Yearbook of Greece*, NSGG, Athens, 2008, p. 42: Table II.1 (at: http://dlib.statistics.gr/Book/GRESYE_01_0002_00060.pdf) (last visited: 31 August 2016)*; ELSTAT, *Greece in figures*, ELSTAT, Piraeus, 2014, p. 4: Table 2 (at: www.statistics.gr/portal/page/portal/ESYE/BUCKET/General/GREECE_IN_FIGURES_2014_EN.pdf) (last visited: 31 August 2016); Eurostat, *News release 173/2013*, 20 November 2013 (at: http://ec.europa.eu/eurostat) (last visited: 31 August 2016).

IV.2. CRIMES OF PRISONERS

The crimes for which the prisoners have been convicted of or have been accused of and have awaited for their trial are presented in the online Statistics in main categories corresponding to the chapters of the Penal Code, and not in detail (Table 5). Thus, since it is not possible to present more detailed information, we

Figure 1. Registered crimes in total, misdemeanours and felonies, convicted persons (1995-2013), convictions to imprisonment (1995-2010), and prison population (flow; 1995-2012) – registered felonies and prisoners, in secondary axis

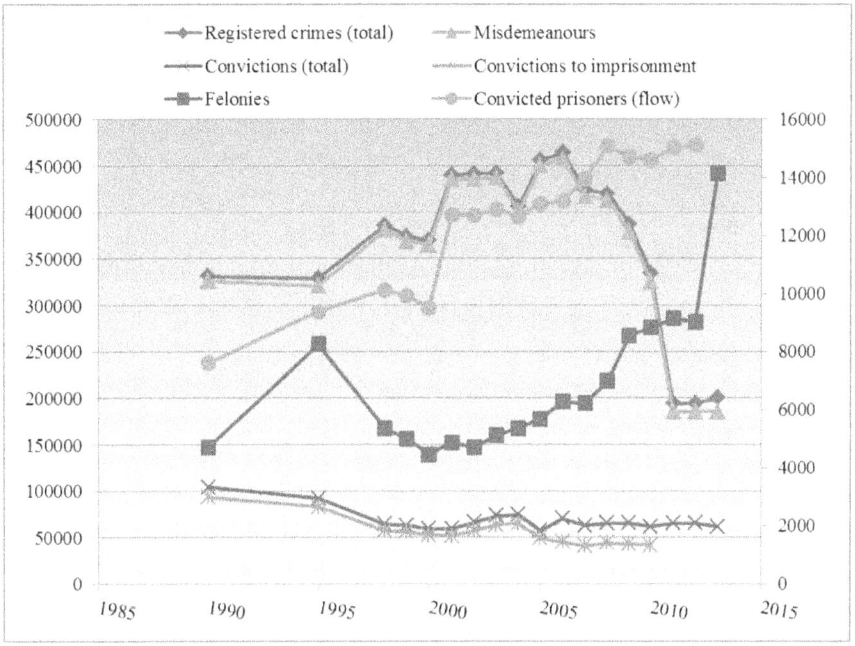

Source: *ELSTAT* Justice Statistics 1990–1996: Table I; 1998–2013: Table B4 available online; Prison Statistics 1990–1996: Table G1; 1998-2012: Table G01AK, E24 available online; ICPS/International Centre for Prison Studies, *2012, 2013 World Prison Brief*, 2014, 2015 (at: www.prisonstudies.org/country/greece) (last visited: 31 August 2016); ICPR/Institute of Criminal Policy Research, *2015 World Prison Brief*, 2016 (at: www.prisonstudies.org/country/greece) (last visited: 31 August 2016); *MPO* 1998/1997: Table 4.

use in Table 5 *Crimes against life* that represent 58-78% of "Violent Crimes", instead of homicides (murders, manslaughters) and serious assaults. *Thefts and robberies*, which represent 83-89% of the "Property Offences", are fortunately described in detail in online Statistics. *Drug crimes* are also described in detail online for the period 1998-2008; however, pre-trial detainees are not included. For this reason we have kept the main crime category i.e. "Special Criminal Laws", of which drug crimes correspond, to approximately 50-60% and put in a special column the numbers of prisoners convicted for drug crimes (Stock) for reasons of homogeneity with the rest of the crime numbers.

Table 5 gives us a detailed overview about the trends in rates, as well as in absolute numbers.

Violations of Special Criminal Laws and property crimes are mostly responsible for imprisonment and a higher increase over the years in absolute numbers and proportionality can be seen. Data for prisoners serving a sentence

Table 5. Convicted prisoners (flow), according to committed crime (in groups) in time series (1980-2010)

Year	Violent crimes	Property crimes	Common dangerous crimes	Other	Violations of Special Criminal Laws	Drug crimes	Military Penal Code	Total prisoners-Flow
1980	2079	2405	156	322	2868	664	356	8186
	25,4	29,4	1,9	3,9	35	8,11	4,3	100
1985	1380	2420	86	147	1722	631	443	6198
	22,3	39	1,4	2,4	27,8	10,18	7,1	100
1990	1316	2567	90	98	3264	1174	253	7588
	17,3	33,8	1,2	1,3	43	15,47	3,3	100
1995	1519	3111	109	89	4200	1872	349	9377
	16,2	33,2	1,2	0,9	44,8	19,96	3,7	100
1998	1735	5076	93	131	6792	2389	85	10130
	17,1	50,1	0,9	1,3	67	23,58	0,8	100
1999	1622	4719	106	120	6827	2502	15	9910
	16,4	47,6	1,1	1,2	68,9	25,25	0,2	100
2000	1397	3850	98	107	6424	2249	19	9519
	14,7	40,4	1	1,1	67,5	23,63	0,2	100
2001	1949	4846	112	155	9368	3362	16	12687
	15,4	38,2	0,9	1,2	73,8	26,5	0,1	100
2005	2281	5338	120	209	9905	3047	16	13082
	17,4	40,8	0,9	1,6	75,7	23,29	0,1	100
2006	2390	5337	109	212	10015	4261	7	13170
	18,1	40,5	0,8	1,6	76	32,35	0,1	100
2007	2314	5355	152	272	10661	4727	12	13964
	16,6	38	1,1	1,9	76,3	33,85	0,1	100
2008	2354	5862	129	309	11299	4720	10	15074
	15,6	38,9	0,9	2	75	31,31	0,1	100
2009	2192	5810	119	358	11494	4635	4	14719
	14,9	39,5	0,8	2,4	78,1	31,49	0	100
2010	2564	6715	152	393	10791	4243	6	14598
	17,6	46,03	1	2,7	73,9	29,07	0	100

Source: *ELSTAT* 1998-2011: Table G01AK available online.

for violations of drug legislation–which are included in the crime group of Special Criminal Laws–are presented in a separate column. We also see from Table 5 that the rate of drug crimes in relation to the rest of the crimes of each year significantly increases over the years. Between 1980 and 2001 they have more than tripled from 8.11% to 26.63% despite amendments to leniency over the years, moderately increasing afterwards from 26.5%-33.8% between the years

2005-2010. Yet their increase in comparison with the previous year is much higher between 2001 and 2007 and ranges from 10.9% to 49.5%, followed by a slight drop after 2008 (0.1%-8.4%). The development of Violations of Special Criminal Laws and Drug crimes are essentially identical (Table 5). Crimes against life show a similar increasing trend to property crimes (thefts and robberies) but on much lower level.

IV.3. SENTENCES SERVED BY PRISONERS

Concerning the sentence served by the prisoners it would be useful to compare the respective rates in time series. From Table 6 we see that the convicted prisoners serving prison sentences for misdemeanours from one to five years have decreased dramatically over the years (48.1-7.4%), and have increased the rates of prisoners serving sentences over five years (28.9-62%). More impressive is the picture when we include in the first group the proportion of prisoners who were serving sentences from one to 12 months. So the rate of all those serving a prison sentence up to five years in 1980 was 64.6% of the prison population, in 1990, 57.5%, in 2006, 33.9%, in 2011 was 28.3%, and in 2014, 9.7%.

Table 6. Distribution of convicted prisoners (stock) in % according to the length of their sentence (1980-2014)

Year	Prisoners in % according to serving sentence (stock)			
	1-12 months	**1-5 years**	**5-20 years**	**Life**
1980	16.5	48.1	28.9	6.5
1990	10.3	47.2	36.8	5.7
1996	7.7	24.3	51.8	16.2
2003	11	17.6	62	9.5
2006	14.5	19.4	57.1	9
2011	16.8	11.5	62	9.7
2014*	2.3	7.4	80	10.3

Source: *ELSTAT* 1980, 1990, 1996: Table G1; 2006, 2011: Table G06.2 online

* *Ministry of Justice* 2014, unpublished.

The rate of prisoners who serve a life sentence follow a less impressive trend compared with the previous group, but in any case it is growing (Table 6). The absolute numbers of prisoners serving life sentences in Greece are still of the highest in the EU. Although the 2012 data for lifers regarding Greece are not included in the Overview Table 7 of the *CoE* 2012[20], comparing the data of 2014 provided by the Ministry of Justice with those of the rest EU countries in 2012, it seems that Greece has the fourth highest amount of prisoners serving life sentences after the UK, Germany, and Italy, while the rate per 100,000 inhabitants rises to nine persons. However, this does not mean that they will remain in prison for life. They will be probably released earlier than in other European countries, apart from certain cases such as the 17 November members convicted of terrorism.

Statistics on releases each year show that more and more were released early, either because of parole, or work and beneficiary counting of their sentence, or had part of their sentence converted. Consequently, there was a noticeable and steady decline in the proportion of released prisoners who had served their maximum sentence, from 31% in 1980, to 19.8% in 1990, 8.8% in 2000, 3.7% in 2005, and again to 8.3% in 2011 with a fluctuation in the meantime.[21] E-monitoring, as an alternative for early release, started to be implemented in May 2015. Fifty convicted prisoners from five prisons, 50 juvenile prisoners from the main juvenile prison, 100 people on remand and 50 detainees or convicted prisoners from the prison hospital (*PD* 62/2014, Article 7[1])[22] were meant to test the e-monitoring system, yet, until July 2016, after one year, only six prisoners have been willing to be electronically tagged, five remand and one convicted (see more below).

IV.4. ALTERNATIVES TO IMPRISONMENT

Criminal and Prison Laws (alias: Correctional Code/GCC) formally provide five alternatives to imprisonment, while in practice four are used, and two of them are mostly preferred. In detail, the laws foresee a) the suspension of the prison sentence, b) the conversion of prison sentence to fine, c) the segmented serving of imprisonment, which has been previously replaced by fines and the offender cannot afford the payment, during weekends and holidays (GCC, Article 64), d) community service, and e) electronic monitoring. Originally, the third and fourth

20 Marcelo F. Aebi & Natalia Delgrande, *Council of Europe Annual Penal Statistics SPACE I: Survey 2012*, Strasbourg: Council of Europe, 2014, p. 98 (at: http://wp.unil.ch/space/files/2014/05/Council-of-Europe_SPACE-I-2012-E_Final_140507.pdf) (last visited: 31 August 2016).

21 Other reasons for early releases are because of acquittal by the appellate court, merging and conversion of sentences, as well as the rescinding of the court's decision or cessation of the sentence because of serious illness or irreparable damage to the prisoner's health.

22 PD/Presidential Decree (62), *About the operation of e-monitoring for pre-trial detainees, convicted prisoners and prisoners on leave, and its pilot use*. Government's Gazette A105, 29 April 2014*; see also G4S, *Information about the Project. Pilot Implementation of E-Monitoring of Prisoners on Remand, Convicted Prisoners and Prisoners on Leave*, 15 May 2015 (at: www.ministryofjustice.gr/site/Portals/0/uploaded_files/uploaded_11/Enimerosi_gia_to_ergo.pdf) (last visited: 31 August 2016).*

alternatives were foreseen for sentences of up to 18 months, but the segmented serving of imprisonment (c) has not been used at all, while community service (d) is provided for higher sentences of three years following the limits of conversion, and lately of five years (GPC, Article 82[1,5]). In December 2013, 1,523 persons were serving their sentence in the community in common welfare organizations.[23]

Regarding suspension, the Criminal Law foresees either the mandatory or the discretionary suspension of a prison sentence which is not longer than three years (mandatory up to one year- previously up to six months, discretionary up to three years); the court must or can order the suspension of the sentence which cannot be lower than one and longer than three years – until recently it could not be lower than three and longer than five years (GPC, Article 99).

Until the 1990s, conversion of imprisonment to a punitive fine (alias: pecuniary penalty) was possible only for sentences up to 12 months; the limits were further increased to 18, then to 24 months and finally to three years. Thus, with sentences of imprisonment up to three years, a person can either serve the sentence or pay a cash penalty at a daily rate (GPC, Article 82, paragraph 1, 2). Mandatory is the conversion of prison sentence up to 12 months (GPC, Article 82, paragraph 1). Every day of imprisonment or detention is converted to 5-100 euro, depending on the financial situation of the person, while the Ministers of Justice and Finance can decrease or increase the limits on the amount (GPC, Article 82, paragraph 1).

The Criminal as well as the Prison Law foresee conditional release (parole) with and without supervision and several amendments have broadened the opportunities for early release from prison (GPC, Articles 100, paragraph 1, 105, paragraph 1). Conditional release is mandatory, unless the court with a specific reasoning based on the behaviour of the prisoner during custody, regards the continuance of custody absolutely necessary (GPC, Article 106[1]). According to Criminal Law (Article 110, paragraph 2), the Prison Directorate is not required to justify its decision for the early release of a prisoner, though it has to justify its denial of conditional release after the expiry of the required minimum period of custody. In that case a report of the prison social service is required (GPC, Article 110, paragraph 2).[24]

Electronic monitoring was issued by Law 4205 in November 2013 and the Ministry of Justice after a call of tender contracted with G4S in November 2014.

---

23 Marcelo F. Aebi & Julien Chopin, *Council of Europe Annual Penal Statistics SPACE II: Persons serving non-custodial sanctions and measures. Survey 2013*, Strasbourg: Council of Europe, 2014, p. 17: Table 1.1 (at: http://wp.unil.ch/space/files/2011/02/Council-of-Europe_SPACE-II-2013-E_Final_150205.pdf) (last visited: 31 August 2016).

24 See more in Effi Lambropoulou, 'Correctional Policy in Greece: Law in Action', in: Peter J.P. Tak & Manon Jendly (eds), *Prison Policy and Prisoners' Rights*, International Penal and Penitentiary Foundation, Nijmegen: Wolf Legal Publishers, 2008, p. 391-406.

In May 2015, an 18-month pilot program for 250 prisoners was started whereby the lifers are excluded (Law 4356/2015, Article 39).[25] The cost is €15 per day paid by each tagged offender. If he or she cannot pay the amount, the cost is paid by the State (PD 62/2014, Article 2). The charge for 250 persons for the 18 months of the pilot project will be €2,025,000. The unit relays the offender's movements, via satellite, to a control room run by G4S, which has also provided the ankle tags.[26] A three-member committee of high-ranking officers at the Ministry of Justice supervises the program (PD 62/2014, Article 4). E-monitoring is foreseen as a term for conditional release of the convicted (GPC, Article 110B), as a term for detainees who are charged with a felony awaiting their trial (GPPC, Article 282), and as a term for granting furlough to a convicted prisoner with a life sentence or imprisonment of 25 years (GCC, Article 54).

Concerning the first case, the prisoners applying for e-monitoring should have served 2/5 of their sentence or in case of those serving a life sentence, at least 14 years. Juveniles also have the possibility for parole supervision with electronic monitoring devices, if they have served at least 1/3 of their sentence (Law 4205/2013, Article 1). In the previous cases, the prisoners are free to choose the use of e-monitoring or not. In the other two cases –prisoners awaiting trial or those without a final sentence and as a term for granting furlough– e-monitoring is granted either by the court (Law 4205/2013, Article 2B; GPPC, Article 282, paragraph 3) or the prison board respectively, integrated into the eligibility criteria of the prison leave scheme (GCC, Article 55, paragraph 1).

In summary, during the last two decades, there have been several regulations attempted to bring prison overcrowding under control leading to strong criticism by judges and prosecutors. In particular, the recent amendments on early release introduced in April 2015, as well as those issued in August 2016 (Law 4411/2016), were criticized for annulment of the judgments imposed in casu, i.e. in the case provided on the basis of facts and according to law, discrediting the general and special deterrence of punishment, for deconstructing law and sentence enforcement, putting society at risk, and reinforcing the impression of a state operating in discontinuity, self-defeating and not respecting the laws issued by itself, especially in the sensitive field of crime.[27]

---

25 *To Vima*, 'Ready the Electronic Bracelet for Prisoners and Detainees. The Program Starts Today in Cooperation with the Ministry of Justice', 12 May 2015 (at: http://www.tovima.gr/society/article/?aid=703294) (last visited: 31 August 2016).*

26 *Idem; Proto Thema*, 'The Program Has Just Launched. Fee of 375 Euros Monthly to Each Prisoner for Ankle Bracelet', 13 May 2015 (at: www.protothema.gr/greece/article/475479/hreosi-375-euro-miniaios-se-kathe-kratoumeno-gia-to-vrahiolaki/) (last visited: 31 August 2016), 2015b.*

27 *Proto Thema*, 'Prosecutors' Union Against the Bill of Minister of Justice', by Panagiotis Tsimboukis, 1 April 2015 (at: www.protothema.gr/greece/article/464282/kazani-pou-vrazei-i-koinonia-ton-eisaggeleongia-tis-sullivdin-apofulakiseis-kratoumenon-pou-proothei-i-kuvernisi/) (last visited: 31 August 2016), 2015a.*

What is generally needed is a reduction in the length of imposed sentences and the minimum foreseen by law of prison sentences, along with their possibility to be converted to cash penalty, and to early parole so that their successive increase or early release will stop, otherwise punishment and law enforcement will be further discredited. Thus, instead of continuous amendments, decriminalization of certain economic crimes would affect prison overcrowding without degrading justice and putting society at risk; therefore it is advisable to be carried out fairly promptly. Certainly, anti-drug legislation needs a radical reform after a thorough examination of crimes related to drug use and drugs smuggling offering systematically the offenders the alternatives to restitution, community service and eventually e-monitoring. The majority of prisoners convicted for drug crimes serve long sentences and have very high fines to pay as well, making their return to prison inevitable. Consequently, the statutory maximum and minimum (sentences) must be decreased and the parallel imposition of fines abolished.

V. CONCLUSIONS

The Greek criminal law foresees reasonable sentences. The prosecution service and the courts are following the country's judicial tradition showing leniency towards traditional types of crimes and criminals, converting prison sentences into fines, suspending sentences, granting parole and "good time" early release, not only in order to control overcrowding, but also to balance the rising limits of imprisonment. However, it should be noted that they are quite reluctant enforcing new alternatives to prosecution and imprisonment, which can be attributed to their daily routine and its typifications[28], but also to the scepticism of involved parties and distrust towards the alternatives, also consolidating the prosecutors' reluctance.

The EU's directives and conventions regarding new crimes or harder punishment for older crimes have motivated the Greek governments to show strong commitment to fight, for example, international organized crime and terrorism, money laundering, corruption and other economic offences and later on human trafficking, domestic violence, to protect children against sexual exploitation and abuse, racism and xenophobia, since the mid-1990s, by

28 Rüdiger Lautmann, *Justiz-Die stille Gewalt. Teilnehmende Beobachtung und entscheidungssoziologische Analyse*, Frankfurt: Athenaeum, 1972 (new edn. Springer 2011); Graham T. Allison, 'Drei Modelle zur Analyse politischer Prozesse', in: Bernhard Badura (ed.), *Seminar: Angewandte Sozialforschung. Studien über Voraussetzungen und Bedingungen der Produktion, Diffusion und Verwendung sozialwissenschaftlichen Wissens*, Frankfurt: Suhrkamp, 1976, p. 466-502; Tilmann Betsch, 'Wie beeinflussen Routinen das Entscheidungsverhalten? ', 56 *Psychologische Rundschau* 4 (2005), p. 261–270.

introducing advanced and extremely punitive legislation in this respect, as well as to introduce more control bodies. Yet it cannot be ignored that severe sentencing in legislation drags down the sentences of several other crimes. Thus, even though the rates of convictions might not increase, as we saw in section II of the chapter, the prison sentences become longer, the fines higher and cannot be paid-off (section III). This affects the prison population, and in turn, drives governments to again pass laws for increasing the opportunities for early release. The courts work with judges who give longer sentences, so that they cannot be suspended or paid off. It is obvious that we experience a circulus vitiosus manifested also on the regulatory deficit, which has been intensified by the economic situation of the last six years.

A recent example of the presented impasse is that in 2014, when the government passed legislation (Law 4312) to avoid the expense of keeping non-violent offenders in prison while bringing more revenue into the national budget. The law included people convicted of tax evasion, money laundering, submitting declarations with inaccurate sources of wealth, breach of faith or public embezzlement. If the suspect or the convicted returned all the illegally-obtained money before going to court or prior to appeal respectively, he or she would get a mitigated prison sentence. Prosecutors can also offer suspects charged with misdemeanours or felonies carrying a maximum punishment of ten years in prison, the option to pay to stay out of prison. However, due to the present economic crisis, people are in a difficult situation and cannot afford monetary penalties (see also section III).

A year later, a new law (4337/2015) increased prison sentences (minimum two years imprisonment) and fines for the same crimes foreseen by the previous laws (4174/2013 and 2523/1997) regarding tax evasion and debts due to the state, and upgraded law violations after a certain amount of money owed to a serious crime (felony) punishable with minimum five years imprisonment (see also section II).

Coming to an end, there are some practical issues that have to be taken into account for the author to sufficiently justify for which categories of offences a policy of non-custodial sentences or lower prison sentences would be most possible and/or most desirable. These issues are the differential reliability of certain information sources and the inconsequence of detailed statistics.

According to narratives from practitioners and little prison qualitative research[29], the actual time in prison to an unknown number of persons, convicted with sentences of up to 15 years for financial crimes, violations of the

29 Anna Kasapoglou, 'Economic Crisis and Prisoners for Economic and 'White Collar' Crimes. The Effects of Imprisonment on their Social Identity', in: Margarita Gasparinatou (ed.), *Essays in Honor of Prof. Dr. Nestor Courakis*, A.N. Sakkoulas: Athens, Komotini, 2016, p. 2551-2586 (at: www.ant-sakkoulas.gr/periexomena/15-2764-2.pdf) (last visited: 31 August 2016).*

labour welfare legislation, violations of building regulations, embezzlement, contraband, counterfeiting, forgery, unsettled or unsecured public-law debt, breaking customs laws, and (financial) cybercrime[30], is approximately 3-5 years. A part of the above perpetrators of economic crimes are in prison most likely, either due to their inability to pay their fines - to compensate the State or the victim - so imprisonment is the "last resort". Although the increase of the number of convictions that result in imprisonment is not yet reflected in the prison population, taking into account that there is no published data after 2010/2011, the reduction of the statutory term of punishment for such crimes would help the actual serving of sentences and would increase respect for the justice system and the prestige of the state.

After all, we would suggest:

- Specialized branches in ministries to incorporate sufficiently international and EU conventions and directives into customized national laws, and improve the quality of regulatory governance.
- Codification and recasting of regulations in order to eliminate legal ambiguity would be the most necessary step to bring overregulation under control.
- The cooperation of control bodies with the administration should also be improved.
- Decriminalization of certain economic crimes, and promotion of use of plea bargaining in already foreseen cases by law.
- Decrease of the statutory maximum and minimum sentences for economic and drug crimes along with their fines.
- Abolishing either administrative or criminal sanctioning for the same law violations.
- Support of prosecutorial service with assistants.
- Support of Juvenile and Probation service.
- Effective dealing with the practical and legislative problems of mediation, compensation, plea-bargaining and community service in adult as well as in juvenile criminal law, and
- Use of the alternative sentences of community service and e-monitoring more often, especially for non-violent offenders, but not for professional criminals and itinerant criminal groups.

30 *Idem*, p. 2569-2570.

OVERUSING THE CRIMINAL JUSTICE SYSTEM: THE CASE OF IRELAND

Mary ROGAN* & Michael REILLY**

I. INTRODUCTION

This report explores the use of criminalisation, prosecution, and punishment in Ireland. Ireland is currently in an interesting phase of development concerning its penal policy. Over the last five years, Ireland's prison population has fallen, reflecting new strategic priorities for the Government and its criminal justice agencies established in 2011. There has been a move since that time to reduce the use of imprisonment, and has given rise to some efforts at diversion away from the criminal justice system, from the prison system, and through the use of back door strategies to reduce the prison population. There have been fewer developments in the realm of reducing the use of criminalisation itself. Discussions in Ireland, both at the policy and scholarly levels, of the possibilities for legalisation, decriminalisation and policy tolerance are surprisingly limited, although the use of alternatives to prosecution is emerging as a topic of possible reform.

* Associate Professor, School of Law, Trinity College Dublin, Ireland. Corresponding author: mary.rogan@tcd.ie. I am grateful to the following individuals for their very kind assistance in providing information to assist in the writing of this report: Michael Flahive, Assistant Secretary, Department of Justice and Equality, Criminal Law Reform Division, and Kate Mulkerrins, Head of the Prosecution Policy Unit, Office of the Director of Public Prosecutions. I am also most grateful to Aoife Hyde for assistance in preparing the data presented in this chapter.

** At the time of writing, Judge and Inspector of Prisons, Ireland. The views expressed here are not those of the Office of the Inspector of Prisons.

II. OVERUSE OF CRIMINALISATION

The key sources of information for crime rates in Ireland now come from the Central Statistics Office, Ireland's national statistics authority. Until 2006 crime statistics were published by the Irish police force (An Garda Síochána). It should be noted that additional caution, over and above that which should be exercised concerning all official crime statistics, is necessary when examining Irish recorded crime statistics. In 2014, the Central Statistics Office (CSO) suspended publication of crime statistics following a report by the Garda Inspectorate which highlighted concerns about the ways in which crimes and detections were being recorded by members of the police service. Publication was resumed in June 2015, but the CSO continues to recommend caution when examining detection rates in particular.

At the time of writing, more serious concerns have arisen in Ireland about the quality of crime data as supplied to the Central Statistics Office by An Garda Síochána. The effect of this was that the Central Statistics Office suspended publication of Recorded Crime data in March 2017. It was decided to resume publication in 2018. However, it has been decided to publish such data under the category "under reservation", which means, according to the Central Statistics Office that it serves to "indicate to users that the quality of these statistics do not meet the standards required of official statistics published by the CSO".[1]

For this reason, until more certainty about the quality of crime data in Ireland, it has been decided, with regret, not to include this information in the present report.

Ireland does not conduct a national victimisation survey, however, the quarterly national household survey (which asks questions about a wide range of issues) has included questions on one's experiences of being a victim of crime in the previous 12 months (see Figure 1). These questions have not been included in every such survey, but results are available for 1998, 2003, 2006 and 2010. The definitions of crimes used in the survey are not the same as those used in official crime statistics, and the results are therefore not directly comparable to those data.

Ireland is a common law jurisdiction. The vast majority of offences in Irish law are now either created by statute, or consolidated in statute form. Ireland is a member of the European Union and is therefore affected by Union-wide obligations. It is also party to certain international treaties which require certain kinds of conduct to be criminalised. Obligations arising out of membership of the European Union have given rise to a series of pieces of legislation, including the Criminal Justice (Offences relating to Information Systems) Bill, the Criminal

1 Update on the publication of Recorded Crime Statistics, www.cso.ie/en/statistics/crimeandjustice/updateonthepublicationofrecordedcrimestatistics/, last accessed 16 March 2018.

Figure 1. Households classified by whether they were victims of crime (Quarterly National Household Survey, 2008 and 1993)

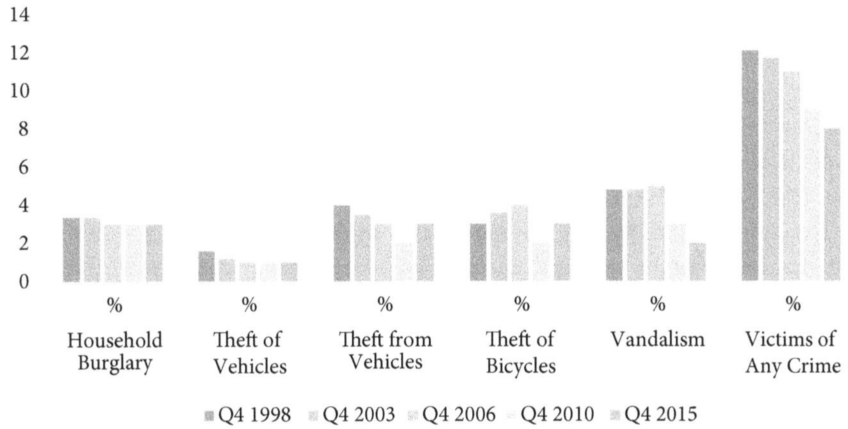

Justice (Corruption) Bill, the Criminal Justice (Counterfeiting) Bill[2], the Criminal Justice (money Laundering & Terrorist Financing) (Amendment) Bill[3], the Cybercrime Bill[4], and the Non-Fatal Offences against the Person Bill. This latter bill is being introduced to ratify aspects of the Istanbul Convention and to modernise the law on domestic, sexual and gender-based violence. The Criminal Justice (Corruption) Bill is also being introduced to meet commitments arising out of membership of the Council of Europe, the Organisation for Economic Cooperation and Development (OECD) and the United Nations, specifically the Council of Europe Criminal Law Convention, the OECD Convention on Combating Bribery of Foreign Public Officials in International Business Transactions and the United Nations Convention against Corruption.

II.1. POSSIBILITIES FOR DECRIMINALISATION, LEGALISATION AND POLICY TOLERANCE

The possibilities for decriminalisation, legalisation and policy tolerance in Ireland tend to revolve around drug offences and prostitution.

There has been some discussion at the official level of the decriminalisation of certain drug offences. In 2015, the Oireachtas (parliament) Joint Committee on

2 This Bill will transpose outstanding elements of Directive 2014/62/EU on the protection of the euro and other currencies against counterfeiting.
3 This is intended to give effect to the fourth EU Money Laundering Directive.
4 This is intended to give effect to provisions of the Council of Europe Convention on Cybercrime 2001 which have not already been provided for in Irish law in order to enable ratification of this Convention.

Justice, Defence and Equality published a report on "a harm reducing and rehabilitative approach to possession of small amounts of illegal drugs".[5] The Committee strongly recommended "the introduction of such an approach, whereby the possession of a small amount of illegal drugs for personal use could be dealt with by way of a civil/administrative response and rather than via the criminal justice route".[6] It was the Committee's view that discretion in the application of this approach should remain with the national police service and health providers concerning how such an individual might be treated. It would therefore be up to the police services to decide whether or not to refer the person for treatment services. The Committee considered that the application of criminal sanctions to certain drug users could be counter-productive, and that the approach should be one which treats people in this position as patients rather than criminals. As part of its research, the Committee analysed the experience in Portugal. It is not clear whether this approach will find favour with the current government, which came into power in 2016.

More movement has been seen in the area of prostitution. The selling of sex, *per se*, is not a criminal offence in Ireland. However, the manifestations of this practice, i.e. loitering with the intention of selling sex, or soliciting sex for financial reward are criminal offences. This position has been criticised for focusing the attention of the criminal law on those selling sex, rather than buying it, but also because it suggests that the only concern of the law is onlookers who might be offended by seeing aspects of the practice.[7]

The present situation in Ireland is, therefore, that exchanging sex for financial reward is not illegal of itself, but the public manifestations of that activity, i.e. solicitation and loitering are.[8] Keeping a brothel is also a crime, as is organising prostitution, coercing or compelling a person to engage in prostitution or to live knowingly on the earnings of prostitution.[9] Legislation was also passed in 2008 concerning human trafficking, which makes it an offence to knowingly solicit or importune a trafficked person for the purposes of prostitution.[10]

A Bill is currently before the Oireachtas (parliament) which proposes to decriminalise loitering with the intention of selling sex, or the solicitation of sex for financial reward. At the time of writing, this Bill had not yet been passed, and

5 Joint Committee on Justice, Defence and Equality, *A harm reducing and rehabilitiative approach to possession of small amounts of illegal drugs* (2015), available at www.drugsandalcohol.ie/24750/1/Committereport.pdf (last accessed August 8 2016).

6 *Ibid.*, at p.10.

7 For a discussion of these arguments, see S Fitzgerad and K McGarry, "Problematizing Prostitution in Law and Policy in the Republic of Ireland" (2016) 3 *Social and Legal Studies* 289-309.

8 Criminal Law (Sexual Offences) Act 1993, sections 6, 7, and 8.

9 Sections 9, 10, 11 of the Criminal Law (Sexual Offences) Act 1993. See further: www.oireachtas.ie/parliament/media/committees/justice/1.Part-1-final.pdf.

10 Criminal Law (Human Trafficking) Act 2008.

is currently in its second stage before the Dáil (the lower house of parliament). Part 3 of this Bill will now criminalise the purchasing of sexual services. The relevant section reads: "a person who pays, gives, offers or promises to pay or give a person (including a prostitute) money or any form of remuneration or consideration for the purpose of engaging in sexual activity with a prostitute shall be guilty of an offence".[11] A person convicted of such an offence will be dealt with by the District Court and will be subject to a 'class E' fine on the first offence, and a 'class D' fine in the case of a second or subsequent offence. The legislation ensures that the person who is providing the sexual service is not subject to an offence. The proposed Bill amends the Criminal Justice Act 1993 by removing the following section from the definition of "solicits" or "importunes": "offers his or her services as a prostitute to another person".[12] At the time of writing, this Bill had yet to pass the Dáil (the lower house of Parliament) but has passed the Seanad (upper house).

This Bill was prompted, at least in part, by the Joint Oireachtas (parliament) committee on Justice, Defence and Equality, which received submissions on the current law and proposals for reform, and travelled to Sweden to examine changes to the law there. The Committee recommended the creation of a summary offence for the purchase of sexual services of another person by means of prostitution, or any request, agreement or attempt to do so, and that the law be clarified so that no offence would be committed by the person who is selling his or her sexual services.[13] It should be noted, however, that there were differences of opinion expressed in the submissions to the joint Oireachtas committee as to the appropriate model to introduce, with some groups opposing the introduction of the Swedish model in Ireland.

Another planned piece of legislation on the topic of decriminalisation concerns blasphemy, currently an offence contained in Bunreacht na hÉireann, the Constitution of Ireland. Article 6.1.1 of the Constitution contains a prohibition on the publication or utterance of blasphemous matter, and makes such publication or utterance an offence punishable by law. Under section 36 of the Defamation Act 2009 provides for the crime of blasphemy and makes a person liable on conviction on indictment for this offence to a fine of up to €25,000.[14] The latest Programme for Government, which contains the priorities for the new Irish government, elected in 2016, contains a commitment to holding

11 Section 20 of the Bill, proposing to insert section 7A into the Criminal Justice (Sexual Offences) Act 1993.

12 Section 1(2)(a) of the Criminal Justice (Sexual Offences) Act 1993. Section 24 of the Criminal Law (Sexual Offences) Bill 2015 removes this definition from the Act of 1993.

13 Joint Oireachtas Committee on Justice, Equality and Defence, *Report on hearings and submissions on the review of prostitution legislation* (2012). Available at: https://www.oireachtas.ie/parliament/media/committees/justice/1.Part-1-final.pdf (last accessed August 8 2016).

14 Section 36(1) Defamation Act 2009.

a referendum to remove the offence of blasphemy from the Constitution.[15] At the time of writing, preliminary work had commenced on the Bill to be put forward in this referendum.[16]

III. OVERUSE OF PROSECUTION

There has been a recent increase in focus on the possible use of alternatives to prosecution in Ireland, and it is likely that it is in this area that we will see most movement in reducing the overuse of the criminal justice system in Ireland in the near future.

Figures relating to the prosecution of crimes in Ireland are described below (see Figures 2 and 3). Figures do not pre-date 2003.

Figure 2. Number of files received by the Director of Public Prosecutions

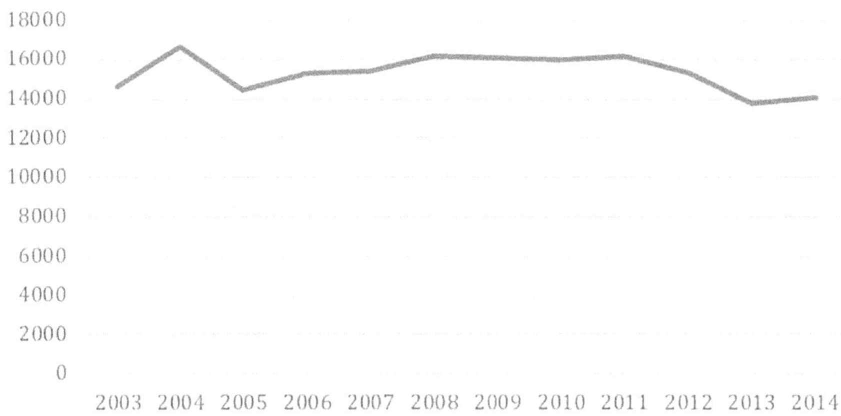

Prosecutions in Ireland can be taken under three main mechanisms: private prosecutions; prosecutions managed by An Garda Síochána (the police force); and those managed by the Director of Public Prosecutions. Private prosecutions are very rare in Ireland, and can only be processed by the District Court. If prosecution before a higher court is required, the Director of Public Prosecutions must take over the proceedings, if she so wishes.

The office of the Director of Public Prosecutions (DPP, or 'the Director') was established in Ireland by the Prosecution of Offences Act, 1974. This provides for

15 A referendum is needed for any change to the Constitution of Ireland.

16 The content of the proposed amendment can be found at: www.merrionstreet.ie/MerrionStreet/en/ImageLibrary/20160607LegislationProgramme.pdf (last accessed 8 August 2016).

Figure 3. Outcomes of referrals to the Director of Public Prosecutions 2012-2014

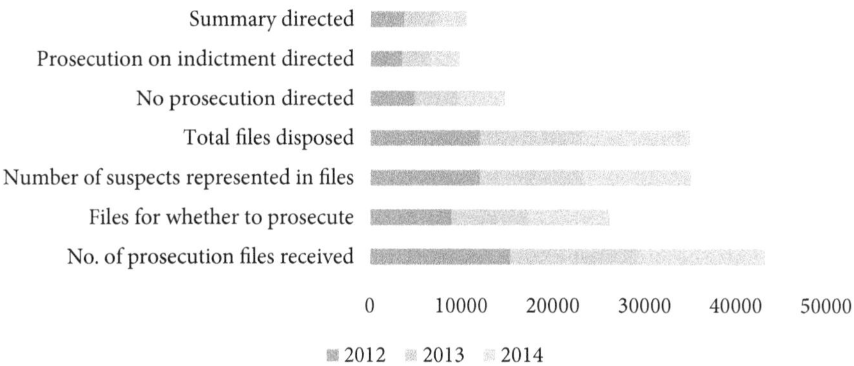

the statutory independence of the Director.[17] The prosecution system in Ireland is governed by a combination of the Constitution of Ireland, 1937, the 1974 Act and common law principles. The DPP has no investigate function, its powers are purely of prosecution.

An important distinction in Irish law is between offences tried on indictment, or indictable offences, and offences tried summarily or summary offences. Summary offences are dealt with in the District Court, and attract penalties of no more than one year in prison. Indictable offences are tried in the Circuit Court, the Special Criminal Court, and the Central Criminal Court and attract higher penalties. Indictable offences are tried before a judge and jury, while summary offences are dealt with by a judge sitting alone. A further category of offences are known as hybrid offences or triable-either-way offences, which can be dealt with in either court, when certain conditions are fulfilled.[18]

The DPP has the power under the 1974 Act to prosecute offences both on indictment and summarily. Under Article 30.3 of the Constitution of Ireland (Bunreacht na hÉireann) all indictable offences must be prosecuted in the name of the Attorney General, with some limited exceptions. Summary offences are prosecuted by An Garda Síochána, under the supervision of the Director of Public Prosecutions. The DPP gives specific directions in such cases when requested. In practice, most summary cases are presented by members of An Garda Síochána, who run the entire prosecution. It is the role of the Director to decide whether to charge a person with criminal offences, and what the charges should be.

17 Section 2(3), Prosecution of Offences Act 1974.

18 See further T O'Malley, *The Criminal Process* (Dublin, Round Hall – Thomson Reuters, 2009).

The prosecution of offences in Ireland is governed by principles established by the Director of Public Prosecutions. The *Guidelines for Prosecutors*[19] makes it clear that "a prosecution should be initiated or continued, subject to the available evidence disclosing a *prima facie* case, if it is in the public interest, and not otherwise".[20] These Guidelines further state "it will generally be in the public interest to prosecute a crime where there is sufficient evidence to do so, unless there is some countervailing public interest reason not to prosecute".[21] A *prima facie* case means that there is admissible, substantial and reliable evidence that a criminal offence known to the law has been committed by the suspect. The evidence must be such that a jury, properly instructed on the relevant law, could conclude beyond a reasonable doubt that the accused was guilty of the offence charged".[22] A bare *prima facie* case is not enough. If there is no reasonable prospect of securing a conviction before a reasonable jury or judge, no prosecution should be taken. This involves an assessment of the reliability and credibility of witnesses, the strength of other evidence, and the presence of aggravating or mitigating factors. Prosecutions may be initiated when there is a reasonable prospect of conviction, and where it is in the public interest to prosecute. There must therefore be an assessment of the evidence and other factors before a prosecution may be initiated by the Director of Public Prosecutions.

Until relatively recently, the policy of the Director of Public Prosecutions, which was upheld in several decisions of the Irish courts[23], was not to give reasons for decisions concerning prosecution. Since 2008, the Director of Public Prosecutions has provided reasons in cases where a death has occurred including situations of murder, manslaughter, infanticide, fatalities in the workplace and fatal road traffic accidents. Reasons will be given on request to members of the deceased's family or household, their legal or medical advisers or social workers acting on their behalf, and only if reasons can be given without creating an injustice, e.g. exposing witnesses to injustice by taking their good name or revealing confidential sources.[24] Victims of other crimes can ask the DPP for a summary of the reasons not to prosecute in the case of decisions made since

19 Office of the Director of Public Prosecutions, *Guidelines for Prosecutors* (2010), available at: https://www.dppireland.ie/filestore/documents/GUIDELINES_-_Revised_NOV_2010_eng.pdf (last accessed 8 August 2016).

20 *Ibid.*, at para 4.4.

21 *Ibid.*, at para 4.6.

22 *Ibid.*, at para 4.10.

23 *Monaghan v DPP*, unreported, High Court, Charleton J, March 14 2007; *Dunphy (a minor) v DPP* [2005] IR 585; *Eviston v DPP* [2002] 3 IR 260.

24 Office of the Director of Public Prosecutions, *Policy on the Giving of Reasons for Decisions not to Prosecute* (2008), available at https://www.dppireland.ie/filestore/documents/POLICY_STATEMENT_-_ENG.pdf (last accessed 8 August 2016).

November 2015. If the decision not to prosecute is made by An Garda Síochána, reasons can also be sought from that agency.

III.1. OPPORTUNITIES FOR DIVERSION

At present, there are some structures for diverting individuals from the criminal justice system or to proceedings which can give rise to lower penalties in Ireland. The Director of Public Prosecutions may, for example, give a direction that she will consent to the summary disposal of certain offences automatically, i.e. that the offence can be dealt with by the District Court, which can impose a maximum prison sentence of one year, or two years in the case of multiple offences, and/or a fine of up to €5,000. When an offence is prosecuted on indictment, the possible sanctions are more severe.

An important policy direction from the DPP concerns offences which the DPP has given a blanket consent to summary disposal. This mechanism, therefore, acts to divert such offences from the possibility of more severe sentences. These offences include theft where the property appropriated does not exceed €7,000 in value, burglary where any property taken does not exceed €7,000 in value, handling stolen property where the property does not exceed €7,000 in value. The DPP also elects for summary disposal for offences including those under section 15 of the Misuse of Drugs Act, 1997 for possession of drugs with the intention of selling them or supplying them, where the view of An Garda Síochána is that the value of the drugs does not exceed €1,500 in the case of cannabis or cannabis resin, € 500 in the case of diamorphine, LSD or cocaine, or €1,000 for other drugs. This policy also applies to simple possession of controlled drugs and offences of criminal damage where the property involved does not exceed €7,000 in value. In these cases, the police officer should consider whether the previous record of the person or the multiplicity of offences mean that summary prosecution would be inadequate.[25]

III.2. FIXED CHARGE NOTICES

A particular mechanism for processing road traffic offences outside of the court structures in Ireland is the fixed charged notice scheme. There are currently 550 traffic offences which are the subject of fixed charged notices. Certain offences, including failing to display an insurance disc, driving in a bus lane, or driving a motorcycle without a helmet, allows a person to pay a fixed charge of a fine as an

25 These offences are detailed in General Direction No. 3 from the Director of Public Prosecutions, issued under section 8 of the Garda Síochána Act 2005, available at https://www.dppireland.ie/filestore/documents/General_Direction_No._3.pdf (last accessed 8 August 2016).

alternative to being prosecuted in court.[26] Some public order offences are also subject to this scheme[27], as well as offences under the Intoxicating Liquor Act 2008. Any member of the Garda Síochána or a traffic warden has the authority to issue a fixed charged penalty notice.

The scheme was established under the Road Traffic Act 2002. It enables the police service (An Garda Síochána) to conduct computerised, automated processing of offences provided for under the scheme. A key objective is to reduce the number of cases in the court system. A fixed charge offence may be detected in one of two ways: an intercept or a non-intercept. An intercept occurs when a garda or traffic warden stops an offender at the time of offence. The police officer or traffic warden has the discretion to issue a fixed charge notice or not. A non-intercept is captured either by a safety camera or a speed camera in a garda van. 514,959 fixed charge notices were issued in 2011, 449,403 in 2012 and 393,588 in 2013.[28] Figures on the operation of the system are difficult to come by and there has been no academic analysis of its use.

The highest volume road traffic offences dealt with under the scheme are offences relating to speed, having no tax or no insurance disc, not wearing a seat belt, using a mobile phone while driving and public order offences.[29] Concerns have been expressed about the processes used in cancelling fixed charge penalty notices as well as the efficient management and oversight of the system.[30]

III.3. ADULT CAUTION SCHEME

Since February 1st 2006, an adult cautioning scheme has been in place in Ireland. This scheme was introduced following a report into the prosecution system, known as the 'Nally Report' which recommended the extension of the use of on-the-spot fines and cautioning.[31] This scheme applies to certain offences committed by persons aged 18 years and upwards. It applies where there is evidence of the commission of a criminal offence covered by the scheme, but where the prosecution of the offence is not required in the public interest. A member of the Garda Síochána may decide to administer an adult caution if the offence is of a kind appropriate for a caution, and the alleged offender is deemed

26 These offences are contained primarily in the Road Traffic Acts 1961 to 2014.

27 Criminal Justice (Public Order) Act 1994.

28 Garda Inspectorate, *The Fixed Charge Processing System – A 21st Century Strategy* (Garda Inspectorate, 2014), at p. 30.

29 Garda Inspectorate, *The Fixed Charge Processing System – A 21st Century Strategy* (Garda Inspectorate, 2014).

30 *Ibid.*

31 The Public Prosecution System Study Group, *Report* (chaired by Dermot Nally), available at: https://www.dppireland.ie/filestore/documents/Report_of_the_Public_Prosecution_System_Study_Group.pdf (last accessed 8 August 2016). Judge Michael Reilly was a member of this group.

suitable for consideration. Typically this applies to people without previous convictions, but those with a past criminal record are not automatically excluded from the scheme.

The offences to which the adult caution scheme applies include[32]: intoxication in a public place[33], disorderly conduct in a public place[34], theft of property up to an amount of €1,000, damaging property of up to €1,000 in value[35], and being on a licensed premises during prohibited hours.[36]

For the scheme to apply, there must be *prima facie* evidence of the offender's guilt, the offender must admit the offence, must understand the significance of a caution and give informed consent to being cautioned. Before the offence and the offender are to be considered for a caution, the views of any victims must be sought, if that is reasonably possible. It is not possible for the victim to prevent the administration of a caution, but the victim's views must be taken into account. The scheme is clearly intended to be applied only once too an individual, but there is no formal bar to it being applied to a person who has previously received an adult caution, once the DPP consents.

Adult cautions may only be administered by higher ranking officers, i.e. a Superintendent in charge of a district, known as a District Officer, or an Inspector acting for a District Officer. Other than in exceptional circumstances, it should take place in a police station.

The adult caution is recorded and made known to a court if the person is convicted of a subsequent criminal offence. It is not disclosed to employers or others through requests for vetting.

There has been very limited investigation of the operation of the adult caution scheme in Ireland. A rare example of research into this field was conducted by Tolan and Seymour.[37] This study found that the majority of those in receipt of an adult caution were aged between 18 and 32 years. Analysis for 2010 showed that 43% were between 18 and 22 years and a further 29% were between 23 and 32 years. 73% of those receiving adult cautions between 2006 and 2010 were male. In keeping with the generally poor nature of data collected on the Irish criminal justice system[38] particularly in the case of nationality and ethnic background, this information was not made available to the researchers.

---

32 When initiated, the scheme applied to 14 offences, but this was increased to 20 offences in 2009.

33 Section 4 of the Criminal Justice (Public Order) Act 1994.

34 Section 5 of the Criminal Justice (Public Order) Act 1994.

35 Section 2 of the Criminal Damage Act 1991.

36 Section 17, Intoxicating Liquor Act 1927.

37 Graham Tolan and Mairéad Seymour, "Increasing the potential for diversion in the Irish criminal justice system: the role of the Garda Síochána adult cautioning scheme" (2014) 14(1) *Irish Journal of Applied Social Studies* 60-71.

38 Mary Rogan, "Improving Criminal Justice Data and Policy" (2012) 43(2) *Economic and Social Review* 303–344.

The use of the adult caution scheme has increased considerably since it commenced, with 3,865 incidents being dealt with through it in 2006 and 9,308 in 2010. While the use of the scheme is increasing, in relative terms it remains very much a marginal area of police activity. As Tolan and Seymour have shown, on average, 5.8% of eligible offences are dealt with by way of adult caution each year. The study also found wide geographical variation in the use of the scheme. It was found to be most widely used in the western part of the country, which is more rural, and used less frequently in Dublin, the capital (9.4% and 7% of all eligible offences and respectively).

Of the types of offences most commonly dealt with under the scheme, by far the most common were public order offences (44%) and theft (32%). In the view of Tolan and Seymour there is "considerable scope to increase the use of cautioning for the offences currently included in the scheme".[39]

Data are not published by governmental agencies on the levels of reoffending amongst those who have received adult cautions. Tolan and Seymour conducted such analysis, using the category of "suspected offender" when measuring reoffending. The authors acknowledge this is not the same as reconviction, but is the best measure available. A follow up analysis of those cautioned between 2006 and 2009 identifies that one third came to the attention of the police in this way in the twelve months after committing the offence for which they were cautioned.

Tolan and Seymour conclude that more serious offences could be included in the adult caution scheme and suggest that it should also be used more often in circumstances where a person has a previous conviction. They caution against adding conditions concerning the completion of rehabilitative programmes as part of a cautioning scheme, and suggest that such schemes should be grounded in a policy and practice framework based on the principle of proportionality and only where rehabilitative conditions are appropriate.

Diversion schemes also exist for children. A person under 18 years of age who accepts his or her guilt can be cautioned and subject to supervision by An Garda Síochána's Youth Diversion Office as an alternative to prosecution. As part of the caution, the child may agree to make an apology to the victim, provide compensation, comply with a curfew or take part in some kind of sporting or recreational activity.[40] Another effort to divert children from the criminal justice system was found in the raising of the age of criminal responsibility from 7 to 12 in most cases, and 10 when the offence charged is one of murder, manslaughter or rape.[41]

39 Graham Tolan and Mairéad Seymour, "Increasing the potential for diversion in the Irish criminal justice system: the role of the Garda Síochána adult cautioning scheme" (2014) 14(1) *Irish Journal of Applied Social Studies* 60-71, at p. 66.

40 Part 4 Children Act 2001.

41 Children Act 2001.

III.4. INCREASED FOCUS ON ALTERNATIVES TO PROSECUTION

In 2014, the Minister for Justice and Equality published the report of the Penal Policy Review Group. This group comprised, *inter alia*, the Director General of the Irish Prison Service, the Director of the Probation Service, a High Court judge, senior officials in the Department of Justice and Equality and NGOs working in the areas of victims' rights and penal reform.[42] This group was charged with conducting a comprehensive and strategic overview of penal policy in Ireland. One of its recommendations concerned the increased use of alternatives to prosecution. It recommended that relevant agencies, including the Director of Public Prosecutions and An Garda Síochána review the offences covered by the adult caution scheme with a view to including a wider range of offences.[43] The Review Group also recommended that a programme similar to the Youth Diversion Programme be introduced for young people above the age of 18 with an initial focus on 18-21 year olds. This is currently under consideration by the Irish Youth Justice Service.[44] At the time of writing, no legislative or policy changes have yet been introduced, but the alternatives to prosecution project is continuing its work.[45]

The Law Reform Commission, a body established by statute to keep Irish law under review and to suggest changes, has also explored the possibility of introducing "deferred prosecution agreements" (DPAs) into Irish law. These would apply in the case of financial and corporate crime, and are inspired by developments in the United States. Such an agreement would involve the suspension of a criminal prosecution and an agreement by the corporate body to enter a supervised compliance programme and pay a financial penalty. If the conditions of the agreement are complied with, no prosecution will ensue.[46]

A form of deferred prosecution already exists in the area of competition law. The "Cartel Immunity Programme" seeks to address coordinated anti-competitive behaviour. Individuals or undertakings involved in such activity can apply to the CCPC for immunity from prosecution for certain cartel offences. The Director of Public Prosecutions may grant immunity from prosecution if the

42 Penal Policy Review Group, *Report of the Penal Policy Review Group* (2014). Mary Rogan was a member of this group from February 2014.
43 Recommendation 5, Penal Policy Review Group, *Report of the Penal Policy Review Group* (2014).
44 Recommendation 7, Penal Policy Review Group, *Report of the Penal Policy Review Group* (2014).
45 Personal communication.
46 Law Reform Commission, *Regulatory Enforcement and Corporate Offences: Issues Paper*, (2016), available at: www.lawreform.ie/_fileupload/Issues%20Papers/Issues%20Paper%20on%20Regulatory%20Enforcement%20and%20Corporate%20Offences%20final.pdf (last accessed 8 August 2016).

applicant is the first to apply, and if it gives full cooperation in the investigation of the cartel activities.[47]

IV. OVERUSE OF IMPRISONMENT

Academics and non-governmental organisations have argued that Ireland overuses imprisonment and has a particularly unnecessary reliance on short-term prison sentences.[48] The prison rate in Ireland is at the upper end of the middle range of European countries, being currently around 83.1 per 100,000.[49] See Figure 4. The prison population in Ireland increased dramatically during the 2000s, and particularly between 2005 and 2010. Subsequently, the prison population has recorded falls. The reasons for this are not entirely clear, but the fall follows statements from the Penal Policy Review Group that the prison population should be brought down.[50]

Figure 4. Committals to prison 2010-2015

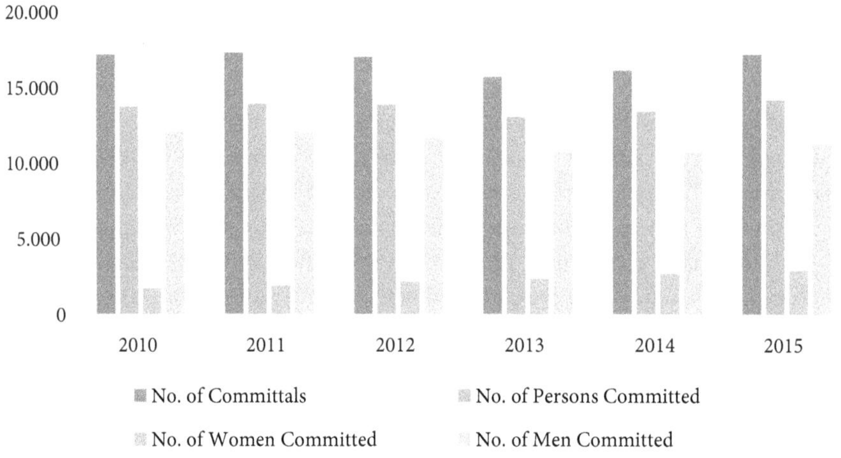

47 Office of the Director of Public Prosecutions, *Cartel Immunity Programme* (2015), available at: https://www.dppireland.ie/filestore/documents/Cartel_Immunity_Programme_[updated_20_Jan_2015].pdf (last accessed 8 August 2016).

48 See, for example, Tom O'Malley, "Time Served: the impact of sentencing and parole decisions on the prison population" (2010) *Paper presented to the Irish Penal Reform Trust, June 28 2010*; Irish Penal Reform Trust, *Community Sanctions* (Irish Penal Reform Trust, 2010); Ian O'Donnell, "Imprisonment and Penal Policy in Ireland" (2004) 43(3) *Howard Journal of Criminal Justice* 253-266.

49 Marcelo Aebi, Mélanie Tiago and Christine Burkhardt, *SPACE I – Council of Europe Annual Penal Statistics: Prison populations survey 2014* (Council of Europe, Strasbourg, 2016).

50 Recommendation 8, Penal Policy Review Group, *Report* (2014).

The Irish prison system is characterised by a high number of committals for short sentences (under six months' imprisonment) (see Figures 5 and 6). The majority of committals are for non-violent offences. The top five offence groups in sentenced committals are: road and traffic offences; offences against the government, justice procedures and organised crime (which includes non-compliance with a direction of a police officer); public order and social code offences; and theft and related offences.

Figure 5. Committals under sentence by sentence length 2010-2015

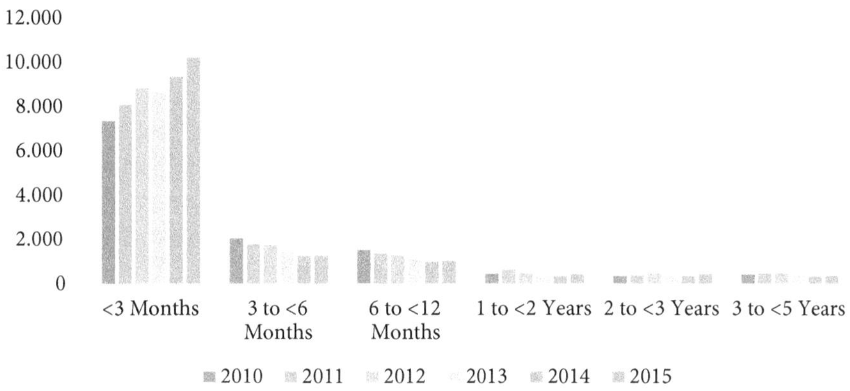

Figure 6. Sentenced committals by sentence length 2010-2015

It is difficult to assess whether judges in Ireland are using imprisonment unnecessarily, or underusing alternatives to custody. This is because empirical research into Irish sentencing practice remains limited, though is growing. That research is presented in this section. Ireland has not enshrined a statement of principle that imprisonment should be a measure of last resort within its legislation for adult offenders, though such a position is in legislation concerning children.[51]

IV.1. PRISON AND DEFAULTING ON A FINE

Perhaps the most high profile example of a clear overuse of imprisonment in Ireland concerns imprisonment for defaulting on a fine imposed by a court. Prior to the commencement of the Fines Act 2014, a person who failed or refused to pay a court-ordered fine, for whatever reason, was liable to be committed to prison. Such committals made up the vast majority of all committals to prison for several years. In 2014, over 55% of all committals were for defaulting on a fine.[52] In 2015, 9,883 committals were for non-payment of a court-ordered fine, which represented an increase of 10% from the previous year.

These high levels of committals, and, indeed the fact that people could be committed to prison for defaulting on fines at all, have been subject to a great deal of criticism.[53] The Fines Act 2010 was introduced to make it more difficult to send a person to prison for failing to pay a fine. The relevant provisions were never commenced and another piece of legislation, the Fines (Payment and Recovery) Act 2014 was then passed. This latter piece of legislation was commenced only in 2016.[54] This legislation permits the payment of court-ordered fines by instalment, and ensures that imprisonment will be a sanction of last resort. Other sanctions, including recovery orders and community service, must be attempted first.

IV.2. ALTERNATIVES TO PRISON

Several alternatives to imprisonment exist in Irish law and practice. The Probation Act 1907 provides for the possibility for a person to avoid conviction, even when the facts are proven.[55] A judge may also impose a probation order, which is supervised by members of the Probation Service. Community service orders were introduced in Ireland by the Criminal Justice (Community Service) Act 1983. This legislation was amended in 2011.[56] Judges are now required to consider community service when they would otherwise consider a sentence of up to twelve months' imprisonment. This amendment was introduced with the

51 Children Act 2001.
52 Irish Prison Service, *Annual Report 2014* (Irish Prison Service, 2014).
53 See, for example, Irish Penal Reform Trust, "IPRT welcomes commencement of fines legislation" (press release) (Irish Penal Reform Trust, 2016).
54 Fines (Payment and Recovery) Act 2014 (Commencement Order), S.I. No. 6/2016.
55 Section 1(1)(ii) Probation Act 1907.
56 Criminal Justice (Community Service) (Amendment) Act 2011.

explicit goal of increasing the numbers of people diverted from custody into a non-custodial alternative.[57]

When community service is imposed, a prison sentence is attached, which will activate if the conditions for community service are broken. The maximum number of hours which may be imposed is 240, and the order must be completed within one year. Those completing community service engage in work beneficial to the community, such as removing graffiti, painting, and maintaining public spaces. Under the legislation, the Probation Service must assess the individual as being suitable for community service work, and must confirm to the judge that suitable work is available. The individual must also agree to the imposition of a community service order.

O'Hara and Rogan have found evidence that judges attach a larger alternative prison sentence to a community service order than would otherwise be imposed if imprisonment was imposed directly.[58] This suggests judges do not have full confidence in the effectiveness or credibility of community service orders. O'Hara and Rogan have also found of variation based on geography in the imposition of community service or short term prison sentences, and that in the case of individuals sentenced for drug offences, there was some evidence of up-tariffing.[59]

A further alternative to custody in Ireland is the suspended sentence. This involves a judge imposing a prison sentence, but that sentence will not take effect if certain conditions are abided by. These conditions might include keeping the peace, or attending a particular treatment programme. If those conditions are broken, the sentence of imprisonment may be activated. In 2016, the High Court found that aspects of then applicable legislation governing suspended sentences was unconstitutional.[60] Legislation is to be introduced to provide a new basis for the suspended sentence.

The courts also have the power of 'binding over'. This longstanding power involves the court requiring the person to keep the peace and be of good behaviour. The individual enters a recognisance or guarantee agreeing to comply with these conditions. A financial guarantee is required and if the conditions are not kept, the money may be forfeited and a sentence of imprisonment imposed. Judges may also make use of the 'Court Poor Box'. An individual may agree to

57 Department of Justice and Equality, "Commencement of Criminal Justice (Community Service) (Amendment) Act 2011" (press release), available at: www.justice.ie/en/JELR/Pages/PR11000185 (last accessed 8 August 2016).

58 Kate O'Hara and Mary Rogan "Examining the use of community service orders as alternatives to short prison sentences in Ireland" (2015) 12 *Irish Probation Journal* 22-46.

59 *Ibid.*

60 *Moore and others v Director of Public Prosecutions, Ireland and the Attorney General* [2016] IEHC 244.

Figure 7. Total number of offenders dealt with in the community during each year 2011–2015

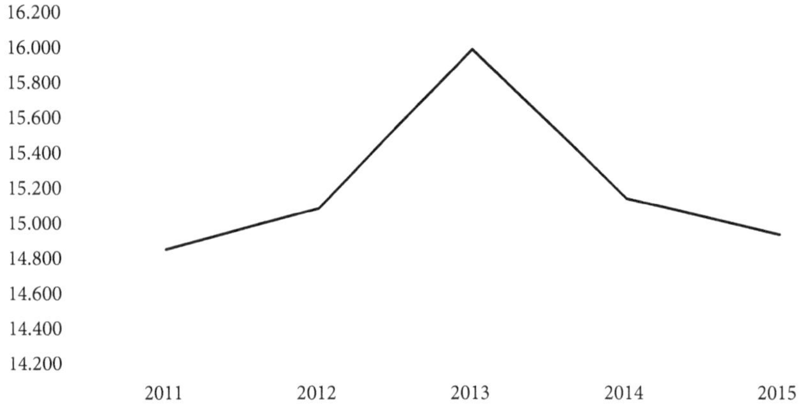

pay a sum of money into this poor box, usually to avoid a conviction.[61] There is no statutory basis for this scheme, but it is well established practice.

Compensation is also provided for under Irish law.[62] It may be imposed instead of another form of sanction, or in addition to another kind of sanction.

For adults, restorative justice is a possibility. Restorative justice programmes are limited to particular geographical locations at the time of writing.

As noted above, data on the Irish criminal justice system are limited. Though data collection and quality is showing some signs of improvement, the nature of the data collected at present means it is not possible to assess whether or not imprisonment is in fact being used when alternatives could otherwise be. It is true to say that there is additional capacity within alternatives and that they could be used more often than is currently the case.[63] It is also the case that the numbers of community service orders has actually decreased since the introduction of legislation designed to give rise to increased use of such sanctions.[64] However, it is contestable as to whether this represents an increasing use of imprisonment, or whether there has been a decrease in the use of all sanctions. See Figures 7 and 8.

---

61 See further, Law Reform Commission, *Report on the Court Poor Box: Probation of Offenders* (Law Reform Commission, 2005).

62 Section 6, Criminal Justice Act 1993.

63 Personal communication.

64 From 2,738 in 2011 to 2,569 in 2012 to 1,935 in 2015, *Annual Reports* (Probation Service).

Figure 8. Number of probation orders and community service orders for each year 2005–2015

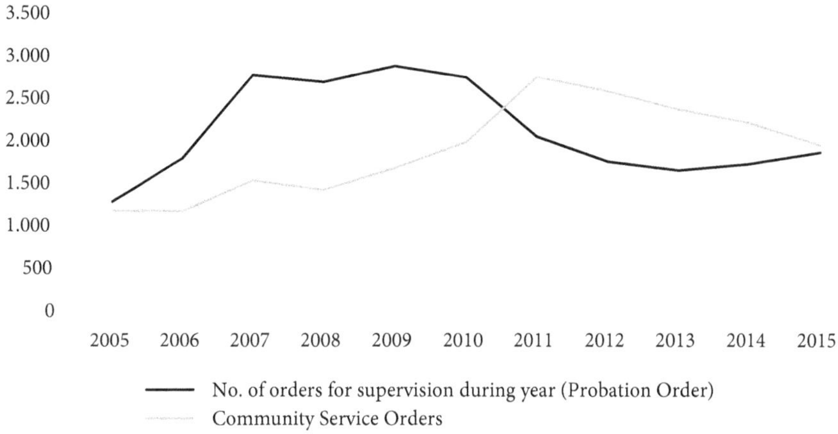

IV.3. MANDATORY SENTENCING

Mandatory sentencing is a feature of Irish law. The mandatory penalty for murder is life imprisonment, though release is possible from such a sentence. In the late 1990s there was a political push towards more use of mandatory sentencing, which resulted in the introduction of a presumptive minimum sentence of ten years for the possession of drugs with a value of €13,000 or more with the intention of selling or supplying those drugs.[65] This controversial sentence has not, however, been adopted by the judiciary entirely as the legislature planned. Under the legislation, the presumptive minimum sentence may be departed from where there are extraordinary excusatory circumstances. In practice, this has been held to include a guilty plea, and the circumstances in which the presumptive minimum sentence have been applied have been more limited than might have been expected.[66] There has also been commentary to the effect that this sentence has had the effect of recalibrating sentencing more generally, and giving rise to an uplift in the sentencing for other offences.[67] This has not been

65 Section 15A Misuse of Drugs Act 1977.

66 Patrick McEvoy, *Research for the Department of Justice on the criteria applied by the Courts in sentencing under s. 15A of the Misuse of Drugs Act 1977 (as amended)* (2005), available at: http://www.inis.gov.ie/en/JELR/Research.pdf/Files/Research.pdf (last accessed August 8 2016). Further analysis of sentencing under section 15A can be found in: Kelley Mackey, Analysis of Sentencing for Possession and Importation of Drugs for Sale or Supply (Dublin, Judicial Researchers' Office, 2013), available at: www.irishsentencing.ie/en/ISIS/Analysis%20of%20Sentencing%20for%20Drug%20Offences,%20Mar%202014.pdf/Files/Analysis%20of%20Sentencing%20for%20Drug%20Offences,%20Mar%202014.pdf (last accessed 8 August 2016).

67 Irish Penal Reform Trust, *Mandatory Sentencing* (Irish Penal Reform Trust, 2013),

tested empirically to date, however. Mandatory sentencing has also been introduced for some firearms offences.[68] Both the Law Reform Commission and the Penal Policy Review Group have recommended that no further mandatory sentences be introduced into Irish law.[69]

Ireland does not have mandatory sentencing guidelines. The Penal Policy Review Group examined the possibility of introducing such guidelines in legislation and declined to recommend it, preferring, instead, that the lead role in developing sentencing guidelines be taken by the judiciary at present. There is evidence that the Court of Appeal, the second most senior court in Ireland, is seeking to develop more guidance in sentencing through the development of precedent.[70] The independence of the judiciary and the extensive discretion held by sentencers in Ireland has been viewed as a mechanism of resistance to punitivism in the Irish criminal justice system.[71]

IV.4. WOMEN IN THE IRISH CRIMINAL JUSTICE SYSTEM

The number of women being sent to prison has been steadily increasing in Ireland in the past decade or so. The driving force behind this change is unclear, and whether it is a result of more criminal activity by women, more prosecutions of women or more women being sentenced to prison than was previously the case is not known. The number of women sentenced to a community service order has fallen between 2011 and 2015.[72] The Irish Prison Service and Probation Service have launched a joint strategy aimed at addressing offending by women in particular. This strategy seeks to develop an approach to offending by women which emphasises alternatives to custody and gender-sensitive non-custodial alternatives. The Penal Policy Review Group has also advocated an approach for female offenders which is non-custodial in focus. It is of note that this group considered that Ireland needs to break with the notion that prison is the only real form of punishment for all those sentenced by the courts.[73]

---

68 Section 15 Firearms Act 1925, as inserted by s.42 Criminal Justice Act 2006.

69 Law Reform Commission, *Report: Mandatory Sentences* (Dublin, Law Reform Commission, 2013). Recommendation 34, Penal Policy Review Group, *Penal Policy Review Group Report* (2014).

70 *DPP v Ryan* [2014] IECCA 24; *DPP v Z* [2014] 1 IR 613 ; *DPP v Fitzgibbon* [2014] 1 IR 627.

71 Shane Kilcommins et al., *Crime, Punishment and the Search for Order in Ireland* (Dublin, Institute of Public Administration, 2004).

72 *Annual Reports,* Probation Service.

73 Recommendation 32.

V. BACK DOOR STRATEGIES IN IRELAND

There are no irreducible sentences in Irish law. Individuals can be sentenced to life imprisonment, and may spend the entirety of their lives in prison, but the possibility of release exists. Life sentences and determinate sentences of eight years or more are subject to review by the Parole Board. At the time of writing, this body has a purely advisory role, with the decision-making power vested in the Minister for Justice and Equality, a member of the Executive. A life sentence is mandatory in the case of a conviction for murder. Where a person is convicted of the murder of *inter alia* a police officer, prison officer, a mandatory sentence of 40 years' imprisonment applies.

Members of the Parole Board, who make recommendations to the Minister for Justice and Equality, concerning release for all life sentence prisoners and all those serving over eight years, are appointed by the Minister. The Parole Board does not have a foundation in statute. The Penal Policy Review Group has recommended that the Parole Board be placed on a statutory footing, with the power to direct release. At present, recommendations of the Parole Board tend to be followed by the Minister, but need not be. In 2014, the Parole Board made recommendations in the case of 86 prisoners, and in 82 of those cases the recommendations were accepted in full. Four recommendations were accepted conditionally or in part.[74]

The first opportunity for a person serving a life sentence to be reviewed by the Parole Board is at the seven year point. It is clear that the average time spent in prison by a person on a life sentence in Ireland has increased considerably over the last decade. It is now the case that life sentence prisoners spend an average of 17 or 18 years in prison before being recommended for release, whereas in the late 1990s, the average length of time spent in prison was around 7 years.[75] Griffin and O'Donnell argue that the average length of sentence served by 'lifers' in Ireland is vulnerable to the political climate.

Remission is a central feature of Irish prison law. Remission is the complete ending of a sentence at a fixed point. The Prison Rules 2007[76] are the foundational rules governing all aspects of prison life. Under rule 59 they allow for two types of remission: standard, set at 25% of the sentence, and enhanced, up to 33%. Prisoners sentenced to life imprisonment can seek release under a

---

74 Parole Board, *Annual Report 2014* (Parole Board, 2014), available at: http://justice.ie/en/JELR/Parole%20Board%20Annual%20Report%202014 %20(English).pdf/Files/Parole%20Board %20Annual%20Report%202014 %20(English).pdf (last accessed 8 August 2016).

75 See further Diarmuid Griffin and Ian O'Donnell, "The Life Sentence and Parole" (2012) 52(3) *British Journal of Criminology* 611-629.

76 S.I. No. 252 of 2007.

different regime, *via* the Parole Board. Remission does not apply to such sentences.[77] Remission is the complete ending of a sentence at a reduced point.

It used to be the case that a prisoner had to be serving a sentence of one month to be entitled to remission, but that restriction was abolished by the Prison (Amendment) Rules 2014.[78] It is not possible for a court to impose a sentence purporting to exclude remission.[79]

Enhanced remission is a concept introduced by the Prison Rules 2007[80], through rule 59(2). This rule allows for up to one third remission for prisoners. Prisoners may therefore be eligible for release of between one quarter and one third of a sentence. The conditions are essentially that the Minister for Justice and Equality must be satisfied that the prisoner is less likely to reoffend and better able to reintegrate, by examining certain factors including the prisoner's engagement in authorised structured activity. Following a series of cases which sought to clarity the application of the rule, the Prison Rules (Amendment) (No. 2) of 2014[81] was introduced. The revised rule now states that:

> (2) (*a*) A prisoner who has engaged in authorised structured activity may apply to the Minister for enhanced remission.
>
> …
>
> (*d*) Where the Minister receives an application under subparagraph (*a*), the Minister shall, as soon as practicable thereafter –
>
> (i) if he or she is satisfied that the prisoner, having regard to the matters referred to in subparagraph (*f*) is less likely to re- offend and better able to re-integrate into the community, notify the prisoner of his or her decision to grant enhanced remission to the prisoner and the period of enhanced remission of sentence which is to apply, or
>
> (ii) notify the prisoner of his or her decision to refuse the prisoner's application and the reasons for the refusal.
>
> …

The factors to which the Minister must have regard are stated as follows:

> (*f*) The Minister shall, when making a decision in respect of an application under subparagraph (*a*), have regard to the following matters:
>
> (i) the manner and extent to which the prisoner has engaged constructively in authorised structured activity;

77 For a consideration of the factors which influence the Parole Board's decision-making concerning life sentenced prisoners, see Diarmuid Griffin, "The Release and Recall of Life Sentence Prisoners: Policy, Practice and Politics" (2015) 53(1) *The Irish Jurist* 1-35.

78 S.I. No. 385 of 2014.

79 *O'Brien v. Governor of Limerick Prison* [1997] 2 ILRM 349.

80 S.I. No. 252 of 2007.

81 S.I. No. 385 of 2014.

(ii) the manner and extent to which the prisoner has taken steps to address his or her offending behaviour;
(iii) the nature and gravity of the offence to which the sentence of imprisonment being served by the prisoner relates;
(iv) the sentence of imprisonment concerned and any recommendations of the court that imposed that sentence in relation thereto;
(v) the period of the sentence served by the prisoner;
(vi) the potential threat to the safety and security of members of the public (including the victim of the offence to which the sentence of imprisonment being served by the prisoner relates) should the prisoner be released from prison;
(vii) any offence of which the prisoner was convicted before being convicted of the offence to which the sentence of imprisonment being served by him or her relates;
(viii) the conduct of the prisoner while in custody or during a period of temporary release;
(ix) any report of, or recommendation made by—
    (I) the Governor of, or person for the time being performing the functions of the Governor in relation to, the prison concerned,
    (II) the Garda Síochána,
    (III) a probation officer, or
    (IV) any other person whom the Minister considers would be of assistance in enabling him or her to make a decision on an application under subparagraph (*a*).

V.1. BRINGING DOWN THE IRISH PRISON POPULATION

The efforts to reduce the prison population in Ireland have involved the introduction of a new backdoor strategy. The Irish Prison Service and Probation Service launched a scheme in 2013 entitled "Community Return". This scheme arose out of a recommendation from the group set up by the Irish government to review a decision to build a very large prison.[82] This group suggested that a back door strategy be adopted to reduce the then growing prison population. "Community return" was subsequently introduced. This scheme involves a person serving up to eight years' imprisonment being eligible for release at the half year point, following a risk assessment. Such a person is released into the supervision of the Probation Service and completes work in the community. Once the conditions are abided by, the person will remain out of prison. Approximately 700 people were released on the community return scheme in 2015, which is a

82 Thornton Hall Review Group, Report (Thornton Hall Review Group, 2011), available at: www.justice.ie/en/JELR/ThorntonReviewReportRedacted.pdf/Files/ThorntonReviewReportRedacted.pdf (last accessed 8 August 2016).

significant number in the context of an annual daily prison population of around 3,500.[83]

Community return is perhaps the most concrete back door strategy to bring down the prison population since the development of an official government position that the rising numbers in prison were problematic. This recognition is evident in the report of the Penal Policy Review Group, which recommends the reduction in the prison population to the lowest possible level consistent with public safety. This desire is evident across party lines. In 2011, the Joint Oireachtas (parliamentary) Committee on Justice, Defence and Equality established a sub-committee on penal reform which published a report in 2013. This report recommended the adoption of a 'decarceration strategy' by the Government, with the specific goal of reducing the prison population by one-third over a ten-year period. It also recommended that all sentences for under six months which were imposed for non-violent offences, be commuted and replaced with community service orders. A further recommendation was to increase standard remission from one-quarter to one-third of a sentence, and to introduce an incentivised remission scheme of up to one half. This report achieved a cross-party consensus. To date, however, its recommendations have not formally been adopted by government.

Amnesties or collective pardons have not been used by the Irish government since independence in 1922. Under the Constitution (Bunreacht na hÉireann), there is a power, vested in the President, to issue a pardon. Article 13.6 grants the President "the power to commute or remit punishment imposed by any court exercising criminal jurisdiction", and permits this power to be conferred on other authorities by law. The power of commutation has been used in the past to convert sentences of death to sentences of 40 years' imprisonment for individuals who had been found guilty of 'capital murder', in this case murder of serving members of the police service (An Garda Síochána) at a time when the death penalty was the sanction prescribed for that offence.[84]

V.2. MINIMISING PRISONISATION WITHIN THE PRISON ESTATE

There are two open prisons in Ireland, both of which are for men only. One such prison is in the south-east of the country and the other in the north-west. The former, Shelton Abbey, has an average daily prison population of around 95, while the latter holds around 100 people.[85]

83 Probation Service, *Annual Report 2015* (Probation Service, 2015).
84 See *Callan v Ireland* [2013] 2 IR 267.
85 See www.irishprisons.ie for daily population figures.

A consistent criticism of the Irish penal estate is the lack of provision for more open conditions, and the inappropriate use of higher levels of security than is necessary. The Penal Policy Review Group has recommended the greater use of open prison conditions and, in particular, the introduction of an open prison for women. At the time of writing, plans were being put in place to develop a new open centre for women.[86]

VI. CONCLUSION

There are signs that Ireland is taking steps to reduce the overuse of imprisonment, with some emerging evidence that it is also attempting to reduce the use of criminalisation and prosecution in some areas. There is evidence of an increased desire at governmental level for a greater use of alternatives to imprisonment and the continuing reduction of the prison population. There are further signs that an increased use of alternatives to prosecution is also likely to be seen in the coming years, though this is likely to be in the area of very minor offences, or else for corporate or financial crime. In the area of criminalisation, most momentum is currently behind legislative change in the area of prostitution. It is not clear that there is a sustained campaign to reduce the use of criminalisation of the use of drugs or drug related offences.

Following a period of sharp and continuing growth in the prison population, Ireland is now an example of a country which has taken concrete and determined steps to reduce the numbers in custody. It is perhaps in the use of back door strategies, particularly community return, that this policy has been most successful and may be most instructive for other countries seeking to follow its example.

86 Penal Policy Review Group, *Report of the Penal Policy Review Group* (2014).

OVERUSE IN THE CRIMINAL JUSTICE SYSTEM IN JAPAN*

Taro MORINAGA**

I. INTRODUCTION

If asked whether there is any considerable "overuse" in the criminal justice system, an average criminal judge or prosecutor in Japan will probably answer, "I don't think so", or, "I've never thought of that." Some defence lawyers or bar associations may argue that there is overuse of arrest or pre-trial detention, but I doubt that they feel there is any serious problem of overuse of criminalization, prosecution or imprisonment. Similar replies can be expected from lawmakers and drafters, and they may add, "We are very cautious with criminal law legislation. We are always exercising utmost care in order to prevent such problem from arising." As I will discuss below, statistics do not show any notable signs or symptoms of any serious overuse.

Although there may be dissenting opinions, it seems to me that the problem of overuse in the criminal justice system has not, at least so far, become a major concern in the Japanese society. Overuse seems to have been fairly well controlled. But having been exposed to this question on this occasion, I started thinking that Japan may have simply been lucky. Few people think that there is overuse in the criminal justice system, but is Japan really qualified to say that the current situation is something that has been achieved by conscious efforts to avoid unwanted overuse? Isn't the fairly satisfying situation just a coincidental

* The contents hereof and the opinions expressed herein are those of the author and do not necessarily reflect the understanding or opinion of any Japanese state or governmental agency or institution, or any private organization whatsoever. The author is solely responsible for contents hereof, which are based merely on the author's personal knowledge and experience as an average legal professional qualified only in the jurisdiction of Japan.

** Government Attorney, Tokyo High Public Prosecutors Office and, at the time of writing this chapter, Deputy Director of Asia and Far East Institute for the Prevention of Crime and the Treatment of Offenders (UNAFEI).

result of a combination of different factors, environment or, maybe, legal or social tradition? So I do not dare to say that Japan has consciously controlled the problem of overuse and succeeded, and I do not deny the potential risk of overuse that may rise at any time in the future. However, I would like to say that, currently, there seems to be no major concern about overuse, and there have surely been a variety of elements in the criminal justice system and practice that led to this favourable situation. Taking a quick look at those elements may still be worthwhile.

II. OVERUSE OF CRIMINALIZATION

Under the Constitution of Japan, there are currently 1,959 laws[1] in force (as of 1 December 2015) out of which some 940 laws[2] carry penal provisions. The basic statute concerning substantive criminal law is the Penal Code (Law No. 45, 24 April 1907, as amended), of which the general provisions apply to every offence stipulated in other statutes as well. Unlike some other countries that require that all penal provisions be set forth in the penal code, the Japanese legal system allows penal provisions to be stipulated in different laws. The law expressed in the Penal Code is called "penal law" in the narrow sense, and the laws expressed in the provisions of laws other than the Penal Code are referred to as "special penal law". Special penal law can be further divided into two categories: (1) statutes enacted simply for the purpose of punishing certain conduct not stipulated in the Penal Code and (2) a group of provisions which form a part of a certain statute of which the main purpose is not necessarily punishment of a certain conduct but, based on specific necessity, has some penal provisions. A typical example of the former which is frequently applied in daily practice would be the Act on Prevention and Punishment of Theft and Robbery (Law No. 9, 22 May 1930), and an example of the latter would be the Company Act (Law No. 86, 26 July 2005, as amended), a very big statute which has twenty articles relating to criminal punishment out of 979 articles in total.

As an exception to Article 31 of the Constitution, which requires penal provisions to be prescribed in laws only, local self-governments such as prefectures, cities, and townships having their own assemblies are allowed to include penal provisions in their ordinances insofar as such provisions do not

1 Here, the word "law" refers to formal, normative legal documents, i.e., any statute enacted by the National Diet having general binding effect. Some are titled "Law", while others bear the name "Code" or "Act". English translations of important Japanese laws are available on the website of the Ministry of General Affairs (at: www.japaneselawtranslation.go.jp/?re=02) (last visited: 9 December 2016).

2 The exact number seems to be 943 according to quick research, but this is not an officially recognized figure so stating a precise number has been avoided.

come into conflict with national laws and the prescribed punishment does not exceed the limit of imprisonment for two years.[3] A well-known example of such penal clauses is the prefectural ordinances punishing public nuisance such as violent or indecent behaviour in public, like physical sexual harassment not reaching the level of forcible indecency as prescribed in art. 176 of the Penal Code.

Thus, a large range of conduct is criminally punishable. Starting with murder, robbery and arson all the way down to minor offences like littering or urinating in public spaces, it looks as though, in Japan, every kind of wrong or indecent human act or behaviour is treated with criminal punishment. Even in the areas of administrative law, as well as civil and commercial law, penal provisions are widely used as means to secure implementation and to achieve expected outcomes.

One reason behind this may be the reluctance to resort to administrative sanctions, which is a history-related tendency. Before the end of World War II in 1945 when Japan was an empire and not yet a democratic state, the executive branch had much more power than today, and the judiciary was not supposed to intervene in the area of state administration. Administrative sanctions were widely used without any judicial scrutiny, which naturally led to frequent and serious infringement of human rights. After the democratization under the new constitution, with the rapid spread of liberalism, there was a reactive mood against the administrative power, and not only the scholars and legal professionals but also the lawmakers became allergic to administrative sanctions. They thought it would be much better to limit the power of the executive branch to lay down sanctions as much as possible and to shift the imposition of penalties on citizens, however small and insignificant they may be, from the administrative area to the criminal justice area. The prevailing view was that qualified, impartial prosecutors and judges should handle such cases in accordance with the very strict procedural rules. Therefore, even minor misconduct, which in some other jurisdictions would not be considered a criminal offence and would be dealt with through administrative sanctions, is treated as a criminal offence in Japan.

Another characteristic of Japanese substantive criminal law is the rather wide range of penalties. A simple theft can be punished with a fine not exceeding 500,000 yen[4] or imprisonment with labour from one month up to ten years (Article 235 Penal Code). One convicted of murder may face a punishment of more than 5 years' imprisonment up to the death penalty (Article 199 Penal Code). So, theoretically, one can go to jail for ten years for shoplifting of one piece of chocolate cake, while a murderer may enjoy suspension of execution of

3 Article 94 of the Constitution of Japan and art. 14, Paragraph 3 of the Law on Local Self-Government

4 Approximately 4,600 USD or 4,000 EUR.

sentence[5] and go free after the guilty verdict. Reading the penal provisions only, one might argue that the Japanese criminal justice system is irrational, if not ridiculous. However, and of course, such ridiculous situations never happen in reality. The rule of proportionality is always observed by the courts, prosecutors and also by the police. A first-time shoplifter will never come to court; he or she will rarely be arrested and face prosecution. What I would like to mention here is that the criminal legislation in Japan places great trust in the prosecution and the judiciary, and the judicial system as a whole. It seems that it has been almost a tradition of law-making in Japan since the modernization in late nineteenth century: the legislators grant a wide range of discretion to the judiciary, expecting adequate decisions and proportionate sentencing based on the actual circumstances of each specific case.[6]

Whether to regard these characteristics of Japanese criminal law as an "overuse" seems to be a matter of perception. Given the vast variety of penal provisions, one might argue that this is simply too much, but when taking a closer look, it becomes clear that none of the provisions are unnecessary and they all will probably withstand scrutiny when challenged in court as a constitutional issue.[7] The Cabinet Legislation Bureau[8] and the Legislation Bureaus of the House of Representatives and House of Councillors, with their duty to review and approve draft laws, are generally careful and capable enough to avoid the

5 Although suspension of execution can only be granted in case of a sentence not exceeding 3 years of imprisonment (Article 25 Penal Code), the judge has the discretion to halve the penalty if he or she deems it proper to do so under the given circumstances (Article 66 Penal Code); therefore, when the judge selects the minimum penalty for murder, which is 5 years, and halves it, the defendant will be eligible for suspension of execution.

6 But it is not that lawmakers are always indifferent about the risk of misuse or overuse. Sometimes, when they enact laws carrying penal provisions in a controversial area, which can easily result in serious, unwanted infringement of fundamental human rights and freedoms such as the freedom of expression when misused, they insert provisions reminding the judiciary and law enforcement that they should be careful in the application of that statute. One example may be the "Act on Regulation and Punishment of Acts Relating to Child Prostitution and Child Pornography, and the Protection of Children"(Law No. 52, 26 May 1999, as amended), which says in Article 3 "In the application of this Act, care shall be taken not to improperly infringe upon the rights and freedoms of citizens relating to academic research, cultural and artistic activity and press, and the Act should not be abused for other purposes deviating from the original purpose which is to protect children from sexual exploitation and sexual abuse and to support their rights."

7 Japan does not have a constitutional court. Instead, all courts are vested with power of judicial review. Article 81 of the Japanese Constitution says: "The Supreme Court is the court of last resort with power to determine the constitutionality of any law, order regulation or official act". It is an established interpretation of this provision that the existence of the word "last resort" here implies that the lower courts also have the power to exercise judicial review, although the decision of the Supreme Court is the final one.

8 For the organization and function of the Cabinet Legislation Bureau see at: www.clb.go.jp/english/ (last visited: 9 December 2016).

embarrassing situation of having laws they have approved be struck down as unconstitutional by a court of law.

Now, in contrast to the variety and number of crimes and offences stipulated in laws and ordinances, the number of crimes and offences committed in reality is quite modest. Japan is known as a country with low criminality. The latest data shows that, in the year 2013, 1,917,929 penal code offences were reported, the crime rate – the number of reported penal code offences per 100,000 inhabitants (the total number of inhabitants is 127,298,000) – being 1,507 cases.[9] Historically, the crime rate continued to reach record highs every year from 1998 (2,127) to 2002 (2,897), but since 2003 the crime rate has steadily declined.

As to what crimes are burdening the criminal justice system the most, the top five penal law offences reported in 2014 were: theft (897,259 cases – 50.9%), negligence in vehicle driving resulting in injury or death (550,258 cases – 31.2%), destruction of property (126,818 cases – 7.2%), fraud (41,523 cases – 2.4%) and assault not resulting in injury (32,327 cases – 1.8%).[10] In the special penal law area, Road Traffic Act violations rank at the top, representing the vast majority of persons referred to prosecutors with a number of 327,327 persons (77.8%), followed by violation of the Stimulant Drugs Control Act with 17,633 persons (4.2%), violation of the Minor Offences Act with 8,949 persons (2.1%), violation of the Waste Management Act with 6,585 persons (1.6%) and violation of the Firearms and Swords Control Act with 5,228 persons (1.2%).

Given the modest crime situation reflected in the data discussed above, the law enforcement and the judiciary in Japan do not seem to be overburdened, although there are certainly busy aspects of their work. There is currently no significant call or pressure for decriminalization, legalization or policy-based tolerance. Several crime trends have drawn the attention of practitioners,

---

9 For details, see the English version of Research and Training Institute, White Paper on Crime 2014, Ministry of Justice (at: http://hakusyo1.moj.go.jp/en/63/nfm/n_63_2_1_1_1_0.html) (last visited: 9 December 2016). The data in the White Paper on Crime 2015, of which the English version is still not available, shows that the crime rate has further decreased to the level of 1,762,912 reported offences, the crime rate being 1,387 per 100,000 inhabitants.

10 However, the top five offences in the penal law offences area *cleared and referred to the prosecution* were: i) negligence in vehicle driving causing injury or death (68.8%), ii) theft (14.0%), iii) assault resulting in injury (4.9%), iv) fraud (2.1%), and v) embezzlement and criminal breach of trust (2.0%), showing a significant difference from the number of *reported* cases. This reflects the fact that many of the reported offences such as theft, simple assault or destruction of property tend to remain unresolved, or insignificant enough to be treated as minor offences (see footnote 13 below) and not referred to the prosecution.

researchers and lawmakers but it is doubtful that these trends would be dealt with by decriminalization[11] or policy-based tolerance[12] in any jurisdiction.

One area as to which there may be arguments for decriminalization could be drug abuse. In contrast to many other nations, Japan imposes criminal punishment on simple drug use and possession of small amounts of drugs in addition to trafficking or possession of a significant amount. There may be criticism against the Japanese way, saying that drug users or abusers should be treated as patients by medical institutions rather than being treated as offenders by criminal justice institutions; the criminal justice institutions should handle drug traffickers, i.e., the suppliers, and should leave the consumers alone. But Japan firmly rejects such argument. It has been Japan's established policy that the drug consumers should also be punished because they are the ones that create the demand, motivate the suppliers and enrich them by paying them money which ultimately funds organized crime. Thus far, there have been no major movements within Japan in favour of decriminalization of drug use, except for some insignificant and unconvincing arguments that marijuana smoking should be legalized. However, these arguments have not attracted much attention.

On the contrary, Japan has been facing increased foreign and domestic pressure towards criminalization. Along with the incredibly rapid development in the information technology area, Japan had to cope with cybercrime by enacting a series of cyber-related laws including penal provisions. In addition, frequent media reports of gut-wrenchingly tragic traffic accidents caused by irresponsible attitudes of professional drivers caused huge public fury and led to new legislation severely punishing dangerous driving under the influence of controlled substances, etc. International criticism led to the criminal punishment of simple possession of child pornography. In order to join the OECD anti-corruption treaty, Japan criminalized the bribing of foreign officials. There is also a long-lasting debate whether to criminalize conspiracy as a premise for ratifying the two major UN criminal justice conventions, the UN Convention against Transnational Organized Crime (UNTOC) and the UN Convention against Corruption (UNCAC). These days, there is also international pressure on Japan to criminalize hate speech.

11 What can be regarded as the largest decriminalization in the post-war history of criminal justice in Japan is the shifting of traffic rules violations from the criminal justice area to the administrative area (the "ticket" system) in 1968. This system was obviously designed to relieve the criminal justice system from the huge and rapidly growing burden of dealing with minor traffic violations.

12 One form of policy-based tolerance in Japan can be seen in the system of what is called "minor offences disposition", under which the police may drop minor cases such as first-time shoplifting or harmless assault cases in accordance with guidelines prescribed by the chief prosecutors of district prosecutors' offices. The police must report their disposition to the district prosecutors' office by submitting a list of dropped cases at the end of each month.

Thus, at least for the time being, it looks like there is little room for decriminalization or legalization in the legal system of Japan; it seems that there is greater inclination towards criminalization. But as long as the lawmakers, drafters and relevant practitioners maintain their basic concepts and notions with respect to criminal law, overuse will be less of a problem. These basic concepts include approaches such as the fundamental principle of "restraint"[13], which applies to every aspect of both substantive and procedural criminal law, limiting the creation and administration of criminal law and limiting its application as only a "last resort" to protect society. Further, it may be said that, in Japan, control against overuse of such an expanding penal system not only relies on careful legislative work but also simultaneously on actual administration of criminal justice, and due control is realized by an effective combination of these two mandates for the state. And after all, restraint is also exercised as a matter of due process of law, which is enshrined in Article 31 of the Japanese Constitution.

III. OVERUSE OF PROSECUTION

When it comes to the matter of prosecution including the issue of coercive measures in criminal investigation, there is even less risk of overuse. The problem of "over-prosecution" seems to have been solved quite long ago in the imperial era. This issue has a direct connection with the transformation of the Japanese prosecution system: to be a little more precise, the shift from the legality principle to the expedience principle.

After the transition from a feudal warlord (*samurai*) state into a monarchy in 1868, Japan adopted a French–German style legal and criminal justice system in which the principle of legality was one of the important elements of the justice system based on nineteenth century-style liberalism. The principle of legality was reflected in the criminal procedure laws of 1880 and 1890. However, these laws had a serious side effect, which was the overcrowding of prisons. In order to cope with this situation, the Justice Minister at that time issued a directive in 1885 to the effect that minor offences under a certain level need not be processed as criminal offences, and that is said to be the beginning of the introduction of the expedience principle in Japan. With the rising trend of prosecutors engaging themselves deeper and deeper in criminal investigations, prosecutors became increasingly selective in prosecuting crimes, and this eventually led to the de facto suspension of prosecution. Such practice was endorsed by a circular issued

13 As used herein, the term "principle of restraint" may differ in meaning or context from when used by scholars or law professionals in jurisdictions other than Japan. In this paper, the term corresponds to the Japanese concept of the "principle of restrained use of penal law", an established principle in Japanese jurisprudence.

by the Legal Affairs Office of the Ministry of Justice in 1918 referring to a non-prosecution decision within the discretion of a prosecutor, and, finally, under Article 279 of the 1922 Criminal Procedure Code, the prosecutors could refrain from prosecution if it was "deemed unnecessary in light of the personal character, age and background of the accused as well as the nature and circumstances of the offence and the aftermath of the offence", although the prescribed procedure was an inquisitorial, German-style procedure. This provision was inherited by the current Criminal Procedure Code[14], which adopted an Anglo-American style adversarial system under which the expedience principle seems to be a matter of course.

Taking a quick look at statistics[15], the changes mentioned above can be observed. Before the Justice Minister's directive in 1885, for example in 1884, out of 182,777 cases disposed of by the prosecution, 130,112 cases were formally prosecuted, showing a prosecution rate of 71%. The prosecution rate thereafter did not drastically drop, because the directive was just instructing not to treat minor wrongdoings as criminal offences and not necessarily advising prosecutors to drop cases. But it began to fall slowly and steadily, and by 1918 when the Ministerial circular endorsing discretionary non-prosecution was issued, the prosecution rate had already dropped to 57%. After the circular, for example in 1920, only 85,701 cases were prosecuted out of 295,071, the prosecution rate being 29%. After World War II and the democratization of Japan, for example in 1950, out of 1,907,053 cases disposed of by the prosecution, 523,434 cases were prosecuted, resulting in a prosecution rate of 27%.

The prosecution rate is understandably affected by the overall crime situation and trends, crime rate, social circumstances and the perception of crime by the general public, as well as the criminal justice policies of that time. Coming closer to today, in the year 2000 when the crime rate for penal law offences was climbing, out of 2,625,359 persons whose cases were disposed of by the prosecution[16], 1,035,182 persons were prosecuted, showing a rather high prosecution rate of 39%, which may be understood as partially reflecting the police and prosecutions' sense of crisis as to the rising crime rate. But after that, prosecution rates declined again gradually during the first decade of the twenty-first century by 10% to 29%, further dropping to 26% in 2014 when out of

---

14 Art. 248 Criminal Procedure Code (Law No. 131, 10 July 1948, as amended): "Where prosecution is deemed unnecessary owing to the character, age, environment, gravity of the offence, circumstances or situation after the offence, prosecution need not be instituted".

15 Unless otherwise indicated, the statistical figures appearing in this part and the next part are drawn from Ministry of Justice, *Annual Report of Statistics on Prosecution for 2014* (only available in Japanese).

16 Please note that from 1951, there is no more official data as to the number of cases available. Current statistics are based on the number of persons processed.

1,427,664 suspects disposed of by the prosecution, 377,539 suspects were prosecuted.

The relatively low rate of prosecution may be a reflection of the fairly developed "diversion" scheme in Japan. Here I would like to use the word "diversion" in a broad sense, i.e., any lawful measure taken by the authorities to let a criminally accused person drop out of the formal procedural pathway leading to punishment by incarceration.

The possibility for proper diversion starts at the earliest stage of the criminal justice procedure, right after the suspect is identified. At the earliest stage, there is the "minor offences" disposition by the police as already referred to in one of the footnotes above. In cases falling under the minor offences category, the police officer does not arrest the suspect; the officer conducts a routine, quick investigation and just gives a warning to the suspect that he or she should never do the same thing again. The procedure ends there, except that the incident will be included in the monthly report submitted to the district prosecutors' office. In 2014, 73,907 suspects were disposed of by this system.

Another system that may be conceived as diversion at the earliest stage is the ticketing system of minor traffic rules violations, under which, as one of the rare exceptions in Japan where administrative penalties are generally disliked, the handling of such violations are shifted to the administrative area under certain conditions. This system was introduced in 1968 in order to cope with the rapid increase of traffic rules violations in those days that were brought about by "motorization" of the Japanese society. For instance, speeding not exceeding 30km/h above the speed limit will be handled in accordance with administrative procedures conducted by the police on the spot. The suspect will receive a "ticket" from the police officer, and after receiving via post the slips for payment of the fixed administrative fine, he or she just has to go to the nearest bank to pay the amount due. But if the suspect does not consent to the procedure, then the case is assigned to the criminal justice system, and if the suspect wishes, it is his or her constitutional right to go to trial. The data for 2014 shows that there were 6,717,978 tickets issued for minor traffic rules violations, a number which is more than 4.5 times of the total number of criminal cases accepted by the prosecution in the same year.

Although the police commence criminal investigation by their own initiative and it is their duty to do so, they are not allowed to close any case by themselves. Once they start a criminal investigation, they have to refer the case to the prosecutor (Article 246 Criminal Procedure Code. The "minor case disposition" as mentioned above is an exception to this general rule based on the proviso of the same article). And when the police arrest a suspect[17], they have to bring the suspect to the prosecutor within 48 hours together with relevant documents and evidence showing probable cause. Then the prosecutor has to decide, within 24 hours, whether to apply to the judge for a detention warrant or release the suspect. If the prosecutor applies for a detention warrant and the judge is, upon hearing the suspect's allegations, satisfied that there is probable cause and necessity to hold the suspect, the judge issues a detention warrant based on which the suspect will be detained for a period of ten days. The detention period may be extended by further decisions by the judge for a period not exceeding ten days. Within the period of detention, the prosecutor has to decide whether to formally charge the suspect or to release him/her.

Once a criminal case is referred to the prosecutor, there is another opportunity for diversion. As already discussed, the Japanese prosecution does have wide discretion based on the expedience principle and prosecutes only a part of the cases referred to them. The rest of the cases end in non-prosecution, out of which a substantial amount is disposed of by way of "suspension" of prosecution in accordance with Article 248 of the Criminal Procedure Code. Going back to the 2014 data and taking a closer look, prosecutors disposed of cases related to 1,427,664 suspects in total. 377, 539 suspects were prosecuted. Out of the rest, that is 1,050,125, non-prosecution amounted to 772,277[18]; out of this number, 701,081 suspects were diverted from the process by suspension of prosecution.

Although the number of prosecuted suspects, 377,539, looks rather big, there is yet another opportunity for diversion in the final disposition by the prosecutors. Out of the total number of prosecuted suspects, 90,840 persons became defendants and went to formal trial. The rest were referred for "summary prosecution", a procedure at the summary court for imposing fines not exceeding one million yen.[19] So, the overall formal prosecution rate, in other words, the

17 Of course, the police and prosecutors do not arrest every criminal suspect. If it seems that there is no problem in proceeding without any arrest, they prefer to do so. The statistics for 2014 show that, out of 342,530 suspects (this number excludes suspects of traffic violations and other traffic related offences) as to whom final dispositions were made, 125,595 suspects were arrested by the police and 172 suspects by the prosecutors.

18 Other than that, 1,311 suspects were put under temporary halt of proceedings (most of them are suspects that cannot be located or are seriously ill), and 276,587 were either sent to another district or referred to juvenile courts for alternative or protective procedures.

19 Summary courts are the first-instance courts with limited jurisdiction over minor offences. They have exclusive jurisdiction over cases which deserve fines not exceeding 1 million yen (approx. 9,200 USD or 8,000 EUR) to be dealt in accordance with the summary procedure, a non-oral, *in camera* proceeding in which the defendant does not appear at court at all. The judge simply reviews the case file, and if he/she is satisfied with the guilt of the defendant, imposes an appropriate fine. This procedure requires the consent of the defendant. If the defendant does not give consent or revokes it, the proceeding will automatically be converted into an ordinary public trial.

percentage of criminally accused persons who had to appear at a formal trial, was only 6.3% in 2014.

Recently, a notable change in practice regarding the treatment of offenders is in progress in Japan. Although Japanese prosecutors had placed much importance on the possibility of rehabilitation without incarceration of the alleged offender (especially those who admit guilt) as an element to be considered when making decisions as to whether they should prosecute the case, in the past, they were generally indifferent about what concrete treatment methods or measures were best for the suspects or defendants to lead them to rehabilitation and prevent their re-offending. But recently, with the growing number of offences such as theft and fraud committed by the elderly (most of them are minor cases like shoplifting or the so-called "eat and run", i.e., leaving the restaurant without paying the bill) and the considerably high recidivism rate of these people, which seems to be connected with poverty and isolation from society, the entire criminal justice administration started to focus on social reintegration and prevention of recidivism, a movement in which the prosecution was also expected to play an important role. Prosecutors throughout Japan started a concerted effort with the help of relevant institutions such as the probation offices to divert – again, making full use discretionary power vested in them by Article 248 CrPC – such elderly offenders as much as possible to community-based treatment using every possible alternative such as support by public and private social welfare institutions instead of prosecuting them in court. Even after prosecution, it became common for prosecutors to recommend that the court impose suspended execution combined with probation rather than straightforward imprisonment. The outcome of such efforts has yet to be evaluated carefully, but this seems to be another measure against overuse. But again, what is noteworthy is that the prosecution in Japan did not necessarily think of the issue of overuse here – their main focus was how to suppress recidivism, and the countermeasures they applied would have, coincidentally and simultaneously, the effect of reducing the risk of overuse.

IV. OVERUSE OF IMPRISONMENT

Alleged perpetrators who do not deserve to be diverted at an earlier stage reach the courtroom. Despite the pious efforts of defence lawyers, in 2014, only 116 defendants were acquitted and 320 defendants had their cases dismissed. The conviction rate was 99.5%, just as it had been for decades, which may be an astonishing figure for scholars and legal professionals who are not very familiar with Japanese practice.

However, even if found guilty, the court is also ready to provide a chance for the convicts to rehabilitate in the community. Under certain conditions, the court may suspend the execution of imprisonment sentences that do not exceed the limit of three years.[20] If the convict does not re-offend within the suspension period of up to five years as determined by the court, the effect of the sentencing will become null and void with the lapse of such period, and the convict will never be incarcerated.

Statistics for 2014 show that out of 55,709 defendants sentenced to imprisonment, 33,206 defendants were granted suspension.[21] Thus, the percentage of defendants formally prosecuted and actually punished by the court in some way was 63%, among them 25% with actual imprisonment. If asked what the chance is for the accused to face incarceration, the answer will be "it depends, but in 2014 it was 1.5%." Again, this may be a matter of perception, but regarding these statistics as signs of overuse of imprisonment would be difficult.

Looking at the prisons, statistics[22] show that during 2014, prisons accepted 21,866 new inmates, 19,744 male offenders and 1,216 female offenders. The top five offences committed by those incarcerated were: i) theft (7,183 – 33%), ii) violation of the Stimulant Drug Control Act (6,016 – 28%), iii) fraud (1,827 – 8%), iv) violation of the Road Traffic Act (1,033 – 5%) and v) assault resulting in injury (890 – 4%).

At the end of 2014, there were 52,860 inmates (48,484 male and 4,376 female) incarcerated in prisons all over Japan.[23] The top five offences for which they are doing time are: i) theft (14,051 – 26%), ii) violation of the Stimulant Drug Control Act (13,538 – 26%), iii) fraud (4,186 – 8%), iv) robbery resulting in injury or death (3,434 – 6%) and v) murder (3,170 – 6%).

Although Japanese prisons tend to hold the inmates for a period close to the period determined by the court[24], a recent trend to allow more early release on parole can be observed, which may be viewed as being a reflection of the crime situation becoming rather modest in recent years. Taking a look at the past ten years, the parole rate, which had continued to fall from 2005 to 2010, showed an upward turn in 2011 and is now steadily rising. Data shows that in 2014, out of 24,684 inmates released from prisons, 13,925 were released on parole, the parole rate being 56.5%; less than half of the prisoners serve full sentences.

Another noteworthy development in Japan may be that the recent amendments to the Penal Code and relevant laws adopted a system of "partial

20 See Articles 25 to 27-7 of the Penal Code. Technically, suspension may also be granted to defendants sentenced to fines, but in practice, this is very rare (only two examples in 2014).

21 As to the remaining figure, i.e., 35,131 defendants at trial, 22,475 were sentenced to imprisonment with a definite term, 28 to life imprisonment and 7 to death. The rest consists of defendants sentenced to fines only. Please note that these figures are figures of the first instance judgments, which may have been challenged through the appellate process.

22 The Annual Report of Statistics on Corrections for 2014, Volume I, Ministry of Justice

23 The occupation rate of prisons and detention facilities at the end of 2014 was 67.1%. Currently, the problem of overcrowding seems to have been resolved.

24 A vast majority of inmates serve more than 75% of the sentenced prison term.

suspension of execution". Up to now, judges have only been able to suspend the execution of the sentence in whole, or have the defendant incarcerated for the whole period of the determined sentence. But as of 20 May 2016, the judges may opt to suspend the execution of a part of the sentence – the sentencing may read: "The defendant is hereby sentenced to 3 years' imprisonment with labour. The court hereby suspends the execution of the remaining period of said punishment after two years of the sentence has been served". This system was introduced with the aim of filling the gap between the actual imprisonment and suspension of execution and authorizing the judge to choose something in between. It is expected that this system will contribute to the enhancement of offender rehabilitation with a more flexible administration of criminal penalties.

V. CONCLUSION

If someone asked me to characterize the Japanese criminal justice in one phrase, "lots of penal provisions very carefully used" would be my answer at least for now. It seems to me that, at least at the moment, the problem of overuse is fairly well controlled. So far, so good. But again, I do not deny the possibility that, once the sound legal mind and common sense shared by relevant authorities and the general public starts to erode or get twisted in some way, there may be a risk of overuse. With the rising fear of terrorism, organized crime or new types of crimes rapidly spreading, I think that no one can be certain that the situation will not deteriorate such that someone becomes overzealous and begins to misuse the existing system and practice. If it ever happens, it may be caused by the characteristic of the Japanese criminal justice system in which the statutes place trust in and allow the prosecutors and courts to exercise a large amount of discretionary power, which has so far been regarded as a virtue. Therefore, although I am definitely in favor of the current style of Japanese criminal justice administration, I believe that everyone involved therein should be again reminded of the vulnerability of the Japanese system, and, bearing that in mind, should consciously continue efforts to avoid such unwanted risks of overuse or abuse, especially focusing on human capacity building in the legal field. After all, any system is operated and administered by human beings.

In Japan, there is an old proverb about "a hereditary treasure sword" — meaning a sword handed down from generation to generation, of course a deadly weapon, which should be possessed to serve as deterrence but should never be drawn. I hope that many penal provisions will become "treasure swords" that become unnecessary for us as prosecutors to wield.

TENDENCIES OF OVERUSE IN CRIMINAL LAW POLICY AND CRIMINAL LAW ENFORCEMENT IN THE NETHERLANDS

Paul Mevis*

I. INTRODUCTION: TENDENCY TO A 'TOUGH IN CRIME' POLICY WITH SOME EXCEPTIONS

In order to shed light on aspects of the use and overuse in the criminal law system, policy and law enforcement in the Netherlands[1], one can see several more or less dualistic developments. The major trend is clear: there is a strong call to emphasize the possibilities for criminal liability, criminal prosecution and sanctioning. The general approach is highly politically driven; politicians want to be 'tough on crime'. For instance, as a reaction to terrorism, this tendency might be understood as being driven by developments in society. The call for a certain change in substantive criminal law and in the possibilities for investigating computer crimes is louder nowadays as well. This accentuated use of criminal law does not necessarily need to be characterized as 'overuse'. Other aspects and changes tend more towards this qualification, especially where changes in criminal law politics are driven by other factors than what is necessary within a rational-pragmatic, evidence-based approach and policy.

This focus has dominated changes in legislation and criminal law politics in the Netherlands over the last decades in a way that has been characterized as a development towards a '*totaal strafrecht*'[2]; a firm and omnipresent criminal law

---

* Professor for criminal law and criminal procedure at the Erasmus University Rotterdam (mevis@law.eur.nl) and Dutch member of the IPPF/FIPP. The author wishes to thank ms. Sari Eckhardt, student-assistent, for her support.

1 For an outline: P.J.P. Tak, *The Dutch criminal justice system*, Nijmegen: Wolf Legal Publishers 2008.

2 A.H. Klip, 'Totaalstrafrecht', *DD* 2010/34.

enforcement that at any time and in any situation guarantees the effective application of severe and strict criminal law sanctions, including possibilities for further effective control of behaviour of the criminal after the execution of sanctions. Although this tendency is not typical for the Netherlands alone, the impression is that there is more focus on this policy in the Netherlands than in other European countries. The call for a 'tough on crime'-policy is not evidence-based on higher crime rates in the Netherlands. On the contrary, crime rates are falling and people, if questioned in detail, even feel more safe in the Dutch society. But these ('alternative'?) facts hardly seem to 'confuse' the mind of policymakers who are convinced that criminal law enforcement should be more firm and strict to do justice to the 'legitimate rights and interests of victims of crime' and to ensure that the Dutch society as a whole will be more 'safe'. The latter aspect refers to the use of criminal law, criminal policy and law-enforcement as a preventive mechanism in the 'risk-society'. In the Netherlands, the role and influence of the victims of crime especially has led to a change in criminal law policy in recent years. The general accepted (political) aim is that criminal law enforcement should be an effective reaction to crime towards all parties concerned, including the victim and the society as a whole. Over the last few years, the notion has widely been accepted that criminal prosecution should do justice in and to the interests of the victim. They have (and use) more possibilities to interfere with the process of criminal law enforcement in separate cases. In this approach, the interests of the accused and/or convicted citizen (for instance, the right to fair trial of the accused and the right to resocialization and rehabilitation of the convicted citizen) are no longer the central interest of criminal law policy, but are reduced to *one* of the interests at stake, amongst others.

In the next section some main examples of this mainstream tendency towards firmer criminal law enforcement will be described. Focus will also be on the few examples that might be qualified as a certain (little) 'counter current'.

II. SUBSTANTIVE CRIMINAL LAW

II.1. TERRORISM, MONEY LAUNDERING AND OTHERS: THE 'VLUCHT NAAR VOREN' (HEADLONG RUSH) AND 'OVERINCLUSIVE' CRIMINAL LAW

As such, it is not surprising that especially terrorism and the technical possibilities for computer crimes have led to an increasing call for substantive criminal law in this field. The typical aspect here is the tendency to use criminal law to avoid a terrorist or cybercrime attack.[3] The result is substantive criminal law that more than ever criminalizes all kinds of behaviour that is (only) connected to acts of preparation of terrorist attacks. Under Dutch criminal law, not only a terrorist crime as such is a(n) (aggravated) crime, but also the attempt to commit a crime, and the preparation for a terrorist crime is a punishable act. As a result of the Council of Europe Treaty against terrorism[4] and the EU-Framework Decision of 28 November 2008[5], under Dutch law, even all kinds of taking part in training for terrorism is classified as a separate criminal offence.[6] The criminal liability in these earlier stages of preparation of a terrorist attack has been expanded under Dutch criminal law in such a way that the further guideline in this direction by the recent EU proposal on combatting terrorism[7] seems not to call for any change in substantive Dutch criminal law. 'We' have already gone further than was required by earlier instruments.

This tendency to accept an early stage of criminal liability (the headlong rush) made this kind of criminal law more 'salonfähig' (acceptable) in other fields of substantive criminal law.[8] If this is an adequate instrument in the 'war against terrorism', the next step is to declare the fight against drugs as a 'war against drugs'. Under this qualification 'more' criminal law is 'of course' necessary and allowed; 'we' can hardly afford to 'lose' a war. Consequently, in 2015, a change in the Dutch Drugs Act came into force. It qualifies all types of acts of preparation of illegal hemp growing as a separate crime, punishable with imprisonment up to three years and/or a fine up to 82,000 euros. It is by no means certain that we need this kind of legislation because existing laws have shown to be insufficient. Another recent and remarkable example of such a tendency towards 'overuse' and 'overinclusive' criminal law can be found in recent legislation in the field of money laundering. Interpreting the original crime of money laundering, the Supreme Court tried to avoid double criminal responsibility of an offender by

---

3 A recent comparative overview of the widening tendency in substantive criminal law dealing with computer-crimes can be found in: Q. Wang, *A comparative study of cybercrime in criminal law: China, US, England, Singapore and the Council of Europe* (dissertation Erasmus University Rotterdam), Rotterdam 2016.

4 Warsaw, 16 May 2005, *Trb.* 2006, 34.

5 Council Framework Decision 2008/919/JHA of 28 November 2008 amending Framework Decision 2002/475/JHA on combating terrorism.

6 Section 134a of the Dutch Penal Code (DPC) reads: "Any person who intentionally obtains or attempts to obtain for himself or another person means or information for the commission of a terrorist offence or a serious offence for the preparation or facilitation of a terrorist offence, or gains knowledge or skills for that purpose or imparts this knowledge or these skills to another person, shall be liable to a term of imprisonment not exceeding eight years or a fine of the fifth category".

7 Proposal for a Directive of the European Parliament and of the Council on combating terrorism and replacing Council Framework Decision 2002/475/JHA on combating terrorism, 2/12/2015, COM/2015/0625.

8 M.J. Borgers, *Vlucht naar voren* (inaugural lecture Free University Amsterdam), The Hague: Boom Juridische uitgevers 2007.

being prosecuted for illegally obtaining goods or property such as money for instance, by theft and for laundering those same goods (self-laundering). The Supreme Court excluded double criminal liability in this case. The legislator overruled the Court with a new and explicit, separate crime of 'simple money laundering', characterized by the fact that it deals with laundering the results of someone's own crime. Avoiding overuse, that is avoiding double criminal liability after this change of law has to be found in a profound policy of criminal prosecution by the public prosecutor service or in the application by the judge of the statutory rules on the concurrence of offences, Article 55 para 1[9] and Article 56[10] DPC especially.

II.2. 'MORAL' CRIMES; SEXUAL OFFENCES, 'MEIN KAMPF'

One might see a slightly different tendency if one looks at the trends in more 'moral' crimes. On the other hand, we can see the same tendency. Out of a certain 'fear for the strange' or 'fear for the other', Dutch politics decided to forbid the 'burqa' in the more or less public surroundings such as hospitals, public transport, education, healthcare and buildings of governmental institutions like town halls, and so forth.[11] About ten years ago, this kind of legislation was declined because of the stigma of being 'discriminative' legislation. On the other hand, in the near future, the definition and scope of sexual offences will be part of political discussion again.[12] In the sixties and seventies of the last century, the scope of these crimes was limited to criminal acts protecting against violence and protecting minors in their sexual orientation and development, including protection against temptations created by themselves. Moral interests are more or less excluded. That will be the approach for legislation in the future too, although it is considered necessary to redefine crimes like grooming, sextortion, and so forth, in order to provide a better protection of minors. The protection of minors sometimes leads to a very unwelcome criminal prosecution in cases of

9 "If an offence is punishable under more than one criminal provision, only one of these provisions shall apply. Where these provisions differ, the one which carries the severest punishment shall apply".

10 "If several offences are related in such a way that they have to be considered as one continuous act, notwithstanding the fact that each in itself constitutes a serious offence or a minor offence, only one criminal provision shall apply. Where these provisions differ, the one which carries the severest punishment shall apply".

11 *Kamerstukken II* 34349.

12 K. Lindenberg & A.A. van Dijk, *Herziening van de zedendelicten?* (WODC report), Groningen: Uitgeverij Paris 2015, with a summary in English (at: https://www.wodc.nl/binaries/2392-volledige-tekst_tcm28-73306.pdf) (last visited: 27 June 2017).

'consensual sexting' between minors.[13] As we saw above in the example of 'overinclusive criminal law' in the case of money laundering, the legislator trusts the prosecute to take the appropriate decision not to prosecute in these cases, instead of creating adequate substantive criminal law provisions to avoid criminal liability. It would not be that surprising if more strict moral opinions in Dutch modern society might have an influence as well. Especially the complex and unclear meaning of 'indecency' and the inconsistent way in which this aspect is an element of the definition of (some) sexual offences, will lead to a discussion about the scope of 'indecency' in the modern, multi-cultural society. Furthermore, the wide acceptance under Dutch criminal law of public nude recreation, a system that does allow local communities to forbid nude recreation, is a notorious element in existing Dutch criminal legislation on this point.

Of special interest are some initiatives to decriminalize certain acts in the field of public expressions. In 2014[14] the separate crime of blasphemy was abolished. A similar initiative is under discussion to abolish the crime of 'majesty insult'; the insult of a head of state whom we are not at war with and who is therefore considered as 'friend'.[15] A third initiative that is being discussed in Dutch politics is the proposal to widen the limits of the crimes of (public) hate speech and restrict criminal liability to expressions that form a direct incitement to hatred on grounds of race, religion, sexual orientation, etc. The initiative more or less has followed a Supreme Court decision from 2009[16], in which it was decided that an insulting expression for a group of people does not immediately include the crime of insult for all members of the specific group. A degrading expression about a certain religion is therefore not a discriminating expression for all members of that religion, because of their religion only (as a substantive part of the crime of 'hate speech' in art. 137c of the Dutch Criminal Code). The discussion to limit the scope of this and other hate speech-crimes is combined with a discussion whether it would be necessary to create a separate crime for the denial of genocide.[17]

An interesting element in the discussion on the scope of certain crimes and the impact of substantive criminal law is the influence of 'Europe', which includes the Council of Europe and the European Union. The latter tended for some years to approach all sorts of problems and topics in Europe (such as trafficking of drugs, weapons, people and/or their organs, pollution, racism, child pornography, fraud and other forms of transnational crimes), in a way that often

---

13 Supreme Court of the Netherlands, 9 February 2016, ECLI:NL:HR:2016:213, *NJ* 2016/257 annotated by N. Rozemond.

14 Act of 23 January 2014, *Stb.* 2014, 39.

15 *Kamerstukken II*, 34 456.

16 Supreme Court 10 March 2009, ECLI:NL:HR:2009:BF0655, *NJ* 2010/19 annotated by P.A.M. Mevis

17 *Kamerstukken II* 30579.

included a call for firm substantive criminal law in the member States. Due to a certain 'Euro-scepsis', in recent documents one can find a more reluctant approach to the promises of EU-driven substantive criminal law. As far as the Council of Europe is concerned: on the one hand, there is jurisprudence of the European Court on Human Rights in Strasburg, where it emphasizes the so called 'positive treaty obligation' that, in the view of the court, might call for a firm substantive criminal law approach in some cases (rape for instance) to protect the interests of others as protected in the European Convention.[18] This approach is not without its critics and recently it was argued that especially this theory of positive treaty obligations would not support - but does seriously *challenge* - the criminal law approach as vital and necessary instrument in the 'war against drugs'.[19] As part of the current against the mainstream, it might be worthwhile to sum up the observations concerning substantive law with the conclusion that the European Convention on Human Rights forces the (Dutch) courts to judge whether a substantive criminal law provision is – in a specific case – 'necessary in a democratic society'. That Dutch courts take their task seriously in this respect might be illustrated by a recent decision of the Amsterdam Court of Appeal.[20] Given, amongst other reasons, the possibilities to find the text of the book on the internet, the Court ruled that the criminal provision prohibiting a bookshop to have Adolf Hitlers 'Mein Kampf' present for selling is no longer 'necessary in a democratic society'. In other words, there is 'no pressing social need' to apply this provision in the specific case. The bookshop-owner was acquitted. The Supreme Court accepted the decision.[21]

III. CRIMINAL INVESTIGATION, PRE-TRIAL DETENTION AND SANCTIONING ILLEGALLY OBTAINED EVIDENCE

The possibilities for criminal investigation have been widely expanded over the recent years in Dutch criminal procedure. That does not mean that all changes should be qualified as 'overuse'. Electronic developments have led to possibilities for criminal investigation of computers and obtaining data stored in it. As such, it

18 ECHR 4 December 2003, 39272/98 (M.C. v. Bulgaria); ECHR; ECHR 10 October 2016, Appl. nr. 16143/20 (G.U. v. Turkey).

19 P.H.P.H.M.C. Van Kempen & M.I. Fedorova, *International law and cannabis II. Regulation of cannabis cultivation and trade for recreational use: positive human rights obligations versus UN Narcotic Drugs Conventions* (WODC report), Deventer: Kluwer 2016 (at: https://www.voc-nederland.org/persberichten_pdf/Internationaal_recht_en_Cannabis_II.pdf) (last visited: 27 June 2017) (summary in English available).

20 Amsterdam Court of Appeal 1 February 2016, ECLI:NL:GHAMS:2016:299.

21 Supreme Court 14 February 2016, ECLI:NL:HR:2017:220.

is understandable that the possibilities for the use of DNA are codified in adequate criminal law procedures. Making use of new technics possible in criminal investigation, it is also a possibility to limit and control the use of it. But there is a classic point of overuse in Dutch criminal law for which the Netherlands has been criticized from the perspective of the European Convention on Human Rights. The topic concerns the use of pre-trial detention in the Netherlands. On the one hand, the codified law allows pre-trial detention in the investigation of a large number of crimes, including minor crimes. However, that possibility as such does not lead to a breach of the European Convention. But it is important to note that in the Dutch practice of alternatives to the deprivation of liberty are hardly used.[22] The urge to impose pre-trial detention is shown from the fact that the total number of detainees consists of a large number of pre-trial detainees. In fact, they do not differ much from each other. The pre-trial detainees displayed as a part of the total group of detainees gives the following percentages: 2011 49%, 2012 49%, 2013 47%, 2014 43% and 2015 43%.[23]

In most cases, any order for pre-trial detention will lead to deprivation of liberty. The Code on Criminal Procedure contains a provision for 'bail', but that is a 'silent' part of the code; it is never used in practice. The code also contains possibilities for the suspension on remand. This provision is used, but only in minor cases. There is no general rule for the judge to investigate, discuss and allow alternatives for pre-trial detention before ordering the deprivation of liberty.[24] Given the broader tendency of changing from deprivation of liberty to forms of restrictions of liberty (see below), the actual initiative to modernize the Code of Criminal Procedure plans to include effective remedies to improve practice in a better use of alternatives for pre-trial detention or at least the use of deprivation of liberty in this context. There is a certain EU approach in this respect as well. The so called 'Green Paper on detention' from 2011[25] did – so far

22 J.H. Crijns, B.J.G. Leeuw & H.T. Wermink, *Pre-trial detention in the Netherlands: legal principles versus practical reality* (research report Universiteit Leiden), Den Haag: Boom Juridisch 2016; P.J.P. Tak, 'Pre-trial detention in the Netherlands: improvements are still mandatory', in: P.H.P.H.M.C. van Kempen (ed.) *Pre-trial detention. Human rights, criminal procedural law and penitentiary law, comparative law/Détention avant jugement. Droits de l'homme, droit de la procédure pénale et droit pénitentiaire, droit comparé,* Cambridge, Antwerp, Portland: Intersentia 2012.

23 Dienst Justitiële Inrichtingen, *Gevangeniswezen in getal 2011-2015,* Den Haag: Ministerie van Veiligheid en Justitie 2016.

24 Moreover, a recent urge to speed up proceedings, especially the criminal prosecution of people who attacked public law officials, allow pre-trial detention just for the only purpose to have the accused present in the court procedures, given that these procedure will take place no longer than 17 days and 15 hours after the arrest.

25 European Commission, *Green paper: Strengthening mutual trust in the European judicial area – a green paper on the application of EU criminal justice legislation in the field of detention,* Brussels 2011, COM(2011) 327.

– not lead to any further EU regulation[26], but it is clear that too large differences in rules, procedures and practice concerning pre-trial detention in the member-states can be a serious threat to the cooperation in criminal matters based on mutual trust and mutual recognition in the EU. Given the expanded possibilities for (strict controlled) forms of restrictions of liberty (see below), this change, although significant, does not necessarily lead to a less strict or firm criminal law enforcement on this point.

The expanding possibilities for criminal investigation and the codification of possibilities to breach fundamental rights and liberties of citizens brings one to another point that can be qualified as 'overuse'. Under the Dutch law of criminal procedure, it was (and partly is) accepted that the interests of effective criminal law enforcement should, under specific circumstances, resign and give way to the protection of other vital interests, such as the legal professional privilege of doctors and others. Another restriction was the traditional option that illegally obtained evidence – under certain conditions – should not be used as evidence against the accused. This approach is the result of the Rule of Law implication that a fair and legitimate criminal process calls for the exclusion of information and evidence if it turns out that this information and evidence was gained with methods that are found outside the codified possibilities for the organs of criminal investigation. But due to the notion that someone 'who did it' should no longer 'profit' from these kinds of 'mistakes' and that an acquittal on this kind of 'formal' grounds would not be acceptable for society as such, and 'the' victim especially, the Dutch Supreme Court reduced the possibilities for the exclusion of evidence (and for some other sanctions) tremendously in recent years. Even to a level that is criticized by lower courts and in literature. It can be expected that the above-mentioned actual review of the Dutch Code on Criminal Procedure will more or less 'restore' fundamental constitutional relations on this point.[27]

IV. PROSECUTION; POSSIBILITIES TO PROSECUTE

In the Dutch criminal procedure, the power to prosecute resides exclusively with the prosecution service. The prosecution service is not obliged to prosecute every crime brought to its attention. There is a wide range of discretion in which the

26 There is only the Council Framework Decision 2009/829/JHA of 23 October 2009 (Publ. L. 294/20) on the application, between Member States of the European Union, of the principle of mutual recognition to decisions on supervision measures as an alternative to provisional detention.

27 It is as such a bit strange that the European Court on Human Rights as a general approach, so far refuses to step to the opinion that the use of evidence obtained in breach of art. 8 of the Convention does as such not breach the 'fair trial'-provision of Article 6 of the Convention.

prosecution may decide to drop a case, not only when there is not enough evidence, but also 'for reasons of public interest'.

Ever since the sixties, it has been accepted that within this broad room for manoeuvre, the discretionary power of the prosecution service was – and in fact is used - *not* to prosecute, not only in separate crimes and cases, but also in categories of crimes. The decision not to prosecute is based on the considerations of general policy and public interest. The use of this discretion is based and structured by published national prosecution guidelines. To name only two examples: first, the famous Dutch 'coffee shop policy'[28] and second, the Dutch euthanasia and assisted suicide policy.[29] Both are the outcome of this rather pragmatic use of criminal policy. Selling soft drugs in a coffee shop is a crime, just as euthanasia and assisted suicide is. But these crimes will not be prosecuted if the owner of the coffee shop or the physician who committed euthanasia complies with certain criteria. In case of the coffee shop, the owner must, in addition to compliance with other criteria, not sell hard drugs or alcohol nor soft drugs to minors. As far as euthanasia is concerned, every case of euthanasia or assisted suicide is a crime, even when committed by a physician. But if the 'end of life decision' of the physician meets the due care criteria of the law that can shortly be referred to as the 'Dutch euthanasia law', then, based on a published guideline, there will be no prosecution of the physician. It is left to the so-called 'Euthanasia Review Committees' to give the preliminary decision whether the criteria indeed were met.

In terms of the 'use and overuse', this modality, in which the Public Prosecution Service plays an important role as a policy-maker, as an actor of criminal law enforcement policy in general, shows a rather pragmatic approach in which criminal liability, that is, the use of criminal law to define an act as a crime, is used, not aiming in the first place at prosecuting, but at controlling certain behaviour in society by *not* prosecuting categories of crime as long as certain criteria are met. The possibility of criminal prosecution, based on the criminal liability as such, is used as a 'threat', as a deterrent, to ensure that people comply with the criteria. The coffee shop owner commits a crime if he sells soft drugs to minors. Consequently, his coffee shop can be closed down immediately. Similarly, the physician who does not meet the criteria laid down in the euthanasia law can be prosecuted for a crime against the life of another person.

---

28 See for a description: M. van Ooyen & E.R. Kleemans, 'Drug policy: the "Dutch" model', *Crime & Justice* 2015, 44.

29 See for a description: A. van der Heide, 'Physician-Assisted Dying in the Netherlands', in: G.D. Borasio et al (ed.) *Assistierter Suizid: Der Stand der Wissenschaft*, Heidelberg: Springer Berlin 2017 and M. Lindemann & P.A.M. Mevis, 'Recent developments in the legislation and case-law on euthanasia and assisted suicide – a comparative analysis of the situation in Germany and the Netherlands', *Annual Review of Law and Ethics* 24, Berlin: Duncker & Humblot 2016.

We can see this phenomenon nowadays in the so-called 'houses of public interest and public safety' (veiligheidshuizen). These are more or less 'round table' institutions in which the prosecutor discusses criminal cases regarding problematic offenders, such as young offenders, addicted offenders, hooligans, offenders in the outer sphere of criminal groups, or offenders with psycho-social problems with representatives of all types of organizations, for example the local police, youth care workers, local probation and welfare services and such others. The aim is to choose the best way to help the offender to prevent recidivism. This best way is of course not necessarily criminal prosecution. The prosecutor will waive prosecution under the condition that the offender accepts help.

The weak aspect of this pragmatic, rather reluctant use of criminal prosecution is that it only exists as long as society and politics accept it. The system is not protected against a more intrusive, 'aggressive' criminal policy that no longer accepts a reluctant use of the possibilities of criminal prosecution. On the contrary, it calls for a resolute and decisive approach in which effective criminal prosecution is seen as a necessity to protect the society. And that is exactly what happened in the mainstream in criminal law policy in the Netherlands over the last two decades in general.[30] Effective criminal law enforcement has become a major focus of attention of Dutch politics. Political parties and politicians use criminal law topics for their political campaign. As one can expect, that is a guarantee for overuse as politicians call for criminal prosecution; waiving prosecution is no longer accepted. Non-prosecution is seen as an exception that requires justification. The decision of the prosecution service not to prosecute in specific cases, for instance in cases of violence against officials of law enforcement, has even led to questions and debate in Parliament.

Two important factors do increase this tendency. The first is the role and influence of (the political attention for) the victims of crime, as described above. As a result, criminal prosecution is more or less seen as a right of the victim in 'his' or 'her' case, in which he or she can speak out in court and/or demand for compensation of damages from the offender. In this approach, it is difficult for the victim to accept that 'his' case is dropped by the prosecutor for reasons of public interest. This is illustrated by the fact that the legal option for the victim to appeal against the decision *not* to prosecute, threatens to break down under its case-load. This position of the victim may also be an explanation for why mediation in criminal cases, seen as an option to avoid criminal prosecution, is not a frequently used option. However, there is an explicit provision in the Dutch Code on Criminal Procedure that calls for the use of mediation, if appropriate.

30 The 'exception' is that in cases of euthanasia the actual debate in Dutch society tends to decriminalize more cases of euthanasia based on an broader influence of a right to self-determination.

The second factor is that, until some ten to fifteen years ago, it was the prosecution service itself that opposed strongly a popular policy-driven influence towards the need for prosecution and to accept the decision not to prosecute only in exceptional cases. The prosecution service used to state that its role on (the Dutch part of) this planet was to protect criminal law enforcement against too general, far too easy, political and popular-based calls for 'firm' law enforcement. It tried to make clear that a careful decision by an independent body whether to prosecute or not in a certain criminal case, would make the difference between 'law enforcement under the Rule of Law' and calling for revenge. But unfortunately, those days are behind us.

Nowadays, the public prosecutor service even tends to embrace and support the political emphasis on law enforcement by criminal prosecution. This approach has resulted in several changes in Dutch criminal law. There are no longer time limits for the prosecution of crimes carrying a statutory prison sentence of more than twelve years. The Supreme Court ruled recently that the prosecution does not lose its right to prosecute even in cases in which the right to be heard in court 'within a reasonable time' (Article 6 ECHR) is exceeded extremely.[31] A very important and fundamental change of law came into force in 2008: the introduction of the so-called 'penal order', or 'punishment order' by the prosecutor's office. This punishment order allows the public prosecutor service to impose sentences and orders, without prior intervention by the courts. The possibility to use the punishment order is limited to crimes carrying a statutory prison sentence of no more than six years. The introduction of this punishment order is under the danger of becoming an element of 'overuse' in prosecution, especially because the implementation of a punishment order does not require the decision of a public prosecutor in person. The order can also be imposed by other members of the public prosecutors service, when mandated by a prosecutor.

This means that if you were to attend a dance festival in the Netherlands, you might find at the festival location not only a branch of the local coffee shop, but also of the local prosecutor's office for imposing punishment orders on festival visitors who commit a crime at the festival venue. This 'festival arrangement' from the local public prosecutor's office even includes the possibility to pay the imposed fine immediately at the festival spot, with a credit card for instance. In the latter case, there is no possibility anymore to take the case to court afterwards. Also, it is not prescribed that the unsuspecting citizen should be informed about this consequence before he or she is invited to pay the imposed fine.

In terms of overuse, the public prosecutor's office developed an approach of all kinds of less-severe daily, common minor crimes. This approach has been

31 As indicated above describing the Supreme Courts approach towards the sanctioning of illegally obtained evidence, this general exclusion of this sanction too, is not accepted by all lower courts.

brought under the officially used umbrella of the one liner 'as soon and as effective as possible' (and – thus – not necessarily 'as carefully as possible'[32]). This policy aims at realizing at least some kind of deterrent reaction, and in many cases a sentence imposed by a punishment order, to every crime as soon as possible afterwards and, if possible, by avoiding 'the long way of prosecution' before the criminal courts, leading to a sentence that – in the view of the prosecution service – might be too light. The broad use of the punishment order helps to 'avoid' these last mentioned 'disadvantages' of criminal prosecution, as long as the sentenced person does not take his case to court by way of appeal against the punishment order.

The instrument of the punishment order, allowing the public prosecutor's office to impose sanctions on its own authority, is a very important instrument for the realization of this 'as soon as and as effective as' policy. More and more cases are being dealt with by means of such a punishment order. According to the Central Bureau of Statistics, in 2009 some 4,850 (2% of the pending cases) were dealt with by punishment order. The number of cases decreased to 11,125 (5%) in 2010, 24,230 (10%) in 2011 and 35,700 (16%) in 2012. Then it stabilized: 35,015 (17%) in 2013, 34,475 (16%) in 2014 and 28,055 (15%) in 2015.

Nevertheless, there is a significant restriction. The most used sanction imposed by a punishment order is a fine. And although it is also possible to impose instructions and other forms of restriction on liberty, it is not possible to impose any form of deprivation of liberty. One of the few provisions in the Dutch Constitution that concerns criminal law, explicitly states that imprisonment or other forms of custodial sanctions as criminal sanctions, may only be imposed by a judge. Thus, although the punishment order is an increasingly used instrument of criminal law enforcement, it has not led to an overuse of custodial sanction. One may have the impression that minor cases, had they been prosecuted, may have been sanctioned with a short-term imprisonment, might, in the actual approach, be dealt with by way of punishment order that does not allow short-term imprisonment. Nevertheless, there is also a tendency to prosecute and take cases which are just above the bottom line of severity to court in order to use the increased number of sanction modalities that Dutch courts have nowadays to impose all kinds of instructions and other orders to put offenders under a regime of restricted liberty, imposing at the same time the possibility of immediate arrest of the offender if he does not adhere to the instructions. For this last possibility, the above-mentioned constitutional provision makes a decision of a judge necessary. That brings us at some significant changes in the sanction-system.

---

32 There is research that the punishment order is applied in cases that would not lead to a conviction (most times because of a lack of evidence) if these cases would have been brought to court. G. Knigge & C.H. de Jonge van Ellemeet, *Beschikt en gewogen* (report of the general prosecutor at the Supreme Court), Den Haag: De Groot 2014.

V. OVERUSE IN THE SANCTION SYSTEM

Looking for tendencies in the Dutch sanction system that might be considered forms of overuse, some specific developments need to be examined.

V.1. INCREASE OF MAXIMUM, MINIMUM SANCTIONS, NAMING AND SHAMING

The maximum sanction for all types of crimes have been 'reviewed' over the recent years, which has lead in all cases to an increased maximum. The general maximum of (temporary) imprisonment has been increased from 20 to 30 years, and there is a debate whether it should be 40 years. The extended maximum is used in practice; imprisonment for a period between 20 and 30 years has been applied in (a very few) cases. Research about the negative effects of long-term imprisonment are denied; applying long-term imprisonment in the Dutch legal system is not bound to any specific legal substantive or procedural safeguard.[33] The possibilities to forbid an offender the further professional practice if he or she committed crimes during that practice have been widened; there is an element of 'naming and shaming' in this legislation. Political initiatives for a general system of minimum sanctions for all specific crimes[34] have been debated, but have not been accepted so far.

There is one specific exception to this: according to Article 22c DPC, certain crimes should, in the view of the legislator, not be punished with a community service order, but with imprisonment. Judges are avoiding the strict application of this rule in cases where they think a community service order is an appropriate sanction. The topic is discussed as part of the constitutional relation between the legislator under the legality-principle responsible for the sanction system as such, and the (independent) judiciary responsible for a fair sanction in every separate case. The exception discussed here is a breach in the traditional broad room for manoeuvre in sanctioning by judges in the Dutch legal system. Nevertheless there can be no doubt about the legitimacy of the legislature to limit this room for manoeuvre as such. The problem is that the law does not leave any room for any exception.

33 P.A.M. Mevis, '(Te) lang opsluiten? De wettelijke begrenzing van de maximumduur van de gevangenisstraf', *DD* 2012/1.

34 Dutch law has a general minimum for every separate sanction (such as one day imprisonment) and a specific maximum for each crime (for instance 15 years imprisonment for manslaughter)

V.2. SUPERVISION – RESTRICTION OF LIBERTY

The most significant change in the Dutch sanction system is the broad introduction of all types of modalities for sanction arrangements that might be characterized as a 'well controlled restriction of liberty', especially in the direction of 'controlling' the accused, convicted or ex-convicted citizen in order to 'prevent' him from reoffending, or at least in controlling him in this respect. This development, as such, has been widely spread in Europe in recent years.[35] In Dutch law one might find the possibility to order an accused not to commit any new crime or to stay away from the victim or from certain areas or places, such as football stadiums, as part of conditional suspension of pre-trial detention, suspended conviction, suspended execution of imprisonment or as a separate order of the court by way of criminal safety measure or, as a matter of fact, as an order of the Public Prosecutor. Three typical Dutch general complementary provisions may tend to the qualification of a certain overuse of this modality. Firstly, most times the judge who gives the order may impose rather strict forms of electronic monitoring, controlling whether the citizen under the order complies with it. Secondly, in many cases, the judge will order deprivation of liberty (custodial sentence) in case the citizen under the order will break the conditions. Because of this already ordered, subsidiary form of deprivation of liberty, the police can immediately arrest somebody if the electronic monitoring system or the probation service (or any other controlling body) or the victim signals that he or she is breaking the order. The arrest is based on the already ordered custody for this case by the judge who then, after the arrest, has to decide whether the custody can be accepted and prolonged. Thirdly, in some cases the sentencing judge can allow the immediate execution of his decision, that is, ordering that the execution of this part of his decision is possible, even though the accused has appealed against the verdict as such. Only on the request of the accused, the appeal court might overrule the decision of the lower court on this point.

The most significant change in this respect of overuse by implementing possibilities for long-term controlling of a citizen who committed a crime is the triple-modality that was accepted by Dutch Parliament in 2015.[36] In short, the law introduces three modalities for indeterminate supervision of dangerous offenders.[37] The first is the introduction of an indefinite period of conditionally terminated TBS-safety measure for mentally disturbed offenders. The second is

35 F. McNeill & K. Beyens, *Offender Supervision in Europe*, UK: Palgrave Macmillan 2013.

36 Act of 25 November 2015, *Stb.* 2015, 460, effective from 1 January 2018 (some parts from 1 January 2017).

37 For a more detailed description and critics: S. Struijk & P.A.M. Mevis, 'Legal constraints on the indeterminate control of 'dangerous' sex offenders in the community: the Dutch perspective', *Erasmus Law Review* 2016, 2.

the possibility for the courts to extend the probation period after conditional release from imprisonment for certain crimes of violence even continuously for up to two years, each time again. Consequently, any offender sentenced to an unconditional imprisonment of at least one year may, in principle, be life-long supervised by prolonged court decision. The third aspect of the Bill introduces a separate supervisory safety measure. The sentencing judge has to apply this measure. But the idea is that the execution will only start once an imposed TBS measure or prison sentence is (un)conditionally terminated. At that moment, a new and separate court decision for the execution of this sanction is necessary. It is for the court to decide whether the actual situation after imprisonment or TBS is such that the previously measure imposed must be enforced. On the one hand, the legal framework guarantees that a court decision is necessary to assess the question whether the application and extension of these legal possibilities is necessary. But there are no further substantive or procedural guarantees to prevent the application of this new framework to be disproportionate from a human rights perspective.[38] There is no sufficient research and evidence underlying the practical need or effectiveness of these provisions, nor are there well-accepted instruments for adequate risk assessment to select the 'dangerous' offenders adequately. The Dutch legal system will have to lean on the proper application of the new measures by the judiciary. Judges bear great responsibility in balancing all interests of fair justice and acceptable sanctioning in this respect. The problem is that the public and political upheaval with criminal law enforcement is partly based on a popular driven 'attack' on the judiciary for their 'reluctance' in sentencing. The judiciary is no longer 'protected' by politics in the necessity of reluctant, proportionate sanctioning as part of a legitimate sanction system that, under the rule of law, represents a vital element of *general* interest. Reluctant sanctioning judges are rather seen as a threat to public safety.

VI. EXECUTION OF SANCTIONS

Given the tendencies described above, it can hardly be surprising that the approach of a popular-politics driven, firm approach can be found in the field of the execution of (custodial) sanctions as well. Three significant aspects can be highlighted here that bear the danger of a certain 'overuse'.

38 S. Struijk & P.A.M. Mevis, 'Legal constraints on the indeterminate control of 'dangerous' sex offenders in the community: the Dutch perspective', *Erasmus Law Review* 2016, 2.

VI.1. LESS SIGNIFICANT POSITION OF REHABILITATION AND RESOCIALIZATION

Rehabilitation and resocialization has never been a constitutional guarantee in the Dutch sanction system. There was a provision in the Dutch act concerning the execution of imprisonment stating 'the execution of the custodial sentence is made subservient to the offenders' rehabilitation as much as possible'. That provision is still there, but it has been amended. In the new version it is expressively mentioned that the interests of the safety of society and of victims and survivors of crime should be taken into account as well. These interests are therefore, in legal terms, made of equal value to the interests of the convicted person, especially their resocialization. The application of detainees for resocialization is made conditional to their 'good' behaviour in prison. Given this change in law, the Ministry of Safety and Justice took over the principle responsibility for the arrangements of the execution of every individual sanction. Based on a strict 'what works?'- approach, resocialization in prison facilities is limited to the 'selected category' of willing 'privileged' prisoners who have 'proved' in their behaviour to accept their responsibility and are expected to be able to use resocialization facilities 'adequately'. Others are kept on a more 'sober regime'. There is an element of inhuman treatment in this approach where the expectation is that prisoners are capable of acting appropriately in this system of 'resocialization as an offer and a choice'. The rehabilitation and resocialization is not seen as a necessary offer to all detainees as a vital element of legitimate (execution of) imprisonment. Those who are incapable of changing their behaviour are left behind as 'unwilling', leading for instance to consequences that certain facilities and freedoms will not be allowed and conditional release might be postponed. There is an element of *overuse* in this approach where, along these lines of reorganizing the execution of custodial sanctions, adequate resocialization is only seen as a right of the inmate (that can be limited) instead of a true and thorough possibility to get a convicted citizen to change his or her behaviour by not committing crimes anymore after execution of criminal sanction as a vital, general interest of society as such. From a perspective of 'effective' execution of sanctions towards true reducing reoffending, it is a not that the best approach.

VI.2. THE BLIND ALLEY OF LIFETIME IMPRISONMENT

The most significant example of this politically-driven, 'blind alley' approach lies in the recent 'escapades' of the lifetime imprisonment under Dutch law. The story is as unbelievable and therefore significant as short. The Dutch system has accepted lifetime imprisonment ever since the actual Criminal Code came into force in 1886. When applied, it was, up to some decades ago, common policy that the government would take the initiative to consider pardoning the convicted person after a long-term imprisonment. There can be hardly any doubt whether the European Court on Human Rights would accept this system as sufficient. The Court accepts lifetime imprisonment under the ECHR, it just calls for a system in which the sanction of lifetime imprisonment must be reducible de jure and de facto, 'meaning that there must be both a prospect of release for the prisoner and a possibility of review'.[39] However, Dutch politics have changed. In the popular-driven wish for firm law enforcement, the simple possibility for any form of review of life time imprisonment was abandoned; 'lifetime is lifetime'. That approach was, of course, not acceptable for the European Court on Human Rights. Based on (its own interpretation of) the jurisprudence of that Court, the Dutch Supreme Court ruled in July 2016[40] that, given the breach of Article 3 of the Convention in the way of *execution* of lifetime imprisonment, the *application* of this sanction will be no longer possible under Dutch law. The politically-driven, firmer approach to lifetime imprisonment has therefore led to a certain end in the use of this sanction! The government is (finally) rethinking its position and there will be a certain restoration of a review procedure of some kind. It is doubtful whether the approach that has been published so far, will meet the criteria of the Strasburg Court. There is still a difference in approach where the Government wants to use a review procedure (the idea is: after 25 years imprisonment) as the first moment to decide whether resocialization activities should be allowed and initiated. The Strasburg Court, on the other hand, has called for these types of activities to be formed on the first day of the execution of the sanction, not only to keep the regime 'bearable', but also in the approach that the (necessary) review procedure can only be effective if the 'lifetimer' is given appropriate possibilities to work on resocialization (and prove his capability in this respect) before and in the run up to the (possible) review of applied lifetime imprisonment.

VII. CONCLUSION

To conclude, the 'landscape' differs. One can say that in general, there is a broad popular driven policy for a stronger criminal law enforcement. One can find elements of that policy especially in the changes in the sanction system and in the approach of criminal procedure. Sanctions that include possibilities to control

39 See recently the summary of the general principles established in the Court's case law on life sentences in ECHR (Grand Chamber) 17 January 2017, ECLI:CE:ECHR:2017:0117JUD005759208 (*Hutchinson v. UK*), par. 42-45.

40 Supreme Court 5 July 2016, ECLI:NL:HR:2016:1325, *NJ* 2016/348 and already in Supreme Court 16 June 2009, ECLI:NL:HR:2009:BF3741, *NJ* 2009/602.

accused and convicted citizen in their behaviour, are popular. However, a huge threat and tendency to overuse of criminal prosecution is the no longer rational-based prosecution policy and a lack of protection against political influence on criminal prosecution in the direction of 'firm' law enforcement in all cases. The threat is amplified by the fact that the public prosecutor service tends to embrace the popular-based approach rather than to 'protect' criminal prosecution against a politically-driven 'overuse'. Especially the position and influence of the victim and his or her interests (as defined by policymakers) allow the move towards a criminal law enforcement in which the accused and his/her right to a fair trial is no longer central and the main focus. Resocialization and rehabilitation have to be discovered and restored again in Dutch sanction politics, as has the necessity for an appropriate review procedure for life-timers. The popular approach has shown to be a 'blind alley' towards Strasburg; it has died (if you wish: in beauty) there. On the other hand, the upcoming review of the Code of Criminal Procedure will be used to address the problem of the overuse of pre-trial detention. Moreover, Dutch courts and politics are more critical of some 'moral' crimes, for instance, whether these provisions are 'necessary in a democratic society' as provided by the European Convention on Human Rights.

OVERUSE IN THE CRIMINAL JUSTICE SYSTEM IN NEW ZEALAND

Yvette TINSLEY & Warren YOUNG*

I. INTRODUCTION

In recent years, New Zealand has seen a decline in both recorded crime and the number of prosecutions. However, in the same period, the prison population has continued to climb. In this chapter, we examine the reasons for New Zealand's high per capita prison population and illustrate that attempts to reduce prosecution have not filtered through to affect rates of imprisonment.

In Part II, we outline the trend of a declining crime rate over the last decade, and note that criminalisation is almost exclusively reserved for behaviour involving harm to individuals or the community. However, the rate of real crime is almost certainly much higher than the numers recorded, as is illustrated in victim surveys conducted by the Government. In common with comparable jurisdictions such as England and Wales, there has been an increase in quasi-criminal offences and orders over the past decade, and we examine two examples of these. These alternatives to criminalisation sit alongside police practice and discretion, which allow for tolerance in areas such as the possession of illicit drugs.

New Zealand's expedience-based prosecution process contains no centralised prosecution service, but instead relies on the police to initiate most prosecutions.

In Part III we examine prosecution trends and the offences prosecuted in the greatest numbers, as well as the process of prosecutions for both minor and more serious offences. Since 2010, greater efforts have been made by New Zealand

* Dr. Y. Tinsley LLB (Hons), PhD is professor at the School of Law of Victoria University of Wellington, New Zealand.
Dr. W. Young BA, LLB, PhD, is a policy and law reform consultant in Wellington, New Zealand. He has been Deputy President of the New Zealand Law Commission, a Deputy Secretary for Justice and a Professor of law.

Police to consider alternatives to prosecution, but we argue that these have had little impact on the prison population or on rates of imprisonment.

In Part IV, we argue that the overuse of imprisonment in New Zealand can be seen to be a result of longer nominal and effective sentences imposed. This in turn has been driven by both government policy and the public mood, as affected by the media and pressure groups. Alongside a high per capita prison prison population sits an extensive system of non-custodial penalties. Despite some restrictions, in general judges have a relatively wide discretion when imposing sentences. We conclude by noting the rather blunt mechanisms open to Government to reduce imprisonment in the current system and the consequent likelihood of continued overuse of imprisonment in New Zealand.

II. OVERUSE OF CRIMINALIZATION

II.1. TRENDS IN CRIMINAL OFFENDING

In recent years, the rate of recorded crime in New Zealand has been declining. This is despite the general population in New Zealand rising in the same period of time, from an estimated 4,136,000 in December 2005 to 4,513,100 by the end of 2014.[1] As a small country, New Zealand takes its obligations as an international citizen very seriously, and tends to take fairly rapid steps to criminalise conduct where required to enable ratification of international treaties or other conventions and agreements (for example, bribery of foreign officials, money-laundering, and transnational crime). However, there is little evidence to suggest that the fulfilment of its obligations changes the number of offences to any noticeable extent. Usually, such offences are covered by extant criminal offences already, and if not it is conduct that rarely occurs in New Zealand.

As is shown in Table 1[2], although the number of offences recorded by police between 2006 and 2014 reduced as an overall figure, there were variations across offence types. In particular, the number of recorded sexual offences increased across the decade. As a percentage of all recorded offences, sexual offences therefore saw a steady increase, particularly after 2011.[3] This is likely to be due to

1 Figures generated from population estimates at: Statistics New Zealand, *Infoshare* (at: www.stats.govt.nz/infoshare/) (last visited: 20 October 2016).

2 Data for 2006-2014 is shown for recorded and resolved offences in this part of the chapter. From 2015, New Zealand Police changed the method by which they record crime. Figures from before 2015 are not directly comparable with the new statistics. See New Zealand Police, *New Recorded Crime Victim Statistics* (at: www.police.govt.nz/sites/default/files/publications/rcvs-stakeholder-briefing.pdf) (last visited: 20 October 2016).

3 Sexual offences comprise a small percentage of total recorded offences, but this rose from 0.67% in 2006 to 1.16% in 2014, a 70% increase, see Data from Statistics New Zealand (at: http://nzdotstat.stats.govt.nz/WBOS/Index.aspx) (last visited: 26 May 2016).

public concern and changes in police investigation and recording of sexual offences, rather than to actual increases in offending.[4] Aside from minor fluctuations, the levels of other offence types as a percentage of total recorded offences remained fairly stable. This demonstrates that the fall in recorded offences was a general trend, rather than the result of policy change in relation to particular offence types.

Table 1. Recorded offences in New Zealand by offence type, 2006-2014*

	2006	2007	2008	2009	2010	2011	2012	2013	2014
Homicide	98	91	102	127	97	83	68	83	66
Acts intended to cause injury	34545	39475	42035	45375	44515	42278	40851	39447	39944
Sexual offences	2838	2831	2795	2912	3016	3466	3512	3919	4056
Dangerous or Negligent Acts	752	752	785	749	859	979	1022	787	737
Abduction, Harassment etc.	10757	12416	12719	14473	14157	12947	12476	13763	15024
Robbery and related offences	3060	2894	2826	2828	2641	2447	2199	2178	2140
Burglary and related offences	61437	58230	59326	61405	59323	59518	52937	52247	53265
Theft and related offences	153460	145465	140858	144780	136932	135442	119476	121035	119323
Fraud, Deception etc.	12917	12430	14604	13314	9726	8010	8013	7997	9037
Illicit Drug Offences	19224	19084	20631	24923	22994	20738	20792	16069	16543
Weapons and Explosives Offences	7838	7376	7291	7763	7074	6362	6063	5675	5791
Property Damage	57075	61016	61759	62636	58483	51984	48901	45577	40358
Public Order Offences	38521	41819	42981	46945	46105	42969	42522	35850	26751
Offences Against Justice	20181	21150	21075	21790	19084	17404	15797	14425	16085
Miscellaneous Offences	1434	1355	1596	1385	1339	1429	1384	1359	1269
TOTAL	424137	426384	431383	451405	426345	406056	376013	360411	350389

* Data from Statistics New Zealand (at: http://nzdotstat.stats.govt.nz/WBOS/Index.aspx) (last visited: 26 May 2016). Note that if an offence that occurred within a given year is recorded 15 days or more after the end of a year it will not appear in the official statistics for that year.

4 Following a Commission of Inquiry Report into Police Conduct in 2007, (Department of Internal Affairs, *Report of the Commission of Inquiry into Police Conduct* (at: https://www.parliament.nz/resource/0000055162) (last visited: 26 May 2016)), until 2017 New Zealand Police has been subject to monitoring of the implementation of the Commission's recommendations, a number of which relate to the investigation of sexual offences.

It should be noted that in New Zealand recorded offence statistics are presented in broad categories, meaning that a number of different crimes are contained within each category. The recording to the end of 2014 is over-inclusive in that it records both actual offences and offences recorded for charging purposes only. This means that a charge could be recorded, withdrawn and re-filed, and thereby record two offences when only one was committed.

They are also under-inclusive, in that they exclude offences where police decide that initial attendance is sufficient to address the matter and do not record it as an offence.[5] The offending categories that are most prevalent have remained stable over the last decade. Table 2 illustrates the ten types of criminal offending most often committed in New Zealand in the period 2006-2014.

Table 2. Most prevalent criminal offences in New Zealand (average number of recorded offences 2006-2014)*

Theft and related offences	135197
Burglary and related offences	57521
Property Damage	54199
Acts intended to cause injury	40941
Public Order Offences	40496
Illicit Drug Offences	20111
Offences Against Justice	18555
Abduction, Harassment and Other Offences Against the Person	13192
Fraud, Deception and related offences	10672
Weapons and Explosives Offences	6804

* Data from Statistics New Zealand (at: http://nzdotstat.stats.govt.nz/WBOS/Index.aspx) (last visited: 26 May 2016). Averages rounded to the nearest whole number.

Table 2 illustrates that property offences are consistently the most prevalent offences committed in New Zealand, with theft, burglary and criminal damage comprising the top three offence types committed. However, these are not the offences that are most likely to be resolved by police. New Zealand police statistics include the offences for which there are apprehensions and some form of resolution, including by way of prosecution, warning and diversion. As can be seen in Table 3, these illustrate that all forms of property offending are amongst

5 New Zealand Police, *New Recorded Crime Victim Statistics* (at: www.police.govt.nz/sites/default/files/publications/rcvs-stakeholder-briefing.pdf) (last visited: 20 October 2016).

the least likely types of offences to be resolved.[6] Typically, such offences are more likely to be reported (often in order to support an insurance claim). However, apprehensions of offenders can be difficult in such cases, as offenders will have often left the scene when the crime is discovered. In addition, property offending such as burglary and deception may be serial crimes which can take longer to resolve.

Table 3. Average percentage of offences resolved 2006-2014, by offence type*

Offences Against Justice	92.99%
Illicit Drug Offences	92.73%
Homicide and related offences	91.46%
Weapons and Explosives Offences	91.06%
Public Order Offences	86.68%
Acts intended to cause injury	80.96%
Miscellaneous Offences	71.14%
Abduction, Harassment and Other Offences Against the Person	67.72%
Dangerous or Negligent Acts Endangering Persons	67.09%
Sexual Assault and related offences	57.28%
Fraud, Deception and related offences	52.35%
Robbery and related offences	42.13%
Property Damage	29.27%
Theft and related offences	23.32%
Burglary and related offences	14.84%

* Data from Statistics New Zealand (at: http://nzdotstat.stats.govt.nz/WBOS/Index.aspx) (last visited: 26 May 2016).

Unsurprisingly, the offences that are most often resolved in New Zealand are those that are typically witnessed by others, or that result in the apprehension of offenders during the offending, such as possession of drugs and offences involving breaches of public order.

As in all comparable jurisdictions, the recorded crime levels represent only a percentage of actual crime. At each stage of the criminal justice process there is attrition, including choices to report, police decisions to record as an offence, police decisions as to prosecution and so on. Therefore statistics based on recorded offences, such as prevalence figures and resolved rates for offending, are also flawed. The government has attempted to generate a more complete picture

6 There is some undercounting of resolutions where offences are recorded towards the end of the year and are then resolved a few weeks into the following year, as these will not appear as resolved in official statistics.

of the level of crime in New Zealand than police recorded statistics allow, by the introduction of a victim survey. This survey, called the New Zealand Crime and Safety Survey (NZCASS) was carried out in 2006, 2009 and 2014 in relation to crime experienced in 2005, 2008 and 2013.[7] It is a face-to-face laptop based survey of almost 7000 randomly chosen people, and it is conducted in participants' homes. It collects information about participants' experiences of crime, including levels of victimisation, reactions to experiencing crime, the needs of victims, and crime trends. The NZCASS only surveys people over the age of 15 years, and it does not record commercial crimes, victimless crimes (such as drug offences) or crimes where the victim is unable to report (such as homicides). NZCASS aims to measure how much crime gets reported to police, and therefore asks participants if incidents were reported. However, responses about reporting are not verified with police records, and there is no accurate way to do so. Because of these differences in approach between police recording of crime and the NZCASS, the survey is not directly comparable to police recorded crime statistics except in relation to thefts of and from vehicles, burglary, robbery and assaults.[8] The 2014 survey estimated that 31% of all crime, and 24% of interpersonal violent crime, is reported to police.[9] This result is consistent with the previous survey results. In 2014, the NZCASS results estimate that 1.9 million incidents of crime were committed.[10] While subject to sampling bias, the NZCASS therefore suggests that true rates of offending in New Zealand are much higher than the number of offences reported to, and recorded by, police.

II.2. ALTERNATIVES TO CRIMINALIZATION

In New Zealand there is little evidence that there are criminalised behaviours which could be dealt with in another way. Most offences involve behaviour which causes harm to individuals or risks to the community. This means that there are few truly 'victimless' or purely moral offences. Those offences which were based in morality have gradually been legalized or decriminalised, most recently in

7 The main findings report from the latest survey can be downloaded at: Ministry of Justice, *2014 New Zealand Crime and Safety Survey* (at: www.justice.govt.nz/assets/Documents/Publications/NZCASS-201602-Main-Findings-Report-Updated.pdf) (last visited: 20 October 2016).

8 These offences comprised 43% of reported offences in the 2014 survey: Ministry of Justice, *Reporting Crime* (at: www.justice.govt.nz/justice-sector-policy/research-data/nzcass/survey-results/reporting-crime/) (last visited: 20 October 2016).

9 Ministry of Justice, *Reporting Crime* (at: www.justice.govt.nz/justice-sector-policy/research-data/nzcass/survey-results/reporting-crime/) (last visited: 20 October 2016).

10 Ministry of Justice, *New Zealand Crime and Safety Survey – Main Findings Summary Pamhplet* (at: www.justice.govt.nz/assets/Documents/Publications/NZCASS-Main-Findings-Summary-Pamphlet.pdf) (last visited: 20 October 2016).

relation to prostitution. The Prostitution Reform Act 2003[11] aimed to create a framework that safeguards sex workers' rights. Whilst prostitution itself was not illegal, a number of associated behaviours were criminal offences. The Act has replaced these with a system of regulation.[12]

However, there are a number of areas where policy innovations have led to quasi-criminal offences which act as preventive mechanisms that sit outside the criminal law. They are introduced to address the risk that individuals may commit a crime, do not require that any criminal offence is actually committed, and are officially deemed to be civil orders. Such orders are becoming more numerous in common law jurisdictions. They have been likened to Trojan horses and described as "stealth sanctions" because of the involvement of law enforcement officers, and because the breach of civil orders is sometimes used to justify criminal penalties.[13] Simester and Von Hirsch have suggested that they blur the difference between civil and criminal law, because they use the civil law to condemn wrongdoing and risk "loss of clarity of the criminal law's distinctively moral voice".[14] Two examples of quasi-criminal or hybrid orders introduced in recent years in New Zealand are Police Safety Orders and the expansion of civil pecuniary penalty orders.

a. Police Safety Orders

Police Safety Orders were introduced in 2010, and 19,470 orders were issued between 1 July 2010 and 31 December 2012. The use of the orders has increased over time, with orders being issued in 14% of all family violence cases attended by police. They seek to address the risk of family violence, harassment and intimidation at an early stage, in order to prevent escalation to more serious criminal offending. They are issued where there is insufficient evidence of an offence but the officers attending think that action is necessary to ensure the

---

11 Prostituion Reform Act 2003, s 3 (at: www.legislation.govt.nz/act/public/2003/0028/latest/DLM197821.html).

12 For a review of the Act, see Gillian Abel, Lisa Fitzgerald & Cheryl Brunton, *The Impact of the Prostitution Reform Act on the Health and Safety Practices of Sex Workers*, Department of Public Health and General Practice, Christchurch: University of Otago, 2007 (an e-copy of the report can be found at: www.otago.ac.nz/christchurch/otago018607.pdf) (last visited: 20 October 2016). See also Paul Bellamy, *Prostitution law reform in New Zealand*, Parliamentary Library Research Paper 2012/05, 2012.

13 Andrew Ashworth, 'Editorial: In Favour of Community Safety', *Criminal L.R.* (1997), p. 769-770; [1997] *Crim. L.R.* 769, 770; R M White, ''Civil Penalties': Oxymoron, Chimera and Stealth Sanction', 126 *LQR* (2010), p. 593.

14 Andrew Simester & Andreas von Hirsch, 'Regulating Offensive Conduct', in: Andrew Simester & Andreas von Hirsch (eds), *Incivilities: Regulating Offensive Behaviour*, Oxford: Bloomsbury, 2006, p.189.

safety of the people at the address. An order may last for up to five days.[15] The person bound by the order must leave the premises named in the order for its duration, even if they normally live there. The police may detain the bound person for up to two hours to issue and serve the order and there is no right of appeal. If the order is breached, the person may be arrested and brought before the court, although no criminal charges will eventuate from the breach itself. Although a 2014 evaluation commissioned by New Zealand Police was largely positive about the operation of Police Safety Orders[16], there is concern that they may be issued where there is no safety risk, or instead of an arrest in cases where there has been violence. The requirement for the bound person to leave the residence raises issues of financial and emotional hardship for both children and adults involved, including the potential for other government agencies to become involved in their lives. The inability to appeal raises concerns about due process protections for those subject to the orders.

b. Pecuniary penalty orders

Civil pecuniary penalty orders are punitive measures that avoid the mechanisms of the criminal trial. The penalties can be substantial, and are paid to the Crown, yet are imposed on the civil standard of proof without the protections afforded to defendants in a criminal trial.[17] In a recent report on the increasing use of civil penalties, the Law Commission noted the ad hoc nature of their growth and the resulting lack of a coherent set of guiding principles.[18] The majority of existing penalties have been introduced recently – after 2000 – and aim to deter commercial wrongdoing. Their benefits include savings for the government agency involved, the court system and the defendant, and they often allow defendants to admit liability without also admitting to criminal activity. Some pecuniary penalties are true alternatives to criminal offences, being stand-alone civil offences.[19] Others work in parallel ways with criminal offences depending on mens rea – these are enforced as a criminal offence when the act is performed with intent or recklessness, or by way of a pecuniary penalty where no intent or recklessness is proved.[20] Both individuals and body corporates may be subject to the penalties. Given the breadth of penalties in number and character, there is

15 New Zealand Police, *Police Safety Orders* (at: http://www.police.govt.nz/advice/family-violence/police-safety-orders) (last visited: 20 October 2016).
16 Elaine Mossman, Venezia Kingi & Nan Wehipeihana, *An Outcome Evaluation of Police Safety Orders*, Wellington: New Zealand Police, 2014.
17 It is unclear whether pecuniary penalties amount to an "offence" for the purposes of New Zealand Bill of Rights Act 1990, s 25, which provides for criminal procedure protections.
18 New Zealand Law Commission, *Pecuniary Penalties: Guidance for Legislative Design*, Report 133, Wellington, 2014.
19 See, for example: Unsolicited Electronic Messages Act 2007.
20 Hazardous Substances and New Organisms Act 1996, ss 109 and 124B.

little surprise that they have been described as "a grave form of state-imposed punishment."[21] The Law Commission recommended a series of reforms to aid consistency, including the need for oversight from the Ministry of Justice prior to the creation of new penalty provisions; the creation of a specific chapter in the Legislative Design and Advisory Committee guidelines; and the drafting of model provisions by the Parliamentary Counsel Office. These have been accepted in principle by the Government, but at the time of writing little progress has been made.

II.3. OTHER POSSIBILITIES FOR POLICY-BASED TOLERANCE AND EDUCATION

Although there is generally little evidence of criminalisation of behaviours that could be dealt with differently in New Zealand, a major exception can be found in the approach to small scale drug possession and use. Whilst imprisonment of drug offenders is mostly reserved for cultivation, sale and importation of drugs, possession and use is still subject to the criminal justice regime. The governing statute, the Misuse of Drugs Act 1975, is focused on prohibition and control. This is in contrast to the harm minimisation approach in the National Drug Policy.[22] There is some evidence of a changing approach in New Zealand to the implementation of the law as to possession. A study of arrests and prosecutions for cannabis possession between 1991 and 2008 by Wilkins and Sweetsur suggests that there was a substantial decline in arrests, prosecutions and convictions for cannabis use in the decade before their study was published. They also report an increase in the availability of alternatives to conviction such as diversion (see below) and the court outcomes of 'discharge without conviction' and 'convicted and discharged'.[23] The apprehensions for cannabis use and possession bear out that this is a continuing trend, falling from 318 apprehensions per 100,000 of the population in 2000 to 119 apprehensions per 100,000 of the population in 2014.[24] However, there is no documented policy approach to tolerance, and as such the principles and criteria for exercising tolerance of small scale possession and use is

---

21 New Zealand Law Commission, *Pecuniary Penalties: Guidance for Legislative Design*, Report 133, Wellington, 2014, p. 6.

22 The most recent National Drug policy can be accessed at: Ministry of Health, *National Drug Policy 2015 to 2020*, August 2015 (at: www.health.govt.nz/system/files/documents/publications/national-drug-policy-2015-2020-aug15.pdf) (last visited: 20 October 2016).

23 Chris Wilkins & Paul Sweetsur, 'Criminal justice outcomes for cannabis use offences in New Zealand, 1991–2008', 23 *International Journal of Drug Policy* 6 (2012), p. 505-511.

24 Data from: Statistics New Zealand, *Annual Apprehensions for the Latest Calendar Years (ANZSOC)* (at: http://nzdotstat.stats.govt.nz/wbos/Index.aspx?DataSetCode=TABLECODE7407#) (last visited: 26 May 2016).
If offences including possession of paraphernalia are included, the relevant apprehension rates are 450 per 100,000 population in 2000 and 165 per 100,000 population in 2014.

rather opaque. In 2011, the Law Commission recommended a presumption against imprisonment and the introduction of a mandatory cautioning scheme for personal possession and use offences. Cautions would be issued where users acknowledged responsibility for the offence, and opportunities for accessing treatment would be provided. Treatment would not be enforced for possession, but attendance at a brief intervention would be a condition after the first, second or third caution, depending on the 'class' of drug the user possessed. After a set number of cautions, the user would be prosecuted.[25] This scheme would have offered an explicit set of rules by which policy-based tolerance could be practiced, but it has not been adopted by the Government.

III. OVERUSE OF PROSECUTION[26]

III.1. TRENDS IN THE USE OF PROSECUTION

As a percentage of total recorded offences, New Zealand appears to prosecute a relatively small percentage of offences, between 23% and 26% annually over the last decade. Table 4 sets out the offences resolved, prosecuted and convicted as a percentage of total recorded offences. It shows that since 2006, between 56% and 60% of all resolutions of recorded offences are prosecutions. However, because of the difference between police recording practices and prosecution and conviction statistics, these figures are misleading. Police records are offence-based, whereas prosecution and conviction statistics are case-based. This makes comparisons of rates of detected and prosecuted crime difficult to make, since Police may prosecute an offender for some but not all of the offences that are recorded in relation to an incident. The rate of prosecutions across all offence types, therefore, is almost certainly higher than Table 4 suggests.

Table 4 also illustrates that after 2011, the number of offences prosecuted and convicted has been falling, although the percentage of prosecuted offences that results in a conviction has been rising over the same period. This may suggest that prosecution is increasingly likely to be reserved for cases where there is the greatest prospect of a conviction.

The total number of offences prosecuted in the period 2000-2015 is shown in Table 5, illustrating the offence types prosecuted in the highest numbers over the period. The table also shows what percentage each offence type is of the total

25 New Zealand Law Commission, *Controlling and regulating drugs: A review of the Misuse of Drugs Act 1975*, Report 119, Wellington, 2011.

26 The process discussed in this chapter relate to adult offending. There is a different process where the offender is a child or young person: see Alison Cleland & Khylee Quince, *Youth Justice in Aotearoa New Zealand - Law, Policy and Critique*, Wellington: LexisNexis, 2014; Nessa Lynch, *Youth Justice in New Zealand*, Wellington: Thomson Reuters, 2016.

Table 4. Percentage of recorded offences resolved, prosecuted and convicted, 2006–2014*

	2006	2007	2008	2009	2010	2011	2012	2013	2014
Total # recorded offences	424137	426384	431383	451405	426345	406056	376013	360411	350389
Total # resolved offences	185227	194768	201419	215618	202545	190820	176853	158042	145367
% resolved of all recorded	43.67%	45.68%	46.69%	47.77%	47.51%	46.99%	47.03%	43.85%	41.49%
Total # prosecuted offences (all outcomes)	105346	113396	121811	127033	119510	106607	98826	90061	82011
% prosecuted of all recorded	24.84%	26.59%	28.24%	28.14%	28.03%	26.25%	26.28%	24.99%	23.41%
% prosecuted of all resolved	56.87%	58.22%	60.48%	58.92%	59.00%	55.87%	55.88%	56.99%	56.42%
Total # convicted offences	81917	88363	95041	99716	95377	87120	80833	74461	68446
% convicted of all recorded	19.31%	20.72%	22.03%	22.09%	22.37%	21.46%	21.50%	20.66%	19.53%
% convicted of all resolved	44.23%	45.37%	47.19%	46.25%	47.09%	45.66%	45.71%	47.11%	47.08%
% convicted of all prosecuted	77.76%	77.92%	78.02%	78.50%	79.81%	81.72%	81.79%	82.68%	83.46%

* Data from Statistics New Zealand (at: http://nzdotstat.stats.govt.nz/WBOS/Index.aspx) (last visited: 26 May 2016).

number of prosecutions across the whole period, and an average (mean) of the number prosecuted in each offence type yearly. While traffic offences and offences against justice have been the two types of offence prosecuted in the highest numbers each year in the period 2000-2015, and robbery and homicide the smallest numbers of prosecutions, there has been variability in the numbers for other offence types relative to each other. This may represent changes in policy focus. For example, public order offences began and ended the period as the seventh and eighth most numerous offence type prosecuted, but in the middle of the period rose to the offence type with the third highest number of prosecutions.

The offences prosecuted in the highest numbers are also those most likely to result in conviction in New Zealand, with 88% of traffic offences and 75% of offences against justice resulting in a conviction. This reflects the nature of such offences, which often involve cogent evidence (for example from police witnesses or official records) and relatively minor offending.

Table 5. Number of offences prosecuted by offence type 2000-2015*

	Total outcomes 2000-2015	Average (yearly mean) outcomes 2000-2015	Percentage of outcomes from total
Traffic offences	816912	51057	18.96%
Offences against justice	702017	43876	16.29%
Theft and related offences	427966	26748	9.93%
Acts intended to cause injury	396575	24786	9.20%
Fraud, deception and related offences	353521	22095	8.20%
Public order offences	339021	21189	7.87%
Illicit drug offences	303567	18973	7.04%
Acts endangering persons	259938	16406	6.03%
Property damage	180669	11292	4.19%
Miscellaneous Offences	142163	8885	3.30%
Burglary and related offences	136543	8534	3.17%
Weapons offences	81125	5070	1.88%
Sexual offences	73638	4602	1.71%
Other offences against the person	70927	4433	1.65%
Robbery and related offences	21589	1349	0.50%
Homicide and related offences	3142	196	0.07%
TOTAL OFFENCES	4309313	269332	100.00%

* Data from Statistics New Zealand (at: http://nzdotstat.stats.govt.nz/WBOS/Index.aspx) (last visited: 26 May 2016).

III.2. THE PROSECUTION PROCESS

Unlike most Commonwealth countries, New Zealand does not have a centralised prosecution service or Director of Public Prosecutions. Any person may institute a prosecution for an offence, except for a minority of offences which require the prior consent of the Attorney-General (for example, offences concerning judicial corruption and bribery of judicial or law enforcement officers).[27] Every prosecution is commenced by way of filing a charging document at the District Court. It must contain information about the charge, name of person charged and filing the document and, except for private prosecutions, the name of the relevant agency.

27 Crown Law, *Statutory Offences Requiring the Consent of the Attorney-General* (at: www.crownlaw.govt.nz/assets/Uploads/Prosecution-Guidelines/statutory-offences-2013.pdf) (last visited: 20 October 2016).

In practice, most criminal proceedings are initiated by the police.[28] They act independently when deciding to conduct investigations and prosecutions. Police prosecutors can be uniformed officers, qualified lawyers, or both, but the police prosecutions section is separate from the investigative arm of the police. The officer in charge of the case will make the decision to charge and prepare the original charging document, and the Police Prosecutions Service is then tasked with reviewing and handling the case.[29]

The most serious offences, and less serious cases where the defendant is able to and does elect trial by jury, are deemed to be Crown prosecutions.[30] In these cases, the police take initial responsibility for the progress of the prosecution. They hand the case over to the Crown Solicitors from an early stage of court proceedings.[31] Crown Solicitors are independent from police, are private practitioners appointed by the warrant of the Governor-General, and are supervised by the Deputy Solicitor-General.[32] Although police make the initial decision to prosecute, Crown solicitors and prosecutors are independent of the police and have discretion as to what charges should be pursued at trial. Responsibility for Crown prosecutions rests with the Attorney-General, but by convention he or she does not play any active role, and the prosecution functions are performed in practice by the Solicitor-General.

The New Zealand prosecution process operates under the opportunity or expedience principle. The decision to prosecute is based on an assessment of evidential sufficiency and the public interest in prosecution. Guidelines have been issued by the Crown Law Office to assist prosecutors in making their decisions.[33] The evidence which can be adduced in court must be sufficient to provide a reasonable prospect of conviction. Guideline 5.3 of the Prosecution Guidelines provides that:

> A reasonable prospect of conviction exists if, in relation to an identifiable person (whether natural or legal), there is credible evidence which the prosecution can adduce before a court and upon which evidence an impartial jury (or judge), properly directed in accordance with the law, could reasonably be expected to be satisfied beyond

28 There are a variety of other enforcement agenices (for example, Customs, Inland Revenue, Immigration and Fisheries) that also lay charges and conduct prosecutions themselves.

29 New Zealand Police, *Police Prosecution Service Statement of Policy and Practice*, July 2013 (at: www.police.govt.nz/sites/default/files/publications/pps-statement-of-policy-and-practice.pdf) (last visited: 20 October 2016), p. 10.

30 Crown Prosecution Regulations 2013, regulation 4.

31 For detailed information, see: Crown Prosecution Regulations 2013, regulation 5.

32 There are sixteen Crown Solicitors who hold warrants for different regions in New Zealand and oversee the Crown prosecution work in that region. They delegate work to Crown Prosecutors.

33 The Prosecution Guidelines can be accessed at: Crown Law, *Solicitor-General's Prosuection Guidelines*, 1 July 2013 (at: www.crownlaw.govt.nz/assets/Uploads/Prosecution-Guidelines/prosecution-guidelines-2013.pdf) (last visited: 20 October 2016).

reasonable doubt that the individual who is prosecuted has committed a criminal offence.

It can therefore be seen that, rather than being focused on the intrinsic merits of the case, in practice the evidential test is largely predictive. It takes into account admissibility of the evidence and any likely legitimate defence. The evidential test must be satisfied before the public interest test is considered. This means that prosecutions will not go ahead unless there is a reasonable prospect of conviction by a properly instructed jury applying the law, even in cases where there is considerable public interest in prosecution.

If a case passes the evidential sufficiency test, the prosecutor will consider whether the prosecution is required in the public interest. Not all offences for which there is sufficient evidence are prosecuted.[34] Generally, the more serious the charge and the stronger the evidence to support it, the less likely it will be that it can properly be disposed of other than by prosecution. Other public interest considerations in favour of prosecution include (but are not limited to) whether the offence involved[35]:

- serious violence, financial loss or risk;
- previous convictions;
- prevalent offending;
- premeditation;
- organised crime;
- vulnerable victims;
- abuse of trust;
- 'hate crime';
- group offending; or
- corruption.

Conversely, public interest considerations against prosecution include where[36]:

- the Court is likely to impose a very small or nominal penalty;
- there was minor loss or harm from a single incident;
- it is unlikely to be repeated;
- there has been a long passage of time between an offence taking place and the likely date of trial unless the offence is serious, newly reported or the result of a long investigation;

34 There are exceptions to the general proposition that it is not the rule that cases where there is evidential sufficiency must proceed: as a matter of policy, some offence types must proceed where there is sufficient evidence, most notably offences involving driving with excess breath or blood alcohol.

35 Crown Prosecution Regulations 2013, regulation 5.8.

36 Crown Prosecution Regulations 2013, regulation 5.9.

- prosecution is likely to have a detrimental effect on the physical or mental health of a victim or witness;
- the defendant is elderly, young or ill;
- the defendant has no previous convictions;
- loss or harm has already been rectified;
- there are issues of national security;
- or proper alternatives to prosecution are available.

There is no indication in the Guidelines as to the prioritisation or balancing of these factors. If the decision is taken that there should not be a prosecution, there may be occasions where it may be re-opened, such as where a reassessment of the decision shows that it was wrong or where more evidence is found.

If the decision is made to prosecute, since July 2013 case management discussions under sections 55 and 56 of the Criminal Procedure Act 2011 explicitly allow plea arrangements to be made. The advantage of such arrangements is the avoidance of a contested trial, which is said to be better for complainants and witnesses, saves court time and money, and allows for defendants to take advantage of a sentencing discount for pleading guilty. In reaching an arrangement, the charges must reflect the essential criminality of the conduct and allow sufficient scope for sentencing. Prosecutors must not proceed with unnecessary additional charges or a more serious charge with a view to securing a negotiated plea. They must also avoid agreeing to a plea of guilty to an offence not disclosed by the evidence, or to a guilty plea on the premise that the prosecutor will support a specific sentence.[37] No arrangement should be reached where the public interest favours proceeding on the charges as originally laid. Complainants should be told about plea discussions and can make their views known to the prosecutor. The prosecutor may not depart from the terms of an arrangement unless he or she has been materially misled by any information, and the Crown Solicitor agrees.

III.3. ALTERNATIVES TO PROSECUTION AND OPTIONS TO REDUCE PROSECUTION FURTHER

As part of the Policing Excellence Strategy, New Zealand Police introduced the Prevention First operating model[38], which has resulted in an increase in the types and use of alternatives to prosecution. As at the end of 2015, police reported a

37 Crown Prosecution Regulations 2013, regulation 18.

38 State Services Commission, *Formal Review of the New Zealand Police*, September 2012 (at: https://www.ssc.govt.nz/sites/all/files/pif-police-review-sept12.PDF) (last visited: 20 October 2016).

reduction of 16% in overall crime since 2009.[39] Two alternatives to prosecution, adult diversion and pre-charge warnings, are widely utilised by police, and restorative justice practices are becoming more frequent, although mainly at the pre-sentence stage rather than as an alternative to prosecution. In addition, police has introduced a new strategy to respond to the over-representation of Māori as both victims and offenders. Although alternatives to prosecution may reduce the numbers of offences prosecuted, because the current options are reserved for lower level offending they are unlikely to reduce imprisonment. Pre-charge alternatives to prosecution that could operate for more serious offending, such as restorative justice, are being considered by the government.[40] However, the form any such alternatives would take is not yet clear.

a. Diversion

Once formal proceedings are initiated, the police may offer a defendant 'diversion', whereby a conviction is avoided. Diversion should only be used when there is sufficient evidence to file a charging document. This means that diversion is not a true alternative to prosecution, as the initial steps to prosecute are taken. Diversion is reserved for more minor offences and favours first time offenders, although since 2013 police policy allows it to be used for recidivist offenders. Defendants must admit responsibility for the offence, agree to the diversion process, and agree to complete the requirements of diversion that are imposed. If diverted, the defendant attends a first appearance in court, where the case is adjourned. The requirements imposed must be proportionate to the offence, achievable within the adjournment period, and 'appropriate' in that they must be directed towards reparation, rehabilitation or both.[41] They may include letters of apology, reparation, meeting with the victim, counselling or community service. If the diversion requirements are carried out, police offer no evidence in court, and the prosecution is withdrawn or dismissed. There is some concern that diversion has a net-widening effect, resulting in prosecutions which would not have been pursued without the scheme being in place. It is a discretionary process operated by police, and is sometimes inconsistent in its application.

---

39 These figures appear in the 2016-2020 Strategic Plan: New Zealand Police, *New Zealand Police Four Year Plan*, May 2016 (at: www.police.govt.nz/sites/default/files/publications/strategic-plan-2016-2020-four-year-plan.pdf) (last visited: 20 October 2016).

40 Such alternatives were recommended in research regarding sexual offending and alternative trial processes: see Elisabeth McDonald & Yvette Tinsley (eds), *From Real Rape to Real Justice*, Wellington: Victoria University Press, 2011; New Zealand Law Commission, *Alternative Models for prosecuting and trying criminal cases*, IP30, Wellington, 2012; New Zealand Law Commission, *The Justice Response to Victims of Sexual Violence: Criminal Trials and Alternative Processes*, Report 136, Wellington, 2015.

41 New Zealand Police, *Adult Diversion Scheme Policy* (at: www.police.govt.nz/sites/default/files/publications/adult-diversion-scheme-policy.pdf) (last visited: 20 October 2016).

b. Pre-charge warnings

Pre-charge warnings are alternative resolutions that operate post-arrest and pre-charge. They act to divert offenders from prosecution in cases where there is evidential sufficiency to prosecute. They can be used for offences with a maximum penalty of less than 6 months' imprisonment. In such cases prosecution may not be in the public interest, because the time and cost of prosecution is seen to be disproportionate to the offending. Pre-charge warnings cannot be offered in relation to family violence offences and methamphetamine offences. They can only be offered to offenders over the age of 17 years. A recent review of pre-charge warnings by the Independent Police Conduct Authority found that warnings may assist in reducing reoffending by offenders who have not previously been before the courts, either because they respond to the fact that they have been given a second chance, or because they avoid the stigma arising from a court appearance and conviction. However, it also found that there was considerable inconsistency in decision-making within and between Police districts.[42] Between February and April 2016, 3189 pre-charge warnings were issued in New Zealand, meaning that pre-charge warnings were issued in 37% of all eligible cases.[43] Pre-charge warnings were more likely to be given to non-Māori offenders than to Māori offenders: since Māori are more likely to be repeat offenders, the eligibility criteria operate to exclude them more often. If a warning is issued, it is not recorded as a criminal conviction, but the fact of the warning is held on record.

c. Community Justice Panels

Community justice and iwi panels (Māori indigenous community panels), like pre-charge warnings, are a form of pre-charge alternatives to prosecution. They operate for offences where a pre-charge warning is not seen to be a sufficient response, but where there is no public interest to proceed with prosecution. Panels consist of one police staff member (who manages the referral process) and community members such as church leaders, sports coaches and school teachers. Panels conduct a hearing, from which they impose conditions for the offender. Outcomes focus on restitution, accountability and education, including conditions such as apologies, community service, financial reparation, donations, essays and referrals to treatment or support services. Four panels are currently in operation: one community justice panel and three iwi panels. The panels have not

42 Independent Police Conduct Authority, *Review of Pre-Charge Warnings*, 14 September 2016.
43 Independent Police Conduct Authority, *Review of Pre-Charge Warnings*, 14 September 2016, p. 7-8.

yet been rolled out nationally, despite the initial pilot period concluding in 2015.[44]

If the conditions imposed by a community justice panel are complied with, no criminal conviction is recorded, but the fact that the offender went through a community justice panel process is kept on file. The same New Zealand Police Alternative Resolutions criteria apply to these panels as to pre-charge warnings. Offenders must admit guilt and be over 17 years of age, and there must be evidential sufficiency for prosecution. Contrary to the criteria, panels have been allowed to consider some cases involving family violence, and some that have a higher maximum penalty than six months' imprisonment, although the majority of offences involved dishonesty, property damage, disorder, cannabis use and possession, and driving offences.[45]

d. *Turning of the tide*

The representation of Māori as both victims and offenders is disproportionate to their numbers in the general population. Police have recently introduced "Turning of the Tide", which is a joint strategy between police and Māori that contains six targets across areas involving first time offenders, repeat offenders, repeat victims, and fatal and serious crashes.[46] As part of the strategy, police aim to reduce offending by young, first-time and repeat offenders. The strategy acknowledges the long term, societal issues contributing to Māori offending and victimisation. If a true partnership with Māori is achieved, the strategy has potential to expand and enhance alternatives to prosecution for Māori.

IV. OVERUSE OF IMPRISONMENT

IV.1. TRENDS IN THE USE OF IMPRISONMENT

New Zealand has for a long time had a high per capita prison population by international standards. In 2015 it stood at 191.8 prisoners per 100,000 of

---

44 Gaining consistency of approach is difficult, but there appears to be significant community support for continuation of the panels in the areas where they already operate: New Zealand Law Society, *Justice Panels: Innovative way to achieve justice*, 11 February 2016 (at: https://www.lawsociety.org.nz/lawtalk/lawtalk-archives/issue-881/justice-panels-innovative-way-to-achieve-justice) (last visited: 20 October 2016).

45 New Zealand Police, *Community Justice Panel in Christchurch: An Evaluation*, November 2012 (at: www.police.govt.nz/sites/default/files/publications/community-justice-panel-christchurch-pilot-evaluation-report-nov-2012.pdf), p. iii.

46 New Zealand Police, *New Zealand Police Four Year Plan*, May 2016 (at: www.police.govt.nz/sites/default/files/publications/strategic-plan-2016-2020-four-year-plan.pdf) (last visited: 20 October 2016).

Table 6. Prison population 2000–2015*

Year	Total Prison Population	Total Population	Rate per 100,000 population
2000	5661	3,860,200	147
2001	5985	3,887,000	154
2002	6048	3,951,200	153
2003	5826	4,027,700	145
2004	6556	4,088,700	160
2005	7420	4,136,000	179
2006	7595	4,186,900	181
2007	7771	4,230,700	184
2008	7887	4,271,100	185
2009	8326	4,318,200	193
2010	8816	4,370,200	202
2011	8587	4,407,400	195
2012	8618	4,435,600	194
2013	8597	4,442,048	194
2014	8571	4,509,700	190
2015	8821	4,600,000	192

* Data from: Statistics New Zealand, Yearbook Collection: 1893-2012 (at: www.stats.govt.nz/browse_for_stats/snapshots-of-nz/digital-yearbook-collection.aspx) (last visited: 5 May 2016); Department of Corrections, Prison Statistics, (at: www.corrections.govt.nz/resources/research_and_statistics/quarterly_prison_statistics.html) (last visited: 5 May 2016); Statistics New Zealand, 2012 Yearbook population tables (at: www.stats.govt.nz/browse_for_stats/snapshots-of-nz/yearbook/people/population/yearbook-pop.aspx) (last visited: 5 May 2016).

population, a slight decline from the record high of 202.7 per 100,000 in 2013. In 2013 New Zealand had the seventh highest prison population rate out of 34 OECD countries[47], and more recently the World Prison Brief produced by the Institute for Criminal Policy Research ranked New Zealand 68 out of 221 countries.[48]

As Table 6 demonstrates, there has been a particularly pronounced rise in the prison population in the last 15 years, from 5,661 in 2000 to 8,821 in 2015. There were particularly large increases between 2003 and 2005, and again between 2008 and 2010.

---

47 Statista *Incarcaration Rates in OECD Countries 2012/2013* (at: https://www.statista.com/statistics/300986/incarceration-rates-in-oecd-countries/) (last visited: 20 October 2016).

48 World Prison Brief – Institute for Criminal Policy Research *Highest to Lowest – Prison Population Rate* (at: www.prisonstudies.org/highest-to-lowest/prison_population_rate?field_region_taxonomy_tid=All) (last visited: 20 October 2016).

This increase in the prison population has been against the backdrop of a long term decline in recorded crime and a more recent reduction in the number of prosecutions and convictions (see Tables 1 and 4). As a result, the official prediction from the Government in 2011 was that the prison population would begin to decline.[49] As Table 1 shows, the trend until 2014 accorded with this prediction, but the initial decrease has since reversed, and in 2015 the population reached an all-time record level of 8,821. As at the time of writing (September 2016), it stood at 9,789.[50]

The most significant contribution to the increase in the prison population has come from an increase in the remand population (those in custody awaiting trial or sentence). In fact, as Table 7 shows, apart from a significant increase between 2004 and 2005, the sentenced prisoner population rate per 100,000 has remained fairly constant since 2000, while the remand prisoner population rate has undergone a remarkable increase from 18.3 per 100,000 to 46.2 per 100,000. As a result, the proportion of the prison population comprising remand prisoners has almost doubled.

On the face of it, therefore, sentenced prisoners have made a relatively small contribution to the increase in the prison population. However, this is a little misleading. In New Zealand, by virtue of section 82 of the Parole Act 2002, any periods spent on remand in custody are automatically deducted from the time served under a prison sentence when the date of release is being calculated. It follows that an increase in the use or length of custodial remands will reduce the time that offenders spend in custody as sentenced prisoners. If the number and length of prison sentences were remaining constant, therefore, an increase in the remand population would actually result in a decline in the sentenced prisoner population. This has not happened; there has in fact been a small increase. It can therefore be concluded that either the number or the length of prison sentences, or both, have increased over the 15-year period.

IV.2. REASONS FOR THESE TRENDS

Historically, New Zealand's high prison population rate compared with other countries has generally had more to do with average length of detention than the numbers being sent to prison on remand or under sentence.[51]

Although New Zealand's prison population saw a steady growth from the beginning of the 1970s, it was in the period following the passage of the Criminal

49 Ministry of Justice, Justice Sector Forecast 2011-2021, 30 September 2011.

50 Department of Corrections, *Prison facts and statistics – September 2016*, 30 September 2016 (at: http://corrections.govt.nz/resources/research_and_statistics/quarterly_prison_statistics/prison_stats_september_2016.html) (last visited: 20 October 2016).

51 See Warren Young & Mark Brown, 'Cross National Comparisons of Imprisonment', 17 *Crime and Justice: An Annual Review of Research* (1993), p. 1-49.

Table 7. Sentenced and remand prison population 2000–2015*

Year	Sentenced Prisoners Per 100,000 Population	Sentenced Prisoners as Percentage of Prison Population	Remand Prisoners per 100,000 Population	Remand Prisoners as Percentage of Prison Population
2000	128	87.5	18	12.5
2001	131	85.0	23	15.0
2002	126	82.4	27	17.6
2003	120	83.2	24	16.8
2004	131	81.5	30	18.5
2005	147	81.9	32	18.1
2006	149	82.0	33	18.0
2007	143	78.1	40	21.9
2008	143	77.5	42	22.5
2009	151	78.3	42	21.7
2010	158	78.4	44	21.6
2011	154	79.0	51	21.0
2012	152	78.5	42	21.5
2013	164	80.9	39	19.1
2014	150	78.8	40	21.2
2015	146	75.9	46	24.1

* Data from: Statistics New Zealand, Yearbook Collection: 1893-2012 (at: www.stats.govt.nz/browse_for_stats/snapshots-of-nz/digital-yearbook-collection.aspx) (last visited: 5 May 2016); Department of Corrections, Prison Statistics, (at: www.corrections.govt.nz/resources/research_and_statistics/quarterly_prison_statistics.html) (last visited: 5 May 2016); Statistics New Zealand, 2012 Yearbook population tables (at: www.stats.govt.nz/browse_for_stats/snapshots-of-nz/yearbook/people/population/yearbook-pop.aspx) (last visited: 5 May 2016).

Justice Act 1985 that imprisonment rates began to increase markedly. It was only 80 per 100,000 in 1981 and 89 per 100,000 in 1987, but by 2000 it had risen to 147 per 100,000. The major driver of this increase in the prison population was the increase in the length of both the nominal and the effective sentence[52] imposed on those receiving prison sentences. These harsher sentencing practices were particularly pronounced for violent and sexual offenders.

The further increase in the prison population since 2000 has largely reflected the same pattern, at least in relation to sentenced prisoners. During this period,

52 The "nominal" sentence is the length of sentence specified by the Court, whereas the "effective" sentence is the time actually served after taking into account release on the early statutory release date or on parole.

penal debate and penal policy have reflected many of the ingredients of what Tony Bottoms termed "populist punitiveness".[53]

Politicians have made law and order, and the need for tougher sanctions in response to crime, a key platform in election campaigns. In doing so, they have been responding (and in some cases contributing) to media commentary that is seen as an indicator of the public mood.[54]

The first tangible indicator of this new wave of popular punitiveness was a citizens' initiated referendum in the 1999 General Election, with the question: "Should there be a reform of our justice system placing greater emphasis on the needs of victims, providing restitution and compensation for them, and imposing minimum sentences and hard labour for all serious violent offences?" Notwithstanding the multi-faceted nature of this single question, it was put to the general public and resulted in a 91.75% vote in favour. That was followed by the emergence of various citizen-based lobby groups, the most notable being the ironically named Sensible Sentencing Trust. Although the Trust subsequently masqueraded as a victim support group, its primary express function was to lobby politicians for tougher sentencing and bail laws. Its primary spokesperson became the first port of call for the media looking for comment on any crime or law and order issue.

The key components of the Government's response to these perceived indicators of public mood were the enactment of the Sentencing Act 2002, the Parole Act 2002 and the Bail Act 2002.

The Sentencing Act 2002 actually contained relatively few provisions that were explicitly designed to lead to tougher sentencing. There were increases in the minimum terms to be served by those receiving a sentence of life imprisonment for murder, and the eligibility criteria for the sentence of preventive detention (an indeterminate sentence for high risk offenders) were widened. But the primary thrust of the statute was to spell out in detail the purposes and principles of sentencing and the aggravating and mitigating factors that dictate the choice of sentence. In this respect, the Act largely codified the pre-existing law that had been developed through the decisions of the Courts (termed in New Zealand the "common law").

Similarly, the Parole Act 2002 did not in itself make the granting of parole more difficult. It did for the first time make the risk of re-offending the only criterion in determining release on parole, but if this had been implemented as intended it is doubtful whether it would have resulted in prisoners serving a greater proportion of their sentence. It also enabled the Parole Board to keep

53 Anthony E. Bottoms, 'The Philosophy and Politics of Punishment and Sentencing', in: Chris Clarkson & Ron Morgan (eds), *The Politics of Sentencing Reform*, Oxford: Clarendon Press, 1995, p. 15-49.

54 John Pratt & Marie Clark, 'Penal Populism in New Zealand', 7 *Punishment and Society* 3 (2003), p. 303-322.

offenders in prison for the full term of their nominal sentence, whereas previously this had required an application to the Court. However, this was counterbalanced by a widening of parole eligibility to allow offenders to be released on parole after one third of their sentence, compared to the previous one half. The overall impact on the prison population of the reforms made by the Parole Act 2002 might therefore have been expected to be relatively neutral.

In fact, there was little immediate impact on the sentenced prisoner population following the 2002 legislative reforms, as is evident from Table 2. That was to be expected, since any change in sentencing practice would take a little time to impact on the prison population. But it soon changed, with an upward trend emerging by 2004. To the extent that this reflected any change in sentencing practice, this was arguably primarily due to the public and political climate that followed the citizens' initiated referendum and surrounded the implementation of the legislative reforms, which impacted on judicial practice and led to more conservative sentencing. That more conservative climate had a greater impact on the length of sentence than on the number of prison sentences imposed.

Although prison sentences as a proportion of total sentences remained more or less constant at 9-11% throughout the period 2002-2015, there was an increase of 29% in actual numbers between 2002 and 2009 as a result of an increase in the total volume before the courts. There was then a drop of 20% between 2009 and 2015 as a result of the introduction of policies and practices designed to keep minor offenders out of court (see above). In contrast, between 2002 and 2015, the sentenced prisoner population experienced a steady upward growth of 16%, reflecting the cumulative impact of a growth in average sentence length, particularly for more serious offences.

The much greater impact on the prison population came from the dramatic increase in the remand population after 2000. This was attributable more to the numbers being remanded in custody than the length of remand: between 2000 and 2006 receptions into prison on remand increased by 44%.[55]

However, while the Bail Act 2002 introduced some restrictions that limited the grant of bail, it again largely codified the common law, as with the Sentencing and Parole Acts. Much of the increase in the number of remands after 2000 can therefore again be attributed to the political and public climate surrounding the passage of the legislation rather than the content of the law itself. That is reflected in the fact that the number of defendants being remanded in pre-trial custody began to rise well before the legislation came into force.

The same cannot be said for subsequent legislation. The Bail Act 2002 has been amended no less than five times since its original enactment – in 2007,

55 Statistics New Zealand, *Adults convicted in court by sentence type – most serious offence calendar year* (at: http://nzdotstat.stats.govt.nz/wbos/Index.aspx?DataSetCode=TABLECODE7353) (last visited: 10 September 2016).

2008, 2009, 2011 and 2013. These amendments have progressively introduced a range of presumptive rules against the granting of bail, on the basis of the nature of the offence they are accused of committing and their previous criminal history.[56]

This has arguably led to an unduly risk adverse approach to defendants who have not yet been found guilty of an offence but are presumptively denied bail because of the characteristics of the group to which they belong rather than an individualised risk assessment. The further 7% increase in the numbers being remanded in custody between 2007 and 2010 were probably a direct result of the impact of these legislative changes.

IV.3. THE USE OF PRISON AND OTHER SENTENCES

In view of New Zealand's comparatively high prison population, it is perhaps surprising that internationally it has one of the most developed systems of alternative sanctions. The Sentencing Act 2002 stipulates an ascending hierarchy of tariff punishments that are designed as alternatives to imprisonment. These are:

- Home detention: a sentence for up to 12 months involving electronic monitored detention in a specified residence for 24 hours a day subject to leave for authorised purposes such as employment, attendance at a rehabilitation programme or medical appointments.
- Community detention: a sentence for up to 12 months involving an electronically monitored curfew in a specified residence for up to 12 hours a day.
- Community work: a sentence requiring the completion of up to 400 hours community work within 12 months of the date of sentence.
- Monetary penalties: either a fine or a sentence of reparation (compensation to the victim) or both.

In addition, the legislation provides for two rehabilitative sentences that may be combined with a tariff punishment:

- Intensive supervision: supervision by a probation officer that involves one or more special conditions including a requirement to undertake residential treatment programme.
- Supervision: supervision by a probation officer for up to 12 months, that may (but does not need to) involve special conditions including a requirement to undertake a non-residential treatment programme.

---

56 For a summary of these restrictions, see Warren Young, 'Pre-trial Detention in New Zealand', in: P.H.P.H.M.C. van Kempen (ed), *Pre-trial Detention*, Cambridge: Intersentia, 2012, p. 559-584.

The range of alternatives to imprisonment has progressively expanded with the passage of time. Home detention was made a sentence in its own right in 2002 and is available only if a judge has already determined that a sentence of two years imprisonment or less would otherwise be appropriate. Community detention and intensive supervision were both introduced in the Sentencing Amendment Act 2007 to provide a wider array of non-custodial options for sentencing judges.

Not surprisingly, therefore, imprisonment constitutes only a small proportion of total sentences: just over 11%. As Table 8 shows, about 75% of total sentences comprise monetary penalties or community-based sentences (community detention, community work, supervision and intensive supervision). By far the most common community-based penalty is community work, with 15,739 sentences of this type in 2015.[57]

Table 8. Types of sentences

	2011		2012		2013		2014		2015	
	Number	**%**	**Number**	**%**	**Number**	**%**	**Number**	**%**	**Number**	**%**
Prison	8370	9.6	7911	9.8	7477	10	7454	10.9	7278	11.4
Home Detention	2800	3.2	3013	3.7	2959	3	2812	4.1	2755	4.3
Community-based penalties	32128	36.9	30648	37.9	27783	37.3	26325	38.5	24710	38.8
Monetary penalties	33250	38.2	29560	36.6	27537	37	24199	35.3	21724	34.1
Other	10572	12.1	9701	12	8705	11.7	7656	11.2	7279	11.4
Total	87120	100	80833	100	74461	100	68446	100	63746	100

Notes:
Prison: Life imprisonment, Preventive Detention and Imprisonment
Home detention: Home Detention
Community-based: Community Detention, Community work, Intensive Supervision, Supervision
Monetary penalties: Fine, Reparation/Restitution
Other: Disqualification from Driving, Other, Conviction and Discharge

Source: Statistics New Zealand, *Adults convicted in court by sentence type – most serious offence calendar year* (at: http://nzdotstat.stats.govt.nz/wbos/Index.aspx?DataSetCode=TABLECODE7353) (last visited: 10 September 2016).

It can be seen from Table 8 that, in the last five years, the number of prison sentences imposed has substantially decreased – from 8,370 to 7,278. However, this mirrors the fall in the total number of convictions in that period. As a

57 Statistics New Zealand, *Adults convicted in court by sentence type – most serious offence calendar year* (at: http://nzdotstat.stats.govt.nz/wbos/Index.aspx?DataSetCode=TABLECODE7353) (last visited: 10 September 2016).

proportion of total sentences the use of imprisonment has actually increased – from 9.6% to 11.4%.

This does not in itself point to the emergence of a more punitive sentencing regime over that period. Most of the decline in the total number of convictions has resulted from the introduction of "alternative resolutions" before Court, notably pre-charge warnings (see above). These alternative resolutions particularly focus on minor crimes that would otherwise result in a token penalty such as a small fine. The average seriousness of offences resulting in a conviction has accordingly increased, with a corresponding increase in the average severity of the sanction.

Nevertheless, it is notable that the number of prison sentences has significantly fallen during a period when the prison population has increased to a record level. This reinforces the fact, as noted above, that the increase in the prison population is largely attributable to the increase in remands in custody and the ongoing cumulative impact of increases in sentence length in the preceding decade.

IV.4. THE SENTENCING REGIME

New Zealand has a relatively permissive sentencing regime. Although there has been a recent legislative pattern of placing greater restrictions on the breadth of the sentencing judge's discretion, these restrictions have been piecemeal and largely ineffective; judges still have a very wide measure of discretion as to the severity of the sentence for any particular offence.

The statutory restrictions or guidelines that do exist take the following four forms.

a. *Maximum penalty*

The main legislative mechanism for providing guidance as to the expected quantum of punishment is the maximum penalty prescribed for each individual offence – for example, 10 years' imprisonment for burglary. Section 8(c) of the Sentencing Act 2002 requires the judge to impose the maximum penalty prescribed for the offence if the offending is within the most serious of cases for which that penalty is prescribed, unless circumstances relating to the offender make that inappropriate.

However, since offences typically cover a range of behaviour of widely varying seriousness and culpability, and the maximum penalty is reserved for the hypothetical worst class of case, it is generally a poor guide to the expected sentence in day-to-day sentencing practice for the ordinary run of cases. The vast majority of sentences imposed for a particular offence therefore have little apparent relationship with it. Moreover, there is no systematic mechanism for revising maximum penalties. Where offences have been on the statute book for a long time and have not been revised, therefore, the maximum penalty may be outdated and not in accordance with contemporary mores.

b. Presumptive mandatory or minimum sentences

While there are no mandatory or minimum sentences that remove judicial discretion altogether, there are a number of "presumptive" mandatory or minimum sentences. These are presumptive because they are always accompanied by a caveat that enables the judge to depart from them in particular circumstances. For example:

- Section 128B(2) of the Crimes Act 1961 requires that a person convicted of sexual violation must be sentenced to imprisonment unless, having regard to the particular circumstances of the offence and the offender, the Court thinks that the person should not be sentenced to imprisonment.
- Section 12 of the Sentencing Act 2002 requires that, where there has been loss of or damage to property caused by the offence, the Court must impose a sentence of reparation unless it is satisfied that the sentence would result in undue hardship for the offender or the dependents of the offender, or that any other special circumstances would make it inappropriate.
- Section 102(1) of the Sentencing Act 2002 requires that an offender who is convicted of murder must be sentenced to imprisonment for life unless, given the circumstances of the offence and the offender, a sentence of imprisonment for life would be manifestly unjust.
- Section 104 of the Sentencing Act 2002 requires that an offender who is convicted of the worst murder must be sentenced to life imprisonment with a minimum term before parole eligibility of at least 17 years, unless the circumstances of the offence and the offender would make that manifestly unjust.

These types of provisions leave a considerable degree of flexibility for judges to determine the appropriate sentencing outcome, since terms such as "undue hardship", "manifestly unjust" and "circumstances relating to the offender" are undefined and left to judicial interpretation.

c. "Two strikes" and "three strikes" laws

As a specific form of presumptively mandatory sentencing, New Zealand has since 2010 had its own form of "two strikes" and "three strikes" legislation.[58]

58 Stencing Act 2002, ss 86A-86H, as inserted by section 6 of the Sentencing and Parole Reform Act 2010.

Under this regime, offenders who are convicted of a serious violent offence, committed when they were aged over 18, must receive a first warning as to the consequences of further offending. If they are convicted of a further serious violent offence, they must receive a final warning, and serve the full term of a determinate prison sentence without the possibility of parole. If they are then convicted of a third such offence, they must be sentenced to the maximum penalty for that offence, unless the court determines that this would be manifestly unjust, and serve the full term without the possibility of parole. In the case of a conviction for murder after a first or final warning, the offender must be sentenced to life imprisonment without the possibility of parole unless the court determines that this would be manifestly unjust. Not surprisingly, given the breadth of the offences that come within the definition of "serious violent offence", the courts have so far found manifest injustice following the legislative presumption in the vast majority of cases.

d. *Statutory purposes and principles*

Finally, the Sentencing Act 2002 prescribes the main purposes and principles of sentencing, and the aggravating and mitigating factors that should be taken into account. These are primarily set out in section 7, 8 and 9 of the Act, and are in large part designed to ensure that the sentence is proportionate to the seriousness of the offence and the culpability of the offender. As noted above, section 10A of the Act also provides a hierarchy of tariff sentences, which is subject to the overarching statutory principle in section 8(g) that the Court must impose the least restrictive outcome that is appropriate in the circumstances.

However, there are significant limitations to the effectiveness of these statutory provisions in ensuring proportionality and the least restrictive outcome. First, there is no prioritisation of the various purposes of sentencing set out in section 7: sentencing judges can pick and choose the purpose that they believe is appropriate to the particular case as they want. Secondly, the principles include a range of matters that go beyond seriousness and culpability. Finally, the principles, and the aggravating and mitigating factors, dictate how a sentence for one offence should relate to another, but they provide no guidance as to the actual quantum apart from the maximum penalty, which as noted above generally bears very little relationship to day to day sentencing practice.

e. *Wide judicial discretion*

As a result, in the New Zealand system the quantum of punishment has been largely left to the courts; judges have relatively few external constraints in determining the custodial or non-custodial sentence they think appropriate within the maximum penalty.

The main mechanism for determining sentencing levels and imposing enforceable constraints on disproportionate outcomes is therefore review by appellate courts. Both prosecution and defence have a broad right of appeal; appellate courts are able to allow the appeal not only if there has been an error in the sentence imposed, but if they conclude that a different sentence should have been given. In reaching those appellate decisions, the courts have developed an elaborate body of case law that dictates not only the methodology that judges are required to follow in deciding on the appropriate sentence, but also the appropriate sentencing levels in classes of case.

In relation to methodology, the Court of Appeal has stipulated that judges should go through a notional four step process in determining the final sentence:

- The first step is to determine the sentencing starting point by assessing the seriousness of the offence and the culpability of the offender. This should take into account the aggravating and mitigating factors relating to the offence, before allowance is made for aggravating and mitigating factors personal to the offender. This is the "starting point" that identifies the sentence proportionate to seriousness and culpability.
- The second step is to consider whether overall the offence is aggravated or mitigated by the offender's particular personal circumstances, including previous criminal convictions, to the extent that it requires a variation from the starting point.
- The third step is then to provide discounts for a guilty plea or for assistance to the authorities (the amount of the discounts being fairly closely prescribed in percentage terms).
- The final step is to determine whether there are any special circumstances in the individual case (such as the promptings of mercy or rehabilitative prospects that will be enhanced by an alternative sentence) that justify a departure from the tariff sentence produced by the first three steps.

A failure to follow this methodology will lead an appellate court to consider the matter afresh.

As well as this sentencing methodology, the other major enforceable constraint to achieve proportionality in sentencing can be found in tariff decisions of appellate courts that analyse sentencing levels for a particular type of offence across a range of cases when deciding an individual appeal. The most systematic example of such decisions are guideline judgments produced by the Court of Appeal. These provide guidance about sentencing levels for a particular offence or class of offence, generally expressed as a sentencing range set out in bands. For example, in a leading guideline judgment[59] in relation to offences of serious violence with intent, the Court prescribed three overlapping bands of

59 *R v Taueki* [2005] 3 NZLR 372; (2005) 21 CRNZ 769.

prison sentence length depending on the presence of specified aggravating factors: 3 to 6 years for offending at the lower end of the spectrum with no or few aggravating factors; 5 to 10 years for offending with two or three aggravating factors; and 9 to 14 years where there are three or more aggravating factors and the combination of such factors is particularly grave.

However, appellate decisions are limited in their ability to ensure proportionality in sentencing. They are reliant upon submissions from prosecution and defence counsel and generally do not have the full range of information that one would expect in order to enable the court to reach an informed decision. Guideline judgments by the Court of Appeal are largely confined to the more serious cases resulting in significant terms of imprisonment. It is difficult to find guideline judgments for offences of lesser seriousness. Appeals against sentence for such offences are often heard by the High Court at a local level, giving rise to the potential for considerable inconsistency between one area and another. Not surprisingly, therefore, New Zealand sentencing practice is characterised by substantial inconsistency in practice between one Court and another (and to a lesser extent between one judge and another) in the extent to which imprisonment is used for lower level offences.

For example, in a recent study of sentencing practice for aggravated drink driving between District Court circuits, Goodall and Durrant[60] found substantial variations in sentencing practice. After controlling for a large number of relevant variables, they found that, by comparison with the circuit with the lowest incarceration rate, offenders were at least twice as likely to be incarcerated in 14 other circuits and in four of those circuits were more than 10 times as likely to be incarcerated. They argued that the existing system settings (the legislative framework and the availability of appeal) do not overcome the challenges created by the complexity, uncertainty and time pressure, breadth of discretion, and the relative isolation faced by the judges. In response to these challenges, sentencing judges have to formulate local sentencing policies. While they take a similar approach to offence seriousness and criminal history variables, this is not sufficient to achieve consistency of sentencing. Thus "the system works effectively in terms of informing judges about what factors to take account of but not how give effect to those factors. The consequence is that the threshold for incarceration is set at different levels in different places. In the absence of system-wide guidance local rules of thumb or guidelines have developed."[61]

60 Wayne Goodall & Russil Durrant, 'Regional variation in sentencing: The incarceration of aggravated drink drivers in the New Zealand District Courts', 46 *Australian & New Zealand Journal of Criminology* 3 (2013), p. 422–447.

61 *Idem*, p. 444.

V. CONCLUSION

Despite a falling recorded crime rate and considerable efforts to offer alternatives to prosecution, New Zealand continues to overuse imprisonment. While the legislature in New Zealand has had a direct impact on the numbers being held in pre-trial detention through restrictive bail laws, the sentencing regime in contrast largely leaves it to the judiciary to determine sentencing levels. If Parliament (the elected representatives who are accountable to the public through the ballot box) wishes to decrease the use of imprisonment, the legislative tools that it uses to do so are limited such measures as amendments to maximum penalties or the introduction of new sentence types or mandatory or presumptive sentences for a particular offence. These mechanisms are blunt, generally of limited impact and often counterproductive. Apart from the inconsistency in sentencing already noted, this gives rise to two significant public policy problems.

First, it causes what Ashworth has called a "democratic deficit"[62]: unelected judges, who are necessarily removed from the political arena and only indirectly responsive to community concerns, largely determine the severity of punishment for categories of offending, and thus effectively dictate fundamental matters of sentencing policy. That is at odds with the proper separation of powers in a modern democracy.

Secondly, it largely removes any ability for the cost effectiveness of different sentencing options to be analysed. Judges, including those sitting in appellate courts, are largely reliant upon submissions from counsel and generally do not have access to the range of information that would enable them to undertake such an analysis.

As a result, there is no ability for the government to make trade-offs between, or to assess the relative merits of expenditure on, the administration of sentences and expenditure in other areas. As Young and King noted[63]:

> ... the Government must meet whatever resource demands the sentencing system imposes on it, with little ability to influence the scale of those demands. There is no effective mechanism for considering, and no opportunity for public input into, whether the limited resources are most appropriately directed to the administration of sentences or other criminal justice activities like policing or offender rehabilitation, or even to other areas of social policy such as health and education.

---

62 Andrew Ashworth, *Sentencing and Criminal Justice*, Cambridge: Cambridge University Press, 2005.

63 Warren Young & Andrea King, 'The Origins and Evolution of Sentencing Guidelines: A Comparison of England and Wales and New Zealand', in: Andrew Ashworth & Julian Roberts (eds.), *Sentencing Guidelines: Exploring the English Model*, Oxford: Oxford University Press, 2013, p. 202-217.

In recognition of these problems, the New Zealand Law Commission in 2006 recommended the establishment of a Sentencing Council, comprising a mix of judicial and non-judicial members.[64] In brief, the remit of this Council would have been the development of guidelines for specific offences and offence types prescribing presumptive sentences for "categories" or "bands" of seriousness. These guidelines would have been the subject of a cost-effectiveness analysis and would have been dependent on the approval of Parliament.

The Government of the day, concerned about the rapidly rising prison population, decided to implement that recommendation, and Parliament subsequently enacted the Sentencing Council Act 2007 that came into effect in 2008. However, before there was an opportunity for the Sentencing Council to be established, there was a change of government in late 2008, and the new Government that came to power decided that it did not support a Sentencing Council. As a result, it took no steps to set a Council up, and at the time of writing (September 2016) was in the process of repealing the legislation. Ironically, the Government's lack of support stems from two apparently contradictory concerns: that a Sentencing Council would undermine judicial independence; and that the development of detailed sentencing policy by such a body would usurp the role of Parliament (notwithstanding the fact that Parliament had been given a critical role in approving the guidelines).

The present position is therefore that the prison population in New Zealand continues to rise, and in the last year has risen rapidly. As noted above, much of this can be attributed to more restrictive bail laws, over which Parliament has exercised significant control. However, there is no equivalent mechanism to change sentencing levels. If the Government wishes to bring down those levels and reduce the size of the sentenced population (and they have occasionally suggested that they would like to do so), they have only indirect and ineffective tools at their disposal to do. Sadly, therefore, a reduction in at least the sentenced prison population seems unlikely any time soon.

64 New Zealand Law Commission, Sentencing Guidelines and Parole Reform, Report 94, Wellington, 2006.

OVERUSE IN THE CRIMINAL JUSTICE SYSTEM IN NIGERIA

Uju AGOMOH*

I. INTRODUCTION

In Nigeria, the criminal justice system is predicated on the notions that the suspect's, accused or defendant's dignity must be recognized and that generally the suspect or defendant/accused is considered innocent until proven guilty by a court of competent jurisdiction.[1] Unfortunately, violations of these fundamental procedural rules have become rampant in Nigeria.[2] Such violations obviously obstruct defendant's human rights and most essentially threaten the very foundation of the Nigeria criminal justice system.[3]

The prison population in Nigeria has therefore been described as a mixed grill consisting of adult males and females, young persons, criminal and civil lunatics, pregnant women, debtors, detainees and first offenders. About 70% of the people admitted to prison are awaiting trial or are being remanded in custody. Nigeria currently has a total of 241 prisons.[4] In some of these prisons, the percentage of persons awaiting trial is as high as 80 to 97% of the total prison population.[5] The majority of these awaiting trial persons (ATPs) end up waiting

* Dr. Uju AGOMOH is Executive Director of the Prisoners' Rehabilitation And Welfare Action (PRAWA), as well as the President of the International Correctional and Prisons Association, Africa Chapter (ICPA –Africa). She can be contacted via: uagomoh@prawa.org.

1 Leonard C. Opara, 'The Law and Policy in Criminal Justice System and Sentencing in Nigeria', 4 *International Journal of Asian Social Science* 7 (2014), p. 886-897 (at: www.aessweb.com/journals/5007) (last visited: 15 June 2016).

2 *Idem.*

3 *Idem.*

4 Nigerian Prisons Service Statistics Database (at: www.prisons.gov.ng/about/statistical-info.php) (last visited: 15 June 2016).

5 Uju Agomoh, *Criminal Justice Reform: Does the Punishment Fit,* Discussion Paper on Penal Policy and Non-Custodial Measures presented at the Nigerian Bar Association 4th Criminal Justice Reform Conference in Kastina 16–18 June 2014.

months or even years before their trial starts and consequently fall victim of what has been termed the human rights crisis of our time: the overuse of pre-trial detention.

Many of these ATPs do not need to be there, but are held on charges linked to minor, nonviolent offenses. Others should have been tried, or released: people like Hyginus Ajibo, a Nigerian who was accused of murder and spent almost 17 years in pre-trial detention until he was released on bail in 2014. Not surprisingly, it is the poor who make up the vast majority of those held in pre-trial. The poor are more likely to come into conflict with the law, more likely to be detained pending trial, and less able to afford the keys to pre-trial release: a bribe, bail, or a lawyer.[6]

Factors identified as resulting in the high percentage of ATPs and elongating their stay awaiting trial include delays in the administration of justice, overuse of prison sentences, over criminalization and inadequate utilization of both police and court bail. However, not all detention is irrational or unlawful. Persons who present a genuine risk of flight or are likely to endanger witnesses or the community can be detained before trial, in the absence of reasonable alternatives. Pre-trial detention when applied properly and sparingly plays an important role in a balanced criminal justice system. In Nigeria, after decades of incarceration, cutting down on the number of persons behind bars who face trial is deemed a national imperative.

II. OVERUSE OF CRIMINALIZATION

Nigeria has a population of 186.7 million people, based on the latest United Nations estimates; see Table 1.[7]

The findings of a crime victimization survey conducted by CLEEN Foundation in 2013 with a population sample consisting of 11,518 Nigerians equally distributed among male and female adults aged 18 years and above from all the 36 States in the country and the Federal Capital Territory indicate trends analysis of criminal victimization in Nigeria as follows[8]:

6 Why the Overuse of Pre-trial Detention is an Overlooked Human Rights Crisis- Open Society Foundations (at: www.opensocietyfoundations.org/voices/why-overuse-pretrial-detention-overlooked-human-rights-crisis) (last visited: 15 June 2016).

7 Population of Nigeria 2016 and historical (at: www.worldometers.info/world-population/nigeria-population/) (last visited: 15 June 2016).

8 Public Presentation of Findings of the National Crime Victimization and Safety Survey, 2013 by CLEEN Foundation (at: www.cleen.org) (last visited: 15 June 2016). CLEEN Foundation, with the support from the Macarthur Foundation, has been conducting Crime Victimization Surveys in Nigeria since 2005. The findings are meant to assist the government, police and the entire criminal justice administration system to better understand emerging trends in crime and safety

Table 1. Population of Nigeria (2016 and historical)

Year	Population	Yearly % change	Yearly change	Migrants (net)	Median age
2016	186,987,563	2.63%	4,785,601	−60,000	18
2015	182,201,962	2.71%	4,555,444	−60,000	18
2010	159,424,742	2.69%	3,962,688	−60,000	18
2005	139,611,303	2.59%	3,346,916	−34,000	18
2000	122,876,723	2.53%	2,890,380		

Source: Population of Nigeria 2016 and historical (at: www.worldometers.info/world-population/nigeria-population/) (last visited: 15 June 2016).

a. Robbery

Experience of robbery has increased from 17% in 2012 to 18% in 2013. When disaggregated by States (see Figure 1), the results of the 2013 survey showed that Kaduna State recorded the highest at 43%, followed by Akwa-Ibom State (42%) and Cross River State (39%), while Jigawa (5%) and Kano (3%) were among the states with the lowest incidence of robbery. The survey also revealed that security in the home remains a key challenge, as 37% of robberies occurred in the homes of respondents; another 26% occurred near the home, while 9% took place in the workplace or school.

b. Rape and attempted rape

As Figure 2 shows, 5% of respondents stated that they had been raped or been victims of attempted rape. The analysis according to geopolitical zones shows that the South has the highest incidence with 10%, followed by the North East (6%). The South West and North West recorded 4% each. The North Central recorded 3% and South East had the lowest score of 1%. The incidence of rape has been on the increase from 3% in 2011 to 5% in 2013. When victims were asked where the rape occurred, 36% said it happened near their own homes; 19% said it occurred at their homes and 13% said it occurred in the school or work place. Again the challenge of security and safety in the homes is explicitly exhibited in rape case. Respondents were further asked how widespread the incidence of rape was: 10% believed it was very widespread, 33% said it happened occasionally, 48% believed it was non-existent while 9% said they do not know.

---

in Nigeria and consequently, to refine and deploy improved strategies to resolve the country's current challenges of security and safety.

Figure 1. Robbery by State

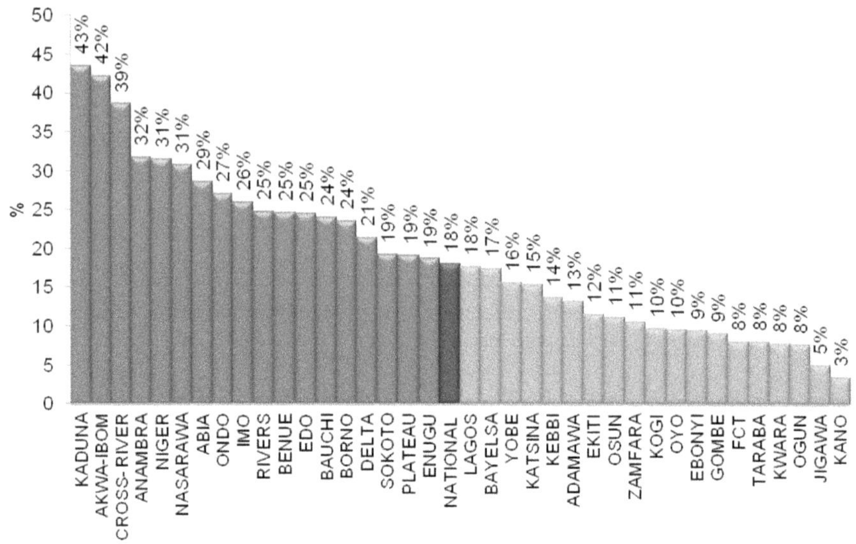

Figure 2. Rape/Attempted rape

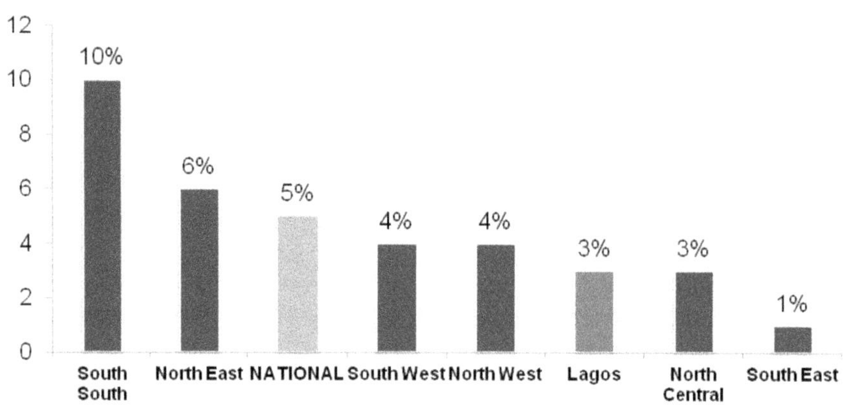

c. *Kidnapping and attempted kidnapping*

A total of 3% of the respondents interviewed nationwide said that they had been victims of kidnapping or attempted kidnapping; see Figure 3. The South West had the highest incidence of kidnapping with 5%, followed by the South East and South with 4% each. The North West and North East each had an incidence of 3%, with the lowest being North Central at 2%.

Figure 3. Kidnapping/Attempted kidnapping

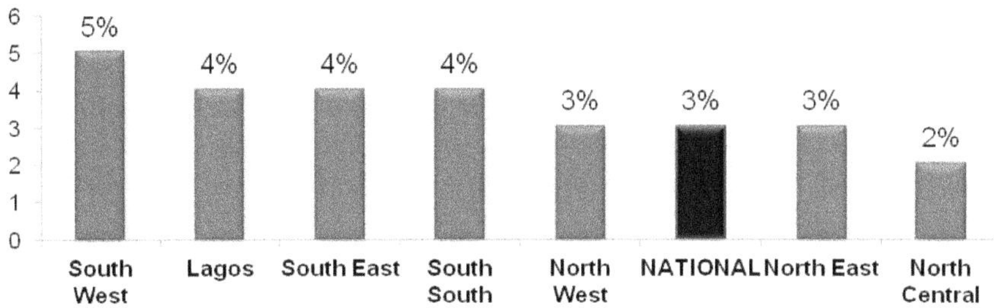

d. Physical assault

33% of respondents said they had been victim of physical assault in the 2013 survey. Some states, Enugu (84%), Ebonyi (77%), Rivers (58%), and Anambra (50%) recorded 6 a high incidence of physical assault compared to other states such as Ogun (38%), Taraba (36%), Lagos (35%) and Kogi (34%). The FCT recorded an increase from 15% in 2012 to 24% in 2013. Some states such as Kano recorded a decrease from 14% in 2012 to 3% in 2013. In Niger State, physical assault fell from 68% in 2012 to 6% in 2013; and in Jigawa State, it fell from 23% in 2012 to 8% in 2013. See Figure 4.

Figure 4. Physical assault by State

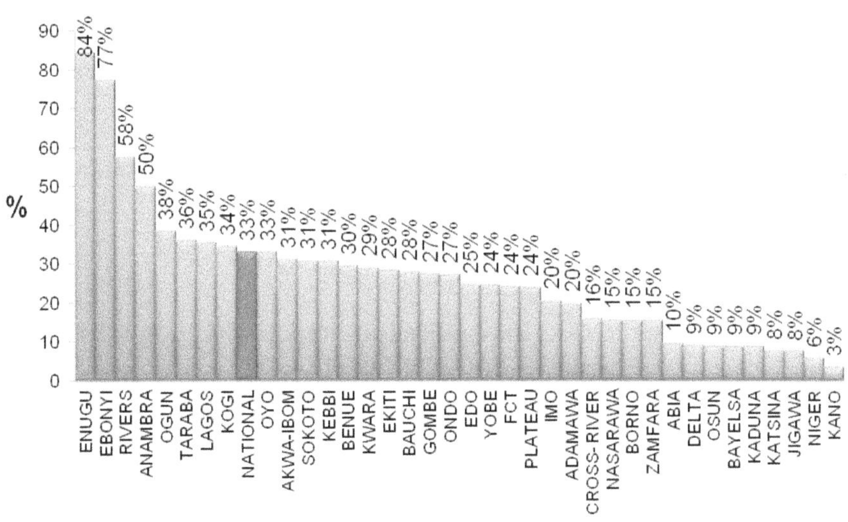

e. Domestic violence

Nearly one in every three respondents (30%) admitted having been a victim of domestic violence. Over the last 3 years, there has been an increase in domestic violence. There was a progressive increment from 21% in 2011 to 31% in 2012 with a 1% decrease in the 2013 survey to 30%. The findings of the 2013 survey revealed that domestic violence ranks amongst the top four most common victimizations in Nigeria. Prevalence is highest in the South East with 43% followed by the South West and the North East with 35% each. The South-South recorded a 26% incidence while the North Central and North West recorded the lowest with 19% each.

f. Attempted murder

5% of respondents stated that they were victims of attempted murder. This indicated an increase from the 3% recorded in 2012. As Figure 5 shows, the highest was in the North East (8%), followed by the South and North West with 7% each, the South West (6%), North Central (3%) and South East (2%) had the lowest incidence in this analysis.

Figure 5. Attempted murder

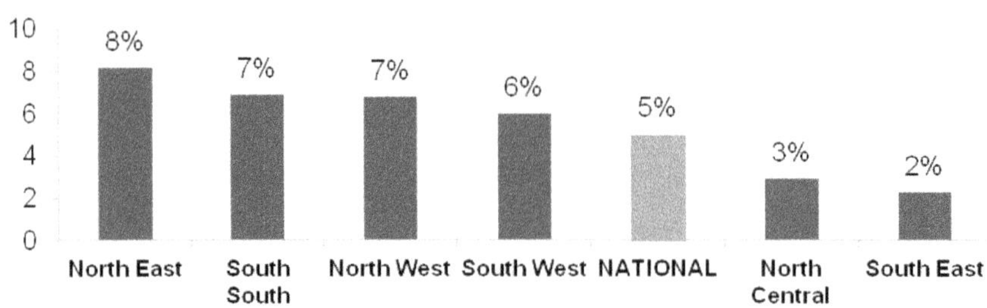

g. Theft of mobile phone

Over all, nearly one in every two respondents, that is 45%, reported being a victim of theft of mobile phone. Theft of mobile phones remains the number one crime committed in Nigeria. At the State level (see Figure 6), Taraba ranks highest at 64%, followed by Kwara, Abia, Lagos, at 59%, 57%, 55% respectively, while Kaduna, Ekiti, Nasarawa and Plateau all had scores of 54% each. Lowest ranking were Ogun and Yobe with 23% and 22% respectively.

Figure 6. Theft of mobile phones

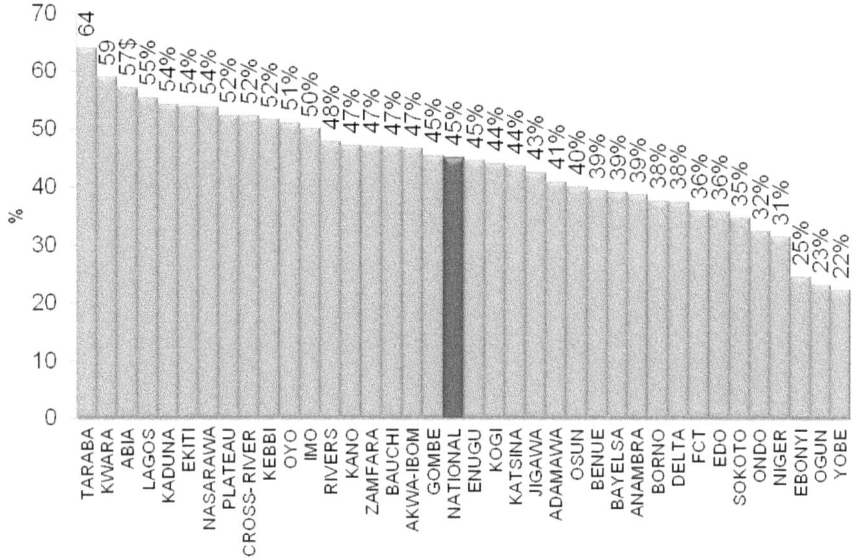

h. *Car theft*

The Survey revealed that 4% of respondents have had their cars stolen in the past one year. The highest incidence of car theft occurred in the North West (6%), followed by the South (5%); see Figure 7. The North East and South West recorded 4% and 3% respectively, while the South East and North Central recorded 2% and 1% respectively. 35% of cars were stolen in victims' homes, 34% near victims' homes, 19% elsewhere and 12% at their work place or school.

Figure 7. Car theft

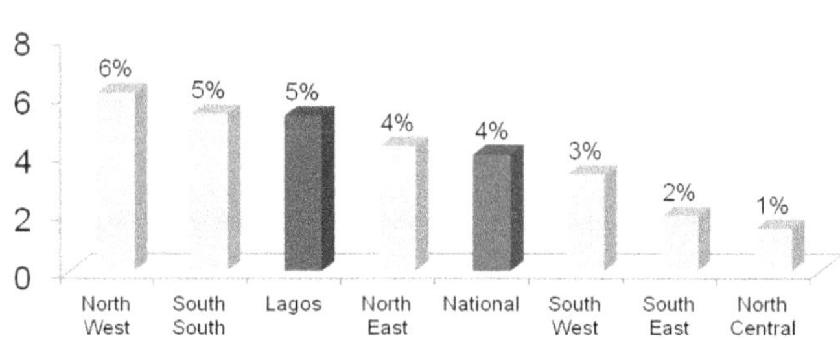

i. *Armed violence other than robbery*

Armed violence (Figure 8) entails the use of weapons and physical force to inflict, or attempt to inflict injuries on another. The results of the survey indicated that

4% of respondents were victims of armed violence. The highest incidence was in the North East with 11%, followed by the South with 9%. For the other regions, the North Central and North West recorded 3% while the South West and South East recorded 1%.

Figure 8. Armed violence by region

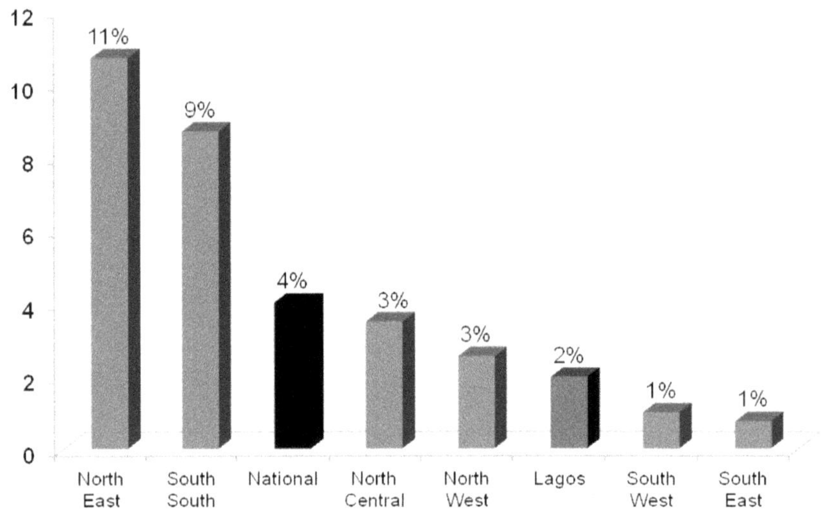

Going by the outcome of the above survey, the criminal justice system is burdened with the following categories of crime

- Theft of mobile phones at 45%;
- Physical assault at 33%;
- Robbery at 18%;
- Attempted murder at 5%;
- Rape/Attempted rape at 5%;
- Armed violence other than robbery at 4%;
- Car theft at 4%;
- Kidnapping at 3%.

Two related aspects of societal management – the environment and traffic – constantly present a puzzle for policymakers in Nigeria. In many respects, Nigeria's attempts at environmental sanctity presents celebrated contradictions for the justice system. For many years the country had no legal structure for environmental management. When it eventually developed such a structure, its 'commitment' to the process was evidenced by the signing of a plethora of international protocols, aptly followed by numerous domestic legal enactments.

In the same manner, traffic in Nigeria is quite chaotic, as in most African cities. This is not without cause. First, driver training and an effective licensing system to support it are near absent. Most of the roads are in bad shape and the attitude of road users remains a sore point for policymakers. Despite the best efforts of several regimes, management of road usage remains challenging across most of Nigeria.

Interestingly, while the environment remains a major concern for governments at different levels, the emphasis and/or ranking of environmental issues in the hierarchy of needs among ordinary Nigerians is an issue which needs to be examined further. While there are no questions that the environment should be adequately taken care of, the extent to which this should be prioritized over and above day-to-day needs of the common man, whose daily concerns are basic and rudimentary, possibly presents what has been a continued struggle between the people and institutions of governance. In some instances, the very poor do rely on environmentally degrading activities to survive. For example, Section 18(f) of the Enugu State Waste Management Agency law considers it an offense to "sell or display or offer or carry for sale any goods or article of trade in a road junction or at any place prohibited by the authority pursuant to this law or any other law". The high informality of business ventures in which many Nigerians are engaged and which manifest in makeshift kiosks and roadside hawking among other practices often pits them against such laws. In other instances, the sheer trouble of bothering about the environment, when several other survival challenges contend for available time and other resources, is considered difficult to manage by the citizen. Consequently, frictions between policy stance on the environment and the behaviour of citizens are rife. Such contradictions, interestingly, have given opportunity for law enforcement agents, both regular and ad hoc, to confront, and be confronted by, citizens whose actions and inactions seemingly serve against sustainable environment or policy pronouncements to that effect. Thus, following the spate of environmental awareness and the trends at both the Federal and international levels, Enugu State one of the states in the south east region of Nigeria established the Enugu State Waste Management Agency [ESWAMA] based on CAP 75 Revised Laws of Enugu State 2004. The Agency has a mandate to arrest and prosecute all cases of violation of the Enugu State Laws in relation to Waste Management and Disposal. There is also an ESWAMA Court which has jurisdiction to adjudicate on all Enugu State Waste Management and Disposal Cases and to proffer sanctions where necessary.

On its part, traffic management remains a headache. With little training on handling, rights of way, parking and other requirements of conventional road usage, most roads remain dotted with parked vehicles that reduce the size of the road by half, cut off other users and drastically slow down traffic. In other instances, avoidable collisions regularly lead to road blockades that double commuting time, stress both the road and its users and reduce time available for productive work. This is a problem to both commuters and traffic authorities. In

Enugu state, a state in the south east region of Nigeria, the Ministry of Transport, for example, liaises with the Enugu State Capital Territory Development Authority and engages a private firm, Easy Park, all in a bid to control traffic in the city. However, traffic offenses are universally considered minor. Without improving the education of road users, force-based enforcement and incarceration are used to combat these offenses, which seems an overreaction trying to tackle the situation. In these cases, accused persons, who for varied reasons are unable to afford penalties, usually in the form of fines, are remanded in prison custody. But also, the Ministry of Transport assiduously engages itself alongside a host of 'amorphous' employees and agents to utilize its power to impound vehicles of offenders who violate traffic offenses. The outcome is a constant marketplace along roadsides, where negotiations about implications of diverse traffic offenses and options for dealing with offenses go on continually between suspected offenders and law enforcement officials and their agents. The implication of this for understanding the blossoming culture of impunity remains largely understudied.

Sitting as arbiter between law enforcement and the citizen is the justice system, more specifically the courts and the prison system. Unfortunately, the justice system is saddled with a number of challenges already, not the least the very low speed of dispensation of justice. The first recourse to the justice system for environmental issues followed the infamous 'Koko Toxic Waste' saga in 1988. Subsequently, virtually all states of the Nigerian Federation have enacted one or more laws to regulate practices affecting the environment as well as to mete out punishment for those whose activities are considered inimical to environmental sustainability. Likewise, for traffic sanity, the Federal Government established the Federal Roads Safety Commission, tasking it with education of road users and controlling speed and quality of vehicles that ply the road. But here, both the making and interpretation of the laws for environmental and traffic safety seem to are in need for a significant upgrade. The fact that the criminal justice system in Nigeria requires significant overhaul is no news, especially when it comes to the terms and conditions for incarceration of offenders. What calls for concern in this regard, is the high percentage of detainees who are in prison for offenses that may be considered light and 'non-incarcerable' (especially environmental and traffic). As can be expected in a federal system, the practice of such incarceration and severity of the challenge it poses for citizen-government relationship, vary from one state to another.

There seem to be areas of mismatch between offense and punishment may actually be imposing undue costs to both the state and the people, instead of having a deterrent effect. In particular, given the already burdened system as well as the nature of the offenses it tries, there are indications that both the law enforcement and court system focus unduly on extraction of rents from suspected parties. More so, there are indications that the manner of dispensation of justice in both ESWAMA and Traffic Mobile Courts may actually be adding to the cost of maintaining an already ailing justice system. The Prisoners' Rehabilitation and Welfare Action (PRAWA), with support from the DFID funded Justice for All Programme (J4A), embarked on a research in 2014 with the following aims and objectives:

To:

- Assess the legal provisions of environmental and traffic offenses, their respective implications and options for improving them.
- Provide evidence on the manner of enforcement of environmental and traffic offenses and assess implications of those methods used for environmental sustainability, effective traffic management and relationship of the citizenry to the state and costs and burdens of governance.
- Assess the prosecution and treatment of environmental and traffic crime offenders in Enugu State and the implications of these prosecutions for the prison system.
- Evaluate to what extent alternatives could be implemented, aimed to divert environmental and traffic offenders away from prison custody, thereby reducing costs for both the individual and the state.
- Gather information and evidence to facilitate advocacy and dissemination of best practices in the treatment of environmental crime offenders including supporting the use of non-custodial measures.

Generally, sanctions for environmental and traffic offenses can be either administrative or criminal, and they differ in two important aspects. Administrative law relies on regulations and uses primary pecuniary fines, while the criminal sanctioning regime relies on police, public prosecutors and courts. The latter involves severe penalties such as incarceration and heavy court-imposed fines that are entered in an offender's criminal records. The key problem for both supporters and detractors of the merits of both sanctions for environmental policy is a lack of empirical evidence to support either position. Almer and Goeschl[9] tried to fill this gap on criminal sanctions for environmental offenses, by providing an empirical examination of the deterrent effect based on an economic model of environmental crime. The study uses dynamic panel data approach in relation to the German penal code for environmental crime and punishment. In his seminal paper on the economics of crime, Becker researched to what extent empirical data support the unconfirmed hypothesis that criminal sanctions are successful in deterring environmental crime, determine the individual contributions of different components of the sanctioning regime to the deterrence effect and explore some of the specificity of environmental crime in

9 Christian Almer and Timo Goeschl, 'Environmental crime and punishment: empirical evidence from the German penal code', *Land Economics*, vol. 86, nr. 4, (2010), p. 707-726.

order to learn more about the role of political economy variables in enforcement.[10] The study finds that criminal sanctions do have the deterrent effect intended by policy makers. This finding lends support to the fact that criminal sanctions are effective in combating environmental offenses and is in line with the emerging consensus on criminal sanctions in general.[11] It also concludes that the probability of being tried rather than being convicted provides the most significant deterrent and that political economy factors are statistically significant drivers of reported environmental crime rate.[12]

Faure and Visser surveyed the empirical evidence on the economic analysis of the instruments for the control of environmental pollution.[13] The study notes that environmental law is often categorized as administrative law, but in practice the whole body of environmental law is, to a large extent, also criminal law. Thus, in environmental law attention has been paid to the way in which the law should use penal sanctions to deter environmental pollution, but environmental criminal law had never been subjected to an economic analysis. The goal of the paper therefore was to provide an overview of the way in which traditional theories on the economics of crime have been applied to environmental criminal law, addressing within this framework the manner in which the literature on the economics of crime relates to environmental pollution. The paper attempts to provide a survey of the literature concerning the way in which criminal law has been and can be used in the fight against environmental pollution, aimed at accessing the optimal penalties for environmental pollution. The paper notes that economists have paid a lot of attention to the optimal instrument to be used in environmental policy[14], with a lot of trust placed in such facilities as emission trading and taxes. However, the reality of environmental law in many countries was and still is very different with respect to command and control systems, which determine environmental actions and the violation of environmental regulations is backed up by criminal sanctions. Indeed, with few exceptions (Cohen[15]), environmental criminal law has rarely been subjected to an economic analysis. It notes the striking gap between the (modest) economic research into

10 G.S. Becker, 'Crime and Punishment: an Economic Approach', in: N.G. Fielding, A. Clarke, R. Witt (eds), *The Economic Dimensions of Crime*, Palgrave Macmillan, London 1968, p. 13-68.

11 Steven D. Levitt and Thomas J. Miles, 'Economic Contributions to the Understanding of Crime', Annual Review of Law and Social Science, vol. 2 (2006), p. 147-164; Christopher Cornwell and William N. Trumbull, 'Estimating the Economic Model of Crime with Panel Data', The Review of Economics and Statistics, Vol. 76, No. 2 (1994), p. 360-366.

12 PRAWA/J4A Research Report on ESWAMA and Traffic Offenders in Enugu State.

13 Michael G. Faure and Marjolein Visser, 'Law and Economics of Environmental Crime: a Survey', in: Hans Sjögren and Göran Skogh (eds), *New Perspectives on Economic Crime*, Edward Elgar 2004, p. 57-75.

14 With reference to Neil Gunningham and Peter Grabosky, *Smart regulation: designing environmental policy*, Oxford: Clarendon Press 1998.

15 M.A. Cohen, 'Optimal environmental strategy to prevent oil spills: an application of a principle-agent model with moral hazard', Journal of Law and Economics, vol. 30 (1987), 23-51; M.A.

environmental crimes as in Dewees et al.[16] and environmental criminal law, which is heavily influenced by criminal legal dogmatics. The study notes that the economic theory on the use of criminal law can also be applied to environmental pollution. Thus, it can be concluded that given the relatively low probabilities of detection, other means than civil law measures, like paying of fine and undoing the wrong that was done, should be used to deter environmental pollution.[17]

Nigeria, the populous, oil-rich but underdeveloped African country, faces some environmental problems. Thus, Ladan identified what he considered the four most important of these problems – ensuring sustainable industrial production and effective treatment of industrial effluents, preventing and reversing desertification which is a major problem in the Northern Nigeria, managing forest, wildlife and natural resources besides timber products and combating floods and inland and coastal erosion.[18] The study notes that in Nigeria, industrial effluents are poorly managed while deforestation affects non-wood products such as medicines, food and paper that are derived from wood. Meanwhile, hunting causes loss of wildlife, thus the need to protect species and areas that are of scientific, recreational or aesthetic value. The study sets itself a number of goals including to examine the nature and scope of access to environmental justice, to analyse the role of the judiciary in promoting the rule of law in regard to principles 10 of the Rio Declaration, to determine the nature of environmental litigation, to examine judicial approach to some of the common problems that arise in the different types of environmental litigation, including issues of jurisdiction, burden of proof and judicial remedies and to highlight judicial approach in other jurisdictions. The study notes that it has been demonstrated that peculiar facts of Nigeria's socio-economy, culture and law impose a duty on the judiciary to take an activist, critical and creative stance in order to prompt or ensure effective environmental management especially by public bodies, as well as to create an atmosphere for the development of a public ethic of and participation in environmental conservation and justice. It notes that

---

Cohen, 'Environmental crime and punishment: legal/economic theory and empirical evidence of enforcement of federal environmental statutes', *Journal of Criminal Law and Criminology*, vol. 82, (1992), p. 1054-1108; M.A. Cohen, 'Criminal penalties', in: Tom Tietenberg (ed), *Innovation in environmental policy, Economic and legal aspects of recent developments in environmental enforcement and liability*, Aldershot: Edward Elgar 1992, p. 75-108; M.A. Cohen, 'Criminal law as an instrument of environmental policy: theory and empirics' in Hayes, A. (ed.), *The law and economics of the environment*, Cheltenham, UK and Lyme, US: Edward Elgar 2001, p. 198-216.

16 Don Dewees, David Duff and Michael Trebilcock, *Exploring the domain of accident law, taking the facts seriously*, New York: Oxford University Press 1996.

17 Michael G. Faure and Marjolein Visser, 'Law and Economics of Environmental Crime: a Survey', in: Hans Sjögren and Göran Skogh (eds), *New Perspectives on Economic Crime*, Edward Elgar 2004, p. 57-75.

18 Muhammed Tawfiq Ladan, 'Review of NESREA Act 2007 and Regulations 2009-2011: A New Dawn in Environmental Compliance and Enforcement in Nigeria', *Law Env't & Dev. J.*, vol. 8 (2012), p. 116-140.

not much is undertaken in the area of judicial enforcement of environmental laws in Nigeria by way of prosecution of offenders. But there is quite some civil litigation, mostly involving oil spillage or pollution and these involve substantial claims. But in environmental offenses offenders do not seem to face any commensurate amount of criminal prosecution. It also observes that quite a number of environmental actions which affect human health are not pursued, and if pursued, not with the same vigour and ambition as actions in spillage or pollution. This partially reflects the incentives facing economic agents in Nigeria, but may also reflect a lack of awareness on the part of the society of issues in environmental litigation. The study recommends enlightenment of the people on their legal rights within their immediate environment.

A number of other studies have enquired into different aspects of the specifics of the environment or traffic systems, the judiciary and/or administration of punishment for those that violate these systems. For example, Skinnider attempts to discuss the technical issues of victimization in environmental crimes by looking at emerging forms of crime that have a significant impact on the environment and identifying the key issues and challenges from the perspective of the victims that require further study and action.[19] The study notes that environmental crime is one of the most profitable and fastest growing areas of international criminal activity and that it is often perceived as "victimless". Consequently, there has been little attempt to describe the actual prevalence and consequences of victimization as a result of environmental crime. In particular, the complexity of victimization – in terms of time, space, impact, and who or what is victimized – is one of the reasons why governments and the enforcement community have trouble in finding proper responses to the challenge.[20]

III. OVERUSE OF IMPRISONMENT

People are incarcerated for various reasons, crimes and offenses and the duration of incarceration also depends on the specifics of the offense actually committed and the legal system of such a community. These crimes and offenses range from theft to kidnapping, fraud, extortion, forgery, robbery, rape, murder, manslaughter, etc. In a country like Nigeria, where justice is often denied, there are so many people in the Nigerian prisons that ought not to be there. A statistics released by the Nigerian Prisons Service on 31 October 2014 revealed the following facts about incarceration rate (see Tables 2, 3, 4 and 5).

19 Eileen Skinnider, Effect, *Issues and Challenges for Victims of Crimes that have a Significant Impact on the Environment*, United Nations 2013.

20 Idem, p. 1.

Table 2. Prison population

	Male	Female	Total	% of total inmate population
Convicted prisoners	17,280	264	17,544	32
Unconvicted prisoners	38,685	892	39,577	68
Total	55, 965	1, 156	57, 121	100

Table 3. Number of convicted prisoners

	Male	Female	Total	% of total convicts
Short term (< 2 years)	7,900	92	7,992	48
Long term (≥ 2 years)	7,279	134	7,413	41
Condemned convicts (death row)	1,559	29	1,588	8
Lifers	542	9	551	3
Total	17,280	264	17,544	100

Table 4. Percentage of male/female detainees

	Male	Female	Total	% of total inmate population
Convicted Prisoners	17,667	212	17,879	28
Unconvicted Prisoners	44,432	831	45,263	72
Total	62,099	1,043	63,142	100

The Nigerian Prisons Service Statistics as 31 March 2016 is also presented below as follows: Total Number of Prisons is 241 with a total installed capacity is 50,153.

Table 6 shows various kinds of criminal offenses, their frequency count and percentages. It showed that 10 respondents representing 28.6% were in prison as a result of stealing, 6 respondents representing 17.1% were in prison as a result of murder-related cases, 5 respondents representing 14.3% were in prison as a result of fraudulent acts such as 419 (as called in Nigeria) and economic-related crimes, while 4 respondents representing 11.4% committed drug-related crimes. The table further showed that only 2.9% of the respondents were in prison as a result of robbery and bribery respectively. Figure 9 gives further representation of Table 6.

In some legislation, the word sentence and judgment are used interchangeably. However, under the criminal justice system in Nigeria sentencing means the prescription of a particular punishment by a court to someone convicted of a crime. Thus, after an accused person or defendant has pleaded guilty or has been found guilty during the trial or prosecution process,

Table 5. Number of convicted male/female prisoners

	Male	Female	Total	% of total convicts
Short term (< 2 yrs)	8,003	85	8,088	45.2
Long term (≥ 2 yrs)	7,603	96	7,699	43.1
Condemned convicts (death row)	1,653	27	1,680	9.4
Lifers	408	4	412	2.3
Total	17,667	212	17,879	100

SUMMARY
Total inmate population is 63,142
Total number of convicted prisoners is 17,879 (28% of total inmate population)
Total number of unconvicted prisoners is 45,263 (72% of total inmate population)
Total number of male inmates is 62,099 representing 98% of the total inmate population
Total number of female inmates is 1,043 representing 2% of the total inmate population
According to a study conducted to identify among others the common criminal offenses that lead people to prison in Nigeria (Adeola Shobola & Taiwo O. Ajeigbe, 'Inmates Incarceration and Family Support as Precursors of Prison Recidivism in Nigeria', 11 *European Scientific Journal* 34 (2015), p. 500-501), using a counselling rehabilitation group of 13 male and 22 female inmate volunteers from one of the prisons in Nigeria showed that stealing out of other reasons was the most common reason for being in prison (28.6%).

Table 6. Frequency/Percentage in terms of nature of criminal offenses

Nature of offense	Frequency	Percentage
Stealing	10	28.6
Murder-related cases	6	17.1
Fraudsters	5	14.3
Drug-related cases	4	11.4
Conspiracy of fraud	3	8.6
Cyber crime	3	8.6
Impersonation	2	5.7
Robbery	1	2.9
Bribery	1	2.9

the presiding judge or magistrate then renders a judgment of conviction and thereby sets a date aside for sentencing.

The court must pronounce a sentence for every count of the offense for which a defendant is convicted.[21] Whenever a court pronounces more than one sentence

21 Oyediran & Ors v. The Republic [1967] N.M.L.R. 122; Yesufu v. Inspector-General of Police [1960] L.L.R. 140.

Figure 9. Frequency/Percentage in terms of nature of criminal offenses

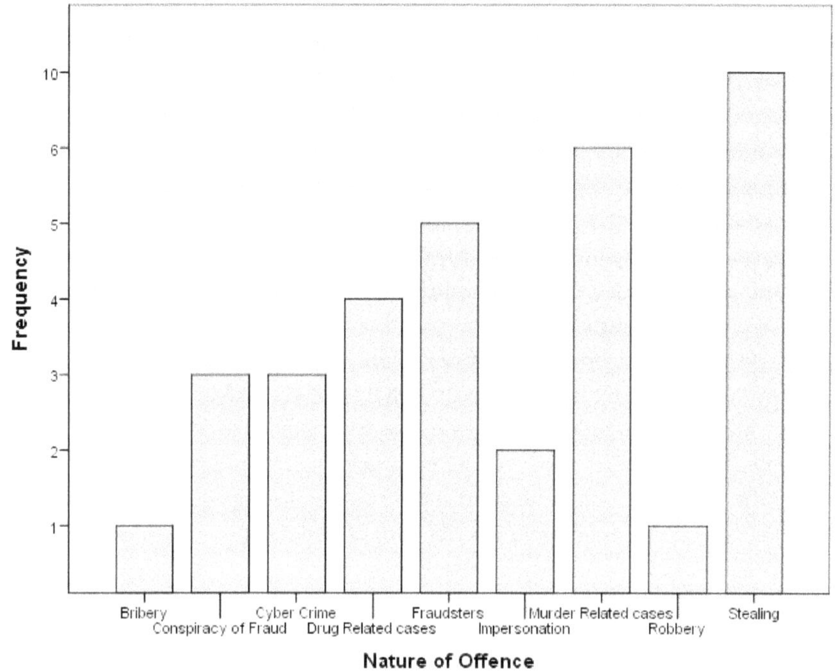

in a trial, it may direct or order that the sentences should run concurrently or consecutively. A concurrent sentence is a sentence which is to be served at the same time as another sentence imposed, at the same proceedings or at different proceedings. A consecutive sentence is separate sentence(s) (each additional to the other) imposed upon a defendant who has been convicted on a charge or information containing several counts each sentence being made to begin at the expiration of another.[22] If upon the pronouncement of its sentences, the court is silent on whether the sentences are to run concurrently or consecutively, the sentences will run concurrently.

The prescribed sentence for any offense is the maximum sentence which the law creating the offense prescribes. However, in imposing sentences, a court has discretion to impose a less severe sentence than the prescribed punishment or a fine in lieu of a sentence of imprisonment. The discretion of the court to impose a sentence, which is less severe than or different from the prescribed penalty, is limited in three instances as follows:

22 Bob Osamor, *Fundamentals of Criminal Procedure Law in Nigeria*, Abuja: Dee-Sage Nigeria, 2004, p. 377.

- Mandatory Sentences: the court cannot impose less than or a penalty different from the mandatory penalty prescribed for an offense. The death penalty for instance is not permissive but mandatory for capital offenses; therefore the court does not have the discretion to impose any penalty other than the death penalty upon conviction for a capital offense. The court's discretion is limited absolutely
- Minimum Penalties: where the law which creates the offense prescribes the minimum penalty for offenders upon conviction, the discretion of the court is relatively limited. The court can impose a higher penalty but cannot impose a penalty a penalty less than the minimum. So also where the minimum penalty is a term of imprisonment, the court cannot impose a fine in lieu of imprisonment.
- Penalties without option of a fine: where the law which creates an offense prescribes a penalty without option of a fine, upon conviction, the court does not have the discretion to impose a fine in lieu of or as an option to the prescribed penalty.[23] However, where a law prescribes a penalty and is silent on the option of a fine, the court has discretion to impose a fine in lieu of or as an option to the penalty prescribed for offenders upon conviction.

Table 7 captures a list of minor offenses and the applicable punishments, including the legal provision on alternative to imprisonment:

Table 7. List of minor offenses and applicable punishments

s/n	Offenses & Sections	Terms of punishment	Alternative term to imprisonment
1	S. 106 – Unlawful assembly	One year	None
2	S. 115 – Forcible entry in a manner likely to cause breach of peace.	One year	None
3	S. 117 – Affray	One year	None
4	S. 119 – Fighting in a prize-fight or subscription to or promotion of prize-fight.	One year	None
5	S. 120 – Threatening violence during the day	One year	None
6	S. 121 – (1) unlawful processions	Six months for officer bearing or wearing firearms, bows & arrows etc… One month for each of the other persons.	None None

23 Dada v. Board of Customs & Excise 1982 (2) N.C.R 79.

s/n	Offenses & Sections	Terms of punishment	Alternative term to imprisonment
7	S. 123 – Public servant abstraction or making copy of any document of property of his employer without authority.	One year	None
8	S. 127 – Public offices receiving property to show favour.	Six months	None
9	S. 137 – Impersonating soldiers or police.	One year	None
10	S. 138 – Unlawful wearing the uniform of Nigeria forces.	One month	Or fine of 10 Naira
11	S. 152 – Preventing witness duly summoned to attend Court from attending court.	One year	None
12	S. 158 – Advertising a reward for the return of stolen or lost property.		Fine of 100 Naira
13	S. 168 – Prison officers accessory to breaches of discipline	Six months	And a fine of 100 Naira
14	S. 169 – Taking prohibited things into or out of prison	Six months	And a fine of 100 Naira
15	S. 174 - Obstructing offices of courts of justice	One year	Or to a fine of 200 Naira
16	S. 182 – Neglect to aid in suppressing riot.	One year	None
17	S. 183 – Neglect to aid in arresting officers.	One year	None
18	S. 188 – Disturbing Religious Worship.	2 months	Or to a fine of 10 Naira
19	S. 191 – Being present at or making poison for unlawful trial by ordeal.	One year	None
20	S. 206 (1) Procuring defilement of women by threats or fraud or administering drugs.	Six months	Or to a fine of 100 Naira
21	S. 228 (4) unlawful gaining.	Three months	Or to a fine of 10 Naira
22	S. 232 penalty for running betting house.	One year	And to a fine of 1000 Naira
23	S. 234 (a) (b) (c) (d) & (e) offices relating to lotteries.	A period not exceeding six months	Or to a fine not exceeding 100 Naira
24	S. 247 (a) (b) (c) & (d) – Idle and disorderly person.	One month	None
25	S. 248 (a) – (f) Rogues and Vagabonds.	Three months (for first offices) or one year imprisonment for every subsequently office.	None
26	S. 249 Bringing contempt on uniform of the Nigeria force	Three months	Or to a fine of 40 naira
27	S. 281 – Attempting to commit suicide.	One year	None
28	S. 303 – Negligent acts causing harm	Six months	
29	S. 391 – Pretending to exercise witchcraft or tell fortunes.	One year	None
30	S. 392 – Obtaining registration by false pretence.	One year	None
31	S. 396 – Having possession of thing reasonable suspected of having been stolen.	Six months	Or to a fine of 200 Naira

s/n	Offenses & Sections	Terms of punishment	Alternative term to imprisonment
32	S. 397 – Penalty for being in possession of stolen goods.	Six months	Or to a fine of 200 Naira
33	S. 399 – unlawfully using animals or vehicles without the consent of the owner.	One year	Or to a fine of 40 Naira
34	S. 400 – Suspicion of stealing animals.	None	Fine of 100 Naira
35	S. 467 - 468 Malicious breach of contract.	Six months	Or to a fine 100 Naira
36	S. 478 – Offices of cruelty to animals	Six months	Or to a fine of 40 Naira
37	S. 487 – Entering ship or wharf without ticket	One month imprisonment in default of fine.	Liable to a fine of 4 Naira or in default to imprisonment for one month

Source: PRAWA/J4A Research Report on Diversion From Prison Custody through Alternative to Imprisonment.

The recently enacted Administration of Criminal Justice Act in Nigeria which merged the provisions of two principal legislations guiding criminal procedure in Nigeria, the Criminal Procedure Act (applicable in the south) and the Criminal Procedure Code into one principal federal Act which is intended to apply uniformly in all federal courts across the entire Federation and at the same time also preserves the existing criminal procedures.

The innovative provisions contained in the Act include: the provision for alternative sentences other than prison custody, such as community service[24], parole[25], and suspended sentences[26], as a way of reducing prison congestion and overuse of imprisonment

Below are the findings of the research conducted by PRAWA on diversion from prison custody through alternatives to imprisonment in 3 prisons located in Enugu a state in the south east of Nigeria.

Table 8. Age distribution of short-term convicts in the three prisons in Enugu State

Age Distribution of Short-Term Convicts in Enugu, Nsukka and Oji River Prisons		
Age	**Under 18 years**	**18 years and above**
Occurrence	3	107
Percentage	2.73%	97.27%

24 Section 460 of the Administration of Criminal Justice Act.
25 Section 468 of the Administration of Criminal Justice Act.
26 Section 460 of the Administration of Criminal Justice Act.

From Table 8, 97.27% of the persons convicted in prisons in Enugu State for short-term sentences are 18 years and above, while 2.72% of the persons are below 18 years.

Table 9. Gender distribution of short-term convicts in the three prisons in Enugu State

Gender Distribution of Short-Term Convicts in Enugu, Nsukka and Oji River Prisons		
Gender	**Male**	**Female**
Occurrence	108	2
Percentage	98.19%	1.81%

Table 9 shows that 98.19% of short-term convicts in the three prisons in Enugu State are male, whereas 1.81% of them are female.

Table 10. Occupational distribution of short-term convicts in the three prisons in Enugu State

Occupational Distribution of Short-Term Convicts in Enugu, Nsukka and Oji River Prisons			
Occupation	**Jobless**	**Menial job**	**Skilled job**
Occurrence	26	81	3
Percentage	23.63%	73.63%	2.72%

From Table 10, 23.63% of short term convicts in the three prisons in Enugu State had no occupation, while 73.63% were engaged in menial jobs. However, only 3 persons representing 2.72% of the total number of short-term convicts in the three prisons were involved in skilled jobs. See also the numbers in Table 11.

Table 11. Aggregate duration for short-term convicts in the three prisons in Enugu State

Name of Prison	Enugu prison	Nsukka prison	Oji River prison	Total
No. of short-term convicts	74	14	22	110
Aggregate duration of prison sentence (in months)	1543	252	400	2195
Aggregate duration spent in prison custody before conviction (in months)	100	59	52	211

Figure 10. Analysis of application of fine to short-term convicts

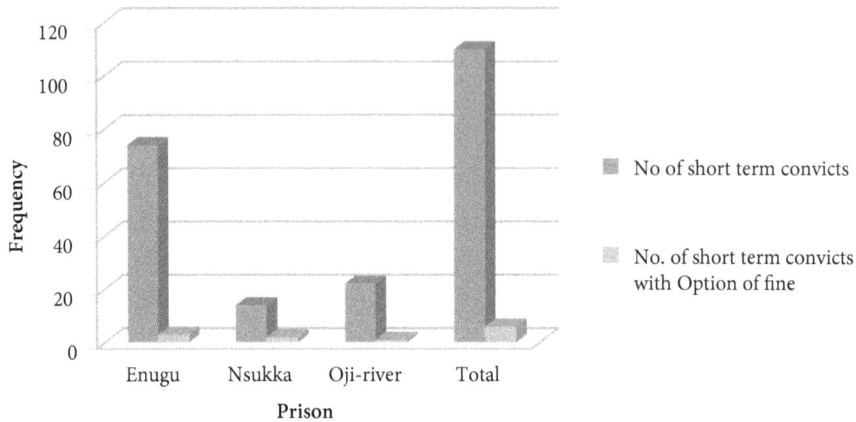

Table 12. Application of alternatives to imprisonment

Prison	Enugu	Nsukka	Oji River	Total
No. of short-term convicts with sentence under 3yrs	74	14	22	110
No. of short-term convicts with option of fine	3	2	1	6 (5%)
No. of short-term convicts without option of fine	71	12	21	104 (95%)
No. of short-term cases with option of fine who took it	1	1	0	2
Value of money of the option of fine	N310,000	N30,000	N15,000	N355,000
Application of other alternative to imprisonment	Nil	Nil	Nil	Nil

Table 12 indicated that only 6 convicts out of 110, representing 5% of short term convicts in the three prisons in Enugu State received alternative to imprisonment conviction through option of fine, while the remaining 104 convicts representing 95% were to serve their punishment in prison custody. However, only 2 of the 6 beneficiaries of alternative to imprisonment sentence were able to take the option. See also Figure 10.

Table 13. Persons admitted in prison for minor offenses (awaiting trial and convicted)

Prison	Enugu	Nsukka	Oji-river	Total
Number of minor offenses	102	84	52	238
ATP	65	65	40	170 (71.43%)
Convicted	37	19	12	68 (28.57%)

It is worth noting that the arguments for non-custodial sanctions essentially mirror image of the arguments against imprisonment.

(i) Firstly, they are considered more appropriate for certain types of offenses and offenders.

(ii) They can be said to be more humane.

(iii) They are generally less costly than sanctions that involve imprisonment.

(iv) By decreasing the prison population, they help reduce prison overcrowding and by doing so facilitate the effective administration of prisons and encourage appropriate time and resources for correctional treatment of those who remain in prison. Reducing the number of cases that have to be processed in prison decreases the workload of the prison administration.

(v) They offer a range of alternative and flexibilities for the court. For a wide range of petty offences (cf. Table 13), imprisonment would not even be considered, as they are not seen to "merit" imprisonment. On the other hand, non-custodial sanctions are deemed appropriate for certain type of offenders, or offenders with certain characteristics, such as first time offenders, or offenders with certain characteristics. Also, the assessment of appropriateness is also connected with the offender's willingness to participate in a non-custodial program, the ties of the offender to the community (for example, family and employment), and the availability of the necessary resources for non-custodial programs (e.g. the supervisors, the availability of space in the programs, even the technological infrastructure).

(vi) Non-custodial sanctions seem to provide opportunities for the application for a wider range of programs than institutional treatment. For these reasons, it can be argued that they care and serve the purpose of the individualization of punishment and treatment than imprisonment.[27]

(vii) Non-custodial sanctions do not hinder readjustment to society and may indeed facilitate this. Prisons have difficulties in preparing offenders held in detention for effective reintegration back into the community. It is important to note that every prisoner (except if he or she dies in prison or is sentenced to life imprisonment) will some day be released into society. When people are imprisoned/incarcerated they are likely to lose their jobs, accommodation, social ties, etc. – all the factors necessary to effectively reintegrate into the community. The assumption is that the greater use of non-custodial sanctions will reduce recidivism given that with non-custodial measures the above factors are usually not destroyed while the person continues to serve his/her sanction.

---

27 See Elías Carranza, Nicholas J.O. Liverpool & Luis Rodríguez-Manzanera, 'Alternatives to Imprisonment in Latin America and the Caribbean' in: Uglješa Zvekić, Alternatives to imprisonment in comparative perspective, Chicago: Nelson-Hall Publishers, p. 384-438.

(viii) Non-custodial measure encourages restorative justice and benefits victims as well as offenders. Odinkalu & Agomoh[28] and Mediation UK[29] researched mediation between the victim and the offender and stated some of the benefits which stem from this approach as follows:
   - For victims:
     - Learn about the offender
     - Ask the offender questions
     - Express their feelings and needs about the crime
     - Receive an apology and/or appropriate reparation, and
     - Try to educate the offender(s) concerning the effects of their offenses.
   - For the offenders:
     - Take responsibility for their crimes
     - Become more aware of the effects of their crime on the victim
     - Reassess their future behaviour
     - Apologize and/or offer appropriate reparation
     - Experience a sense of forgiveness and of 'making it right'
     - To reconcile with society and the community instead of being excluded and alienated (it provides an alternative method of conflict resolution).

Given that the majority of the prison population in Nigeria are ATPs, one may argue that there is no need for the consideration of adoption of non-custodial measures in Nigeria. The focus should rather be on how to speed up the criminal justice process and address the critical issues relating to pre-trial justice. Whilst it is important to address the above, the following is recommended:

(i) The promotion of non-custodial measures and the use of these will effectively balance the cycle as we speed up the pre-trial process. We also need to have available alternatives to utilize as disposition measures for those that will be found guilty. More so, increasing the speed and quality of justice will necessarily lead to an increase in conviction rate. Also, if we do not ensure that non-custodial sanctions are utilized especially as contained in the new ACJ Act, we will continue to be a state with a high prison population, overcrowding in detention centres, high costs and stress on human and other resource – all we would have gained is to shift the pendulum from ATPs to sentenced prisoners.

---

28 Anselm Chidi Odinkalu & Uju Roseline Chiemeka, 'Victimology and the Criminal Justice System in Nigeria', 3 *Journal of Human Rights Law and Practice* 3 (1993), p. 114-136.

29 Mediation U.K., *Victim/Offender Mediation: Guidelines for Starting a Service*, Bristol: Mediation UK, 1994.

(ii) That we also utilize non-custodial measures at the pre-trial stage in a creative way. This will help to fast track the process and will only apply to those offenders who have accepted that they have committed an offense. This approach was the basis of the Gacaca process in Rwanda, which helped Rwanda reduce its prison population from over 130,000 (following the genocide) to about 65,000 and is still pushing for further reduction. This effort was complimented by the adoption of Community Service *(Tigi)*. Again, it is worth noting that in terms of Rwanda this was applied to serious offenses, such as murder/genocide. Also in South Africa, non-custodial measures were introduced at the pre-trial phase to effect diversion amongst youth offenders.[30] As the presenter argued elsewhere[31], there are criteria that will assist the decision with respect to which cases can be disposed off at the pre-trial stage with non-custodial measures:
- What is the type and seriousness of the offense (is it appropriate for a non-custodial sanction to apply)?
- Is public interest not violated by not proceeding with the trial?
- Is the available evidence sufficient to obtain conviction?
- Does the offender admit guilt that he or she committed the offense?
- What are the needs of the victim and the views, feelings and desire of the victim towards the scheme?
- What is the attitude of the offender?
- What is/are the expected gain(s) in utilizing the scheme?

(iii) The attempt made to provide some legislative frameworks for non-custodial measures, as was done by Lagos, Anambra, and Ekiti, is that States should be replicated by other States. Also the reflection of these in the new Administration of Criminal Justice Administration Act, which was recently passed by the National Assembly, is highly recommended. However, more needs to be done towards the effective implementation of its provisions.

(iv) Judicial conferences and seminars as well as professional associations should assist in clarifying sentencing objectives and guidelines. They could stipulate the criteria and principles that permit the comparison of various sanctions and the standardization of their use. These conferences and associations need not be limited to judicial personnel; they could be expanded to include corrections personnel and other persons responsible for the administration of sentences.

---

30 See L. Muntingh, 'A Quantitative Survey of Two NICRO Diversion Projects: Pre – Trial Community Service and the Peninsula Youth Offender Programme', in: L. Muntingh (ed.), *Perspectives on Diversion*, Research Series, Nr 2, NICRO: Cape Town, 1995, p. 6-29.

31 U.R. Agomoh, *Decongesting The Nigerian Prisons And Police Cells: A Handbook of Practical Strategies for the Remand Population*, Lagos: PRAWA, 1996, p. 28-29.

(v) Guidelines should also be developed for prosecutors and the judiciary to help them with the decision whether or not to prosecute, with the selection of the appropriate sanction. For non-custodial sanctions to become the norm, this should start with the process of professional socialization and in the curriculum of law schools. Indeed, specific attention should also be paid to the training of the practitioners responsible for the implementation of the sanctions and for the coordination between criminal justice agencies and other agencies involved in the implementation of these sanctions in the community.

(vi) More research is needed on the normative structure that determines the availability and applications of non-custodial sanctions. With regard to sentencing, research is needed on the factors considered by the sentencing judge or magistrate in deciding whether or not to award a custodial or non-custodial sanction. Research on changes in attitudes (showing the causes and extent of such changes) will be of assistance in the introduction or expansion of non-custodial sanctions. Evaluation research focusing on the effectiveness of various non-custodial sanctions for different types of offenders with different characteristics, keeping in mind the severity of the crimes as well as its effect on reduction of recidivism and costs will also be of great help.

(vii) The State and local communities need to provide the necessary resources and financial support for the development, enforcement and monitoring of non-custodial sanctions. We need to ensure that the necessary infrastructures for the implementation of non-custodial sanctions are put in place. Given that the success of many non-custodial sanctions depends to a large extent on the interaction between the community and the offender, special measures should be adopted to sensitize the community to the benefits and crime control potential of non-custodial sanctions. Civil Society Organizations such as NGOs, Faith Based Organizations, volunteer and citizens' associations should be involved in the implementation of non-custodial sanctions or in the provision of any necessary support to the relevant government agencies in the implementation of non-custodial measures. Doing this may also help to decrease the costs that may be associated with the implementation of these measures.

IV. CONCLUSION

In Nigeria there is an overuse of criminal justice – overuse of criminalization of offense, over use of prosecution, overuse of prison. Strangely, the prison is mainly utilized as the statistics indicate for pre-trial detainees. In addition, the power of arrest and detention is a power that is exercised currently by about 19 agencies in Nigeria. Unfortunately, no centralized database exists of the people held in prisons or detention centres. The Administration of Criminal Justice Act has provisions for non-custodial measure but their application is currently limited, since only 3 out of the 36 States in the country have passed the law (the Federal Capital Territory has as well) and even where these measures apply, not much has been achieved by way of implementation. Finally, those who end up in the justice system through informal mechanisms (e.g. community based reconciliations, fine and compensation) are not captured in official statistics.

Coordination as well as addressing root causes of crimes in any criminal justice intervention with structured and regular mechanisms for review and oversight as well as comprehensive approach will guarantee greater success of reforms in the criminal justice sector. Reforms should be coordinated. Steps should be taken to capture the statistics and data of everyone entering the criminal justice system. A proper interface and support between the formal and informal justice system as well as greater use of non-custodial measures is recommended. Imprisonment and detention always need to be used as a last resort, including in pre-trial stage.

OVERUSE IN THE CRIMINAL JUSTICE SYSTEM IN POLAND

Lech K. Paprzycki & Małgorzata W. Wąsek-Wiaderek*

I. INTRODUCTION

In Poland criminal acts are classified as criminal offences ("przestępstwa") and petty or administrative offences ("wykroczenia"). A criminal offence can take the form of felonies (zbrodnie) of misdemeanors (występki). Felonies are criminal acts that can be committed only intentionally and are subject to the penalty of at least three years of deprivation of liberty. Misdemeanors may also be committed unintentionally if the law so provides. Misdemeanors include fiscal offences. Criminal offences are regulated in the Criminal Code of 1997 (Journal of Laws 1997, No. 88, item 553, with amendments; thereafter referred to as "the CC"). The basic act regulating petty or administrative offences is the Petty Offences Code of 1971 (consolidated text: Journal of Laws 2015, item 1094 with amendments; thereafter referred to as "the POC"). Fiscal offences and petty fiscal offences are regulated in the Fiscal Penal Code of 1999 (consolidated text: Journal of Laws 2013, item 186 with amendments). Although the three codes are the basic acts for criminal justice, many criminal offences and petty or administrative offences are provided for in various statutes regulating may aspects of living in society. The number of criminal offences regulated out of the Criminal Code and Fiscal Penal Code is much higher than offences provided for in both codes. For example, more than 300 various types of offences against business transactions and economic turnover are defined in almost 60 statutes regulating economic turnover in Poland.[1]

* Dr. Lech Krzysztof Paprzycki (1947) is former President of the Criminal Chamber of the Polish Supreme Court.
Dr. Małgorzata Wąsek-Wiaderek is professor at the John Paul II Catholic University of Lublin.

1 Robert Zawłocki, *Ekspertyza prawna obejmująca uzasadnienie na użytek projektu ustawy ograniczającej prawo karne w obrocie gospodarczym [Opinion containing justification for the draft*

This chapter does not concern petty and administrative offences. Although they are criminal acts, they do not constitute crimes. The most severe penalty that may be imposed for petty or administrative offences is the arrest (areszt), which means deprivation of liberty for a period not less than 5 days but not exceeding 30 days. Other sanctions are: limitation of liberty, a fine and a reprimand. Persons convicted for petty or administrative offences are not registered in the National Crime Register except for those sentenced to the penalty of arrest.

Some criminal acts directed against property may be classified as criminal offences or petty offences. It depends on the value of property being subject of a given offence. Pursuant to Article 119 of the POC "Whoever takes away someone else's movable item or appropriates it and the value of this item does not exceed ¼ of the minimum monthly salary, is subject to the penalty of arrest, limitation of liberty or a fine. The same threshold of value of property applies to the offence of: 1) a theft of timber (Article 120 of the POC; Article 290 of the CC); 2) handling stolen items (Article 122 of the POC, Article 291 of the CC) and 3) destruction or damage of someone else's item (Article 124 of the POC, Article 288 of the CC). The above mentioned acts are criminal offences only if the value of property exceeds ¼ of the minimum monthly salary which is at present 462.5 PLN (about 105 EUR). They are named "halved criminal offences".

The first section of this chapter contains the general characteristic of crimes reported in Poland since 2000 and the most important changes in the structure of crime. It also identifies the groups of crimes which burden the criminal justice system the most and reflects the academic discussion on the possible decriminalization in certain groups of offences. The second section elaborates on principles governing prosecution in Poland as well as available legal means discharging prosecutorial organs from the duty to investigate every offence. The last section is devoted to the problem of extensive use of penalty of imprisonment in Poland and the amendments of the Criminal Code aimed at lowering incarceration rate in our legal system.

II. OVERUSE OF CRIMINALIZATION

The number of crimes committed in Poland has decreased since 2003. In 2003 the police registered the highest number of crimes during the last 15 years. Since then the number of crimes has decreased from 1,466,643 per year to 1,077,817 in 2013. Table 1 shows the number of crimes registered by the police and public

statute limiting criminal law in economi turnover], elaborated on 29 February 2012 for the Ministry of Justice, unpublished.

prosecution office.[2] However, data concerning 2014 and 2015 do not contain the number of criminal acts committed by minors. Furthermore, due to changes in the manner of reporting crimes in Poland, data for 2014 and 2015 are not precise and are estimates.

Table 1. Number of registered crimes 2002–2015

Year	Number of crimes	Number of crimes per 100,000 inhabitants
2000	1,266,910	3,278.2
2001	1,390,089	3,597.4
2002	1,404,229	3,672.9
2003	1,466,643	3,839.9
2004	1,461,217	3,827.2
2005	1,379,962	3,616.1
2006	1,287,918	3,377.5
2007	1,152,993	3,025.0
2008	1,082,057	2,838.9
2009	1,129,577	2,960.6
2010	1,151,157	3,014.5
2011	1,159,554	3,003.8
2012	1,119,804	2,906.0
2013	1,077,817	2,799.4
2014	915,081[3]	2470.6
2015	833,281	2165.6

The structure of crimes has not changed very much since 2000 until today. In 2002 various crimes against property constituted 63.4% of all crimes reported in Poland. The second most frequently reported crimes were traffic offences (11.8%). However, in this group of crimes operating motor vehicle while under influence of alcohol or other intoxicants prevailed and constituted 10.3% of all crimes. 5.1% of all crimes reported in 2002 were offences against reliability of documents; 3.4% constituted offences against family and guardianship; the same amount of 3.4% of all reported offences constituted crimes against sexual freedom and decency. Crimes defined in the Act of 29 July 2005 on

2 See data concerning the period 2000-2013 as presented by Beata Gruszczyńska, 'Przestępstwa stwierdzone', in: Andrzej Siemaszko (ed), *Atlas przestępczości w Polsce 5*, Warszawa: Oficyna Naukowa, 2015, p. 12.

3 Number of crimes in 2014 and 2015 as reported by the Police (at: www.policja.pl/pol/aktualnosci/121461,Rok-2015-bardziej-bezpieczny.html?search=234333738) (last visited: 30 May 2016).

Counteracting Drug Addiction (consolidated text: Journal of Laws of 2016, item 224; thereafter referred to as "the CDA") constituted 2.6% of all reported crimes in 2002 while crimes against life and health of a person amounted to 2.4% of all crimes.

In 2012, like in 2002, crimes against property were the most frequently reported offences and amounted to 53.5% of all cases; see Table 2. The number of traffic offences increased to 13.9% of all offences. Operating motor vehicle while under influence of alcohol or other intoxicants amounted to 11.9% of all reported crimes. The third largest group were crimes regulated by the law on counteracting drug addiction (6,8% of all reported offences). The number of crimes concerning drugs was more than doubled in comparison to 2002. Crimes against reliability of documents constituted 4,1% of all reported cases, while the number of crimes against sexual freedom and decency increased to 3.9% of all cases. 2.9% of all reported cases were crimes against family and guardianship.[4]

In the following years the structure of crimes was very similar.[5]

Table 2. Types of crimes

	2013	2014	2015*
Crimes against property	52.9%	53.8%	
Offences against public safety and safety of transport (including operating motor vehicle while under influence of alcohol or other intoxicants)	13.4%	10.1%	9.2% (only crimes against safety of transport)
Crimes regulated by the law on counteracting drug addiction	6.7%	5.7%	
Crimes against reliability of documents	4.1%	6.6%	
Crimes against the activities of state institutions and local government	3.9%	4.0%	
Crimes against the family and guardianship	3.4%	3.9%	

* Exhaustive data not available.

During the last 15 years crimes against property have been the most frequently reported offences. These are: property theft; theft by breaking in; appropriation of a movable item or property right; theft of call units; fraud; robbery; theft followed by the use of force or threat of its immediate use; theft by extortion; destruction

4 Beata Gruszczyńska, 'Przestępstwa stwierdzone', in: Andrzej Siemaszko (ed), *Atlas przestępczości w Polsce 5*, Warszawa: Oficyna Naukowa, 2015, p. 16.

5 Data elaborated on the basis of: 1) *Rocznik statystyczny RP 2014* [*Statistical Yearbook of the Republic of Poland 2014*], p. 147-148 (at file:///C:/Users/MWW/Downloads/rocznik-statystyczny-rp-2014.pdf) (last visited: 30 May 2016).
2) *Rocznik statystyczny RP 2015 [Statistical Yearbook of the Republic of Poland 2015]*, Warszawa 2015, p. 76-77; (at: http://stat.gov.pl/files/gfx/portalinformacyjny/pl/defaultaktualnosci/5515/2/10/1/publ_oz_rocznik_statystyczny_rp.pdf) (last visited: 30 May 2016).

or damage of someone else's item; taking motor vehicle without consent with the purpose of using it for a short period of time; theft of timber and handling stolen items. Every year since 2000 thefts were the most frequently reported crimes against property. For example, in 2002 thefts constituted 35.4% of all offences against property, while theft by breaking in 34.2%. In 2012, 38.5% of all property crimes were thefts, while thefts by breaking in constituted 21.3% of all property offences.[6]

In 2013 and 2014 the number of registered thefts decreased due to changes in the POC. As was mentioned in the Introduction chapter, certain criminal acts against property are the so called "halved criminal offences." Thus, they may be crimes or petty offences depending on the value of property being subject of the act. The Law of 27 September 2013 (Journal of laws 2013, item 1247, with binding force as from 8 November 2013) provided that criminal acts as defined in Article 119, 120, 122 and 124 of the POC were petty offences and not crimes when the value of property had not exceeded ¼ minimum monthly salary. Before this amendment petty offences comprise only acts against property of value not exceeding 250 PLN (about 56 EUR). The purpose of this amendment was to lower the number of criminal acts of insignificant social harmfulness which were classified as crimes. As a result of the amendment, in 2014 the number of thefts classified as criminal offences decreased by 19.1% in comparison to 2013. At the same time the number of thefts classified as petty offences increased by 16.3%.[7] Although the amendment did not cause decriminalization of petty thefts, it decreased the number of registered crimes against property and resulted in lowering sanctions imposed for these offences.

It should be stressed that the scope of criminalization in Poland has been extended over the last 11 years due to the obligation to implement European Union law (previously conventions and framework decisions, currently directives) into the national legal system. This process has been only one element of wider process of internationalization of the Polish criminal law.[8] Poland has to implement many Council of Europe conventions, as well as UN conventions providing for the obligation to criminalize certain acts. Due to the limited scope of this chapter, below are presented only the main areas affected by the criminalization stemming from the EU law. Europeanization contributed to extending criminalization of corruption in the public sector and introduction of

6 Beata Gruszczyńska, 'Przestępstwa stwierdzone', in: Andrzej Siemaszko (ed), *Atlas przestępczości w Polsce 5*, Warszawa: Oficyna Naukowa, 2015, p. 31.

7 *Raport o stanie bezpieczeństwa w Polsce w 2014 r. [Report on the state of security in Poland in 2014]* Ministry of Internal Affairs, p. 54-55.

8 Celina Nowak, 'The Europeanisation of Polish Substantive Criminal Law: How the European Instruments Influenced Criminalisation in Polish Law', 3 *New Journal of European Criminal Law* (2012), p. 365-366.

new types of corruptive criminal acts in private sector corruption.[9] Although human trafficking has been penalized in Poland since 1930s, the new extended definition of human trafficking was introduced to the CC in 2010 as a result of implementation of the Framework Decision 2002/629/JHA of 19 July 2002 on combating trafficking in human beings.[10] Obligation to implement EU law resulted also in introduction to the CC of the "crime of terrorist character".[11] The catalogue of crimes against sexual freedom and decency has to be extended in order to implement EU directive 2011/92/EU of the European Parliament and of the Council of 13 December 2011.[12] According to the new, very controversial Article 199 § 3 of the CC, introduced by the law of 4 April 2014[13], sexual intercourse with a minor (a person under 18) in exchange of material or personal benefits, is subject to the penalty of deprivation of liberty for between 3 months and 5 years.[14] Furthermore, EU law supported by UN or Council of Europe conventions influenced the scope of criminalization of illegal drug dealing[15], money laundering, illegal migration, fraud, acts directed against environment[16] and cybercrimes.[17]

Unfortunately quite often implementation of the EU law to the Polish criminal law is based on the presumption that the provisions of EU law imposing obligation to sanction certain conduct shall be reflected in the new separate types of criminal offences despite the fact that prohibited conduct had been criminalized before under the general rules provided in the CC. There is also a tendency to use criminal law as the most effective tool to sanction certain obligations stemming from the EU law although other measures (for example administrative ones) could be more useful to achieve the goal.

9 *Idem*, p. 367.
10 Arkadiusz Lach, 'Penalizacja handlu ludźmi w prawie polskim' [Criminalisation of human trafficking in the Polish law], in: Agnieszka Grzelak, Michał Królikowski & Andrzej Sakowicz (eds), *Europejskie prawo karne*, Warszawa: C.H. Beck Publishing, 2012, p. 322-324.
11 Article 115 § 20 of the CC. See, Krzysztof Wiak, *Terrorism and criminal law*, Lublin: Wydawnictwo KUL, 2012.
12 Directive on combating the sexual abuse and sexual exploitation of children and child pornography, and replacing Council Framework Decision 2004/68/JHA, Official Journal of the European Union L 335, 17 December 2011, p. 1.
13 Journal of Laws 2014, item 538.
14 See critics of this provision: Jarosław Warylewski, 'Komentarz do art. 199 kodeksu karnego', in: R. A. Stefański (ed), *Kodeks Karny. Komentarz*, Warszawa: C.H. Beck Publishing, 2015, paragraph E.1.
15 Mateusz Zreda, 'Nielegalny handel narkotykami', in: Agnieszka Grzelak, Michał Królikowski & Andrzej Sakowicz (eds), *Europejskie*..., *p.* 327-336
16 See Valsamis Mitsilegas, Malgosia Fitzmaurice & Elena Fasoli, *Fighting Environmental Crime in Poland: A Country Report Work*, London 2015 (at: http://efface.eu/sites/default/files/EFFACE_Fighting%20Environmental%20Crime%20in%20Poland.pdf) (last visited: 23 May 2016).
17 See Eleonora Zielińska, 'Europeizacja i harmonizacja prawa karnego w ramach Unii Europejskiej, in: Tadeusz Bojarski (ed), *System Prawa Karnego. Źródła prawa karnego*, vol. II, Warszawa: C.H. Beck Publishing, 2011, p. 347-419.

The criminal policy in Poland has changed since the recent parliamentary election in October 2015. In accordance with the current opinion of the governing political party "Law and Justice", the criminal law in Poland shall be more severe. The new Minister of Justice several times underlined that penalties for certain crimes shall be strengthened. This tendency is evidenced by the fact that since the beginning of 2016 the new Parliament has extended the time limits for prescription of punishability of crimes[18] and has increased sanctions for giving false testimony and providing false expert opinion for the purpose of legal proceedings.[19] Furthermore, the possibility to discontinue criminal proceedings upon the motion of the victim who was compensated by a suspect (Article 59a of the CC) was abolished by the new Parliament (see section III).

Summarizing, currently in Poland there is no social or political tendency to decriminalize certain acts. The prevailing political opinion is that criminalization shall be extended. One shall also mention that the increased criminalization of last few years very often had its sources in the need to implement EU legal instruments.

However, it is worth underlining that since many years, academics have analyzed the social disadvantages of criminalization of the possession of small amount of drugs. The first Act on drug abuse of 1985 did not provide for a penalty for possession of drugs. In 1997 such offence was introduced to the Polish legal system. However it did not apply to possession of small amounts of drugs solely for personal use. Pursuant to the current wording of Article 62 of the CDA, possession of narcotic drugs or psychotropic substances is subject to penalty of deprivation of liberty for a term up to 3 years (paragraph 1). In case of possession of a considerable quantity of narcotic drugs or psychotropic substances, the perpetrator is subject to the penalty of deprivation of liberty for between 1 year and 10 years (paragraph 2). Only in case of lesser gravity, the perpetrator shall be subject to a fine, the penalty of limitation of liberty or deprivation of liberty for a term up to 1 year (paragraph 3). It should be explained that soft drugs like marijuana or hashish are also included into the list of psychotropic substances prohibited by the CDA.

In the resolution of the 27 January 2011 the Supreme Court resolved the discrepancies in the interpretation of Article 62 of the CDA and stated that even possession of small amounts of drugs and exclusively for personal use falls within the ambit of Article 62 of the CDA.[20] Before this date some courts argued that

18 The Act of 15 January 2016, Journal of Laws 2016, item 189.

19 The Act of 11 March 2016, Journal of Laws 2016, item 437.

20 I KZP 24/10, published in: Orzecznictwo Sadu Najwyższego. Izba Karna i Wojskowa (thereafter referred to as OSNKW) 2011, no. 1 item 2.

possession of small amounts of drugs for personal use does not constitute a crime under Article 62 of the CDA.[21]

Since 2005 drug possession crimes have been the most frequently reported offences under the CDA. Every year these offences constituted more than 45% of all drug offences. For example in 2014 offences defined in Article 62 of the CDA constituted 53.9% of all drug offences, while in 2013 51.8%.[22] Between 2000 and 2013 the total amount of yearly reported drug offences increased from about 20 000 to about 70 000.[23]

Some authors are of the opinion that criminalization of the possession of small amounts of drugs solely for personal use is contrary to the proportionality principle expressed in Article 31 paragraph 3 of the Polish Constitution.[24] It is stressed that the crucial aim of criminalizing possession of drugs, it is combating drug trafficking, has not been reached. Statistics confirm this conclusion since most of persons convicted for the possession of drugs are young consumers of soft drugs whose acts are classified under Article 62, paragraph 3, of the CDA (as "cases of lesser gravity").[25] As transpires from the report of the Institute of Public Affairs, about half of representatives of law enforcement agencies and judiciary are of the opinion that Article 62 of the CDA is not a useful tool in fighting drug trafficking (48% of police officers, 60% of prosecutors, 45% judges and 56% of probation officers).[26] Others underline that the law does not prohibit using drugs. Consequently possession of drugs only for personal use shall not be penalized.[27]

On 9 December 2011 the amendment of the CDA entered into force.[28] It introduced Article 62a of the CDA, which allows for discontinuation of criminal proceedings concerning offences defined in Article 62, paragraph 1 or 3 of the

21 See *inter alia* Judgment of the Supreme Court of 21 January 2009, II KK 197/08, published in: OSNKW 2009, no. 4, item 30; judgment of the Wrocław Court of Appeal of 17 November 2005, II AKa 288/05, published in: Orzecznictwo Sądów Apelacyjnych 2005, no. 5, item 26.

22 Raport o stanie bezpieczeństwa … 2014, p. 137.

23 Beata Gruszczyńska, 'Przestępstwa stwierdzone', in: Andrzej Siemaszko (ed), *Atlas przestępczości w Polsce 5*, Warszawa: Oficyna Naukowa, 2015, p. 41.

24 Mateusz Klinowski, 'Ustawa o przeciwdziałaniu narkomanii a konstytucyjna zasada proporcjonalności', 'Prokuratura i Prawo' 2 (2009), p. 69-84.

25 *Idem*, p. 71. See also K. Krajewski, 'Prawo karne wobec narkotyków i narkomanii: ustawodawstwo polskie na tle modeli regulacji dotyczących narkotyków', 20 Alkoholizm i Narkomania 4 (2007), p. 434.

26 Ewelina Kuźmicz, 'Drug policy in Poland – time for a change', Analyses and Opinions 2010, no. 13/110, Institute of Public Affairs (at: http://www.isp.org.pl/uploads/analyses/1718781744.pdf) (last visited: 23 May 2016).

27 Magdalena Kornak, Glosa do uchwały SN z dnia 27 stycznia 2011 r., I KZP 24/10, Lex/el. 2011. See also: Witold Klaus, Irena Rzeplińska & Dagmara Woźniakowska-Fajst, 'Punitywność? Kierunki zmian w polskiej polityce kryminalnej', in: Andrzej Rzepliński, Irena Rzeplińska, Maria Niełaczna & Paulina Wiktorska (eds), *Pozbawienie wolności – funkcje i koszty. Księga Jubileuszowa Profesora Teodora Szymanowskiego*, Warszawa: Wolters Kluwer Publishing, 2013, p. 311.

28 Act of 1 April 2011, Journal of Laws 2011, no. 117, item 678.

CDA in case of possession of small amount of drugs solely for personal use if the imposition of the penalty on the offender would be purposeless due to circumstances of the commission of the offence and insignificant social harmfulness of the act. On the basis of new Article 62a of the CDA public prosecutors discontinued 2145 criminal proceedings in 2012 and 3132 criminal proceedings in 2013.[29]

III. OVERUSE OF PROSECUTION

The Polish criminal procedure is based on the principle of legalism (Article 10 of the Code of Criminal Procedure, Journal of Laws of 1997, no. 89, item 555 with amendments, thereafter referred to as "the CCP"). Thus, all organs responsible for the prosecution of offences (the police, public prosecutors) are obliged to institute and conduct preparatory proceedings. They are not free to drop out the investigation. For this reason plenty of cases, including these concerning offences of insignificant social harmfulness, must be adjudicated by criminal courts instead of being resolved out of courts.

The Polish legal system provides only a few exceptions to the principle of legalism. These are:

1) Possibility to discontinue the criminal proceedings due to negligible social harmfulness of the prohibited act. Article 1, paragraph 2 of the CC states that a prohibited act of negligible social harmfulness does not constitute a crime. The degree of "social harmfulness" shall be assessed in accordance with the following criteria, as defined in Article 115, paragraph 2 of the CC: type and nature of the infringed legal interest, the extend of inflicted and anticipated damage, the manner and circumstances of the commission of the act, the importance of duties violated by the perpetrator, as well as the form of the intent, the perpetrator's motivation, the type of violated safeguard rules and the degree of such violation. Pursuant to Article 17, paragraph 1(3) of the CCP the proceedings shall be discontinued if the harmfulness of the criminal act is negligible.
2) Possibility to discontinue the criminal proceedings in view of penalty imposed on the accused for another offence. Pursuant to Article 11 of the CCP, the criminal proceedings concerning misdemeanors punishable by a penalty of deprivation of liberty for up to five years may be discontinued, if the imposition of the penalty on the offender would be obviously purposeless

29 Piotr Kubaszewski, *Nowelizacja ustawy o przeciwdziałaniu narkomanii w trzy lata po jej wejściu w życie – raport z praktyki stosowania,* Helsinki Foundation of Human Rights, Warszawa, 2014, p. 15 (at: www.hfhr.pl/wp-content/uploads/2014/12/HFPC_nowelizacja_upn_09122014.pdf) (last visited: 23 May 2016).

in view of a penalty finally imposed for another offence and provided that such a discontinuation is not contrary to the interest of the victim. If the penalty for the other offence has not yet been decided by a final judgment, the proceedings may be suspended. The suspended proceedings should be discontinued or resumed within three months of the date at which the judgment concerning the other offence became final.

3) The opportunity to discontinue the proceedings conditionally for a probation period not less than 1 year and not exceeding 3 years. It applies to offences subject to penalty of deprivation of liberty not exceeding 5 years. The proceedings may be discontinued conditionally only by the court if the perpetrator's guilt and social harmfulness of the act are not substantial, the circumstances of the committed crime are indubitable, and due to the demeanor of the perpetrator, who has not been previously sentenced for an intentional crime, his characteristics, personal conditions and previous way of life, it is reasonable to expect that, in spite of the discontinuation of the proceedings, he will respect the legal order, especially by not committing a crime (Article 66 of the CC).
4) The above described possibility to discontinue the criminal proceedings concerning the offence defined in Article 62, paragraph 1 or 3 of the CDA (possession of drugs solely for personal use).

The CCP provides for mediation in criminal cases. However, it should be underlined that a settlement reached in mediation does not terminate the criminal proceedings. While deciding on bringing a case before the court, the prosecutor should take the content of a settlement agreement into consideration. Moreover, the court should take into account the results of the mediation while delivering the judgment. Pursuant to Article 53, paragraph 3 of the CC while imposing a penalty, the court shall take into consideration the positive results of the mediation between the victim and the perpetrator or the settlement they have reached during the proceedings held before a court or a public prosecutor.

Although the Polish criminal procedure allows for different forms of consensual proceedings, none of them may result in resolving the criminal case out of the court. Even if the penalty is settled by the public prosecutor and the suspect at the pre-trial stage of the proceedings, the bill of indictment or the motion for conviction has to be submitted to the court for adjudication. If indictment is accompanied by settlement, the case is not submitted to the hearing but adjudicated at the session of the court without conducting evidentiary proceedings.

Very important measure of restorative justice was introduced to the Polish law by the amendments of the CC and the CCP which entered into force on 1 July 2015. Unfortunately, it was removed from our legal system by the act of 11 March 2016 amending the CC and the CCP as from 15 April 2016. Pursuant to Article

59a of the CC, in force since 1 July 2015 until 15 April 2016, if a suspect (the accused) reconciled with the victim, in particular as a result of mediation, and repaired the material or moral damages, criminal proceedings shall be discontinued at the request of the victim. The above provision applied only to minor offences (misdemeanors) subject to the penalty of deprivation of liberty not exceeding 3 years and also to offences against property subject to the penalty of deprivation of liberty not exceeding 5 years. Furthermore, this institution of restorative justice could not be applied to suspects previously convicted for intentional, violent crime.

It is worth stressing that the discontinuation of criminal proceedings on the basis of Article 59a of the Criminal Code could be initiated only by the victim and could be decided by the public prosecutor. Thus, this measure provided for the very useful tool to terminate the proceedings out of court, already at the pre-trial stage, after full compensation of the victim by the suspect. The motion of a victim could be refused only exceptionally, when discontinuation of the proceedings would be contrary to the aims of imposition of penalties, as defined in Article 53 of the CC. Once refused at the pre-trial stage of the proceedings, the victim's motion for discontinuation of criminal proceedings could be submitted to the court at the judicial stage of the proceedings.

The new institution of restorative justice has been strongly criticized by some authors, mainly by public prosecutors. They argued that this measure of avoiding conviction and its consequences was available only for rich people.[30] Others pointed to the risk that suspects would exert pressure on victims in order to get discontinuation of criminal proceedings.[31] Those who accepted the new institution underlined that it permitted to mitigate the social conflict caused by the committed crime without the need to apply state means of force and it served to satisfy victim's claims.[32]

We regret that Article 59a was removed from the Criminal Code. It had a chance to become the effective tool to terminate many criminal proceedings concerning offences against property which, as indicated above, every year are the most frequently reported offences in Poland. Currently all such cases must be brought to the court. Of course various consensual proceedings may be applied to examine such cases. However, there is no legal basis for discontinuation of the

30 See Ewa Ivanova, *Bogatemu przestępcy postępowanie umorzą i jeszcze za to zapłacą*, Dziennik Gazeta Prawna of 25 May 2015 (at: http://prawo.gazetaprawna.pl/artykuly/874359,bogatemu-przestepcy-postepowanie-umorza-i-jeszcze-za-to-zaplaca.html) (last visited: 23 May 2016).

31 Arguments of supporters and opponents of this institution are presented by: Kamil Trybek, 'Pozytywne i negatywne aspekty umorzenia na podstawie art. 59a KK', 19 *Kwartalnik Krajowej Szkoły Sądownictwa i Prokuratury* 3 (2015), p. 58-71.

32 Ryszard A. Stefański, 'Umorzenie restytucyjne odstępstwem od zasady legalizmu', in: Barbara Dudzik, Jakub Kosowski & Ireneusz Nowikowski (eds), *Zasada legalizmu w procesie karnym*, vol. I, Lublin: Wydawnictwo, 2015, p. 425.

proceedings out of court. Moreover, the abolished measure offered speedy compensation to victim and gave the chance to activate mediation in criminal proceedings. Its scope was defined correctly. Criminal proceedings concerning crimes against property of insignificant value as well as these concerning traffic accidents (unintentional inflicting a medium bodily harm subject to the penalty of deprivation of liberty not exceeding 3 years) should mainly aim at providing compensation to victims.

The existing exceptions to the principle of legalism do not offer the adequate legal framework for combating the overuse of prosecution in Poland. Table 3 shows that the number of investigations and inquiries discontinued on the bases of Article 11 of the CCP, Article 17, paragraph 1(3) of the CCP and Article 62a of the CDA as well as the number of motions for conditional discontinuation of proceedings is very low in comparison to the number of indictments brought to the court every year.

Table 3. Number of discontinued investigations and inquiries

	2000	2001	2002	2003	2004	2005	2006	2007
Initiated preparatory proceedings							–	885738
Terminated preparatory proceedings	1370000	1512000	1516000	1535000	1542000	1500000	1375000	1304326
Cases brought to the courts							–	406134
Bill of indictments brought to the courts	241000	374000	391000	402000	415000	434000	429000	358541
Motions for conditional discontinuation of the proceedings brought to the courts	7000	7000	8000	8000	9000	11000	10 000	9437
Discontinued preparatory proceedings							812 338	586231
Preparatory proceedings discontinued on the basis of Article 11 of the CCP							–	76
Preparatory proceedings discontinued on the basis of Article 17, paragraph 1 (3) of the CCP							6491	6068
Preparatory proceedings discontinued on the basis of Article 62a of the CDA	0	0	0	0	0	0	0	0
Preparatory proceedings discontinued due to non-disclosure of a suspect	714000	702000	682000	694000	682000	619000	519591	301127

[33]	2008	2009	2010	2011	2012	2013	2014	2015
Initiated preparatory proceedings	–	814255	797681	803807	768117	762620	682113	556231
Terminated preparatory proceedings	944000	964658	1170068	1187030	1142529	1133037	1049190	834287
Cases brought to the courts			388972	397346	377839	354 885	297836	265173
Bill of indictments brought to the courts	370000	385073	375839	382160	361266	338 058	282347	179612
Motions for conditional discontinuation of the proceedings brought to the courts	11000	10895	11667	13 928	15286	15589	14129	15 444
Discontinued preparatory proceedings	445099	458086	445809	430 396	415433	429 919	406466	271018
Preparatory proceedings discontinued on the basis of Article 11 of the CCP	–	–	77	101	99	55	53	55
Preparatory proceedings discontinued on the basis of Article 17, paragraph 1 (3) of the CCP	6084	–	5178	4 848	4 979	6 174	5391	4 771
Preparatory proceedings discontinued on the basis of Article 62a of the CDA	0	0	0	0	2 145	3 132	4273	5 754
Preparatory proceedings discontinued due to non-disclosure of a suspect	167199	181694	181625	171 344	159 730	149 784	137376	81 102

As transpires from the available data, persons suspected of offences against property constitute the majority of all suspects (35.5% in 2002; 32.8% in 2012). The second most frequent accusations concern offences against public safety and safety of traffic (28.7% of all suspects in 2002; 29.6% – in 2012). In this group prevail persons suspected of driving motor vehicle while under influence of alcohol or other intoxicants (25.4% of all suspects in 2002; 25.7% of all suspects in 2012). Both in 2002 and 2012 the third largest group of suspects were persons accused of offences against family and guardianship (8.2% of suspects in 2002; 6.0% of suspects in 2012). Persons suspected of offences against life and health constituted 6.3% of all suspects in 2002 and 5.7% in 2012. In 2002 persons suspected of drug offences constituted only 2.4% of all suspect while in 2012 –

33 Table elaborated on the basis of the yearly reports of the General Public Prosecution Office (at: http://pk.gov.pl/sprawozdania-i-statystyki/strona,6.html) (last visited: 23 May 2016). Not all requested data are available in the reports.

5.9% of all suspects. Thus, in 2012 more persons were suspected of drug offences than of offences against life and health.[34]

Statistics confirm that suspects accused of thefts by breaking in and thefts constitute the largest group. In 2012 there were 151.6 persons suspected of thefts per 100 000 inhabitants in Poland. With reference to thefts by breaking in this number amounted to 62.4; with reference to taking part in a brawl or a beating this rate was 45.1; for robbery 31.2; for drug offences 76.1; for causing bodily harm 25.2; for rape 1.8.[35]

IV. OVERUSE OF IMPRISONMENT

The CC provides for the following penalties: 1) fine; 2) limitation of liberty; 3) deprivation of liberty; 4) deprivation of liberty for 25 years; 5) deprivation of liberty for life. See the numbers in Table 4.

A fine is imposed in daily rates. As a rule, the number of daily rates shall not amount to less than 10 and more than 540. Depending on perpetrator's income, his personal and family conditions, the value of one daily rate may not amount to less than PLN 10 and more than PLN 2 000 (2.2 EUR – 460 EUR).

The penalty of limitation of liberty has evolved since entry into force of the CC in 1998. Until 1 July 2015 it could be imposed for a period no less than one month and not more than 12 months. It could be performed as unremunerated, supervised work for community purposes for 20 to 40 hours per month or as a deduction of 10 to 25% of monthly remuneration for work for a court-designated community purpose. The person performing this penalty was obliged not to change the place of permanent residence without the court's consent and to give explanations regarding the course of serving of the penalty. The law of 20 February 2015, with binding force as from 1 July 2015[36], extended the catalogue of forms of execution of the penalty of limitation of liberty by: 1) the electronic supervision of the perpetrator and 2) imposition of certain obligations on the perpetrator. Before this amendment "imposition of certain obligations" did not constitute the independent form of the penalty of limitation of liberty but could be imposed in addition to the above-mentioned two forms of this penalty. Furthermore, on 1 July 2015 the possible maximum period of execution of the penalty of limitation of liberty was extended to two years. The amendments introduced in 2015 were aimed at stimulating the courts to use this penalty instead of penalty of imprisonment. However, the criminal policy has changed

34 Andrzej Siemaszko, 'Podejrzani', in: Andrzej Siemaszko (ed), *Atlas przestępczości w Polsce 5*, Warszawa: Oficyna Naukowa, 2015, p. 65.

35 *Idem*, p. 73-83.

36 Journal of Laws of 2015, item 396.

since the last parliamentary election and has resulted in the immediate amendments of the CC. The laws of 11 March 2016[37] reduced the possible methods of execution of the penalty of limitation of liberty to these existing before 1 July 2015.

The penalty of deprivation of liberty may be imposed for a period no less than 1 month and no more than 15 years. This penalty occurs in the CC in variety of configurations. Predominantly misdemeanors are subject to the penalty of deprivation of liberty for between 3 months and 5 years (about 90 offences defined in the CC). Frequently misdemeanors are subject to the penalty of imprisonment between 1 month and 3 years (about 80 offences in the CC) and between 1 month and 2 years (about 80 cases in the CC). In about 50 cases the Criminal Code provides for the penalty of deprivation of liberty between 1 year and 10 years. Also about 50 offences are subject to imprisonment between 6 months and 8 years.[38] As was mentioned in the *Introduction*, felonies are penalized with the penalty of deprivation of liberty for a period no less than 3 years.

Before amendments of 2015, enforcement of all the above described penalties could be conditionally suspended for a test period (from 2 to 5 years – in case of the penalty of deprivation of liberty and from 1 to 3 years in case of conditional suspension of a fine or of a penalty of limitation of liberty – Articles 69 and 70 of the CC). As a rule the conditional suspension could be applied only to the penalty of deprivation of liberty not exceeding 2 years. However, in consensual proceedings Article 343, paragraph 2 of the Code of Criminal Procedure provided a separate legal basis for suspension of a penalty of deprivation of liberty not exceeding 5 years for a longer test period, nor exceeding 10 years. Before 2015 the suspended sentence of imprisonment had been frequently imposed by the courts for relatively long test periods. As transpires from the statistics, this penalty was imposed in about 60% of all cases. This resulted in the high number of suspended sentences being enforced due to breaking of conditions of the test period. As transpires from data collected by the Ministry of Justice, about 50% of all prisoners were placed in prison in order to execute the sentence of deprivation of liberty which was originally imposed as a suspended sentence. Moreover, before 2015 approximately 400 000 people were sentenced to imprisonment with conditional suspension of its execution two or three times. There were perpetrators who had been sentenced to suspended penalty of deprivation of liberty more than 20 times. In August 2012 in Poland were 667 persons sentenced at least 8 times to the suspended penalty of deprivation of

37 Journal of Laws 2016, item 437; Journal of Laws 2016, item 428.

38 Michał Królikowski & Robert Zawłocki, 'Prawo karne', Warszawa: C.H. Beck Publishing, 2015, p. 326.

liberty.[39] Thus, probation system proved to be ineffective and generated high prison population. It is stressed in the literature that in practice suspended sentence of deprivation of liberty is not a real probative measure since only in about 30% of cases courts order the offender to comply with certain obligations when suspending a custodial sentence.[40] Moreover, in 2014 about 70,000 convicted persons awaited placement in prison to serve the final sentence of deprivation of liberty.[41]

As a result of the above tendencies and despite the principle of priority for non-confinement penalties, as expressed in Article 58, paragraph 1 of the CC, the number of prisoners per 100,000 inhabitants (incarceration rate) in Poland is very high and one of the highest in Europe.[42] In 2012 it amounted to 200.2 (77,147 prisoners). This is an unquestionable evidence of excessive severity of the Polish criminal law.[43] Moreover, high incarceration rate resulted in overcrowding of penal institutions in the first decade of the 21st century.[44] The detention conditions have improved during the last few years[45], however the incarceration rate is still very high and amounts to 201 (77,371 inmates, including detainees).

The majority of convicts serve the sentence of imprisonment for offences against property. On 31 December 2015 65,900 prisoners were serving the sentence of imprisonment finally imposed. 52.3% of them were convicted for crimes against property. 11,093 persons were convicted for thefts by breaking in (16.8% of all prisoners); 9,371 convicts served the sentence finally imposed for robberies (14.2%); 5561 prisoners were convicted for thefts (8.4%); 4,571 persons served the sentence for offences against safety of transport (6.9%); 4,383 for manslaughters (6.6%); 3,776 – for physical or mental maltreatment of an immediate family member or a dependent person (5.7%) and 3001 – for non-

39 See written reasons of the draft law no. 2393 submitted to the Parliament of VII term (at: www.sejm.gov.pl) (last visited: 20 May 2016).

40 Irena Rzeplińska & Paulina Wiktorska, 'Controlling Criminality', in: Konrad Buczkowski, Beata Czrnecka-Dzialuk, Witold Klaus, Anna Kossowska, Irena Rzeplińska, Paulina Wiktorska, Dagamara Woźniakowska-Fajst & Dobrochna Wójcik, *Criminality and Criminal Justice in Contemporary Poland. Sociopolitical Perspectives,* Ashgate Publishing, 2015, p. 112.

41 Jan Skupiński, 'Problem alternatyw pozbawienia wolności w obecnej i przyszłej polskiej polityce kryminalnej (uwagi końcowe)', in: Jolanta Jakubowska-Hara & Jan Skupińki (eds), *Alternatywy pozbawienia wolności w polskiej polityce karnej*, Warszawa: Scholar Publishing, 2009, p. 310.

42 Irena Rzeplińska & Paulina Wiktorska, 'Controlling Criminality', in: Konrad Buczkowski, Beata Czrnecka-Dzialuk, Witold Klaus, Anna Kossowska, Irena Rzeplińska, Paulina Wiktorska, Dagamara Woźniakowska-Fajst & Dobrochna Wójcik, *Criminality and Criminal Justice in Contemporary Poland. Sociopolitical Perspectives,* Ashgate Publishing, 2015, p. 108.

43 Jan Skupiński, 'Problem alternatyw pozbawienia wolności w obecnej i przyszłej polskiej polityce kryminalnej (uwagi końcowe)', in: Jolanta Jakubowska-Hara & Jan Skupińki (eds), *Alternatywy pozbawienia wolności w polskiej polityce karnej*, Warszawa: Scholar Publishing, 2009, p. 309.

44 See, inter alia, ECtHR, Judgment of 22 October 2009, *Orchowski v. Poland*, Appl. 17885/04.

45 Currently only 86,6% of places availabe in the whole penitentiary system are occupied (at: http://sw.gov.pl/Data/Files/001145jkol/3.06.2016r.-informacja-o-zaludnieniu-jednostek-penitencjarnych.pdf) (last visited: 3 June 2016).

Table 4. Structure of penalties in Poland*

	Total number of convicted persons	Sentenced to the penalty of deprivation of liberty**	Sentenced to the suspended penalty of deprivation of liberty	Sentenced to the penalty of limitation of liberty	Sentenced to the fine
2000	222,815	30,748(13.8%)	143,497(64.4%)	14,796	33,699
2001	315,013	37,076(11.8%)	184,819(58.7%)	28,507	64,475
2002	365,326	35,898 (9.8%)	214,485(58.7%)	39,156	75,698
2003	415,933	36,698 (8.8%)	233,055(56.0%)	52,763	93,274
2004	513,399	49,129 (9.6%)	278,338(54.2%)	71,887	111,491
2005	504,281	43,136 (8.6%)	291,409(57.8%)	67,254	100,968
2006	462,937	42,549 (9.2%)	272,653(58.9%)	57,918	88,407
2007	426,377	37,764 (8.9%)	257,141(60.3%)	47,091	82,988
2008	420,729	38,615 (9.2%)	250,774(59.6%)	40,643	89,011
2009	415,272	38,030 (9.2%)	243,974(58.8%)	43,524	88,236
2010	432,891	39,706 (9.2%)	251,087(58.0%)	49,692	92,329
2011	423,464	41,075 (9.7%)	239,076(56.5%)	49,611	93,571
2012	408,107	41,815 (10.2%)	224,185(54.9%)	50,730	91,296
2013	353,208	39,786 (11.3%)	195,348(55.3%)	41,287	76,759
2014	295,353	35,722 (12.1%)	163,534(55.4%)	33,009	63,078

* With reference to data for 200-2012: Marek Marczewski, 'Skazania i orzeczone kary', in: Andrzej Siemaszko (red.), *Atlas przestępczości*, Warszawa: Wydawnictwo, 2015, p. 102. Data concerning 2013 and 214: Prawomocne skazania osób dorosłych w latach 1946-2014, Ministry of Justice, Warszawa 2015 (at: http://isws.ms.gov.pl/pl/baza-statystyczna/publikacje/) (last visited: 1 June 2016).

** Including penalty of deprivation of liberty for life and for 25 years.

support (non-execution of a statutory or court-ordered duty to take care of an immediate family member or of another person – 4.6% of all prisoners).[46] In previous years the tendency was very similar. In 2013 52% of all convicts served the sentence of imprisonment for crimes against property, 12% – for crimes against life and health, 10% – for crimes against a family. Among all convicted for crimes against property 30% were punished for thefts by breaking in and 30% – for robberies.

The main purpose of the above-mentioned amendments of the Criminal Code of 2015 was to decrease the use of penalty of imprisonment and to activate

46 Elaborated on the basis of: *Roczna informacja statystyczna za 2015 r.* document published by the Ministry of Justice, p. 11 (at: http://sw.gov.pl/Data/Files/001c169lidz/rok-2015.pdf) (last visited: 23 May 2016).

a fine and the penalty of limitation of liberty as effective tools of criminal policy.[47] For this reason the so-called mixed penalty was introduced. It is a combination of a short-term imprisonment not exceeding 3 or 6 months and the penalty of limitation of liberty. Such mixed penalty may be imposed in every case concerning misdemeanor subject to penalty of deprivation of liberty (Article 37b of the CC). Furthermore, pursuant to Article 37a of the CC, in cases concerning offences subject to penalty of imprisonment not exceeding 8 years, the court may impose a fine or the penalty of limitation of liberty instead of the penalty of deprivation of liberty. At the same time the opportunity to suspend the sentence of deprivation of liberty were reduced. Currently courts may only suspend enforcement of the sentence of deprivation of liberty not exceeding 1 year. This applies also to consensual proceedings.

As already mentioned, in March 2016 the new amendments to the CC were adopted which may further increase prison population. The new law reduced the number of available forms of serving the penalty of limitation of liberty. Furthermore, it removed Article 59a from the Criminal Code, which could offer an effective tool to lower the number of persons convicted for offences against property. The recent amendments deleted also Article 60a of the CC. Consequently, the courts have been deprived of the possibility of reducing the penalty in exchange for an procedural agreement on grounds other than those that can be used in ordinary criminal proceedings. It can be expected that this will decrease the number of cases adjudicated in consensual proceedings and thus will increase the overall length of criminal proceedings. However, the Law of 11 March 2016 did not remove Article 37a and 37b from the CC. Both provisions allow to impose non-custodial sentences for majority of misdemeanors, in particular for offences against property that cause the greatest burden for the prison system.

In our opinion the modification of criminal policy shall concern mainly non-violent offences against property and offences against safety of transport which usually are subject to the penalty of deprivation of liberty not exceeding 5 years. Desirable change in the practice could involve more frequent use of conditional discontinuation of the proceedings in this group of cases. In 1 July 2015 the scope of this probative measure was extended and it may apply to offences subject to the penalty of deprivation of liberty not exceeding 5 years, while before this date, as a rule, it could be applied to offences punishable by up to 3 years of imprisonment.

Furthermore, the fine accompanied by compensation for victims shall be the basic sanction imposed for property crimes and road traffic offences. Jan Skupiński pointed to two crucial reasons for failure to apply this penal measure in

47 See Maciej Małolepszy, 'Kilka uwag na temat reformy systemu sankcji', *Prokuratura i Prawo* 11 (2015), p. 34-36.

practice. The first one was the wording of Article 58, paragraph 2 of the CC which was deleted from the Code on 1 July 2015. According to this provision a fine was not imposed if it was reasonable to expect that the perpetrator would not pay the fine due to his financial situation. The second reason was the lack of knowledge of procedural organs about the real financial situation of the accused.[48] The amendments of the CCP introduced in 2015 have improved the system of gathering information about suspects. Consequently both obstacles to impose fines more frequently have been removed.

As was underlined above, as a result of recent changes of the Criminal Code, the Polish law does not provide for out-of-court settlements in criminal matters. Thus, the criminal proceedings cannot be discontinued by the public prosecutor upon the motion of the victim who had been compensated by the suspect. Unfortunately this measure of restorative justice introduced to the Criminal Code in 2015 was abolished by the Law of 11 March 2016.

V. CONCLUDING REMARKS

The criminal justice system in Poland is now in transition. On 1 July 2015 entered into force the Act modifying the principles of imposition of penalties and penal measures. Directives of court sentencing have been changed in order to increase the number of non-custodial penalties, in particular the fine and the penalty of limitation of liberty. In addition, the new measure of restorative justice was introduced to the Criminal Code. It is too early to assess the impact of these changes on the criminal justice system. However, the recent amendments of the Criminal Code adopted in 2016 seem to reverse the above trend in criminal policy.

48 Jan Skupiński, 'Problem alternatyw pozbawienia wolności w obecnej i przyszłej polskiej polityce kryminalnej (uwagi końcowe)', in: Jolanta Jakubowska-Hara & Jan Skupińki (eds), *Alternatywy pozbawienia wolności w polskiej polityce karnej*, Warszawa: Scholar Publishing, 2009, p. 315.

OVERUSE IN THE RUSSIAN CRIMINAL JUSTICE SYSTEM

Yakov GILINSKIY*

I. INTRODUCTION

It is well known that the criminal justice system in the Soviet Union was needlessly repressive. It featured the death penalty and massive political crackdowns, especially during the Stalinist period. Gorbachev's perestroika made the system significantly more humane. Unfortunately, over the past fifteen to twenty years, the criminal justice system in Russia has gradually become increasingly repressive. Russian law enforcement is still dominated by repressive approaches, as I will show in more detail below.

II. OVERUSE OF CRIMINALIZATION

The new Russian Federal Criminal Code (1996) was relatively moderate in terms of the number of the actions and practices it criminalized. However, the original version criminalized such acts as "giving offence" (Article 130), "disorderly conduct" (Article 213), "imprudent property destruction or damage" (Article 168), as well as numerous so-called economic crimes, which were often only shady business practices, for example, knowingly false advertising (Article 182), illegal business (Article 181), and illegal loans (Article 176).[1] These practices should have, in fact, been classified as misdemeanours or civil wrongs, not criminal offenses.

* Yakov Gilinskiy (1934), PhD, Dr. of Law (habil.), is Professor of Criminal Law at the St. Petersburg's Juridical Institute of the Academy of the General Prosecutor's Office of Russian Federation; Head of Department of Criminal Law, the Russian State Pedagogical University, St. Petersburg; Dean of Faculty of Law, the Baltic Institute of Ecology, Policy and Law.

1 *Ugolovnyi kodeks Rossiiskoi Federatsii* [Criminal code of the Russian Federation] (1996) (Moscow: Prospekt, 2016).

The Russian national legislature, the State Duma, has gradually criminalized more and more actions and practices, potentially making every citizen a criminal. For example, among many other actions, "offending the feelings of religious believers" (Article 148, as amended in 2013), "illegal entry into a secured area" (Article 215.4, adopted in 2015), "undesirable organizations" (Article 284.1, adopted in 2015), and "repeated violations of regulations for organizing and holding rallies, demonstrations, marches, and pickets" (Article 212.1, adopted in 2014) have been criminalized.

All of this has opened up huge opportunities for prosecuting any and all Russian citizens, as evidenced by the following criminal cases.

On 19 February 2012, five young women from the art group Pussy Riot performed the so-called punk prayer "Mother of God, Drive Putin Away" at Christ the Saviour Cathedral in Moscow. On 5 March 2012, three of the young women in the group (Nadezhda Tolokonnikova, Maria Alyokhina, and Yekaterina Samutsevich) were arrested. On 17 August 2012, they were convicted of "disorderly conduct motivated by religious hatred or enmity" (Article 213.2) and sentenced to two years in prison.[2] The conviction was even more egregious, because there had been no concrete evidence a crime had been committed. The defendants had not employed weapons or used other objects as weapons during the commission of their non-crime, and they had not, in fact, been motivated by religious enmity, as the prosecution had (falsely) argued. The defendants had attempted to stage a contemporary art performance. Amnesty International declared all three women prisoners of conscience.

On 3 December 2015, Muscovite Ildar Dadin was sentenced to three years in prison under Article 212.1 of Criminal Code, because in August 2014, September 2014, and January 2015, respectively, he had been involved in pickets that had not been authorized by Moscow city hall. This verdict aroused indignation among the civil rights community as a violation of the freedom of expression.[3]

March 2016 saw the trial of Viktor Krasnov, who in 2014 had posted the phrase "There is no God" on his personal page on the Russian social network VKontakte. In 2015, Krasnov spent a month in a psychiatric hospital, where he underwent a forensic psychiatric examination. Krasnov was accused of "offending the feelings of religious believers" (Article 148.1 of the Criminal Code).[4]

2 "Prigovor po delu Pussy Riot" (Verdict in the Pussy Riot case) (at: https://ru.wikisource.org/wiki/%D0%9F%D1%80%D0%B8%D0%B3%D0%BE%D0%B2%D0%BE%D1%80_%D0%BF%D0%BE_%D0%B4%D0%B5%D0%BB%D1%83_Pussy_Riot) (last visited: 12 March 2016).

3 "Delo Dadina" (The Dadin case) (at: http://memohrc.org/special-projects/delo-dadina) (last visited: 10 March 2016).

4 "'Boga net'– srok est': delo Viktora Krasnova" (There is no God, but there is a sentence: the case of Viktor Krasnov), *Krym.Onlain*, March 6, 2016 (at: http://crimea-news.today/russia/russia_4900.html) (last visited: 10 March 2016); "Khristos ostanovilsia v Stavropole" (Christ stopped in Stavropol), *Novaia Gazeta,* 4 March 2016 (at: www.novayagazeta.ru/society/72093.html) (last visited: 11 May 2016).

Criminal charges are pending against artist Pyotr Pavlensky for his numerous politically engaged art performances.[5]

These are only a few examples. In reality, there have been many, many more such cases over the past several years.

As is shown in Table 1, there was an increase in the numbers of crimes and the per capita crime rate until 2006. Beginning in 2007, the numbers and rates decreased, but this was due less to law enforcement and more to the global trend in the reduction of numbers of crimes and crime rates that has occurred in all countries since the late 1990s and early 2000s.

Theft accounted for the greatest percentage of all crimes (over 40%). Along with robbery and armed robbery, such crimes accounted for 50% of all crimes reported during the period in question. In second place were crimes related to illegal drug trafficking (over 10%). Murder, grievous bodily harm, and rape accounted for two to two and a half per cent.[6] So-called other crimes constituted more than 40%. It is clear that many of these crimes pose no great danger to society. They are not, in fact, crimes, and should be decriminalized.

Too many people are prosecuted for crimes related to drug trafficking; see Table 2. This is due to excessive criminalization of such practices, including the illegal acquisition, storage, transportation, manufacturing, and processing of narcotic drugs, psychotropic substances, and their *analogues*; violation of traffic rules while transporting narcotic drugs or psychotropic substances; the illegal acquisition, possession or transportation of narcotic drugs, psychotropic substances, and their precursors; inducement to consume narcotic drugs, psychotropic substances, and their *analogues*; and illicit cultivation of plants containing narcotic drugs, psychotropic substances, and their precursors (Articles 228, 228.1, 228.2, 228.3, 228.4, 229, 230, and 231, respectively, of the Russian Federal Criminal Code). Many of these alleged crimes should be decriminalized. Moreover, it is unacceptable to criminalize any actions *by analogy*.

Many Russian experts have written about excessive criminalization. Luneev argues, "It should be clear that, in the legislative process, offenses that might be classified as administrative offenses or [...] matters of civil law."[7] As Korobeev writes, "In general, the 1996 Criminal Code [...] suffers from a pronounced excess of criminalization."[8]

---

5 "Ugroza. Pavlenskii. Dveri" (The threat, Pavlensky, the doors), *Mediazona*, 11 November 2015, (at: https://zona.media/story/ugroza/) (last visited: 12 March 2016).

6 See, e.g., *Prestupnost' i pravonarusheniia*, 2014, p. 12.

7 V.V. Luneev, 'Ugolovnoe zakonodatel'stvo i obshchestvenno opasnye realii' [Criminal law and anti-social realities], in: V.G. Grafskiĭ, *Gosudarstvo i pravo na rubezhe vekov* [The state and the law at the turn of the century, Moscow: nstitut gosudarstva i prava RAN, 2001, p. 87.

8 A. Korobeev, 'Ugolovno-pravovaia politika: problemy spravedlivosti v Ugolovnom kodekse 1996 goda' [Criminal law policy: issues of justic in the 1996 Criminal Code], in: *Predmet ugolovnogo*

Table 1. Numbers of reported crimes and crime rates (per 100,000 people) in Russia, 1990-2015*

Year	Number of crimes	Crime rate
1990	1,839,451	1,242.5
1991	2,173,074	1,463.2
1992	2,760,652	1,856.5
1993	2,799,614	1,887.8
1994	2,632,708	1,778.9
1995	2,755,669	1,862.7
1996	2,625,081	1,778.4
1997	2,397,311	1,629.3
1998	2,581,940	1,759.5
1999	3,001,748	2,026.0
2000	2,952,367	2,028.3
2001	2,968,255	2,039.2
2002	2,526,305	1,754.9
2003	2,756,398	1,926.2
2004	2,893,810	2,007.2
2005	3,554,738	2,499.8
2006	3,855,373	2,700.7
2007	3,582,541	2,519.0
2008	3,209,862	2,260.5
2009	2,994,820	2,112.0
2010	2,628,790	1,852.6
2011	2,404,807	1,682.9
2012	2,302,168	1,607.8
2013	2,206,249	1,539.6
2014	2,190,578	1,500.4
2015	2,352,100	1,605.5

* Data on crime in the Russian Federation has been drawn from various editions of the yearbooks *Prestupnost' i pravonarusheniia. Statichestichii sbornik* (Crime and offenses: a statistical yearbook) (Moscow: Russian Federal Interior Ministry and Justice Ministry), and *Sostoianie prestupnosti v Rossii. Ezhegodnik* (The state of crime in Russia: a yearbook) (Moscow: Russian Federal Interior Ministry).

prava i ego rol' v formirovanii ugolovnogo zakonodatel'stva Rossiiskoi Federatsii (The subject of criminal law and its role in shaping Russian federal criminal legislation), Saratov, 2002, p. 10.

Table 2. Crimes related to drug trafficking, 2000–2015

Year	Number of crimes
2000	243,572
2001	241,598
2002	189,576
2003	181,688
2004	150,096
2005	175,241
2006	212,019
2007	231,218
2008	232,600
2009	238,527
2010	222,564
2011	215,214
2012	218,974
2013	231,462
2014	253,500
2015	234,800

Source: *Prestupnost' i pravonarusheniia*, 2000–2015.

As we can see, there is no pronounced trend with respect to these crimes. This is due, in particular, to the fact that the number of reported crimes depends on the work of the police and the Russian Federal Drug Control Service (FSKN).

More than ten thousand people are convicted every year for crimes related to drug trafficking. Of these, between 40% and 49% are sentenced to prison.[9] People convicted of these crimes constituted 22% of all prisoners in 2014.[10] Such a large number of people are convicted of drug trafficking-related crimes and imprisoned because, first, many actions that are not, in fact, crimes have been criminalized without sufficient grounds. Second, the police can easily find and arrest drug addicts through their networks of informers and "solve" such "crimes," thus padding the statistics measuring their effectiveness as law enforcers. Many lawyers, criminologists, and narcologists have argued for the decriminalization of many offenses related to drug trafficking. But the State Duma and police need to "intensify the fight" against drug use and drug trafficking, and they thus prevent these offenses from being decriminalized.

9 *Prestupnost' i pravonarusheniia*, 2014, p. 173.
10 *Council of Europe Annual Penal Statistics*, 2016.

Many so-called economic crimes should be decriminalized, for example, illegal loans (Article 176 of the Criminal Code), unlawful use of insider information (Article 185), evasion of customs duties (Article 194), and tax evasion (Article 198). All these actions should be subject to administrative or civil law. However, the State Duma is no hurry to decriminalize such offenses, either.

III. OVERUSE OF PROSECUTION

Overuse of prosecution was always a problem in the Soviet Union, and it has continued to be a problem in post-Soviet Russia. This is particularly clear when we compare the level of prisoners (number of prisoners per 100,000 people) in different countries. Russia for many years ranked first or second in the world, after the United States. Unfortunately, various sources have published different statistics for the same years.

In 2007, the countries with the highest prison population rates (per 100,000 people) were the United States, Russia, Belarus, Belize, the Bahamas, Georgia, and Grenada. The countries with the lowest prison population rates in 2007 were Nepal, Nigeria, Mali, Sierra Leone, Andorra, and Iceland.[11] See Table 3.

We can see a general trend: an increase in the number of convicted criminals, including those sentenced to prison, from 1990 until 2001, followed by a decline. The percentage of persons sentenced to imprisonment increased from 66% in 1990–1992 to 87.6% in 2003, but dropped to 56% in 2013. Moreover, during the entire period in question, approximately half of those people convicted of crimes served suspended sentences and did not do real prison time, so long as they did not violate the conditions set of their parole as set down by the court.

The percentage of offenders convicted of various crimes is presented in Table 4. We can see that most offenders were convicted of theft, followed by those convicted of drug-related crimes. Armed robbery came in third.

The proportion of so-called white-collar crimes is negligible. But this is the outcome of very high latency, of the fact that crimes are not reported. For example, according a study led by Inshakov, the latency coefficient for bribery and graft is above seventy to seventy-five.[12]

11 Stefan Harrendorf, Markku Heiskanen & Steven Malby (eds), *International Statistics on Crime and Justice,* Helsinki: HEUNI, 2010; Roy Walsmley, *World Prison Population List,* London: International Centre for Prison Studies, Kings College London, School of Law, 2006, p. 164–165.

12 S.M Inshakov (ed), *Teoreticheskie osnovy issledovaniia i analiza latentnoi prestupnosti* (Theoretical bases of the study and analysis of latent crime), Moscow: IuNITI-DANA, 2012, p. 521–524.

Table 3. Prison population rates (per 100,000 people) in different countries

Countries	1990/1991	1994/1995	2000/2001	2004/2005	2007	2012
Australia	83	94	113	126	130	129
Austria	90	78/92	84	107	107	104
Belarus	253	496	554	335	468	438
Belgium	59	74	83	88	90	111
Bulgaria	84	99	124	129		145
Canada	111	118	123	107		117
Czech Rep.	80	160	188	170	182	215
Estonia	281	300	327	339		258
Finland	68	59	60	66	67	59
France		89	80	92	85	117
Germany		81	97	98	95	85
Great Britain	88	95	129	141	148	152
Hungary	119	124	173	165		177
Italy	45	89	96	102	77	111
Japan	38	37	47	49	65	54
Lithuania	238	344	304	234	239	334
Netherlands	46	66	94	123	128	68
Poland	131	160	147	211	230	218
Russia	485	571	681	577	613	501
Spain		102	114	142		147
Sweden	61	65	69	81	74	68
USA	465	554	685	738	762	730

Source: Gordon Barclay, Cynthia Tavares et al., 'International comparisons of criminal justice statistics 2001', *Home Office Statistical Bulletin* 12 (2003); Yuri Aleksandrov, 'Legal Practice', *Nevolia* 38 (2014), p. 4–15; Stefan Harrendorf, Markku Heiskanen & Steven Malby (eds), *International Statistics on Crime and Justice*, Helsinki: HEUNI, 2010; Roy Walsmley, *World Prison Population List*, London: International Centre for Prison Studies, Kings College London, School of Law, 2006; *World Prison Brief*, Highest to Lowest - Prison Population Total (at: www.prisonstudies.org/highest-to-lowest/prison-population-total) (last visited: 10 April 2016).

Criminologists and experts in the field of criminal law have written extensively about excessive prosecution in Russia.[13]

13 A.E. Zhalinskii, *Ugolovnoe pravo v ozhidanii peremen* (Criminal law on the verge of change), Moscow: Prospekt, 2009, p. 6–95; A.E. Zhalinskii, *Izbrannye trudy. T. I. Kriminologiia*, Moscow: Vysshaia shkola ekonomiki, 2014; Iakov Gilinskii, *Kriminologiia. Teoriia, historiia, empiricheskaia baza, sotsial'nyi kontrol'* (Criminology: theory, history, empirical basis, social control), St. Petersburg: Alef-Press, 2014, p. 446–511; A.M. Iakovlev, *Sotsiologiia prestupnosti* (Sociology of crime), Moscow: Sodeistvie novyi vek, 2001, p. 204–211.

Table 4. Percentages of offenders convicted of various crimes

Type of crime	2000	2002	2004	2006	2009	2010	2012	2013
Murder	1.6	2.3	2.5	2.0	1.5	1.5	1.3	1.3
Grievous bodily harm	3.0	4.4	5.3	4.5	4.0	4.0	4.2	4.1
Rape	0.5	0.7	0.8	0.8	0.5	0.5	0.4	0.4
Disorderly conduct	4.5	5.6	0.9	0.6	0.3	0.2	0.2	0.2
Robbery	2.3	3.1	3.2	3.1	2.2	2.1	1.8	1.6
Armed robbery	5.5	6.9	8.7	9.5	7.7	7.3	6.1	5.5
Extortion	0.6	0.6	0.6	0.6	0.5	0.4	0.3	0.4
Theft	50.6	32.7	36.5	32.6	29.5	30.0	30.3	29.1
Fraud	1.4	1.2	2.1	3.6	3.6	3.4	3.2	3.4
Embezzlement	1.3	1.1	1.4	1.3	1.2	1.1	0.9	1.0
Bribery	0.1	0.2	0.2	0.5	0.6	0.6	0.5	0.7
Drug-related crimes	8.4	11.1	7.5	8.6	11.8	12.4	14.4	14.8

Source: *Prestupnost' i pravonarusheniia.*

We can see a general trend: an increase in the number of convicted offenders, including incarcerated offenders, from 1990 until 2001, followed by a decline; see Table 5. The percentage of persons sentenced to imprisonment increased from 66% in 1990–1992 to 87.6% in 2003, and dropped to 55.9% in 2013. Moreover, during the entire period in question, approximately half of those people convicted of crimes served suspended sentences and did not do real prison time as long as they did not violate the conditions of their parole as set down by the court.

Prison terms are very long under Russian criminal law. Interestingly, the Russian Criminal Code of 1926 (when the country was already part of the Soviet Union) stipulated maximum prison terms of ten years (Article 28). According to the Criminal Code of 1960, the maximum prison term was fifteen years (Article 24). The current Criminal Code of 1996 increased the maximum prison term to twenty years (Article 56), and it stipulates life imprisonment (Article 57) in certain cases. Repeat offenses could draw sentences of up to thirty years in prison, but in 2013 this was increased to thirty-five years. These are very long terms of imprisonment, much higher than those imposed by courts in Europe and Japan.

Of course, criminal law stipulates other penalties not involving deprivation of liberty: fines, community service, corrective labour, restriction of liberty, and arrest, among others (Article 44). But they are employed rarely or not at all, such as arrest. For example, during the period 2003–2014, 6–15% of all convicted offenders were fined; 7–10% were sentenced to compulsory work; 4–10%, to corrective labour; and 0.2–0.9%, to restriction of liberty. Especially unacceptable

Table 5. Number of crimes recorded in Russia, crime rate (per 100,000 people), number of convicted offenders, and number of imprisoned offenders

Year	Number of crimes	Crime Rate	Convicted Offenders	Number /% of prisoners
1990	1,839,451	1,242.5	537,643	355,975/66.2
1991	2,173,074	1,463.2	593,823	390,161/65.7
1992	2,760,652	1,856.5	661,392	434,103/65.6
1993	2,799,614	1,887.8	792,410	568,549/71.7
1994	2,632,708	1,778.9	924,754	632,763/68.4
1995	2,755,669	1,862.7	1,035,807	769,588/74.3
1996	2,625,081	1,778.4	1,111,097	863,846/77.7
1997	2,397,311	1,629.3	1,013,431	860,075/84.9
1998	2,581,940	1,759.5	1,071,051	894,435/83.5
1999	3,001,748	2,026.0	1,223,255	996,611/81.5
2000	2,952,367	2,028.3	1,183,631	898,126/75.9
2001	2,968,255	2,039.2	1,244,211	1,050,527/ 84.4
2002	2,526,305	1,754.9	859,318	735,299/85.6
2003	2,756,398	1,926.2	773,920	678,182/87.6
2004	2,893,810	2,007.2	793,918	673,032/84.8
2005	3,554,738	2,499.8	878,893	726,712/82.7
2006	3,855,373	2,700.7	909,921	733,474/80.6
2007	3,582,541	2,519.0	916,479	712,033/77.7
2008	3,209,862	2,260.5	914,541	No data
2009	2,994,820	2,112.0	892,360	630,789/70.7
2010	2,628,790	1,852.6	845,071	573,115/67.8
2011	2,404,807	1,682.9	782,274	509,341/65.1
2012	2,302,168	1,607.8	739,278	428,228/57.9
2013	2,206,249	1,539.6	735,605	411,337/55.9
2014	2,190,578	1,500.4	746,270	
2015	2,352,100	1,605.5	762,556	

Source: *Prestupnost' i pravonarusheniia*, 1990–2015; *Sostoianie prestupnosti v Rossii*, 1990–2015.

from my viewpoint is the fact that deprivation of liberty (incarceration) is actively applied to juveniles (children aged fourteen to seventeen). Thus, over the same period, 16–21% of convicted juvenile offenders were sentenced to actual prison time; 40–50% were given suspended sentences; 1.1–3.4% were sentenced to restriction of liberty; 1–2%, to corrective labour; 13–22%, to compulsory work; and 10–12%, to fines.[14]

14 *Prestupnost' i pravonarusheniia*, 1990–2015.

IV. OVERUSE OF IMPRISONMENT

The latest Russian Federal Criminal Code (1996) contains quite stern forms of punishment: the death penalty, life imprisonment, deprivation of liberty for a maximum of twenty years; in case of a partial or full merger of the terms of deprivation of liberty into the assignment of punishment by an accumulation of penalties, the maximum total term of deprivation of liberty may not exceed thirty years, and for cumulative sentences, thirty-five years (Article 56). In all previous Russian Criminal Codes, including during the Stalin regime, there were no such punishments as life imprisonment and thirty-five-year sentences. A moratorium on the death penalty has been in effect since 1997, but the Russian parliament (the State Duma) has never ratified it.

In addition, Russian prisons and pre-trial detention facilities are notorious for their poor and dangerous living conditions. They serve poor quality food and provide inadequate health care. Numerous penalties (including time in so-called punishment cells and solitary confinement) are handed out liberally in most places of incarceration for a variety of real and imaginary "infractions." Defendants awaiting trial and suspects under investigation are placed in so-called pressure cells to extract confessions of guilt.[15] Mass beatings are common. Life in Russian penitentiaries (prisons and so-called correctional colonies) is unbearable, and the possibilities for "rehabilitation" are non-existent. There is an extensive academic and activist literature on the depressing conditions in Russian jails, prisons, and penal colonies.[16]

The widespread use of torture results from number of factors.[17] Torture is employed to obtain confessions from suspects in pre-trial detention facilities as well as to punish "habitually bad behaviour" in prisons. There is a general lack of professionalism among police investigators and prosecutors due to low salaries, poor supervision, and better officers transferring to business and private security

15 Pressure cells can be found in all places of imprisonment. In such cells prisoners selected by the administration beat torture and rape other prisoners to obtain information from them or to make them compliant to the needs of the administration.

16 Liudmila Al'pern, *Son i iav' zhenskoi tiur'my* (The dream and reality of women's prisons), St. Petersburg: Aleteia, 2004; Mary McCauley, *Children in Custody: Anglo-Russian Perspectives*, London: Bloomsbury, 2009; Lev Ponomaryov (ed), *Rossiiskii gulag: ubiistva i pytki, No. 1* (The Russian gulag: murder and torture, no. 1), Moscow: Vestnik "V zashchitu prav zakliuchennykh," 2006 (at: http://library.khpg.org/files/docs/1431091341.pdf) (last visited: 13 May 2016); Nikolai Shchur (ed), *Monitoring primeneniia pytok v ugolovno-ispolnitel'noi sistemy Cheliabinskoi oblasti* (Monitoring the use of torture in the penal system of Chelyabinsk Region), Chelyabinsk: Ural'skii demokraticheskii fond, 2013 (at: http://uraldem.ru/wp-content/uploads/2013/08/Chel_pytki_monitor1.pdf) (last visited: 13 May 2016); *Polozhenie zakliuchennykh v Rossii segodnia* (The condition of prisoners in Russia today), Moscow: Moskovskaia Khel'sinskaia gruppa, 2003.

17 For more detail, see Yakov Gilinskiy, 'Torture by the Russian Police: An Empirical Study', 12 *Police Practice and Research*, 2 (2011), p. 163–171.

firms. Instead of investigating cases thoroughly and using the objective evidence available to them, investigators resort to shortcuts, using threats, fraud, provocations, and torture to obtain confessions. Torture is also associated with a culture of corruption in which it is considered normal for investigators and prosecutors to take bribes. High-ranking officials also encourage the use of torture to solve cases and improve "clean-up" rates (the percentage of cases solved), an important criterion for evaluating a law enforcement agency's performance. Furthermore, torture and the use of cruel and inhumane punishment go unpunished. In practice, law enforcement officers are almost never criminally prosecuted for torturing detainees. There are also a number of law officers with a sadistic outlook who take pleasure in torturing people. Violence and torture are also venerable Russian traditions stretching from the police and gendarmerie of Tsarist Russia to the crackdowns and purges of the Soviet regime. The final and main cause is the total absence of so-called political will on the part of authorities to put an end to the routine use of torture.

In Russia, I led a group that did an empirical study of torture in five regions: St. Petersburg, Pskov, Nizhny Novgorod, the Komi Republic, and Chita. Surveys of prisoners were carried out in two regions: Komi (197 convicts) and Chita (150 convicts). Prisoners were questioned only about whether they had experienced torture before conviction and imprisonment. This was essential to exclude answers dealing with conditions in penal institutions. In Komi, 39% of convicts claimed to have been subject to unlawful or unjustified cruel physical treatment or the threat of such treatment, including 10.1% who said that mistreatment was "systematic." In Chita, the percentage of convicts who said they had been subjected to unlawful or unjustified cruel physical treatment or threats of such treatment was 61.3% (including 21.3% systematically). Furthermore, 40% of those interviewed in Komi, and 56.7% in Chita, said they had been subjected to unlawful physical coercion to confess or incriminate themselves or other persons, or to make them refuse to testify.

In terms of methods of physical abuse, forcing detainees into physically excruciating positions (stretching, hanging, handcuffing, etc.) were most prevalent: 29.4% in Komi, and 43.4% in Chita. The next most prevalent method was beating: 26.4% in Komi, and 44.6% in Chita. The main categories of law enforcement torturers were as follows: criminal police and detectives, 29.4% in Komi, and 42.0% in Chita; prosecutors, 7.1% in Komi, and 11.3% in Chita; and senior police officers, 10.7% in Komi and 16.0% in Chita.[18]

Inadequate medical care or incarceration of terminally ill people, who by law should be exempted from punishment, may be de facto torture. Thus, on 6 April

---

18 *Sotsiologia nasiliia. Proizvol pravokhranitel'nykh organov glazami grazhdan* (The sociology of violence: law enforcement abuse as witnessed by people), Nizhny Novgorod: Komitet protiv pytok, 2007.

and 9 April 2016, prisoners Maria D. and Oksana S. died in a prison hospital in St. Petersburg. Oksana had been suffering from fourth-stage (terminal) cancer, but had not been released to die on the outside.[19] Neither of the young women had been convicted for violent or other serious crimes, but for distributing drugs. Did they deserve to die in prison for such crimes?

V. CONCLUSION

As I have shown above, Russia is generally plagued by an overuse of criminalization, prosecution, and imprisonment. Of course, the circumstances in today's post-Soviet Russia are better than they were in the Soviet Union, but they are much worse than in Western Europe, Australia, and Japan. Finland has one of the most liberal and democratic judicial and penal systems, which I have studied both via the scholarly literature[20] and by visiting prisons in the cities of Helsinki and Turku.

Overcoming the overuse of criminalization, prosecution, and imprisonment should solve two fundamental problems. First, it would make relations in society more humane. Second, it would reduce the numbers of excluded and marginalized people who are afflicted by crime, alcohol abuse, drug addiction, and suicidal behaviour. We usually forget that by sending people to prison, society gets back people even poorer in social, moral, and mental terms.

Criminal policy, criminal law, penitentiary law, and law enforcement are in need of fundamental reform in Russia. All actions and practices that pose no great danger to society should be decriminalized and regulated by administrative and civil law. The independence of courts must be a real fact of life, and not just something proclaimed but only honoured in the breach. The death penalty should be abolished from the list of penalties, the maximum period of imprisonment reduced, and the practice of imposing long prison terms done away with. Alternative penalties (fines and various types of community service) should be applied more widely. Conditions in prisons should not violate basic human rights, and they should be places where nutritious food and decent medical care are available. Torture must be absolutely rooted out of the police and the penitentiary service. Unfortunately, all of these things will become possible only if the political and economic circumstances in Russia are fundamentally changed.

---

19 Vera Chelishcheva, 'Nakazanie smert'iu' (Death penalty), *Novaia Gazeta*, 13 April 2016, p. 18–19.

20 Iskender Isaveev (ed), *Ot "strany tiurem" k obshchestvu s ogranichennym prichineniem boli. Finskii opyt sokrashcheniia chisla zakliuchennykh* (From a "country of prisons" to a society that inflicts a limited amount of pain: Finnish know-how in reducing the number of prisoners), Helsinki: National Research Institute of Legal Policy, 2012.

OVERUSE IN THE CRIMINAL JUSTICE SYSTEM IN SPAIN

Deborah García Magna*

I. INTRODUCTION

The Spanish penal system is strongly established on the principle of legality and comes from a codification tradition, based on the classical liberal criminal law, which could be classified as a procedural justice system. As a fundamental principle of modern continental criminal law, the principle of legality implies that in our system both behaviours considered criminal and the punishments to be imposed (with minimum and maximum limits) are previously and explicitly set out in the law[1], including all facts to be taken into account when sentencing: degrees of participation and execution of crime, concurrent offences, mitigating and aggravating circumstances, exoneration of criminal liability, etc.[2] Law also contains provisions on how imposed penalties are enforced, and under which conditions this enforcement can be suspended or a penalty can be replaced, as well as cases in which parole and open regime can be granted.[3] Spanish judges are bound by some rules that limit the room for discretion in the imposition of sanctions, and their subsequent enforcement.[4] In addition, in recent years there is a tendency to carry out penal reforms very often. During its twenty years of existence, the Spanish penal code has already been modified more than 30 times,

* Deborah García Magna is assistant professor of Criminal Law at the University of Malaga, Spain.

1 LO 1/2015 (Organic Law 1/2015), of 23 November 2015, of the Penal Code (hereinafter referred to as PC), and special criminal laws.

2 Articles 61 to 79 PC.

3 Articles 80-94 bis of the PC; LO 1/1979 (Organic Law 1/1979), of 26 September 1979, General Penitentiary Law; and RD 190/1996 (Royal Decree 190/1996), of 9 February 1996 approving the Prison Regulations.

4 J.M. Tamarit Sumalla, 'Sistema de sanciones y política criminal. Un estudio de Derecho comparado europeo', *Revista Electrónica de Ciencia Penal y Criminología* 9 (2007), p. 1-40, studies different indicators of punitiveness and flexibility, concluding that Spain has a rigid system both in books, and in action.

on an average of more than one penal reform by year. Most of them have increased punitiveness by widening the categories of crimes, raising the penalties, and making the penitentiary system less flexible, especially for some criminal offences[5], all leading to a very high prison population.

The results of a recent thorough study of each stage of the Spanish penal system show that the model of law and order is displacing the procedural justice system.[6] As a result, it is unlikely that decriminalization policies will be carried out in the immediate future. As it will be highlighted in this report, although there are no alarming crime figures in Spain and experts consider it appropriate to decrease punitive pressure in some areas, it seems that this could only happen for utilitarian reasons, within a context of economic crisis that makes it unsustainable to maintain such a high prison population.

II. OVERUSE OF CRIMINALIZATION

II.1. REALITY OF CRIME IN SPAIN

Spain does not have high crime rates, as it can be seen in the comparative analysis between neighbouring countries showing that the Spanish crime rate is far below the EU-15 average (Figure 1). The available data on offences recorded by the police show that there was a slightly rising trend from 2000 to 2008, followed by a downward period that lasts until now (Figure 2).

It is highly desirable to supplement police data with information provided by other measuring instruments, such as victimization surveys.[7] Although Spain has only participated in the 1989 and 2005 waves of the International Crime Victim Survey[8], there are more recent data at a national level, which show low crime figures and a slightly declining trend, even for the period between 2000 and 2005, where police figures are slightly ascendant.[9]

Regarding crimes that burden the criminal justice system the most, as they are grouped in the official statistics, crimes against property stand first, especially larceny and burglary representing more than half of all crimes (51.3%). They are

5 J.L. Díez Ripollés, 'Rigorismo y reforma penal. Cuatro legislaturas homogéneas (1996-2011)', *Boletín Criminológico*, 141 and 142 (2013).

6 D. García Magna, *El modelo penal de la seguridad ciudadana y su implantación en el sistema penal español*, Dissertation, University of Malaga, 2015.

7 As evidenced in M. Aebi & A. Linde, 'El misterioso caso de la desaparición de las estadísticas policiales españolas', 12 *Revista Electrónica de Ciencia Penal y Criminología* 7 (2010), p. 1-30, official statistics have many flaws.

8 *European Sourcebook of Crime and Criminal Justice Statistics*, 5th edition, 2014, p. 342.

9 E. García España, J.L. Díez Ripollés, F. Pérez Jiménez, M.J. Benítez Jiménez & A.I. Cerezo Domínguez, 'Evolución de la delincuencia en España. Análisis longitudinal con encuestas de victimización', *Revista Española de Investigación Criminológica (REIC)* 8 (2010), p. 9.

Figure 1. Compared crime rates in EU-15 (2014)

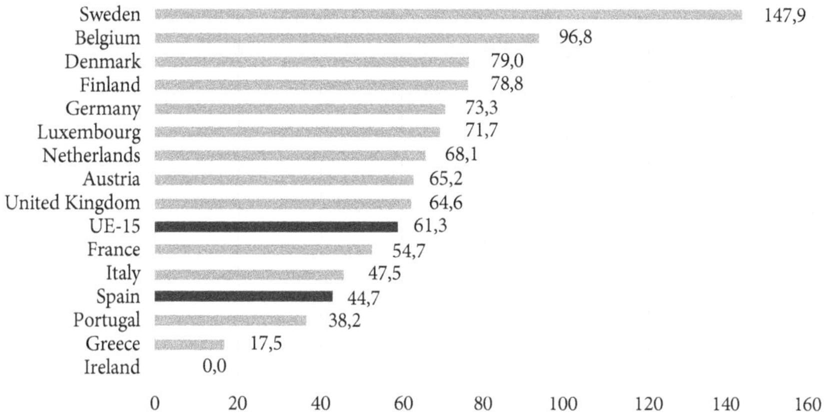

Source: Ministry of Home Affairs. Annual Statistics, 2014.

Figure 2. Crime rate in Spain (Crimes / 1000 population) 2000-2015

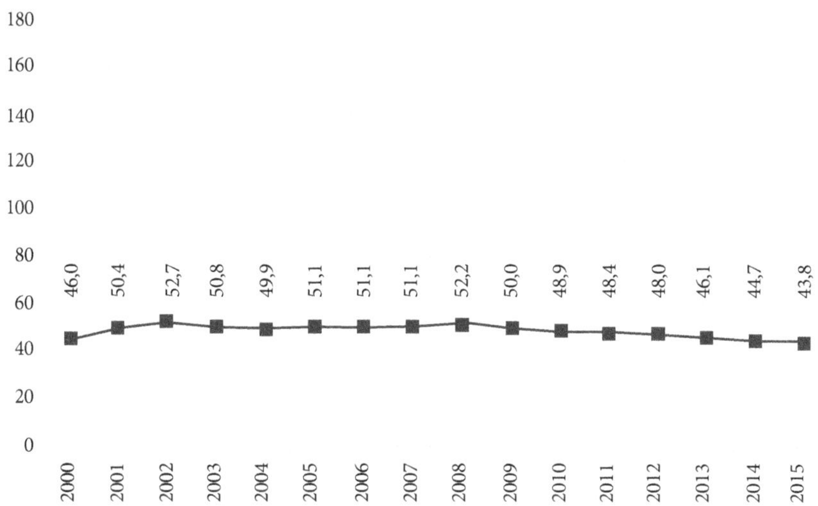

Source: EUROSTAT and Ministry of Home Affairs.

followed in second place by crimes against persons, including homicide and murder (0.7%), injuries (9.6%), gender-based violence (3.7%) and crimes against freedom (5.2%). The third place is occupied by crimes against public safety, which contain drug offenses (0.6%) and traffic offenses (2.4%). The fourth and the fifth position go to crimes against public order and the administration of justice, followed by other crimes whose representation is lower (forgery, 0.9%; crimes against sexual freedom, 0.4%; and felonies against relatives, 0.5%). According to disaggregated data, this classification varies slightly, as shown in Figure 3.

Figure 3. Most frequent crimes (2014)

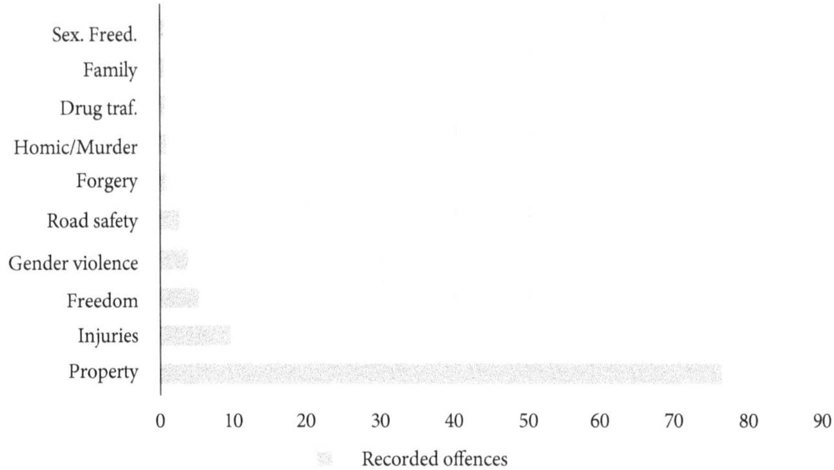

Source: Ministry of Home Affairs.

II.2. FACTORS INFLUENCING THE CRIMINALIZATION OF BEHAVIORS: SUPRANATIONAL OBLIGATIONS AND PRESSURE GROUPS (POPULIST DYNAMICS)

In Spain, as in many other countries, the legislative initiative is influenced by several factors, beyond the actual need for criminal protection. Especially some areas are more prone to populist dynamics and more likely to incorporate the discourses of pressure groups, in particular, of the victims. On the other hand, Spain has assumed some supranational commitments that determine legislative processes, where two situations can be distinguished: obligations that must be transposed into national legislation, and those that serve as a pretext for the national legislator to carry out broader reforms than the ones required by international standards.

On the first issue, recent empirical research about framing and agenda-setting show that populist criminal policies are based on rather emotional than rational arguments[10], and their proposals often disregard or neglect what citizens

10 Studies on attitudes towards crime show that Spaniards are not particularly punitive. Among others, D. Varona Gómez, '¿Somos los españoles punitivos? Actitudes punitivas y reforma penal en España', *Indret* 1 (2009), p. 1-31.

really need and claim.[11] As the purpose is to obtain electoral gains, decisions often focus on the short-term view, where the media plays a key role.[12] In short, politicians use public opinion as a criterion to measure the level of attention on a particular issue, thus justifying punitive measures or inaction in certain areas.

It is therefore necessary to refer specially to pressure groups influencing the criminal legislative decision-making in Spain. That includes victims[13], judiciaries, practitioners and legal experts[14], think tanks linked to political parties[15], associations positioning themselves as representatives of public morals[16], stakeholders looking for business opportunities[17], and even other States acting as

---

11 Regarding the three vertices of the triangle of decision making: politicians, media and public opinion, see, among others, J.J. Medina Ariza, 'Discursos políticos sobre seguridad ciudadana en la historia reciente de España', in: Fernando Pérez Álvarez (ed), *Serta: in memoriam Alexandri Baratta*, Salamanca: Ediciones Universidad de Salamanca, 2004, p. 1299-1320; H. Criado Olmos, '¿Qué temas destacan los partidos? El discurso del PP y el PSOE durante las campañas de 1996 y 2000 en España', 63 *Revista Internacional de Sociología* 41 (2005).

12 Among others, C. Rechea Alberola & E. Fernandéz Molina, *Los discursos sobre seguridad ciudadana y lucha contra la delincuencia en la prensa española*, Instituto Universitario de Investigación sobre Seguridad Interior, 2006; M. García Arán & L. Peres-Neto, 'Discursos mediáticos y reformas penales de 2003' in: M. García Aran & J. Botella Corral (eds), *Malas noticias. Medios de comunicación, política criminal y garantías penales en España*, Madrid: Tirant lo Blanch, 2008; L. Pozuelo Pérez, *La política criminal mediática. Génesis, desarrollo y costes*, Madrid: Marcial Pons, 2014, among others.

13 A.I. Cerezo Domínguez, *El protagonismo de las víctimas en la elaboración de las leyes penales*, Madrid: Tirant lo Blanch, 2010, p. 35, shows that victims receive a different treatment depending on whether they are members of a victims association or not. In any case, there are numerous examples of penal reforms that have been carried out due to the mobilization of the victims, especially when it comes to: sexual crimes and murders committed against minors (e.g. Mari Luz Cortés and the reform of 2010: LO 5/2010, or Marta del Castillo and the reform of 2015: LO 1/2015), terrorism (after huge demonstrations organized by associations of victims, and meetings with members of the Government), violent juvenile crimes (e.g. Sandra Palo and the reforms of 2003 and 2006: LO 15/2003 and 8/2006), and gender violence (following the pressure of feminist groups on the drafting of various laws, including LO 5/2010). A different view of feminist pressure groups can be found in M.L. Maqueda Abreu, '¿Es la estrategia penal una solución a la violencia contra las mujeres? Algunas respuestas desde un discurso feminista critico', *Indret* 4 (2007), p. 10, p. 10.

14 Grupo de Estudios de Política Criminal (Group of Studies on Criminal Policy, GEPC), the platform Otro Derecho penal es posible (Other Criminal Law is Possible), the professional association Jueces para la Democracia (Judges for Democracy), etc., but unfortunately, legislators do not usually listen to the experts.

15 For example, the Foundation for Analysis and Social Studies (FAES) is linked to the popular party (PP) and the Foundation for Progress and Alternatives (IDEAS) is linked to the socialist party (PSOE).

16 In areas with a strong ethical component, such as abortion, euthanasia and genetic manipulation, ecclesiastical institutions are a real pressure group (e. g. the Episcopal Conference), as are some associations such as the Family Forum, the Right to Live platform, or Family and Human Dignity, among others.

17 Last reform (LO 1/2015), for example, has incorporated compliance programs in the field of liability of legal persons, and has given a more relevant role to private security guards in crimes against public order.

lobbyists and imposing their criminal policy approach through mandatory international conventions.[18]

Regarding the second issue, an analysis of the 30 reforms of the current Penal Code has been carried out, in order to identify references to supranational commitments. It is noteworthy that 14 of them explicitly refer to conventions and jurisprudence of international courts, whereas 5 mention the legislation and jurisprudence of other countries. As regards the content of the laws (analysis of the preambles), there are 69 specific references to European or international legislation, 11 to comparative legislation or jurisprudence, and 3 to the European Court of Human Rights.[19] Sometimes the reforms are very punitive because the supranational instruments so demand.[20] Other times these instruments are used by the national legislator to carry out a reform that goes beyond what is required.[21]

II.3. OPPORTUNITIES FOR LEGALIZATION, DECRIMINALIZATION OR POLICY-BASED TOLERANCE OF CERTAIN BEHAVIORS

The high media attention of the legislative phase may lead to a double strategy: while reforms on crimes that shake public opinion and receive major media coverage are usually very punitive (such as terrorism or sexual offenses), other reforms pass unnoticed and can even reduce penal intervention (as it has recently happened with drug offences in Spain, through LO 5/2010).

18 This has happened, for example, in the United States regarding the field of drugs or intellectual property, as evidenced in P. Rando Casermeiro, 'La influencia de los grupos de presión en la política criminal de la propiedad intelectual. Aspectos globales y nacionales', 17 *Revista Electrónica de Ciencia Penal y Criminología* 3 (2015), p. 23 et seq.

19 D. García Magna, *El modelo penal de la seguridad ciudadana y su implantación en el sistema penal español*, Dissertation, University of Malaga, 2015, p. 197 et seq.

20 For example, Framework Decision 2004/68/JHA, that provides a very broad concept of child pornography (Article 189 PC); Framework Decision 2008/919/JHA on preparatory acts and participation in terrorist offenses (Articles 572, 575, 578 and 579 PC); Directive 2008/99/EC on the protection of the environment that may be violating the principles of legality and ultima ratio of criminal law (Article 326 PC); Framework Decision 2008/913/JHA on hate crimes, which could undermine the principle of subsidiarity (Article 510 PC); Directive 2011/36/EU, on combating trafficking in human beings, that impose the same minimum penalty as the one established by Directive 2014/62/EU for offenses of counterfeiting (Articles 177a and 386 PC), violating the principle of proportionality.

21 For example, the Spanish regulation on hate crimes (Article 510 PC) is broader than the provisions of the Framework Decision 2008/913/JHA; the regulation of both confiscation (Article 127a PC) and genetic profile (Article 129 bis PC), is more extensive than the Directive 2014/42/EU and the Council of Europe Convention held in Lanzarote, 2007, respectively; the regulation of terrorism (Article 577 PC) is more punitive than in UN Security Council Resolution 2178 /2014; or the age of sexual consent is not fixed in the Council of Europe Convention for the protection of children against exploitation and sexual abuse of 2007, despite what the reform LO 1/2015 might sustain.

There are three ways of reducing punitive pressure: legalization (the conduct is declared legal, even under certain conditions), decriminalization (the conduct is no longer a crime, but is still forbidden under non-criminal legislation) and permissiveness or policy-based tolerance (the conduct still constitutes an offence but is expressly permitted by the prosecution and the administrative authorities on the basis of documented policy).

According to some scholars, some behaviours should be excluded from the criminal legislation under certain circumstances. This is the case for abortion, the regulation of which has recently been modified from an indications system into a mixed term-based and assumptions system.[22] Authors also consider the possibility of legalizing euthanasia under certain conditions and guarantees, making a wider interpretation of the right to life that includes the recognition of the right to die with dignity.[23] Scholars have also proposed the possibility of legalizing some offences of drug trafficking, concurring with a paradigm shift in the United States and Latin America, where it seems that the drug problem is now considered more as a public health issue rather than a matter of public safety. This has given way to certain proposals of risk mitigation measures through the regulation of controlled use of drugs.[24] On the other hand, several scholars have pointed out the convenience of legalizing some minor offences against property or imposing non-custodial measures when no violence or intimidation has been used.[25] Some scholars also believe that juvenile criminal law should have its own catalogue of crimes, of less extension than the penal code

22 In favor of the time-limit system, J. Ropero Carrasco, 'La insuficiencia del sistema de indicaciones en el delito de aborto', LVI *Anuario de Derecho Penal y Ciencias Penales* (2003), p. 240 et seq.; José Luis González Cussac & Isabel Valldecabres Ortiz, 'El Anteproyecto de Ley Orgánica de salud sexual y reproductiva y de la interrupción voluntaria del embarazo', *Revista Xurídica Galega* 59 (2008), p. 18; P. Laurenzo Copello, *Dogmática y Política Criminal del aborto*, Valencia: Tirant lo Blanch, 2012, p. 101 et seq.

23 Thus, Grupo de Estudios de Política Criminal (GEPC), *Una alternativa al tratamiento jurídico de la disponibilidad sobre la propia vida*, Madrid: Tirant lo Blanch, 1991; J.L. Díez Ripollés, 'Eutanasia y Derecho', *Anuario de Filosofía del Derecho* (1995), p. 85, who considers preeminent the willingness of the affected; M. García Arán, 'Eutanasia y disponibilidad de la propia vida', *Cuadernos de Derecho Judicial* (1995), p. 26, refers to the presumption of consent when the subject may not be able to consent himself; F. Rey Martínez, *Eutanasia y derechos fundamentales*, Centro de Estudios Constitucionales, 2008 p. 88.

24 Report of the European Parliament, Afet-Eurolat, 'Europa y América Latina, la lucha contra la droga y el narcotráfico', 2012, p. 12 et seq. See also: www.theguardian.com/us-news/2016/mar/29/barack-obama-drug-addiction-health-problem-not-criminal-problem. In favor of legalizing policies, among others, Grupo de Estudios de Política Criminal (GEPC), *Una alternativa a la actual política criminal sobre drogas*, 1991; F.J. Álvarez García, 'La necesidad de un cambio de paradigma en el tráfico de drogas: la urgencia de su legalización', *Cuadernos de Política Criminal* 105 (2011), p. 200; J. Muñoz Sánchez, 'La relevancia penal de los clubes sociales de cannabis: Reflexiones sobre la política de cannabis y análisis jurisprudencial', 17 *Revista Electrónica de Ciencia Penal y Criminología* 22 (2015), p. 3 et seq.

25 As proposed, for example, in the report of the Observatorio del Entorno Penitenciario (Observatory of Prison Environment - Network of Social Organizations of the prison

for adults which is currently the one applied to underage offenders between 14 and 18 years old.[26]

As regards the option of decriminalization, and following the proposals of some experts[27], the latest reform of the Penal Code (LO 1/2015) has eliminated some misdemeanours and moved them to the field of administrative law.[28] However, many of these behaviours are still subject to criminal law, currently classified as minor offences.

In any case, whether the choice is legalization or decriminalization, crime figures in Spain indicate that the punitive pressure could be reduced and still be providing effective protection of society. For example, by looking at the low number of offenses of drug trafficking (Figure 5), it would be justified to decriminalize certain behaviours amongst fully capable adults, and to regulate only those that could cause damage to minors and vulnerable people. In the same vein, some penal offences against road safety, which are already adequately regulated in administrative law, could also be decriminalized.[29]

On the other hand, in the Spanish legal system there are only few examples of explicitly formulated rules, principles and criteria under which some sort of permissiveness could be applied regarding the criminal conduct on behalf of the prosecution and the administrative authorities. Recently, the Criminal procedural law has been modified to incorporate the principle of opportunity regarding some minor offences.[30] Indeed, some studies on the differences in police pursuit or sentences imposed by judges regarding several crimes reveal that in some categories of crimes there seems to be a tendency to be less punitive or rigorous.

---

environment, ROSEP), 2016, p. 15-16. Criticizing the reform of the offence of theft by the LO 1/2015 that established new aggravating circumstances and changed the misdemeanor into a felony, J. Del Carpio Delgado, 'Sobre la innecesaria reforma de los delitos de hurto. A propósito del Anteproyecto de 2012 de reforma del Código penal', 16 *Foro Nueva Época* 2 (2013), p. 83-137.

26 Among others, B. Cruz Márquez, 'Presupuestos de la responsabilidad penal del menor: Una necesaria revisión desde la perspectiva adolescente', in *Anuario de la Facultad de Derecho de la Universidad Autónoma de Madrid* 15 (2011), p. 256.

27 The Consejo General del Poder Judicial (General Council of the Judiciary), in plenary session of June 28, 2012, issued a report entitled "Propuestas para la reducción de la litigiosidad", p. 46 et seq., recommending the decriminalization of certain misdemeanors that could be regulated by civil or administrative law, and giving jurisdiction to Jueces de Paz (magistrates in the Spanish law system) to hear some of the minor criminal offences.

28 For example, LO 4/2015 (Organic Law 4/2015), of 30 March 2015, for the protection of public safety.

29 Regarding the offense of driving without a license, F. Miró Llinares, 'El 'moderno' Derecho penal vial y la penalización de la conducción sin permiso', *Indret* 3 (2009), p. 28, believes it should at most be imposed as an aggravating circumstance.

30 Articles 963.1.1ª and 964.2ª Criminal Procedure Law (RD of 14 September 1882), hereinafter referred to as CPL), will be analyzed in the following section.

In any case this is not explicitly documented, except for certain jurisprudential interpretations in areas such as drug trafficking and planning-breach.[31]

In closing, it cannot be confirmed that reforms reducing punitive intensity have increased the vulnerability of the population. Indeed, if we look, for example, at two of the few reforms that have softened the criminal intervention (abortion and drug trafficking, both of 2010), it can be found that the number of crimes in these areas has not risen since then.[32]

III. OVERUSE OF PROSECUTION

III.1. POLICE AND JUDICIAL PROSECUTION IN SPAIN

As noted in section 2, Spanish crime rate has remained at low levels throughout the period analysed, showing a slight upward trend until 2008, and a descending one until the present (Figure 2). Available data on prosecution and police effectiveness (clear-up rate, arrests and sentenced people) show generally coincident trends. The arrest rate has been steadily rising, with isolated descending periods (between 2000 and 2003, 2008 and 2010, 2011 and 2013). The evolution of the percentage of cleared-up crimes is much more stable and slightly upward, with soft decreases between 2000 and 2001, and 2011 and 2012 (Figure 4). The percentage of sentenced people on the total of detainees is markedly upward until 2008 and then descending, especially from 2010, with a slight upturn in 2014 (Figure 5).

---

31 P. Laurenzo Copello, 'Violencia de género y derecho penal de excepción: entre el discurso de la resistencia y el victimismo punitivo', *Cuadernos de Derecho Judicial* 9 (2007), p. 31-74; e. Larrarui Pijoan, *Criminología crítica y violencia de género*, Madrid: Trotta, 2007, p. 70 et seq., both note the reluctance of the courts to apply the felony of habitual mistreatment, as occasional minor offenses have also high penalties. Regarding allowance in drug trafficking when the amount is insignificant, see STS 920/2013 (Spanish Supreme Court, Judgment 920/2013), 11 December (ROJ STS 5868/2013), among many others. J.M. Garcés Peregrina, 'La evolución jurisprudencial de los delitos urbanísticos en la provincia de Málaga', *Jueces para la Democracia* (2014), p. 126-152, shows the low sentences imposed on planning-breach crime. D. García Magna, *El modelo penal de la seguridad ciudadana y su implantación en el sistema penal español*, Dissertation, University of Malaga, 2015, p. 223 et seq., shows how crimes of money laundering, planning-breach or against public finance are less prosecuted and receive lower penalties than those of drug trafficking or against property.

32 According to the Spanish Ministry of Health, since 2011 there has been a decline in the number of abortions, despite the fact that the current law allows the termination of pregnancy at up to 14 weeks, not being necessary to allege any reason, as established by Articles 13 and 14 of the LO 2/2010 (Organic Law 2/2010), of 3 March 2010, of sexual and reproductive health (http://www.mspsi.gob.es/profesionales/saludPublica/prevPromocion/embarazo/home.htm). According to the Ministry of Home Affairs, drug offences have not increased, despite the reduction of penalties and the new specific mitigating circumstance included in Article 388 PC in 2010.

Figure 4. Crimes solved (% of reported offences) (2000-2014)

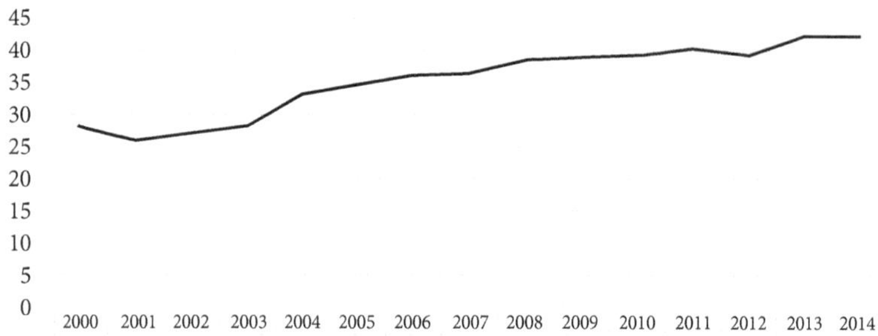

	2000	2001	2002	2003	2004	2005	2006	2007	2008	2009	2010	2011	2012	2013	2014
Crimes solved (%)	27,6	25,9	27	28,1	32,6	34,5	35,8	36,2	38,3	38,6	39,1	39,9	39,1	41,9	42,4

Source: Ministry of Home Affairs.

Figure 5. Condemned (% of detainees) (2000-2014)

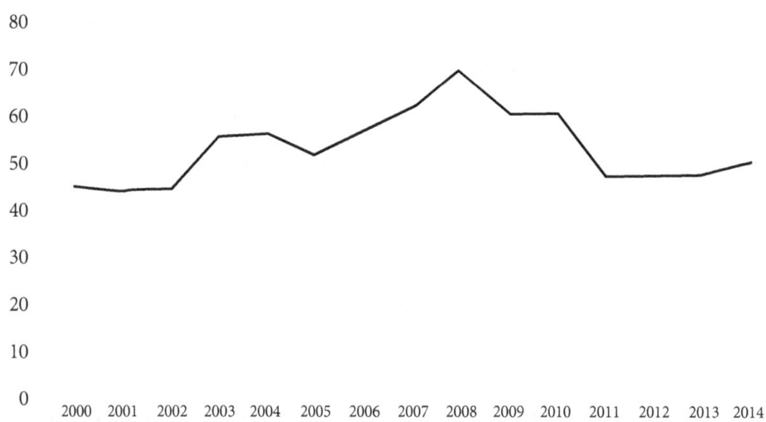

	2000	2001	2002	2003	2004	2005	2006	2007	2008	2009	2010	2011	2012	2013	2014
% Condemned	45,3	44,8	45,3	55,9	56,7	51,9	56,8	62,1	69,7	61,2	61,1	47,3	47,9	48	50,6

Source: Ministry of Home Affairs and Spanish Statistical Office (INE).

The distribution of sentences by type of crime (Figure 6) follows this order: crimes against road safety (34.8%), crimes against property (23.2%), injuries (12.2%), drug trafficking (4.6%), crimes against freedom (3.9%), crimes against sexual freedom (0.9%) and homicide/murder (0.5%). It is noteworthy that crimes against road safety, which are in fifth place according to police data (as seen in section 2.1), are however those who receive the most sentences.

Figure 6. Distribution of sentences for types of crime (2014)

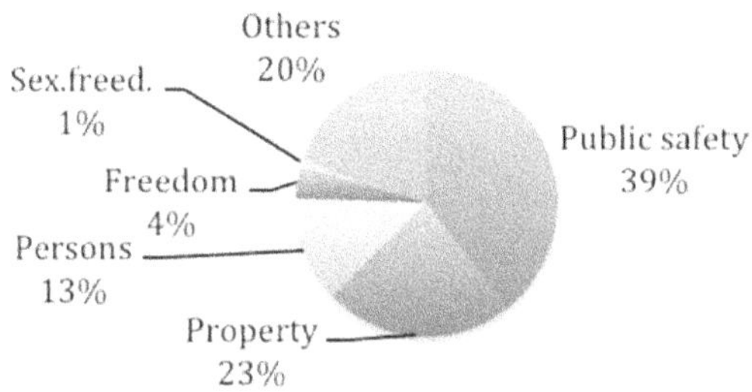

Source: Spanish Statistical Office (INE), 2014.

III.2. DETERMINANTS OF PROSECUTION IN SPAIN. ALTERNATIVES TO PROSECUTION IN THE SPANISH LEGAL SYSTEM

The principle of legality is a fundamental pillar of the Spanish legal system and the general rule is that all reported crimes must be pursued.[33] Thus, most offences under the Spanish penal code are "public". A small part are "semi-public", i.e., they may only be prosecuted if there is a prior complaint of the injured party (e.g. some sexual offences), but once filed and if the prosecution has already started, authorities proceed as if it were a public offense. Finally, there are some "private" crimes that can only be prosecuted if the complainant initiates the proceedings (e.g. libel).

Nevertheless, there are some alternatives to prosecution in line with the principle of discretionary prosecution, which was first established on the plea bargain in abbreviated procedure, and, later, in speedy trials.[34] In reality, this kind of agreements is not penal mediation, because among other things, parties are not placed on an equal footing.[35]

A recent procedural reform has included the option for the public prosecutor to request the dismissal of the procedure for reasons of discretionary prosecution

33 Article 259 et seq., CPL.

34 Articles 787 and 801, CPL. Circular Fiscalía General del Estado 1/1989, 8 March, III.C, (Report of the Public Prosecutor Office 1/1989) notes that the principle of consensus mean a socializing attitude that "as far as possible should not be disturbed either by continuing the process, or by submission to the stigmatization of the trial".

35 Scholars criticize the high number of trials that end with a plea bargain (in 2011 between 48% and 68%), without the taking of evidence and therefore without sufficient guarantees. Thus, Sáez Valcárcel, R., "Juicios rápidos, condenas negociadas, órdenes de alejamiento y deterioro del proceso penal", in *Jueces para la Democracia*, 49 (2004), pp. 3-8.

in the case of minor offences.[36] Furthermore, according to the same reform, the public prosecutor´s proposal can become the final sentence when the defendant agrees.[37] In both cases, however, the victim does not intervene. In our system there is only place for dejudicialization in the field of juvenile criminal law, through mediation, negotiation, and reconciliation, even before the penal procedure begins. In the process of adult criminal conduct, all the possibilities are situated within the procedure, once it has already begun.[38] In the absence of specific regulation on mediation, the Consejo General del Poder Judicial (General Council of the Judiciary) has carried out several pilot tests.[39]

The suspension of the sentence, the mitigating circumstance of damage repair[40] and the replacement of the penalty are also alternative ways to resolve the conflict but cannot be compared to mediation, even if the judge may rule that the suspension of the sentence is subject to compliance with the agreement reached under mediation.

Most scholars consider that the implementation of mediation would be desirable for minor and less serious offences (those punishable by up to 5 years of imprisonment). In addition, existing experiences show that it is easier to reach agreement on crimes against property than on violent crimes. It is often discussed whether mediation would be possible in crimes of abstract danger, those without an individual victim, and serious crimes (including terrorism).[41] Another area where mediation could be implemented is the enforcement of sentences, including any kind of crime.[42] Many authors criticize that crimes that reach mediation are usually always the same: family or neighbourhood minor conflicts.[43] In reality the draft reform of the criminal procedure law did not set

36 Articles 963.1.1ª and 964.2ª CPL, modified by LO 41/2015, provided that in addition to the low gravity of behavior, there isn't a significant public interest in prosecuting the offense. See also the report of the Public Prosecutor's Office, Circular 1/2015.

37 Article 803 bis, CPL, called "process by acceptance of decree", and also "criminal admonition procedure".

38 A. Del Moral García, *La mediación en el proceso penal. Fundamentos, problemas, experiencias, Madrid: Netbiblo,* 2010, p. 49-69, speaks of 'legal recognition' regarding juvenile justice, and 'anomie' in adult criminal proceedings.

39 For a review of many of them, see J.A. Cruz Parra, *La mediación penal. Problemática y soluciones*, Granada: Autopublicacionlibros.com, 2015.

40 Damage repair have exculpatory effects in a few crimes (offenses against public finances and Social Security, 305 et seq.).

41 J.I. Echano Basaldua, 'Mediación penal entre adultos: ámbito de aplicación en atención a la clase de infracción', *Cuadernos penales José María Lidón* 9 (2013), p. 157-204.

42 J. Ruiz Sierra, 'Víctima y mediación penal', *Noticias Jurídicas*, 29 October 2015.

43 M.V. Cervelló Donderis, *Módulo IV. Características de la Mediación Penal*, Valencia: Alfa Delta Digital, 2013, p. 51-87.

limits to mediation by type of crime, placing in the hands of the prosecutor to decide whether or not it was appropriate, depending on the nature of the act.[44]

The GEPC, a group of scholars and practitioners experts on criminal policy, has also produced a report[45] in which they propose a single regulation for plea bargain in crimes punishable by up to 5 years of imprisonment or deprivation of rights. In addition, they suggest that the defendant should be involved in the process to reach an agreement, and that its content must not necessarily be totally included in the sentence, as the judge could reduce liability or even acquit it. This could prevent serious disproportion between the proposed and rejected punishment during the negotiation, and the one that is finally requested by the prosecutor.

IV. OVERUSE OF IMPRISONMENT

IV.1. PRISON REALITY

Despite the fact that Spain does not have high crime rates, there is a very high prison population (Figure 7), as seen in European comparative analysis for 2015, where it ranks third just below UK and Portugal (Figure 8). There is not a high number of persons entering prison (Figure 9), and the percentage of prison sentences imposed among the total number of convictions is variant (Figure 10). That indicates that both law in books and law in action explain this situation. On one hand, there has been an abusive use of imprisonment provisions in the criminal Code, with very long penalties for crimes against property and related to drugs, which are the most represented in prison (Figure 11). On the other hand, few paroles are granted (Figure 12). As a result, Spain has one of the longest average prison stay in Europe (Figure 13).

44 Proposed articles of the Criminal Procedure Law, drafted by the Institutional Commission created by the agreement of the Consejo de Ministros (Spanish Council of Ministers), 2 March 2012: Book II, Title VI, Articles 143-146.

45 Grupo de Estudios de Política Criminal, *Una alternative a algunas previsions penales utilitarias. Perdón, prescripción, dilaciones indebidas y conformidad procesal*, Madrid: Tirant lo Blanch and GEPC, 2014, p. 46 et seq.

Figure 7. Evolution of crime rate and prison rate (2000-2015)

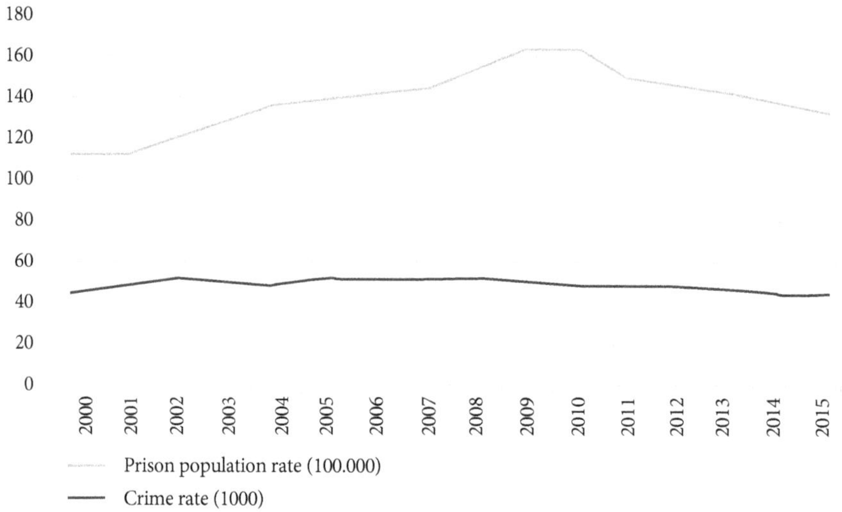

Source: ROSEP, from EUROSTAT and Ministry of Home Affairs.

Figure 8. Compared prison population rate UE-15(2015)

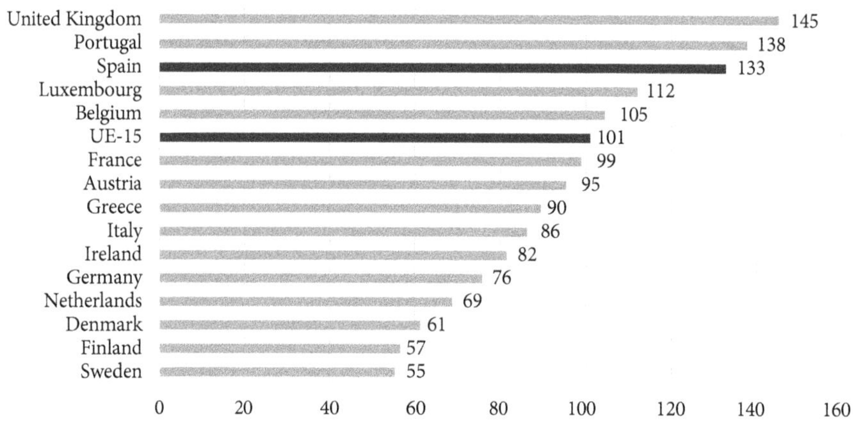

Source: ROSEP, from the International Centre for Prison Studies.

Figure 9. Compared entries in prison / 100.000 population (2012)

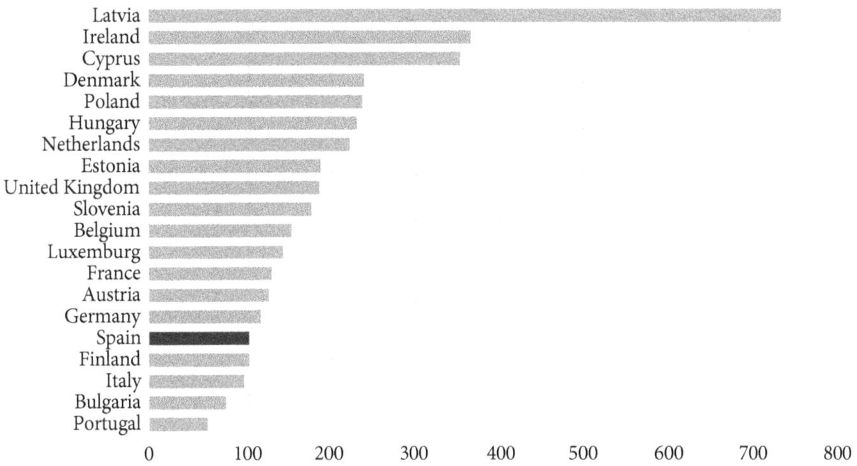

Source: Annual Penal Statistics of the Council of Europe, SPACE I 2013.

Provided by Díez Ripollés, J.L.

Figure 10. Prison sentences (% total sentences) (2000-2014)

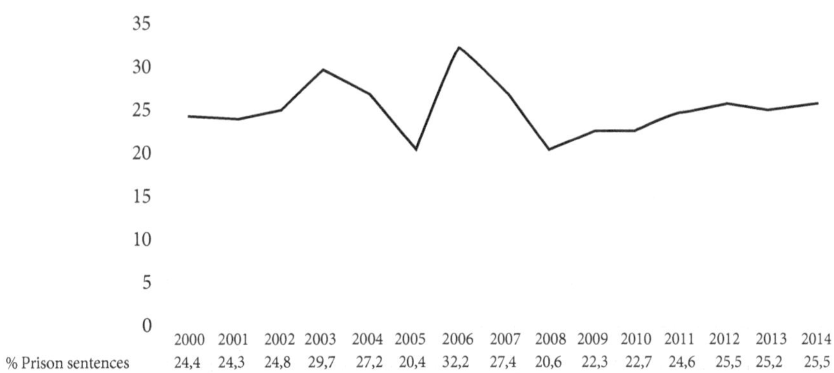

Source: Spanish Statistical Office (INE), 2014.

Figure 11. Crimes represented in prison (2015)

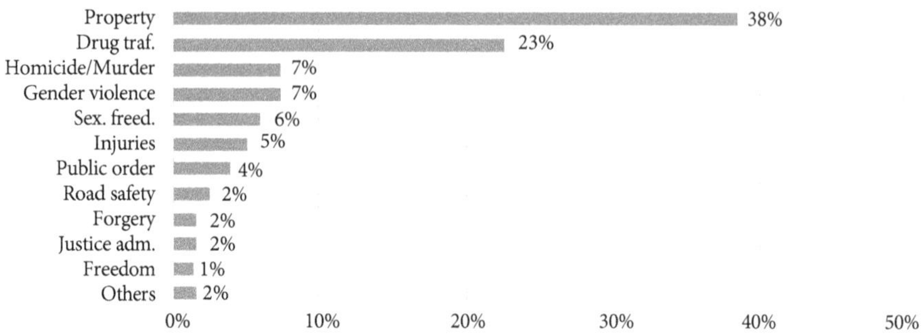

Source: Ministry of Home Affairs, General Directorate of Penal Institutions.

(Secretaría General de Instituciones Penitenciarias).

Figure 12. Granting of paroles (1997–2013)

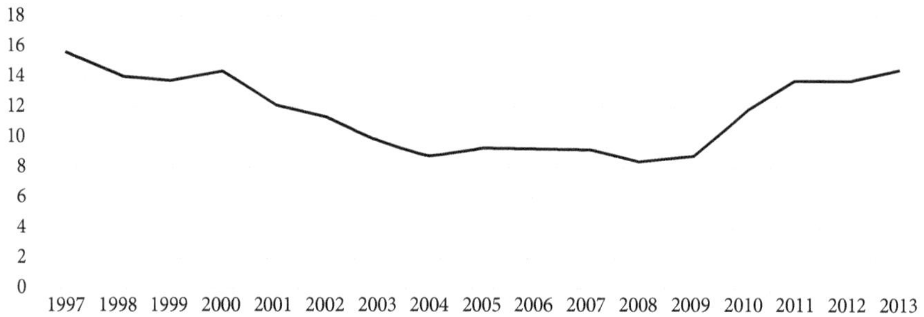

Source: Annual Penal Statistics of the Council of Europe, SPACE I 2013.

Provided by Díez Ripollés, J.L.

Figure 13. Average prison stay in Europe (months), 2012

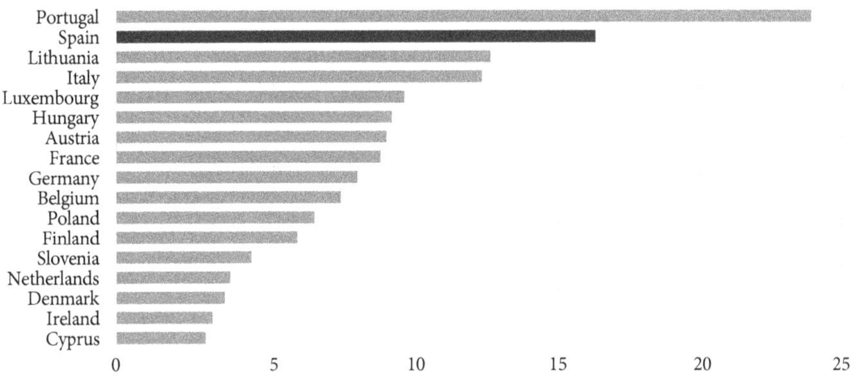

Source: Annual Penal Statistics of the Council of Europe, SPACE I 2013.

Provided by Díez Ripollés, J.L.

IV.2. LIMITATIONS TO THE JUDICIAL DISCRETION ON THE IMPOSITION AND ENFORCEMENT OF PRISON SENTENCES. ALTERNATIVES TO IMPRISONMENT IN THE SPANISH PENAL SYSTEM

As indicated at the beginning of this report, the Spanish penal code establishes one or more penalties for each offence, with maximum and minimum limits, and includes mandatory rules to determine the length of the sentence, depending on the degree of intervention and execution of crime, the aggravating or mitigating circumstances, etc. Once these rules are applied, judges only have limited discretion to decide about the sentence (or the type of sanction in those few offences that may be subject to alternative penalties). Judges also have the power to decide on the replacement and suspension of enforcement of a penalty, albeit reforms carried out in 2003 and 2015 have incorporated very strict requirements, decreasing judicial discretion in these areas.[46] In addition, given the low figures in paroles and alternative to custody measures granted, it seems that neither legislator nor courts are eager to apply non-custodial responses to crime.

As noted above, our penal code establishes very strict penalties, whereas the system of determination and enforcement of sentences is not very flexible either, which explains the long average length of prison stay and the high rates of prison

46 LO 15/2003 and LO 1/2015. It can be said that replacement of penalties has virtually disappeared (except for the expulsion of foreigners), and parole is now a form of suspension of enforcement rather than a stage of serving prison sentences. Thus, now when there is a violation of conditions imposed to grant parole, the convicted person must return to prison to serve the full time remaining, without discounting the time spent outside.

population. Since crime rates are low, it would be possible to mitigate the sanctions and apply more alternative non-custody measures, especially for the crimes that are most represented in prison, such as offences against road safety, drug trafficking, or against property without the use of violence. In any case, it is not enough simply to change laws, but it is also necessary that judges take that consideration into account.[47]

As recent reports suggest, if prison population corresponded to the real crime rate in Spain, according to European data, the rate of prison population would be halved.[48]

V. CONCLUSIONS

As this report has shown, Spain has a stable and low crime rate, compared to neighbouring countries. The most represented crimes in the criminal justice system, not only regarding the number of arrests but also on the basis of imprisonment convictions and prison serving, are offences against property, especially thefts and burglaries. Crimes of drug trafficking are not among the most committed, but surprisingly are among the most represented in prison. The rate of Spanish prison population is one of the highest in the European Union, and so it is the average time spent in prison. As this report has noted, this is mainly because the penal code provides imprisonment penalty for most of the crimes, with especially high penalties regarding those crimes that are most represented in prison. Even if courts usually impose penalties at their minimum limit, the rigidity of the enforcement system makes it difficult to apply alternatives to custody (replacement and suspension). In addition, only few paroles are granted, therefore prisoners often remain in prison until they have fully served their sentences.

The reality of the Spanish crime does not justify many of the punitive reforms of the last years. The few changes that have resulted in lower intervention (drug trafficking or abortion) have not led to an increase in crime, so it seems that the

47 According to J.M. Tamarit Sumalla, 'Sistema de sanciones y política criminal. Un estudio de Derecho comparado europeo', *Revista Electrónica de Ciencia Penal y Criminología* 9 (2007), p. 11, the Spanish legislator does not seem to want to introduce alternative to custody measures in offences against property because of the criminological reality of such crimes. Moreover, M. Aebi, N. Delgrande & Y. Marguet, 'Have community sanctions and measures widened the net of the European criminal justice systems?', 17 *Punishment & Society* 5 (2015), p. 588 et seq., point out that the provision in the law of alternative sentences to prison, is not generating a reduction in the rate of prison population, but actually is expanding the criminal justice system to behaviours that were previously outside the criminal law, instead of apply them to those already carrying prison penalties.

48 Report of the Observatory of prisons environment (Network of social organizations of the prison environment, ROSEP), 2016, p. 71 et seq.

same strategy could be applied to other crimes. These policies could be transferred to other countries with similar crime profiles. Furthermore, limiting judicial discretion could be positive, in a sense, as it would prevent excesses in sentencing, even in the Spanish rigid system in which minimum limits are high. As regards penitentiary establishments, there are some positive experiences that could be transferred to other systems: the construction of numerous social integration centres, the creation of "wards of respect" in prisons, the high percentage of treatment and occupational programs, and the low proportion of pre-trial detainees in relation to other countries.[49]

Regarding alternative to custody measures, there is a lack of legal provisions, combined with the scarcity of resources to implement them. For example, in the field of crimes against road safety, the reform of 2007 included community service as alternative penalty to prison, which resulted in an excessive number of community service sentences that could not be enforced because they were statute-barred. In 2010, a new reform included the fine as an alternative to both prison and community service, which led to a decrease in the number of community service sentences.[50] Said evidence shows the lack of foresight of legislator in law-making processes.

High rates of prison population confirm that custody penalties are central in the Spanish penal system. One might wonder whether the recent reform that has introduced life imprisonment can be understood as the culmination of a constantly aggravating trend[51], or, on the contrary, the future holds new and unsuspected rules and practices entailing even harsher responses to crime. The reality is that this trend toward more severe penalties is unsustainable in both humanitarian and economic terms as several comparative reports have pointed out.[52] In fact, in recent years, prison overcrowding seems to be taking its toll, hence the reforms that led to a slight relief in prisons.[53] Only time will tell if this is a consistent trend or just a brief respite before continuing with the same policies.

49 E. García España & J.L. Díez Ripollés, *Realidad y política penitenciarias*, Madrid: Tirant Lo Blanch, 2012.

50 LO 15/2007, November 30; LO 5/2010, June 22.

51 E. García España & J.L. Díez Ripollés, *Realidad y política penitenciarias*, Madrid: Tirant Lo Blanch, 2012

52 J. Samuels, N. La Vigne & S. Taxy, *Stemming the tide: Strategies to reduce the growth and cut the cost of the federal prison system*, Urban Institute, 2013, p. 1-62; M. Aebi, 'El coste del encarcelamiento en España y Europa', Conference University of Málaga, 18 November 2013.

53 As E. García España & J.L. Díez Ripollés, *Realidad y política penitenciarias*, Madrid: Tirant Lo Blanch, 2012, p. 240, shows some experts believe that these penitentiary reforms were basically carried out in order to improve the image of the Spanish penal system in Europe and to reduce economic costs, at a time when prison population rates had reached shocking figures.

RECOURT-ON DE MANIÈRE EXCESSIVE AU SYSTÈME PÉNAL EN SUISSE ?*

André KUHN** & Matteo SOLCÀ***

I. INTRODUCTION

Lorsque l'on traite de la question du recours excessif au droit pénal, il nous semble utile de subdiviser le processus pénal en plusieurs phases. L'excès peut en effet d'abord être *législatif*, c'est-à-dire le recours abusif par le législateur lui-même au droit pénal pour tenter de régler des problèmes sociaux. L'excès peut ensuite provenir de l'usage que la justice fait du droit pénal qui lui est mis à disposition par le législateur, usage abusif qui peut être le fait d'une *autorité d'instruction* appliquant le principe de la légalité des poursuites à outrance et ne laissant que trop peu de place à l'opportunité des poursuites, d'une *autorité de jugement* préférant certaines peines sévères – souvent privatives de liberté – à d'autres plus proportionnées – plutôt restrictives de liberté, voire pécuniaires seulement – ou encore d'une *autorité d'exécution des peines* qui mise davantage sur la neutralisation des condamnés que sur leur resocialisation. La présente contribution traite successivement de ces diverses formes de recours excessif au système pénal au regard de la situation helvétique.

Le contexte politico-juridique suisse présente certaines particularités qu'il s'agira de mettre en relation avec l'utilisation du système pénal. Si chacune des

* Certaines parties du présent texte – et surtout les idées qui y sont véhiculées – ont déjà été publiées par l'un ou l'autre des auteurs dans des écrits antérieurs. De surcroît la même contribution a fait l'objet d'une publication dans la *Revue internationale de criminologie et de police technique et scientifique* (RICPTS 1/2018). Là où certains utiliseront peut-être la notion ridicule d'«auto-plagiat», les auteurs considèrent qu'il s'agit plutôt d'un phénomène positif, puisqu'il permet de toucher des lectorats variés et qu'il est le reflet d'un mode de pensée logique, cohérent et surtout constant.

** Professeur de criminologie et de droit pénal à l'Université de Neuchâtel.

*** Collaborateur scientifique à l'Ecole des sciences criminelles de l'Université de Lausanne.

parties du présent article reviendra tour à tour sur ces spécificités, il nous semble néanmoins utile de restituer, ici déjà et de manière générale, le contexte helvétique. La Suisse est un pays d'un peu plus de huit millions d'habitants répartis dans 26 cantons souverains, formant un Etat fédéraliste basé sur un système dit de *démocratie parlementaire*. On parle dans le cas helvétique de *démocratie directe* dans la mesure où l'ensemble du corps électoral peut, par l'intermédiaire du référendum ou de l'initiative populaire, déclencher une procédure permettant d'adopter, de supprimer ou de réviser une disposition constitutionnelle au niveau communal, cantonal ou fédéral. De plus, s'il revient à la Confédération de fixer les dispositions générales en termes de normes pénales, l'organisation judiciaire et la mise en application de ces normes demeurent du registre des cantons. Il existe donc en Suisse 26 ministères publics cantonaux distincts et un ministère public de la Confédération, ce qui peut engendrer de grandes différences entre les cantons en matière d'application de la loi. Ce n'est par ailleurs que très récemment que la Confédération s'est dotée d'une procédure pénale unifiée pour l'ensemble de son territoire. L'organisation policière, elle aussi, est cantonale. S'il existe une police fédérale dont les tâches relèvent davantage de la gestion des menaces globales pour le pays, la détection, l'enregistrement et la dénonciation des infractions pénales est du ressort des cantons. C'est ainsi qu'une importante autonomie est laissée aux différents corps de police cantonaux en ce qui concerne leur organisation, mais également quant aux priorités qu'ils se fixent. Il existe donc de grandes disparités inter-cantonales en termes d'infractions enregistrées en fonction de la proactivité de leurs polices respectives. Nous aurons, tout au long de cet article, l'occasion de revenir sur ces spécificités propres au contexte helvétique.

II. RECOURS EXCESSIF AU DROIT PÉNAL EN MATIÈRE DE CRIMINALISATION

II.1. CONSIDÉRATIONS GÉNÉRALES

L'évolution du droit pénal est faite d'une multitude d'abolitions d'interdits «désuets» (tels que la fornication, le concubinage, l'homosexualité, l'avortement, la prostitution, etc.) et d'un nombre non moins considérable de nouvelles criminalisations (telles que l'abus de carte bancaire, la soustraction ou la détérioration de données informatiques, l'utilisation frauduleuse d'un ordinateur, le blanchiment d'argent, etc.). La question de savoir laquelle de ces deux tendances prédomine n'est pas simple à résoudre. Dans la littérature, il est fait mention du fait que «la plupart des modifications de la législation pénale concernent l'adoption de nouveaux interdits plutôt que la suppression d'incriminations existantes».[1] Il semble d'ailleurs s'agir du résultat d'une longue évolution qui, depuis plusieurs siècles, fait continuellement émerger de nouvelles situations mettant en danger les biens juridiques d'autrui. C'est ainsi qu'avant l'existence du papier, il n'y avait pas lieu de légiférer sur le faux dans les titres et avant l'existence des nouvelles technologies, il ne serait venu à l'idée de personne de criminaliser certains comportements découlant de leur usage. De manière similaire, les infractions de mise en danger concrète et – surtout – abstraite étaient inconnues il y a quelques siècles en arrière et se sont développées ces dernières décennies sous l'effet de la multiplication des situations «dangereuses» post révolution industrielle.[2] Plus récemment, il semble toutefois que l'évolution quantitative du droit pénal Suisse ait été bien plus modeste et en tout cas beaucoup plus faible que celle d'autres formes de droits, telles que le droit administratif et le droit civil. C'est ainsi qu'en 1951, 6% des pages de la législation fédérale suisse interne relevaient du droit pénal, alors que lors du dernier relevé, en 1982, le droit pénal ne représentait plus que 3,5% de l'ensemble de la législation.[3] Ce résultat ne doit toutefois pas nous faire omettre que, durant la même période, le nombre d'actes législatifs contenant des dispositions pénales a augmenté de quelque 15% (passant de 102 en 1951 à 117 en 1982) et le nombre de pages de la législation fédérale consacrées au droit pénal a crû d'une vingtaine de pourcents (passant de 538 en 1951 à 647 en 1982).[4]

En 2016, en épluchant la législation fédérale, on trouve 246 lois contenant des dispositions pénales (soit une augmentation de quelque 140% depuis 1951 et d'environ 110% depuis 1982) pour 1'376 pages consacrées au droit pénal (soit, là aussi, un accroissement d'environ 155% depuis 1951 et de quelque 112% depuis 1982). Notons toutefois que l'augmentation récente du nombre de textes légaux contenant des dispositions pénales est largement dû à une explosion de très courtes ordonnances consacrées au respect par la Suisse des sanctions internationales imposées par le Conseil de sécurité des Nations Unies à un nombre grandissant d'Etats, dispositions pénales ne trouvant que très rarement application. Quant à l'accroissement du nombre de pages consacrées à la législation pénale, il est en partie influencé par l'unification au niveau fédéral de la procédure pénale dans un code comptant pas moins de 164 pages à lui seul. De manière plus générale, la législation pénale représente aujourd'hui quelque 4% du droit fédéral interne en Suisse.

---

1 Martin Killias, André Kuhn & Nathalie Dongois, *Précis de droit pénal général*, Berne : Stämpfli, 4ème édition, 2016, p. 26-27, n° 143.

2 Martin Killias, André Kuhn & Nathalie Dongois, *Précis de droit pénal général*, Berne : Stämpfli, 4ème édition, 2016, p. 26-27, n° 501.

3 Martin Killias, Marcelo Aebi & André Kuhn, *Précis de criminologie*, Berne : Stämpfli, 3ème édition, 2012, p. 348, n° 810.

4 Martin Killias, 'La criminalisation de la vie quotidienne et la politisation du droit pénal', 129 *Revue de Droit Suisse* 4 (1995), p. 369-458, plus précisément p. 371-372, n° 203.

Récemment, un juge fédéral a par ailleurs ouvertement critiqué le fait que la société d'aujourd'hui délègue au droit pénal de plus en plus de domaines de la vie sociale, domaines qui auraient pu – et donc dû – trouver une solution par une autre voie.[5] A titre d'exemple, il mentionne l'excès de vitesse, qui est typiquement un acte qui pourrait sans aucune difficulté être régulé par des développements techniques[6], ce qui nécessiterait toutefois un peu de courage politique.

II.2. LE CAS DE LA SUISSE

Nous nous proposons dans cette partie d'illustrer le cas helvétique en mettant en évidence les infractions enregistrées par la police de manière à pouvoir proposer un aperçu des comportements criminalisés les plus fréquemment constatés en Suisse.

Afin de dresser le panorama des actes pénalement punissables les plus recensés, il est intéressant de distinguer dans un premier temps, à travers les infractions enregistrées par la police, la part que le Code pénal représente en comparaison aux autres lois fédérales contenant des dispositions pénales, telles que la Loi sur la circulation routière (LCR; art. 90-103). Malheureusement, bien que nous sachions que la LCR représente pratiquement 50% des condamnations pénales prononcées en Suisse (57'580 condamnations[7] contre 59'799 pour les autres lois), nous ne disposons pas des données concernant le nombre d'infractions enregistrées par la police.

Ainsi, lorsque l'on se réfère aux infractions enregistrées par la police en Suisse, il est difficile de mesurer la proportion que représente la LCR parmi les infractions enregistrées tout en soupçonnant que celle-ci constitue une part importante – voire prépondérante – au regard du nombre important de condamnations qu'elle suscite (cf. graphique 1). Pour le surplus, le graphique 2 permet de donner un aperçu de la proportion des infractions au Code pénal enregistrées par la police par rapport à d'autres lois fédérale (LCR exceptée).

Nous constatons en premier lieu que la majorité des infractions recensées par la police sont des infractions au Code pénal. Il est par ailleurs intéressant d'observer que, dans la statistique policière, la tendance des deux dernières années montre que, si les infractions au Code pénal sont en diminution (–7%), celles relatives à la Loi sur les stupéfiants (LStup) comme celles en lien avec la Loi sur les étrangers (LEtr) augmentent (respectivement +6% et +7%). Il est donc particulièrement intéressant de prendre en considération ces autres lois fédérales contenant des dispositions pénales que sont la LStup et la LEtr.

---

5 Niklaus Oberholzer, in *NZZ am Sonntag* 3 janvier 2016, p. 9.

6 A ce propos, voir André Kuhn, 'Décriminaliser la circulation routière, est-ce vraiment impossible ?', 3 *Revue Interdisciplinaire de Circulation Routière* 2 (2011), p. 23-26.

7 Les contraventions ne sont pas prises en compte dans la présente statistique malgré le fait que, dans certains cas, elles puissent également faire l'objet d'une inscription dans le casier judiciaire.

Graphique 1. Evolution du nombre de condamnations selon le type de loi

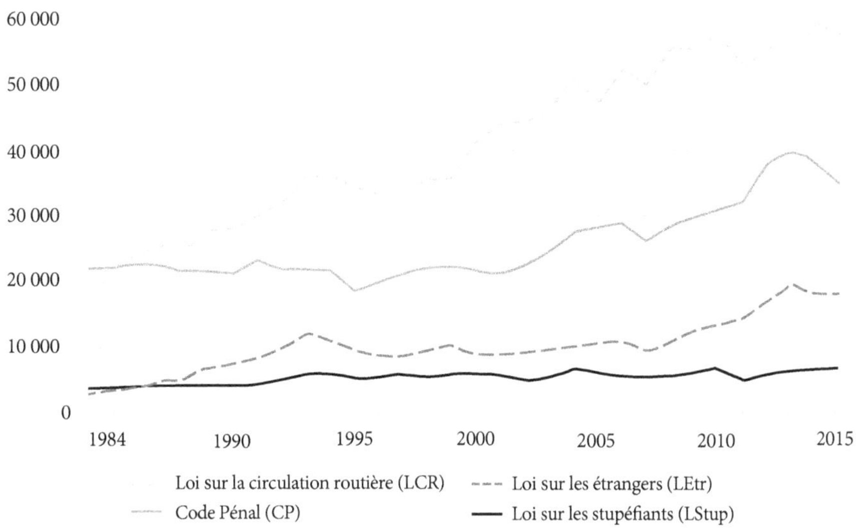

Source : Office fédéral de la statistique, Neuchâtel 2016.

Graphique 2. Répartition des infractions selon les lois (hormis LCR, 2015)

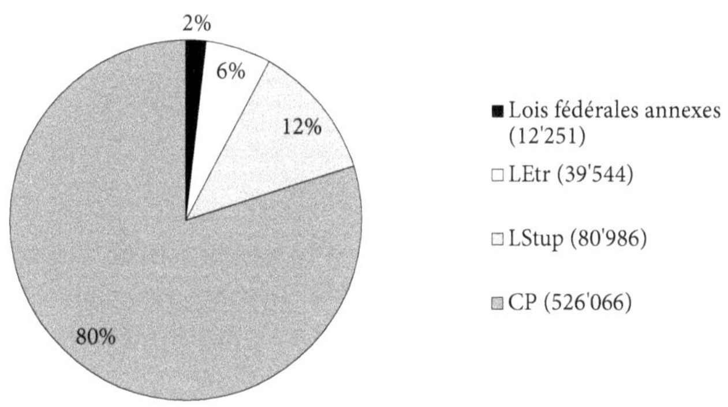

Source : Office fédéral de la statistique, Neuchâtel 2016.

En ce qui concerne plus spécifiquement les infractions au Code pénal, le graphique 3 nous donne des indications quant à la nature des infractions les plus souvent enregistrées par la police en Suisse. Les infractions au patrimoine y apparaissent comme très largement majoritaires. Ces infractions au patrimoine, dans plus de la moitié des cas (186'708 cas, soit 50,4% des infractions au patrimoine concernant 2015), sont des vols sans violence (les vols de véhicules n'étant pas compris dans cette catégorie). Autrement dit, si l'on fait abstraction des infractions à la LCR, le vol est, de loin, le crime le plus couramment enregistré en Suisse par la police.

Graphique 3. Répartition des infractions au CP enregistrées par la police (2015)

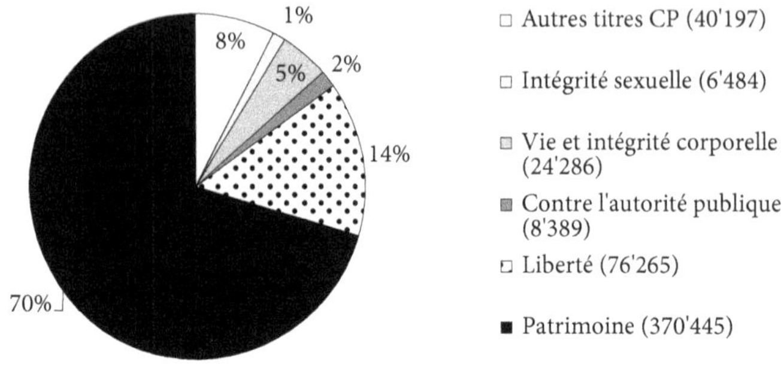

Source : Office fédéral de la statistique, Neuchâtel 2016.

Graphique 4. Répartition des infractions à la LStup enregistrées par la police (2015)

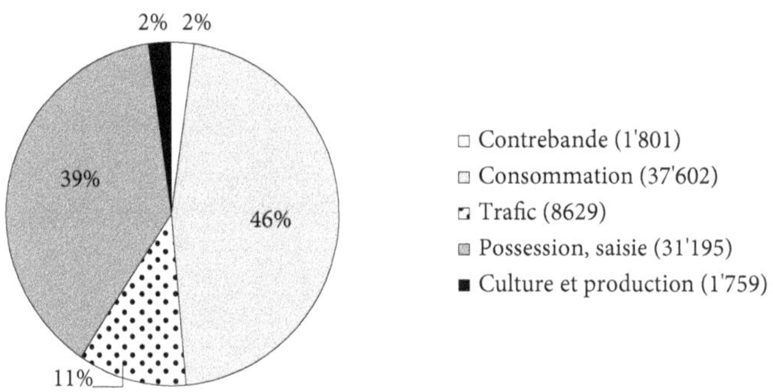

Source : Office fédéral de la statistique, Neuchâtel 2016.

Concernant la LStup, la consommation et la possession de stupéfiants apparaissent comme étant les infractions les plus nombreuses, représentant à elles seules plus de 80% du nombre total d'infractions enregistrées en la matière (Graphique 4).

Enfin, en ce qui concerne la LEtr, le graphique 5 présente les infractions les plus couramment enregistrées par la police et identifie l'entrée et le séjour illégal comme prédominants et représentant plus de 2/3 des infractions enregistrées.

Comme nous l'évoquions précédemment, les polices cantonales sont dotées d'une grande autonomie. Il existe ainsi d'importantes disparités en termes de fréquences des infractions enregistrées par la police selon le canton, disparités qui relèvent certainement autant des réalités locales que des priorités que se fixent les polices dans une perspective proactive. Si l'on analyse de plus près les fréquences des infractions à la LStup, les différences cantonales observées s'expliquent en partie à travers certains éléments propres à leurs situations sociodémographiques. Certains cantons sont principalement composés de régions rurales peu peuplées,

Graphique 5. Répartition des infractions à la LEtr enregistrées par la police (2015)

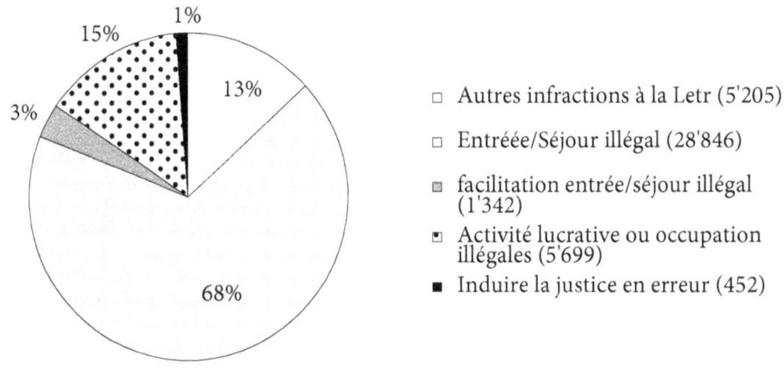

Source : Office fédéral de la statistique, Neuchâtel 2016.

alors que d'autres sont principalement faits de centres urbains à forte densité de population. Il en résulte des fréquences d'enregistrement de la criminalité liée aux stupéfiants allant du simple au quintuple en fonction de l'endroit où l'on se situe. En revanche, les disparités inter-cantonales concernant les infractions à la LEtr enregistrées par la police semblent plus difficiles à expliquer à partir des spécificités des populations locales. Un canton comme Genève, présentant des caractéristiques sociodémographiques similaires au canton de Bâle-Ville (canton frontière, canton-ville de type urbain), enregistre des taux presque trois fois plus importants d'infractions à la LEtr. Dans ce cas-ci, les spécificités sociodémographiques ne sont pas en mesure d'expliquer ces grandes différences qui doivent au contraire être interrogées à travers l'activité de la police elle-même.

II.3. REMARQUES FINALES

Aucune guerre n'a jamais servi la paix! Pourquoi en irait-il autrement en matière de criminalité ? Si la guerre contre le crime avait la moindre chance d'éradiquer ou de faire diminuer la criminalité, nous vivrions déjà depuis longtemps dans une société sans crime. En effet depuis plusieurs milliers d'années, l'être humain édicte des lois interdisant de tuer autrui. Pourtant, aujourd'hui comme hier, on constate que certains individus commettent des homicides. On doit donc se demander si la loi pénale elle-même bénéficie encore d'une légitimité, la société n'ayant en effet pas besoin de lois pour savoir qu'un meurtre est inadmissible. Ainsi, certains criminologues proposent l'abolition pure et simple de cette loi et donc une société sans droit pénal. Ces abolitionnistes avancent notamment que les sanctions informelles (soit celles qui ne sont pas prévues par une loi) seraient suffisantes pour réguler notre société. D'autres, en revanche, estiment qu'elles seraient insuffisantes. Cette seconde conception est aujourd'hui, en Suisse, dominante, raison pour laquelle le législateur édicte encore et toujours des lois à caractère pénal en imaginant régler des problèmes sociaux dont on ignore souvent la source mais que l'on croit pouvoir combattre efficacement par cette entremise. Criminaliser un comportement procure certainement le sentiment de s'attaquer à un problème et donne surtout bonne conscience alors qu'en réalité, toute criminalisation équivaut à un aveu d'échec d'une politique sociale. Ce n'est en effet que parce que d'autres moyens de résoudre un problème social échouent que l'on criminalise. C'est ainsi notamment que la consommation de stupéfiants n'est pas un problème pénal, mais un problème de santé publique géré de façon désastreuse par le politique, que la criminalisation de la migration est un aveu d'échec face à l'incapacité de gérer un problème migratoire dont la source réside souvent hors de nos frontières et qu'il ne serait pas nécessaire de criminaliser la circulation routière si des politiques de prévention adéquates étaient enfin mises en œuvre.

Ce panorama des infractions à caractère pénal les plus couramment enregistrées par la police nous permet de dégager quelques éléments concernant l'impact qu'une potentielle décriminalisation de certains comportements pourrait avoir sur la fréquence des infractions enregistrées par la police. Nous constatons tout d'abord que si le Code pénal est bien une source de criminalisation importante, certaines autres lois contenant des dispositions pénales engendrent également un nombre important de délits enregistrés. Nous constatons par ailleurs qu'au sein même de ces différentes bases légales, un nombre restreint de délits représente une part très importante de la criminalité. Ainsi, en décriminalisant un petit nombre de comportements, la Suisse pourrait potentiellement réduire de manière importante le nombre d'infractions pénales enregistrées. De plus, les disparités régionales en termes de fréquence des infractions enregistrées nous montrent à quel point le contexte fédéraliste permet aux polices cantonales de garder une autonomie importante dans l'exercice de leur activité.

Enfin, mentionnons encore qu'une autre manière de surutiliser le droit pénal à travers la criminalisation de certains comportements, est de prévoir – tout étant égal par ailleurs – un allongement des délais de prescription. Si nous n'avons pas eu l'occasion de développer cet aspect dans le présent article, mentionnons néanmoins à ce propos que la Suisse a adapté ses délais de prescription à plusieurs reprises durant les 15 dernières années (en 2002, 2006, 2011, 2013 et 2014), et ce à chaque fois dans le sens d'un allongement, voire en prévoyant l'imprescriptibilité de certaines infractions (souvent d'ailleurs à travers le processus de l'initiative populaire).

Finalement, la question de savoir si le développement de la densité législative exerce une influence sur le taux de criminalité a également fait l'objet de développements intéressants dans la littérature.[8] Il semblerait ainsi que l'inflation des lois pénales ne cause pas systématiquement un accroissement du nombre de crimes

8 A ce propos, voir Martin Killias, Marcelo Aebi & André Kuhn, *Précis de criminologie*, Berne : Stämpfli, 3ème édition, 2012, p. 346-352, n° 807-813.

commis. Il n'existerait dès lors pas de corrélation entre le taux de criminalité et la densité législative d'un Etat.

III. RECOURS EXCESSIF À LA MISE EN ACCUSATION

III.1. CONSIDÉRATIONS GÉNÉRALES

Selon le principe du caractère impératif de la poursuite pénale, l'Etat doit engager des poursuites à chaque fois que les conditions en sont réalisées. C'est ainsi que lorsqu'il existe des indices permettant de présumer que les éléments constitutifs d'une infraction pénale sont réalisés, les autorités de poursuite sont tenues d'ouvrir une action pénale.[9] Ce principe, dit de la *légalité des poursuites*, est pourtant quelque peu édulcoré par celui de l'*opportunité des poursuites*, selon lequel les autorités pénales peuvent - voire parfois doivent - renoncer à une poursuite pénale lorsque certaines conditions sont remplies. Il en va notamment ainsi dans bon nombre d'Etats lorsque la culpabilité de l'auteur et les conséquences de son acte sont peu importantes, lorsque l'auteur a réparé le dommage causé et que l'intérêt du lésé et l'intérêt public à le poursuivre et le sanctionner sont peu importants, lorsque l'auteur a été personnellement atteint par les conséquences de son infraction et qu'il en a déjà suffisamment souffert, et enfin lorsque la poursuite d'une infraction ne serait pas propre à modifier de façon significative la situation juridique d'un prévenu.

C'est ainsi qu'un système dominé par le principe de la légalité produira un grand nombre de condamnés coupables de délits de peu de gravité, puisque toute enquête doit – en théorie du moins – y être poursuivie jusqu'à la condamnation dès que des indices permettent d'admettre la culpabilité du prévenu. En revanche, un système de procédure plus sélectif, dominé par le principe de l'opportunité, permet aux autorités de ne poursuivre que les affaires dépassant un certain seuil de gravité.[10] L'application plutôt stricte du principe de la légalité des poursuites – tel que pratiqué en Allemagne et au Japon – étant propre à mettre en marche le processus pénal bien plus souvent qu'une application plus large du principe de l'opportunité des poursuites – tel que pratiqué aux Etats Unis et aux Pays-Bas –, il en découle tout naturellement un nombre plus élevé de mises en accusation.

---

9 A moins évidemment qu'une condition de poursuite (liée notamment à la prescription ou à la plainte pénale) ne soit pas réalisée. Il en va par exemple ainsi lorsque l'infraction n'est poursuivie que sur plainte et qu'aucune plainte n'a été déposée.

10 A ce propos et sur les effets – notamment sur la criminalité féminine – de ces deux politiques criminelles différentes, voir Martin Killias, Marcelo Aebi & André Kuhn, *Précis de criminologie*, Berne : Stämpfli, 3ème édition, 2012, p. 90-95, n° 4090-4095.

III.2. LE CAS DE LA SUISSE

En Suisse[11], le Code de procédure pénale instaure le principe de la légalité de la poursuite pénale, sous réserve de quelques motifs d'opportunité. En application de ce principe, l'autorité pénale – soit en général la police et le ministère public – a l'obligation de mettre en œuvre l'action publique à chaque fois qu'il existe des indices suffisants de commission d'une infraction pénale. Ce principe de la légalité est toutefois tempéré par la loi elle-même, dans laquelle on trouve un certain nombre d'exceptions reposant sur le principe de l'opportunité. Ce dernier permet ainsi de mettre un terme à l'action pénale par une décision de non-entrée en matière ou de classement, quand bien même la procédure révélerait des soupçons suffisants de la commission d'une infraction. Le principe de l'opportunité des poursuites est expressément placé dans les mains du ministère public – à l'exclusion de la police – dans la phase de la procédure préliminaire et des tribunaux dans la phase de jugement.

Les motifs d'opportunité retenus peuvent être regroupés en quatre catégories :

- Lorsque la loi permet ou impose de renoncer à toute poursuite pénale. La loi cite notamment (et lorsque certaines conditions sont réalisées) l'absence d'intérêt à punir des infractions bagatelles, la réparation du dommage et l'atteinte directe de l'auteur par les conséquences de son acte.
- Lorsque la poursuite aboutirait à la fixation d'une peine additionnelle insignifiante. Ce motif d'opportunité repose donc avant tout sur un principe d'économie de procédure et prévoit que lorsque parmi plusieurs infractions, certaines apparaissent à ce point accessoires qu'elles n'auront pour ainsi dire pas d'effet sur la fixation de la peine, il y a lieu d'en prononcer le classement.
- Lorsqu'une poursuite pénale menée à l'étranger à raison des mêmes faits a eu lieu. Là aussi, il s'agit d'un motif d'opportunité reposant, d'une part, sur un principe d'économie de procédure, mais d'autre part aussi sur la règle *ne bis in idem*.
- Lorsque l'intérêt d'une victime âgée de moins de 18 ans au moment des faits l'exige impérieusement (par exemple en raison du risque de suicide du mineur) et que celle-ci consent au classement de l'affaire.

La spécificité suisse s'exprime également à travers la diversité de l'activité des ministères publics cantonaux. Il est d'ailleurs intéressant de constater que les procureurs généraux sont, dans certains cantons, élus par le peuple, alors qu'ils le sont par les pouvoirs législatif ou exécutif dans d'autres. Au demeurant, les exigences liées à la formation que doivent avoir suivi les candidats pour être éligibles à ce poste ne sont pas forcément les mêmes dans tous les cantons. L'absence de

11 Pour des détails sur le sujet, voir Yvan Jeanneret & André Kuhn, *Précis de procédure pénale*, Berne : Stämpfli, 2013, p. 201-202, n° 519.

Graphique 6. Evolution de l'effectif des détenus selon le type de détention

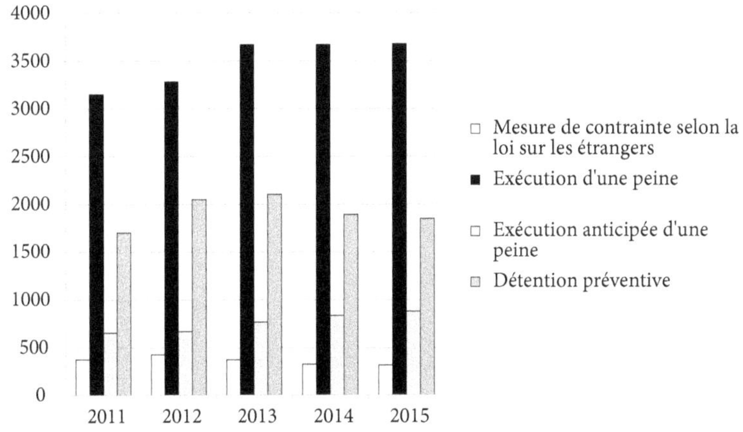

Source : Office fédéral de la statistique, Neuchâtel 2016.

statistiques au niveau national concernant l'activité des différents ministères publics cantonaux empêche de constater objectivement le polymorphisme que semble revêtir l'activité des différentes entités cantonales, mais les diverses formes de nomination n'en apparaissent pas moins comme un indicateur en lui-même de l'absence d'uniformité au niveau fédéral. L'utilisation différentielle de la détention avant jugement (anciennement appelée détention préventive) est un autre indice de ces disparités inter-cantonales. Les graphiques 6 et 7 illustrent la part importante que la détention avant jugement représente sur l'ensemble des privations de liberté, mais également les différences extrêmes dans l'utilisation de la détention avant jugement dans les différents cantons.

Le type de populations placées en détention avant jugement est également un élément intéressant à mettre en évidence. On constate au graphique 8 que les étrangers sans titre de séjour sont très largement surreprésentés parmi les personnes placées en détention durant l'instruction. Cela s'explique en partie par le fait que, pour prononcer ce genre de détention, l'autorité d'instruction doit prendre en considération trois éléments-clés, soit le risque de fuite, le risque de collusion et le risque de réitération. C'est probablement dans le premier de ces éléments (risque de fuite) que les ministères publics puisent l'essentiel de leur argumentation pour maintenir des prévenus étrangers en détention. La différence inter-cantonale en termes d'usage de la détention avant jugement pourrait donc éventuellement être mise en relation avec le nombre d'étrangers résidant dans ces cantons. Néanmoins, à situation identique en la matière, les cantons de Genève et de Bâle (tous deux frontaliers) ne font pas du tout usage de la détention avant jugement dans les mêmes proportions.

Graphique 7. Détentions avant jugement selon le canton en 2015 (nombres absolus, 2015)

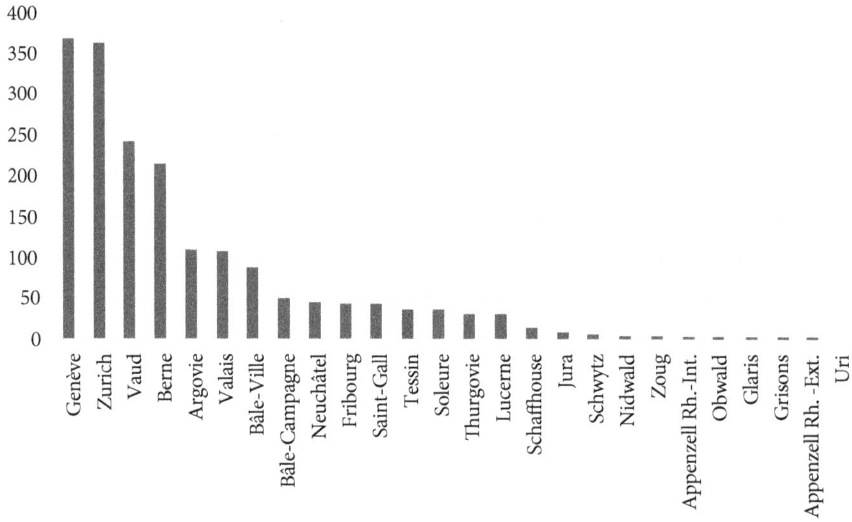

Source : Office fédéral de la statistique, Neuchâtel 2016.

Graphique 8. Détention avant jugement selon le statut de séjour (2015)

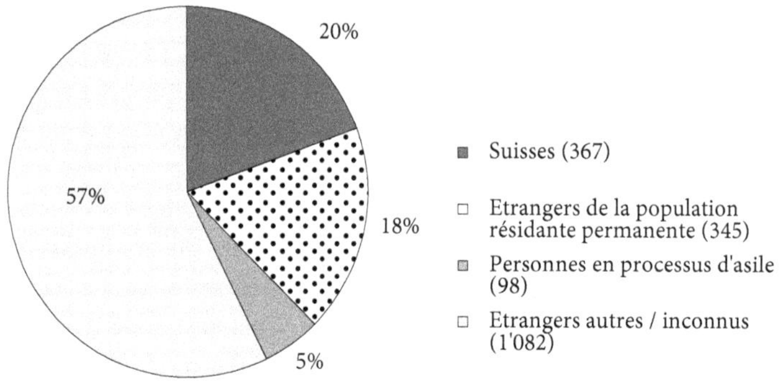

Source : Office fédéral de la statistique, Neuchâtel 2016.

III.3. REMARQUES FINALES

Nous l'avons mentionné plus haut, la Suisse connaît le principe de la légalité des poursuites, quelque peu édulcoré par certaines exceptions reposant sur le principe de l'opportunité. Sachant par ailleurs qu'une application plutôt stricte du principe de la légalité des poursuites est propre à mettre en marche le processus pénal bien plus souvent qu'une application plus large du principe de l'opportunité des poursuites, une diminution du nombre de poursuites pénales en Suisse pourrait être obtenue en élargissant les possibilités de classer certaines affaires en opportunité.

Constatant par ailleurs que la diversité de l'activité des ministères publics cantonaux engendre de grandes différences en matière de mise en détention avant jugement d'un canton à l'autre, une certaine uniformisation serait probablement la bienvenue, ne serait-ce que pour satisfaire le principe fondamental de l'égalité de traitement des prévenus. Une telle uniformisation pourrait éventuellement passer par une certaine uniformisation de l'organisation judiciaire au niveau national – ce qui nécessiterait toutefois que les prérogatives cantonales soient affaiblies et irait ainsi à l'encontre des principes du fédéralisme helvétique –, mais surtout par une immixtion beaucoup plus forte du Tribunal fédéral – notre Cour Suprême – dans les décisions de mise en détention avant jugement et une application plus large des mesures de substitution à la détention avant jugement, pourtant expressément prévues par le Code de procédure pénale.

Finalement, une dernière manière de tenter de diminuer le recours à la mise en accusation serait d'enfin introduire dans la législation pénale suisse une procédure tirée de la justice restaurative, telle que la médiation pénale.[12] Cette dernière permettrait en effet de résoudre certains conflits en amont et donc d'éviter d'initier le processus pénal ordinaire. Une telle procédure de médiation avait été proposée par le Conseil fédéral (soit le Gouvernement suisse)[13], mais rejetée par le Parlement au moment des délibérations autour de l'unification de la procédure pénale.[14]

IV. RECOURS EXCESSIF À LA PRIVATION DE LIBERTÉ

IV.1. CONSIDÉRATIONS GÉNÉRALES

La prison, en tant que peine, peut être surutilisée de deux manières très différentes : d'une part si l'on envoie trop de personnes en établissement pénitentiaire et, d'autre part lorsque les durées des peines sont trop importantes. Le *stock* pénitentiaire dépend en effet du *flux* d'entrées et de la *durée* des séjours. En d'autres

12 A propos de la médiation pénale en Suisse, voir – entre autres – André Kuhn, 'La médiation pénale', *Journal des Tribunaux* 2002, p. 99-109, ainsi que Camille Perrier, *La médiation en droit pénal suisse : étude de la législation suisse relative à la médiation pénale à la lumière des droits français, allemand et belge*, Bâle : Helbing Lichtenhahn, 2011. Concernant plus généralement la justice restaurative, voir la conclusion de la présente contribution.

13 FF 2006 1057, plus particulièrement p. 1252-1253 et 1469-1470.

14 Sur les raisons – principalement politiques et financières – de ce rejet, voir Catherine Faller, 'Historique de la médiation pénale dans le Code de procédure pénale suisse : de son introduction à sa suppression', 127 *Revue pénale suisse* 1 (2009), p. 18-39.

termes, d'une part, rien ne sert d'infliger une peine privative de liberté lorsqu'une autre peine est également possible et que l'on peut en attendre le même résultat en termes de récidive potentielle et, d'autre part, rien ne sert de prévoir de longues durées de détention lorsque des privations de liberté plus courtes sont également possibles ou lorsque les programmes de resocialisation ne sont mis en œuvre que durant les dernières années de l'exécution de la peine.

Historiquement, cette thématique n'est pas nouvelle, loin s'en faut. En effet, avec les débuts de la peine d'enfermement apparaissent également ses détracteurs. C'est ainsi que, en 1864 déjà, partant de l'idée que la privation de liberté est parfois un «mal nécessaire» qu'il faut toutefois éviter à chaque fois que cela est envisageable, Bonneville de Marsangy[15] écrit dans ses conseils et propositions au législateur :

> «Le juge doit se borner à prononcer l'amende toutes les fois, qu'eu égard au délit en lui-même ou au caractère du coupable, l'amende peut suffire à la répression; et il ne doit y ajouter l'emprisonnement qu'au cas de nécessité absolue... Une des règles consiste à ne jamais édicter ou prononcer la peine privative de liberté là où la peine pécuniaire suffit à la répression».

Il s'agit donc d'éviter l'emprisonnement autant que possible et de lui substituer des sanctions dont les effets personnels et sociaux seraient moins lourds. Quatre années plus tard, en 1868, Edouard Desprez[16] va encore plus loin que la simple limitation de la privation de liberté et écrit :

> «L'Emprisonnement est un moyen radicalement mauvais et qui doit être abandonné complétement».[17]

Néanmoins, depuis que la liberté a été érigée en bien suprême dans le courant du XVIIIème siècle, l'enfermement – représentant la perte de cette liberté – est progressivement devenu le châtiment judiciaire par excellence. Ainsi, dans la grande majorité (pour ne pas dire dans la totalité) des systèmes pénaux européens, la peine privative de liberté est aujourd'hui la peine de référence en matière pénale.

---

15 Bonneville de Marsangy, *De l'amélioration de la loi criminelle en vue d'une justice plus prompte, plus efficace, plus généreuse et plus moralisante*, tome II, Paris : Cosse et Marchal, 1864, p. 253 et 258. Par ailleurs, il est à noter que Bonneville de Marsangy n'est pas à l'origine de cette manière de penser; en effet, Cesare Beccaria, (*Des délits et des peines*, Milan, 1764, § XV) écrivait un siècle auparavant : «Parmi les peines, et dans la manière de les appliquer en proportion des délits, il faut donc choisir les moyens qui feront sur l'esprit du peuple l'impression la plus efficace et la plus durable et, en même temps, la moins cruelle sur le corps du coupable».

16 Edouard Desprez, *De l'abolition de l'Emprisonnement*, Paris : Dentu, 1868, p. 202.

17 Par ailleurs, Desprez indique dans son avant-propos (p. I) que «En parlant de l'*Emprisonnement*, nous prenons le mot dans son sens le plus étendu, et non pas dans son acception spéciale et juridique. Nous comprenons sous la même dénomination, non seulement l'Emprisonnement correctionnel, mais encore la Réclusion et les Bagnes».

La dimension des populations carcérales ainsi créées est généralement mesurée par le *taux de détention*, obtenu en rapportant le nombre de personnes détenues – à une date donnée ou en moyenne annuelle – au nombre d'habitants. Ce taux permet d'obtenir des informations quant à l'effectif et à la structure des populations carcérales à un moment déterminé; cette statistique est dès lors dite de «*stock*».[18] Il est toutefois important de noter que l'effectif de ces populations résulte de mouvements (d'entrée et de sortie) considérables. Ces derniers sont pris en compte par ce que l'on appelle les statistiques de «*flux*».[19] Celles-ci se réfèrent à la notion dynamique d'*entrées* en prison plutôt qu'à la notion plus statique de personnes qui *sont* en prison.

Nous nous trouvons donc en présence de deux indices voisins – et souvent confondus – qui recouvrent pourtant des notions très différentes. Afin d'obtenir une vision plus dynamique des populations carcérales étudiées, il peut parfois être intéressant de mettre en relation ces deux indices. On doit alors faire intervenir une troisième notion qui est celle de la *durée* des peines. On peut en effet considérer que le nombre de personnes détenues (qui sont en prison) dépend du nombre de personnes incarcérées (qui entrent en prison) et de la durée des détentions. En d'autres termes, le stock est une composition du flux et de la durée[20] :
Stock = Flux * Durée

Nous parlerons de «*substituts* à la privation de liberté» lorsque nous entendons faire référence à toutes les mesures propres à diminuer, soit le flux des incarcérations, soit la durée des détentions. Cette terminologie a l'avantage de recouvrir aussi bien les mesures permettant d'éviter l'incarcération de certaines personnes (flux) que celles propres à diminuer la durée de la détention.

Afin de simplifier la problématique des substituts à la privation de liberté, nous avons tenté de la rendre accessible sous la forme d'un schéma (Graphique 9). A chacune des extrémités des branches de cet arbre des possibles en matière de substituts à la privation de liberté sont énumérées des mesures qui semblent propres à diminuer le nombre des incarcérations ou la durée des détentions.

Dans un premier temps, cet arbre fait une distinction entre les substituts à l'incarcération (à savoir les mesures permettant d'éviter à certaines personnes d'entrer en prison) et les substituts à la détention (à savoir les mesures qui, sans éviter l'entrée en prison, permettent à des détenus d'éviter de devoir rester enfermés). Les substituts à l'incarcération se résument principalement à deux mesures :

18 Le taux de détention s'exprime généralement par un nombre de détenus pour 100'000 habitants.
19 Sur la nuance entre le «flux» et le «stock», cf. également André Kuhn, *Détenus : Combien ? Pourquoi ? Que faire ?*, Berne : Haupt, 2000, p. 11-14.
20 Pour davantage de précisions à ce sujet, cf. Pierre Tournier, 'Detention stocks, flows and durations : Modes of turnover of prison populations in Europe', in : HEUNI (eds), *Prison Population in Europe and North America : Problems and Solutions*, Strasbourg : Conseil de l'Europe, 1997, p. 67-91.

Graphique 9. Arbre des possibles en matière de substituts à la privation de liberté

Conception : Pierre Tournier et André Kuhn, 1997.*

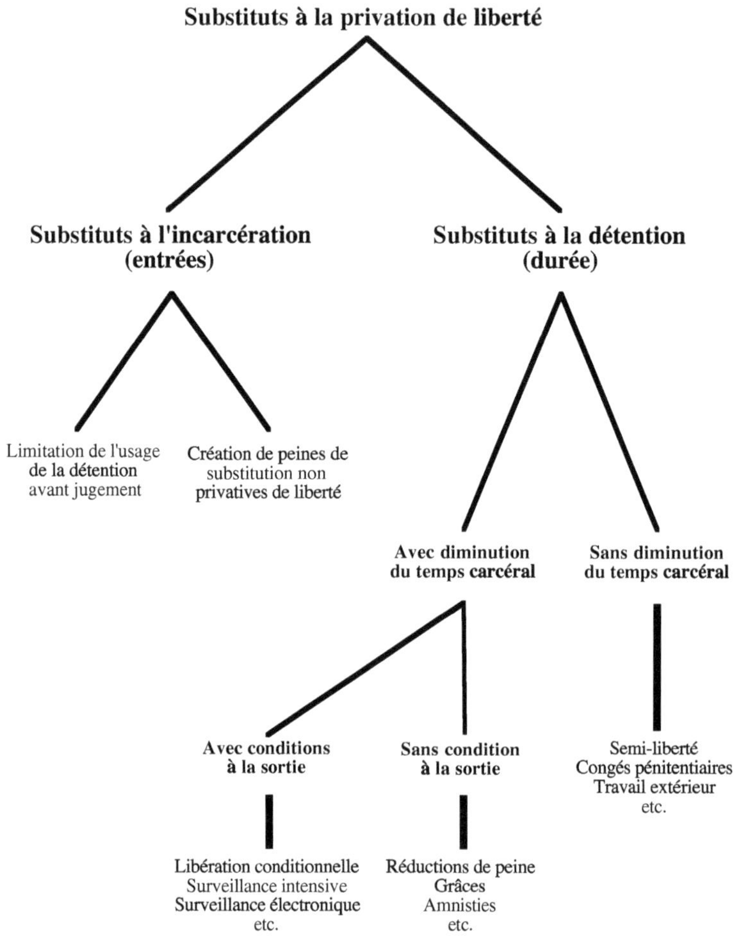

* Conceptualisation entreprise dans le cadre des travaux préparatoires qui ont mené à l'adoption, le 30 septembre 1999, de la Recommandation n° R (99) 22 concernant le surpeuplement des prisons et l'inflation carcérale; cf. «*Rapport sur le surpeuplement des prisons et l'inflation carcérale*» élaboré par le PC-CP avec l'aide des Experts scientifiques André Kuhn, Pierre Tournier et Roy Walmsley, Strasbourg : Conseil de l'Europe, 2000, p. 13-94, en particulier p. 67.

la limitation de l'usage de la détention avant jugement par des normes rendant la mise en détention préventive plus difficile, et la création – ou l'extension – de peines de substitution à la privation de liberté (telles que le sursis à la condamnation ou à l'exécution de la peine prononcée, le travail d'intérêt général, la peine pécuniaire, l'interdiction de conduire, la confiscation, les arrêts à domicile, l'interdiction d'exercer un métier, etc.). Ces peines sont dites *restrictives* de liberté.

Parmi les substituts à la détention, on trouve ceux qui entraînent une diminution du temps carcéral (la peine à purger devenant moins longue), et ceux qui n'interviennent pas sur la durée effective de la peine, mais qui sont néanmoins des mesures d'allégement pour les détenus. Il s'agit essentiellement de la semi-liberté, des congés pénitentiaires, des travaux que certains détenus sont amenés à effectuer à l'extérieur de la prison, etc. Si ces substituts à la détention sans diminution du temps carcéral ne modifient en réalité pas le taux de détention, les détenus étant toujours comptés comme présents, ils réduisent toutefois le temps à passer derrière les murs et permettent de préparer la sortie de prison, augmentant ainsi les chances d'insertion post-carcérale.

Finalement, parmi les substituts à la détention avec diminution du temps carcéral, on trouve les retours à la liberté soumis à une/des condition(s)[21] résolutoire(s) ou suspensive(s), et les retours à la liberté sans condition, tels que les réductions de peine, les grâces et autres amnisties.

IV.2. LE CAS DE LA SUISSE

Comme mentionné en introduction, l'usage abusif de la privation de liberté peut être appréhendé à travers l'activité de deux organes de la justice pénale. On peut en effet analyser l'usage de l'enferment à travers l'activité de l'*autorité de jugement* qui favoriserait des peines privatives de liberté au détriment d'autre peines plus proportionnées. On peut également l'interroger à travers les pratiques de l'*autorité d'exécution des peines*, qui, quant à elle, miserait davantage sur la neutralisation du condamné au détriment de sa resocialisation.

Tout d'abord, mentionnons que, malgré la limitation de l'usage des courtes peines privatives de liberté (soit des peines de moins de 6 mois) depuis 2007, le taux de détention est resté relativement stable, voire a même légèrement augmenté depuis l'entrée en vigueur de la nouvelle législation, passant de 75 à 83 détenus pour 100'000 habitants (Graphique 10).

Or, un des objectifs de la révision 2007 du Code pénal était précisément de remplacer les peines privatives de liberté de moins de six mois par des peines pécuniaires ou du travail d'intérêt général de manière – entre autres – à faire diminuer ce taux de détention. Si cet objectif a été atteint dans le cas des peines privatives de liberté inférieures à un mois (baisse de près de 100% pour les peines avec sursis et de 77% pour les peines fermes), il n'en demeure pas moins que les séjours carcéraux de moins de un mois représentent toujours une part importante des peines privatives de liberté exécutées en Suisse (Graphique 11).

S'agissant des peines de un à six mois, le recul entre 2007 et 2015 est par contre relativement faible (–32% pour les peines avec sursis et –19% pour les peines fermes). Cela est dû notamment au fait qu'une grande partie de ces peines

21 Si la condition n'est pas ou plus remplie, le libéré devra retourner en prison.

Graphique 10. Evolution du taux de détention pour 100'000 habitants

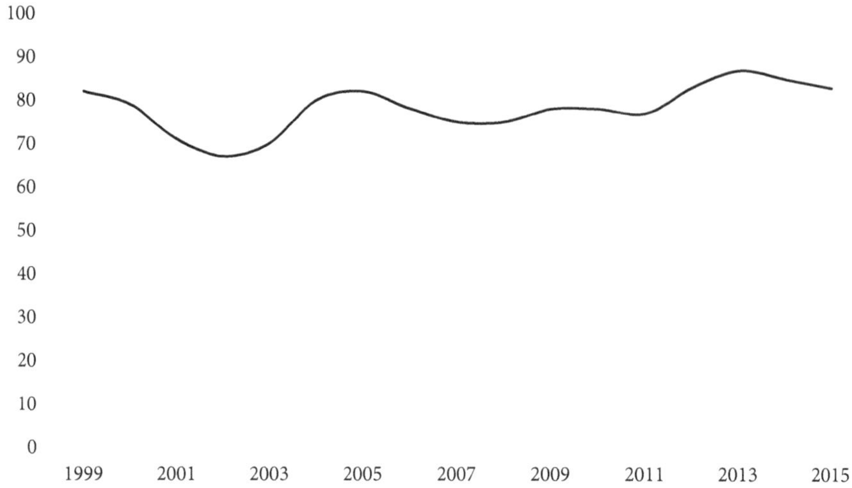

Source : Office fédéral de la statistique, Neuchâtel 2016.

Graphique 11. Durée moyenne des exécutions de peines privatives de liberté (2015)

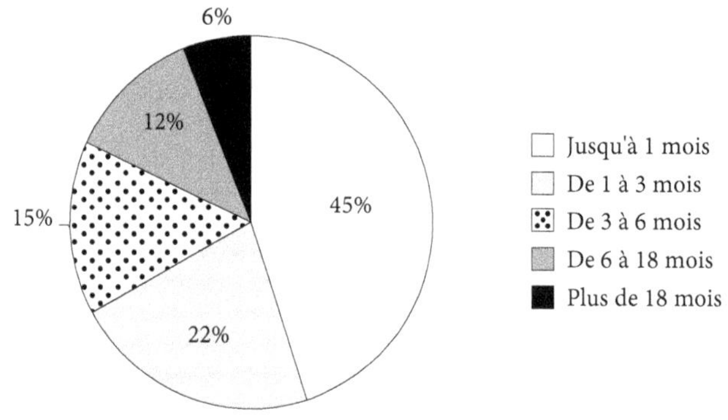

Source : Office fédéral de la statistique, Neuchâtel 2016.

concerne des personnes étrangères sans statut de séjour (80% des condamnations à une peine privative de liberté ferme de un à six mois), ce qui rend plus difficile l'exécution d'une peine pécuniaire ou d'un travail d'intérêt général. Encore une fois, comme pour la détention avant jugement, les étrangers sans titre de séjour semblent être plus souvent incarcérés que les autres. Mais l'augmentation de la population carcérale pourrait également s'expliquer par le fait qu'en contraignant les juges à prononcer des peines pécuniaires pour les condamnations de moins de 6 mois, le système a probablement poussé ces derniers à augmenter leur punitivité en prononçant des peines plus longues augmentant ainsi le stock de détenus.

Toujours concernant l'activité de l'autorité de jugement, l'analyse des statistiques de condamnation permet de mettre en évidence les types de crimes les plus réprimés pénalement. On constate que, comme mentionné précédemment, la LCR représente environ la moitié des condamnations pénales pour crimes et délits en Suisse[22] (Graphique 12).

Graphique 12. Condamnation selon le type de loi (2015)

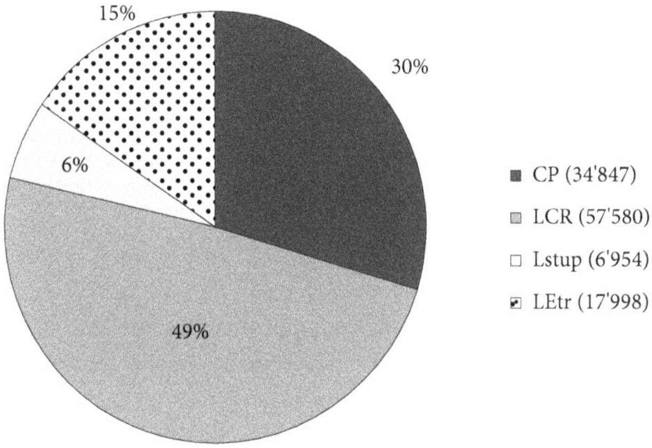

Source : Office fédéral de la statistique, Neuchâtel 2016.

Au-delà de ces statistiques de condamnation, il n'existe en Suisse que peu d'informations relatives à l'incarcération, particulièrement en ce qui concerne les types de délits pour lesquels une personne est incarcérée. Néanmoins, les Statistiques Pénales du Conseil de l'Europe nous fournissent quelques informations à ce sujet (Graphique 13). A leur lecture on constate l'importance du nombre de personnes exécutant une peine privative de liberté pour des délits en lien avec la LStup proportionnellement à la part des infractions enregistrées par la police en la matière. Si les infractions à la LStup ne représentent qu'un pourcentage relativement faible des délits enregistrés par la police (environ 12%) et une part encore moins importante des condamnations pénales (moins de 10%), elles concernent près d'un quart (23,1%) des motifs d'exécution d'une peine privative de liberté en Suisse et constituent la catégorie de délits la plus représentée en détention! Malheureusement, cette statistique ne permet pas de faire émerger la part que représentent les infractions à la LEtr et à la LCR parmi les personnes condamnées à des peines d'enfermement, ces deux catégories étant incluses dans la sous-catégorie autres types de délit.

22 Pour rappel, les contraventions sont exclues de cette analyse.

Graphique 13. Exécution de peines privative de liberté selon le type d'infraction (2013)

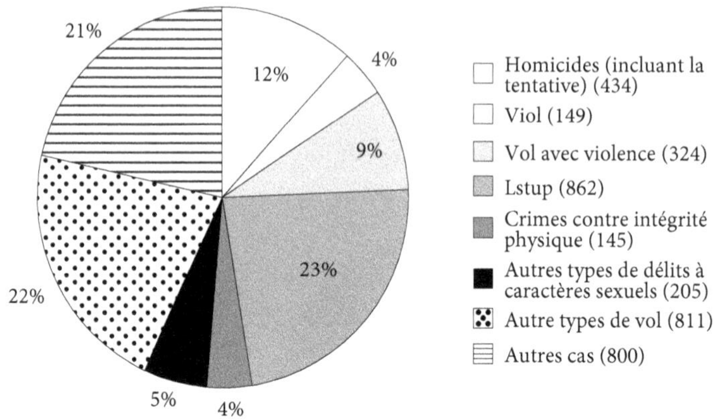

Source : Council of Europe Annual Penal Statistics, SPACE I, Prison Population Survey, 2013.

Concernant les caractéristiques de la population incarcérée, on constate à la lecture des données que les étrangers sont largement surreprésentés dans les statistiques pénitentiaires : ainsi plus de 2/3 des personnes en détention ne sont pas suisses. Cela pourrait s'expliquer par le fait que ces personnes semblent remplir les critères permettant aux tribunaux de leur infliger des courtes peines privatives de liberté en accord avec la modification du Code pénal de 2007. Cependant la lecture longitudinale des données disponibles en la matière semble montrer que cette augmentation de la part des étrangers parmi le nombre total de détenus est antérieure à la modification légale de 2007 (Graphique 14).

Le système de sanctions suisse est largement centré sur la peine privative de liberté et ses substituts qui interviennent principalement lors de l'exécution et sont utilisés de manière très limitée. Ainsi, lorsque l'on interprète les données en lien avec *l'autorité d'exécution des peines*, on constate la part de plus en plus faible que représente la semi-détention (soit la forme d'exécution qui consiste à pouvoir travailler dans la société libre tout en passant ses nuits et ses moments de loisirs en détention) dans les formes d'exécution de la sanction. La semi-détention y apparaît comme en net recul depuis les années nonante alors que l'exécution ordinaire de la peine privative de liberté augmente, apparaissant toujours plus comme le mode d'exécution de référence (Graphique 15).

En dehors des peines (généralement à durées déterminées), le système de sanctions suisse connaît encore des mesures privatives de liberté dont la durée est indéterminée. C'est ainsi que certains détenus malades et/ou représentant un danger particulier pour la société peuvent se voir imposer un traitement des troubles mentaux, un traitement des addictions ou un internement. Ces mesures pèsent sur le système carcéral par leurs durées généralement longues davantage que par leur nombre. En effet, comme en attestent les graphiques suivants (graphiques 16

Graphique 14. Proportion d'étrangers en exécution de peine privative de liberté

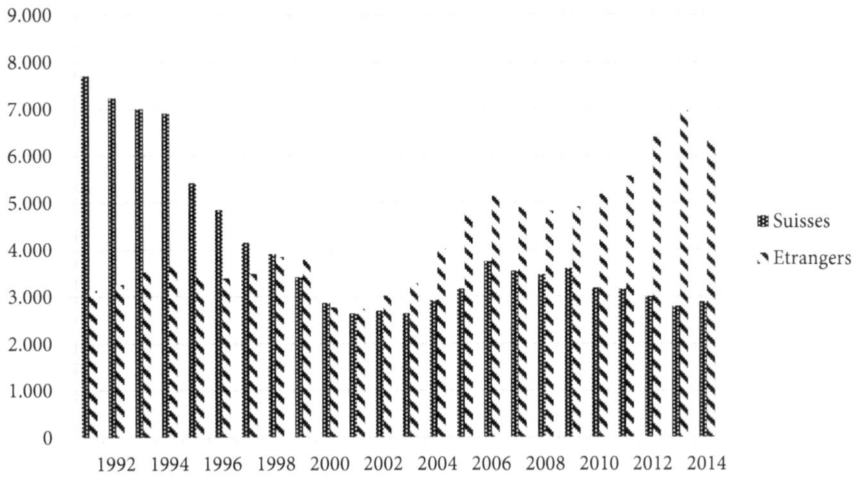

Source : Office fédéral de la statistique, Neuchâtel 2016.

Graphique 15. Evolution des formes d'exécution de la sanction

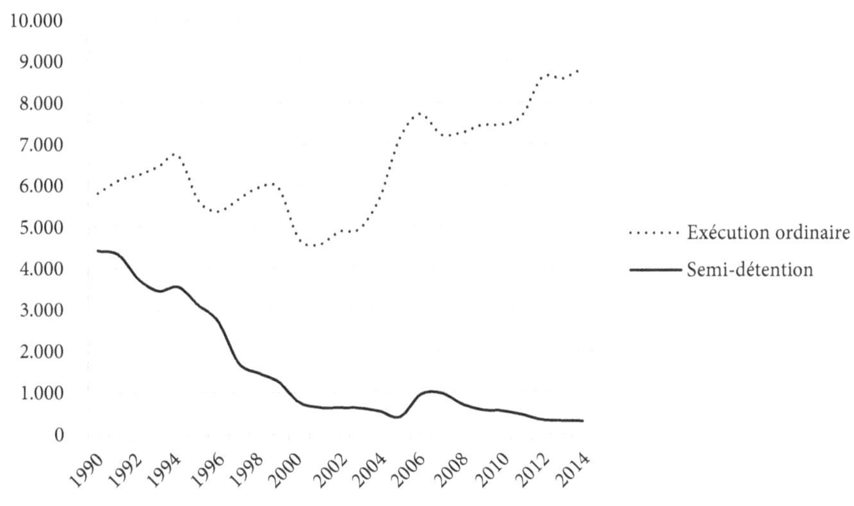

Source : Office fédéral de la statistique, Neuchâtel 2016.

et 17), l'effectif moyen de personnes incarcérées en vertu d'une mesure a tendance à diminuer alors que les durées moyennes et médianes de ces incarcérations augmentent drastiquement.

Graphique 16. Evolution des mesures prononcées, selon le type de mesure

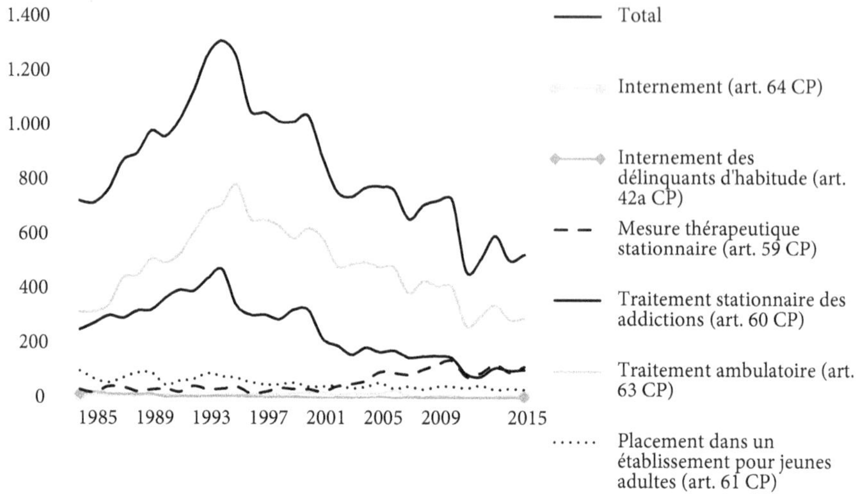

Source : Office fédéral de la statistique, Neuchâtel 2016.

Graphique 17. Exécution de mesures, durée moyenne et médiane de la détention (en jours)

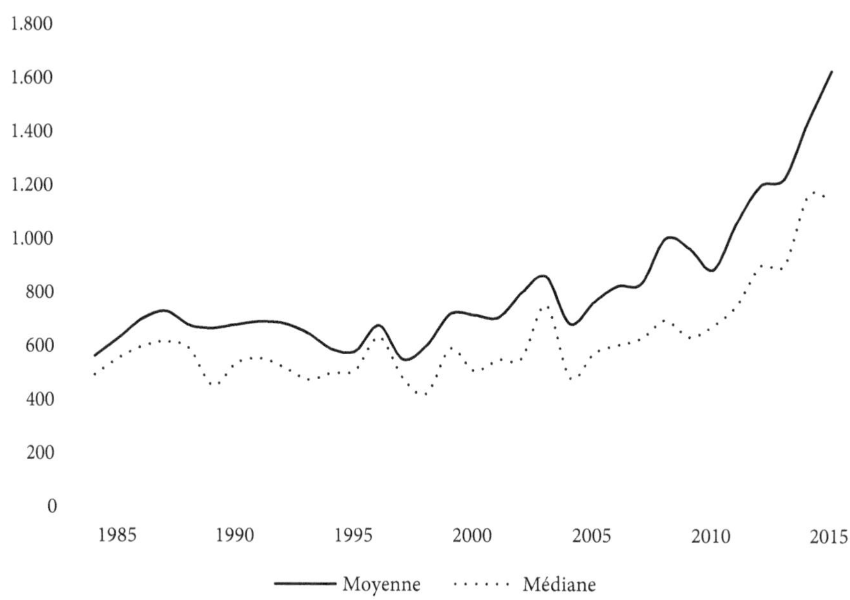

Source : Office fédéral de la statistique, Neuchâtel 2016.

IV.3. REMARQUES FINALES

En admettant que la sanction pénale reste nécessaire malgré les développements présentés au chapitre II, le droit des sanctions doit idéalement devenir un droit de l'accession à la capacité de vivre en société sans commettre d'infractions. Pour qu'il en soit ainsi, il est indispensable que chaque sanction soit toujours adaptée à la situation particulière de l'individu qu'elle touche. En d'autres termes, d'un droit de l'*acte*, le droit pénal doit devenir un droit de l'*auteur*, c'est-à-dire un droit non plus tourné vers l'infraction commise dans le *passé*, mais vers l'*avenir* de l'individu sanctionné.

La sanction doit donc être *personnalisée*. Pour y parvenir, en plus de la nécessité d'élargir la palette des sanctions[23] à la disposition des juges, nous proposons que le système de sanctions soit subdivisé en deux phases distinctes. L'idée serait ainsi de créer un système pénal à deux étages[24], avec un juge de siège qui se prononce essentiellement sur la *durée* de la peine et un juge d'application des peines qui se prononce ensuite sur le *type* de peine. Au tribunal, le juge, au lieu de prononcer un type de peine pour une certaine durée, ne se prononcerait plus que sur la *durée* de la peine. Il prononcerait ainsi sa peine en «unités pénales» en fonction de la culpabilité – ou plutôt de l'état et des besoins[25] – du délinquant.

Le juge aurait également le pouvoir de prononcer l'ajournement de ces «unités pénales», si les conditions de l'ajournement de la sanction sont remplies. S'il prononce l'ajournement, la procédure s'arrête là et le délinquant est condamné à un certain nombre d'«unités pénales» avec sursis. Si par contre le juge ne prononce pas le sursis, le dossier est renvoyé à un juge d'application des peines, à qui il revient de prononcer le *type* de peine le mieux adapté au délinquant. Ce juge d'application des peines sera tenu par le *quantum* de la peine, mais aura un large

23 A ce propos, voir par exemple les propositions de Yvan Jeanneret, André Kuhn & Laurent Moreillon, 'Quel droit pénal pour demain ?', in : Marcel A. Niggli, José Hurtado Pozo & Nicolas Queloz (eds), *Festschrift für Franz Riklin*, Zurich : Schulthess, 2007, p. 137-151, contribution dans laquelle les auteurs proposent – outre une extension de l'opportunité des poursuites et l'introduction du système de l'ajournement de la peine – le travail d'intérêt général réparateur, la flexibilisation des peines existantes, l'assignation à résidence, l'interdiction de conduire, la peine panachée, *etc.* A ces peines, on pourrait encore ajouter bon nombre d'autres sanctions «originales» permettant de sanctionner l'infraction par la peine la mieux à même de faire réfléchir l'auteur et d'éviter sa récidive. Nous pensons ici, à titre d'exemple, à l'interdiction d'exercer une profession, l'interdiction de conduire, la publication du jugement, la confiscation du matériel de ski et à l'interdiction de se rendre sur un domaine skiable pour un skieur ayant causé des lésions corporelles ou un homicide par négligence en skiant de manière imprudente et en fonçant dans un autre utilisateur des pistes, *etc.*

24 A ce propos, voir André Kuhn, *Détenus : Combien ? Pourquoi ? Que faire ?*, Berne : Haupt, 2000, p. 207-215.

25 A ce propos, voir par exemple Loïc Parein, *La fixation de la peine : de l'homme «coupable» à l'homme «capable»*, Bâle : Helbing & Lichtenhahn, 2010, p. 191-240, auteur qui parle du délinquant comme d'un individu «submergé» qu'il s'agit de «libérer», créant par là même le concept de «droit pénal libérateur».

pouvoir d'appréciation, puisque la palette des sanctions qu'il aura à sa disposition sera très grande.

Dans certaines limites légales, le juge d'application des peines transformera donc chaque «unité pénale» soit en un jour-amende, soit en un jour de travail d'intérêt général, soit encore en un jour de détention, en un jour d'assignation à résidence, *etc.*

On peut même aller jusqu'à imaginer que ce juge d'application des peines puisse panacher et subdiviser la peine globale en une partie de peine à subir en détention et une seconde partie qui serait, par exemple, transformée en travail d'intérêt général. On pourrait aller encore plus loin et imaginer que le juge d'application des peines ait lui aussi le pouvoir d'assortir une partie de la peine, voire la peine dans sa totalité, d'un sursis.

Ce juge d'application des peines aurait comme obligation première de faire correspondre la sanction aux besoins réels du condamné et donc de répondre à l'exigence de personnalisation ou d'individualisation de la peine. Un tel système permettrait même une sorte de double individualisation, puisque le juge de condamnation prononcerait lui aussi sa peine en tenant compte de la situation personnelle du condamné.

Dans les faits, cette proposition reviendrait à passer d'un système où un seul juge décide de la culpabilité et de la peine dans son ensemble avant de laisser à une autorité (souvent administrative) le soin de prendre les décisions quant au mode d'exécution de cette peine, à un système dans lequel tout est judiciarisé. C'est à un magistrat qu'il reviendrait de se prononcer sur la culpabilité et sur le *quantum* de la sanction et c'est encore à un magistrat qu'il reviendrait de déterminer le type de sanction et le mode d'exécution.

Le fait de transférer la décision quant au type de sanction du juge de siège à un juge d'exécution des peines est une garantie pour qu'il ne soit pas tenu compte du type de peine que l'on inflige lorsque l'on en prononce le *quantum*. De surcroît, un tel système laisse le soin du choix du genre de sanction à un spécialiste de la matière, soit à une personne dont les compétences devront être davantage psychologiques et/ou psychiatriques que juridiques.

En résumé, les décisions à prendre dans le processus pénal sont des décisions (1) quant à la culpabilité, (2) quant au *quantum* de la peine, (3) quant au type de peine, et (4) quant au mode d'exécution.

Aujourd'hui, le juge se prononce d'abord sur la culpabilité; dans un second temps, il prend une décision d'ensemble sur le type et le *quantum* de la peine, avant de se prononcer éventuellement sur le sursis; enfin, l'autorité d'exécution de la peine se détermine sur le mode d'exécution. Dans le système proposé, le juge de siège se prononce sur la culpabilité, sur le *quantum* de la peine et éventuellement sur son ajournement, puis c'est à un juge d'application des peines qu'il appartient de se prononcer sur le type de peine et sur le mode d'exécution.

Quant à la publicité du jugement, elle doit s'arrêter au *quantum* de la peine. En effet, le fait de ne publier que le *quantum* retire au juge d'application des peines la pression de l'opinion publique sur sa décision quant au type de peine. Cette dernière pourra donc être totalement adaptée au délinquant. C'est d'ailleurs également le seul moyen de faire comprendre de façon générale que la privation de liberté n'est définitivement plus la colonne vertébrale du système de sanctions.

En guise de conclusion, nous pensons qu'il n'est pas exagéré de prétendre que, pour améliorer la situation carcérale d'un Etat, ce dernier doit absolument être audacieux, ce que la Suisse n'est manifestement pas. Jacqueline Bernat de Celis[26] le disait :

> «C'est à une évolution générale des mentalités qu'il faudrait travailler si l'on voulait vraiment, en politique criminelle, faire du neuf».

Par ailleurs, on attribue souvent à Einstein cette phrase ô combien intelligente selon laquelle «*on ne peut pas résoudre un problème au même niveau de pensée que celui qui a permis de le créer*». Comme nous l'avons vu, il n'est pas insoutenable de prétendre que le système pénal est davantage un problème en soi qu'une solution aux problèmes sociaux qu'il est censé résoudre; il devient donc urgent de le repenser. Le repenser ne veut toutefois pas forcément dire qu'il suffit de remplacer les peines privatives de liberté par d'autres sanctions, mais peut-être faudrait-il revenir aux fondamentaux; nous allons le tenter dans notre conclusion.

V. CONCLUSION

Le présent article a tenté de présenter de manière succincte les éléments pouvant faire penser à une surutilisation du système pénal en Suisse. Il a tout d'abord mis en évidence le fait qu'un nombre restreint d'actes criminalisés représentait une part importante des délits enregistrés et que parmi ces comportements problématiques, un certain nombre pourraient être traités sans avoir recours au système pénal. La spécificité du fédéralisme helvétique a également été mise en exergue. Elle se traduit par une grande diversité dans l'activité des divers organes étant amenés à faire respecter la loi. En effet, parmi les comportements proscrits, certains semblent faire l'objet d'une attention particulière en fonction du lieu où l'on se situe et indépendamment des caractéristiques endémiques. *A contrario*, certains délits que l'on sait pourtant récurrents dans notre pays, comme le blanchiment d'argent, semblent bénéficier d'un certain laxisme au regard de la rareté des cas instruits. Ces différences cantonales se traduisent notamment par l'usage

26 Jacqueline Bernat de Celis J., 'Pourquoi les tribunaux français appliquent-ils si peu les peines dites «de substitution» ?', 7 *Archives de Politique Criminelle*, Paris : Pedone, 1984, p. 239.

extrêmement variable de la détention avant jugement. Une variabilité de l'action pénale qui concerne également la population à laquelle elle s'attaque. Ainsi, les étrangers semblent largement plus enclins à subir une période de privation de liberté que la population locale, qu'il s'agisse d'ailleurs de détention avant jugement ou d'exécution de peine. Concernant l'autorité de jugement, nous avons constaté que le taux de détention, tout comme la durée moyenne de l'enfermement sont à la hausse dans notre pays. En y regardant de plus près, nous avons pu mettre en évidence le fait que les infractions à la LStup pèsent lourd dans l'enfermement quand bien même cette catégorie d'infraction n'est que minoritairement enregistrée par la police. Enfin, concernant les formes d'exécution de la sanction, nous constatons que les autorités d'exécution des peines semblent de moins en moins enclines à octroyer aux condamnés des allégements de régime, en particulier à travers le régime de semi-détention dont l'usage se fait de moins en moins fréquent.

Mais au-delà de la simple remise en question de la criminalisation de certains actes, et de la manière dont ils sont traités par les ministères publics et les autorités de jugement puis d'exécution des peines, c'est peut-être également vers une autre forme de justice qu'il serait bon de se tourner. Il existe en effet deux grandes formes de justice à travers le monde. La première prévoit que le crime est une offense contre l'Etat et ses lois; que la justice se concentre donc sur l'établissement de la faute qui a été commise dans le passé, afin de mesurer la dose de souffrance à infliger à l'auteur; cette justice est recherchée au cours d'un duel entre adversaires, duel lors duquel l'accusé est opposé à l'Etat; finalement, on évalue cette justice pénale en fonction de la bonne application – et donc du respect – des règles matérielles et formelles en vigueur. Cette forme de justice pénale – que nous connaissons bien, puisqu'elle constitue le fondement de notre système pénal actuel – est généralement appelée la «justice *rétributive*» ou, plus métaphoriquement, la «*justice du glaive*»[27], notion faisant référence au fait que notre droit pénal suppose l'existence d'intérêts individuels distants les uns des autres, le conflit intervenant lorsque les intérêts des uns se rapprochent trop de (voire empiètent sur) ceux des autres. La justice est ainsi appelée à trancher le point de rencontre avec le glaive et à replacer les intérêts de chacun sur une balance afin de rétablir l'équilibre.

La seconde manière de prendre en charge les comportements ressortant de la déviance criminalisée envisage le crime comme une offense contre des gens et des relations; dans cette conception, la justice – ouverte sur l'avenir – s'efforce d'identifier les besoins de chacun afin de trouver un remède à la situation, de réparer les

27 Métaphore empruntée à Anne-Catherine Salberg & Julien Knoepfler, 'Le Glaive, le miroir et l'Autre. Expériences de médiation transculturelle en Suisse romande', in : Pierre Centlivres & Isabelle Girod (eds), *Les défis migratoires*, actes du 4e colloque CLUSE, Neuchâtel : Seismo, 2000, p. 518-527, plus particulièrement p. 526.

dommages et de restaurer les relations; elle encourage le dialogue et l'accord mutuel et donne à l'auteur et à la victime un rôle central; finalement, on évalue cette justice en fonction du résultat, soit de l'étendue de la prise de conscience et de la «guérison» des individus et des relations. Cette forme de justice – relativement peu connue sous nos cieux actuellement, mais largement répandue dans d'autres cultures[28] – est généralement appelée la «justice *restaurative*»[29] ou, métaphoriquement, la «*justice de l'aiguille*»[30] et considère que les divers intérêts individuels s'imbriquent et forment les fibres d'un tissu social. Le conflit correspond alors à un éloignement des intérêts individuels, soit à une déchirure de ce tissu social. Telle une couturière munie d'un fil et d'une aiguille, la justice doit alors recoudre les intérêts séparés par la crise.

Ces deux conceptions montrent clairement que la justice est un concept polysémique et qu'il est donc possible de rendre justice de plusieurs façons. Nos tribunaux appliquent la «justice du glaive»[31], alors que d'autres sont plus sensibles à une forme de «justice de l'aiguille». Si notre logique judiciaire se propose de trancher un litige en donnant raison à l'une des parties en conflit au détriment de l'autre, la seconde conception vise, quant à elle, à permettre aux parties de trouver

---

28 Principalement en Océanie, en Afrique, en Amérique du Sud et au nord de l'Amérique du Nord. A ce propos, voir notamment André Kuhn & Camille Perrier, 'Quelle importance accordons-nous aux modes amiables de règlement des conflits ?, in : Nadja Capus & Jean-Luc Bacher (eds), *Strafjustiz zwischen Anspruch und Wirklichkeit – Le système de justice pénale : ambitions et résultats*, Berne : Stämpfli, 2010, p. 217-244, plus précisément p. 227ss.

29 Cette justice est parfois appelée «réparatrice», en référence à l'aspect réparateur des préjudices de cette forme de justice, et parfois «restauratrice» ou «restaurative», en référence au terme anglophone «*restorative justice*» et à la volonté de restaurer des relations intersubjectives; à ce propos, voir Catherine Rossi, 'Le modèle québécois des Rencontres Détenus-Victimes', *Les Cahier de la justice* 2 (2012), p. 107-126, plus précisément p. 107.

30 Métaphore empruntée à Koffi Kumelio A. Afande, 'Les sanctions pénales en Afrique : entre tradition et modernité', in : Volker Dittman, André Kuhn, Renie Maag & Hans Wiprächtiger (eds), Entre médiation et perpétuité : Nouvelles voies dans la lutte contre la criminalité, Rüegger, Coire, 2002, p. 275-295, plus précisément p. 277.

31 Selon l'histoire telle qu'il est de coutume de la conter dans nos Facultés de droit européennes, de vengeance privée, la justice aurait passé aux mains de l'État, en conséquence de quoi la victime aurait progressivement perdu sa place au procès pénal au profit de cet État. Il est donc logique que, dans cette conception de la justice, le crime soit perçu comme une atteinte à l'État plutôt qu'à la victime. Cela ne laisse évidemment que peu de place à une justice couturière. Mais ne serait-il pas opportun de revoir quelque peu nos fondements historiques ? La vengeance privée était-elle véritablement la première forme de justice existante ? Comment expliquer que, dans des contrées aussi éloignées les unes des autres et en des temps où les contacts entre peuples de continents différents étaient inexistants, l'Afrique, l'Océanie et l'Amérique du Nord ont connu des modes de résolution des conflits aussi semblables que la palabre, la conférence et le cercle (à ce propos, voir par exemple André Kuhn & Camille Perrier, 'Quelle importance accordons-nous aux modes amiables de règlement des conflits ?, in : Nadja Capus & Jean-Luc Bacher (eds), *Strafjustiz zwischen Anspruch und Wirklichkeit – Le système de justice pénale : ambitions et résultats*, Berne : Stämpfli, 2010, p. 217-244, ainsi que Assouman Bamba, 'Les États africains à l'école du pardon purificateur de l'arbre à palabre', LXVI *Revue Internationale de Criminologie et de Police Technique et Scientifique* 2 (2013), p. 152-168) ? La première forme de justice n'aurait-elle pas peut-être plutôt été amiable que vengeresse ?

– si possible consensuellement – une solution à leur conflit grâce à l'intervention d'un tiers qui sera davantage médiateur[32] que juge.

Le système de justice étant construit comme une poupée russe, les pièces intérieures ne méritent un traitement que lorsque la pièce principale existe. Si le problème de la criminalisation était résolu, plus de problème de justice et d'exécution des sanctions. C'est donc bien sur le chapitre II qu'il est important de s'attarder.

Finalement, à ceux qui ne pourraient concevoir une société sans prison, sans sanction et sans loi pénale, il est utile de rappeler qu'il fut un temps, pas si lointain, où l'aveu était nécessaire pour condamner un individu et où le «bon» fonctionnement du système était dépendant de l'existence de la torture pour obtenir (ou extirper) cet aveu. En ce temps-là, une société sans torture n'était simplement pas concevable… Si l'on avait dit à des pénalistes de l'époque que, au XXIème siècle, on pourrait condamner un individu sans qu'il avoue son méfait, ils auraient simplement répondu que nous sommes des barbares, puisque nous prenons le risque de condamner des innocents… Avec l'œil averti d'un humain du XXIème siècle, nous regardons pourtant le droit de nos aïeux avec condescendance. Mais quel regard portera l'humain du XXVème siècle sur les pratiques pénales – dont fait partie l'enfermement – de ses propres aïeux ?

Rien n'est donc éternel… ni la prison, ni les sanctions formelles, ni même le droit pénal probablement… Une chose est en effet certaine, et notre système pénal ne l'a manifestement pas encore compris : «On ne peut garantir la vie en donnant la mort, on ne peut défendre la liberté en enfermant des milliers d'individus, on ne peut refuser la violence en utilisant la violence»[33]; notre droit pénal est donc indubitablement destiné à se réformer en profondeur, voire à disparaître.

---

32 A propos de la médiation pénale, voir – entre autres – André Kuhn, 'La médiation pénale', *Journal des Tribunaux* 2002, p. 99-109, ainsi que Camille Perrier, *La médiation en droit pénal suisse : étude de la législation suisse relative à la médiation pénale à la lumière des droits français, allemand et belge*, Bâle : Helbing Lichtenhahn, 2011.

33 Catherine Baker, *Pourquoi faudrait-il punir ?*, Lyon : Tahin Party, 2004, p. 176-177.

OVERUSE OF THE CRIMINAL JUSTICE SYSTEM IN TAIWAN

Rong-Geng LI*

I. INTRODUCTION

In Taiwan, some actions may have been unnecessarily criminalized at the legislative level, and extremely heavy punishments have been imposed on some offences. Furthermore, prosecutors do not have much power to decide whether or not to prosecute certain cases. Therefore, over-prosecution exists in Taiwan's criminal justice system. According to statistical data, overcrowding in prisons has been an issue for a long time. However, the Taiwanese government is aware of the problem and is taking measures to solve it by revising and enacting related statutes. This paper aims to address the problem concerning the overuse of the criminal justice system in Taiwan. In addition, the paper discusses how Taiwan is showing improvements in its attempt to resolve the problem at hand.

II. OVERUSE OF CRIMINALIZATION

II.1. THE ANNUAL NUMBER OF CRIMES

A total of 297,676 crimes occurred in 2015, which involved 270,817 offenders. In the same year, Taiwan's population was 23,492,074, indicating that 1,268.71 cases and 1,154.23 offenders existed per 100,000 people in Taiwan in 2015. From a long-term perspective (2000 to 2015), on average, a total of 423,302 cases

* Dr. Rong-Geng Li is professor of Criminal Procedure and Criminal Law at National Taipei University, Taiwan. Dr. Li obtained his LL.M. and S.J.D. degrees from Indiana University-Bloomington in 2006 and 2008.

(including 231,167 offenders) occurred annually.[1] During that period, the average population was about 22,953,810.[2] Thus, about 1,857.56 cases and 1,006.74 offenders existed per 100,000 Taiwanese annually, on average. The number of cases is greater than that of the offenders because one case means that an offender commits a crime. Therefore, when an offender commits two crimes, it adds up to two cases. The aforementioned data are further presented in Table 1.

Table 1. Number of crimes

	Population	Cases	Offenders	Cases /100,000	Offenders /100,000
2000	22,276,672	438,520	181,614	1,976.69	818.65
2001	22,405,568	490,736	180,527	2,196.56	808.05
2002	22,520,776	503,389	185,751	2,240.95	826.91
2003	22,604,550	494,755	158,687	2,192.80	703.32
2004	22,689,122	522,305	176,975	2,306.30	781.46
2005	22,770,383	555,109	207,425	2,442.21	912.57
2006	22,876,527	512,788	229,193	2,246.76	1,004.20
2007	22,958,360	491,815	265,860	2,146.03	1,160.08
2008	23,037,031	453,439	271,186	1,971.67	1,179.19
2009	23,119,772	386,075	261,973	1,672.88	1,135.14
2010	23,162,123	371,934	269,340	1,607.25	1,163.91
2011	23,224,912	347,674	260,356	1,499.01	1,122.54
2012	23,315,822	317,356	262,058	1,363.78	1,126.14
2013	23,373,517	298,967	255,310	1,280.66	1,093.65
2014	23,433,753	306,300	261,603	1,308.77	1,117.79
2015	23,492,074	297,676	270,817	1,268.71	1,154.23
Average	22,953,810	424,302	231,167	1,857.56	1,006.74

One noteworthy observation from Table 1 is that the numbers of offenders have not evidently changed since 2007. In contrast, the number of cases show a consistent decreasing pattern. This means that the law and order situation in Taiwan has shown consistent improvement over the years.

1 Ministry of the Interior, 5.1 Offenses Handled by Police Organizations, 2016 (at: http://sowf.moi.gov.tw/stat/month/m5-01.ods) (last visited: 18 February 2016).

2 Directorate-General of Budget, Accounting, and Statistics, Executive Yuan, Number of Villages, Neighborhoods, Households and Resident Population, 2016 (at: http://sowf.moi.gov.tw/stat/month/m1-01.ods) (last visited: 18 February 2016).

II.2. TOP FIVE CRIMES IN TAIWAN

In the past few years, the top five crimes in Taiwan have been quite consistent. In 2014, among all cases sent by the police to the district prosecutor's offices, the most frequently occurring crimes were offences against public safety (10.7%), offences related to narcotics (6.3%), injury (5.0%), larceny (3.9%), and fraud (3.9%).[3] The data are highly similar to those recorded in other years, with slight differences in the last two rankings for fraud and larceny. For instance, in 2012, the top three crimes were offences against public safety (8%), those related to narcotics (7.1%), injury (4.8%), fraud (4%), and larceny (3.9%).[4] In 2013, the rankings were almost the same: offences against public safety (9%) was the most committed crime that year, followed by offences related to narcotics (6.7%), injury (4.8%), larceny (3.9%) and fraud (3.6%).[5] These data are further presented in Table 2.

Table 2. Top 5 crimes

	Top 1	Top 2	Top 3	Top 4	Top 5
2014	Offences against public safety (10.7%)	Offences related to narcotics (6.3%)	Injury (5%)	Larceny (3.9%)	Fraud (3.9%)
2013	Offences against public safety (9%)	Offences related to narcotics (6.7%)	Injury (4.8%)	Larceny (3.9%	Fraud (3.6%)
2012	Offences against public safety (8%)	Offences related to narcotics (7.1%)	Injury (4.8%)	Fraud (4%)	Larceny (3.9%)

With respect to offences against public safety and injury, a few things should be mentioned. In 1999, the legislature revised the Criminal Code and criminalized driving under the influence of alcohol, narcotics, or medication (Article 185-3). That provision was codified in the chapter of "Offenses Against Public Safety (Chapter 11)." Since then, offences against public safety have become the most commonly occurring crime in Taiwan. In addition, negligently causing injury to another person is deemed a criminal offence that is punishable according to the Criminal Code (Article 284). In other words, injury with intention and negligent injury are both considered criminal offences. Meanwhile, traffic accidents often result in a large number of negligent injuries. As these accidents commonly occur

3 Ministry of Justice, *2014 Justice Annual Statistical Report 18*, 2015 (at: www.rjsd.moj.gov.tw/rjsdweb/book/Book_File.ashx?book_id=31_1) (last visited: 26 February 2016).

4 Ministry of Justice, *2012 Justice Annual Statistical Report 18*, 2013 (at: www.rjsd.moj.gov.tw/rjsdweb/book/Book_File.ashx?chapter_id=31_7_1) (last visited: 26 February 2016).

5 Ministry of Justice, *2013 Justice Annual Statistical Report 18*, 2014 (at: www.rjsd.moj.gov.tw/rjsdweb/book/Book_File.ashx?chapter_id=66_7_1) (last visited: 26 February 2016).

in people's daily lives, injury has become the third most common crime in Taiwan.

II.3. PROBLEMATIC OBLIGATION TO CRIMINALIZE CERTAIN ACTIONS

a. *Post-Martial Law period*

After more than 38 years, President Li Den-hui declared the end of Martial Law in 1987. However, the current version of the Criminal Code still shows influences of that period of time. For example, the Preface of the Constitution of the Republic of China states that "The National Assembly of the Republic of China, by virtue of the mandate received from the whole body of citizens, in accordance with the teachings bequeathed by Dr. Sun Yat-sen in founding the Republic of China, …… does hereby establish this Constitution ……" In this case, the Preface does not obligate the legislature to penalize a person insulting Dr. Sun Yat-sen. The Criminal Code, however, punishes a person who, with the purpose of insulting the founder of the Republic of China, Dr. Sun Yat-sen, openly damages, removes, or dishonours his portrait, shall be sentenced to imprisonment for not more than one year, short-term imprisonment, or a fine of not more than three hundred yuan (Article 160, Sec. 2). That provision has an announcement effect, rather than a practical one. In fact, no person has yet to be prosecuted or found guilty of this crime since the enactment of the Criminal Code in 1928.

b. *Societal obligation to criminalize certain acts*

In some cases, the society obligates the legislature and even the courts to criminalize or increase penalties for certain actions. Such societal influence usually demands the legislature and courts to criminalize more actions, which should not be penalized nor incur heavier punishments for offenders. Two cases highlight such societal influence.

The "White Rose Movement"

In 2010, the defendant, Lin Yi-Fang molested a six-year old girl, whom he found wandering alone. Lin then held the victim in one arm, and inserted his finger into the victim's vagina. Lin was arrested after the police arrived. The court, however, found that Lin's act was not against the will of the victim. Therefore, he was found guilty of having sexual intercourse with a person under the age of fourteen (Sec. 1, Article 227), instead of forcibly having sexual intercourse with a minor (Item 2,

Sec. 1, Article 222). Consequently, the court meted out a lighter punishment and sentenced Lin to imprisonment for three years and two months.[6]

Not long after the Lin case, a Supreme Court case involving a minor victim raised public attention. In this case, the victim was a three-year-old girl. The defendant, Wu Jing-yi, took the victim to his place and proceeded to insert his finger, glasses, and a straw into the victim's vagina. The victim felt extreme pain and cried out for the assailant to stop. In this case, the high court convicted the defendant of forcibly having sexual intercourse with a person under the age of fourteen.[7] The defendant appealed his case. Unfortunately, the Supreme Court held the opinion that the evidence showing the victim's involuntary participation in the act was insufficient; that it was unclear whether Wu had sexual intercourse with the victim against her will, or Wu simply took advantage of the victim's mental immaturity, which made resistance against forced sexual intercourse impossible. Therefore, the Supreme Court reversed the original judgment and remanded the case to the original court for a retrial.[8]

For many people, these verdicts were simply unacceptable. Within a very short period of time, those who were outraged by these rulings established the "Justice Alliance."[9] One of their main claims was that the finding of facts was unreasonable. In the Lin case, the court convicted the defendant of having sexual intercourse with a person under the age of fourteen, but not forcibly so, because there was no evidence showing such conduct against the victim's will. In the Wu case, the Supreme Court reversed the original judgment that convicted the defendant of forcibly having sexual intercourse with a person under the age of fourteen. The Supreme Court did so because the evidence was insufficient to prove that the defendant's conduct was against the victim's will. Neither the court in the Lin case nor that in the Wu case held that no evidence showed that the acts were committed against the victims' will. Amidst these rulings, several questions emerged: Why did the courts consider that the defendants' acts were forced upon the victims? How could those victims not be forced to have sexual intercourse? Why did the courts require evidence to show involuntariness? Especially considering the fact that those victims were merely six and three years old, they were too young to realize the meaning of sexual intercourse and had no ability to show or not show consent for such conduct. Moreover, they were mentally vulnerable and unable to explicitly show involuntariness.[10] Therefore, it should be noted that having sexual intercourse with children should be considered an act

6 99 Su-Zi No. 422 (Kaohsiung District Court, 2010).

7 97 Shang-Su-Zi No. 1008 (High Court of Kaohsiung, 2008).

8 99 Tai-Shang Zi No. 4894 (2010).

9 Zhou Mei-Hui, *Protest against*, United Daily News, 25 September 2010, A18.

10 Zhou Mei-Hui, *The Judgment was a Thorn on Hearts*, United Daily News, 4 September 2010, A3.

that is done against the victim's will; hence, the public prosecutor should not be required to prove that material element.[11]

On 25 September 2010, a demonstration by the so-called "White Rose Movement" was staged on Ketagalan Boulevard in front of the Presidential Palace. About 20,000 people from all over Taiwan joined the demonstration to call for judicial reform, the removal of incompetent judges, and better protection of children.[12]

Actually, the Wu and Lin cases were accurately ascertained by the judges according to the related provisions of the Criminal Code. Specifically, in order to convict a defendant of forcibly having sexual intercourse with a person under fourteen (Item 2, Sec. 2, Article 222), the public prosecutor has to prove that the conduct was against the will of the victim. A defendant may only be convicted of having sexual intercourse with a person under the age of fourteen (Sec. 2, Article 227), rather than forcibly having sexual intercourse with a person under fourteen (Item 2, Sec. 2, Article 222), if there is no evidence showing involuntariness on the part of the victim. In the Lin case, the victim was six years old and might have no knowledge about sexual activities at all. The court could not convict the defendant of forcibly having sexual intercourse with a person under the age of fourteen because no evidence showed that the defendant's conduct was against the victim's will. In the Wu case, the victim was three years old and might not have realized the meaning of sexual activities. According to the evidence provided by the public prosecutor, the defendant either forcibly had sexual intercourse with the victim, or took advantage of the victim's mental immaturity, which made resistance against sexual intercourse impossible. The Supreme Court reversed the judgment and remanded the case because the public prosecutor did not provide sufficient evidence proving that the defendant's conduct was against the victim's will beyond a reasonable doubt. Therefore, those judgments were rendered in accordance with the material elements of related provisions.

The Resolution of the Supreme Court

As a result of mounting public pressure resulting from the Lin and Wu cases, the Supreme Court made very significant interpretations of the aforementioned provisions. On 7 September 2010, the 7th resolution by the Criminal Divisions Conference of the Supreme Court was delivered. The following points were included in this landmark resolution:

---

11 Wang Wen-Ling, *People in Rage*, United Daily News, 2 September 2010, A10.

12 Zhou Mei-Hui & Li Ming-Xian, *Oppose Judges, Protection of Children, Ma Heard the Appeals of White Rose*, United Daily News, 26 September 2010, A1.

a. A person shall be convicted of having sexual intercourse with another person under the age of fourteen (Sec. 1, Article 227) if the latter is over the age of seven but under the age of fourteen.
b. A person shall be convicted of forcibly having sexual intercourse with another person (Item 2, Sec. 1, Article 222) if such person is under the age of seven.
c. A person shall be convicted of forcibly having sexual intercourse with another person (Item 2, Sec. 1, Article 222) if the latter is over the age of seven but under the age of fourteen, and the act is against his/her will.
   In other words, an offender shall be convicted of forcibly having sexual intercourse with another person if the latter is under the age of seven, regardless of whether the act committed is against the will of the victim. That resolution was obviously made in response to the demands of those behind the Justice Alliance and the White Rose Movement as well as to pacify other organizations that expressed dissatisfaction regarding the rulings on the Wu and Lin cases.[13] However, despite this noble act, the Supreme Court committed a violation of the legality doctrine (Nulla poena sine lege).[14] The Criminal Code provides that a conduct is punishable only when expressly so provided by the law at the time of its commission (Article 1). In both cases, being against the will of the victim is a material element of forcibly having sexual intercourse with a person under the age of fourteen (Item 2, Sec. 1, Article 222). That resolution, however, did not consider whether an offender's conduct is against the victim's will, thereby viewing all people having sexual intercourse with females/males as committing acts against the victims' will.
d. Opportunity to decriminalize certain offences
   Offences related to narcotics and abortion are good examples to be considered when discussing the decriminalization of certain offences. The decriminalization of narcotic use resulted from the realization of that conduct, whereas policy-based tolerance mainly resulted from the prevailing societal culture and atmosphere.

c. *Offences related to narcotics*

According to the data provided by the Ministry of Justice, offences related to narcotics comprised the second most common crimes in Taiwan for a long time. The offenders usually violate provisions of the Narcotics Hazard Prevention Act

13 Wang Cai-Li, *Gathering on Ketagalan Boulevard Tomorrow Evening*, United Evening News, 24 September 2010, A8. Those organizations included The Garden of Hope Foundation, Modern Woman's Foundation, and Jing-Chuan Child Safety Foundation. They are all non-governmental organizations dedicating themselves to the improvement of benefit of children and women.

14 Lin Dong-mao, Criminal Law 2-75 (2012); Chen Zi-ping, 1 Criminal Law: Kinds of Offenses 227-28 (2015).

(NHPA). The rising number of drug-related offenders have brought heavy pressure upon Taiwan's criminal justice system, including the police, prosecutors, courts, and prisons. Officers in the system have to spend most of their resources, time, and energy on handling drug-related cases. Meanwhile, an increasing number of studies have shown that people who use drug, narcotics, or other controlled substances need therapy, rather than criminal punishment. In other words, to prevent the use of narcotics, therapy may be considered a more effective solution than punitive measures.

In the past, the legislature considered instances of drug use as regular crimes and punished the offenders with regular criminal penalties. The history of the decriminalization of drug use in Taiwan may be traced back to the use of opium. Opium was once imported at large numbers into Taiwan, even resulting in two opium wars with Great Britain in 1840 and 1856. In addition, Taiwanese society has also acknowledged the problems and crimes caused by drug use. As mentioned above, however, heavy and strict punishments could not solve the drug problem nor reduce the number of drug users.

However, when the NHPA was enacted in 1998, it changed the public's basic attitude towards drug users for that Act declared drug users as "patient–criminals." Hence, although the use of Category 1 or 2 drugs still constituted a crime according to the NHPA, rather than criminal punishment, observation, rehabilitation, and addiction treatment were imposed (Article 20, 1998).[15] The Constitutional Court's decision also explained that, under the NHPA, the actions of first-time narcotics users and second-time offenders abstaining from drug use after rehabilitation still constituted crimes, although their sentences may be revoked.[16]

In 2003, the NHPA was revised, and the periods of observation and rehabilitation were extended. In addition, an offender should be released immediately if he or she underwent observation and rehabilitation and showed no signs of continuing narcotics use (Article 20, 2003). In addition, a non-prosecution order shall be delivered by the prosecutor (Article 23, 2003). The 2003 revision of the NHPA simplified the criminal process of narcotics use and built upon the policy of compulsory rehabilitation in rehabilitation centres. In other words, NHPA adopted less protective probation to narcotics use. The legislature also took the position that rehabilitation is more effective for addiction treatment than protective probation.

In 2008, the NHPA was revised again. Other than the non-prosecution option, the prosecutor may also order a rehabilitation treatment as a deferred prosecution pursuant to CCP (Article 24). After that revision, the NHPA adopted a two-track model: first, the prosecution is deferred to rehabilitation by the

15 The general explanatory note of the NHPA revision (2003.7.9).
16 Judicial Interpretation No. 544 (2002).

prosecutors, and second, the observation, rehabilitation, and compulsory treatment is imposed by the courts. In general, the NHPA continued to expand the decriminalization of narcotics use, treat those users as patients, rather than criminals, and recommend addiction treatments, rather than impose criminal penalty.

In 2009, the legislature decriminalized the using of Category 3 and 4 narcotics, such as ketamine and mephedrone. The use and possession of Category 3 or Category 4 narcotics of less than 20 grams no longer constitute a crime (Articles 11 and 11-1). That revision demonstrated that the NHPA officially recognized drug use and/or drug addiction as an illness rather than a crime. In fact, drug users were usually not responsive to criminal punishment and require addiction treatment instead.

The evolution of narcotics-related criminal justice is rather lengthy. At present, the NHPA employs non-criminal measures for narcotics users and decriminalizes some of them as a result of changes in the legislature and public perception, that is, drug use is an illness and not just a crime.

d. *Abortion*

The Criminal Code states that a pregnant woman who, by taking drugs, causes her abortion shall be sentenced to imprisonment for not more than six months, short-term imprisonment, or a fine of not more than one hundred yuan. A woman who permits another to cause her abortion shall be subject to the same punishment (Sec. 1 and 2, Article 288). Moreover, whether for personal gain or not, a person who commits abortion with the consent of a pregnant woman shall also be punished for said act (Sec. 1, Article 289, and Sec. 1, Article 290). The Criminal Code also punishes a person who publicly advertises a method or object to be used for abortion or someone who offers his or her service or that of another to perform an abortion (Article 292). From those proceeding provisions, it is apparent that abortion constitutes a crime. However, it is almost impossible for a woman to be arrested, prosecuted, or punished because she has had an abortion.[17]

First of all, the legislature enacted another statute that created a backdoor, through which a pregnant woman is allowed to have an abortion "legally." The Genetic Health Act (GHA) provides that induced abortion may be conducted for a pregnant woman, subject to her own accord, if she has been diagnosed or if it proven that pregnancy or childbirth is likely to affect her mental health or family life (Sec. 1, Article 9). Those elements of such a provision are extremely vague. After all, a pregnancy or childbirth always affects a woman's mental health or family life. Almost all pregnant women who caused their own abortion argued

17 Gan Tain-gui, 1 Criminal Law: Kinds of Offense 78 (San-ming 2009).

that pregnancy or childbirth resulted in some kind of impression on their mental health or family life. That provision, therefore, has turned into a justification for abortion. In fact, since the Criminal Code was enacted in 1928, there had been less than 50 cases involving a pregnant woman seeking an abortion (Sec. 1 and 2, Article 288), and less than 25 cases involving an abortion with a pregnant woman's consent or request whether for or not for gain (Sec. 1, Article 289, and Sec. 1, Article 290). Moreover, in practice, there has never been any case involving a public advertisement of a method or object that can be used for abortion and offering of services to conduct abortion (Article 292).

On the one hand, according to the Criminal Code, abortion is a crime, but on the other hand the legislature enacted the GHA to justify it, thus resulting in abortion-related acts being rarely punished. What is the reason for this? One important reason is that abortion is considered as something that is very personal. One person should not interfere with another person's decision with respect to abortion. The legislature, however, still feels morally obligated to protect foetuses. Thus, the Criminal Code has provisions to punish abortion-related actions. Ironically, the GHA also justifies all of them.

II.4. POSSIBILITY OF DECRIMINALIZATION

From the preceding discussion, it could be concluded that the less the likelihood that an offence can harm others or the whole society, the greater the chance for it to be decriminalized. Abortion is an appropriate example to explain this principle. Abortion is usually considered as a personal affair with a consequence that does not cause any harm to others. The legislature, therefore, enacted the GHA to *de facto* legalize a pregnant woman's abortion even though the Criminal Code still has provisions to punish such an act. Moreover, whether there is a victim involved whenever the crime of abortion is committed remains a debatable issue. As it is impossible for foetuses to argue for themselves, such offences as abortion are more likely to be decriminalized or at least tolerated based on a policy.

Another possibility, through which an offence can be "legalized," is the factual pressure placed over the criminal justice system. Narcotics use is legalized because the society has realized that it is an illness rather than a crime. Meanwhile, another reason to facilitate the deregulation of drug use is the excessive number of prisoners involved in drug-related cases, which is more than the capacity of Taiwan's prison facilities. Overcrowded prisons have forced the government and the legislature to face the reality of drug use.

II.5. THE PRACTICAL METHOD OF DECRIMINALIZATION

Based on previous experience, the practical and realistic course of action, through which to decriminalize certain actions, is to make appeals to the legislature or the executive organizations. The revision of statutes and modification of policies are mainly made by the legislature and the government. However, many changes in criminal policies are initiated by the society and motivated by non-governmental organizations, which are typically more aggressive than the government. After the negotiation, discussion, and compromise between those two parties, a solution that is acceptable to both can be achieved. That solution could not only decriminalize certain offences but also provide the society with effective protection.

III. OVERUSE OF PROSECUTION

III.1. PROSECUTED CRIMES PER YEAR

In 2014, 192,915 cases were prosecuted, which included 219,121 defendants.[18] From 2002 to 2014, 164,993 cases and 192,975.62 defendants were prosecuted per year, on average.[19] These statistical data are further presented in Table 3.

III.2. THE TOP FIVE OFFENCES

From 2002 to 2014, the top five crimes sent to the district prosecutors' offices were all the same, but in different orders; see Table 4. In 2014, 108,422 defendants committing offences against public safety, the most common crime to have occurred that year (20.87%), were sent to the district prosecutors' office. The second most common crime comprised offences related to narcotics (65,724 defendants, 12.65%), followed by injury (63,027 defendants, 12.13%), fraud (58,365 defendants, 11.24%), and larceny (46,131 defendants, 8.89%). From 2002 to 2014, on average, the most common crime brought to the district prosecutors'

18 Ministry of Justice, *2014 Justice Annual Statistical Report Chart 3-4*, 2015 (at: http://www.rjsd.moj.gov.tw/rjsdweb/book/Book_File.ashx?chapter_id=122_23_1) (last visited: 7 March 2016).

19 Ministry of Justice, *2014 Justice Annual Statistical Report Chart 3-4*, 2015 (at: http://www.rjsd.moj.gov.tw/rjsdweb/book/Book_File.ashx?chapter_id=122_23_1) (last visited: 7 March 2016); Ministry of Justice, *2013 Justice Annual Statistical Report Chart 3-4*, 2014 (at: http://www.rjsd.moj.gov.tw/rjsdweb/book/Book_File.ashx?chapter_id=66_23_1) (last visited: 7 March 2016); Ministry of Justice, *2012 Justice Annual Statistical Report Chart 3-4*, 2013 (at: http://www.rjsd.moj.gov.tw/rjsdweb/book/Book_File.ashx?chapter_id=31_23_1) (last visited: 7 March 2016).

Table 3. Prosecuted crimes per year

Year	Cases	Defendants
2002	125,289	153,003
2003	113,004	136,258
2004	118,851	139,454
2005	134,624	158,817
2006	158,889	189,943
2007	188,422	221,486
2008	199,374	231,813
2009	187,179	216,540
2010	187,424	218,443
2011	182,051	211,783
2012	176,379	203,760
2013	180,508	208,262
2014	192,915	219,121
Average	164,993	192,976

office comprised offences related to narcotics (74,086 defendants, 15.74%), followed by offences against public safety (66,476 defendants, 14.13%), fraud (63,999 defendants, 13.6%), injury (50,918 defendants, 10.82%), and larceny (48,995 defendants, 10.41%). Further statistical data are shown below.

III.3. THE LEGALITY PRINCIPLE

The R.O.C. Code of Criminal Procedure was enacted in 1935, serving as the foundation of the basic structure of the current CCP.[20] The R.O.C. Code of Criminal Procedure of 1935 was revised in 1967 and was renamed "The Code of Criminal Procedure." The legislature followed the fundamental concept of the inquisitorial system, revising the Code of Criminal Procedure of 1967. In 1997, Taiwan began to change its criminal justice system and revised hundreds of provisions included in the CCP. The most significant change is the abandonment of the inquisitorial system and the adoption of the adversarial one. Many inquisitorial provisions are still left in the CCP, because the basic structure has yet to be revised. The legality principle applied to prosecution is one such provision.[21]

20 Yuan-Sheng Huang, 'A Study of the Chinese Supreme Court's Criminal Procedure Decisions During the Period of 1912–1914', 61 *NCCU Law Review* 36 (1999), p. 47–48.

21 Wang Jaw-perng et. al, 1 Criminal Procedure 595–96 (2015).

Table 4. Top 5 offences

	Top 1	Top 2	Top 3	Top 4	Top 5
2002	57,254 (15.31%) Offences related to narcotics	46,141 (12.34%) Larceny	40,384 (10.8%) Offences against public safety	39,487 (10.56%) Injury	34,139 (9.13%) Fraud
2003	55,748 (15.68%) Offences related to narcotics	43,897 (12.35%) Larceny	37,038 (10.42%) Injury	36,073 (10.15%) Offences against public safety	34,070 (9.58%) Fraud
2004	70,331 (18.4%) Offences related to narcotics	46,045 (12.05%) Larceny	43,048 (11.26%) Fraud	42,082 (11.01%) Offences against public safety	33,644 (8.8%) Injury
2005	87,659 (20.38%) Offences related to narcotics	52,024 (12.09%) Larceny	46,634 (10.84%) Offences against public safety	45,360 (10.54%) Fraud	37,173 (8.64%) Injury
2006	77,749 (16.25%) Offences related to narcotics	64,433 (13.47%) Fraud	53,229 (11.13%) Larceny	52,977 (11.07%) Offences against public safety	43,390 (9.07%) Injury
2007	87,992 (17.16%) Offences related to narcotics	82,028 (16%) Fraud	63,790 (12.44%) Offences against public safety	53,488 (10.43%) Larceny	41,944 (8.18%) Injury
2008	90,688 (17.47%) Fraud	84,943 (16.36%) Offences related to narcotics	66,243 (12.76%) Offences against public safety	57,301 (11.04%) Larceny	43,860 (8.45%) Injury
2009	105,120 (20.22%) Fraud	74,046 (14.24%) Offences related to narcotics	72,933 (14.03%) Offences against public safety	48,590 (9.34%) Injury	Larceny (9.03%) 46,973
2010	86,274 (16.39%) Injury	79,785 (15.16%) Offences related to narcotics	77,024 (14.63%) Offences against public safety	53,707 (10.2%) Fraud	50,621 (9.62%) Larceny
2011	84,583 (17.08%) Offences against public safety	77,672 (15.38%) Offences related to narcotics	60,496 (11.98%) Fraud	58,696 (11.62%) Injury	49,149 (9.73%) Larceny
2012	81,635 (16.62%) Offences against public safety	73,775 (14.84%) Offences related to narcotics	61,490 (12.37%) Injury	60,447 (12.16%) Fraud	46,398 (9.33%) Larceny
2013	91,408 (18.35%) Offences against public safety	70,438 (14.14%) Offences related to narcotics	61,325 (12.31%) Injury	55,086 (11.06%) Fraud	45,540 (9.14%) Larceny

	Top 1	Top 2	Top 3	Top 4	Top 5
2014	108,422 (20.87%) Offences against public safety	65,724 (12.65%) Offences related to narcotics	63,027 (12.13%) Injury	58,365 (11.24%) Fraud	46,131 (8.89%) Larceny
average	74,086 (15.74%) Offences related to narcotics	66,476 (14.13%) Offences against public safety	63,999 (13.6%) Fraud	50,918 (10.82%) Injury	48,995 (10.41%) Larceny

With respect to the prosecution, the CCP provides that if the evidence obtained by a public prosecutor in the course of an investigation is sufficient to show that an accused is suspected of having committed an offence, the prosecutor shall initiate a prosecution.[22] Accordingly, the prosecutor has no discretion to decide whether to prosecute or not if the obtained evidence is sufficient. In order to prosecute criminals and protect innocence, it has been argued that prosecution is governed by the legality principle. That principle, moreover, also prevents the government from interference with individual cases.[23]

Despite the fact that the prosecution is governed by the legality principle, the CCP still has several provisions that allow prosecutors not to prosecute certain cases. The scope, however, is very little and severely limited. To date, three categories of non-prosecution cases exist.

The first category of non-prosecution cases does not provide prosecutors with any discretion not to prosecute a case if the obtained evidence is sufficient. The CCP provides that a ruling not to prosecute shall be made if one of the following circumstances exists:

(1) a final judgment has been rendered;
(2) the period of statute of limitation has already expired;
(3) there has already been an amnesty;
(4) a law enacted after the commission of an offence abolishes the punishment;
(5) the complaint or request in offences chargeable only upon complaint or request has been withdrawn or the time within which a complaint may be filed has expired;
(6) the accused is dead;
(7) the court has no judicial power over the accused;
(8) the act is not punishable;
(9) the punishment is remitted under law; and
(10) the suspicion of an offence having been committed is insufficient.

22 Sec. 1, Article 251 of the CCP.

23 Lin Yu-xiong, Prosecutors 17–18 (1999).

The CCP requires a prosecutor not to prosecute a case if one of the aforementioned circumstances exists, since a court will render a judgment of not-guilty if any of those circumstances is applicable.[24] That provision, therefore, does not authorize prosecutors not to prosecute any case; it merely permits prosecutors not to prosecute certain cases when a guilty judgment cannot be rendered.

The second category of non-prosecution cases are misdemeanours. The CCP provides that a prosecutor may make a ruling not to prosecute if the offence is a misdemeanour specified in Article 376 of the CCP, and the prosecutor considers it appropriate after having considered the factors stated in Article 57 of the Criminal Code[25], although that provision applies to misdemeanours only. However, the scope of such a provision is rather limited; it does not offer prosecutors a wide discretion not to prosecute.

The third category is that the prosecution will not affect the execution of a sentence. The CCP states that a prosecutor may make a ruling not to prosecute if a defendant commits several offences for one of which a final judgment of a more severe sentence has been received, and the prosecutor considers that the prosecution for another offence will not substantially affect the execution of the sentence. The application of that provision is not limited by crimes. In other words, a prosecutor could make a ruling not to prosecute a suspect committing a misdemeanour or felony under that provision. However, the application of this category of non-prosecution requires that the defendant must have committed several offences, a final judgment of a more severe sentence has been made to one of them, and prosecution for another offence will not affect the execution of the sentence. That provision, therefore, is limited to a very narrow scope, and prosecutors do not have wide discretion not to prosecute.

III.4. ALTERNATIVES TO PROSECUTION

a. *Deferred prosecution*

Other than prosecution and non-prosecution, a prosecutor may decide to make a ruling of deferred prosecution. Deferred prosecution may apply to more cases than non-prosecution does. Thus, deferred prosecution eases the problem caused by the legality principle applying to the prosecution.

The CCP states that a prosecutor may provide a ruling of deferred prosecution if the defendant has committed an offence other than those punishable with death penalty, life imprisonment, or with a minimum punishment of imprisonment for not less than three years; in such cases, the

24 Articles 300, 301, 302 and 303 of the CPP.
25 Article 253 of the CCP.

public prosecutor, after considering the matters specified in Article 57 of the Criminal Code and the maintenance and protection of public interest, deems that a deferred prosecution is appropriate. Hence, the prosecutor shall set up a period for the deferred prosecution not more than three years and not less than one year.[26]

In making a ruling on deferred prosecution, a public prosecutor may require the defendant to comply with or perform certain items within a limited period of time, such as apologize to the victim, make a written statement of repentance; pay to the victim an appropriate sum as compensation for property or non-property damages; pay a certain sum to a governmental account or a designated non-profit or local self-governing organization; perform 40- to 240-hour community services to a designated non-profit, local self-governing organization, or community; complete drug addiction treatment, psychotherapy and counselling, or other appropriate treatments; comply with the necessary order for the protection of the victim's safety; and comply with the necessary order for the prevention of recommitting the offence.[27]

b. Summary procedure

The CCP has the "summary procedure," in which a defendant may plead guilty, the prosecutor may have an agreement with him or her, and he or she may consequently receive a more lenient judgment. The summary process is an alternate option for prosecutors not to initiate a regular prosecution.

The CCP states that a court of first instance may pronounce a sentence through a summary judgment without a common trial procedure upon the request of the prosecutor if the defendant's confession in the investigation process or other existing evidence is sufficient for such to determine a defendant's offence. The sentence pronounced through the summary procedure is limited to the suspension of a sentence; a sentence of limited imprisonment and detention, whose commutation to a fine may be ordered; or payment of a fine.[28] In other words, the summary procedure does not apply to crimes with minimum statutory penalty that cannot be suspended. Furthermore, the summary procedure applies to minor crimes only.

When a defendant confesses during an investigation process in cases to which a summary procedure is applicable, he or she may also express his or her willingness to the prosecutor the scope of sentence he or she would undertake. If the prosecutor consents, records shall be made, and the defendant's statement shall serve as the basis for requesting the court to pronounce a sentence or

26 Sec. 1, Article 253-1 of the CCP.
27 Sec. 1, Article 253-2 of the CCP.
28 Article 449 of the CCP.

suspension of a sentence.[29] Under the proceeding circumstance, the court generally pronounces a judgment within the scope of sentence or suspension of sentence requested by the prosecutor.[30] The summary process, accordingly, served as a bargaining process practiced before 2004. In that procedure, a prosecutor may file a motion for a summary judgment, rather than initiate prosecution when the defendant makes a confession during the investigation process.

c. *Bargaining process*

Another alternative procedure to prosecution is the bargaining process. Different from the summary procedure, the bargaining process applies to crimes except for those that are punishable by capital punishment, life imprisonment, a sentence of more than three years, or is adjudicated by the court of appeal as the court of first instance. Mainly, the bargaining process applies to a broader scope of cases compared with the summary procedure.

According to the CCP, excluding crimes that are punishable by capital punishment, life imprisonment, a sentence of more than three years, or is adjudicated by the court of appeal as the court of first instance, once a case has been prosecuted by a prosecutor or applied for a summary judgment, the prosecutor may, before closing his or her oral arguments in the court of first instance or before the summary judgment and after consulting with the victim, act on his or her own discretion or, upon the requests of the defendant or his or her agent or attorney approved by the court, negotiate with the defendant outside the trial procedure. Once both parties involved reach an agreement and the defendant pleads guilty, the prosecutor may request the court to deliver its judgment pursuant to the bargaining process. The following items are included in the negotiation between the prosecution and the defendant:

1. The defendant accepts the scope of sentence or accepts the sentence to be placed under probation.
2. The defendant shall apologize to the victim.
3. The defendant shall pay a certain amount of compensation.
4. The defendant shall pay a certain amount to the government treasury, designated public interest organizations, or local autonomous organizations.[31]

29 Sec. 1, Article 451–1 of the CCP.
30 Sec. 4, Article 451-1 of the CCP.
31 Sec. 1, Article 455-2 of the CCP.

Except for circumstances under which the court may not pronounce a bargaining judgment[32], the court shall adjudicate the case within the scope of bargaining agreement without oral argument. The sentence pronounced by the court under a bargaining judgment is limited to a suspension of sentence, limited–under two years, detention, or payment of a fine.[33]

The bargaining process is an alternative option for the prosecution even though a prosecutor may request the court to make a bargaining judgment only after the cases have been prosecuted or applied for a summary judgment. In practice, most prosecutors and defendants who want the courts to render a bargaining judgment often reach an agreement during the investigation process. In this case, the prosecutor initiates prosecution and requests the court to prove the negotiation outside the trial procedure if the defendant pleads guilty in the investigation process.

III.5. POSSIBLE OFFENCES THAT CAN BE EXCLUDED FROM PROSECUTION

In practice, a prosecutor may choose alternatives to prosecution (non-prosecution, deferred prosecution, application of summary judgment, or request to make bargaining judgment) based on several reasons. First, a victim's consent plays a crucial role; it is an essential element of the case even though consent is not a material element of the alternatives to prosecution. A prosecutor is more willing to choose alternatives to prosecution when the defendant consents to compensate for the victim's damage, and both the victim and the defendant are able to reach an agreement. Actually, it is almost impossible for prosecutors not to prosecute a defendant if the victim does not give consent and the defendant does not reach an agreement with the victim. This is because the victim may file an application for reconsideration to the non-prosecution or deferred prosecution if it is made without the victim's consent.[34] In addition, a victim's consent also influences the courts' decision. Courts are more willing to accept the request for a summary judgment or bargaining process if the victim gives his or her consent.

Second, case loading may also affect a prosecutor's decision on whether to initiate prosecution. For instance, driving under the influence has been at least the fourth most prosecuted crime since the Criminal Code revised and criminalized this act in 1999. The amount of cases involving DUIs was so large and overwhelming that prosecutors were unable to handle other cases. Offices of

32 Where the bargaining was not made out of the defendant's free will, the bargaining agreement is obviously inappropriate or unfair, or the court deems proper to pronounce punishment remitted or case dismissed, the court may not render a bargaining judgment. *See* Sec. 1, Article 455-4 of the CCP.

33 Sec. 2, Article 455-4 of the CCP.

34 Article 256 of the CCP.

district prosecutors have thus implemented a policy wherein a ruling of deferred prosecution may be made if the defendant is a first-time offender and the offence causes no harm to another person.[35]

III.6. THE PRACTICAL STRATEGY TO DECREASE THE NUMBER OF PROSECUTED CASES

In order to decrease the number of prosecutions, the most effective method is to adopt the expedience principle in prosecution, which provides prosecutors the discretion to decide whether cases should be prosecuted or not. The expedience ensures not only the appropriate treatment for each individual case, but also the proper distribution of the very limited resources of law enforcement agencies. However, because of the tradition of the inquisitorial system, the adoption of the expedience principle is extremely difficult, if not impossible. Thus, the expansion of the scope of non-prosecution and deferred prosecution is a more practical option. Non-prosecution and deferred prosecution should be applied to more minor offences. In addition, even though victims' opinions are important, prosecutors should have greater discretion to decide whether or not to make a ruling of non-prosecution or deferred prosecution. At present, victims' opinions have a *de facto* binding effect on the prosecutors. A prosecutor does not have a choice not to prosecute an offender even though the prosecutor knows that the case complies with the requirements of non-prosecution or deferred prosecution and that the offender involved should not be prosecuted.

IV. OVERUSE OF IMPRISONMENT

IV.1. CRIMINALS IN PRISON FACILITIES

As Table 5 shows, in 2014, various prison sentences were imposed upon 112,706 defendants.[36] Those prisoners exceeded the capacity of all prison facilities by 16.2%.[37] From 2002 to 2014, 108,614.23 defendants served sentences in prisons

35 *See* Mou Pei-yu, *The Standard for Non-prosecution to DUI Raised*, United Daily News, 11 July 2013, B1.

36 Ministry of Justice, *2014 Justice Annual Statistical Report Chart 4-3*, 2015 (at: http://www.rjsd.moj.gov.tw/RJSDWEB/book/Book_File.ashx?chapter_id=122_48_1) (last visited: 7 March 2016).

37 Ministry of Justice, *2014 Justice Annual Statistical Report Chart 4-1*, 2015 (at: http://www.rjsd.moj.gov.tw/RJSDWEB/book/Book_File.ashx?chapter_id=122_45_1) (last visited: 9 March 2016).

per year, on average.[38] During that period, prisons suffered from overcrowding. On average, the percentage of excess was 14.37%.[39] From these data, it can be assumed that overcrowding in prison facilities have been a serious problem in the criminal justice system for a very long time. The proceeding statistical information further explains this phenomenon.

Table 5. Criminals in prison

	Prisoner	Percentage of excess
2002	85,621	6.8%
2003	85,495	9.9%
2004	94,672	8.7%
2005	102,384	15.1
2006	113,738	18.6
2007	109,940	1.2
2008	118,567	15.1
2009	122,008	17.0
2010	119,327	19.6
2011	116,957	18.8
2012	115,553	21.1
2013	115,017	18.7
2014	112,706	16.2
Average	108,614	14.37

38 Ministry of Justice, *2014 Justice Annual Statistical Report Chart 4-3*, 2015 (at: http://www.rjsd.moj.gov.tw/RJSDWEB/book/Book_File.ashx?chapter_id=122_48_1) (last visited: 7 March 2016); *Ministry of Justice, 2013 Justice Annual Statistical Report Chart 4-3*, 2014 (at: www.rjsd.moj.gov.tw/RJSDWEB/book/Book_File.ashx?chapter_id=66_48_1) (last visited: 7 March 2016); Ministry of Justice, *2012 Justice Annual Statistical Report Chart 4-2*, 2013 (at: www.rjsd.moj.gov.tw/RJSDWEB/book/Book_File.ashx?chapter_id=31_45_1) (last visited: 7 March 2016).

39 Ministry of Justice, *2014 Justice Annual Statistical Report Chart 4-1*, 2015 (at: www.rjsd.moj.gov.tw/RJSDWEB/book/Book_File.ashx?chapter_id=122_45_1) (last visited: 9 March 2016); Ministry of Justice, *2013 Justice Annual Statistical Report Chart 4-1*, 2014 (at: www.rjsd.moj.gov.tw/RJSDWEB/book/Book_File.ashx?chapter_id=66_45_1) (last visited: 9 March 2016); Ministry of Justice, *2012 Justice Annual Statistical Report Chart 4-1*, 2013 (at: www.rjsd.moj.gov.tw/RJSDWEB/book/Book_File.ashx?chapter_id=31_44_1) (last visited: 9 March 2016).

IV.2. TOP 10 CRIMES

From 2010 to 2014, most prisoners were convicted for offences involving narcotics. Second were those sentenced because of larceny. These top two numbers remained constant, but the 3rd to 10th positions varied every year.[40] The top 10 offences committed by prisoners, the number of prisoners annually, and the corresponding percentages are provided in Table 6.

Among all these prisoners, the author personally holds those who committed homicide to have the highest degree of responsibility for their imprisonment. They are closely followed by those who committed sexual offences, injury, robbery, and those who committed offences related to the Controlling Guns, Ammunition, and Knives Act. The basic idea is that the greater the degree of harm caused by an offence to another person, the greater the responsibility of the offenders to undergo imprisonment.

IV.3. THE IMPOSITION OF PRISON SENTENCES

In the Criminal Code, each offence has its own minimum sentence. Punishments for several offences committed before a judgment is finalized shall be combined.[41] In combining punishments for several offences, the punishment for each offence shall be pronounced separately, and the execution of a period shall be fixed at not less than the longest period of these punishments and not more than the sum of the periods of these punishments, but shall not exceed thirty years.[42] However, no matter how heavy the sentence is, a court still has the ability to reduce the sentence. The Criminal Code states that a punishment may be reduced at discretion if the circumstances of the commission of the offence are so pitiable that even the minimum punishment is considered too severe.[43]

Apart from the reduction of sentences by the court, it may also suspend the sentence rather than impose a prison sentence upon the defendant. The probation system only applies to minor crimes. The Criminal Code provides that a punishment of imprisonment for not more than two years, short-term imprisonment, or payment of a fine may be suspended for not less than two years but not more than five years if the following conditions are met: (a) probation is considered appropriate and (b) no previous sentence to imprisonment has been imposed for an intentional offence, or no sentence to imprisonment for an intentional offence has been imposed pronounced within five years after

40 Ministry of Justice, *2014 Justice Annual Statistical Report Chart 4-15*, 2015 (at: www.rjsd.moj.gov.tw/RJSDWEB/book/Book_File.ashx?chapter_id=122_60_1) (last visited: 9 March 2016).

41 Article 50 of the Criminal Code.

42 Item 5, Article 51 of the Criminal Code.

43 Article 59 of the Criminal Code.

Table 6. Top 10 crimes in prisons

	2010			2011			2012			2013			2014		
	Rank	Amount	Percentage	Rank	Amount	Percentage	Rank	Amount	Percentage	Rank	Amount	Percentage	Rank	Amount	Percentage
Narcotics-related offences	1	24,480	42.9	1	25,257	43.9	1	26,326	44.9	1	26,779	45.7	1	26,683	46.3
Larceny	2	5,613	9.8	2	5,757	10.0	2	5,461	9.3	2	5,144	8.8	2	4,821	8.4
Offences against public safety	8	1,880	3.3	7	2,074	3.6	7	2,693	4.6	5	3,523	6.0	3	4,585	8
Robbery	3	5,544	9.7	3	5,178	9.0	3	4,867	8.3	3	4,572	7.8	4	4,166	7.2
Sexual offences	6	2,624	4.6	5	2,946	5.1	4	3,401	5.8	4	3,709	6.3	5	3,726	6.5
Homicide	5	2,895	5.1	6	2,825	4.9	6	2,721	4.6	7	2,611	4.5	6	2,514	4.4
Offences related to the Controlling Guns, Ammunition, and Knives Act	4	3,277	5.7	4	3,087	5.4	5	2,952	5.0	6	2,655	4.5	7	2,395	4.2
Fraud	7	1,976	3.5	8	1,701	3.0	8	1,648	2.8	8	1,524	2.6	8	1,467	2.5
Injury	9	1,264	2.2	9	1,207	2.1	9	1,246	2.1	9	1,267	2.2	9	1,130	2
Forgery	10	940	1.6	10	998	1.7	10	1,037	1.8	10	974	1.7	10	921	1.6

completing execution or remission of a previous sentence to imprisonment for an intentional offence.[44]

IV.4. ALTERNATIVES TO IMPRISONMENT

Two main alternatives to imprisonment exist within Taiwan's criminal justice system: commutation to a fine and commutation to community service. The Criminal Code provides that, in an offence that carries a maximum principal punishment of not more than five years of imprisonment, if the offender is sentenced to imprisonment for not more than six months or amounting to a short-term imprisonment, the punishment may be commuted to a fine. Commutation to a fine, however, does not apply to those cases in which the commutation is manifestly of little corrective effect, or the legal order cannot be maintained.[45]

If an offender is pronounced to be imprisoned for less than six months and the commutation to a fine is not applicable, the court may commute the imprisonment to community service.[46] Therefore, similar to the commutation to a fine, commutation to community service also applies to minor crimes only.

IV.5. POSSIBLE OFFENCES FOR WHICH NON-CUSTODIAL SENTENCES CAN BE IMPOSED

Based on a very practical reason, offences related to narcotics would be the best possible cases of crimes for which non-custodial sentences or lower sentences can be imposed. From the last revisions of the NHPA, it could be concluded that the legislature's attitude towards the use of narcotics has been changed. The legislature has realized that narcotics users are more patient than criminals. Penalties cannot effectively stop them from using narcotics over and over again; rather, what they really need is effective treatment. Therefore, the NHPA has been revised for several times, such that the latter versions already decriminalize the use of certain narcotics and addiction treatments are adopted to replace criminal penalty for all related offences.

One practical reason is overcrowding in prison facilities. Right now, prisons are filled with offenders who have been sentenced to imprisonment for offences related to narcotics. The large number of narcotics-related prisoners has resulted in heavy pressure on correction institutes. Therefore, this practical reason could be an opportunity for the government to face the reality of drug users and employ more non-custodial measures to rectify their actions.

---

44 Sec. 1, Article 74 of the CCP.
45 Sec. 1, Article 41 of the CCP
46 Sec. 3, Article 41 of the CCP.

IV.6. REALISTIC METHOD TO DECREASE IMPRISONMENT

The Criminal Code sets up a minimum sentence to each crime. Parole, probation, commutation to a fine, and commutation to community service are all regulated by that Code. Though courts and the correction authorities are empowered to decrease imprisonment in some cases, this power is rather narrow and limited. The extension of reduction of imprisonment is mainly governed by statutes. Therefore, in order to decrease imprisonment and solve problems resulting from the imposition of over-strict penalties, the more practical method would be the revision of related statutes. The legislative body is also an ideal place, in which to balance the necessary protection of society and the imposition of the proper criminal penalty.

V. CONCLUSION

Currently, the criminal justice system in Taiwan is overused, as too many actions are criminalized and penalized. The legislature and courts are under rising pressure from Taiwan society to impose heavier penalties for certain offences or to criminalize certain actions. Nevertheless, the legislature may have been aware of that problem, still enacting or revising statutes to ease it. According to the statistical data, a high percentage of criminals were prosecuted. This results from the legality principle. The CCP has the option to go for non-prosecution or deferred prosecution. Prosecutors, however, have little discretion. A prosecutor shall initiate prosecution if the evidence is sufficient to prove the defendant guilty. As to the summary procedure and bargaining process, they apply to minor crimes only. Prosecutors are so burdened that they may not have sufficient resources and time to handle felonious cases. Even though the adoption of the expedience principle may fundamentally solve that problem, the practical method to decrease the number of prosecution is still to expand the application of alternatives to prosecution.

Overcrowded prisons have become a serious issue in Taiwan. Courts have the discretion to reduce sentences and suspend sentences for minor crimes, whereas the Criminal Code allows the commutation of sentences to a fine or community service. Those alternatives to imprisonment apply to minor crimes only. Therefore, statistical data show that overuse of imprisonment has been a problem for a long time. The realistic course of action to solve this problem is to revise statutes because alternatives to imprisonment and the deduction of imprisonment are regulated by the legislature.

Even though Taiwan suffers from the overuse of its criminal justice system, there are indicators that the legislature has been aware of that problem. Several statutes have been revised and enacted because the legislature already identified where the problem lies along with the nature of certain actions, such as narcotics use. Therefore, it can convincingly be concluded that Taiwan is on the right track to solve problems resulting from the overuse of the criminal justice.

OVERUSE AND UNDERUSE OF THE UNITED STATES CRIMINAL JUSTICE SYSTEM IN THE AREA OF BUSINESS CRIMES

Edgardo Rotman*

I. INTRODUCTION

The United States criminal justice system is plagued with instances of both overuse and underuse. The concept of "overuse" includes overcriminalization through excessive and overbroad criminal statutes and regulations, as well as staggering imprisonment rates.[1] "Underuse" is usually exemplified by underenforcement of violent street crimes, particularly in deprived urban neighborhoods.[2] In the area of business crimes, also called "white-collar crimes" since the pioneer studies of Edwin Sutherland[3], both overuse and underuse acquire different dimensions and specific characteristics. In general terms,

* Senior Lecturer in International and Comparative Law, *Emeritus*, University of Miami School of Law.

I thank Professor Elliott Manning for providing valuable information.

1 According to Douglas Husak, in *Overcriminalization*, New York: Oxford University Press, 2004, p. 3 "the most important characteristics of both federal and state systems of criminal justice in the United States during the past several years are the dramatic expansion in the substantive criminal law and the extraordinary rise in the use of punishment." Moreover, a considerable amount of this overcriminalization is unjust because it is "inflicted for conduct that should not have been criminalized at all."

2 Alexandra Natapoff, 'Underenforcement', 75 *Fordham Law Review* 3 (December 2006), p. 1715.

3 Edwin Sutherland coined the phrase in 'White-Collar Criminality', 5 *American Sociological Review*, (February 1940). He defined white-collar crime as "a crime committed by a person of respectability and high social status in the course of his occupation" in *White-Collar Crime: The Uncut Version*, New Haven: Yale University Press, 1983, p. 7. This first definition was followed by many others (*see* Stuart Green, 'The Concept of White Collar Crime in Law and Legal Theory', 8 *Buffalo Criminal Law Review* 101 (2004), p. 104. White-Collar crimes are also called indistinctly business, economic, or financial crimes.

overuse is characterized by an excessive number of criminal provisions often lacking definitional clarity and sufficient *mens rea* requirements. Paradoxically, this type of overuse of the criminal justice system coexists with a historical trend towards underusing criminal justice regarding white-collar offenders by overlooking their actions or benefitting them with privileged treatment. While these phenomena of overuse and underuse coexist, the prevalence of one or the other is cyclical. This paper will explain both overuse and underuse in the field of business crimes, as well as the cycles of prevalence of one or the other in recent times. Overuse will be dealt specifically under the label of overcriminalization of business crimes and underuse will be addressed as underenforcement of criminal justice towards white-collar offenders based on preferential treatment.

II. OVERCRIMINALIZATION OF BUSINESS CRIMES

According to Todd Haugh, the proliferation of criminal provisions has occurred more frequently in the area of corporate and white-collar crime than in other fields. He underscores that white-collar crime generated the biggest expansion of federal law during the 1970s and 1980s, followed by a new phase of overcriminalization at the beginning of the twenty-first century with the enactment of the Sarbanes-Oxley Act.[4] Overcriminalization takes the form of thousands of criminal statutes and regulations scattered throughout the federal code and thousands of regulations in the area of business-related criminal law.[5] There is a panoply of criminal pitfalls, particularly in the area of international business transactions.[6]

Besides this quantitative form of overcriminalization, even more problematic is the overcriminalization in the qualitative sense, which consists of enacting criminal offenses too broad in scope, poorly defined, and overlapping.[7] Stephen F. Smith considers that the real problem with overcriminalization is qualitative and not quantitative and that the courts have worsened the situation by interpreting

4 Todd Haugh, 'Overcriminalization's New Harm Paradigm', 68 *Vanderbuilt Law Review* (2015), p. 1206.

5 Ellen S. Podgor, 'Laws Have Overcriminalized Business Behavior', The New York Times, 10 November 2013, (at www.nytimes.com/roomfordebate/2013/11/10/prosecuting-executives-not-companies-for-wall-street-crime/laws-have-overcriminalized-business-behavior) (last visited: 30 July 2016).

6 William M. Hannay, 'Introduction', in: William M. Hannay (ed.), *International Trade: Avoiding Criminal Risks*, New Hampshire: Butterworth Legal Publishers, 1991, p. xxi: Bruce Zagarias, 'Avoiding Criminal Liability in the Conduct of International Business', 21 *William Mitchell Law Review* (1996), p. 749- 838.

7 Stephen F. Smith, 'Overcoming Overcriminalization', 102 *Journal of Criminal Law and Criminology* 3 (2012), p. 540.

criminal statutes too broadly.[8] In the particular field of securities fraud, scholars challenged broad judicial interpretations on constitutional grounds in the 1980s[9], but without any apparent consequences.

II.1. THE LACEY ACT AS A PARADIGM OF OVERCRIMINALIZATION

The Lacey Act constitutes a paradigmatic instance of overcriminalization in the American justice system. Iowa Congressman John Lacey introduced the Act in 1900 in the House of Representatives. At the time, the Act aimed at the preservation of game and wild birds by making it a federal crime to poach game in one state with the purpose of selling it in another. Because Lacey was very concerned about reversing a decline of the wild bird population caused by the action of bird poachers, he introduced to Congress a law by which the violation of state game law would trigger a violation of United States federal law. The Lacey Act was the first federal wildlife conservation statute, narrowly targeting the interstate sale of poached game. During the century since its enactment, the Lacey Act was amended several times, expanding its protection to amphibians, crustaceans, mollusks, and then to indigenous plants, fish, and other forms of wildlife. Since the original Lacey Act did not apply to fish, in 1926 Congress enacted the Black Bass Act, which prohibited the transportation of such fish when sold, purchased, or possessed in violation of state or territorial law, as well as those killed illegally. It contained fines and short-term prison sentences. The 1981 amendments updated the Lacey Act from its original purpose, combining the Black Bass Act with the Lacey Act into one statute that covered both wildlife and fish. Moreover, the Lacey Act was extended to indigenous plants enumerated on endangered species lists.[10] The 2008 amendments to the Act included wood and timber products.[11]

The main reasons why the Act is regarded today as the "poster child of overcriminalization"[12] is the inclusion of foreign laws as predicate laws that

8 *Id.*

9 Daniel J. Bacastow, 'Due Process and Criminal Penalties under Rule 10b-5: The Unconstitutionality and Inefficiency of Criminal Prosecutions for Insider Trading', 73 *Journal of Criminal Law and Criminology* 1 (Spring 1982), p. 96; Steven B. Duke, 'Legality in the Second Circuit', *Yale Law School Legal Scholarship Repository* (1983), p. 911.

10 C. Jarrett Dieterle, 'The Lacey Act: A Case Study in the Mechanics of Overcriminalization', 102 *The Georgetown Law Journal* (2014), p. 1290.

11 Mathew S. White, "Overcriminalization Based on Foreign Law: How the Lacey Act Incorporates Foreign Law to Overcriminalize Importers and Users of Timber Products," 12 *Washington University Global Studies Law Review* (2013), p. 386.

12 Isaac Gorodetski, "A Poster Child for Overcriminalization: The History of the Lacey Act", 10 April 2014 (at www.pointoflaw.com/archives/2014/04/a-poster-child-for-overcriminalization-the-history-of-the-lacey-act.php) (last visited: 27 August 2016).

would trigger a Lacey Act violation, the weakening of the *mens rea* requirements and the considerable increase in penalties. The amendments made in 1935 included the introduction in the United States' stream of commerce of game and other wildlife instances that happened to be in violation of the laws of foreign countries. This extension encompassed an unquantifiable number of foreign laws: with a single sentence in a single legislative act, Congress could "make it a crime to violate any and every law of every nation on earth."[13] The violation of foreign laws as a predicate for the violation of the Lacey Act made this law a trap for the unwary, especially after the weakening of the *mens rea* requirements in the 1981 amendments, lowered from "knowingly and willfully" to merely "knowingly". In addition, the 1981 amendments substantially increased the penalties. The maximum penalty for felonies was raised to $20,000 and/or five years imprisonment, while the penalties for misdemeanor violations were set at $10,000 and/or up to one-year of imprisonment.[14] Today due care violations result in forfeiture plus up to one year sentence and/or a fine of $100,000 for individuals and $200,000 for corporations. Knowing violations result in forfeiture and a five-year sentence and/or a fine of $250,000 for individuals and $500,000 for corporations.[15]

II.2. EXAMPLES FROM THE LACEY ACT

A prototypical case of overcriminalization in the context of the Lacey Act is *United States of America v. David Henson McNab, et al.*, 324 F.3d 1266 (11th Cir. 2003). The defendants were a Honduran citizen, David McNab, and three Americans, Abner Schoenwetter, Robert Blandford and Diane Huang. McNab operated a fleet of fishing vessels with which he was engaged in the business of fishing spiny tail lobsters off the coast of Honduras.

This case was initiated by an anonymous facsimile informing the National Marine Fisheries Service ("NMFS") that McNab's cargo transport vessel would arrive in Bayou La Batre, Alabama, with a shipment of lobsters containing undersized lobster tails in violation of Honduran law. In March of 1999, NMFS

13 Brian W. Walsh, 'Doing Violence to the Law: The Over-Federalization of Crime', cited by C. Jarrett Dieterle, 'The Lacey Act: A Case Study in the Mechanics of Overcriminalization', 102 *The Georgetown Law Journal* (2014), p. 1298.

14 Lacey Act Amendments of 1981 (P.L. 97-79, 95 Stat. 1073, 16 U.S.C. 3371-3378, approved November 16, 1981, and as amended by P.L. 100-653, 102 Stat.

15 16 U.S.C. § § 3373-74; *see also* USDA Animal and Plant Health Inspection Service Plant Protection and Quarantine, *Lacey Act Primer and Updates*, August 2013, p. 8 (at https://www.aphis.usda.gov/plant_health/lacey_act/downloads/LaceyActPrimer.pdf) (last visited August 27, 2016). The statutory provisions of 16 U.S.C. § 3373(d)(1) actually state that the fine should be no more than $ 20,000. However, under 18 U.S.C.§ 3571, which raises the maximum permissible fines for federal criminal offenses, the maximum fines for violations to the Lacey Act attain the figures reproduced in the text of this paper.

agents discovered that there were undersized lobster tails in the shipment and that the cargo was processed in bulk plastic bags rather than packed in boxes as required by Honduran law. In addition, the United States officials determined that the defendants had violated the prohibition of harvesting and destruction of lobster eggs. The United States officials seized the lobster shipment and in the next month its agents communicated with Honduran officials who confirmed that there was a 5.5-inch size limit for lobster tails and that all catches had to be reported to Honduran authorities. There were two resolutions establishing the size limit and the obligation to pack the lobster tails in boxes and a regulation prohibiting the harvesting and destruction of lobster eggs. The United States made repeated efforts to ascertain whether these Honduran laws were valid. Later, Honduran officials traveled to Alabama to meet with government prosecutors and investigators who provided written statements that the resolutions regulating the lobster fishing industry were valid, including the regulation that prohibited the harvesting of egg bearing lobsters. After hearing testimony from Honduran officials at a pre-trial hearing, the district court upheld the validity of the Honduran Laws upon which the Lacey Act was premised.[16] This holding was made despite strong expert witness evidence produced by the defense. Two law professors, both experts in Honduran law, and other Honduran officials demonstrated the invalidity of the law used in this case to support the Lacey Act violations.[17]

The language of the Lacey Act that informed the Court's decision is: "[I]t is unlawful for any person to 'import, export, transport, sell, receive, acquire, or purchase' any fish or wildlife 'taken, possessed, transported, or sold' in violation of a domestic or foreign law."[18] The Court found that the defendants were in violation of the Honduran resolutions and regulations encompassed by the phrase "any foreign law" in the Act.

The defendants contended that the Honduran laws that served as predicates for their convictions were invalid and never had the effect of law because they were promulgated improperly. The resolutions at play had been repealed in 1995, prior to the time period covered by the indictment and the provision that prohibits the harvesting and destruction of lobster eggs had been repealed retroactively in 2001.

At the time of the appeal, the Honduran government had changed its original position and maintained that the laws prohibiting the lobster shipments were either invalid or had been repealed retroactively. Moreover, the Honduran courts ruled that the laws, upon which the convictions of the defendants were based,

16 Ellen S. Podgor, 'A New Dimension to the Prosecution of White Collar Crime: Enforcing Extraterritorial Social Harms, 37 *McGeorge Law Review* 1 (2005), p. 8.

17 *Id.*

18 16 U.S.C. § 3372(a).

were null and void. However, the U.S. 11th Circuit Court of Appeals upheld the conviction in a 2-1 decision on the basis that the Honduran laws were valid at the time of the violations. David McNab was convicted and sentenced to eight years of imprisonment despite the fact that the Attorney General of Honduras declared that there was no violation of Honduran laws.[19] The indictment included conspiracy, money laundering, and smuggling, charges that could not have been brought without the Lacey Act violation.[20] The 11th Circuit Court of Appeals considered as a "matter of first impression" to "decide whether our courts are bound by a foreign government's new representations regarding the validity of its laws when its new representations are issued only post-conviction and directly contravene its original position upon which the government and our courts relied and the jury acted."[21] The majority of the Court reacted to what they called a shift in position of the Honduran government considering that "[t]here must be some finality with representations of foreign law by foreign governments."[22] The majority concluded that these foreign laws "were valid and legally binding during the time period covered by the indictment."[23] Judge Fay's dissenting opinion underscored that there was never "unanimity" or "agreement" on the validity of one of the resolutions, later challenged successfully by McNab in a Honduran court, where it was found "null and void."[24] Judge Fay pointed out that the Attorney General of Honduras and top government officials deemed this judgment retroactive and that it should not have been ignored just because its acknowledgment would have caused some frustration or inconvenience.

It is paradoxical that years later, under another statute, the fishing of undersized fish, red groupers in that case, became the fact pattern of a Supreme Court case signaling an important retreat from overcriminalization.[25]

Another example that contributed to the view that the Lacey Act is a "poster child of overcriminalization"[26] was the matter concerning the Gibson Guitar Corporation. In August 2011, this firm was raided by federal agents who seized a large number of guitars and valuable materials, causing Gibson an estimated loss of $2 to $3 million in lost products and productivity. The raid was based on warrants executed by the United States Fish and Wildlife Service to investigate suspicions that Gibson had illegally imported ebony and rosewood from India in violation of the Lacey Act.[27] The legal basis of the raid was that the Company had

---

19 Podgor, (note 17) at p. 3.

20 *Id.* at p. 5.

21 *United States v. McNab*, 331 F.3d 1228, 1232 n.2 (11th Cir. 2003).

22 Podgor (note 17) at p. 10.

23 *Id.*

24 *Id.* at p. 11.

25 *See* Section IV of this paper ("Retreats from Overcriminaliztion and Underenforcement: The Story of the Two Yates").

26 Gorodetski (note 13).

27 Dieterle, (note 11) at p. 1280.

violated Indian export laws regulating wood products. Although Gibson denied at all times that it had violated Indian laws in the exportation of wood, the Company settled the case in Summer 2012 in a deferred prosecution agreement in which the federal government declined to criminally prosecute Gibson.[28] The agreement contained a $300,000 penalty plus a $50,000 payment to the National Fish and Wildlife Foundations for educational programs. In addition, Gibson agreed to withdraw its claims to the wood seized during the criminal investigation and ended up spending $2.4 million in legal fees on top of the penalties. After the settlement, Gibson's CEO expressed that the Company felt compelled to settle considering the time-consuming and expensive nature of proving their case at trial.[29]

III. UNDERENFORCEMENT RESULTING FROM PREFERENTIAL TREATMENT OF WHITE-COLLAR OFFENDERS

The trend towards overcriminalization at the quantitative and qualitative levels coexists with a traditional tendency exempting corporate offenders from criminal punishment or giving them preferential treatment. Historically, business crimes were generally underestimated and received less punishment than the ones reserved for the crimes committed by the "dangerous classes,"[30] whether against persons or property. The motivation of business criminals is influenced by a society galvanized by the guiding idea of overriding economic progress.[31] In 1901, Laschi wrote that an "undefined feeling of complicity leads the public opinion to admire, approve, and absolve the great financial adventurers".[32] Similarly, Marc Ancel affirmed that public opinion "tolerates economic crimes and tends to admire the perpetrators. Even the victim seems to encourage and even provoke the offense."[33] Such responses are captured by the comment made by a fraudster to Lombroso: "the fever of the business world that pushes us to

---

28 *Id.* at p. 1285.

29 *Id.*

30 This expression was taken by sociologists and criminologists from Charles Loring Brace, *The Dangerous Classes of New York*, New York: Wynkoop & Hallenbeck, 1872.

31 Edgardo Rotman, 'La Criminalidad Financiera en el Siglo XIX', *Revista de Derecho Penal y Criminologia* (1969), p. 231.

32 Rodolfo Laschi, *Le crime financier dans la sociologie criminelle, l'histoire et le droit*, Paris : Masson & Cie, (1901), p. 107. In this respect, La Bruyère said: "if the financier fails, the nobleman says about him- he is a bourgeois, a nobody, a shameless person- but if he is successful, they ask him for the hand of his daughter," Jean de la Bruyère, *Les Caractères*, Paris: Garnier Frères, 1960, p. 160.

33 Marc Ancel, 'Preface', in: Enrique Aftalion, *Derecho Penal Economico*, Buenos Aires: Abeledo-Perrot, 1959, p. 11.

deceive, also pushes our victims to be deceived."[34] Robert K. Merton explains how the "reluctant admiration expressed frequently in private and not seldom publicly, of these 'shrewd, smart, and successful' men is a product of a cultural structure in which the sacrosanct goal virtually consecrates the means."[35]

In 1975, Michel Foucault viewed the criminal justice system as a mechanism devised not to eliminate crimes but to manage them in a socially differential way by emphasizing the crimes of the poor and concealing the illegalities of the powerful.[36] Delmas-Marty suggests that Foucault's vision was reinforced by economic and financial globalization, in which criminal risk "becomes part of the totality of business risks, morally tolerated and without bringing about the stigmatization that characterized common criminality".[37] In her view, the long-standing tolerance towards white-collar criminals is buttressed today by codes of conduct, peer evaluations, and other forms of self-regulation because these allow business-related misdeeds to remain contained within the bounds of the business community and resolved by its own players.[38]

Considering the absence of prosecutions against high-level officers after the 2008 subprime mortgage crisis, one of the justifications has been the fear of collateral damages. This fear was reinforced by the fresh memory that a mere indictment meant the death penalty for one of the five top accounting firms of the world. Arthur Andersen LLP was charged in 2002 with accounting fraud and obstruction of justice for shredding Enron's accounting documents to conceal its wrongdoings. Arthur Andersen's indictment led to bankruptcy and the loss of 28,000 jobs. This precedent, together with the general avoidance of collateral damages to stockholders and employees were often cited to justify the multiplication of deferred prosecution (DPAs) and non-prosecution (NPAs) agreements. Although proven meaningful in certain cases, these agreements have been frequently misused by shifting "from the prosecution of high-level individuals to entering into 'cosmetic' prosecution agreements with their

---

34 Laschi, *supra* note 33, at p. 113; *see also* David Mills & Robert Weisberg, 'Corrupting the Harm Requirement in White Collar Crime', 60 *Stanford Law Review* 1345 (March 2008), p. 1375, where they point out that the victim of corporate crime can be seen as a cohort of the perpetrator who ended up on the wrong end of the deal.

35 Robert K. Merton, *Social Theory and Social Structure*, New York: The Free Press, 1968, p. 196.

36 Michel Foucault, *Discipline and Punish: The Birth of the Prison*, New York: Vintage Books, 1979, p. 89.

37 Mirielle Delmas-Marty, 'Aplanir le terrain de jeu' in 'Les Figures de l'Internationalisation en Droit Pénal Des Affaires' *Revue de Science Criminelle et de Droit Pénal Comparé* (2005), p. 735.

38 *Id.* p. 735. Compare, however, with Ulrich Sieber, "The Forces Behind the Harmonization of Criminal Law", in: Mireille Delmas-Marty, Mark Pieth, and Ulrich Sieber (eds), *Les chemins de l'harmonisation pénale (Harmonizing Criminal Law)*, Paris: Société De Législation Comparée, 2008, p. 408, who points out that soft-law mechanisms for harmonizing law led to a higher degree of harmonization, and favor implementation and enforcement devices.

companies."[39] The abuse of DPAs and NPAs constitutes, therefore, a modern example of underenforcement resulting from preferential treatment of white-collar offenders.

Deferred prosecutions originated in the 1930s as a way of helping juvenile offenders.[40] Pre-trial diversion for first-time offenders who had committed relatively minor offenses is a rehabilitative tool to avoid the de-socializing effects of imprisoning juveniles. These agreements usually entail acceptance of responsibility for the misconduct by the perpetrator, who agrees to seek counseling or treatment, and perform community service.[41] Similarly, the government agreed to either defer prosecutions or decline them altogether if companies that had committed various business crimes not only paid substantial fines, but also took transformative corporate governance measures and reinforced compliance programs. DPAs and NPAs were used from the 1980s in isolated cases, but were increasingly applied after 2001.[42] These agreements were officially promoted by the Department of State (DOJ) after the new "Principles of Federal Prosecution of Business Organizations" issued by Deputy Attorney General Larry Thompson in 2003 stated that cooperation and voluntary disclosure could merit granting of not only immunity or amnesty, but also pre-trial diversion.[43]In 2008 the Justice Department endorsed deferred and non-prosecution agreements in the section of its revised guidance regarding collateral consequences. Deputy Attorney General Mark Philip pointed out in his memorandum on "Principles of Federal Prosecution of Business Organizations" that these agreements not only avoided collateral consequences on innocent third parties but also could help restore "the integrity of a company's operations and preserve the financial viability of a corporation that has engaged in criminal conduct."[44] These virtues have been overshadowed by abuses that generated a growing criticism of prosecution agreements. David M. Uhlmann considers that some prosecutors have sacrificed criminal prosecutions too readily for "non-criminal alternatives that include otherwise attractive settlement terms."[45]He points out that in those cases the Justice Department's motivation for pursuing deferred or non-prosecution agreements "has been far less high-minded than concern for collateral consequences or a desire for cooperation or structural reform." Instead,

39 Jed S. Rakoff, 'Justice Deferred is Justice Denied' 19 February 2015 (at: www.nybooks.com/articles/2015/02/19/justice-deferred-justice-denied/) (last visited: 27 August 2016) reviewing Brandon I. Garrett's *Too Big to Jail: How Prosecutors Compromise with Corporations*, Cambridge: The Belknap Press of Harvard University Press, (2014).

40 *Id.* at p.1

41 David M. Uhlmann, "Deferred Prosecution and Non-Prosecution Agreements and the Erosion of Corporate Criminal Liability," 72 *Maryland Law Review* 4 (2013), p. 1304.

42 *Id.* at p. 1307.

43 *Id.* at p.1311.

44 *Id.* at p.1295.

45 *Id.* at p.1325.

Uhlmann notes the agreements are pursued based on what amounts to a cost-benefit analysis concluding that the agreement would achieve the same or better financial penalties, factual admissions, corporate cooperation, and structural reforms without investing the investigative, prosecutorial or judicial resources that might be needed in a corporate prosecution.[46]

This form of underenforcement, which undermines the deterrent and educational value of criminal law, may be understood but not justified by the specific procedural and evidentiary obstacles inherent in this kind of prosecution. "[P]rosecuting white collar crime presents problems that most street crime does not—it is harder to investigate, harder to prove, and harder to deter."[47] Likewise, Mary Kreiner Ramirez points out that "proving accounting fraud through numerous witnesses, financial experts, and hundreds of documents is substantially more complicated than proving the average drug deal on the street."[48]

Paradoxically, the difficulties of convicting corporate offenders have been an argument not only for underenforcement but also for overcriminalization. Prosecutorial challenges have led to the enactment of overlapping statutes when charging individuals, as well as deliberately vague definitions and disproportionately harsh penalties to strengthen enforcement powers and force plea bargaining or pre-indictment settlements.

IV. CYCLICAL ASPECTS

In the first sixteen years of this century the pendulum has periodically swung between the prevalence either of overuse or underuse. At the dawn of the century, following a period of financial deregulation that culminated in a financial market crisis, the United States was shaken by gigantic accounting frauds, of which the most damaging were Enron and WorldCom. In contrast with the traditional judicial attitude regarding white-collar crimes, the perpetrators were punished to the full extent of the law.[49] Congress's prompt reaction to these scandals was the Sarbanes-Oxley Act of 2002 that radically transformed corporate governance in the United States. The Act created gatekeeper liability for corporate leaders (inclusive of the lawyers who had to certify the accounting documents),

46 *Id.* at p. 1295.

47 Haugh, (note 5) at p. 1206.m

48 Mary Kreiner Ramirez, 'Prioritizing Justice: Combating Corporate Crime from Task Force to Top Priority', 93 *Marquette Law Review* 3 (2010), p. 991.

49 For example, the Chief Executive Officer of WorldCom, Bernard Ebbers, was sentenced in 2005 to a twenty-five year prison term and Jeffrey Skilling, former Enron Corporation Chief Executive Officer, was sentenced to twenty-four years of imprisonment that were later reduced to fourteen years.

whistleblowing provisions, a supervisory institution, the Public Company Accounting Oversight Board (PCAOB), and increased the penalties from a maximum of five years to twenty years of imprisonment.

The Sarbanes-Oxley Act and its effects were criticized in the United States[50] and abroad[51] as being excessively punitive and making it too expensive for foreign corporations to list their securities in the United States stock markets. Lucien Dervan addresses what he considers a new round of overcriminalization by identifying two types of rationales[52]: increasing the penalties considerably with general deterrent purposes, and creating vague and overlapping criminal provisions "to provide prosecutors with the tools necessary to ensure that creative and sophisticated white collar criminals are brought to justice in larger numbers."[53] His article contains an empirical study showing that the supposed increase of penalties resulting from overcriminalization due to the Sarbanes Oxley Act is elusive. On the other hand, this type of overcriminalization may have created further incentives to waive the defendant's right to trial and plead guilty, thus showing a symbiotic relationship between overcriminalization and plea bargaining.[54] This conclusion may be extended to pre-indictment settlements such as deferred prosecution agreements and non-prosecution agreements allowing large corporations to avoid the "ignominy of criminal convictions."[55] As Uhlmann adds, "[t]here were no prosecutions at all—deferred or otherwise—for the worst financial crisis since the Great Depression, even though financial institutions and officials within those companies took unnecessary risks and engaged in conduct that imperiled the global economy."[56]

The 2008 mortgage subprime crisis was caused, in large part, by fraudulent behavior on the part of banks and rating agencies. Dubious mortgages portrayed as sound risk and packaged as esoteric financial instruments were used to deceive

50 Lucian E. Dervan, 'White-Collar Over-criminalization, Deterrence, Plea Bargaining, and the Loss of Innocence' 101 *Kentucky Law Journal* 723 (2013).

51 Bernd Schünemann, 'The Sarbanes-Oxley Act of 2002: A German Perspective, 8 *Buffalo Criminal Law Review* 35; Klaus Tiedemann in *Wirtschaftsstrafrecht: Einfürung und Allgemeiner Teil*, Munich, Franz Vahlen, (2014), p. 31 calls the penalties imposed to the responsible for the financial scandals at the beginning of the century "draconian" and situates the Sarbanes-Oxley Act in the context of a typical policy concentrated on deterrence.

52 Dervan, (note 51), at p. 723.

53 *Id.* at p. 724.

54 *Id.* at p. 745.

55 David M. Uhlmann, 'The Pendulum Swings: Reconsidering Corporate Criminal Prosecution', *University of Michigan, Michigan Law, Public Law and Legal Theory Research Paper Series* (August 2015), p. 1, adding that the Criminal Division of the Justice Department entered these types of agreements in more than two-thirds of the corporate cases resolved between 2010 and 2012.

56 *Id.* at p. 2.

the public.[57] These subprime mortgages of questionable creditworthiness were marketed as securities of very low risk and rated "AAA" with the complicity of rating agencies. Large financial institutions received, not only great economic benefits and subsidies, but also an implicit exemption from criminal statutes.[58] One of the most prominent critics of this lack of prosecution is Jed S. Rakoff, who underscored that the wide-spread conclusion was that "fraud at every level permeated the bubble in mortgage-backed securities…and if the Great Recession was…the product of intentional fraud, the failure to prosecute those responsible must be judged one of the more egregious failures of the criminal justice system in many years."[59]

The criticism against the absence of prosecutions after the financial crisis led to another pendulum swing towards the criminal prosecution of corporate crimes as recently as 2014, when the Justice Department brought prosecutions against Credit Suisse and BNP Paribas for currency manipulation.[60] Further, in 2015, the Justice Department also prosecuted JP Morgan Chase, Citicorp, Barclays, Royal Bank of Scotland, and UBS.[61]

V. RETREATS FROM OVERCRIMINALIZATION AND UNDERENFORCEMENT: THE STORY OF THE TWO YATES

In recent times, the stabilizing forces at the extremes of the pendulum swings between the opposite phenomena of overuse and underuse are represented by a case and a memo, both coincidentally designated under the same last name, Yates, after John Yates, a small-town fisherman from Holmes Beach, Florida; and Sally Quillian Yates, the United States Deputy Attorney General.

The case pushing back the pendulum from the extreme of overcriminalization is *Yates v. United States*. The facts of the case are the following: The fisherman, John Yates, was convicted for violating the 18 U.S.C. § 1519 of the Sarbanes-Oxley Act. This anti-shredding provision was conceived to prevent obstructions of justice situations similar to those of Arthur Andersen, LLP, which shredded the accounting records of Enron. According to this provision, it is a crime to destroy a record document, or tangible object with the

57 Jed S. Rakoff, 'The Financial Crisis: Why Have No High-Level Executives Been Prosecuted?' 9 *New York Review of* Books, January 2014 (at: www.nybooks.com/articles/2014/01/09/financial-crisis-why-no-executive-prosecutions/) (last visited: 27 August 2016).

58 Nizan Geslevich Packin, 'Breaking Bad? Too Big-To-Fail Banks Not Guilty as Not Charged', *91 Washington University Law Review* 4 (2014), p. 1090; *See also* Ramirez, (note 49) at p. 868.

59 Rakoff, (note 58).

60 Uhlmann, (note 56) at p. 3.

61 *Id.*

intent to obstruct a federal procedure. The courts applied this provision targeting corporate malfeasance to Yates, who had thrown overboard a crate of undersized red groupers after a federal agent inspected his catch and instructed him to keep the fish in ice until the ship returned to port.[62] A jury found him guilty determining that Yates destroyed tangible objects as defined under the Sarbanes-Oxley Act, and the 11th Circuit Court of Appeals affirmed. The Supreme Court granted certiorari on the question of whether Yates was deprived of fair notice that the destruction of fish fell within the meaning of the Sarbanes-Oxley provision. Justice Ginsburg, joined by Chief Justice, John Roberts, Justice Breyer and Justice Sotomayor concluded that a "tangible object" within § 1519 does not cover the defendant's situation and should be circumscribed to corporate accounting information. It is important to emphasize, however, that in her dissenting opinion, Justice Kagan, expressly addressed the issue of overcriminalization and excessive punishment in the U.S. Code. She criticized § 1519 as "bad law, too broad, and undifferentiated, with too-high maximum penalties, which give prosecutors too much leverage and sentencers too much discretion."[63]

On the other side of the pendulum, the memo written by Sally Quillian Yates constitutes a push back from outrageous underuse. On 9 September 2015 she issued her Memorandum to United States attorneys, including six directives or guidelines to ensure that individuals are held accountable for corporate wrongdoing.[64] According to the first directive corporations must provide to the DOJ all relevant factors about the individuals involved in corporate misconduct as a condition to be eligible for any cooperation credit. The second guideline requires prosecutors to develop a plan to prosecute individuals from the inception of the investigation, while the third one instructs prosecutors to explore every possible potential remedy, civil or criminal, to decide what is the best method to hold an individual accountable, directing criminal and civil attorneys to be in constant communication with each other to achieve such goal. The remaining prosecutorial principles are to avoid granting immunity to individuals in their settlements with corporations except when there are extraordinary circumstances or the existence of an express policy; to include a clear plan to resolve individual cases when dealing with a corporation, while memorializing any declination regarding individuals and finally, that civil attorneys must pursue culpable individuals as well as the corporations, without considering the quantity of the revenue but rather focusing on the long term deterrence of the individuals involved.

---

62 Haugh, (note 5) at p. 1193.

63 *Yates v. United States*, 135 S.Ct. 1074 (2015), p. 1101.

64 Memorandum from Sally Quillian Yates, Deputy Attorney General, to All U.S. Attorneys, Et Al., 'Individual Accountability for Corporate Wrongdoing 2-3, 9 September 2015 (at: www.justice.gov/dag/file/769036/download/) (last visited: 27 August 2016).

Michael P. Kelly and Ruth E. Mandelbaum[65] consider that the pressure exerted by the memo on prosecutors may lead them to adopt expansive interpretations of the statutes, in collision course with judicial decisions such as the Supreme Court adjudication in *Yates v. United States*[66], which recognizes their true, narrow meaning. Except for this extreme and unlikely hypothetical situation, inconsistent with the declarations of the Memo's author[67], the anti-overcriminalization efforts are not incompatible with the Memo. The retreat from scandalous underenforcement of federal criminal law does not affect the judicial reaction against overcriminalization but on the contrary tends also to stabilize the pendulum by correcting situations of blatant underenforcement, contributing thus to a more just criminal repression. Inadequate law enforcement undermining the citizen's confidence in the rule of law[68]does not require expansive interpretations equally damaging to the public image of the criminal justice system.

It is not that the Justice Department has not prosecuted individuals. It has done so to "a non-insignificant number of executives or employees, even after it has secured settlements from the companies in those cases."[69] However, the Yates Memo followed a disproportionate larger number of settlements involving billions of dollars and admissions of guilt.[70] The Memo was also preceded by concerns from some senators, federal judges, and public interest groups.[71] Even senior Justice Department officials voiced a variety of concerns about the prosecution agreements, especially after noting that the stock prices for some companies had increased in value after settlement announcements.[72]

65 Michael P. Kelly & Ruth E. Mandelbaum, 'Are the Yates Memorandum and the Federal Judiciary's Concerns About Over-Criminalization Destined to Collide?', 53 *American Criminal Law Review* 899 (2016).

66 *Yates v, United States* (note 64).

67 In Katelyn Polantz, 'Yates challenges Critics of the Justice Department's White-Collar Investigations Policy' Deputy Attorney General Sally Yates said, "Our goal is not to collect corporate heads. Our goal is to get to the bottom of who did what and if there are culpable individuals, hold them accountable." www.nationallawjournal.com/id=1202757274797/(last visited 30 August 2016).

68 Ramirez (note 49), at p.911 ff. points out the negative effects of underenforcement after the subprime mortgage crisis on the financial markets and on public trust.

69 Kelly & Mandelbaum, (note 66) at p. 903.

70 *Id.* at p. 900.

71 *Id.* at p. 904

72 *Id.* at p. 902.

VI. CONCLUSIONS

Overcriminalization in the area of white-collar crime multiplies the number of traps for the unwary, leads to disparate and disproportional punishment and increases prosecutorial powers with overlapping and vague statutes that allow prosecutors to extract false guilty pleas and even usurp legislative functions. Overcriminalization ultimately creates a climate of unfairness that not only undermines faith in the rule of law, but may also be criminogenic by delegitimizing the criminal justice system in potential offenders' eyes, thus justifying their rationalizations to engage in criminal behavior.[73]

On the other end of the spectrum, underenforcement of criminal law poses similar fairness problems and can "foster resentment and disrespect for the law among otherwise law-abiding members of the community and reduce social incentives to obey the law."[74] The failure to prosecute big corporations after the subprime mortgages financial crisis had "a corrosive effect on the fabric of democracy and our shared belief that we are equal in the eyes of the law."[75]

The Supreme Court in its decision in *Yates v. United States*, as in other recent cases[76], has begun to rectify the trend by federal courts to broadly interpret poorly defined crimes, a trend which often resulted in making defective federal criminal statutes worse. Stephen S. Smith affirms that, "courts share a large share of the blame for overcriminalization, given their penchant to construe ambiguous criminal statutes broadly."[77] *Yates* overthrew lower courts' interpretations of the words "tangible objects" in 18 U.S.C § 1519 out of their corporate accounting context -an interpretation that had transformed a fishing regulatory violation into a serious felony.

By combating ambiguous, overlapping and vague criminal statutes as troublesome forms of overcriminalization, *Yates* made an important contribution towards the respect of the rule of law. The decision better adapts the interpretation of criminal federal statutes to the true nature and spirit of criminal law, by protecting vital social values with precise definitions that fairly warn citizens and preclude the possibility of disparate enforcement.

Likewise, at the other extreme of the spectrum, the *Yates Memo* contributes to the respect of the rule of law and restores criminal law to its specific function

---

73 Tod Haugh, (note 5) at pages 1213 ff. explains in detail the criminogenic effects of overcriminalization, including a perspicacious analysis of the rationalizations leading to the fisherman John Yates ' criminal behavior at p. 1229 ff.

74 Natapoff, (note 3) at p. 1716.

75 Report prepared by the Office of Senator Elizabeth Warren, 'Rigged Justice: 2016: How Weak Enforcement Lets Corporate Offenders Off Easily' (January 2016), p. 1.

76 Kelly and Mandelbaum,(note 66) at ps. 922 ff. mention among others *Bond v. United* States 134 S.Ct. 2077 (2014); and *Skilling v. United States* 561 U.S. 358 (2010).

77 Stephen Smith (note 8) at p. 539.

in a democratic society. The Memo instructs United States attorneys to undertake their specific task to go after both individuals and corporations that have violated criminal law norms that protect the public from corporate wrongdoing.

A policy of excessive use of deferred and non-prosecution agreements to avoid collateral consequences or the uncertainty and challenges of criminal trials in the complex area of business, politicizes the rule of law and fosters disparate treatment. But as Sharon E. Foster points out, "the rule of law cannot be applied like a categorical imperative,"[78]and a certain degree of prosecutorial discretion is always necessary. Prosecutors face a balancing act: if collateral consequences and critical social needs are ignored the law becomes barren, but "if collateral consequences are considered in a disparate fashion so as to create a perception of injustice, the rule of law becomes barren."[79]

After extensive studies of prosecutorial settlements, Brandon L. Garrett concludes that the problems faced by prosecutors in corporate cases are double-edged given that today corporate prosecutions are both over-and underused. Garrett provides insight into a prosecutor's dilemma when faced with the prospect of such prosecutions, as well as normative advice about how to preserve the integrity of the rule of law: Prosecutors should not "offer a company an alternative to prosecution because they think they have a weak case"[80] In these instances they should abstain from prosecuting altogether. "But it is also troubling if prosecutors bring strong cases against egregious corporate violators only to then settle for reduced fines and superficial compliance."[81] Garrett believes that such overly lenient settlements of corporate prosecutions send a corrosive "too big to jail" message to industry and to the public that "undermines the legitimacy of the criminal law."[82]

In complex areas of the law such as the one that regulates the business world there is no room for an absolute and rigid justice. The Supreme Court decision in *Yates,* as well as the *Yates* Memo, tends to counter the extreme pendulum swings between the phenomena of overuse and underuse, both incompatible with the respect of the rule of law. The *Yates* decision curtails the inherent unfairness of over-enforcement of business-related criminal law; on the other hand, the *Yates* Memo curtails outrageous underenforcement. Both contribute to bringing the scales of justice to a state of equilibrium.

---

78 Sharon E. Foster, 'Too Big to Prosecute: Collateral Consequences, Systemic Institutions and the Rule of Law,' in *Review of Banking & Financial Law*, Vol. 34, (2014-2015) p. 655, 711.

79 *Id.* at 712.

80 Brandon L. Garrett, *Too Big to Jail: How Prosecutors Compromise with Corporations*, Cambridge: The Belknap Press of Harvard University Press (2014), p. 286.

81 *Id.*

82 *Id.*

The International Penal and Penitentiary Foundation: history and purpose

International efforts to harmonize criminal justice policy date back to the nineteenth century, when representatives of various European nations met periodically to exchange information and to consider common standards in the treatment of offenders. In 1872, cooperation took a step forward when an International Prison Commission (IPC) was set up to collect national prison statistics and make recommendations for prison reform in Europe. When the League of Nations was formed in 1919, it saw as part of its mandate the promotion of the rule of law in the international community. The IPC became affiliated with the League and continued to hold conferences, meeting in 1925, 1930 and 1935. In the latter year, the IPC became the International Penal and Penitentiary Commission (IPPC).[1] When the new United Nations was created in 1945, it incorporated crime prevention and standards of criminal justice into its policy-setting role. In December 1950, the IPPC was dissolved, to be replaced by the International Penal and Penitentiary Foundation. The IPPF is a foundation governed by the Swiss Civil Code and created on the 5th of July 1951. The Foundation shall have as its aim to promote studies in the field of the prevention of crime and the treatment of offenders, especially by scientific research, publications and teaching. The IPPF strives to foster the rule of law and internationally recognized human rights standards.

See for further information at: www.ru.nl/ippf

---

1 See: United Nations, *The United Nations and Crime Prevention*, New York: United Nations, 1991, p. 3-4.

La Fondation internationale pénale et pénitentiaire: histoire et objectif

Les efforts internationaux entrepris pour harmoniser la politique pénale et pénitentiaire remontent au 19e siècle, quand des représentants de plusieurs Etats européens ont commencé à se réunir périodiquement pour échanger de l'information et élaborer des standards communs dans le domaine du traitement des délinquants. En 1872, la coopération s'intensifia avec l'instauration de la Commission Pénitentiaire Internationale (CPI), chargée de réunir des statistiques nationales sur la prison et de formuler des recommandations pour la réforme des institutions carcérales en Europe. Instituée en 1919, la Société des Nations s'est vue confier le mandat de promouvoir des règles de droit en la matière auprès de la communauté internationale. La CPI devint affiliée à la Société des Nations et continua d'organiser des conférences et rencontres, en 1925, 1930 et 1935, avant de devenir la Commission Internationale Pénale et Pénitentiaire (CIPP).[1] Quand en 1945, à la suite de la Société des Nations, fut créée l'Organisation des Nations Unies, cette dernière maintint parmi ses objectifs principaux la promotion de la prévention du crime et de standards en matière de justice criminelle. En décembre 1950, la CIPP fut dissoute et remplacée par la Fondation internationale pénale et pénitentiaire. Instituée le 5 juillet 1951, la FIPP est une fondation, au sens des articles 80ss du Code civil suisse. La Fondation a pour but d'encourager les études dans le domaine de la prévention du crime et du traitement des délinquants, notamment par la recherche scientifique, les publications et l'enseignement. L'IPPF s'efforce de promouvoir l'état de droit et les normes internationales des droits de l'homme.

Voir pour plus d'informations: www.ru.nl/ippf

1 Traduction libre tirée de: United Nations, *The United Nations and Crime Prevention*, New York: United Nations, 1991, p. 3-4.

The IPPF Series

The International Penal and Penitentiary Foundation (IPPF) has a long history and can trace its roots back to 1872. It shall have as its aim to promote studies in the field of the prevention of crime and the treatment of offenders, especially by scientific research, publications, teaching and international colloquiums.

The IPPF's members are from around the world, are recognized experts in penal and penitentiary matters, and are either high judges, high officials of the prison system, or university professors.

Recent publications of the IPPF regard, e.g., "Prison policy and prisoners' rights", "Minorities and cultural diversity in prison", "Pre-trial detention", "Prevention of reoffending; the value of rehabilitation and the management of high-risk offenders", and "Women in Prison; The Bangkok Rules and Beyond".

Les activités de la FIPP

La Fondation internationale pénale et pénitentiaire (FIPP) est une institution dont les origines remontent à 1872. Elle vise à promouvoir les études dans le domaine de la prévention de la criminalité et le traitement des délinquants, plus particulièrement en menant des recherches scientifiques, en éditant des publications, des cours et par l'organisation de colloques internationaux.

La FIPP compte des membres dans le monde entier, tous experts reconnus dans les matières pénale et pénitentiaire: hauts magistrats, hauts fonctionnaires du système pénitentiaire ou professeurs d'université.

La FIPP a entre autres récemment publié « Politiques pénitentiaires et droits des détenus », « Minorités et diversité culturelle en prison », « Détention avant jugement », « Prévention de la récidive; valeur de la réhabilitation et gestion des délinquants à haut risque », et « Femmes en Prison ; Les règles de Bangkok et au-delà ».

www.ingramcontent.com/pod-product-compliance
Ingram Content Group UK Ltd.
Pitfield, Milton Keynes, MK11 3LW, UK
UKHW051846100926
8556IPUK00005B/471